DATE DUE			
May 1 '77			
PJul 6 '77			
Dec 15 7 B B			
Nov 2 79			
Jan 20 '81			
Apr 24 '81			

DEVIANCE

Deviance

STUDIES IN THE PROCESS

OF STIGMATIZATION AND

SOCIETAL REACTION

SIMON DINITZ

RUSSELL R. DYNES

ALFRED C. CLARKE

New York

OXFORD UNIVERSITY PRESS

London   1969   Toronto

Copyright © 1969 by Oxford University Press, Inc.
Library of Congress Catalogue Card Number: 69-17761
Printed in the United States of America

PREFACE

In some circles, it is currently popular to condemn collections of readings as non-books. We feel that bringing together interesting and significant articles on a particular topic serves a legitimate purpose, not only as an instructional device but also as a medium for the dissemination of a broader understanding. What follows here is not a random collection of articles, but a selection that was guided by our particular view of the concept of deviance. In Part I we have attempted to outline this view. The readings included were chosen for their relevance to this view of deviance, and for their ability to illuminate it. Since the selected articles touch on every major aspect of deviance, the book can be used alone as an integrated set of readings, or it can be used as a supplement to other text treatments.

The over-all objective of the selections is to place deviance in the social context, rather than outside it—to see deviance as human, not inhuman, behavior. Since deviance seems to hold intrinsic interest for many people, it is unfortunate that most accessible information about the subject emphasizes melodrama, not knowledge; eccentricity, not commonness; peculiarity, not universality. By our selections we hope to encourage the reader to do some unconventional thinking about the conventional wisdom of deviance. Too often, people seek simple answers rather than increased understanding. Many forms of simplistic answers are widespread. There have been many pat genetic explanations—poor genes, "bad seed," inherited tendencies. There have been even more pat psychological explanations—weak super-egos, possessive mothers, sexual frustrations. While genes, mothers, and sex are interesting topics of conversation, they provide little understanding of deviance. As sociologists we feel the kind of understanding most meaningful, but as yet less prevalent in the conventional wisdom, is sociological. Since we have chosen readings that are primarily sociological in nature, we have departed from, and thus challenged, much of the conventional wisdom of deviance.

We had another major criterion of selection: we wished to emphasize critical issues of deviance as they appeared to us at the close of the 1960's. While we have included some historical materials, the major emphasis is on current issues. Unfortunately, today's problems often

v

6

take a somewhat different, often disguised, form a few years later. For example, we have felt that the illustration we chose for a specific manifestation of alienation, the hippie, might be declining in prominence in American society. Specific forms will change. Alienation, however, will be expressed in some other way in another time. Such changes in specific forms we must expect, so it is perhaps impossible to be completely up to date. Even out of date, we still have much to learn from yesterday's problems since they have continuity to the present.

Besides these guidelines, we used several other criteria in the final process of choosing from the hundreds of articles we considered. In general, we have included articles dealing with broad conceptual issues. We wanted to raise questions, not to reinforce answers. Consequently, we have excluded a number of valuable studies on specific and delimited topics. For example, we have chosen to deal with the *concept* of mental illness rather than included delimited studies on particular clinical symptoms.

We have also used summaries that provide inventories of current knowledge. In this connection we have drawn heavily on the President's Commission on Law Enforcement and the Administration of Justice. The reports of this commission are the collective products of persons who are both concerned and knowledgeable about their topics. In addition to these summaries, we have selected a few articles on the basis of their interest and the vividness of their content and style. Some journalists are adept at writing on social science subjects, and some social scientists do not always provide models of clarity in their exposition. While interest and style rather than professional identification were occasionally emphasized, this does not mean that we sought the lowest common denominator in style. Simplicity can reflect lack of understanding, and style should never be confused with cleverness. Complex ideas often require complex exposition. The reader, then, will find various levels of difficulty.

After the selection process, each article was carefully edited. Material not central to the main thrust of the topic was eliminated. Footnotes were also eliminated. The functions of footnotes—to acknowledge intellectual ancestry, to add supporting evidence, and to suggest further enquiry— are not crucial to a volume of this kind. Each writer has many intellectual ancestors, only some of whom become footnoted. We can offer here as a substitute our general footnote of appreciation to those, past and present, acknowledged and unacknowledged, who have attempted to understand human behavior. Even with the absence of footnotes, we hope the readings will encourage those who read this book to seek out other sources to extend their knowledge. A library card file is one acceptable substitute for footnotes.

In making our own final footnote, we wish to thank the many authors for their willingness to have their work included, even with our editing. Too, we wish to thank Cathy Ball for her skill in keeping track of our continuing discussion, the selection process, and the final preparation of the manuscript.

S.D.
R.R.D.
A.C.C.

Columbus, Ohio
January 1969

CONTENTS

THE CONCEPT OF DEVIATION

1 DEVIANCE, NORMS, AND SOCIETAL REACTION

Human deviance is just as characteristic of society as conformity is. Every human group, no matter how cohesive, stable, and well integrated, must somehow respond to such problems as mental illness, violence, theft, and sexual misconduct, as well as to other similarly difficult behaviors. Problems of deviance inevitably are defined as being a real or perceived threat to the basic and core values of the society. For whatever reasons, some persons act, at times at least, in so bizarre, eccentric, outlandish, abhorrent, dangerous, or merely unique and annoying a manner that they cannot readily be tolerated. Thus, every society must somehow deal with its saints and sinners, its kooks and clowns, and its dependent, disruptive, inadequate, and aberrant members.

Understanding deviance involves, at a basic minimum, at least three dimensions. First, it is apparent that every society defines behaviors that are to be labeled as deviant and proscribed as undesirable. Second, since deviance may be "commonplace," and even widespread, some explanations or theories must be offered for the existence and persistence of such deviant behavior in the face of negative social sanctions. Third, there would be little reason to define, sanction, and explain deviance without also doing something to, for, or with the deviant in order to correct, deter, prevent, and/or punish him. Every society, then, defines, explains, and acts with regard to deviance.

DEVIANCE AND NORMS

It is necessary to initiate our discussion of deviance by giving attention to norms. Without reference to norms, it is impossible to talk about deviation, since norms provide the baseline, the standard, the unit against which deviation is defined, measured, and sanctioned.

Sumner, the early American sociologist, was the originator of the widely quoted phrase, "the mores can make anything right." It is also true that the mores (norms) can make anything wrong and deviant. Group norms can establish almost any form of behavior, from the most innocent to the most harmful, as deviant. By the same token, norms can even "purify" and legitimize destructive behavior, such as waging war, as not only acceptable but even highly honorific. Because of such normative definitions, variations in norms over time and across societies make it impossible to speak of deviance in universal or absolute terms. What is sinful or criminal to one era and to one society may well be revered at another time or in another society. Nevertheless, regardless of the specific content of behavior, the essential nature of deviance lies in the departure of certain types of behavior from the norms of a particular society at a particular time. Deviance is always and irrevocably normative.

Norms are the *should's* and *should not's* in society. They evolve out of the experience of people interacting within society. In turn, they guide, channel, and limit future relationships. So integral a part of human life are norms that many are unaware of their pervasiveness. Most persons are oblivious to the importance of norms in giving substance and meaning to human life. The reason for this lack of awareness is that norms become so internalized as a part of personality that people take them for granted. Norms are seldom consciously thought about unless they are challenged by contact with persons conforming to another normative order—perhaps "foreigners," "hillbillies," or "outsiders." This "unconscious" quality of norms arises from the fact that persons are rewarded for behaving in certain ways and punished for behaving in other ways until behavior according to the norms becomes almost automatic.

Within every society, norms tend to cluster around the major, recurrent activities in which its members are involved. Such norms are often called social institutions. For example, what is called "the family" is in actuality a complex set of norms that regulates relations between the sexes, legitimizes children, prescribes methods for their socialization, determines the boundaries of the family unit, regulates sexual behavior, provides for a division of labor, and guides the complexities of day-to-day activities. While each specific family unit may be unique in certain ways, depending on the individuality of its members and their interaction, there is an element of commonness among all families within a society. These commonalities stem from the normative proscriptions. In the same context, we can also talk of economic, legal, religious, educational, and political institutions as each being a cluster of norms.

The way norms function can best be understood, however, in contrasting societal contexts. It is useful to contrast the nature of the normative order of modern industrial societies with that of the more traditional societies of the past. Such a contrast will suggest that the nature of deviation would be somewhat different in the two types of societies.

In traditional folk societies, the norms are generally simple. There is a limited range of possibilities for human action, so the rules necessary are also limited. Too, the norms tend to be tied together in a "neater" package. Family life, educational life, and economic life are so closely related that they are difficult to separate. The norms that govern a father and son working in a field are, at the same time, familially, educationally, and economically important. Were the son to violate a norm, the negative sanctions, i.e. punishments, for this violation would be immediate and certain. The specific deviant act by the son, however, would be considered in terms of his "whole" personality, his total actions, past and present. His behavior would be seen as "bad," but the son would not likely be considered a deviant *person* because of such isolated action.

TRADITIONAL FOLK SOCIETIES	MODERN INDUSTRIAL SOCIETIES
simple set of norms	complex set of norms
internalized norms	imposed norms
integrated norms	lack of integrated norms
immediate and certain sanctions	uncertain and delayed sanctions
deviant behavior seen as one part of total behavior	deviant behavior seen as characteristic of total person

The situation is quite different in modern societies. The normative order becomes more and more complex since there is greater diversity within the society itself. Social life becomes more segmentalized. Family behavior is separated from educational and economic behavior and the norms regulating these several areas often become inconsistent and lack integration. Since the society is more impersonal, the sanctions for the deviant act are neither certain nor immediate. Since the society is segmentalized, deviant acts in one segment very often stigmatize the *person* in others. The norms and sanctions in modern industrial societies, then, are quite different from those of the more traditional societies.

It it useful to indicate briefly some of the forces which have created such normative differences between traditional and modern societies. While many factors have combined to create these results, one way to summarize them is in terms of the "silent" revolutions as they have affected American society.[1] Among these we mention revolutions in industry, mobility, science, and organization. These social forces have transformed the physical and material existence of mankind, and have altered, disrupted, and changed the earlier normative order. One might suggest that, just as traditional societies had a type of social organization that minimized deviance, modern societies have developed a normative order and a social organization that facilitate deviance. For example, the

---

[1] For a more extensive treatment see Russell R. Dynes, Alfred C. Clarke, Simon Dinitz, and Iwao Ishino, *Social Problems, Dissensus and Deviation in an Industrial Society* (New York: Oxford University Press, 1964), Chapter 2, "The Development of an industrial Society."

Industrial Revolution has changed man's relationship to the world of work. Earlier systems of norms, based on a state of perpetual scarcity of goods and need for manpower, no longer fit in a world of complex technology and relative affluence. The traditional yoke of hard physical labor has been lifted—first by the introduction of the machine, then by the factory, later by mass production techniques, and in more recent years by the development of servomechanisms and automation, which allow workerless factories. To a world used to physical labor, these changes have had tremendous impact on traditional norms of work. Those who dreamed of leisure in the future have found the future already here.

The mobility revolution has shaken the historic normative patterns in several respects. First, the tremendous geographic mobility in this century has been without parallel. This age may yet be designated by future historians as the century of the "refugee"—voluntary and involuntary. Vast floods of refugees fleeing from war, persecutions, and economic catastrophes—as well as immigrants searching for greater opportunity—have moved across the world. Too, there have been continual internal migrations. There has been a shifting of populations from East to West, to the point that in California a "native" is defined as one who has lived there for five years. In addition to this shift westward, rural to urban migration has altered the United States, changing it from an overwhelmingly rural society to a metropolitan society. There has also been the continuous shift of the Negro out of the South and into Northern and, lately, Western urban areas. The movement of Mexican braceros and "wetbacks," the Appalachian (hillbilly) migrations, and the Puerto Rican and Cuban group settlements in metropolitan New York and Florida, respectively, continue to alter the population mosaic. Another less visible aspect of the mobility revolution is taking place: millions of families move and resettle every year in different cities, counties, and states. Whereas most people formerly lived and died within a fifty-mile radius of their birthplace, now the typical American often feels underprivileged unless he has traveled widely, or frequently moved from place to place.

All of this geographical mobility has had its normative consequences. Internal migrations have shattered the continuity of life in the small community, and traditional norms, which arise from intimate face-to-face interaction with the same persons over many years, cannot be sustained under such conditions. This decline of the small stable community raises the interesting question of how to maintain expected—normative—behavior when the "expecters," that is, the community, and the expectations are changing. The primary problems of today are urban ones—congestion, slums, pollution, the emergence of the "black core and the white ring," the confrontation of the rich and the poor, the inability of local governments to cope with a mobile population, etc.

The mobility revolution can also be seen as movement in "social space," that is, social mobility. In stable social settings, people "fit in" on the basis of status ascribed to them—according to their age, sex, and/ or family position. In the past, men were often faced with permanent inequalities that came from such ascription. For example, the Negro in America has had—and still has—the problem of overcoming such placement because of his race. In industrial societies, however, achievement replaces ascription as a norm and as a value. Fitting in now involves notions such as "climbing and achieving." Norms which were functional to the older ascribed system do not fit in social structures geared to achievement. In societies that emphasize achievement, however, there are new psychological and social costs, particularly for those who do not or cannot achieve—the "failures." For example, in more traditional societies, the older person was often given high status by virtue of his age; but in societies in which achievement is a principal value around which status and prestige are organized, the older person often cannot achieve and therefore is assigned low status. Indeed, all who are nonproductive and economically dependent, whether aged or not, tend to be viewed with disdain. When nonachievement is considered to be willful and purposeful, as is sometimes imputed to the unemployed, the school dropout, or the hippie, the lack of achievement is considered to border on the deviant. The point here is that in a society geared to achievement, those who cannot or do not wish to achieve have difficulty in finding a place.

Although the scientific revolution did not specifically alter interaction among people, it undermined traditional concepts of knowledge and truth. Man's understanding of his world and his approach to knowledge have become so radically different that previous dogmas, taboos, beliefs, and norms have lost their immediacy. Science as a way of life, as a secular religion, as a mode of thought, as a system for obtaining and systematizing information, has superseded previous approaches. The possibilities of understanding, prediction, and control of the physical, biological, and social worlds continue to stir the imagination. Science is a method of achieving and a system for integrating knowledge; yet the knowledge science has already achieved has created racial problems which we cannot overcome using our existing norms.

The scientific mode of thought spawned the "hardware" revolution, which is directed toward man's unquenchable desire for gadgets and products. The scientific "genie" in its various applications has transformed everything from man's conception of the universe to woman's role in the marital partnership. No aspects of life have remained untouched. Everything from ultimate destruction to ultimate destiny has been affected by this revolution.

Of the various other silent revolutions, perhaps only the organizational revolution warrants comment here. The growth of mass society is characterized by the phenomenal development of large-scale and complex organizations. Man still has illusions about his uniqueness, individuality, and captaincy of his fate. But, like the interchangeable components in the industrial machine, he has become specialized, bureaucratized, and expendable. Having so laboriously developed norms more applicable to an earlier setting of face-to-face relationships, his problem now is how to adapt to a world of mass organization. This point is far from academic. Complex organization gives rise to some very vexing issues for deviance. For example, whereas an individual might be quite reluctant to steal from a parent, or a friend, or a neighbor, what is to keep him from "helping himself" to the property of a large impersonal organization? Where are the controls in such impersonal situations? Even more to the point, criminologists and many others are now concerned with a wholly different kind of criminality—white-collar crime on a massive scale. In a famous conspiracy case, large electrical companies were involved in rigging, bidding, and dividing the "profits" on a percentage basis. Who was guilty of such unlawful acts? Can a corporation be guilty? Or are the executives, the board of directors, the department heads guilty? How far down among personnel in organizations does criminal responsibility extend? The norms governing responsibility and liability of individuals have been considerably distorted by the organizational revolution.

TYPES OF NORMATIVE CHANGE

The foregoing discussion points to only some of the consequences of the silent revolutions that have transformed modern society and have changed the nature of the normative order. The types of change in the normative order that have particular significance for deviance need to be further discussed. Seven types of normative problems will be specified here: (1) norm breakdown; (2) norm conflict; (3) unreachable goal norms; (4) discontinuous norms; (5) impotent and sanctionless norms; (6) evasive norms; and (7) stressful norms.

1. *Norm Breakdown.* Most, or all, of today's most pressing social issues, including those pertaining to deviant behavior, are attributed in some measure to norm breakdown. The clarity, precision, and holding power of historic and traditional norms are no more; new norms are always in the emergent state. As a result, deviant behavior becomes a plausible and common occurrence. Norm breakdown can be illustrated in many ways. The most meaningful, perhaps, is to note that the traditional status role of the adolescent has been shattered. That is, the clus-

ter of norms that guides adolescent behavior no longer possesses clarity. Adolescence is no longer another stage in the life process with clearly defined duties, privileges, and obligations. Today the adolescent is "freed" from traditional family, neighborhood, and community ties. He is also more affluent than ever before and represents a potent economic market. As such, adolescents are style and fashion setters, and a "teenage subculture" has developed and is being perpetuated, a subculture responsive to their particular conditions of life. Teenage argot (language) with its references and allusions now serves as a focus of self-identification for the adolescent, emphasizing his distinctiveness vis-à-vis other age groups. Such distinctiveness is enhanced because the world of work does not need the adolescents' labor; present educational institutions are inappropriate for some; religious institutions can speak to only a few; and the family has lost much of its hold. The norms that once provided the adolescent a context in which he was a responsible and economically productive person, norms characterized by rigid parental discipline, filial piety, and stern sexual morality, with work and thrift as ultimate values, now seem "ancient" to contemporary adolescents. Under such circumstances of norm breakdown and the lack of clarity, delinquency and various other problems are hardly unexpected.

2. *Norm Conflict.* Only in well-integrated societies are the various levels of culture, society, and personality so well meshed that norm conflict is minor. In complex societies, norm conflict becomes inevitable. The demands and expectations are at times antithetical in the different roles people must play. The norms governing conduct in the marketplace, for example, often conflict with those that cover role behavior in the family. It is in terms of this conflict of norms that much deviance, particularly criminal deviance, is to be explained.

Norm conflict is most frequent when different social categories (age, race, religion, sex, occupation, education, area of residence) become the basis of subcultures. In these subcultures, norms develop that frequently clash with those of the larger society. As previously noted, this was one consequence of the breakdown of the older norms that guided adolescent behavior. When the norms of peer group, family, and neighborhood are in conflict with those of other groups and of the larger society, the holding power of each set of norms is weakened.

In dynamic societies, norm conflict is "built into" the system. In such societies, deviant subcultures develop and are maintained. The effect is to support and to perpetuate certain deviance, particularly the criminal types. Too, cases of acute norm conflict provide one basis of explanation for the emergence of such types of deviation as mental illness.

3. *Unreachable Goal Norms.* One consequence of a stable, integrated society is that the goals held out to individuals are reasonable and reach-

able. By following the prescribed pathways, most members can reach the goals they set. Industrial societies, however, present a far different picture. Some of the widespread values are attainable by only a minority of the population. Relatively few can be successful, wealthy, carefree, of high status, or "jet setters." Yet such goals are often accepted as "ideal" norms and as the measure of success. Since lack of attainment (relative failure) is actually the rule rather than the exception, emotional disturbance and social disaffection come to be built into the social order.

Responses to such unreachable goals are varied. Some may reject the goals entirely, e.g. the beatnik. Some may strike out in frustration and grief, as reflected in the slogan "burn, baby, burn" in the Negro ghettos. Others may retreat from life as being too complicated to master or even understand, e.g. the drug addict, the alcoholic. While there are also other reactions, aggressive, escapist, criminal, and rebellious types are potential deviants in a society that makes unreachable goals the goals for everyone.

4. *Discontinuous Norms.* There are few things so continuous as the life cycle, the unfolding and maturation of the person from birth to death. In traditional societies the norms regulating this cycle were continuous. There was a more or less gradual transition facilitated by various rites of passage from one status to another. In industrial societies, by contrast, these transitions go by fits and starts, rather than making a smooth progression from stage to stage. For example, there are two periods in the life cycle which are difficult by definition. The first, adolescence, has already been mentioned. The second, aging, is even more difficult, if only because there is nothing else to grow *into,* as the adolescent grows into early adulthood. One need only observe the treatment of the aged in the mass media to recognize the low estate into which they have fallen. Grandmother strives valiantly to be like granddaughter in everything—from physical appearance (dress, manner) to "cool" conversation. There is no easy shifting of status in the process of physical maturation; there is discontinuity and much tragedy here. Throughout the life cycle there is discontinuity. The demands made on the woman in her roles of housewife and mother are quite different from the demands made on her later, when her children leave home. She has spent her life learning to be a good mother; suddenly she has no one on whom to practice her art. Adequate preparation for the earlier roles may leave her totally unprepared for the roles that she must play in the future. There is some suggestion that at such critical points in the life cycle mental illness may be a common response.

5. *Impotent and Sanctionless Norms.* Some norms, even historically important ones, lose their vigor long before they are replaced by emer-

gent norms. They survive as relics of a world that was. It is interesting that these survivals continue to define normative behavior without being able to control it.

There are many illustrations of impotent and sanctionless norms. While most persons in an industrial society continue to profess some sort of religious identity and commitment, the hold of religious norms on conduct is frequently minimal. The potent norms are more likely to be those from the occupational and economic realms. Religious norms, which were once translated into blue laws, often remain on the books as part of the structure of modern society. Enforcing such norms, however, is quite another matter. While leading citizens make speeches praising the official norms of the society—honesty and other virtues— those very speakers will admit privately that they themselves often do not follow the norms they uphold. Cheating, for example, is deviant; yet it characterizes many areas of society, not merely the classroom. Many believe that, in order to succeed in a tough, competitive world—and success is perhaps our most potent norm—one *must* cheat; hence, cheating is built into the structure itself, just as much as the norm of honesty is. The point in all of this is that deviance frequently occurs in the context of norms that are accepted as binding but, because of the realities they contradict, are violated almost as often as they are observed. The existence of sanctionless norms is yet another facet of the problems of the normative order and deviant conduct.

6. *Evasive Norms.* More self-defeating and at the same time more comprehensible than the sanctionless norms are the evasive norms. By definition, evasive norms are those that permit, encourage, and reward behaviors defined by other norms as being illegal or immoral. These are the so-called loopholes in the norms, which are common in industrial societies. Thus, bribes are reprehensible, but gifts, "flower funds," and a variety of kickbacks are sanctified by the norms of evasion. Gambling is illegal, but bingo and lotteries are not. Extramarital sexual relationships are unacceptable, but prostitution exists *sub rosa*. In one sense, these norms of evasion provide safety valve action, but they also replace positive norms, with the result that deviant conduct, such as prostitution and gambling, becomes institutionalized even if never quite wholly acceptable.

7. *Stressful Norms.* Except possibly in the most isolated and simple of societies, some norms are inevitably more stressful than others. In industrial societies in which status must be achieved, and in which one's "place" is rarely secure, stressful norms are perhaps the rule more than the exception. For example, industrial societies require highly trained specialists. Increasingly greater ability and training are demanded if one is to compete effectively in the system and to run complex and tech-

nologically sophisticated devices. Such expectations become normative, so that there is constant pressure for ever more training and proficiency. Such normative expectations may be reasonable for those who can fit in without undue stress and strain. For many others, such expectations are deleterious and may possibly be correlated with a variety of personality disturbances.

Norms that emphasize pecuniary standards as the measure of man and as the basis of position in the status hierarchy are also a continuing source of frustration. The success-failure orientation is perhaps the central theme in American society. Its stressful potential may be seen in the high incidence of neurosis, alcoholism, coronary heart disease, and psychosomatic impairment. The consequences may be seen in certain types of crime and in the proliferation of evasive norms.

Thus, deviance is defined normatively—always. The normative order defines and creates the limits of acceptable and unacceptable (deviant) conduct. Just as it is impossible to grasp the concept of deviance except in relation to the social definition of what behavior should or ought to be, so the explanation of much of deviant behavior lies, directly or indirectly, in the normative realm. Norm breakdown, conflict, discontinuity, impotence, and stressfulness create the conditions that eventuate in large-scale deviancy.

DEFINITIONS OF DEVIATION

One of the most frustrating and vexing problems concerns the seemingly simple task of defining the terms "deviancy" and "deviant behavior." It is fairly obvious that societies and cultures differ in their definitions of what is deviant. No less pertinent is the fact that definitions of deviation, like styles and fashions, may differ over time within any one society. Yesterday's sinners, rebels, misfits, malcontents, aliens, outsiders, and even criminals may well become the cultural heroes and heroines of history, while the conformists and the nondeviants—those who fit—may be treated in history and literature as deviant. The heroes of many television and movie westerns, for example, would hardly be welcome in person in most American homes today. For these and other reasons, achieving agreement on the definition of what is deviant is extremely difficult.

In the absence of precision in the definition of deviation, let us initially suggest that deviance can be considered as behavior that represents some form of *undesirable difference*. (See Figure 1.) This difference can be viewed in various ways, depending on the nature of the normative referent. What follows here is a discussion of deviation from five different vantage points: (1) the deviant as freak; (2) the deviant as "sinful"; (3) the deviant as criminal; (4) the deviant as "sick"; and (5) the deviant as alienated. Each of these views presents a different yet related view of deviation.

Figure 1

THE NATURE OF DEVIANCE

Type of Deviant	Example of Deviation	Nature of Normative Order	Nature of Deviation
Freak	Midget, Dwarf, or Giant; Ugly, fat, or disfigured person; Mentally retarded person	Physical, physiological, and intellectual ideals	Aberrant in being
Sinful	Sinner, Apostate, Heretic, Traitor	Religious or secular ideologies	Rejects orthodoxy
Criminal	Murderer, Burglar, Embezzler, Addict	Legal codes	Unlawful in action
Sick	Psychotic, Psychoneurotic	Cultural definitions of mental health	Aberrant in action
Alienated	Bum, Tramp, Suicide, Hippie, Bohemian	Cultural ends and/or means	Rejects dominant cultural values

THE DEVIANT AS FREAK

There are those who insist that deviation be used in a precise and literal sense—as variation from the average or norm. In this view, most behavior is distributed more or less along a normal curve. This definition of deviance focuses on the exception, on the "freak" in a statistical sense. The deviant is one who is some distance from the mean, at the extreme ends of the distribution.

Such a definition adds little, however, to understanding of the etiology of deviance or its treatment. It has two basic difficulties. First, it assumes that attitudes, values, and behavior are distributed in a population in the same way as attributes such as height, weight, strength, appearance, and intellect. The terminology used for physical attributes, as tall and taller, cannot be used to describe deviance, as criminal and more criminal. In many areas significant to deviancy, behavior is more likely to be dichotomous rather than continuous. For example, behavior is seen as being either criminal law-abiding, loyal or disloyal, hallucinatory or rational. The second basic difficulty is that, even if behavior were distributed in a continuous fashion, there is no assurance that the extreme ends—the "freaks"—would necessarily be defined as undesirable. For example, in dealing with physical attributes, there are certain persons at the extremes who are defined as unfortunate—the severely retarded, the midget, the female Amazon, the obese person, etc. Others, who are also at the extremes, such as the genius, the seven-foot-tall basketball player, the 300-pound football tackle, and the overendowed female, may be positively valued. Or, again, a physical attribute such as skin color, on one end of a distribution may be positively valued, while on the other end it may be negatively valued. Both ends may be equidistant from the average, or norm. This underscores the point that it is not the extreme, the variation, or the freakishness in itself that defines social deviation; the extreme has to be evaluated by the society in a negative fashion.

THE DEVIANT AS "SINFUL"

The religious-ideological definition of deviance (and of social problems) has traditionally centered on the concepts originally derived from religious terminology: sinner, heretic, and apostate. In the religious context a sinner is one who violates the central proscriptions and ritually proper ways of thinking, being, acting. Whether this is called sinfulness, or the secular equivalent, immorality, the meaning is clear. Commandments, codes, texts, and other types of prescribed norms are the standards against which behavior is judged. The presumption is that the sinner, or the immoral person, *accepts* the doctrines and norms that he *violates*.

The heretic, unlike the sinner, is considered a deviant precisely because he *rejects* some, or all, of the dogma or prescriptions. It is a not the heretic's failure to live up to the prescriptions, but rather his conscious and willful rejection of them as binding norms or standards, that causes concern. The sinner does not reject the Word; the heretic does. Thus, the heretic is invariably considered a far more serious threat to group welfare than the sinner. This suggests that rejection of values and ideological principles is inherently more threatening to the maintenance of social solidarity than is the negative behavior of a person who accepts the norms.

The most devastating form of deviance from this point of view is apostasy, or "ideological treason." This type of deviance involves not only the rejection of the dogma and faith, but also the acceptance of another, "alien" set of principles, norms, and traditions. Every group strives tenaciously to prevent apostasy. To do otherwise courts group destruction. Seen in this light, it is little wonder that various religious groups, particularly in the past, have viewed religious intermarriage as threatening. In the past religious apostasy was subject to the same negative definitions and sanctions as the more familiar forms of secular "treason." In this sense, the ex-communist, the ex-John Bircher, and the defector can be considered deviant since they now reject norms they previously accepted. Thus, the sinner, the heretic, and the apostate, as defined in sacred and theocratic societies, now have secular equivalents in the immoralist and the traitor.

THE DEVIANT AS CRIMINAL

The legal approach to a definition of deviant behavior is embodied in the criminal law. In the legal framework, deviance worthy of concern is a violation of one or more criminal statutes and therefore a crime. Theoretically, at least, all criminal laws prohibit behaviors that are socially harmful, disruptive, or dangerous. Unfortunately, some laws may outlaw acts that are not especially detrimental to society, leading thereby to the development of disrespect for law and legal processes.

Basically there are four types of criminal acts proscribed by law. The first class, *mala in se,* involves acts thought to be intrinsically bad and with little redeeming virtue. There is widespread consensus in the society that such acts are socially intolerable. *Mala in se* crimes include all the major felony offenses from murder to theft, and from incest to treason. Offenses against a person, or theft of or damage to his property, constitute the essence of *mala in se* acts by present legal standards. Legally, the commission of any such acts, whether for the first or tenth time, stamp one as a deviant who must be deterred, punished, and, if possible, reformed.

If the legal definition were wholly restricted to *mala in se* acts, the problem of defining criminal deviance would be simple. That definition is not restricted, however. The second category of illegal acts, *mala prohibita,* is a source of confusion both to the law and to any rational understanding of deviation. *Mala prohibita* acts are not necessarily immoral, abnormal, harmful, unique, or unusual, but they are still illegal. Their illegality stems from the fact that contemporary social life requires a degree of conformity to "rules of the game." Without a degree of such conformity, chaos and anarchy might follow. The law, then, enshrines rules, demands conformity to them, and imposes penalties on those who transgress. Such offenses, usually called misdemeanors, include traffic and parking violations, the breaking of curfew restrictions, petty violations of all types, and other so-called folk crimes. Neither the law nor tradition nor the current social definition of such rules stamps violators of these rules as being necessarily deviant.

In addition to *mala in se* and *mala prohibita* offenses, a third category exists, which can be called *status offenses.* Criminal law is sometimes used as a means of enforcing specific religious and moral conceptions and values; breaking such a law is a status offence. By such laws we create the paradox of having *crimes without victims.* Among the status offences are drug addiction and homosexuality. In status offenses, the *condition* of the person constitutes deviance. Neither necessary harm to others nor willfulness or maliciousness is involved. Nevertheless, the status of homosexual, vagrant, drunk, and drug addict is defined and treated as being criminal.

Equally perplexing is a fourth type of criminal offense. This type might best be viewed as constituting *crimes with willing victims*. In these offenses, the victim may actively seek the criminal service. Examples of crimes with willing victims include abortion, prostitution, and illegal gambling. Status offenses and offenses with willing victims occur in situations in which the values and styles of life of the larger society are superimposed on segments of the society that do not accept them. Such segments, however, may be large enough to constitute subsocieties and subcultures within the larger society.

Compared with those of most other societies, the legal codes in the United States are most unusual. On the one hand, the United States is characterized by a strong tradition of lawlessness and a general disrespect for legal institutions, in part as a carry-over from the frontier tradition and as a historic reaction against autocratic institutions. On the other hand, and not wholly unrelated, various states have attempted to incorporate into criminal law specific conceptions of vice and sin. Thus, such issues as gambling, pornography, lewdness, and abortion recurrently become critical concerns and divisive questions. The definition of pornography, for example, has been the subject of several recent Supreme Court decisions. Criminal law, in becoming involved with what are essentially moral issues, often becomes identified with maintaining a "narrow" moral viewpoint. *Without* agreement on this viewpoint, laws are difficult to enforce. *With* agreement throughout the society, such laws would be unnecessary. In many countries, the relation between morality and criminality is not as troublesome and legal sanctions are not used as the means to achieve morally acceptable behavior.

THE DEVIANT AS "SICK"

Whereas in the legal framework a deviant is defined as the willful violator of various specific criminal laws, in the pathological ("sick") framework the deviant is seen as not being responsible for his conduct. Deviant behavior in this context is viewed as being partly or wholly irrational. In ordinary language, the behavior is "sick" and the deviant is more patient than perpetrator, and more confused than willful. In public usage, the words "deviant" and "crazy" have almost become synonymous.

This approach is based on a disease model of deviance. In this view, just as various human organs may become infected, diseased, or give pathological evidence of impaired functioning and capacity, so also psychic and social behavior may be unhealthy or impaired. Some conditions, such as psychoses, are considered to be intrinsically abnormal and comparable to disease. And sometimes persistent and excessive anxiety, hostility, dependency, aggression, submissiveness, gregariousness, personal isolation, low self-esteem, guilt, remorse, shame, escapism, withdrawal, phantasy life, and many other psychic states and attributes are also labeled pathological and deviant. The central focus in this view is always on internal, intrapsychic symptoms as constituting and reflecting deviance.

The view of deviance as being abnormal, or pathological, has been extremely significant in changing societal reaction from a punitive to a treatment orientation. Thus, before the alcoholic was considered "sick," when he was still defined as a "drunken bum," the idea that alcoholics could be successfully treated made little or no sense. Once the element of willfulness and personal responsibility was removed as a focal concern, the approach to treatment changed. Similarly, this pathological-medical framework has helped alter public attitudes on mental "illness," nonviolent but legally criminal sexual activity, suicide, and a wide range of modes of deviance previously considered criminal.

Despite its utility in reducing some of the stigma of the deviant inherent in public attitudes, the pathological or disease framework does not solve all problems of definition. A number of its assumptions, such as the universal pathology of some intrapsychic symptoms—for example, dissociational states—cannot be proven cross-culturally. In other words, in other societies such dissociational states are "normal." Other assumptions also seem unreasonable. For example, while many physical symptoms can be traced back to specific diseases or disabilities, much deviant conduct has no organic locus at all. While the notion of pathology may be comforting, it is also confusing. As a result, emphasis is now shifting in this view to a definition of "sickness" as unsuccessful and faulty coping behavior rather than symptomatic and pathological conduct.

THE DEVIANT AS ALIENATED

Almost diametrically opposed to the conception of deviance as an individual pathological state is the view that members of modern industrial societies have become "alienated" from the normative order. The classic views of alienation have emphasized certain recurrent themes. In large part, these views have been based on certain Marxian notions about the results of industrialization. In this view the emergence of the modern world has had certain consequences for those individuals who live in it. One consequence is a sense of powerlessness. Modern man feels powerless to determine those events around him as well as powerless to determine his own fate. He is trapped and impotent. As the limits of the "world" increase, decisions are made increasingly at levels more and more remote from him. Another consequence for the individual is that personal meaning is often lost. As traditional belief systems break down, predictability and certainty can no longer be expected in everyday life. Too, the segmentation of modern life makes man alien to himself. Since people have to play different roles in society, seldom can they be "whole" in their activities. They must constantly wear false fronts, but seldom have the opportunity to express themselves as "real" persons. Like puppets, they move as the situation requires, but they cannot anticipate their future actions because the strings are controlled by someone else, someone they do not know. In this view, people become isolated from the values and norms of the society in which they live. And gradually they become alienated.

Even without alienation, there would still be deviants, but the alienated can also be seen in a deviant context since they are estranged from the society in which they live. They are *in* the society but not *of* the society since they do not accept most of the norms the larger society uses as standards.

The theme of alienation is frequently offered as an explanation for suicide, which involves the loss of individual meaning; as a reason for the persistence of certain groupings of persons, the Bohemians, beats, and hippies; and as a reason for the growth and continued attraction of certain mass movements, which some segments of the population hope may give new meaning to their lives.

A discussion of various definitions of deviance is crucial. But this is not the complete picture. Further insight can be obtained by considering the way in which society reacts to types of deviant behavior.

SOCIETAL REACTION—STIGMATIZATION

Inherent in any discussion of human deviance is the threat—real or imagined—of the deviant to the welfare of society. Society responds to this threat in a number of ways. One reaction is fear, anxiety, disgust, and sometimes revulsion. Another response is to evoke various types of social control mechanisms to compel conformity on the part of the deviant and to deter others from pursuing similar modes of conduct. These social control devices range from mild and informal techniques, such as pleading and counseling, to highly formal ones, such as imprisonment and execution. There has been almost no limit to the ingenuity men have shown in creating and institutionalizing different techniques of control. The major consequence of all such control techniques is to stigmatize and isolate the deviant. Stigmatization is inherent in committing a person to a mental hospital, sending a drunk to the workhouse, labeling an individual a homosexual, convicting a criminal, or bringing a teenager into the juvenile court. Stigmatization shifts the focus of deviation from the act itself to the actor. Although it is the *act* of stealing, or the use of heroin, that is illegal, it is the *person* who is the thief or the drug addict. The process of stigmatization publicly defines the person as being unacceptable and reprehensible. This act of labeling is therefore critical. Once an individual has been officially stigmatized—as mentally ill, a sexual offender, a psychopath, a traitor, a mental retardate, a delinquent—the consequences are hard to undo. The "tainted" find it difficult, often impossible, to alter their conception of themselves as being unacceptable. Others find it difficult to accept those once defined as deviant. Although the stigma attached to some forms of psychiatric disorder, alcoholism, and illegitimacy may have lessened in recent years, American society still remains highly intolerant toward these and other forms of deviance.

The stigmatization of the deviant and the isolation imposed on him often force him to seek out social circles which support him but also tend to perpetuate his deviancy. The Bohemian retreats to a particular section of a large community; the addict moves to the world of "needle park"; the homosexual lives in a "gay" world; the criminal has his underworld. Instead of reintegrating such deviants, which is one intent of social control methods, the stigmatization and subsequent isolation tend to reinforce and confirm deviants as "outsiders." Thus, the paradoxical result is that formal control methods, designed to prevent and reform, often lead to the opposite effect. This may be the reason deviancy continues to flourish despite stern attempts at control. It may also account for the greater effectiveness of treatment and rehabilitation that occurs when persons define themselves as deviants, e.g. members of Alcoholics Anonymous or Synanon, than when they are stigmatized through the usual institutional channels and compelled to be "reformed."

Figure 2 illustrates the process of stigmatization, showing the responses of both the society and the deviant. In general, in his contact with others within a society, the deviant experiences predictable reactions —fear, pity, hostility, etc. In turn, others in the society withdraw their affection, which further isolates and rejects the deviant. Too, most societies develop institutionalized ways of reacting to deviance. One way is to protect the deviant. For example, types of protective institutions may be created and types of therapeutic programs developed, e.g. mental hospitals, outpatient clinics, rehabilitation programs, etc. In other instances, forms of punishment may be directed toward the deviant, e.g. expulsion, execution, imprisonment, etc. In part, the "choice" between protection and punishment seems to be based on the social definition of the degree of responsibility an individual has for his own deviance. If it is felt that the person "can't help it," there is a tendency to take a protective attitude; but if it is felt that the individual could "avoid" being a deviant, punishment is likely to follow. As a result of these various reactions, both on the interpersonal and institutional level, there is a tendency

Figure 2

THE PROCESS OF STIGMATIZATION

Type of Deviant	Interpersonal Reactions	Interpersonal Sanctions	Societal Definition of Individual's Responsibility	Institutionalized Forms of Reaction	Resultant Self-Definitions
Freak	↑ Fear, Anxiety, Tension, Pity, Sympathy, Anger, Hostility, Revulsion, Feelings of Aggression, Etc. ↓	↑ Withdrawal of Affection, Shunning, Rejection, Isolation, Ostracism, Ridicule, Laughter, Gossip, Etc. ↓	Minimal	Protection, Rehabilitation	Acceptance of low self-esteem
Sinful man			Total	Punishment, Excommunication, Banishment	Variable, ranging from acceptance of low self-esteem to appeal to higher values
Criminal Man			Total	Punishment, Imprisonment	Variable acceptance of low self-esteem
Sick Man			None	Protection Institutionalization, Therapy	Acceptance of low self-esteem
Alienated Man			Partial to Total	None, Usual integrative mechanisms	Variable, ranging from acceptance of low self-esteem to appeal to higher values

for deviants to develop negative conceptions of themselves. In a few instances, however, the deviant may orient himself to a "higher set of values and norms" which provides self-justification. In other words, the deviant may feel that he is right and the world is wrong. This is a possible outcome, but it is a difficult one to maintain in the face of greater contradictory evidence. The more usual results of the process are stigmatization and the acceptance of low self-esteem—the feeling of being "different and bad."

ISSUES IN DEVIATION

In addition to the problems of definition of deviation, there are a number of issues that are relevant to almost all types of deviation. Some of these will be discussed again toward the end of the book, but it is useful now to indicate some of them since they relate to almost all of the forms of deviation to be discussed in the following pages. These issues are the basis of discussion and conflict over social policy. We will touch on four of them here.

1. *The Nature of Causation.* There is conflict over the nature of causation of deviation. This can be identified as the issue of "hard versus soft" determinism. The "hard" determinists, which would generally include most of the social and behavioral scientists, suggest the "cause" of the deviancy is more or less out of the hands of the deviant himself. Various explanations can be given—poor genes, glands, or body structure; inadequate family, housing, or status characteristics; faulty socialization; inadequate personality characteristics; or a variety of other "causes"—and these may be offered singly or in combination. The causal factors are seen to be "outside" the individual. The "soft" determinists, among them many law enforcement officials and many religionists, often embrace the view that "free will" and personal choice are central and decisive in human motivation. Whatever the "outside" forces are which impinge on the individual, they are not seen as determinate. The "decision" to engage in deviant behavior is seen as a result of conscious choice. This issue is at the base of most discussions of personal responsibility and accountability in deviation.

2. *Effectiveness of Treatment versus Punishment.* Another issue is found in the perennial dispute over the desirability and the effectiveness of treatment versus punishment of the deviant. The discussion arising from this is not an "either-or" matter, but rather one of emphasis. Enforcement people and many in the lay public believe that the only sensible way of dealing with deviants, especially the more serious offenders, is to "lock them up and throw the keys away." Today there is, they insist, far too much coddling of the aberrant. The opposing position is

that repression and suppression, and even the most violent of social responses, have never been successful and that deviancy can no more be extirpated than can conformity. To a judge required to pass sentence, or a parole board that must decide to grant or withhold conditional freedom, this issue is far from academic.

3. *Appropriateness of Methods of Control.* More recently, another major problem has emerged, which centers on constitutional rights (civil liberties) versus societal protection and the legitimacy of enforcement methods in the suppression of deviancy. This point of view, like the others, is a matter of philosophy and ideology, but is often related to everyday specifics. Illustrations of the issues involved are numerous. Is wiretapping a legitimate law enforcement tool and, if so, under what conditions? At what point does "bugging" represent an unwarranted invasion of privacy? Is it legitimate for law enforcement personnel to dress up as females and invite attack from muggers and molesters? Does this constitute "entrapment" or is it sensible and realistic enforcement? What are the rights of a person arrested as to the proper mode of his interrogation, the right to counsel, and the offering of a confession? What about the control of firearms? Should we permit guns to be readily accessible to any and all persons who have the money to obtain them? These are extremely vexing issues and the source of considerable social conflict.

4. *Limits of Public Policy.* Finally, at the public policy level, there is considerable confusion and often violent conflict over the legalization of certain behavior. Should public lotteries and betting parlors be legalized? What ought public policy to be with regard to the newer drugs, such as the hallucinogens? Or, for that matter, should the possession and use of marihuana be made legal, as indeed was the case in the United States prior to 1937? Is abortion homicide, or is the state's concern with the matter only an unwarranted intrusion on personal rights? Are homosexual relationships, conducted in private between consenting adults, criminal and deviant or merely unfortunate and thereby immune from public action? These issues are recurrent themes in the discussion of various types of contemporary deviation.

The collection of readings that follows is designed as an introduction to the topic of deviancy. Because of the scope of material available, the readings are intended to introduce a range of problems rather than to provide an intensive view of any specific type of deviance. The nearly sixty articles in the volume deal with many facets of deviance, from riots and looting to crime, hidden delinquency, abortion, drugs, suicide, and prostitution. We have concentrated primarily on three views of deviance: the *criminal,* the *alienated,* and the *pathological.*

CRIMINAL DEVIATION

2 PROBLEMS IN THE SOCIAL CONTROL OF CRIME

The selections in this chapter deal with three broad interrelated concerns: first, the nature and extent of criminal deviation in the United States; second, the characteristics of those people whose occupation is law enforcement; and, third, the nature of criminal justice in the United States.

In the first selection, former President Lyndon Johnson reviewed for Congress the main points of the National Crime Commission Report. In this stock-taking message of January 1967, the President outlined the magnitude of the crime problem and its economic and social costs. Six major needs are stressed in the report: more emphasis on crime prevention, the improvement of the criminal justice system, more and better trained personnel, a broader range of treatment services, more research on fundamental issues, and more resources for improving the entire system of criminal justice.

In the second contribution, Professor Yale Kamisar seriously disputes the common assumption that the crime problem is increasingly serious. The main thrust of his argument is that the Cassandras of every decade since 1900 have decried the growth of crime, so that the present allegations of a crime increase are hardly novel. What *is* new is that recent Supreme Court decisions have been singled out as the primary cause of the increase. Professor Kamisar dismisses most of these charges as unwarranted and concludes that more effective crime control can only be achieved through social reforms. Although polemical in character, this article is a welcome contrast to the common position that problems of crime have never been worse.

Professor Skolnick is interested in "Why Cops Behave the Way They Do." Policemen develop a "working personality" which is derived from the two chief elements in the police role—danger and authority. Always attuned to potential violence, the "working personality" comes to be characterized by an uncommon degree of suspiciousness, an intolerance for the unusual, a conception of order which stresses regularity and predictability, a distaste for the unconventional, an unusually high degree of occupational solidarity, and an emotional and even political attachment to the status quo. At the same time, this "personality" is subjected to the severe stress occasioned by the hostility of even law-abiding people whose freedom of action the "cop" must sometimes restrain. Equally stressful is the need, as a policeman, to regulate public morality. A "victim" of his role, the policeman comes to think and feel like the minority group member he is.

The final article in this section deals with "Poverty and Criminal Justice." Patricia Wald, an active attorney in Washington, D.C., and a member of several commissions, including the President's Commission on Law Enforcement, starts with three generally typical cases and follows them through various stages in the legal and criminal procedure to determine what difference it makes to the individual in the system if he is poor. The first subject, representing 35 per cent of all arrests in the United States, is picked up and booked for drunkenness and disorderly conduct. The second, a woman, is arrested for shoplifting a ten-dollar dress in a department store. The third is a man accused of being involved in an armed robbery of a liquor store, during which the owner was seriously wounded. Wald, after tracing the possible alternatives at each procedural stage, concludes that "the poor are arrested more often, convicted more frequently, sentenced more harshly, and rehabilitated less successfully than the rest of society."

THE NATIONAL CRIME
COMMISSION REPORT

Lyndon B. Johnson

Two weeks ago [January 1967] I received the report of the National Crime Commission, which I appointed in July 1965, to make the most comprehensive study of crime in the history of our country. That report . . . gives us an extraordinary insight into the nature of crime and criminal justice in America.

It cannot be summarized in a few paragraphs, but several of its findings give us some measure of our task:

Over 7 million people each year come into contact with one of the agencies of criminal justice in America. More than 400,000 are confined on any one day in correctional institutions.

The cost of operating correctional services alone is $1 billion a year.

From the President's Message to the Congress, 90th Congress, 1st Session, House of Representatives, Document 53, January 1967.

Crime's cost to the economy is staggering. Property losses approach $3 billion a year. In many stores the cost of shoplifting and employee pilfering is as high as—in some cases, higher than—the profit margin. The economic cost of white collar crime—embezzlement, frauds, anti-trust violations and the like—dwarfs that of all crimes of violence.

A great deal of crime is never reported to the police. Probably more than twice as many aggravated assaults, burglaries, and larcenies occur, as are reported. In some communities the figure may be 10 times as high.

The incidence of crime is highest in the 15 to 21 age group. 15-year olds commit more of the serious crimes than any other age group, with 16-year olds close behind. More than fifty percent of arrests for burglaries are of youths under 18.

Most crimes of violence are committed by and against people who know each other.

Those who commit crimes of violence more commonly do so against members of their own race. Relatively few major crimes are interracial.

Six principal themes run through the Crime Commission report:

1. *Crime prevention is of paramount importance.*

Prevention of crime means equipping police forces to respond quickly to emergency calls. It means reducing crime opportunities: from theft-proof ignition systems for cars, to stricter controls on the sale of guns, from better street lights and modern alarm systems to tactical deployment of police forces in high crime areas.

But crime prevention also means elimination of the conditions which breed crime. In the words of the Crime Commission,

> there is no doubt whatever that the most significant action, by far, that can be taken against crime is action designed to eliminate slums and ghettos, to improve education, to provide jobs, to make sure that every American is given the opportunities and the freedoms that will enable him to assume his responsibilities. We will not have dealt effectively with crime until we have alleviated the conditions that stimulate it. To speak of controlling crime only in terms of the work of the police, the courts and the correctional apparatus alone, is to refuse to face the fact that widespread crime implies a widespread failure by society as a whole.

2. *The system of criminal justice must itself be just and it must have the respect and cooperation of all citizens.*

So long as perfunctory, mass-production methods prevail in many lower courts, so long as scandalous conditions exist in many jails—where, in 1965, 100,000 children were held in adult jails, and where attempts to rehabilitate are almost non-existent—we cannot achieve full public confidence in the system of criminal justice.

What is required of that system is a profound self-analysis, the willingness to change, and a massive effort to:

Improve the caliber and training of law enforcement, judicial and corrections officials.

Strengthen the capability of police to detect crimes and apprehend those who commit them.

Extend the range and quality of treatment services.

Make full use of advanced scientific methods in the courtroom, to reduce frustrating and unfair delays and to make available to the sentencing judge all necessary information about the defendant.

Provide better counsel for juveniles and for adults who cannot afford to provide their own.

Improve communication and understanding between law enforcement authorities and the urban poor.

So long as we deny police, courts and correctional agencies the resources they need to provide fair and dignified public service, large elements of our population will challenge both the institutions of justice and the values they represent.

What is required of citizens in every community in America is an understanding, not only of the critical importance of first-rate law enforcement, but also of the difficulties under which their police, judges and corrections officials labor today. If local citizens are prepared to cooperate with their own system of justice and to support it with the resources it needs to discharge its duty, those difficulties can be substantially reduced.

3. *Throughout the criminal justice system, better-trained people are desperately needed and they must be more effectively used.*

The Crime Commission found that current personnel practices in most jurisdictions often fail to attract high-caliber men and women. Requiring each new police officer to begin his career as a patrolman makes the lateral entry of better-qualified men almost impossible. There are today few means of tapping the special knowledge and skills of those brought up in slums. Today's single, rigid line of police promotion and service is inefficient. Critical shortages of specially trained policemen, probation and parole officers, teachers, caseworkers, vocational instructors, and group counselors are severely weakening the criminal justice system. . . .

4. *A far broader—and more profound—range of treatment is needed than the present correctional system provides.*

This applies to offenders of all ages, but it is especially true—and particularly important for the young. Since the generation of children about to enter teen-age is the largest in our history, we can anticipate an even sharper rise in juvenile delinquency in the decade to come—unless we make drastic changes in the effectiveness of the criminal justice system, as well as in economic and social conditions.

Many offenders, the young most of all, stand a far better chance of being rehabilitated in their home communities, than in ordinary confinement. Recently, the California Youth Authority concluded a 5-year experiment with various methods of treatment. Convicted juvenile delinquents were assigned on a random basis either to an experimental group where they were returned to their communities for intensive personal and family counseling, or to the regular institutions of correction. The findings to date are dramatically impressive:

Only 28 percent of the experimental group had their paroles revoked.

More than half—52 percent—of those confined in regular institutions later had their paroles revoked.

Falling back into crime was almost twice as great for those treated in regular institutions, as for those treated in the community. And it appears that the community treatment program costs far less than institutional confinement.

On the basis of this California experiment and its other studies, the Crime Commission concludes that local institutions related to the community, each housing as few as 50 inmates, and supported by a wide range of treatment services, should be developed throughout the country.

This will require the commitment of new resources by most communities. In a recent survey of juvenile court judges, 83 percent said that no psychologist or psychiatrist was available to their courts. A full third had neither probation officers nor social workers. Further, if many young offenders are better handled by community agencies other than juvenile courts, the potential of those agencies must be enlarged and fully tapped.

  5. *Access to better information and to deeper and broader research is vital to police and correctional agencies.*

The Crime Commission found little research being done on the fundamental issues of criminal justice—for example, on the effect of punishment in deterring crime, or on the effectiveness of various police and correctional procedures. . . .

  6. *Substantially greater resources must be devoted to improving the entire criminal justice system.*

The Federal government must not and will not try to dominate the system. It could not if it tried. Our system of law enforcement is essentially local: based upon local initiative, generated by local energies and controlled by local officials. But the Federal government must help to strengthen the system, and to encourage the kind of innovations needed to respond to the problem of crime in America.

WHEN WASN'T THERE
A "CRIME CRISIS"?

Yale Kamisar

Are We Losing the War Against Crime? Is the Public Getting a Fair Break? Has the Pendulum Swung Too Far to the Left? Do the Victims of Crime Have Some Rights, Too? Are the Courts Handcuffing the Police?

If there were a hit parade for newspaper and magazine articles, speeches and panel discussions, these topics would rank at the top of the list.

Not only are these questions being raised with increasing frequency, but they are being debated with growing fury. In 1964, one of the most famous police chiefs in the United States, the late William H. Parker of Los Angeles, protested that American police work has been "tragically weakened" through a progressive "judicial take-over." These are strong words, but Boston District Attorney Garrett Byrne, then President of the National District Attorney Association, easily topped the chief with the cry that the Supreme Court is "destroying the nation." [At] or about the same time Messrs. Byrne and Parker were pummeling the High Court, *The Reader's Digest* ran a story entitled: "Take the Handcuffs off Our Police!" Whether or not the courts are handcuffing the police has been a perennial favorite topic for debate. Now, however, an exclamation mark had replaced the question mark. Mr. Murphy's pet line is: "We [the police] are forced to fight by Marquis of Queensberry rules while the criminals are permitted to gouge and bite." As the Bergen, New Jersey, *Evening Record* recently observed, "Mr. Murphy has a smash hit on his hands. The road eats up this stuff." As the same newspaper also pointed out: "If criminals used the Marquis of Queensberry rules they wouldn't be criminals and if police were allowed to gouge and bite they would be criminals."

Not infrequently, one who dares to defend the Court, or simply to explain what the Court is doing and why, is asked which side he is on: the side of law and order—or the side of the robber, the dope peddler and the rapist. Any defense of the Court is an attack on the police. And any attack on the police is an "attack on our American system," perhaps

From Speech delivered at the 28th Conference of the Third Judicial Circuit of the United States, Atlantic City, N.J., September 9, 1965.

even part of "a world-wide campaign by Communists, Communist dupes, and sympathizers."

Today, the course of the Court is clear. Once concerned with property rights much more than with human liberty, it is now the keeper, not of the nation's property, but of its conscience. If heeding the warning that "federalism shoud not be raised to the plane of an absolute, nor the Bill of Rights reduced to a trust" and operating on the premise that to the peoples of the world "the criminal procedure sanctioned by any of our states is the procedure sanctioned by the United States" constitute lending aid and comfort to the criminal element, then the Court is guilty. As Judge Walter Schaefer of the Illinois Supreme Court pointed out in his famous Holmes Lecture of a decade ago, however, many of those safeguards of criminal procedure which we now take for granted came surprisingly late. Whether or not a state had to appoint counsel for an indigent defendant was a question which did not confront the Court until 1932 and it held then that counsel had to be provided only when the defendant was facing a possible death sentence. Whether or not the state could convict a defendant on the basis of a coerced confession was an issue first presented to the Court in 1936 and all the Court was asked to do then was ban confessions extracted by brutal beatings. What was it like in 1910 and 1920 and 1930 when the effectuation and implementation of criminal procedural safeguards were pretty much left to the states themselves? What was it like in the days when, as Dean Erwin Griswold of the Harvard Law School recently pointed out, "some things that were rather clearly there" (in the Constitution) had not yet "been given the attention and effect which they should have if our Constitution is to be a truly meaningful document." Or, if you prefer, what was it like in the "good old days" before the U. S. Supreme Court began to mess up things?

In 1910, . . . the President of the California Bar Association underscored the need for an "adjustment" in our criminal procedures "to meet the expanding social necessity." "Many of the difficulties," he continued, "are due to an exaggerated respect for the individual as the isolated center of the universe. There is too much admiration for our traditional system and too little respect for the needs of society." . . . He proposed (1) that a suspect be interrogated by a magistrate and, if he refused to answer the inquiries, that the state be permitted to comment on this fact at the trial; and (2) that the requirement of a unanimous verdict of guilty be reduced to three-fourths, "except possibly in cases where infliction of the death penalty is involved." This, he pointed out, would still "give the defendant three-fourths of the show," but now, at least, "the public" would have one-fourth.

The following year, 1911, in a hard-hitting *Atlantic Monthly* article entitled "Coddling the Criminal," a New York prosecutor . . . charged that "the appalling amount of crime in the United States compared with other civilized countries is due to the fact that it is generally known that the punishment for crime in America is uncertain and far from severe. . . . According to [the prosecutor], the two law enforcement obstacles which had to be cleared were the protection against double jeopardy and the privilege against self-incrimination. . . .

"The anarchists and criminals of England who are being driven out of that country will find an admirable refuge in the United States and plenty of companions and sympathizers. In America, anarchists, yeggmen, safe-blowers, and members of the Black Hand fraternity already enjoy American hospitality."

So contended the distinguished ex-president of Cornell University, Andrew D. White, that same year, 1911. He noted that 1911 had seen more than a 10 percent increase in homicide over 1910 and that "the number of capital crimes in our country has for many years steadily increased and is now increasing at a greater rate than our population." As evidence of the alarming proportions of the American crime problem he cited the fact that although London's population was two million larger than New York's, there were ten times more murders in New York. How was this possible? According to Mr. White, it stemmed largely from the utilization by the modern criminal, "and, above all, the criminal with money," of procedural safeguards "devised in the Middle Ages to protect the weak against the strong or the serf against the feudal lord."

Eight years later, Hugo Pam, the president of the Institute of Criminal Law and Criminology, also addressed himself to the "crime problem," one which had been greatly aggravated by "the advent of the automobile." As he viewed the situation in 1919, "the boldness of the crimes and the apparent helplessness of the law have embittered the public to the extent that any advance in treatment of criminals save punishment is looked upon with disfavor." Law enforcement officials, he noted, "have repeatedly charged that in the main these serious crimes have been committed by people on probation or parole." It followed, of course, that there was a strong movement afoot to curtail or completely repeal these provisions.

The following year, 1920, and again in 1922, Edwin W. Sims, the first head of the newly established Chicago Crime Commission, added his loud voice to the insistent demand on the part of the public "for action" that will reduce crime. He had a new set of figures: "During 1919 there were more murders in Chicago (with a population of three million) than in the entire British Isles (with a population of forty million)." Moreover, the prosecution had obtained only forty-four convictions as against

336 murders. The situation called for strong words and Mr. Sims was equal to the occasion:

> We have kept on providing criminals with flowers, libraries, athletics, hot and cold running water, and probation and parole. The tender solicitude for the welfare of criminals publicly expressed by social workers conveys to 10,000 criminals plying their vocation in Chicago the mistaken impression that the community is more interested in them than it is in their victims. It would be more helpful if this sympathy was directed to a consideration of the feelings of the widows and children of policemen who are murdered in the discharge of their duty, or to the survivors of those who are victimized by the outlaws.
>
> So much soft-hearted sympathy has been mixed with the application of lawful force that it has become so feeble as to practically lose its effect upon the habitual criminal. There has been too much mollycoddling of the criminal population. . . . It is time for plain speaking. Murderers are turned loose. They have no fear of police. They sneer at the law. It is not a time for promises. It is a time for action. The turning point has come. Decency wins or anarchy triumphs. There is no middle course.

If Edwin Sims were still in fine voice today, he would be much in demand. At home and on the road, he would probably even outdraw Messrs. Byrne, Murphy and Parker. About all Sims would have to do would be to strike "social workers," insert "Supreme Court," and maybe add a paragraph or two about recent Supreme Court decisions. But his era, I repeat, was 1920.

The 1920's were troubled times. In speaking of the need for a National Crime Commission, *The New Republic* of August 26, 1925, declared: "It is no exaggeration to assert that the administration of criminal justice has broken down in the United States and that in this respect American state governments are failing to perform the most primitive and most essential function which society imposes on government." At about the same time, the great criminologist Edwin H. Sutherland reported: "Capital punishment has been restored in four states since the war, and in many places there is a strenuous demand for the whipping post. In almost every magazine we may expect an occasional article on 'the rising tide of crime' or 'cross country crime' or on rallying against crime. . . . Crime commissions are recommending increased severity and certainty of punishment."

Despite an angry realization of the situation in the troubled twenties, the tide of crime was not stemmed. By 1933, the public had become so alarmed at an apparent increase in professional criminality that a U. S. Senate investigating committee, chaired by Royal S. Copeland of New

York, scoured the country for information which could lead to a national legislative solution. According to Chairman Copeland's figuring, from 1850 to 1930 the rate of crime had increased fourfold. "Even disregarding prohibition and many other conditions, taking any other year in a recent period of time will indicate the tremendous increase in the proportion of prisoners to the population." He promised that witnesses would show that the tide of crime was running so strong that "the cost of crime in the United States is about $13,000,000,000. When we consider that the National income is only $50,000,000,000, it means that one dollar out of every four of the peoples' money is spent because of crime and for its suppression and its control." "It is certain," he told a group of New York police officers, that "the rats of the underworld have found ways to crawl through the meshes of the law and to carry on their slimy business in spite of your ardent desires to stop them."

The Detroit hearings brought out that the murder rate in the United States was nine times higher than in England and in Wales, "where they have basically the same Anglo-Saxon institutions," and even twice as high as Italy's, "the home of the Mafia, the 'Black Hand.' " In New York, a witness solemnly declared that "the crime situation in this country is so serious that it approaches a major crisis in our history, a crisis which will determine whether the nation is to belong to normal citizens or whether it is to be surrendered completely to gangster rule." In Chicago, drawing upon his twenty years of experience as a lawyer, prosecutor and municipal judge, a witness concluded that "there is entirely too much worry, consideration and too many safeguards about the criminal's constitutional rights"; . . . "the public should have a break, the people should be put in the saddle." He recommended for the Senate Committee's consideration Illinois's new "reputation vagrancy law, which provides that all persons who are reputed to habitually violate the criminal laws and who are reputed to carry concealed weapons are vagrants." "Under this law," he reported, "we have harassed and convicted . . . numerous mad dogs of the west side." (The following year, the Illinois Supreme Court struck down the law as unconstitutional.)

Senator Copeland told assembled witnesses of his desire for "a frank expression of opinion, no matter how critical you may be of existing institutions," assuring them that "the public sentiment is such that you will be applauded for any information you give, no matter how bitter your criticism may be of conditions as they exist." Most of the witnesses were equal to the challenge.

A Major Homer Schockley urged that "constitutional and statutory guaranties, applicable to the average citizen, be suspended by special court procedure for the person who is known to be an habitual criminal . . . or who habitually consorts with criminals, to the end that the burden of proof of innocence of any fairly well substantiated charge be squarely placed on the accused; that he be tried without the benefit of a jury; and that, if convicted, all of his property and wealth be confiscated except such portion as the accused can prove were honestly gained by honest effort." The presumption of innocence is "fair enough" for the normal person, but not "for the dirty rat whom everybody knows to be an incurably habitual crook."

Citing the recent experience in Toronto, where whippings were said to have broken a wave of jewelry store stick-ups, another witness, New York Police Commissioner Edward Mulrooney, came out for 30 or 40 lashes to be applied at the time the criminal entered prison, others every six months thereafter. Whipping kidnappers, maintained the Commissioner, "is no more brutal than what they meted out to the victim." Noting that it is by way of fine roads built with the aid of the federal government "that many criminals escape and stick up banks," an Indiana superior court judge urged the use of federal troops to patrol these roads.

Lewis E. Lawes, the famous warden of Sing Sing prison exclaimed: "Strip our hysterical reaction in the present emergency and what have you? A confession that our agencies are not keeping step with crime, are falling short of their mark. Yesterday it was robbery, today it is kidnapping, tomorrow it will be something else. With every new crime racket, will come a new hysteria." After delivering these refreshingly sober remarks, Warden Lawes proceeded to disregard his own advice:

> I think I am a liberal, but at the same time, in case of war I would fight for the country, and this is war. I believe if they do not have some form of martial law against this particular group (racketeers and kidnappers) that there will come in . . . lynch law and from lynch law they will have the martial law. . . . It seems to me that this is a war to be stamped out quickly and could be stopped in 60 days if all the authorities get together honestly and let the public know exactly what they are doing. . . . If I were Mussolini I could do it in 30 days. I said 60 days. I mean with governmental influence.

A New Jersey police officer who followed Warden Lawes to the witness stand thought "he struck the keynote when he stated that there was a war, that we were fighting a war and that we needed a Mussolini to pull us out of it." He continued: "I think we should take the bull by the horns and forget our American principles of freedom and have Congress pass legislation registering every person in the United States, just as we did during the war." Many witnesses came out for universal fingerprinting. As the representative of the International Association of Chiefs of Police saw it, "God put [prints] on man's fingers for some reason, and

I believe that it must have been intended for nothing else than to identify one man from another."

Even renowned defense attorney Sam Liebowitz, honored "to be called upon to speak from the viewpoint of the criminal lawyer," seemed to get into the swing of things. He proposed a "national vagrancy law," whereby if a well-dressed crook "cannot give a good account of himself" to a police officer who spots him on the street or in his Cadillac "you take him into the station house and question him, and then take him before a judge. The judge says, 'Prove you are earning an honest living.' " "No honest man need rebel against a thing like that," contended the great criminal lawyer. "If you are earning an honest dollar, you can show what you are doing. . . . It is the crook that sets up the cry of the Constitution, and the protection of the Constitution, when he is in trouble."

Detroit prosecutor Harry Toy agreed that "a national vagrancy act— we call it a public enemy act—is a wonderful thing." Mr. Liebowitz had assumed that a national vagrancy act would require an amendment to the privilege against self-incrimination, but the Detroit prosecutor insisted that such an act "could be framed under the persent Federal Constitution as it now stands." (His own state's "public enemy" law was held unconstitutional by the Michigan Supreme Court a few months later. The following year New Jersey made it a felony, punishable by 20 years' imprisonment, to be a "gangster"; the U. S. Supreme Court struck the law down in 1939 on the grounds of vagueness and uncertainty.)

Chicago Municipal Court Judge Thomas Green plumped for an amendment to the Fourth Amendment, permitting searches of persons "reputed" to be criminals and to be carrying firearms. The reason the framers of the Constitution stressed personal liberty, he explained, was that "there were no gangsters" then. "At that time they did not have these corrupt syndicated and organized rings." "I think personal liberty is a wonderful thing," he hastened to add, "but today the man who takes advantage of personal liberty is the gangster, the gunman, the kidnapper." His colleague, Judge Frank Padden, saw no objection to convicting a man on the basis of evidence taken from his office without a search warrant or "probable cause"; "I do not believe a man's office is like his home."

Buffalo Police Chief Roche, the delegate from the International Association, reported that his police department "is doing as much to save souls as some of the clergy," but unfortunately "a lot of the degenerates" with whom American youth was associating were "protected beyond iron doors and barred windows, according to the interpretation by some shyster lawyers of our Constitution." He complained to the Senate Committee that "even if you beg a police officer to go in [a house of prostitu-

tion] and save your daughter, he will have to say, 'Go get a warrant.' "
(The U. S. Supreme Court did not construe the Federal Constitution as
requiring state courts to exclude illegally seized evidence until 1961 and
in the 1930's and 40's most state courts, including New York's, permitted the use of such evidence.)

Speaking for the International Association, Chief Roche testified that
"we do not believe that it was the intention of the framers of the Constitution to have the 'unreasonable search and seizure' clause apply to
hangouts for criminals, disorderly houses, gambling dens, and places
where the law is being violated, but merely to guard the sanctity of the
home of the decent, law-abiding citizen." He did not clarify how the
police could tell in advance whether the house they were searching belonged to law breakers or "decent" citizens.

The parole and probation systems took a severe pounding. One police
chief claimed it was "demoralizing" law enforcement and pinned it down
as "the cause of the crime wave in the country." Another chief called it
"the worst discouragement the policeman has today" and urged that
parole boards be staffed by "policemen or retired policemen with 10
years' service, men who have had to contend with these criminals and
know their records." A report of the International Association of Chiefs
of Police charged that "many politicians and lawyers who seek the release of criminals shield themselves and their purpose by the secrecy of
the parole office."

Virtually every procedural safeguard caught heavy fire. One witness
called "the right to the 'shield of silence' " (the privilege against self-
incrimination) "the greatest stumbling block to justice and incentive to
crime in all common-law countries." Another maintained that "the present provisions against self-incrimination were intended to protect the
citizen against the medieval methods of torture; and they have become
obsolete in modern life." A report of the International Association of
Chiefs of police listed as "contributing factors to our serious crime problem . . . the resort to injunctions, writs of habeas corpus, changes of
venue, etc., all with a view of embarrassing and retarding the administration of justice." One witness called the Great Writ "the writ of 'hocus-
pocus.' " The "founders of the Republic," it was argued, "never intended
that habeas corpus and bail should be granted to a thug or serious thief."
Judge William Skillman of Detroit Criminal Court maintained that permitting the State to appeal an acquittal "would do much to insure to
society, represented by the State, a fair break in the trial of a lawsuit"
because "the so-called 'former jeopardy clause' . . . has many times
been used as a shield by weak or timid or even a venal judge." A great
many witnesses, including three federal district judges, favored changing
the requirement of a unanimous verdict of guilty in criminal cases to

10-2, 9-3, or 8-4. Captain A. B. Moore of the New York state police proposed that an "expert adviser" or legally trained "technician" sit with and retire to the jury room with the jury "to advise them [on] those technicalities that had been implanted in their minds by a very clever attorney."

So much for the 1910's and 20's and 30's, the so-called golden era when the U. S. Supreme Court kept "hands off" local law enforcement.

When [the late] Chief Parker warns us in our own time that "the police . . . are limited like the Yalu River boundary, and the result of it is that they are losing the war just like we lost the war in Korea," I wonder: *When, if ever, weren't* we losing the war against crime? *When, if ever, weren't* law enforcement personnel impatient with the checks and balances of our system? *When, if ever, didn't* they feel unduly "limited"? *When, if ever, will* they realize that our citizens are free *because* the police are "limited"?

When an official of the National District Attorneys' Association insists in our time: "This country can no longer afford a 'civil rights binge' that so restricts law enforcement agencies that they become ineffective and organized crime flourishes," I wonder: *When, if ever,* in the opinion of law enforcement personnel, *could* this country afford a "civil rights binge"? When, if ever, *wasn't* there a "crime crisis"? When, if ever, *weren't* there proclamations of great emergencies and announcements of disbelief in the capacities of ordinary institutions and regular procedures to cope with them? . . .

I venture to say that today too many law enforcement spokesmen . . . are using different crimes statistics and . . . concentrating on a different target—the U. S. Supreme Court rather than the state courts, parole boards, social workers and "shyster lawyers"—but they are reacting the same way they reacted in past generations. They are reconciling the delusion of our omnipotence with the experience of limited power to cope with the "crime crisis" by explaining failure in terms of incompetence, even betrayal. . . .

As the Wickersham Report of 1931 disclosed, the prevailing "interrogation methods of the 1920's and 30's included the application of the rubber hose to the back or the pit of the stomach, kicks in the shins and blows struck with a telephone book on the side of the victim's head. These techniques did not stem the tide of crime. Nor did the use of illegally seized evidence, which most state courts permitted as late as the 1940's and 50's. Nor, while they lasted, did the "public enemy" laws, or the many criminal registration ordinances stimulated by the Copeland Hearings.

If history does anything it supports David Acheson, who, when U. S. Attorney for the District of Columbia (the jurisdiction which has borne the brunt of "restrictive" court rules), dismissed the suggestion that "the crime rate will go away if we give back to law-enforcement agencies 'power taken from them by federal court decisions' " with the assurance that "the war against crime does not lie on this front. Prosecution procedure has, at most, only the most remote causal connection with crime. Changes in court decisions and prosecution procedure would have about the same effect on the crime rate as an aspirin would have on a tumor of the brain."

Unfortunately this speech was not given the publicity it deserved. Nor were the refreshingly cool, thoughtful remarks of the . . . [then Deputy] Attorney General, Ramsey Clark, who . . . pointed out:

> Court rules do not cause crime. People do not commit crime because they know they cannot be questioned by police before presentment, or even because they feel they will not be convicted. We as a people commit crimes because we are capable of committing crimes. We choose to commit crimes. . . . In the long run, only the elimination of the causes of crime can make a significant and lasting difference in the incidence of crime. But the reduction of the causes of crime is a slow and arduous process and the need to protect persons and property is immediate. The present need for greater protection . . . can be filled not by . . . court rulings affirming convictions based on confessions secured after hours of questioning, or evidence seized in searches made without warrants. The immediate need can be filled by more and better police protection.

Chief Parker . . . expressed the hope that in searching for answers to our crime problem the new National Crime Commission "not overlook the influencing factor of the judicial revolution." The greater danger is that too much attention will be paid to this "revolution."

Critics of the courts are well represented, but not a single criminologist or sociologist or psychologist sits on the nineteen-man commission. These are conspicuous omissions for a group asked "to be daring and creative and revolutionary" in its recommendations. These are incredible omissions for those of us who share the views of the . . . Attorney General that "the first, the most pervasive and the most difficult" front in the war on crime "is the battle against the causes of crime: poverty, ignorance, unequal opportunity, social tension, moral erosion." . . .

Probably the most eminently qualified member of the President's commission is Columbia Law School's Herbert Wechsler, the Director of the American Institute and chief draftsman of the recently completed Model Penal Cade, a monumental work which has already had a tremendous impact throughout the nation. The commission would have gotten off to a more auspicious start if, instead of listening to a criticism of recent court decisions, its members had read (or reread) what Mr. Wechsler, then a young, obscure assistant law professor, once said of other crime conferences of another era of "crisis" (those called by the U. S. Attorney General and other states, including New York, in 1934-36) :

> The most satisfactory method of crime prevention is the solution of the basic problems of government—the production and distribution of external goods, education and recreation. . . . That the problems of social reform present dilemmas of their own, I do not pretend to deny. I argue only that one can say for social reform as a means to the end of improved crime control what can also be said for better personnel but cannot be said for drastic tightening of the processes of the criminal law—that even if the end should not be achieved, the means is desirable for its own sake. I argue, finally, that this should have been the primary message of the crime conferences and that this is the story which the newspapers should have carried.

WHY COPS BEHAVE
THE WAY THEY DO
Jerome Skolnick

A recurrent theme is the effect of a man's work on his outlook on the world. Doctors, janitors, lawyers and industrial workers develop distinctive ways of perceiving and responding to their environment. Here I will concentrate on analyzing certain outstanding elements in the police milieu: danger, authority and efficiency, as they combine to generate distinctive cognitive and behavioral responses in police—a "working personality." There are distinctive recognizable tendencies in police as an occupational grouping. Some of these may be found in other occupations sharing similar problems. So far as exposure to danger is concerned, the policeman may be likened to the soldier. His problems as an authority bear a certain similarity to those of the schoolteacher, and the pressures he feels to prove himself efficient are not unlike those felt by the industrial worker. The combination of these elements, however, is unique to the policeman. Thus, the police, as a result of their social situation, tend to develop ways of looking at the world distinctive to themselves, cognitive lenses through which to see situations and events.

The policeman's "working personality" is most highly developed in his constabulary role of the man on the beat. For analytical purposes

From *New York World Journal Tribune,* October 23, 1966, pp. 12-14. Reprinted by permission.

that role is sometimes regarded as an enforcement speciality, but in this general discussion of policemen as they comport themselves while working, the uniformed "cop" is seen as the foundation for the policeman's working personality. The police, unlike the military, draw no caste distinction in socialization. Every officer of rank must serve an apprenticeship as a patrolman. This feature of police organization means that the constabulary role is the primary one for all police officers, and that whatever the special requirements of roles in enforcement specialities, they are carried out with a common background of constabulary experience.

The process by which this "personality" is developed may be summarized: the policeman's role contains two principal variables, danger and authority, which should be interpreted in the light of a "constant" pressure to appear efficient. The element of danger seems to make the policeman especially attentive to signs indicating a potential for violence and lawbreaking. As a result, the policeman is generally a "suspicious" person. Furthermore, the character of the policeman's work makes him less desirable as a friend, since norms of friendship implicate others in his work. Accordingly, the element of danger isolates the policeman socially from that segment of the citizenry which he regards as symbolically dangerous and also from the conventional citizenry with whom he identifies.

The element of authority reinforces the element of danger in isolating the policeman. Typically, the policeman is required to enforce laws representing puritanical morality, such as those prohibiting drunkenness, and also laws regulating the flow of public activity, such as traffic laws. In these situations the policeman directs the citizenry, whose typical response denies recognition of his authority, and stresses his obligation to respond to danger. The kind of man who responds well to danger, however, does not normally subscribe to codes of puritanical morality. As a result, the policeman is unusually liable to the charge of hypocrisy. That the whole civilian world is an audience for the policeman further promotes police isolation and, in consequence, solidarity. Finally, danger undermines the judicious use of authority.

In attempting to understand the policeman's view of the world, it is useful to raise a more general question: What are the conditions under which police, as authorities, may be threatened? To answer this, we must look at the situation of the policeman in the community. One attribute of many characterizing the policeman's role stands out: the policeman is required to respond to assaults against persons and property. When a radio call reports an armed robbery and gives a description of the man involved, every policeman, regardless of assignment, is responsible for the criminal's apprehension. The *raison d'être* of the policeman and the criminal law, the underlying collectively held moral sentiments which justify penal sanctions, arises ultimately and most clearly from the threat of violence and the possibility of danger to the community. Police who "lobby" for severe narcotics laws, for instance, justify their positions on grounds that the addict is a harbinger of danger since, it is maintained, he requires $100 a day to support his habit, and he must steal to get it. Although the addict is not usually a violent criminal, criminal penalties for addiction are supported on grounds that he may become one.

The policeman, because his work requires him to be occupied continually with potential violence, develops a perceptual shorthand to identify certain kinds of people as symbolic assailants, that is, as persons who use gesture, language and attire that the policeman has come to recognize as a prelude to violence. This does not mean that violence by the symbolic assailant is necessarily predictable. On the contrary, the policeman responds to the vague indication of danger suggested by appearance. . . . Like the animals of the experimental psychologist, the policeman finds the threat of random damage more compelling than a predetermined and inevitable punishment. . . .

However, the policeman may well, as a personality, enjoy the possibility of danger, especially its associated excitement, even though he may at the same time be fearful of it. Such "inconsistency" is easily understood. Freud has by now made it an axiom of personality theory that logical and emotional consistency are by no means the same phenomenon.

However complex the motives aroused by the element of danger, its consequences for sustaining police culture are unambiguous. This element requires him, like the combat soldier, the European Jew, the South African (white or black), to live in a world straining toward duality, and suggesting danger when "they" are perceived. Consequently, it is in the nature of the policeman's situation that his conception of order emphasize regularity and predictability. It is, therefore, a conception shaped by persistent *suspicion*. The English "copper," often portrayed as a courteous, easygoing, rather jolly sort of chap, on the one hand, or as a devil-may-care adventurer, on the other, is differently described by Colin MacInnes, the British suspense writer:

"The true copper's dominant characteristic, if the truth be known, is neither those daring nor vicious qualities that are sometimes attributed to him by friend or enemy, but an ingrained conservatism, an almost desperate love of the conventional. It is untidiness, disorder, the unusual, that a copper disapproves of most of all: far more, even than of crime which is merely a professional matter. Hence his profound dislike of people loitering in streets, dressing extravagantly, speaking with exotic

accents, being strange, weak, eccentric, or simply any rare minority—
of their doing, in fact, anything that cannot be safely predicted."

Policemen are indeed specifically *trained* to be suspicious, to perceive
events or changes in the physical surroundings that indicate the occurrence or probability of disorder. A former student who worked as a
patrolman in a suburban New York police department describes this
aspect of the policeman's assessment of the unusual:

"The time spent cruising one's sector or walking one's beat is not
wasted time, though it can become quite routine. During this time, the
most important thing for the officer to do is notice the *normal*. He must
come to know the people in his area, their habits, their automobiles and
their friends. He must learn what time the various shops close, how
much money is kept on hand on different nights, what lights are usually
left on, which houses are vacant . . . only then can he decide what
persons or cars under what circumstances warrant the appellation 'suspicious.' "

The patrolman in one community I studied closely, and probably in
most communities, has come to identify the black man with danger.
James Baldwin vividly expresses the isolation of the ghetto policeman:

". . . The only way to police a ghetto is to be oppressive. None of the
police commissioner's men, even with the best will in the world, have any
way of understanding the lives led by the people they swagger about in
twos and three controlling. Their very presence is an insult, and it would
be, even if they spent their entire day feeding gumdrops to children. They
represent the force of the white world, and that world's criminal profit
and ease, to keep the black man corraled up here, in his place. The
badge, the gun in the holster and the swinging club make vivid what will
happen should his rebellion become overt. . . .

"It is hard, on the other hand, to blame the policeman, blank, good-
natured, thoughtless and insuperably innocent, for being such a perfect
representative of the people he serves. He, too, believes in good intentions and is astounded and offended when they are not taken for the
deed. He has never, himself, done anything for which to be hated—
which of us has?—and yet he is facing, daily and nightly, people who
would gladly see him dead, and he knows it. There is no way for him
not to know it: there are few things under heaven more unnerving than
the silent, accumulating contempt and hatred of a people. He moves
through Harlem, therefore, like an occupying soldier in a bitterly hostile
country; which is precisely what and where he is, and is the reason he
walks in twos and threes."

While Baldwin's observations on police-Negro relations cannot be dis-
puted seriously, there is greater social distance between police and "civil-

ians" in general regardless of their color than Baldwin considers. . . .

. . . Policemen whom one knows will often express their sense of isolation from the public as a whole, not just from those who fail to share their color. The police I studied were asked, for example, to rank the most serious problems police have. The category most frequently selected was not racial problems, but some form of public relations: lack of respect for the police, lack of co-operation in enforcement of law, lack of understanding of the requirements of police work. One respondent answered:

"As a policeman my most serious problem is impressing on the general public just how difficult and necessary police service is to all. There seems to be an attitude of 'law is important, but it applies to my neighbor—not to me.' "

One policeman related the following incident:

"Several months after I joined the force, my wife and I used to be socially active with a crowd of young people, mostly married, who gave a lot of parties where there was drinking and dancing, and we enjoyed it. I've never forgotten, though, an incident that happened on one Fourth of July party. Everybody had been drinking, there was a lot of talking, people were feeling boisterous, and some kid there—he must have been 20 or 22—threw a firecracker that hit my wife in the leg and burned her. I didn't know exactly what to do—punch the guy in the nose, bawl him out, just forget it. Anyway, I couldn't let it pass, so I walked over to him and told him he ought to be careful. He began to rise up at me, and when he did, somebody yelled, "Better watch out, he's a cop." I saw everybody standing there, and I could feel they were all against me and for the kid, even though he had thrown the firecracker at my wife. I went over to the host and said it was probably better if my wife and I left because a fight would put a damper on the party. Actually, I'd hoped he would ask the kid to leave, since the kid had thrown the firecracker. But he didn't, so we left. After that incident, my wife and I stopped going around with that crowd, and decided that if we were going to go to parties where there was to be drinking and boisterousness, we weren't going to be the only police people there."

All occupational groups share a measure of inclusiveness and identification. People are brought together simply by doing the same work and having similar career and salary problems. As several writers have noted, however, police show an unusually high degree of occupational solidarity. It is true that the police have a common employer and wear a uniform at work, but so do doctors, milkmen and bus drivers. Yet it is doubtful that these workers have so closeknit an occupation or so similar an outlook on the world as do police. Set apart from the conventional world, the policeman experiences an exceptionally strong tendency to find his social identity within his occupational milieu.

When considering how authority influences rejection, the policeman typically singles out his responsibility for enforcement of traffic violations. Resentment, even hostility, is generated in those receiving citations, in part because such contact is often the only one citizens have with police, and in part because municipal administrations and courts have been known to utilize police authority primarily to meet budgetary requirements rather than those of public order. When a municipality engages in "speed trapping" by changing limits so quickly that drivers cannot realistically slow down to the prescribed speed or, while keeping the limits reasonable, charging high fines primarily to generate revenue, the policeman carries the brunt of public resentment.

While traffic patrol plays a major role in separating the policeman from the respectable community, other of his tasks also have this consequence. Traffic patrol is only the most obvious illustration of the policeman's general responsibility for maintaining public order, which also includes keeping order at public accidents, sporting events and political rallies. These activities share one feature: the policeman is called upon to *direct* ordinary citizens, and therefore, to restrain their freedom of action. Resenting the restraint, the average citizen in such a situation typically thinks something along the lines of "He is supposed to catch crooks; why is he bothering me?" Thus, the citizen stresses the "dangerous" portion of the policeman's role while belittling his authority.

Closely related to the policeman's authority-based problems as *director* of the citizenry are difficulties associated with his injunction to *regulate public morality*. For instance, the policeman is obliged to investigate "lovers' lanes," and to enforce laws pertaining to gambling, prostitution and drunkenness. His responsibility in these matters allows him much administrative discretion, since he may not actually enforce the law by making an arrest, but instead merely interfere with continuation of the objectionable activity. Thus, he may put the drunk in a taxi, tell the lovers to remove themselves from the back seat and advise a man soliciting a prostitute to leave the area. But the policeman is apt to cause resentment because of the suspicion that policemen do not themselves strictly conform to the moral norms they are enforcing. Thus, the policeman, faced with enforcing a law against fornication, drunkenness or gambling, is easily liable to a charge of hypocrisy.

The policeman, as a result of the unique combination of the elements of danger and authority, experiences a special predicament. It is difficult to develop qualities enabling him to stand up to danger, and to conform to standards of puritanical morality. The element of danger demands that the policeman be able to carry out efforts that are in their nature overtly masculine. Police work, like soldiering, requires an exceptional caliber of physical fitness, agility, toughness and the like. The man who ranks high on these masculine characteristics is, again like the soldier, not usually disposed to be puritanical about sex, drinking and gambling.

On the basis of observations, policemen do not subscribe to moralistic standards for conduct. For example, the morals squad of the police department, when questioned, was unanimously against the statutory rape age limit, on grounds that as late teenagers they themselves might not have refused an attractive offer from a 17-year-old girl. Neither, from observations, are policemen by any means total abstainers from the use of alcoholic beverages. The policeman who is arresting a drunk has probably been drunk himself; he knows it and the drunk knows it.

Finally, to round out the sketch, policemen are notably conservative, emotionally and politically. If the element of danger in the policeman's role tends to make the policeman suspicious, and therefore emotionally attached to the staus quo, a similar consequence may be attributed to the element of authority. The fact that a man is engaged in enforcing a set of rules implies that he also becomes implicated in *affirming* them. Labor disputes provide the commonest example of conditions inclining the policeman to support the status quo. In these situations, the police are necessarily pushed on the side of the defense of property. Their responsibilities thus lead them to see the striking and sometimes angry workers as their enemy and, therefore, to be cool, if not antagonistic, toward the whole conception of labor militancy. If a policeman did not believe in the system of laws he was responsible for enforcing, he would have to go on living in a state of conflicting cognitions, a condition which a number of social psychologists agree is painful.

This hypothetical issue of not believing in the laws they are enforcing simply does not arise for most policemen. In the course of the research, however, there was one example. A Negro civil rights advocate (member of CORE) became a policeman with the conviction that by so doing he would be aiding the cause of impartial administration of law for Negroes. For him, however, this outside rationale was not enough to sustain him in administering a system of laws that depends for its impartiality upon a reasonable measure of social and economic equality among the citizenry. Because this recruit identified so much with the Negro community as to be unable to meet the enforcement requirements of the police department, his efficiency was impaired, and he resigned in his rookie year.

Police are understandably reluctant to appear to be anything but impartial politically. The police are forbidden from publicly campaigning for political candidates. The London police are similarly prohibited, and before 1887 were not allowed to vote in parliamentary elections, or in local ones until 1893. It was not surprising that one chief of police forbade questions on the questionnaire that would have measured political attitudes. One policeman, however, explained the chief's refusal on grounds that "a couple of jerks here would probably cut up, and come out looking like Commies." . . .

Writing about the New York police force, Thomas R. Brooks suggests a similar interpretation. He writes:

"Cops are conventional people. . . . All a cop can swing in a milieu of marijuana smokers, interracial dates and homosexuals is the nightstick. . . ."

POVERTY AND
CRIMINAL JUSTICE
Patricia M. Wald

The great majority of those accused of crime in this country are poor. The system of criminal justice under which they are judged is rooted in certain ideals: that arrest can only be for cause; that defendants, presumed innocent until shown guilty, are entitled to pretrial freedom to aid in their own defense; that a guilty plea should be voluntary; that the allegations of wrongdoing must be submitted to the truthfinding light of the adversary system; that the sentence should be based on the gravity of the crime, yet tempered by the rehabilitative potential of the defendant; that, after rehabilitation, the offender should be accepted back into the community.

To the extent, however, that the system works less fairly for the poor man than for the affluent, the ideal is flawed.

How *does* the system work for the poor?

On almost any night in any metropolitan jurisdiction in the United States a wide range of arrests is made: petty offenses, serious misdemeanors, felonies, juvenile misconduct. These are typical:

Defendant A is spotted by a foot patrol officer in the skid row district of town, weaving along the street. When the officer approaches him, the man begins muttering incoherently and shrugs off the officer's inquiries. When the officer seizes his arm, A breaks the hold violently, curses the

From The Task Force Report, *The Courts,* The President's Commission on Law Enforcement and the Administration of Justice, 1967, Appendix C, pp. 139-51.

officer and the police. The patrolman puts in a call for a squad car, and the man is taken to the precinct station where he is booked on a double charge of drunk and disorderly [conduct].

Defendant B, a woman, is apprehended for shoplifting a $10 dress in a downtown department store. A store detective who has been watching stops her near the door and finds the dress under her skirt. He calls a police officer who takes her to the precinct for booking on a charge of petty larceny.

Defendant C is charged with holding up a liquor store and seriously wounding the proprietor while making his getaway. His arrest follows an informer's tip and the victim's identification of his mug shot. The mug shot is a leftover from an "investigative arrest" two years before. . . .

All of these defendants are poor. At every stage of the criminal process they will face the cumulative handicaps of poverty.

IN THE STATIONHOUSE

Defendant A's belt is removed to balk any attempts at suicide, and he is put in the drunk tank to sober up.

> His cellmate lies slumped and snoring on the cell's single steel bunk, sleeping off an all-day drunk, oblivious to the shouts. . . . There are at least two men in each 4 × 8 foot cell and three in some. . . . The stench of cheap alcohol, dried blood, urine and excrement covers the cell block. Except for the young man's shouts, it is quiet. Most of the prisoners are so drunk they gaze without seeing, unable to answer when spoken to. There are no lights in the cells, which form a square in the middle of the cell block. But the ring of naked light bulbs on the walls around the cell block throw light into the cells, each of which is equipped with a steel bunk. There are no mattresses. "Mattresses wouldn't last the night," a policeman explains. "And with prisoners urinating all over them, they wouldn't be any good if they did last." The only sound in the cell block is the constant flowing of water through the toilets in each cell. The toilets do not have tops, which could be torn off and broken."

Every half hour or so a policeman checks to see if the inmates are "still warm."

After sobering up, a drunk or disorderly can usually leave the lockup in four to five hours if he is able to post collateral, $10–$25. No matter how many times he has been arrested before, he will not have to appear in court if he chooses to forfeit the collateral. The drunk without money stays in jail until court the next morning. At 6 a.m., the police vans collect the residue of the precinct lockups and take them to the courthouse cell blocks to await a 10:00 arraignment.

Defendant B is booked at the precinct. Her offense is an "open and shut" case with witnesses; she is charged with petty larceny, and the files are checked to see if she has a record. Because of the frequent association among shoplifting, prostitution, and narcotics addiction, she is subjected to a compulsory physical examination. Clean, she is eligible for stationhouse bail of $500. This means cash in the full amount or a $50 premium for a bondsman. She may make one or several phone calls to a bondsman (a list hangs by the pay phone), a friend, relative, or an attorney if she knows one or can pick one out of the yellow pages. But the timing and the number of phone calls are usually a matter of police discretion, and it may be an empty right if no one answers, or if there is no telephone in the rented rooms or tenements of her friends and family. Unable to raise bail, she must await arraignment—any time from an hour to several weeks after booking.

Defendant C, suspected of robbery and aggravated assault, both felonies, is properly warned of his right to remain silent or to consult counsel before any questioning takes place. But he has no right to an appointed lawyer before his first court appearance, and since he cannot afford his own lawyer, his real choice is to keep quiet or sign a waiver of the right not to be questioned. For the present he prefers not to talk.

C's fingerprints and mug shot are taken, and a record check is made for any other arrests in the police files. The FBI is sent a copy of the fingerprints to check for out-of-jurisdiction offenses. He is taken to the hospital for identification by the owner-victim, then back to the liquor store so the police can replay the event and verify the victim's story as well as watch C's reaction. Street witnesses brought to the station point him out as the man they saw running from the store. C is placed in a lineup, made to strike a variety of poses and repeat the words of the holdup man. A blood smear is taken to match against some stains on the sidewalk outside the store. His room is searched for weapons, and ballistics tests are made on a gun found there.

This investigative process, steady or interrupted, may go on for many hours, even days. He is allowed to call or see his family, but their entreaties to tell all, their own woes—"what will happen to me and the kids now"—offer little solace. He may not want to involve others who can help him because they, too, would come under police scrutiny and questioning.

The interrogation (if there is any) and the investigation often precede the actual booking, so he is unsure of what charges are lodged against him. The duration of his custody is open-ended; he is not told how long it will last. If he has not been able to reach a friend or relative, no one knows for sure where he is.

In the back of his mind may linger stories he has heard about police brutality: telephone books which leave no marks, psychological bullying. Only the police are present to hear what he actually says or to observe in what condition he is when he says it. Often, in the tension of the moment and the rush of later events, he forgets what he said. . . .

PRELIMINARY HEARING AND ARRAIGNMENT

Defendant A, charged with drunk and disorderly, is brought into court from the bullpen in a shuffling line of dirty, beat, unshaven counterparts, many still reeking of alcohol. Each spends an average of 90 seconds before the judge, time for the clerk to intone the charge and for the judge to ask if he desires counsel and how he pleads. Rarely does a request for counsel or a "not guilty" break the monotony of muttered "guilties." Lawyers are not often assigned in police court, and anyone who can afford his own counsel will already have been released from jail on bond— to prepare for trial at a later date or to negotiate with the city prosecutor to drop the changes.

Occasionally, an unrepresented defendant will ask for trial. If the arresting officer is present, he will be tried on the spot. There are no jury trials in drunk court. The policeman will testify that the man was "staggering," "his breath smelled of some sort of alcoholic beverage," his speech was "slurred"—"his eyes were bloodshot and glassy." The man may protest that he had only a few drinks, but there are no witnesses to support his testimony, no scientific evidence to establish his alcoholic blood level at the time of arrest, no lawyers to cross-examine the officers. If the defendant pleads not guilty and hopes he can get counsel (his own or court-assigned), he may have his trial postponed a week or two. Meanwhile, he must make bond or return to jail.

Police Court sentencing is usually done immediately after a plea. A few courts with alcoholic rehabilitation court clinics may screen for likely candidates—those not too far along on the alcoholism trail—in the detention pens. Counsel, when available, can ask for a presentence report, but delay in sentencing means jail or bail in the meantime. On a short-term offense it is seldom worth it. . . .

Defendant B, the shoplifter, is arraigned in a misdemeanor court the same morning:

> The audience section of the courtroom is usually jammed with relatives of the defendants involved, and with witnesses and complainants, as well as with defendants themselves who have been released on parole or bail. . . .
>
> The number of reserved seats is usually inadequate for all the attorneys and police involved in the day's cases. As a result, the attorneys usually gather close to the bench; and the police invariably also congregate inside the rail close to the door leading to the detention pen. As each case

is called, the policeman will fetch from the pen the defendant whom he has arrested and bring him before the judge.

B is told of her rights, in a mass of a hundred other accused, crushed into the space between counsel table and spectators "like New Yorkers in a subway at rush hour." Marched slowly to the judge's bench "like assembly line workers in a factory, all parties operate under a climate which makes it appear that nothing may be permitted to interfere with the smooth operation of the line."

When B is before the judge, the clerk reads her a summary statement of the charges against her and recites her rights to trial and counsel, phrased in the words of the pertinent statute or court ruling. "Spoken at high speed, in a dull monotone, phrased in legal jargon, the charges and the rights are frequently unintelligible."

B can plead guilty at her first appearance or ask for a trial. She can also request an adjournment to consult or obtain counsel. . . . Without counsel, defendant B is almost certain to plead guilty.

Even with counsel, however, pressures are strong in a high volume misdemeanor court to plead guilty and hope for, or bargain for, leniency. . . .

After the police have completed their investigation, defendant C is brought before a judge for preliminary hearing. Charged with robbery and aggravated assault, a determination is made on whether he should be bound over to the grand jury. If the police cannot justify the charges, they could be dismissed at this juncture, but if C has already confessed, his admissions can be introduced against him; so can other incriminating post-arrest developments, including lineup identifications, fingerprints, etc. At the preliminary hearing, the defendant has the option of asserting his right to have the government present its case. Appearance of counsel here may be crucial. The defendant may not fully understand that if he waives, he loses one of his best and most effective chances to discover the identity of the government's key witnesses and the nature of the government's evidence. Adroit cross-examination at the preliminary hearing can expose and freeze inconsistencies in testimony before government witnesses have time to reflect and to consult extensively with the prosecution; valuable ground work may be laid for later impeachment at trial.

But the indigent defendant may not always be offered assigned counsel at his first appearance before a judicial officer. Without counsel, few felony suspects are adept enough to probe evidentiary weaknesses by cross-examining prosecution witnesses; few are experienced enough to weigh the pros and cons of taking the stand themselves. Since he has been in police custody from the time of his arrest, the defendant has had no opportunity to line up defense witnesses. Even if, by some extraor-

dinary effort, he succeeded in constructing a plausible defense or in chal-
lenging the government's case, no stenographic record of the preliminary
examination would be available without costly advance arrangements.

Bail in felony cases is ordinarily set for the first time at the preliminary
hearing. For armed robbery and aggravated assault, it may be as high as
$25,000, requiring a $2,500 premium that poor defendants cannot raise.
With no defense lawyer to argue for lower bail, the prosecutor's recommendation will ordinarily stand. Even in cities where projects are operating to release worthy defendants without bail, the indigent's roots in
the community usually must be solid, his record comparatively clean of
past felonies. On the other hand, financial ability to make bail can be a
mixed blessing. It may disqualify him from obtaining assigned counsel
then, or later on arraignment.

When he is bound over to the grand jury, the detained defendant enters a legal limbo. Even if counsel were appointed for the preliminary
hearing, his duties have ceased, and appointment of new counsel awaits
action of the grand jury. Without a lawyer, the defendant can do nothing to affect the grand jury's deliberations or to identify key witnesses.

In jail, the defendant is thrown among convicted criminals. He marks
out his days in idleness. Outside problems proliferate and contacts crum-
ble. He is the target of constant jailhouse advice on "copping a plea"
from fellow inmates. Weeks, months go by, often with no word from the
courts or the lawyers on the progress of his case. If the grand jury finally
declines to indict, his case may be "kicked downstairs" for reinstatement
of misdemeanor charges. This process may take additional weeks while
witnesses are recalled to swear to the new complaint and a new prosecutor assigned to the case. Only when the misdemeanor information is filed
and a new arraignment date set is he notified that the felony charges have
been dismissed.

When an indictment is handed down, the accused felon is brought
from jail for arraignment, this time in the felony court where he will be
tried. Counsel is now offered the indigent defendant. Bail must be reset
by the judge to cover the period until trial, sometimes months away. An
adjournment may be necessary to decide on a plea. Many indigents, energies sapped by prolonged periods in jail, waive counsel and plead
guilty immediately. Yet a plea of not guilty is often necessary to buy time
for negotiating with the prosecutor on reduction of the charges, dropping
some charges in exchange for a plea to others, prosecuting multiple
charges or indictments separately or concurrently. Occasionally only a
token bargaining effort is required because of the pressures of the calendar on the court and prosecutors, but usually defense counsel's success
is comprised of many factors: his reputation and the intensity of his
commitment to the case; his capacity for engaging the prosecution with

pretrial motion and writs; his resources for proceeding to a full-scale trial; his willingness to challenge illegal police or prosecutorial tactics. To bargain expertly, counsel must be able to probe the strengths and weaknesses of the prosecution's case, to realize and fulfill the potential of his own. He must acquire a sure knowledge of all the permutations and combinations of pleas and penalties that are possible under the indictment. Intangibles enter the picture; the defendant must impose full trust in his counsel's strategic judgment, be willing to accept his assessment of the prospects and alternatives. . . .

PREPARATION AND TRIAL

C prepares for trial, although plea bargaining continues up to the time of entering the courthouse. As the momentum of pretail preparation mounts, pressures to compromise increase. Pretrial motions involving full-scale hearings are time-consuming, require extensive research and investigation, and can delay trial for months. Yet they are often the vitals of the defense strategy. The suspect should be taken to the scene of the arrest to replay his account of what happened. Other witnesses to the incident have to be located and their stories recorded. The legal precedents must be researched. New counsel must familiarize himself with any evidence adduced at an earlier preliminary hearing. All of this takes time and money while the defendant languishes in jail. . . .

Tracking down ordinary defense witnesses in the slums to support the defendant's alibi or to act as character witnesses often has a Runyanesque aspect to it. The defendant in jail tells his counsel he has known the witnesses for years but only by the name of "Toothpick," "Malachi Joe," or "Jet." He does not know where they live or if they have a phone. If he could get out and look himself, he is sure he could find them at the old haunts, but his descriptive faculties leave something to be desired. Since a subpoena cannot be issued for "Toothpick," of no known address, counsel sets off on a painstaking, often frustrating, search of the defendant's neighborhood. He stops children at play: he attempts door-to-door conversations with hostile and suspicious slum-dwellers; he haunts the local bars; he even asks the police on the beat for help. If he finally locates the witnesses, they must be "collared" and cajoled into coming to court; otherwise, they will probably ignore a subpoena. They must be reassured—if possible—that there will be no retaliation from police or prosecutors, that they will not themselves be held in jail as material witnesses. Fare for the trip to court must be dredged up from somewhere, lost days' pay replaced. Rarely can they tolerate more than one trip, if their testimony is postponed, they slip back into oblivion.

A defendant in jail cannot help counsel locate witnesses, persuade them to testify, nor restage his story on the actual scene. He is unavailable for spot calls to check details or last-minute conferences to plan strategy; jail may be on the edge of town and the visiting hours inconvenient for busy counsel. . . .

The defendant can have his case tried by a jury or a judge. Detained defendants and those with assigned counsel are more apt to choose a judge; jury calendars are notoriously backlogged, and the penalty for demanding a jury trial may be a stiffer sentence. Adjournments are frequent, and the attrition rate for defense witnesses high. There may be subtler reasons, too, for bypassing a jury. The make-up of many juries is middle-class oriented—small businessmen, accountants, housewives. Slum residents are not so likely to be on the voter registration lists from which the juries are drawn. If they are, they are not attracted to jury duty; usually they cannot afford long absences from their jobs.

The outcome of C's trial depends on a number of factors: his counsel's ability to discredit government witnesses on cross-examination; his successful refutation of scientific evidence or tests; his ability to keep any confessions out of evidence; his success in convincing the judge that the defendant could not be the man involved or that he was somewhere else at the time.

Skillful cross-examination is most effective "when the questions are based on facts rather than on intuition . . . it often takes days or weeks to secure a witness or scientific proof which can destroy a fabricated story. If the fabricated story is not revealed until trial, it may be too late."

But indigent defense counsel must rely too often on spotting surface inconsistencies in a witness's testimony or on comparing testimony on the stand with prior statements made available in the courtroom only after the witness has testified. The statements must then be perused under the impatient eyes of judge and jury while the trial is stalled.

Defense witnesses pose strategic obstacles, even when they actually appear. They are likely to be shabbily dressed, inarticulate, unsophisticated, testy, nervous, and vulnerable to prosecution efforts at impeachment. The effect on a predominantly white-collar jury can be prejudicial.

The defendant himself runs a similar risk. A detained defendant often comes to the courtroom pallid, unshaven, dishevelled, demoralized, a victim of the jailhouse blues. He comes and goes through a special door that the jury soon learns leads to the detention pen beyond. He is always closely accompanied by a police escort or marshal.

A defendant under courtroom guard raises tactical as well as psychological problems. During the trial his lawyer may need to consult with him privately in the courtroom, but his guard is always in range. There can be no productive lunch or recess conferences, no quick trips to locate last-minute rebuttal witnesses, no pretrial warm-ups or post-trial replays. Should surprise witnesses or evidence materialize, the indigent's defense counsel must face such crises alone.

In most cases, the trial will end in a guilty verdict. But even an acquitted defendant often faces debts, no job, broken family ties. Should there be a hung jury and retrial ordered, a transcript of the trial becomes an urgent necessity: to find contradictions in the prosecution's case, to prepare to impeach witnesses, to reevaluate trial strategy. But transcripts for retrial are not routinely provided indigents. Nor is the defendent now likely to be any freer to participate in the crucial work of preparing for his second trial than he was for the first.

After the verdict, the judge can admit the defendant to bail pending sentence, or he can refuse bail altogether. A new bail premium may be necessary to continue his freedom. If he has been detained to this point, it is unlikely that he will be released now. . . .

SENTENCING AND APPEAL

Defendant A, drunk and disorderly, will be sentenced on the spot. The sentence may be suspended if he has no lengthy record. Otherwise, he may be fined $30 (or 30 days) or given a short sentence (10-90 days) in the local jail or workhouse. But even a short jail sentence can play havoc with a marginal offender's precarious existence—day-to-day jobs and rented rooms are gone when he gets back, his tenuous ties to the neighborhood cut.

A poor, petty offender rarely appeals his conviction. Appeal is often discretionary with the courts if the fine does not exceed $50. There is a 3-day limit on filing, and no mention of his appeal right is made in court. Usually, he has no counsel. By the time an appeal would be heard, his sentence is served; a stay would have to be conditional on an appeal bond of perhaps $500-1,000.

Misdemeanant B, convicted of petty larceny, will probably not receive a presentence investigation. If she has counsel, her lawyer can, of course, present his own information and plea to the court, citing her job status, her family responsibilities, her penitent attitude—all the reasons why the court should not disrupt a life with some semblance of normality. An offer to make restitution to the victim for any monetary loss or to pay hospital bills can be effective at this juncture. It may also be impossible if the defendant is impoverished.

In certain kinds of cases, the court will realize that a promise to seek private psychiatric treatment on release holds out a better promise of recovery and safety to the community than a nontherapeutic jail sentence. However, if the defendant or her lawyer can satisfy none of these alternatives, she may go to prison for several months. And any appeal rights may be illusory. Free counsel may not be available on appeal, even in serious misdemeanors.

When felony defendant C appears for sentencing, there will probably be a presentence report in his file. The contents of the report, however, will usually be inaccessible to him or his counsel in accordance with a general policy of nondisclosure. The probation officer will have been to the jail to talk to him and to report his "attitude," "his rehabilitative potential." He will also have been to see his family and friends, employers, neighbors, and enemies. The report will contain a potpourri of their narratives and the investigator's own conclusions. Dedicated counsel may try to supplement this report with an investigation of his own. If possible, he will advance rehabilitation plans for his client in an effort to avoid prison. But often harried by other business, assigned counsel may have to defer judgment to the probation office. For whatever reasons—the defendant's appearance or demeanor, his lack of a job or strong family ties after months in jail—defendants with assigned counsel and defendants detained before trial receive prison sentences more often than the rest.

After sentence, if there is a right to appeal, the indigent must be furnished counsel and a transcript or whatever record is necessary for an adequate appeal. But often there are time limits on how promptly the appeal must be filed, even if counsel has not been appointed. In such cases, the defendant will have to write the petition or file the notice of appeal himself. In any event, he or his lawyer may still have to absorb much of the cost of appeal.

Appeals can prolong the proceedings excruciatingly. Unable to raise new bail, the indigent defendant may languish months in jail—without credit toward his sentence. If he elects to begin serving sentence, he may be sent to a state penitentiary, far from counsel. And successful appeal, while sometimes bringing release, more often means only a new trial and an interminable replay of the whole process. . . .

PRISON, PROBATION, AND PAROLE

Defendant B, the shoplifter, is ultimately granted probation. She will be required to report to a probation officer downtown at the court at his convenience. She must stay in the area. She cannot change jobs, move, alter her marital status without permission, frequent places where liquor is sold, or stay out late. She cannot associate with other law offenders. She must obey all laws. If she does not have a job, she must try "diligently" to get one. Restitution may have to be made. In some counties, the costs of providing her with a legal defense must be repaid as a condition of probation.

In the slum areas where life is lived on the streets and in the bars, where a sizable percentage of local residents are past offenders, the conditions of probation may not be realistic. Probationers, like other slum-dwellers, probably have a greater chance of being "picked up" for a minor street offense because of where and how they live. Now, because of their special status (probationers' names are generally listed at their local precinct), they may attract even closer official attention in areas which police are trying to "keep clean."

Probation officers exercise their discretion as to how to handle "technical violations" in different ways. If the officer and his probationer hit it off well, the officer will hesitate to be rigid, but in many cases the wide social gap between the middle-class officer and his lower-class client inhibits such rapport. The officer can ignore minor rule infractions, recognize the day-to-day pressures of existence, help the probationer to overcome his antiauthority bias. Or he can blow the whistle on every technicality, assuring the probationer's quick return to jail.

If revocation is threatened, the probationer in many jurisdictions will get neither notice nor a hearing. Assignment of counsel to indigent probationers is an accident of jurisdiction. An unrepresented probationer can be refused access to the probation officer's reports or files; confrontation and cross-examination of unidentified accusers may be impossible. Bail may or may not be available during the proceeding. A full-scale probation hearing, like a trial on the main offense, often involves a contest of facts and requires witnesses, evidence, searching cross-examination, for which the indigent is totally without resources.

Defendant C, the indigent hold-up man, has been sentenced to prison. Left behind are a wife and children, snowballing debts. In prison, he can contribute nothing to his dependents' existence. His prison earnings, if any, are meager and are consumed primarily in commissary items—cigarettes, soap, candy. He may be drawn into the prison rackets to earn more. If the prison is distant from his neighborhood, he can expect few visitors to make the time-consuming and expensive trip.

His prison work duty often reflects the same educational and skill deficiencies that plagued him on the outside. He is apt to relate poorly to the prison's middle-class staff.

While in prison, he may try to institute collateral attacks on his conviction by writing judges and public officials his version of how he was wronged. Occasionally such a letter with surface merit will provoke a judge to grant a hearing, but the aid of counsel and supporting investigative resources, seldom available, may be indispensable to success.

At the end of one-third of his sentence, he may petition for parole, and reapply yearly if he is turned down. Parole applications take into account the nature of the man's crime, his pre-prison record, his "institutional adjustment." Even when granted, however, parole may depend on his having a job waiting for him and an approved place to live. A prisoner may wait months after parole has been granted for these conditions to materialize, or until he can be mandatorily released—when his sentence less "good time" is finished.

Back on the street, living on the dole of relatives, or working at a transient job, he starts anew. Parole conditions prevent him from leaving the area, from associating with ex-cons like himself, from carrying weapons, drinking, going to "undesirable places," changing addresses, marrying or cohabiting extramaritally, from driving a car without permission. Because of his record, he cannot work in a bar, restaurant, hospital, and in some places not even in a barber shop. He cannot afford the compensating luxury of further training or education. Old debts have mounted while he was in prison, or he has acquired new debts since his return.

In desperation, some parolees actually ask to be returned; others revert to crime for supplemental income. The parolee can always be sent back to jail for technical violations or new offenses. He is troubled by the threat of police harassment—rightly or wrongly—which can lead to revocation. If he is charged with a new offense, he can go back to prison before, not after, the revocation hearing. He usually has no right to assigned counsel at such a hearing. . . .

CONCLUSION

Poverty breeds crime. The poor are arrested more often, convicted more frequently, sentenced more harshly, rehabilitated less successfully than the rest of society. So long as the social conditions that produce poverty remain, no reforms in the criminal process will eliminate this imbalance. But we can ease the burdens of poverty by assuring the poor those basic procedural rights which our society ostensibly grants all citizens: the right to be represented by competent counsel early enough in the process to preserve other rights; the right to prepare an adequate defense, the right to be free until convicted, the right not to be jailed solely because of lack of money to remit a fine or make restitution, the right to parole, the right to a clean start after prison. In withholding these fundamentals from any citizen, society reveals a poverty of its own.

3 TYPES OF CRIMINAL INVOLVEMENT

The articles in this section were selected not only for their intrinsic merit but also because they indicate the extensive range of acts and behaviors defined as seriously deviant. The readings include selections on murder, rape, check forgery, organized crime and the numbers game, white-collar crime, and criminal tax fraud. Several of the contributions are taken from the 1967 Task Force Reports of the President's Commission on Law Enforcement and the Administration of Justice and, if they are not the last word on the subjects in question, they represent reasonably definitive statements.

In the first article, "Patterns of Violence in San Juan," Professor Wallace describes the nature and characteristics of homicide and aggravated assault. He focuses on the act of violence as an interplay between the perpetrator, the victim, and the audience or spectators. It is hard to fault Wallace's conclusion that violent behavior is a reflection of the social and cultural environment in which it occurs. For this reason, the patterns of violence in Puerto Rican cities are somewhat different from the patterns in American cities. The differences, however, are less impressive than the similarities in the who, when, how, and why of violence.

Until the promising research by Professor Amir of the Hebrew University in Jerusalem, Israel, very little was known about forcible rape as a serious felony offense. This article, "Forcible Rape," is based on an analysis of 646 cases occurring in Philadelphia in a two-year period. The data disprove many misconceptions about forcible rape. The article discusses this problem in terms of the characteristics of offenders and victims, the location of the offense, its planning, degree of violence, victim resistance, victim precipitation of the event, and multiple rapes. As a specific order of violent crime, forcible rape is highly complex, involving far more than a guileless victim and a sadistic, aggressive offender. Instead, an understanding of the dynamics of forcible rape demands an interactional perspective. The event itself is a culmination of a complicated series of interrelationships and signals between the offender(s) and victim in a specific setting.

Quite different from rape as a form of criminal deviation is professional theft. Professional thievery is usually characterized by a high degree of skill—an unnecessary attribute in homicide or rape. To the professional, theft is an occupation and the principal, if not the sole, source of income. Professional thieves share their deviant norms, codes of conduct, and argot. In "The Behavior of the Systematic Check Forger," Professor Lemert uses these characteristics of professional theft as a backdrop against which he describes the former and future life styles of seventy-two systematic check forgers—all but three of whom were serving time in prison when interviewed. While there are certain similarities in occupational habits between the systematic check forgers and more traditional professionals such as con men and pickpockets, the check forger builds his criminal style around a solitary life largely devoid of criminal group contacts. Of relatively high socioeconomic status, well educated, and without other criminal antecedents or associations, the professional bad check passer seems to be a most unusual type of criminal deviant.

A threat to society far more serious than any of the personal forms of criminal deviation, or most of the property offenses, is organized or syndicated crime. Organized crime is built around supplying illegal goods and services—gambling, narcotics, vice—to a substantial segment of the population. More recently, syndicate money has been invested in legal business activities—resorts, construction, real estate—providing organized criminals with legitimate front activities which are especially important for tax purposes. The selection included in this collection, "Organized Crime," is taken from the reports to the President's Commission on Law Enforcement and the Administration of Justice. In addition to a discussion of the illegitimate and legitimate activities of syndicated crime, this article details the internal structure and mode of operation of the twenty-four major syndicate groups or "families" in this country. The "commission" which unifies these criminal families is also described. Although there are more popular and pretentious descriptions of the five thousand or more organized criminals in America, this contribution presents the most authoritative information presently available.

The chief source of revenue for organized crime is gambling. Of the various kinds of gambling, numbers or policy is most closely identified with lower-class status and especially with the Negro. Some estimates indicate that five billion dollars a year are wagered on numbers. While the Italians and Sicilians control the organized syndicate and receive much of the numbers money, the lower echelons of numbers men are Negro. Numbers represent the only significant involvement of the Negro with the ethnically dominated syndicate. "The Numbers Man," as described by Roebuck, is a fascinating type who enjoys high status in the Negro community. Something of a politician and con man, the numbers man often comes from a stable and respectable family setting. Typically nondelinquent as a boy, the numbers man was drawn into the policy game as a means of achieving upward social mobility and perhaps even entering into Negro "society." Viewed from his own perspective and that of his patrons, a numbers man is a professional with high status.

Potentially the most damaging kind of criminal deviation is white-collar crime—damaging not only because it is more costly to society than any other property offense, but also because it undermines trust, and because protection against this form of deviation is impossible. White-collar crime is an outgrowth of modern industrial society. Because it is an emergent problem, traditional criminal law and procedures are unable to control white-collar depredations. In addition, many persons are apathetic about this problem. Neither the deviant nor the public consider milder violations of this nature to be criminal. "White-Collar Crime," another authoritative report on criminal deviation drawn from the President's Commission on Law Enforcement and Administration of Justice, describes the extent and scope of the economic costs and the enforcement problems. The chief illustration of white-collar crime discussed is the almost unbelievable case in which twenty-nine of the major electrical equipment manufacturers conspired to fix prices and divide the market.

The final article in this chapter concerns criminal tax fraud—one of the most widespread of the so-called folk crimes. Attempted by some persons in all walks of life, but chiefly by higher status professionals and businessmen, tax evasion tends to be defined more as a cat-and-mouse game than as criminal deviation—public sympathy is frequently with the violator rather than with the tax collector. No crime better exemplifies white-collar deviation. The section on "Criminal Tax Fraud" was submitted to the President's Commission by the Tax Division of the Department of Justice. It gives a dispassionate and businesslike account of the problem of criminal tax fraud in terms of the offenders, the nature of the offense, the procedural steps in enforcement, and the outcome of prosecution. When one considers that sixty-eight million people file federal tax returns, and so have an opportunity to commit tax fraud, the fact that only 593 defendants were convicted in 1966 is testimony either to the infrequency of this offense or, more likely, to the difficulties of enforcement.

PATTERNS OF VIOLENCE
IN SAN JUAN
Samuel E. Wallace

Violent behavior reflects the social and cultural environment of a society. Who commits the assault, who gets taken to hospital or morgue, who witnessed the event, and the reaction of the community reflect in part how a society is socially structured and what that society considers important. Like other types of behavior, violence does not take place in a vacuum but owes its birth as well as its expression to a number of social and cultural influences.

VICTIM AND AGGRESSOR

Who is the aggressor? Is he young? . . . male? . . . unemployed? . . . uneducated? Where, when, and with what weapon did he commit the assault? What led him to perpetrate violence on another? These questions are crucial, but the study of violence can not be understood through the exclusive study of aggressor alone. What role did the victim play? Did he encourage his aggressor—taunt and provoke him into a fit of anger leading to aggression? Perhaps he actually started the fight, insulting another, initiating the physical conflict and then later losing the battle. Violence between two persons is a type of interaction, subject to the same laws of reciprocal influence in the sequence of events which lead to a violent act. It is therefore necessary to study both victim and aggressor, if the role of each is to be fully appreciated.

Victim and aggressor are the two principal elements in an act of violence, and yet there is a third crucial party, namely, the audience. Who, if anyone, witnessed the violence? What role did they play—supporting and encouraging the aggressor, the victim, or neither? Did they attempt to reconcile the initial conflict and prevent the violence, or perhaps refuse to become involved? Clearly, the role played by the audience is critical, whether it is neutral or actively involved.

Aggressor, victim, and audience make up the social situation, the basic unit of a study of interpersonal violence carried out with the Social Science Research Center of the University of Puerto Rico. Data were collected of 988 situations involving 1,049 victims and 1,189 aggressors.

From *Interdisciplinary Problems in Criminology: Papers of the American Society of Criminology, 1964* (edited by W. C. Reckless and Charles L. Newman), Ohio State University, 1965, pp. 43-48. Reprinted by permission.

The matrix of interpersonal relations which existed between aggressor and victim, between aggressor and those present, and between victim and those present was a primary emphasis.

AGGRAVATED ASSAULT AS INCIPIENT MURDER

The study made another departure from ordinary practice by treating assault with a deadly weapon as an incipient murder. There are many more cases of assault than there are of murder and it is fruitful to ask why the life of the victim was spared in these, but not other cases. The fact that the victim's life was spared might have little if anything to do with the motivations and intentions of the aggressor. Studying aggravated assault also allowed the investigator to interview assault victims and to seek to determine firsthand the victim's participation in the criminal act.

THE SAMPLE

The specific acts of violence included in the San Juan study are all incidents reported to the police, this agency providing the best means to the universe of violent behavior. Seven types of offenses, ranging in severity from aggravated assault to first-degree murder, were studied. All acts of violence were committed during the first five months of 1961. Data were gathered from interviews with most of the victims, some of the eyewitnesses, and in a few cases, from the victim's relatives. Official crime and arrest reports, interviews conducted by the San Juan Homicide Squad, and court records provided additional data. In all cases, the data were secured as soon as possible after the violence occurred—in practice about 5 to 10 days.

The type of approach attempted by the San Juan study is perhaps best indicated by a comparative profile description of aggressor and victim, and then by a glance at the social support components of these situations of violence. The reader should keep in mind that although we refer to the two parties in conflict as victim and aggressor, the term aggressor should not be taken to mean criminal or even police offender, since some of these cases were dismissed immediately upon their presentation in court; other persons were found not guilty; and in some cases the individual noted as the victim by the police in fact turned out, upon closer examination, to be the aggressor.

A total of 1,397 assailants were reported by the victims to the interviewing staff. Of these, 1,189 were officially reported by the police to a magistrate who in turn swore out an order for the arrest of these 1,189 individuals. To this initial 15 per cent loss of assailants between assault and preliminary court action, the additional loss of 615 cases must be added—the number who had not appeared in court one year after the crime had been committed. That is, only 574, or 48 per cent of the aggressors actually appeared in court. Further erosion of cases (not discussed here) takes place during the subsequent trials of the persons apprehended.

THE AGGRESSOR

Using the 574 persons brought into court as our primary source of data, with additional information about the aggressor from the homicide squad interviews with only 51, the following general profile emerges. Crimes of violence in the San Juan metropolitan police area district are overwhelmingly committed by males against other males. Eight of nine of the aggressors were male and four or five victims were male. Research by Verkko has indicated that if the rate of violence is relatively high, the proportionate number of women involved is low. Puerto Rico has a relatively high rate of crimes of violence and conforms to the rule in that women were involved in only half as many cases as that reported for Philadelphia. It is also known from Verkko that as the rate of violence decreases, the proportionate number of women involved increases. In fact, this means that those who become involved in violence remain relatively consistent through time. One reason for the consistency of female involvement is that women seldom assault other women, and the men they assault (or are assaulted by) are typically those with whom they have had, or are having, sexual intercourse. San Juan conforms to all these generalizations.

Violence in San Juan takes place on weekends and on holidays. After a low of 3.5 acts of violence per day on Tuesday and Wednesday, violence begins to climb on Thursday to eventually reach 11.4 acts per day on Sunday, a figure nearly twice the daily median. These acts are relatively low throughout the early morning hours, rise and then fall with lunch-time activities, then increase in the late afternoon and reach a peak between 8 and 10 P.M. Assault typically occurs in public places where liquor is served. The males who commit the aggressions are most often found between the ages of 20 and 24, and males aged 20 to 39 contribute more than half of the acts studied. The male aggressor has had some grade school, is married, and is living with his spouse. He is unemployed in two-thirds of the cases. Perhaps the most interesting statistic available is the aggressor's previous involvement with the police. Prior to the commission of the act which brought these persons within the study group, nearly one half had been charged with the commission of some kind of felony.

THE VICTIM

The profile of the victim parallels that of the aggressor in that the modal case is also between 20 and 24 years of age, but the concentration within a few age brackets is not so pronounced. The median age of the victim exceeds that of the aggressor. Eleven per cent of the victims and 10 per cent of the aggressors were reported to be illiterate and about half had completed some grade school. Only 77 of the 812 victims for which the data were available had completed a high school education or additional schooling.

Twenty-nine per cent of the victims stated that they had never married; 46 per cent were married and [each was] still living with [his] first wife. About one-fourth reported that they had been married two or more times, a figure not much different from that for the aggressors. Whereas two-thirds of the aggressors were unemployed at the time the act of violence was committed, only 38 per cent of the victims fell into this category. It is important to note that this data was reported for the period of time before the act of violence occurred, and that a number of victims lost their jobs through hospitalization.

The details of the activities of the aggressor before he met up with his victim are not known, since victims but not aggressors were interviewed in the study. Information regarding the activities preceding the crime are available for the victim and indicate a gradual transition from private and inaccessible environments to involvement in public places of amusement and entertainment. Twelve hours preceding the crime, half of the victims were in their own homes and one-fourth of them were at work. The remaining 171 cases for which data are available were in bars, someone else's home, on the street, or in a place of amusement, in that order. Three hours preceding the crime, the number in private locations dropped from 84 per cent to 54 per cent. Forty-three per cent of the victims had already met and joined the company of their aggressors. In 90 per cent of the cases there were other persons present in the social situation which eventually culminated in violence.

Not only were victim and aggressor in each other's company before the violence took place, but in the majority of the cases (59 per cent) they were also drinking together. The alcohol consumption of the victim and aggressor is matched by that of the spectators. In over half of the cases where spectators were present, they were also drinking.

Thus the picture emerges of the victim leaving his home or place of work to join his friends at a local bar or perhaps on the street corner. His friends include his aggressor and the two of them spend some time drinking together in the place where the violence eventually occurs. Those present also share in this pattern of alcohol consumption. Since 9 in 10 acts of violence take place in front of an audience, . . . support or non-involvement [of the audience] seems to be critical.

THE AUDIENCE

In about one-fifth of the cases where there is an audience present, a spectator intervened between the initial combatants, and in half of these cases ended up in the hospital himself. The audience more often contains friends of the victim rather than those of the aggressor. In addition to direct intervention, the audience at times encouraged and at times discouraged the ensuing aggression. The importance of the participation of the audience is also indicated by the fact that in the majority of cases the entire sequence of violent behavior was built up from the immediate situation. In other words, violence was usually a product of forces and tensions inherent in the same situation within which the violence occurred, rather than a carryover of previous episodes between victim and aggressor.

THE VICTIM'S CONTRIBUTION TO VIOLENCE

Police, court, and other official and unofficial investigators attempt to determine the participation of the victim in various ways. Although several alternative definitions were employed in the San Juan study, perhaps the best measure within the confines of our own data was that based upon an evaluation by our research staff after all assembled data on each case had been read. According to this staff evaluation, three-fifths of the victims in the San Juan study were considered to have had little or no participation in the commission of the crime. These persons were not guilty of provoking or leading the aggressor to the act of violence which he committed.

In approximately one-fourth of the cases, however, victims and aggressors were considered to be either official or unofficial collaborators. Official collaborators refer to . . . [the victim and the aggressor whom] the police and/or the court considered . . . to be equally involved, and the officials either convicted both, released both, or carried out some other action aimed at both parties. Unofficial collaborators are those with the same characteristics but in these cases the judgment was made by the research staff, rather than by police or court officials. Official collaborators outnumber the unofficial ones by a ratio of two to one.

In about one-tenth of the cases, the staff evaluation considered the person officially charged as the aggressor as practically innocent. Some of these cases were those where A assaulted B but ended up losing the fight. When the police arrived, they took the actual aggressor to the hospital since he was more seriously injured. The person who had successfully defended himself was sent to jail. Since most of these crimes occur among low-income groups who know little about legal defense, and lack the means to afford it, pleas of self-defense were rarely entered and these innocent aggressors served their time in prison with the others.

FORCIBLE RAPE

Monachem Amir

The term "rape" arouses hostile and aggressive feelings in many societies and in many countries. In a number of jurisdictions it is punishable by death. There is sympathy for the victim and hostility toward the offender. Since the crime of rape includes many elements other than sex, judicial decisions relating to punishment and treatment are difficult to render.

This article is based on an empirical study which was designed to explore and disclose the patterns of forcible rape among 646 cases occurring in Philadelphia, Pennsylvania, from January 1 to December 31, 1958, and from January 1 to December 31, 1960. The cases were those in the files of the Morals Squad of the Philadelphia Police Department where all complaints about rapes are recorded and centrally filed.

The emphasis in this study has not been on the psychological dynamics underlying the behavior of the individual offender and his victim but rather on their social characteristics, social relationships, and on the act itself, that is, the *modus operandi* of the crime and the situations in which rape is likely to occur.

The patterns which emerged were derived from a study of 646 victims and 1,292 offenders who were involved in single and multiple rape. Patterns were sought regarding race, marital status, and employment differences, as well as seasonal and other temporal patterns, spatial patterns, the relationships between forcible rape and the presence of alcohol, and the previous arrest record of victims and offenders.

Further questions were raised relating to rape during the commission of another felony, the relationship between the victim and offender, victim-precipitated rape, and unsolved cases of rape. Finally, all of these aspects were related to group rape and to leadership functions in such situations.

SOME MISCONCEPTIONS ABOUT RAPE

Following are some misconceptions about rape disclosed in this study:

1. Negroes are more likely to attack white women than Negro women.

From *Federal Probation*, Vol. XXI, No. 1 (March 1967), 51-58. Reprinted by permission. Dr. Amir is at the Institute of Criminology, The Hebrew University, Jerusalem, Israel.

Rape, we found, is an intraracial act, especially between Negro men and women.

2. Rape reflects a demographic strain due to sex-marital status imbalance in the community. This theory was refuted, along with the derivative assumption about age-sex imbalance which might exist within the general population.

3. Rape is predominantly a hot-season crime. The "thermic law of delinquency" was not confirmed by the present study.

4. Rape usually occurs between total strangers. This assumption was challenged by the analysis of several variables.

5. Rape is associated with drinking. In two-thirds of our cases alcohol was absent from the rape situation.

6. Rape victims are innocent persons. One-fifth of the victims had a police record, especially for sexual misconduct. Another 20 percent had "bad" reputations.

7. Rape is predominantly an explosive act. In almost three-quarters of the cases rape was found to be a planned event.

8. Rape is mainly a dead-end street or dark alley event. Rape was found to occur in places where the victim and offender initially met each other (especially when the meeting was in the residence of one of the participants).

9. Rape is a violent crime in which brutality is inflicted upon the victim. In a large number of cases (87 percent) only temptation and verbal coercion were used initially to subdue the victim.

10. Victims generally do not resist their attackers. As it is commonly believed that almost no woman wants to be deprived of her sexual self-determination, it was surprising to find that over 50 percent of the victims failed to resist their attackers in any way.

11. Victims are responsible for their victimization either consciously or by default. The proportion of rape precipitated by the victim and the characteristics of such acts refute this claim.

FINDINGS OF THIS STUDY

In the following pages are discussed the major significant patterns emerging from the study:

Race. A significant association was found between forcible rape and the race of both victims and offenders. Negroes exceed whites both among victims and offenders in absolute numbers as well as in terms of their proportion in the general population. Negroes have four times their expected number of victims, and the proportion of Negro offenders was four times greater than their proportion in the general population of Philadelphia.

When specific rates by age and sex were calculated on the basis of the "potential" population of each race, it was found that the rates for the Negro victims (on the basis of total Negro female population) is almost 12 times higher than that of the white women who were victims (on the basis of total white female population).

Age. A statistical association existed between age and forcible rape, the age group 15–19 years having the highest rates among offenders and among victims. . . . For victims there is a wider range of "critical" age groups, with the Negro victim rate exceeding that of the white victims in all age groups.

Marital status. After examination of the marital status of both offenders and victims, it was found that both generally were unmarried. The highest rates for victims were in the "dependent" category (below marriageable age and still unmarried).

Occupational status. Examination of the occupational status of the offenders indicated that 90 percent of the offenders of both races belonged to the lower part of the occupational scale. The rate of Negro offenders in the unemployed category was twice as high as the rate of unemployed Negroes in Philadelphia at that time, and five times as high as that of white offenders.

Season. Although the number of forcible rapes tended to increase during the hot summer months, there was no significant association either with the season or with the month of the year. . . . Summer was also found to be the season when multiple rapes were most likely to occur.

Days of the week. Forcible rape was found to be significantly associated with days of the week. We found the highest concentration of rapes (53 percent) to be on weekends, with Saturday being the peak day.

Time of day. A study of the distribution of forcible rapes by hours of the day found the top "risk" hours to be between 8:00 P.M. and 2:00 A.M. Almost half of all the rape events occurred during these hours.

Ecological patterns. The analysis of the ecology of forcible rape reveals that in various areas of Philadelphia there was a correspondence between high rates of crime against the person and the rates of forcible rape. Moreover, those police districts where Negroes are concentrated were also the areas where the rates of forcible rape were highest.

A check was made to determine whether the offenders lived in the vicinity of the victims or the offense. In the majority of cases (82 percent) offenders and victims lived in the same area, while in 68 percent a "neighborhood triangle" was observed, i.e., offenders lived in the vicinity of victim and offense. Also observed was the pattern of "residence mobility triangle," i.e., instances in which the site of the crime was in the area of the residence of the offender but not that of the victim. . . .

Drinking. Unlike previous studies the present one examined the consumption of alcohol by the offender and the victim separately and together. Alcohol was found only in one-third of all the rape events. In 63 percent of the 217 cases in which alcohol was present, it was present in both the victim and the offender.

Alcohol is a factor found to be strongly related to violence used in the rape situation, especially when present in the offender only. In terms of race, it was drinking Negro victims or the offenders who were involved most frequently in violent rapes. Also, alcohol was found to be significantly associated with sexual humiliation forced upon a drinking victim.

Finally, weekend rapes were found to be associated with the presence of alcohol in either the victim, the offender, or both. As an explanation, we offered the fact that Friday is a payday with greater purchase of alcohol and the more intense social and leisure activities.

Previous arrest records of offenders and victims. A relatively high proportion of rapists in Philadelphia (50 percent) had previous arrest records. Contrary to past impressions, it was found that there are slight differences between the races, for offenders or victims, in terms of police or arrest record, although Negro offenders had a statistically significant higher proportion of two or more offenses in their past than white offenders.

When cases of persistence in violating the law were examined, it was found that over 50 percent of those who had an arrest record as adults also had a record as juveniles.

Analysis of the type of previous offenses committed by the offenders revealed that only 20 percent of those who had a past arrest record had previously committed a crime against the person. . . . Among offenders with criminal records, 9 percent had committed rape in the past, and 4 percent had been arrested before for sexual offenses other than rape. . . .

The analysis of the victims' criminal records revealed that 19 percent had an arrest record, the highest proportion of these arrests being for sexual misconduct (56 percent).

The victims' "bad" reputation was explored. It was found that 128, or 20 percent, of the 646 victims had such reputations, with significantly higher proportion of Negro victims having such a reputation. The assumption was made, and later confirmed, that a "bad" reputation, together with other factors such as ecological proximity, was a factor in what was termed "victim-precipitated" forcible rape.

Modus operandi. The analysis of the *modus operandi* was made in terms of processes and characteristics of the rape situation, i.e., sequences and conjunctions of events which enter into the perpetration of the offense. Five phases were distinguished according to offender's behavior, victim's reaction, and situational factors which finally set the stage for the rape event.

In phase one we were concerned with the initial interaction between victim and offender, and the relevant problems such as the meeting place and the degree of planning of the offense. It was found that the most dangerous meeting places were the street, and the residence of the victims or offenders. In one-third of the cases, the offender met the victim at and committed the offense in the victim's home or place where she stayed. . . .

Planning of the act. On the basis of the description of the event by the victim and offender, three degrees of planning were distinguished. Contrary to past impression, the analysis revealed that 71 percent of the rapes were planned. Most planned events were intraracial events when the meeting place was the residence of one of the participants or when the rape was a group affair. Explosive rapes were characterized as being single interracial rapes, with the street as the meeting place.

Location of the event. Phase two concerned itself with the location of the offense and was found to be associated with the place of initial meeting. Thus, when the meeting place was outside the participant's residence, the offense also took place there. Movement of the crime scene was mainly from outdoors to inside. The automobile, was revealed to be the location of the offense in only 15 percent of the cases. A significant association was also found between the location of the rape in the participant's place and use of violence in the commission of the offense, as well as the subjection of the victim to sexually humiliating practices.

Degrees of violence. In phase three we examined various aspects in the actual commission of the offense: Nonphysical methods used to manipulate the victim into submission, the degrees of violence used against her, and sexual humiliating practices which she was forced to endure.

Besides temptation, three forms of nonphysical methods were distinguished: Verbal coercion, intimidation by physical gestures, and intimidation with a weapon or other physical object to force the victim into submission. Combined with verbal coercion, nonphysical aggression was used in the majority of cases (87 percent). . . .

Degrees of violence were classified into three main groups: roughness, beatings (brutal and nonbrutal), and choking. In 15 percent of the 646 rapes, no force was used. Of the cases in which force was used, 29 percent took the form of roughness, one-quarter were nonbrutal beatings, one-fifth were brutal beatings, and 12 percent involved choking the victim. Violence, especially in its extreme forms, was found to be significantly associated with Negro intraracial events and with cases in which the offender was Negro and the victim white. Also, a significant association was found between multiple rape and the use of force in the rape situation and between the latter and the outside as the place of rape.

Sexual humiliation. It was not merely to forced intercourse that the female was subjected in rape, but also to various forms of sexual practices usually defined as sexual deviations. It was found that sexual humiliation existed in 27 percent of all rape cases. . . .

Victim behavior. The behavior of the victim—that is, whether she "consented" or resisted the offender—was, and still is, the basis in determining in the court whether the offender is guilty of forcible rape. This problematic dimension was, therefore, analyzed in the present work.

The varieties of victim behavior have been divided into three groups—submission, resistance, and fight. The analysis revealed that in over half of the rapes the victims displayed only submissive behavior; in 173, or 27 percent, victims resisted the offender; and in 116, or 18 percent, the victims put up a strong fight against their attackers. . . .

Multiple rape. . . . Multiple rape situations were divided into "pair rapes," in which two offenders rape one victim, and "group rapes," in which three or more males rape one victim. Of the 646 cases of forcible rape, 276 cases, or 43 percent, were multiple rapes. Of these cases, 105 were pair rapes and 171 were group rapes. Of 1,292 offenders, 210, or 16 percent, were involved in pair rapes and 712, or 55 percent, participated in group rapes. . . .

Group rape shows a tendency to occur more on weekends and to occur in the evening as well as late at night.

In group rapes, alcohol was more likely to be present, especially in the victim only, while in pair rapes it was more often present only in the offender who was the leader.

A significant proportion of participants in multiple rapes, compared with single-rape offenders, had a previous arrest record either for offenses against the person, for sex offenses other than rape, or for forcible rape. This was true for pair-rape leaders, as compared to their partners, but not for group-rape leaders vis-à-vis their followers.

Turning to the *modus operandi* aspect in multiple-rape situations, it was observed that multiple-rape offenders are most likely to attack victims who live in their area (neighborhood or delinquency triangles). The initial interaction between victims and offenders usually occurred in the street, where the rape also took place. There was little "mobility of crime scene" in multiple-rape situations.

Multiple rapes, especially group rapes, were found to be planned events. Compared to group rapes, pair rapes showed a high proportion of cases of explosiveness or partial planning.

Turning to the problems of intimidation and coercion, it was found that multiple-rape situations, especially group rapes, are characterized by temptation and coercion, with intimidation more used in pair-rape events. The leader was found to be the initiator of the manipulating acts, i.e., he was the first to tempt or to intimidate the victim into submission.

A significant association existed between violence and multiple rapes, especially group rapes. Multiple rapes also are characterized by the greater use of nonbrutal beatings. Extreme violence and brutality characterize the single-rape events, since the lone offender must constantly subdue the victim alone. The leader in pair and group rapes was more violent than his followers, and he was also the one to initiate the beatings.

Group rapes were also found to be characterized by tormenting the victim with perverted sexual practices.

The futility of resistance and fight by the group-rape victim is revealed by the fact that in group-rape situations the victim was more submissive or lightly resisted the offender but was less inclined to put up a strong fight. Pair-rape victims showed no definite pattern in this respect.

For many variables pair rapes and group rapes show some variations from the cluster of patterns which distinguished the multiple-rape situations. We found that in many instances pair rape resembled single rape more than group rape. Thus, it may be better to see pair rapes not as a form of group event but rather as a form of criminal "partnership."

Felony rape. In 76 cases, or 4 percent, of the 646 rape situations, a felony in the form of burglary or robbery was committed in addition to the rape. These cases were mainly single rapes, and especially Negro intraracial rapes. A special trait of felony rape is the age disparity between victim and offender. In more than half of these cases the offender was at least 10 years younger than the victim, especially when the offender was Negro and the victim white. . . .

Victim-offender relationships. Almost half (48 percent) of the identified victim-offender relationships conformed to our definition of "primary" relationships. When the types of primary contacts were further divided into "acquaintanceship" and more "intimate" contacts, the former constituted 34 percent and the latter contributed 14 percent of all types of victim-offender relationships.

A detailed analysis of victim-offender relationships revealed that when primary relationships existed, a relatively large proportion of cases involved Negro victims whose assailants were their close neighbors, or victims who were drinking acquaintances of their white assaulters.

As expected, Negro intraracial events involved mainly close neighbors. White intraracial events occurred mainly between acquaintances who established their relations just before the offense. Again, as expected, acquaintanceships were formed mainly between victims and offenders who were at the same level.

Neighbors met initially in the residence of one of the participants and the rape also took place there. The automobile was the place of rape for those who were intimate.

Although nonphysical means of coercion in its light forms were used between acquaintances, the closer the relationship was between victim and offender the greater was the use of physical force against the victim, and neighbors and acquaintances were found to be the most dangerous people so far as brutal rape was concerned.

As hypothesized, a greater proportion of multiple than single rape was found to take place between strangers. In general, the analysis of the interpersonal relations between victim and offender lent support to those who reject the myth of the offender who attacks victims unknown to him. But equally rejected is the notion that rape is generally an affair between, or a result of intimate relations between, victims and offenders.

Victim-precipitated rape. The term "victim-precipitated," initiated by Wolfgang in his study of homicide, was introduced to refer to those rape cases in which the victims actually—or so it was interpreted by the offender—agreed to sexual relations but retracted before the actual act or did not resist strongly enough when the suggestion was made by the offenders. The term applies also to cases in which the victim enters vulnerable situations charged with sexuality, especially when she uses what could be interpreted as indecent language and gestures or makes what could be taken as an invitation to sexual relations.

Philadelphia data revealed . . . 122 victim-precipitated rapes, which comprised 19 percent of all forcible rapes studies. . . .

Solved and unsolved rape. We distinguished two types of "unsolved" cases: the "undetected"—those cases in which the police could not attribute the recorded offense to any identifiable offender(s), and the "vanished"—those cases about which the police had some information on suspected, identified, or alleged offenders but which suspects were still at large. In 124, or 19 percent, of the rape events the offenders were classified as "undetected" and in 24, or 4 percent, as "vanished." Of 1,292 offenders, 405, or 33 percent, were classified as undetected.

THE NUMBERS MAN

Julian B. Roebuck

Numbers game operators are usually defined as lottery law or policy violators. They are defined by themselves, the police, the underworld and the betting public as numbers men. . . . The numbers game, a variant form of policy, is a special type of *lottery* which constitutes a notorious

From *Criminal Typology: The Legalistic, Physical-Constitutional-Hereditary, Psychological-Psychiatric and Sociological Approaches,* Springfield, Ill.: Charles C Thomas, 1967. Chapter VIII, pp. 136-54. Reprinted by permission.

form of gambling among Negroes in the large metropolitan areas of the Eastern Seaboard and the Midwest. Some have claimed that the numbers game has a certain integrative function for the Negro community, furnishing much of the content of casual conversation, imparting temporal structure to the day and offering a sense of participation in a community-wide institution. It has a widespread patronage among the lower-income and working classes, especially in Negro residential areas. Although only small amounts are generally involved in individual bets, many Negroes who play the game regularly can ill afford to lose. One survey shows that during 1960, almost three out of every eight persons who gambled in this country played the numbers. It is estimated that these 32,000,000 Americans, of whom 14,000,000 were women, wagered the sum of five billion dollars in an effort to hit a lucky number. The numbers game constitutes professional organized crime. It represents the only such area, at present, that Negroes have participated in in large numbers at the higher echelons of organization.

The numbers player bets one cent upward on a three digit number (any combination of numbers from 000 to 999) which he notes on a "slip" and turns over to a "numbers writer," a street numbers bookie (with his wager commonly from ten cents to a quarter), who in turn passes it on to a "pick-up man," and it finally reaches the counting office (the "bank" or "drop") of the numbers ring. At the drop, clerical workers check and tally each individual numbers slip and wager and sift out the slips bearing the winning combination, which is usually determined from pari-mutuel totals at a certain race track. The total payoff figures for the three, five and seven races may be used, or any combination of prices in any three designated races. The last dollar numeral before the decimal is used. The last three digits of the daily total amount bet may also be designated the winning combination. Odds, though varying from one city to another, are usually in excess of 1000 to 1 that any particular combination of three numbers will turn up. The operators pay a winner from 500 to 800 to 1.

THE NUMBERS MAN AS A CRIMINAL TYPE

. . . A qualitative examination of [16 Negro numbers men in the District of Columbia Reformatory at Lorton, Virginia] indicated a stable family background relatively free of emotional conflict, economic deprivation and physical violence. These remarks from one numbers man about his parental family were typical:

> My father worked at the post office as a mail clerk. He retired a few years ago. My mother worked in the government at one time as a clerk. You know, she typed. When us children came along she quit and stayed

home. There were times when things were tight but we managed. We didn't bother with no welfare. We had enough to eat and wear. We had to go to school and keep clean. Also Sunday School. We didn't run the streets either. We stayed at home when we were not at school or at the playground. The old man brought his check home at the end of each month and we all shared alike. He didn't drink it up or live it up with the chicks. He wore the pants in the family, but he wasn't rough. You know he didn't cuss and slap everybody around. He was good to my mother. All in all we had a happy home. If we got out of line they [parents] mostly talked to us and made us stay in the house for a day or two. I never got but two whippings.

In discussing their infrequent juvenile delinquent activities, not one mentioned housebreaking, strong-arm activities, robbery. Involvement in sporadic, unplanned pursuits such as petty thefts from grocery stores were mentioned. Their friends were free of police and juvenile court contact. Accounts of this kind were common:

I had no use for gang boys. Most of them were thugs who lived in the bottom. They never was my kind. I scuffled around with some of them at school. You know, I was no sissy, but I gave them plenty of traveling space and they just left me alone. Sure, I stole a few things as I went through life. I guess everybody does. You know, like a toy or something. I sure had no habit of stealing. My buddies were good boys. We didn't get in trouble with the teachers and we steered clear of cops. . . .

Though the numbers men grew up in non-slum areas, they claimed that their family members and neighborhood acquaintances were tolerant of the numbers game.

My folks were respectable, law-abiding people. None of them went to jail. They knew about the numbers. Man, eveybody knows about the numbers. My mother and father use to play a number now and then. My sister, who went to college, was married to a numbers man. Everybody in the neighborhood knew what the number was each day whether they played one or not. Everybody knew too when somebody hit [won]. Of course my folks didn't like no craps or poker playing. At home we used to joke about dreaming up a good number to play.

In reference to later community adustment, all of these men had strong primary group ties. Eleven maintained strong ties with their first primary group, the parental family; thirteen experienced strong marital ties; the remaining three sustained stable relationships with a paramour.

Their difficulties as adults stemmed from gambling. Though professional gamblers with some understanding of odds and the laws of chance, these men spent much of their leisure time betting at the racetrack, prize fights, poker games and at various other major sports events throughout the Northeast. Betting on horses was their chief recreation. They earned their money from "marks" (numbers players), and at the same time they were "marks" themselves at the race track. Their reactions to this anomaly are illustrated by these comments:

> Money that comes easy, goes easy. Money you win from gambling moves around like ice on top of a red-hot stove. But you know horse racing is the sport of kings. I got to have some fun, you know. Then too, I don't gamble all the money I make from the numbers away.

A sizable portion of their time was spent with attractive young women whom they euphemistically alluded to as "slick chicks," "fine broads," "foxes," and "party girls." They wined, dined and socialized with these women at two plush cocktail lounges situated in a Negro commercial section of Washington, D.C. They passed these girls around among themselves at what they termed "respectable time intervals" (3-6 months). Many of these "playmates" worked in a numbers ring as clerical workers. At times they were actually "kept women," who accepted their roles as companions and sex partners. These remarks were characteristic:

> These chicks as a rule were for real. I mean they would never squeal. They knew we were in the life, and with us they knew they got the best of what there was to get like entertainment, clothes, perfume, booze. Everybody knew who was going with who. The fruit basket would turn over now and then and we would change partners in a nice way, but we didn't get upset and jealous. It was the life. You know we lived it up. We were gentlemen. No girl had to worry about us beating her up or pushing her around. You know many men do slap women around. They understood we were married. They never called us at home. In fact we were all good friends. Some of the chicks worked for us as clerical help.

Their leisure-time nexus of gambling and women seemed to constitute prescribed role playing:

> Well, you know in my business you have to be a sport and a spender. You got to have front. You have to impress the public that you are a man in the know who knows how to live it up. You got to wear sharp clothes, hang out in the best places, set up the boys and girls at the bar with drinks. And you know, give the chicks a break. When these suckers see you swinging out now and then with a fine broad they know you have some money, and they figure they can play their numbers with you safely. This is a competitive business. Of course it's not too hard on me to play the game. My wife understands this. She's been with me now ten years. She isn't going anywhere. Of course she is not happy when I go out and blow a chunk (money) after a big run, but I have to do that. At that time I have to prove I can stand the run.

Their statements demonstrated that the numbers game was a regular, day-by-day occupation and that they were interested in upward mobility in an activity which called for differential responsibility and skills at various levels of performance. As one numbers man reported:

I've made my living by the numbers for years. I started out working for a "numbers writer" twenty years ago as a "runner." He died two years later. I had worked hard and had played him square. The big boy "numbers backer" knew I knew the territory and everybody in it. He also knew I was a pleasant, fast talker and a hard worker who could put on a front. I know to keep my mouth shut when necessary. I could shoot the breeze with the customers about most anything they wanted to talk about . . . you know, sports, gambling, women, even politics. He knew I could also keep my hand out of his bag (steal the backer's take). Five years later he made me a "pick-up man." You see I had a head for figures. I could estimate the normal take in most areas of the city. It was hard for a "writer" to hold out on me cause I knew what the people bet in his area. A few years later the big boy's "head man" was 'busted' [arrested] at the drop and then I got my big break. He called me up to help supervise the drop. Three of us fought it out for "head man" for two years. The competition was keen. I had to be nice to everybody there though I knew some were gunning for me. I really had to be a politician and learn more about numbers too. You know, a little book-keeping and percentages. I also had to get to know the strong and weak points of workers. I had to learn when to recommend hiring and firing certain people. It takes a certain kind of head for figures and a certain kind of personality for numbers. You got to be careful who you hire. You can't afford to hire a "willy" [country boy]. You got to pick a man with some class who knows what's happening, and who knows how to dress and talk right. You got to stay away from gorillas [strong armers] unless you are hiring a bouncer. Finally I made a "head man." After the big boy *was* finally busted I took over as a backer. Not everybody makes it. You can get froze at my level. I was lucky, and I guess I got more class than most people.

Though all these men made their living primarily from numbers, ten of them claimed that at one time or another they had invested money as "silent partners" in what they referred to as legitimate enterprises— bars, liquor stores, tourist homes, poolrooms and used car lots. Five said they owned rental property. The capital for these business ventures was invariably made from numbers. Their general attitude toward legitimate business, money, and the numbers game may be adduced from the following expressions of one numbers man:

What good is a lot of money less it's put to use? Stepping out into business was just like another gamble to me. Many Negro businessmen in this town got their start from working at numbers. Some retire, some don't. If it wasn't for numbers some people wouldn't have jobs and homes. I went into numbers for the same reason other people go into teaching or medicine or anything else. I noticed some outstanding successful people in the game. They attracted me so I went in.

None of them claimed any association with other aspects of the organized underworld, though they were quite familiar with the criminal argot. They asserted only a newspaper knowledge of other underworld activities and admitted to no more than a nodding acquaintance with offenders outside the gambling fraternity. Their criminal companions were usually other numbers men, though they admitted to some association with other types of gamblers, e.g., owners and operators of gambling houses, racetrack bookies, boxing, football and baseball bookies, and "house" card and dice dealers. . . .

The interview material suggested that fifteen of these men were products of the Negro middle class. All were reared in non-slum neighborhoods by respectable parents; twelve graduated from high school; three attended college, ten stated that one or more of their siblings had attended college; twelve stated that their wives attended college; fourteen claimed that their parents had steady, non-laboring jobs; and all mentioned friends and family connections among professionals and semiprofessionals. . . . The men presented themselves as respectable, middle class people who were churchgoers, homeowners, and fathers.

Perhaps, though products of the Negro middle class, these men who lived in the noncriminal as well as the criminal world could best be described as middle and upper class "shadies." But no less a scholar than E. Franklin Frazier lends support to their claim of respectability. He contends that "playing the numbers" has become respectable among members of the Negro middle class and that some members of Negro "society" derive their income from the numbers. He claims further that the Negro middle class is also being recruited from the successful underworld Negroes who have gained their money from numbers and that the sporting and criminal elements are acquiring a dominant position among Negroes.

Regardless of their class position in the Negro community, these men were criminals because they engaged in an illegal racket. They evinced in the interviews the "fast buck" philosophy of the "angle boy" and the professional criminal and expressed negative feelings about all law enforcement machinery, especially the police. Moreover they seemed to have rationalized away their specific form of criminal activity. Gambling to them did not constitute "real" criminal behavior. These assertions by one interviewee were typical:

Why don't the cops spend their time on these hoodlums and leave us numbers men alone. All we do is provide opportunity for people to gamble. You can't stop gambling. We provide a service for which we deserve some return. Hell, we pay 800 to 1 odds. Everybody has his angle. Take you, you got your racket. You probably will write a book. The police have theirs. They will take a red hot stove [accept bribes]. Trying to do away with crooked cops is as easy as dipping all the water out of the Atlantic Ocean with a saucer.

All claimed that the gambling ring for which they worked retained a criminal lawyer on a permanent basis. It is interesting to note that their court records revealed that only four different lawyers (three Negro and one white) were involved in the sixteen different court cases.

Though, according to their reports, the various numbers rings in which they worked competed with each other for personnel and for betting customers, there was no evidence of syndicated numbers activity. On the contrary, the data indicated that the leaders (numbers backers) were local products. There appeared to be a feudal system (minus a king) including several rings, each maintaining its own organizational pattern and its own base of operations and each possessing an individual set of employees. . . .

The arrest histories of these men were comparatively brief (mean: 5.2 per man), and the overwhelming number of their arrests were for lottery law charges. There were a few disorderly conduct charges, usually connected with the presence of the offender in a house dice or card game or in a numbers-counting office and an occasional intoxication charge. Other types of charges were rare. Criminal progression was not in evidence; the arrest histories generally began and terminated with lottery law violation charges. . . .

The numbers men appeared to be in good health and made few somatic complaints. Medical examinations showed that twelve were organically sound, one had diabetes, one had a hyperthyroid condition, and two suffered from mild heart murmurs. They reacted to the interview situation in a friendly and cooperative manner. There were no obvious diagnostic signs of neurosis, psychopathy or psychosis. They appeared to be extroverted and outgoing personalities, who verbalized well at a highly literate level. Neither verbal aggression nor verbal passivity was noted. These men expressed strong emotional ties with friends and family members. Comparatively speaking, they appeared to be sophisticated in reference to the criminal as well as the noncriminal world. Though not regular church attenders, they expressed a strong religious orientation of an orthodox type. They were well poised, confident and self-satisfied. In short, they seemed to relate well and to have well-integrated personalities. . . .

What peculiar constellation of background and personality characteristics disposed them to this and not to other patterns of criminal behavior? The full answer to this question is not known. However, their developmental histories offer some hypothetical clues in this direction. They grew up in home and neighborhood situations which were quite tolerant of the numbers game racket. Parents, friends and acquaintances played numbers. In fact, some of their neighbors and in-laws were numbers men. In a sense they were reared in a cultural milieu where the numbers game constituted a community institution which, though illegal, was not defined as "really criminal." In late adolescence they adopted an adult recreation pattern of drinking, gambling and dancing which they did not conceive of as reprehensible or illegal. Sexually precocious, they began dating early and engaging in promiscuous heterosexual relations. The role of the "sport," the "smoothie" and the "big spender" which was tied in with their early recreation pattern intrigued them. They became interested in "sharp clothes," expensive tastes and what they called "high living." They were surreptitious in these activities because of their desire to please "conventional parents." They avoided juvenile delinquents and juvenile delinquent gang activity. Fighting, stealing, and violence were defined as behavior outside of their life style. They were especially concerned with remaining clear of arrest and police contacts. In a sense they conceived of themselves as . . . "good boys." As young adults they admired the numbers men with whom they came in contact through family and neighborhod acquaintances. They considered some of these racketeers to be outstanding successes in their field. Material success and the way of life of the numbers man that went with this success appealed to them. Consequently they rationalized away the illegal aspects of the numbers game and entered it as a "business pursuit."

This rationalization was probably not too difficult. Perhaps the urban Negro middle class has in part accepted the numbers man. Perhaps he is acceptable because of his money. Material wealth is undoubtedly a great determinant of social status among members of a minority group who are at the bottom of the economic ladder, who have not been stratified into functional social classes until quite recently and who are discriminated against and segregated. In these circumstances the social class lines of urban Negroes are probably fluid. It must also be remembered that the Negro middle and upper classes are much smaller in base and less economically secure than are the white middle and upper classes.

Treatment prospects with such a group of offenders do not appear heartening. Perhaps when the urban Negro comes to be less spatially separated and socially isolated from the remainder of the community, and when his middle and upper class membership increases in size, economic base and security, the numbers man will come to be viewed for what he is, a racketeer. Perhaps then the moral indignation of the Negro community will fall upon him, and all supports for his claim to respectability will be removed. . . .

In prison, the numbers men were generally tractable, pleasant and courteous inmates who were usually liked by other inmates as well as by prison employees. They accepted their time philosophically, and they did not seek special favors. The prison term was viewed as an occupational hazard. In the prison setting they made themselves as unobtrusive as possible. As a rule they were not interested in status within the inmate subculture. Neither "peddler-connivers" nor prison toughs, they seemed to apprcximate in type the "real man" construct suggested by Gresham Sykes—the dignified, composed inmate who does not exploit others and who is able to endure the hardships of incarceration. Their short sentences (usually three years) and their strong primary group ties on the outside perhaps militated against preoccupation with prison status. On the other other hand, they subscribed to the principle that every man has his price, that all occupations are rackets. They saw little use for and they avoided such therapy programs as group counseling, group therapy, and individual therapy. The institution's religious and educational programs were of no interest to them. They appeared to have crystallized their social values and the attitudes which underpinned their specific form of criminal behavior—a behavior which appears to have strong support among their peer groups in "free" society. . . .

Generally, these professional gamblers are model prisoners. To the writer's knowledge, not one "numbers man" has been reported for a serious violation of prison regulations during his sentence at the D. C. Reformatory. They are tractable, pleasant and courteous inmates. They usually competently fill clerical positions as inmate clerks. They are generally liked by other inmates as well as by prison officials. Contrary to what would be expected of the professional criminal, they do not seek special favors. In short, they make "good" adjustments in prison, where they make themselves as unobtrusive as possible. As other professional criminals, they subscribe to the principle that "every man has his price," that all occupations are rackets. In short, they are what is generally referred to in prison slang as "angle boys." For these reasons they should be separated (housing and work details) from nonprofessional criminals in the prison setting.

THE BEHAVIOR OF THE SYSTEMATIC CHECK FORGER

Edwin M. Lemert

. . . The five elements of the behavior system of the thief are as follows: (1) stealing is made a regular business; (2) every act is carefully

From *Social Problems*, 6 (Fall 1958), 141-48. Reprinted by permission.

planned, including the use of the "fix"; (3) technical skills are used, chiefly those of manipulating people; this differentiates the thief from other professional criminals; (4) the thief is migratory but uses a specific city as a headquarters; and (5) the thief has criminal associations involving acquaintances, congeniality, sympathy, understandings, rules, codes of behavior, and a special language.

Altogether 72 persons currently serving sentences for check forgery and writing checks with insufficient funds were studied. Three additional check offenders were contacted and interviewed outside of prison. The sample included eight women and 67 men, all of whom served time in California correctional institutions.

Thirty of the 75 check criminals could be classified as systematic in the sense that they (1) thought of themselves as check men; (2) had worked out or regularly employed a special technique of passing checks; and (3) had more or less organized their lives around the exigencies or imperatives of living by means of fraudulent checks. The remaining 45 cases represented a wide variety of contexts in which bogus check passing was interspersed with periods of stable employment and family life, or was simply an aspect of alcoholism, gambling, or one of a series of criminal offenses having little or no consistency.

FINDINGS

. . . The behavior of the persons falling into the systematic check forgery category qualified only in a very general way as professional crime. In other words, although it is possible to describe these forgeries as *systematic,* it is questionable whether more than a small portion of them can be subsumed as *professional* under the more general classification of professional theft. A point-by-point comparison will serve to bring out the numerous significant differences between systematic forgery and professional theft.

1. FORGERY AS A "REGULAR BUSINESS"

It is questionable whether check men look upon their crimes as a "regular business" in the same way as do members of "other occupational groups" who "wish to make money in safety." In virtually all cases the motivation proved to be exceedingly complex. This fact was self-consciously recognized and expressed in different ways but all informants revealed an essential perplexity or conflict about their criminal behavior. The following statement may be taken as illustrative:

> Nine out of ten check men are lone wolves. Those men who work in gangs are not real check men. They do it for money; we do it for something else. It gives us something we need. Maybe we're crazy. . . .

The conflicts expressed involved not merely the rightness or wrongness of behavior; they also disclosed a confusion and uncertainty as to the possibility of living successfully or safely by issuing false checks. All of the cases, even the few who had a history of professional thieving, admitted that arrest and imprisonment are inevitable. None knew of exceptions to this, although one case speculated that "It might be done by an otherwise respected business man who made one big spread and then quit and retired."

The case records of the systematic check forgers gave clear testimony of this. Generally they had but shortlived periods of freedom, ranging from a few months to a year or two at the most, followed by imprisonment. Many of the cases since beginning their forgery careers had spent less total time outside prisons than within, a fact corroborated by the various law-enforcement officers queried on the point.

Many of the check men depicted their periods of check writing as continuous sprees during which they lived "fast" and luxuriously. Many spoke of experiencing considerable tension during these periods, and two cases developed stomach ulcers which caused them to "lay off at resorts." A number gambled and drank heavily, assertedly to escape their internal stress and sense of inevitable arrest. A number spoke of gradual build-up of strain and a critical point just before their arrest at which they became demoralized and after which they "just didn't care any more" or "got tired of running." The arrests of several men having a very long experience with checks resulted from blunders in technique of which they were aware at the time they made them. Some of the men gave themselves up to detectives or FBI agents at this point.

In general the picture of the cool, calculating professional with prosaic, matter-of-fact attitudes toward his crimes as a trade or occupation supported by rationalizations of a subculture was not valid for the cases in question.

2. PLANNING AS AN ASPECT OF FORGERY

In regard to the second element of professional theft—planning—the behavior of check forgers is again divergent. Actually the present techniques of check passing either preclude precise planning or make it unnecessary. Although systematic check passers undeniably pay careful attention to such things as banking hours, the places at which checks are presented, and the kinds of "fronts" they employ, these considerations serve only as generalized guides for their crimes. Most informants held that situations have to be *exploited as they arise,* with variation and flexibility being the key to success. What stands out in the behavior of systematic check forgers is the rapid tempo—almost impulsiveness—with which they work.

The cases seemed to agree that check forgers seldom attempt to use the "fix" in order to escape the consequences of their crimes. The reason for this is that although one or a small number of checks might be made good, the systematic forger has too many bad checks outstanding and too many victims to mollify by offering restitution. Although the forger may be prosecuted on the basis of only one or two checks, ordinarily the prosecuting attorney will have a choice of a large number of complaints upon which to act. About the best the check forger can hope for through fixing activities is a short sentence or a sentence to jail rather than to prison.

3. TECHNICAL SKILLS

Although the systematic check man relies upon technical skills—those of manipulating others—these are usually not of a high order, nor do they require a long learning period to master. From the standpoint of the appearance of the check or the behavior involved at the time of its passing, there need, of course, be no great difference between passing a bad check and passing a good check. This is particularly true of personal checks, which are at least as favored as payroll checks by check men.

When check men impersonate others or when they assume fictitious roles, acting ability is required. To the extent that elaborate impersonations are relied upon by the forger, his check passing takes on qualities of a confidence game. Most of the check men showed strong preference, however, for simple, fast-moving techniques. A number expressed definite dislike for staged arrangements, such as that of the "out of town real estate buyer" or for setting up a fictitious business in a community, then waiting several weeks or a month before making a "spread" of checks. As they put it, they "dislike the slow build-up involved."

4. MOBILITY

Like the thief, the systematic forger is migratory. Only one check man interviewed spoke of identifying himself with one community, and even he was reluctant to call it a headquarters. Generally check men are migratory within regions.

5. ASSOCIATIONS

The sharpest and most categorical difference between professional theft and systematic forger lies in the realm of associations. In contrast to pickpockets, shoplifters, and con men, whose criminal techniques are implicitly cooperative, most check men with highly developed systems work alone, carefully avoiding contacts and interaction with other criminals. Moreover, their preference for solitude and their secretiveness gives every appearance of a highly generalized reaction; they avoid not only cooperative crime but also any other kinds of association with criminals. They are equally selective and cautious in their contacts and associations with the non-criminal population, preferring not to become involved in any enduring personal relationships.

A descriptive breakdown of the 30 check forgers classified as systematic bears out this point. Only four of the 30 had worked in check passing gangs. Two of these had acted as "fences" who organized the operations. . . .

Three other systematic check forgers did not work directly with other criminals but had criminal associations of a *contractual* nature. One old-time forger familiar with the now little-used methods for forging signatures and raising checks usually sold checks to passers but never had uttered [passed] any of his forgeries. Two men were passers who purchased either payroll checks from a "hot printer" or stolen checks from burglars. Apart from the minimal contacts necessary to sell or obtain a supply of checks, all three men were lone operators and very seclusive in their behavior.

Six of the 30 systematic forgers worked exclusively with one other person, usually a girl or "broad." The check men seemed to agree that working with a girl was equivalent to working alone. These pairs ordinarily consisted of the check man and some girl not ordinarily of criminal background with whom he had struck up a living arrangement and for whom he felt genuine affection. The girl was used either to make out the checks or to pass them. In some cases she was simply used as a front to distract attention. Some men picked up girls in bars or hotels and employed them as fronts without their knowledge.

The remaining 17 of the 30 systematic check forgers operated on a solitary basis. The majority of these argued that contact with others is unnecessary to obtain and pass a supply of checks. Most of them uttered personal checks. However, even where they made use of payroll or corporation checks they contrived to manufacture or obtain them without resorting to interaction with criminal associates or intermediaries. For example, one Nisei check man arranged with a printer to make up checks for a fraternal organization of which he represented himself as secretary-treasurer. Another man frequented business offices at noon time, and when the clerk left the office, helped himself to a supply of company checks, in one instance stealing a check-writing machine for his purposes.

It was difficult to find evidence of anything more than rudimentary congeniality, sympathy, understandings, and shared rules of behavior among the check forgers, including those who had worked in gangs. Rather the opposite seemed true, suspicion and distrust marking their relationships with one another. One organizer of a gang, for example, kept careful account of all the checks he issued to his passers and made them return torn off corners of checks in case they were in danger of arrest and had to get rid of them. Only two of the thirty forgers indicated that they had at times engaged in recreational activities with other criminals. Both of these men were lone wolves in their work. . . .

The two men who had organized gangs of check passers worked with a set of rules, but they were largely improvised and laid down by the fence rather than voluntarily recognized and obeyed by the passers. The other check men with varying degrees of explicitness recognized rules for passing checks—rules learned almost entirely on an individual trial-and-error basis. The informants insisted that "you learn as you go" and that one of the rules was "never use another man's stunt."

Such special morality as was recognized proved to be largely functional in derivation. Thus attitudes toward drinking and toward picking up women for sexual purposes were pretty much the result of individual perceptions of what was likely to facilitate or hamper the passing of checks or lead to arrest. Many of the men stated that since they were dealing primarily with business, professional, and clerical persons, their appearance and behavior had to be acceptable to these people. "Middle class" is probably the best term to describe their morality in most areas.

Careful inquiries were made to discover the extent to which the check men were familiar with and spoke an argot. Findings proved meager. Many of the men had a superficial acquaintance with general prison slang, but only four men could measurably identify and reproduce the argot of check forgery or that of thieves. . . .

INTERPRETATION

. . . In the past forgery was a much more complex procedure in which a variety of false instruments such as bank notes, drafts, bills of exchange, letters of credit, registered bonds, and post office money orders as well as checks were manufactured or altered and foisted off. A knowledge of chemicals, papers, inks, engraving, etching, lithography, and penmanship as well as detailed knowledge of bank operations were prime requisites for success. The amounts of money sought were comparatively large, and often they had to be obtained through complex monetary transactions. The technological characteristics of this kind of forgery made planning, timing, specialization, differentiation of roles, morale, and organization imperative. Capital was necessary for living expenses during the period when preparations for the forgeries were being made. Intermediates between the skilled forger and the passers were necessary so that the latter could swear that the handwriting on the false negotiable instruments was not theirs and so that the forger himself was not exposed to arrest. A "shadow" was often used for protection against the passer's temptation to abscond with the money and in order to alert the others of trouble at the bank. "Fall" money was accumulated and supplied to assist the passer when arrested. Inasmuch as forgery gangs worked together for a considerable length of time, understandings, congeniality, and rules of behavior, especially with regard to the division of money, could and did develop. In short, professional forgery was based upon the technology of the period.

Although precise dating is difficult, the heyday of professional forgery in this country probably began after the Civil War and lasted through the 1920's. It seems to have corresponded with the early phases of industrialization and commercial development before business and law-enforcement agencies developed methods and organization for preventing forgery and apprehending the offenders. Gradually technological developments in inks, papers, protectographs,and check-writing machines made the forging of signatures and the manufacture of false negotiable instruments more difficult. . . . The establishment of a protective committee by the American Bankers Association in 1894, related merchants' protective agencies, and improvements in police methods have made the risks of organized professional forgery exceedingly great.

Check gangs have always been vulnerable to arrest but this vulnerability has been multiplied many times by the large amounts of evidence left behind them in the form of countless payroll checks. Vulnerability is also heightened by the swiftness of communication today. If one person of a check-passing gang is arrested and identifies his associates, it becomes a relatively simple matter for police to secure their arrest. A sexually exploited and angered female companion may easily do the same to the check man. This goes far to explain the extreme seclusiveness of systematic check forgers and their almost abnormal fear of stool pigeons or of being "fingered." The type of persons who can be engaged as passers—unattached women, bar waitresses, drug addicts, alcoholics, petty thieves, and transient unemployed persons—also magnifies the probabilities that mistakes will be made and precludes the growth of a morale which might prevent informing to the police. These conditions also explain the fact that when the forger does work with someone it is likely to be one other person upon whom he feels he can rely with implicit confidence. Hence the man-woman teams in which the woman is in love with the man, or the case of two homosexual girls, or of two brothers check-passing teams.

Further evidence that organized forgery is a hazardous type of crime, difficult to professionalize under modern conditions, is indicated by the fact that the organizer or fence is apt to be an older criminal with a long record, whose handwriting methods are so well known that he has no choice other than to work through passers. Even then he does it with recognition that arrest is inevitable.

A factor of equal importance in explaining the decline of professional organized forgery has been the increasingly widespread use of business and payroll checks as well as personal checks. Whereas in the past the use of checks was confined to certain kinds of business transactions, mostly involving banks, today it is ubiquitous. Attitudes of business people and their clerical employees have undergone great change, and only the most perfunctory identification is necessary to cash many kinds of checks. Check men recognize this in frequent unsolicited comments that passing checks is "easy." Some argue that the form of the check is now relatively unimportant to passing it, that "you can pass a candy bar wrapper nowadays with the right front and story." It is for this reason that the systematic check man does not have to resort to criminal associates or employ the more complex professional procedures used in decades past.

These facts may also account for the presence among lone-wolf check forgers of occasional persons with the identification, orientation, skills, codes, and argot of the thief. Case histories as well as the observations of informants show that older professional criminals in recent decades have turned to check passing because they face long sentences for additional crimes or sentencing under habitual criminal legislation. They regard checks as an "easy racket" because in many states conviction makes them subject to jail sentences rather than imprisonment. Check passing may be a last resort for the older criminal.

The presence of the occasional older professional thief in the ranks of check forgers also may token a general decline and slow disappearance of professional thieving. One professional thief turned check passer had this to say:

> I'm a thief—a burglar—but I turned to checks because it's getting too hard to operate. Police are a lot smarter now, and they have better methods. People are different nowadays too; they report things more. It's hard to trust anyone now. Once you could trust cab drivers; now you can't. We live in a different world today.

THE CHECK FORGER AS AN ISOLATE

The preference of many systematic check forgers for solitary lives and their avoidance of primary-group associations among criminals may also be explicable in terms of their educational characteristics and class origins. The history of forgery reveals that in medieval times it was considered to be the special crime of the clerical class, as indeed it had to be inasmuch as the members of this class monopolized writing skills. It also seems to be true from the later history of the crime that it has held a special attraction for more highly educated persons, for those of higher socio-economic status and those of "refined" or artistic tastes. The basic method of organized forgery is stated to have been invented and perfected in England, not by criminals but by a practicing barrister of established reputation in 1840. . . .

All of this is not to say that less-educated persons do not frequently pass bad checks but rather that the persons who persist in the behavior and develop behavior systems of forgery seem much more likely than other criminals to be drawn from a segment of the population distinguished by a higher socio-economic status. Generally this was true of the systematic forgers in this study. Eight of the 30 had completed two or more years of college. Fourteen of the 30 had fathers who were or had been in the professions and business, including a juvenile court judge, a minister, a postmaster of a large city, and three very wealthy ranch owners. One woman came from a nationally famous family of farm implement manufacturers. Four others had siblings well established in business and the professions, one of whom was an attorney general in another state. Two of the men had been successful businessmen themselves before becoming check men.

The most important implication of these data is that systematic check forgers do not seem to have had criminal antecedents or early criminal associations. For this reason, as well as for technical reasons, they are not likely to seek out or to be comfortable in informal associations with other criminals who have been products of early and lengthy socialization and learning in a criminal subculture. It also follows that their morality and values remain essentially "middle" or "upper" class and that they seldom integrate these with the morality of the professional criminal. This is reflected in self-attitudes in which many refer to themselves as "black sheep" or as a kind of Dr. Jekyll–Mr. Hyde person. Further support for this interpretation comes from their status in prison where, according to observations of themselves and others, they are marginal so far as participation in the primary groups of the prison is concerned. . . .

ORGANIZED CRIME
The President's Commission on Law Enforcement and the Administration of Justice

Organized crime is a society that seeks to operate outside the control of the American people and their governments. It involves thousands of criminals, working within structures as complex as those of any large

From The Task Force Report, *Organized Crime,* 1967, pp. 1-8.

corporation, subject to laws more rigidly enforced than those of legitimate governments. Its actions are not impulsive but rather the result of intricate conspiracies, carried on over many years and aimed at gaining control over whole fields of activity in order to amass huge profits.

The core of organized crime activity is the supplying of illegal goods and services—gambling, loan sharking, narcotics, and other forms of vice —to countless numbers of citizen customers. But organized crime is also extensively and deeply involved in legitimate business and in labor unions. Here it employs illegitimate methods—monopolization, terrorism, extortion, tax evasion—to drive out or control lawful ownership and leadership and to exact illegal profits from the public. And to carry on its many activities secure from governmental interference, organized crime corrupts public officials. . . .

. . . Organized crime affects the lives of millions of Americans, but because it desperately preserves its invisibility many, perhaps most, Americans are not aware how they are affected, or even that they are affected at all. The price of a loaf of bread may go up one cent as the result of an organized crime conspiracy, but a housewife has no way of knowing why she is paying more. If organized criminals paid income tax on every cent of their vast earnings everybody's tax bill would go down, but no one knows how much.

But to discuss the impact of organized crime in terms of whatever direct, personal, everyday effect it has on individuals is to miss most of the point. Most individuals are not affected, in this sense, very much. Much of the money organized crime accumulates comes from innumerable petty transactions: 50-cent bets, $3-a-month private garbage collection services, quarters dropped into racketeer-owned jukeboxes, or small price rises resulting from protection rackets. . . .

Sometimes organized crime's activities do not directly affect individuals at all. Smuggled cigarettes in a vending machine cost consumers no more than tax-paid cigarettes, but they enrich the leaders of organized crime. . . . Even when organized crime engages in a large transaction, individuals may not be directly affected. A large sum of money may be diverted from a union pension fund to finance a business venture without immediate and direct effect upon the individual members of the union.

It is organized crime's accumulation of money . . . that has a great and threatening impact on America. . . . Organized crime exists by virtue of the power it purchases with its money. The millions of dollars it can invest in narcotics or use for layoff money give it power over the lives of thousands of people and over the quality of life in whole neighborhoods. The millions of dollars it can throw into the legitimate economic system give it power to manipulate the price of shares on the stock market, to raise or lower the price of retail merchandise, to determine whether entire industries are union or nonunion, to make it easier or harder for businessmen to continue in business.

The millions of dollars it can spend on corrupting public officials may give it power to maim or murder people inside or outside the organization with impunity; to extort money from businessmen; to conduct businesses in such fields as liquor, meat, or drugs without regard to administrative regulations; to avoid payment of income taxes or to secure public works contracts without competitive bidding.

The purpose of organized crime is not competition with visible, legal government but nullification of it. When organized crime places an official in public office, it nullifies the political process. When it bribes a police official, it nullifies law enforcement. . . .

THE TYPES OF ORGANIZED CRIMINAL ACTIVITIES

CATERING TO PUBLIC DEMANDS

Organized criminal groups participate in any illegal activity that offers maximum profit at minimum risk of law enforcement interference. They offer goods and services that millions of Americans desire even though declared illegal by their legislatures.

Gambling   Law enforcement officials agree almost unanimously that gambling is the greatest source of revenue for organized crime It ranges from lotteries, such as "numbers" or "bolita," to off-track horse betting, bets on sporting events, large dice games and illegal casinos. In large cities where organized criminal groups exist, very few of the gambling operators are independent of a large organization. Anyone whose independent operation becomes successful is likely to receive a visit from an organization representative who convinces the independent, through fear or promise of greater profit, to share his revenue with the organization.

Most large-city gambling is established or controlled by organized crime members through elaborate hierarchies. Money is filtered from the small operator who takes the customer's bet, through persons who pick up money and slips, to second-echelon figures in charge of particular districts, and then into one of several main offices. The profits that eventually accrue to organization leaders move through channels so complex that even persons who work in the betting operation do not know or cannot prove the identity of the leader. Increasing use of the telephone for lottery and sports betting has facilitated systems in which the bookmaker may not know the identity of the second-echelon person to whom he calls in the day's bets. Organization not only creates greater efficiency and enlarges markets, it also provides a systematized method of corrupting the law enforcement process by centralizing procedures for the payment of graft.

Organization is also necessary to prevent severe losses. More money may be bet on one horse or one number with a small operator than he could pay off if that horse or that number should win. The operator will have to hedge by betting some money himself on that horse or that number. This so-called "layoff" betting is accomplished through a network of local, ragional, and national layoff men, who take bets from gambling operations.

There is no accurate way of ascertaining organized crime's gross revenue from gambling in the United States. Estimates of the annual intake have varied from $7 to $50 billion. Legal betting at racetracks reaches a gross annual figure of almost $5 billion, and most enforcement officials believe that illegal wagering on horse races, lotteries, and sporting events totals at least $20 billion each year. Analysis of organized criminal betting operations indicates that the profit is as high as one-third of gross revenue—or $6 to $7 billion each year. While the Commission cannot judge the accuracy of these figures, even the most conservative estimates place substantial capital in the hands of organized crime leaders.

Loan-sharking   In the view of most law enforcement officials loan sharking, the lending of money at higher rates than the legally prescribed limit, is the second largest source of revenue for organized crime. Gambling profits provide the initial capital for loan-shark operations. . . .

Interest rates vary from 1 to 150 per cent a week, according to the relationship between the lender and borrower, the intended use of the money, the size of the loan, and the repayment potential. The classic "6-for-5" loan, 20 per cent a week, is common with small borrowers. Payments may be due by a certain hour on a certain day, and even a few minutes' default may result in a rise in interest rates. The lender is more interested in perpetuating interest payments than collecting principal; and force, or threats of force of the most brutal kind, are used to effect interest collection, eliminate protest when interest rates are raised, and prevent the beleaguered borrower from reporting the activity to enforcement officials. No reliable estimates exist of the gross revenue from organized loan sharking, but profit margins are higher than for gambling operations, and many officials classify the business in the multi-billion-dollar range.

Narcotics   The sale of narcotics is organized like a legitimate importing-wholesaling-retailing business. The distribution of heroin, for example, requires movement of the drug through four or five levels between the importer and the street peddler. . . .

The large amounts of cash and the international connections necessary for large, long-term heroin supplies can be provided only by organized crime. Conservative estimates of the number of addicts in the nation and the average daily expenditure for heroin indicate that the gross heroin trade is $350 million annually, of which $21 million are probably profits to the importer and distributor. . . .

Other Goods and Services   Prostitution and bootlegging play a small and declining role in organized crime's operations. Production of illegal alcohol is a risky business. The destruction of stills and supplies by law enforcement officers during the initial stages means the loss of heavy initial investment capital. Prostitution is difficult to organize and discipline is hard to maintain. . . .

BUSINESS AND LABOR INTERESTS

Infiltration of Legitimate Business   A legitimate business enables the racket executive to acquire respectability in the community and to establish a source of funds that appears legal and upon which just enough taxes may be paid to avoid income tax prosecution. Organized crime invests the profit it has made from illegal service activities in a variety of businesses throughout the country. To succeed in such ventures, it uses accountants, attorneys, and business consultants, who in some instances work exclusively on its affairs. Too often, because of the reciprocal benefits involved in organized crime's dealings with the business world, or because of fear, the legitimate sector of society helps the illegitimate sector. The Illinois Crime Commission, after investigating one service industry in Chicago, stated:

> There is a disturbing lack of interest on the part of some legitimate business concerns regarding the identity of the persons with whom they deal. This lackadaisical attitude is conducive to the perpetration of frauds and the infiltration and subversion of legitimate businesses by the organized criminal element.

Because business ownership is so easily concealed, it is difficult to determine all the types of businesses that organized crime has penetrated. Of the 75 or so racket leaders who met at Apalachin, N.Y., in 1957, at least 9 were in the coin-operated machine industry, 16 were in the garment industry, 10 owned grocery stores, 17 owned bars or restaurants, 11 were in the olive oil and cheese business, and 9 were in the construction business. Others were involved in automobile agencies, coal companies, entertainment, funeral homes, ownership of horses and race tracks, linen and laundry enterprises, trucking, waterfront activities, and bakeries.

Today, the kinds of production and service industries and businesses that organized crime controls or has invested in range from accounting firms to yeast manufacturing. One criminal syndicate alone has real estate interests with an estimated value of $300 million. In a few instances, racketeers control nationwide manufacturing and service industries with known and respected brand names.

Control of business concerns has usually been acquired through one of four methods: (1) investing concealed profits acquired from gambling and other illegal activities; (2) accepting business interests in payment of the owner's gambling debts; (3) foreclosing on usurious loans; and (4) using various forms of extortion.

Acquisition of legitimate businesses is also accomplished in more sophisticated ways. One organized crime group offered to lend money to a business on condition that a racketeer be appointed to the company's board of directors and that a nominee for the lenders be given first option to purchase if there were any outside sale of the company's stock. Control of certain brokerage houses was secured through foreclosure of usurious loans, and the businesses then used to promote the sale of fraudulent stock, involving losses of more than $2 million to the public. . . .

Too little is known about the effects on the economy of organized crime's entry into the business world, but the examples above indicate the harm done to the public and at least suggest how criminal cartels can undermine free competition. . . .

Strong-arm tactics are used to enforce unfair business policy and to obtain customers. A restaurant chain controlled by organized crime used the guise of "quality control" to insure that individual restaurant franchise holders bought products only from other syndicate-owned businesses. In one city, every business with a particular kind of waste product useful in another line of industry sold that product to a syndicate-controlled business at one-third the price offered by legitimate business.

The cumulative effect of the infiltration of legitimate business in America cannot be measured. Law enforcement officials agree that entry into legitimate business is continually increasing and that it has not decreased organized crime's control over gambling, usury and other profitable, low-risk criminal enterprises.

Labor Racketeering   Control of labor supply and infiltration of labor unions by organized crime prevent unionization of some industries, provide opportunities for stealing from union funds and extorting money by threats of possible labor strife, and provide funds from the enormous union pension and welfare systems for business ventures controlled by organized criminals. Union control also may enhance other illegal activities. Trucking, construction, and waterfront shipping entrepreneurs, in return for assurance that business operations will not be interrupted by labor discord, countenance gambling, loan sharking, and pilferage on company property. Organized criminals either direct these activities or grant "concessions" to others in return for a percentage of the profits.

MEMBERSHIP AND ORGANIZATION OF CRIMINAL CARTELS

NATIONAL SCOPE OF ORGANIZED CRIME

In 1951 the Kefauver Committee declared that a nationwide crime syndicate known as the Mafia operated in many large cities and that the leaders of the Mafia usually controlled the most lucrative rackets in their cities.

In 1957, 20 of organized crime's top leaders were convicted (later reversed on appeal) of a criminal charge arising from a meeting at Apalachin, N.Y. At the sentencing the judge stated that they had sought to corrupt and infiltrate the political mainstreams of the country, that they had led double lives of crime and respectability, and that their probation reports read "like a tale of horrors."

Today the core of organized crime in the United States consists of 24 groups operating as criminal cartels in large cities across the nation. Their membership is exclusively men of Italian descent, they are in frequent communication with each other, and their smooth functioning is insured by a national body of overseers. To date, only the Federal Bureau of Investigation has been able to document fully the national scope of these groups, and FBI intelligence indicates that the organization as a whole has changed its name from the Mafia to La Cosa Nostra.

In 1966 J. Edgar Hoover told a House of Representatives Appropriations Subcommittee:

> La Cosa Nostra is the largest organization of the criminal underworld in this country, very closely organized and strictly disciplined. They have committed almost every crime under the sun . . .
> La Cosa Nostra is a criminal fraternity whose membership is Italian either by birth or national origin, and it has been found to control major racket activities in many of our larger metropolitan areas, often working in concert with criminals representing other ethnic backgrounds. It operates on a nationwide basis, with international implications, and until recent years it carried on its activities with almost complete secrecy. It functions as a criminal cartel, adhering to its own body of "law" and "justice" and, in so doing, thwarts and usurps the authority of legally constituted judicial bodies . . .

In individual cities, the local core group may also be known as the "outfit," the "syndicate," or the "mob." These 24 groups work with and control other racket groups, whose leaders are of various ethnic derivations. In addition, the thousands of employees who perform the street-level functions of organized crime's gambling, usury, and other illegal activities represent a cross section of the nation's population groups.

. . . The wealthiest and most influential core groups operate in states including New York, New Jersey, Illinois, Florida, Louisiana, Nevada, Michigan, and Rhode Island. . . .

INTERNAL STRUCTURE

Each of the 24 groups is known as a "family," with membership varying from as many as 700 men to as few as 20. Most cities with organized crime have only one family; New York City has five. Each family can participate in the full range of activities in which organized crime generally is known to engage. Family organization is rationally designed with an integrated set of positions geared to maximize profits. Like any large corporation, the organization functions regardless of personnel changes, and no individual—not even the leader—is indispensable. If he dies or goes to jail, business goes on.

The hierarchical structure of the families resembles that of the Mafia groups that have operated for almost a century on the island of Sicily. Each family is headed by one man, the "boss," whose primary functions are maintaining order and maximizing profits. Subject only to the possibility of being overruled by the national advisory group, which will be discussed below, his authority in all matters relating to his family is absolute.

Beneath each boss is an "underboss," the vice president or deputy director of the family. He collects information for the boss; he relays messages to him and passes his instructions down to his own underlings. In the absence of the boss, the underboss acts for him.

On the same level as the underboss, but operating in a staff capacity, is the *consigliere,* who is a counselor, or adviser. Often an elder member of the family who has partially retired from a career in crime, he gives advice to family members, including the boss and underboss, and thereby enjoys considerable influence and power.

Below the level of the underboss are the *caporegime,* some of whom serve as buffers between the top members of the family and the lower-echelon personnel. To maintain their insulation from the police, the leaders of the hierarchy (particularly the boss) avoid direct communication with the workers. All commands, information, complaints, and money flow back and forth through a trusted go-between. A *caporegima* fulfilling this buffer capacity, however, unlike the underboss, does not make decisions or assume any of the authority of his boss.

Other *caporegime* serve as chiefs of operating units. The number of men supervised in each unit varies with the size and activities of particular families. Often the *caporegima* has one or two associates who work closely with him, carrying orders, information, and money to the men who belong to his unit. From a business standpoint, the *caporegima* is analogous to plant supervisor or sales manager.

The lowest level "members" of a family are the *soldati,* the soldiers or "button" men who report to the *caporegime.* A soldier may operate a particular illicit enterprise, *e.g.,* a loan-sharking operation, a dice game, a lottery, a bookmaking operation, a smuggling operation, on a commission basis, or he may "own" the enterprise and pay a portion of its profit to the organization, in return for the right to operate. Partnerships are common between two or more soldiers and between soldiers and men higher up in the hierarchy. Some soldiers and most upper-echelon family members have interests in more than one business.

Beneath the soldiers in the hierarchy are large numbers of employees and commission agents who are not members of the family and are not necessarily of Italian descent. These are the people who do most of the actual work in the various enterprises. They have no buffers or other insulation from law enforcement. They take bets, drive trucks, answer telephones, sell narcotics, tend the stills, work in the legitimate businesses. For example, in a major lottery business that operated in Negro neighborhoods in Chicago, the workers were Negroes; the bankers for the lottery were Japanese-Americans; but the game, including the banking operation, was licensed, for a fee, by a family member. . . .

There are at least two aspects of organized crime that characterize it as a unique form of criminal activity. The first is the element of corruption. The second is the element of enforcement, which is necessary for the maintenance of both internal discipline and the regularity of business transactions. In the hierarchy of organized crime there are positions for people fulfilling both of these functions. But neither is essential to the long-term operation of other types of criminal groups. The members of a pickpocket troupe or check-passing ring, for example, are likely to take punitive action against any member who holds out more than his share of the spoils, or betrays the group to the police; but they do not recruit or train for a well-established position of "enforcer."

Organized crime groups, on the other hand, are believed to contain one or more fixed positions for "enforcers," whose duty it is to maintain organizational integrity by arranging for the maiming and killing of recalcitrant members. And there is a position for a "corrupter," whose function is to establish relationships with those public officials and other influential persons whose assistance is necessary to achieve the organization's goals. By including these positions within its organization, each criminal cartel, or "family," becomes a government as well as a business.

The highest ruling body of the 24 families is the "commission." This body serves as a combination legislature, supreme court, board of directors, and arbitration board; its principal functions are judicial. Family members look to the commission as the ultimate authority on organizational and jurisdictional disputes. It is composed of the bosses of the nation's most powerful families but has authority over all 24. The composition of the commission varies from 9 to 12 men. According to current information, there are presently 9 families represented, 5 from New York City and 1 each from Philadelphia, Buffalo, Detroit, and Chicago.

The commission is not a representative legislative assembly or an elected judicial body. Members of this council do not regard each other as equals. Those with long tenure on the commission and those who head large families, or possess unusual wealth, exercise greater authority and receive utmost respect. The balance of power on this nationwide council rests with the leaders of New York's 5 families. They have always served on the commission and consider New York as at least the unofficial headquarters of the entire organization.

In recent years organized crime has become increasingly diversified and sophisticated. One consequence appears to be significant organizational restructuring. As in any organization, authority in organized crime may derive either from rank based on incumbency in a high position or from expertise based on possession of technical knowledge and skill. Traditionally, organized crime groups, like totalitarian governments, have maintained discipline through the unthinking acceptance of orders by underlings who have respected the rank of their superiors. However, since 1931, organized crime has gained power and respectability by moving out of bootlegging and prostitution and into gambling, usury, and control of legitimate business. Its need for expertise, based on technical knowledge and skill, has increased. Currently both the structure and operation of illicit enterprises reveal some indecision brought about by attempting to follow both patterns at the same time. Organized crime's "experts" are not fungible, or interchangeable, like the "soldiers" and street workers, and since experts are included within an organization, discipline and structure inevitably assume new forms. It may be awareness of these facts that is leading many family members to send their sons to universities to learn business administration skills. . . .

WHITE-COLLAR CRIME
The President's Commission on Law Enforcement and the Administration of Justice

The term white-collar crime was first popularized by Edwin H. Sutherland in 1939. Until the publication in 1949 of his pioneering study, "White Collar Crime," virtually all criminological literature dealt with

From The Task Force Report, *Crime and Its Impact—An Assessment,* 1967 Chapter 8, pp. 102-108.

ordinary crimes—crimes most prevalent among persons in the lower socio-economic classes. . . .

Sutherland defined white-collar crime as "crime committed by a person of respectability and high social status in the course of his occupation." But the term white-collar crime has generally come to include crimes such as tax fraud, which are not necessarily committed either in connection with an occupation or by persons of "high" social status, but are as a general matter committed by the relatively well-to-do. This definition excludes so-called street crimes, such as burglary, robbery or aggravated assault, which are occasionally, but not generally, committed by persons of means.

As applied to regulatory offenses, the scope of white-collar criminality has expanded in recent years. Until the late 19th century, the economic life of this country was largely unregulated, but over the years it became clear that business enterprise had to be regulated in order to protect both the public and business itself—to maintain standards of health and safety, to assist the poor and ignorant, to obtain decent housing and other necessities, and to maintain the economy at a high level of production. Today virtually every aspect of business life is regulated in some way. There are antitrust laws, food and drug laws, safety and health laws, licensing systems for different kinds of business, housing codes and a multitude of other regulatory statutes. Many of these regulatory laws are enforced, at least in part, by criminal sanctions.

As compared to the [other] offenders, . . . white-collar offenders, by definition, have enjoyed a variety of social and economic advantages. They have received better educations and are better equipped to earn their livings legitimately. Perhaps over-simplifying the distinctive characteristics of such offenders, Sutherland wrote in "Crimes of Corporations" in 1956:

> it is very clear that the criminal behavior of businessmen cannot be explained by poverty, in the usual sense, or by bad housing or lack of recreational facilities or feeble-mindedness or emotional instability. Business leaders are capable, emotionally balanced, and in no sense pathological.

At the outset it is important to recognize the imprecision of the white-collar crime label both as applied to offenders and offenses. Crimes such as employee theft range from pilfering by truck drivers, stock-room personnel or retail salespeople to embezzlement by top executives. Cheating the government can include failure to report tips or other cash receipts and major tax or government contract frauds. And just as burglars range from the relatively successful professional in his 30's or 40's to the 13-year-old amateur from the slums, white-collar offenders include many different types of people. . . .

EXTENT AND SCOPE

There is little systematic data available regarding the incidence of white-collar crime. There are, for example, no consolidated statistics comparable to the FBI's Uniform Crime Reports in the area of traditional crime. Many white-collar crimes are of relatively recent origin. Moreover, it is very difficult to obtain statistics about some types of white-collar crime [and] . . . it is extremely difficult to discover the existence of such crimes as antitrust violations and tax frauds.

Such information as is available, though not systematically compiled, indicates that white-collar crime is pervasive in our society and causes enormous economic and social harm. Congressional investigations have turned up indications of widespread unethical and illegal behavior in various industries. Popular accounts tell of dishonest and unethical practices in the medical and legal professions, the television industry, and among morticians, drug companies and other businesses and professions.

These are corroborated by the few scientific surveys which have been undertaken. Sutherland's investigation of 70 of our largest corporations, published in 1948, suggests that law violation is prevalent in our large business enterprises. He examined the decisions of courts and regulatory commissions under the antitrust, false advertising, patent, copyright, and labor laws as they applied to corporations. During a 45-year period, he found that 980 adverse decisions had been rendered, of which 779 indicated that crimes had been committed. Every one of the 70 corporations had a decision against it and the average number was 14.0. Ninety-eight per cent of the 70 corporations had at least four adverse decisions. About 60 per cent of the 70 corporations had been convicted by criminal courts. They averaged approximately four convictions each. A study of black-market violations during World War II revealed that approximately one in every 15 of the three million business concerns in the country had been punished for serious violations of price regulations. The evidence showed that the total number of violations was much larger than indicated by officially imposed sanctions.

The "Reader's Digest" staff in 1941 sought to document by experimentation the level of white-collar crime in a study of automobile garages, radio repair shops and watch repair shops. Investigators for the magazine disconnected a coil wire in an automobile, a relatively easily diagnosed problem, and then took the automobile to 347 garages in 48 states. Of these, 129 immediately noted the trouble, and either charged nothing or a nominal fee for the work. The remainder—63 per cent of the garages—overcharged, inserted unnecessary parts, charged for work not done or for parts not needed, or took other similar action. Similarly, a radio in excellent working condition was taken to repair shops after one of the tubes had been loosened. Of 304 shops, 109 honestly identified the obvious difficulty, but the rest (almost two-thirds) treated it as a substantial repair problem. And finally, the investigators loosened the small screw that fastens the winding wheel on a watch, and then requested a number of shops to repair it. In almost half of the cases the jewelers charged for cleaning work not performed, and for parts not needed or used.

Commissioner Cohen provided some insight into the amount of tax fraud by noting that in 1964, with the inauguration of dividend and interest reporting by banks and corporations to the taxpayer, there was a 45 per cent increase in this type of income reflected on tax forms, and that 28 per cent more income was collected from these sources. Of course there is no way to determine how much of the unreported income in earlier years was merely overlooked and how much deliberately ignored on the assumption that the Government would be unable to discover the omission.

The most comprehensive survey of attitudes by business executives toward management and corporate practices showed that many believed that unethical conduct and criminal activities are widespread. The sample consisted of executives subscribing to the *Harvard Business Review*. Almost half of the respondents agreed with the statement: "The American business executive tends to ignore the great ethical laws as they apply immediately to his work. He is preoccupied chiefly with gains." Four out of seven believed that businessmen "would violate a code of ethics whenever they thought they could avoid detection."

COSTS

White-collar crime may cause several different types of harm. First, it may and often does cause serious financial losses, sometimes to a single individual or business and sometimes to the entire business community or consumer public. The exact financial loss to the Government caused by tax fraud is difficult to determine but undoubtedly enormous. Estimates of the amount of reportable income that goes unreported each year range from $25 to $40 billion. Some of this is inadvertent, but undoubtedly a sizable amount is deliberate, criminal evasion. The financial loss to the public caused by a single conspiracy in restraint of trade may be untold millions in extra costs paid ultimately by the buying public. It is estimated that the cost to the public annually of securities frauds, while impossible to quantify with any certainty, is probably in the $500 million to $1 billion range. A conservative estimate is that nearly $500 million is spent annually on worthless or extravagantly misrepresented drugs and therapeutic devices. Fraudulent and depective practices in the home repair and improvement field are said to result in $500 million to

$1 billion losses annually; and in the automobile repair field alone, fraudulent practices have been estimated to cost $100 million annually. Individual white-collar criminals are sometimes responsible for losses that are quite beyond the scale of most traditional crime. Billy Sol Estes' $30 million fertilizer swindle and De Angelis' $125-$175 million vegetable oil scandal are two notable examples.

While no reliable estimates can be made of the financial burdens produced by white-collar crime, they probably are far greater than those produced by traditional common law theft offenses—robbery, larceny and burglary. . . .

White-collar crime also does serious damage to our social and economic institutions—although it is extremely difficult to determine the extent of these harms. Thus crimes such as bribery and violation of conflict-of-interest statutes strike deeply at responsible, impartial government. And the damage done by a case such as the celebrated conspiracy of 29 electrical equipment companies to fix prices is not limited to the extra costs paid by their unsuspecting buyers and ultimately the general public. As Judge T. Cullen Ganey declared in sentencing the defendants: "This is a shocking indictment of a vast section of our economy, for what is really at stake here is the survival of the kind of economy under which America has grown to greatness, the free enterprise system."

More broadly, white-collar crime affects the whole moral climate of our society. Derelictions by corporations and their managers, who usually occupy leadership positions in their communities, establish an example which tends to erode the moral base of the law and provide an opportunity for other kinds of offenders to rationalize their misconduct.

The President's Committee on Consumer Interests found that one in 30 of the letters it received from consumers throughout the country conveyed "an attitude of frustration, anger, and displeasure with 'the system.' "

> The most striking feature, in our opinion, is not the allegations of criminal fraud that occasionally have been made to us by correspondents. Rather, it is the sense of unfairness, of disregard of the individual by the organized business community, of lack of effective recourse, and of a feeling that the marketplace is unethical.

Such frustration and discontent with abusive practices may be an important factor underlying some forms of violent crime. The report of the McCone Commission, the Commission appointed by the governor to investigate the Watts riot, included the following:

> The Commission heard recurrent testimony of alleged consumer exploitation in south central Los Angeles: of higher prices being charged

for food there than in other parts of town, of spoiled meat or produce or old bread being sold at the same price as fresh, of high interest rates on furniture and clothing purchases, of shoddy materials at high prices. Complaints were also registered to the effect that there is a bias against the curfew area in the practices of insurance companies and institutional lenders. In a related vein, a number of witnesses advanced the view that there was a vengeance pattern to the destruction of stores in the curfew area, that it was a retribution on merchants who were guilty of consumer exploitation, and particularly on Caucasians who were said to "take from the area but put nothing back into it. . . ."

EFFECTIVENESS OF CRIMINAL SANCTIONS

. . . Most persons convicted of common law crimes are likely to be young and to have serious educational and vocational lacks which rehabilitation programs can help meet. Presumably such programs are far less significant and will often be irrelevant for the white-collar offender.

Furthermore, with respect to many kinds of white-collar offenders long periods of incarceration or supervision are not needed to protect society from further criminality. For example, there appears to be only a negligible amount of recidivism among those convicted of certain white-collar crimes. Thus of the 1,186 persons convicted of criminal tax fraud in 1963 and 1964, only 2 persons were repeat offenders. On the other hand, among some classes of white-collar offenders, such as those guilty of cheating consumers, recidivism may be a serious problem.

There is, unfortunately, no hard evidence available regarding the deterrent effect of criminal sanctions. This was vividly illustrated when in a 1964 tax case the Justice Department was asked to submit a memorandum to the court justifying imposition of a 4-month jail term and a $10,000 fine as a deterrent. The only significant data produced were figures indicating that recidivism among tax violators was minimal, and a case study from Israel which indicated that since 1956, when the government had adopted a program of criminal prosecutions for tax evasion, there had been a graphic increase in the amount of income declared for taxation. . . .

Despite the lack of hard evidence, common sense notions about how people behave support the thesis that the condemnatory and deterrent aspects of criminal sanctions are likely to be peculiarly effective in the white-collar area. Persons who have standing and roots in a community, and are prepared for and engaged in legitimate occupations, can be expected to be particularly susceptible to the threat of criminal prosecution. Criminal proceedings and the imposition of sanctions have a much sharper impact upon those who have not been hardened by previous contact with the criminal justice system. Moreover, white-collar crimes as a class are more likely than common law crimes to be preceded by some deliberation; there is therefore more often an opportunity to calculate the risk objectively.

It appears further that jail sentences, however short, would constitute particularly significant deterrents for white-collar crime. The imposition of jail sentences may be the only way adequately to symbolize society's condemnation of the behavior in question, particularly where it is not on its face brutal or repulsive. And jail may be the only sanction available which will serve as an adequate deterrent. . . .

The Department of Justice believes that imprisonment may often be the appropriate penalty for a clear-cut antitrust violation, such as price fixing. . . .

Significantly, the Antitrust Division does not feel that lengthy prison sentences are ordinarily called for. It "rarely recommends jail sentences greater than 6 months—recommendations of 30-day imprisonment are most frequent."

In tax cases, the Justice Department also considers criminal sanctions, and jail sentences in particular, of significant value as deterrents. It is the Tax Division's policy to recommend jail sentences for all defendants convicted of tax fraud whenever the court requests a recommendation. James V. Bennett, former Director of the Federal Bureau of Prisons, has taken the position that the effort to deter misconduct by imposing relatively harsh penalties, while often a feeble thing in regard to traditional crime, "has had a most benign effect on those who do not like to pay taxes."

But it is clear that the criminal law is not an appropriate means of dealing with all kinds of white-collar misconduct. Since white-collar misconduct usually does not involve an act which, like robbery, burglary or rape, is of a simple and dramatic predatory nature, it is inevitable that one of the critical and difficult issues is determining when the violation is clear-cut enough to warrant use of society's ultimate method of control. A great deal of business is now subject to regulations whose interpretation is not at all clear. . . .

But the law is often adequately unambiguous. The offenders in the *Electrical Equipment* cases were, for example, quite aware that their activities were in violation of the law. As one of the violators testified:

> [I]t was considered discreet to not be too obvious and to minimize telephone calls, to use plain envelopes if mailing material to each other, not to be seen together traveling, and so forth . . . not leave wastepaper, of which there was a lot, strewn around a room when leaving.

The list of executives in attendance at meetings was referred to as the "Christmas card list," and the meetings as "choir practice." The executives filed false travel vouchers in order to conceal their vists to the cities in which meetings were held.

Aside from the question of ambiguity of the violation, it is important to recognize that a decision to use criminal sanctions involves costs and disadvantages which must be analyzed against the gains to be achieved and the alternative methods available to seek compliance. As discussed above, against many types of white-collar offenders application of criminal sanctions is likely to be highly effective in terms of deterrence. But this "economy" of sanction does not argue for an indiscriminate increase in the use of criminal sanctions. Among the economic and social costs involved in using criminal sanctions are the loss of services or serious curtailment of the usefulness of highly productive members of society, and the danger that greatly increased use of the criminal law would dilute its condemnatory effect. And there are many situations in which use of criminal sanctions may not be the most effective means of obtaining compliance with the law. Thus it is apparent that use of the withholding tax scheme has proved an extraordinarily efficient and effective method of preventing tax fraud. This is of course true in other areas of the law as well. Increased use of locks may be far more effective in reducing burglary and auto theft than an increase in police patrol. But the threat of criminal sanctions will often be an economical way to obtain compliance. In the tax area, for example, 80 million income tax returns are filed annually. It would be impractical to audit all of these and investigate all cases in which there was some reason for suspicion. The Tax Division audits only 4 per cent of all returns filed. And the withholding tax scheme, while highly effective, can only ensure that income earned in the course of some regular employment is reported. The Government must therefore depend to a great extent on the deterrent effect of the threat of criminal sanctions.

Careful thought must be given to determining those areas in which use of criminal sanctions is appropriate and in which other means of enforcement will suffice. And sound prosecutorial discretion must be exercised in deciding which cases, among those that might technically involve criminal violations, should be selected for prosecution. . . .

RESISTANCE TO THE USE OF CRIMINAL SANCTIONS

As important as the practical obstacles to effective law enforcement is society's reluctance to impose criminal sanctions upon the white-collar offender. Thus despite the apparent effect of. the *Electrical Equipment* cases, in which seven individual executives received and served jail sentences, since that case no antitrust defendant has been imprisoned. In seven cases since then, involving 45 individual defendants, prison sentences were imposed, but in each case the sentence was suspended. During this time the Government has recommended that, out of 58 cases in which individual defendants were charged with criminal violations, prison sentences be imposed but suspended in seven cases, and imposed and served in 27 cases. The recommendations covered 105 individual defendants. Similarly, Marshall Clinard's study of a variety of rationing and other controls during the second World War revealed that the sentences imposed on OPA violators after conviction were relatively mild.

While little is known of the public attitude toward white-collar crime, it is apparent that the present concern with crime is not directed at white-collar crime but at "crime on the streets." As one executive convicted and sentenced to jail in the *Electrical Equipment* conspiracy said:

> [O]n the bright side for me personally have been the letters and calls from people all over the country, the community, the shops and offices here, expressing confidence in me and support. This demonstration has been a warm and humbling experience for me.

. . . The very characteristics which make white-collar criminals particularly deterrable may make it difficult to obtain the sanctions necessary to deter. They generally have families, an established place in the community, and a spotless record. They often occupy managerial or executive roles in their business and a leadership position in their community.

In the *Electrical Equipment* cases the defendants included several vice presidents of the General Electric Corporation and the Westinghouse Electric Corporation. They were described by a newspaper reporter as "typical business men in appearance, men who would never be taken for lawbreakers." Several were deacons or vestrymen of their churches. One was president of his local Chamber of Commerce, another a hospital board member, another chief fund raiser for the Community Chest, another a bank director, another director of the taxpayer's association, another organizer of the local little league.

The highest paid executive to be given a jail sentence was a General Electric vice president, earning $135,000 a year. He was married, and the father of three children. He had served in the Navy during the second World War, rising to the rank of lieutenant commander, was director of the Schenectady Boy's Club, on the board of trustees of a girls' finishing school, and was a member of the Governor's Temporary State Committee on Economic Expansion in New York. . . .

In addition to the standing of the offenders, there are a number of aspects of white-collar offenses that may encourage public and official reluctance to use criminal sanctions, as well as provide rationalizations for the violators themselves. Thus Cressey's study of embezzlement found rationalization to be an important factor in offenders' patterns of misconduct. They distinguished embezzlement sharply from robbery or theft. He found, for example, that independent businessmen who converted "deposits" which had been entrusted to them because of their business positions, convinced themselves "either (a) that they were merely borrowing the money which they converted, or (b) that the funds entrusted to them were really theirs." It has been argued that use of criminal sanctions to enforce much of the law in this area is inappropriate because the conduct proscribed is "morally neutral." The soundness of some of the regulatory laws that have grown up in recent decades is a subject of continuing debate. And the very fact that they are so recent in comparison with the laws prohibiting such conduct as larceny and assault makes it unlikely that they will enjoy similar acceptance for some time. Many of the defendants in the *Electrical Equipment* cases argued that their behavior, while technically criminal, had really served a worthwhile purpose by "stabilizing prices." They frequently combined this altruistic interpretation with an attempted distinction among illegal, criminal, and immoral acts, expressing the view that what they had done might have been designated by the statutes as criminal, but either they were unaware of such a designation or they thought it unreasonable that acts with admirable consequences should be considered criminal. The fact that the line between legitimate and illegitimate behavior is sometimes fuzzy and seems occasionally arbitrary does not help in obtaining popular support for the law. Thus the fine line between legal tax avoidance and illegal evasion may make it hard for the violator himself or others to accept the appropriateness of criminal sanctions even where the violation is not close to the line.

But most white-collar crime is not at all morally neutral. Most fraud involves preying upon the weak and ignorant; violation of food and drug laws may cause death or serious injury; embezzlement is, very simply, a form of theft; tax fraud involves cheating the Government and, indirectly, other taxpayers.

Reluctance to see criminal sanctions used in the white-collar area derives also from the fact that there is often no particular victim, or group of victims. The harm is not as apparent, and certainly not as dramatic. Where loss is spread throughout society, the harm to any particular individual is minimal. . . .

Moreover, where corporate misconduct is involved, the offenders—and particularly the offenders against whom evidence of guilt can be obtained —act as part of a corporate hierarchy and, ordinarily, follow a pattern of corporate behavior. Individual responsibility is therefore reduced—the offenders are often following orders from above, either explicit or implicit. Moreover, the fact that acts are performed to further the interests of the corporation, and not merely the offenders' personal interests, helps to rationalize misconduct. Thus in the *Electrical Equipment* cases, personal explanations for the acts were, for the most part, sought in the structure of corporate pressures. The defendants almost invariably testified that they came new to a job, found price-fixing an established way of life, and simply entered into it as they did into other aspects of their job. This is illustrative of a pattern that Senator Everett Dirksen of Illinois, during the subcommittee hearings labeled "imbued fraud." There was testimony that, if one employee refused to engage in price-fixing, the responsibility would simply be delegated to another. Prior to imposing sentence in the *Electrical Equipment* cases, Judge T. Cullen Ganey criticized the corporations as the major culprits, but he did not excuse the offenders:

> they were torn between conscience and an approved corporate policy, with the rewarding objectives of promotion, comfortable security, and large salaries. They were the organization or company men, the conformist who goes along with his superiors and finds balm for his conscience in additional comforts and security of his place in the corporate setup.

. . . Application of criminal sanctions in this area raises some of the most delicate and perplexing problems confronting the criminal justice system. The sensitivity of successful members of society to the threat of criminal prosecution is indicative not only of the potential success of criminal sanctions in deterring misconduct, but of their potentially destructive effect upon the offenders. Criminal sanctions may help to educate the public to realize the seriousness of misconduct which is not on its face abhorrent, yet their indiscriminate use in areas where public opinion has not crystallized may seriously weaken the condemnatory effect of the criminal law. Imprisonment may be unnecessary for purposes of rehabilitation and incapacitation, although very effective as a deterrent.

Our goal should be to achieve an "economical" level of criminal sanctions, recognizing that in establishing such a level account must be taken of such intangibles as strengthening public support for the regulatory, revenue or other underlying legislative purpose sought without weakening the criminal law; balancing the effectiveness of criminal sanctions against alternative methods of social control; and maintaining some sense of fair treatment among different classes of offenders touched by the criminal system. . . .

CRIMINAL TAX FRAUD

The President's Commission on Law Enforcement
and the Administration of Justice

We demand compliance with tax laws for an intensely practical reason: Taxes support the Federal Government. In 1966, taxpayers filed more than 104 million tax returns and paid over $128 billion in taxes. Almost 94 cents of each budget dollar came from income, estate, gift, and excise taxes. The Federal income tax alone produced more than 80 percent of budget receipts.

To induce compliance, Congress has crafted a finely calibrated scale of sanctions, ranging from interest on unpaid tax liability, to statutory additions to tax, to civil and criminal penalties. The civil penalties can add from 5 to 100 per cent to the amount of unpaid taxes due. Criminal penalties include felonies and misdemeanors punishable by fine or imprisonment or both. More than 10 separate criminal statutes protect the income tax alone.

THE OFFENDER

Our system of self-assessment and the sheer number of taxpayers make criminal tax fraud a unique white-collar crime. Each taxpayer computes his tax on the basis of facts which he sets out in his return. Annually, some 68 million individuals have an opportunity to commit tax fraud, while few have, for example, the opportunity to embezzle money from a bank.

Criminal tax fraud is committed not mainly by the famous or even by the infamous. The popular impression that celebrities or gamblers and racketeers are the usual subjects of income tax prosecutions is a distortion of publicity. Gamblers and racketeers account for fewer than 10 per cent of such prosecutions, and celebrities are not a visible statistic. If there is a bright line of tax evasion, it divides the self-employed —whose compensation is not subject to withholding and whose opportunity for under-reporting income is thereby increased—from the employee. In 1965, almost two-thirds of those prosecuted for income tax fraud were self-employed. Heading the list of prosecutions were the medical, legal, and accounting professions (20 per cent) followed by the real estate, building and construction trades (6 per cent) and farmers (4 per cent).

From The Task Force Report, *Crime and Its Impact—An Assessment,* 1967, Attachment B, pp. 113-15.

THE OFFENSE

The nature of tax fraud creates unusual difficulties of proof. The crime is usually committed in the privacy of the home or office, without eye-witnesses or physical traces. While many white-collar crimes of misrepresentation have victims who may provide evidence, e.g. competitors, consumers, investors, stockholders, tax fraud has none. The inferences required to prove a tax fraud case must commonly be drawn from events largely independent of the commission of the crime and within control of the offender (increased net worth and expenditures or bank deposits in excess of declared and available resources). In combination, these factors pose formidable obstacles not only to proof of the commission of the crime but also to knowledge of the existence of the crime.

SELECTION, INVESTIGATION AND PROSECUTION

The selection and investigation of criminal tax fraud cases is done within the 58 District Director's offices of the Internal Revenue Service throughout the United States. Within those offices, the Intelligence Division is responsbile for conducting investigations, through its special agents, into possible criminal violations of most internal revenue laws.

Every criminal tax fraud case begins with a lead. Most leads, of course, are obtained from the audit of tax returns. But leads also come from the Internal Revenue Service's data processing centers, from other governmental units, from items appearing in the press, from informants, and from sources developed by Intelligence itself. The leads are evaluated by the chief of the Intelligence Division who determines if a preliminary investigation is warranted. After that investigation, he then decides whether the facts developed call for a full-scale fraud investigation.

The selection of leads to investigate is guided by the desire for uniform enforcement of compliance with the tax laws in all occupations, income groups, and geographic areas. The limited number of agents, however, prohibits strict uniformity. In the 4-year period 1963 through 1966, for example, the number of special agents ranged from 1,691 to 1,721. Preliminary investigations totaled less than 9,000 per year and full-scale investigations around 2,000. In that same period, the number of income tax returns filed increased from 73 million to 80 million, of which, in 1966, about 4 per cent of 3 million were audited. Because every possible case cannot be investigated, the Intelligence Division concentrates on the more aggravated individual cases and on categories of low-compliance taxpayers where prosecution would be most effective in deterring similar violations.

The decision to invoke the criminal process does not rest with the investigator. The odds are 16 to 1 that the case he investigates will not ultimately be prosecuted. Each case that he recommends for prosecution will be reviewed by at least 12 people as it passes through the district and regional levels of the Internal Revenue Service to the Department of Justice, Tax Division, in Washington, and then back to the local level for further review and prosecution by a United States Attorney.

At each of the four levels—district, regional, national, local—the standard of prosecution is the same: whether the evidence is sufficient to indicate guilt beyond a reasonable doubt and whether a reasonable probability of conviction exists. At each level, the taxpayer may obtain a conference. There, the taxpayer is informed of the nature and basis of the charge against him and has an opportunity to make any explanations or to present any evidence he thinks might affect the Government's decision to prosecute. Conferences are held for information rather than for settlement purposes. A criminal tax fraud case will not be settled in return for payment of taxes due, interest, and civil penalties. However, if prior to the investigation or threat of investigation of a criminal tax fraud case, the taxpayer makes a voluntary disclosure and seeks to correct the errors, that fact will be given some weight in deciding whether to prosecute.

THE SIFTING PROCESS

The 2,000 cases that enter the review process after full-scale investigation are sifted through each level with the result that about 600 to 700 emerge as cases commenced in the District Courts. After investigation, the special agent determines whether prosecution is warranted. His decision is reviewed by his group supervisor and by the chief of the Intelligence Division. The criminal aspects of the case are closed if the decision against prosecution is unanimous. Otherwise, the case is transferred from the District Director's office to the Regional Office for review by the Assistant Regional Commissioner for Intelligence. He may recommend further investigation, no prosecution or prosecution. If the latter, the case is forwarded to Regional Counsel and is reviewed by an attorney, a technical advisor and the Assistant Regional Counsel. If they recommend prosecution, the case is transferred to the Department of Justice, Tax Division.

The Justice attorney to whom the case is assigned may also request further investigation or recommend for or against prosecution. His decision is reviewed by the Assistant Section Chief and by the Chief of the Criminal Section, Tax Division. Depending upon the nature of the case and the recommendations of the staff attorneys, the case may also be reviewed by the Second Assistant and by the Assistant Attorney General for the Tax Division. If the Department recommends against prosecution, the case is transferred to Chief Counsel's office, Internal Revenue Service, which may refer the case to Regional Counsel for closing or to the Department of Justice for reconsideration. If the Department recommends prosecution, the case is transferred to the appropriate United States Attorney's office for prosecution. There, a final review is given the case by an attorney and by the United States Attorney or his representative. The United States Attorney's office may advise the Department of Justice that the case should not be prosecuted, but final authority for prosecution rests with the Department.

The extensive review process is largely attributable to the uncertainties surrounding the existence and commission of criminal tax fraud. But comprehensive review also assures taxpayers that indictments for criminal tax fraud, which may seriously affect one's reputation, are not obtained haphazardly. And it assures the Government of a higher percentage of successful prosecutions, thereby increasing their deterrent effect. In 1966, the conviction rate for criminal income tax offenses was 97 per cent. Most defendants plead guilty or *nolo contendere* (*nolo* pleas are accepted over the Justice Department's continuing objection). In cases actually tried, the conviction rate is about 64 per cent.

SENTENCING

Sentencing practices for defendants convicted of income tax evasion vary widely from district to district and from judge to judge. When 54 Federal judges were polled to determine what sentence they would impose on a hypothetical defendant convicted of income tax evasion, they divided almost evenly between incarceration, on the one hand, and probation or fine, on the other. An Internal Revenue Service study of sentencing for income tax fraud for the years 1946 through 1963 shows that the percentage of prison sentences to convictions ranged from zero in South Dakota and 3 per cent in the Western District of Virginia to 88 per cent in the Western District of Washington and 93 per cent in the Western District of Tennessee. In all districts during that period, imprisonment was imposed in only 38 per cent of the cases. And of the 593 defendants convicted of criminal income tax fraud in 1966, 40 per cent received prison terms. Terms of less than one year were imposed on 80 per cent of those imprisoned.

Some of the traditional purposes of sentencing—isolation, rehabilitation—have little application to the typical individual convicted of income tax evasion. Most offenders have no prior record of conviction and do not require isolation from society for its protection. Moreover, severe sentences are not required to rehabilitate the offender. Statistics of the Department of Justice suggest that there is a negligible amount of recidivism. Of the 1,186 persons convicted of criminal tax fraud in 1963 and 1964, only two persons were repeat offenders. The ignominy of indictment, prosecution and conviction rather than the particular type of sentence imposed discourages the ordinary defendant from repeating his crime.

The purpose of sentencing for income tax crimes is to deter others from committing the same offense. As a general matter, the principle of deterrence may be of doubtful validity, but it has been regarded as particularly effective for crimes, such as tax fraud, where rational considerations are predominant. The threat of jail has "a most benign effect on those who do not like to pay taxes." Accordingly, it is our policy to recommend jail sentences for defendants convicted of criminal tax fraud. We follow this policy in the hardest case—where the defendant is a community leader with an otherwise spotless record who has already suffered the disgrace of conviction for income tax evasion. As Judge Skelly Wright has remarked:

> . . . no jail sentence can add to that punishment in any degree. So we say then, why send such a man to jail? And I say to you the answer is that the only real purpose of an income tax sentence is its deterrent value. Unless we use the income tax sentence as a deterrent, we are overlooking one of our responsibilities as Judges.

4 RIOTS AND CRIME

Riots are hardly a recent invention. Even a most cursory glance backward into American history provides convincing evidence of the frequency, explosiveness, and destructiveness of civil disturbances. Race riots can be traced as far back as the eighteenth century. Ethnic and religious riots were the lot of the Irish and the Mormons, to cite but two of many illustrations. Violence on the economic front has flared frequently in the past. As late as the 1930's, labor and management confrontations were bitter, costly, and often exceedingly violent.

But the warfare since 1965 in the inner cores of nearly all major American cities, and many smaller cities as well, is unparalleled and seemingly beyond solution. While violence has always been a concomitant of the shifting strengths of majorities and minorities, the recent convulsions are unique in a number of important respects. In the past, violence was usually triggered by the majority group. Violence to an individual of another skin color was the goal, while looting and property destruction was minimal. At other times, one group might be pitted against another. In the present civil disturbances, there are two additional and very important departures from the past:

(1) The police, and to a much lesser extent the firemen, have become the stand-ins for the majority. "Whitey" is principally a lawman and, in a considerable number of riots, confrontations between policemen and Negro suspects have been a trigger mechanism.

(2) Despite some sniping, a major emphasis is on cleaning out the goods in local business establishments, including those owned by "soul brothers." There is also some burning and firebombing of looted businesses and nearby residences. One unique aspect to all of this is the seemingly carnival atmosphere in which this riot drama is acted out. Riots, according to a good many of the participants and onlookers, are fun.

It would be a serious mistake to assess these civil disturbances merely as a form of mass criminality in which the looting and destruction are only extreme exaggerations of the usual theft and vandalism which routinely occur in the inner city. Surely there is a crime aspect here. But a more meaningful perspective is to see this rioting as a result of the deep-seated despair of the Negro in the urban North. Unless these frustrations are soon alleviated, the scattered city riots may yet deteriorate into a more massive civil war.

The first article in this chapter is excerpted from the section on "Riots and Crime" in the report of the President's Commission on Law Enforcement and Administration of Justice. Summarizing the situation in the "hot" summers of 1964-66, the report states, "Unmistakably, then, the riots were social protest of a sort—a criminal sort. Thousands of acts of assault, of arson, of theft, of vandalism are what a riot is. Putting an end to a riot is a police problem. Almost every riot was touched off by an encounter between the police and a Negro." Mainly, the concern is with the first and pacesetting riot—the Watts conflagration in Los Angeles—in 1965. In an almost blow-by-blow account of the action, the logic of Watts is underscored and a few myths destroyed about who participated and why.

Professor Grimshaw takes the long and cool view of racial violence in the history of the United States in his article, "Lawlessness and Violence in America and Their Special Manifestations in Changing Negro-White Relationships." Apart from discussing our lawless heritage, Grimshaw identifies six major stages (before Watts, Newark and Detroit) in the Negro-white power struggle and suggests that interracial violence took different forms in these different eras. Recent civil disturbances in the black ghettos are thus another phase in the continuing white-black, superordinate-subordinate struggle.

In the distinctive and unmistakable style of *Time,* the third reading is a chronicle of the sequences and events which made the five-day Detroit riot the bloodiest and costliest in fifty years. The Detroit riot holds two special distinctions. More than even Watts or Newark, the civil disturbance in Detroit has become the ineradicable symbol of the Negro revolt. In addition, it occurred in a community which seemingly had made one of the greatest efforts in improving the socioeconomic status of the Negro.

In the article "Looting in Recent Civil Disorders; An Index of Social Change," Professors Quarantelli and Dynes, Co-Directors of the Disaster Research Center at Ohio State University, are concerned with the problem of looting which has been evidenced in various racial disorders since 1965. They point out that looting in such civil disturbances is highly selective; only certain types of consumer goods are looted while other and frequently more valuable property is generally avoided. They also suggest that in these civil disturbances, looting is often positively sanctioned by a segment of the population. While looting is often viewed as simply illegal or meaningless behavior. Professors Quarantelli and Dynes point out that it can be seen as an index of social change since it signals the end of a past normative agreement concerning property rights within the community. Whether it means the initiation of more peaceful ways of instituting change remains to be seen. If not, the continuation of violence and looting may become normative among the lower-class elements of the population.

RIOTS AND CRIME

The President's Commission on Law Enforcement and the Administration of Justice

It is tempting to describe the riots that flared up in the ghettos of some 20 cities during the summers of 1964, 1965, and 1966 as "senseless." It is also unenlightening. To be sure, there were respects in which the riots made little sense. Few of the policemen or white passersby whom the rioters assaulted were people against whom they had specific personal grievances. The great majority of the casualties of the riots—the dead, the injured, and the arrested—were rioters. Some of the property the rioters destroyed belonged to them or their neighbors; a poignant journalistic vignette of the Watts riot in Los Angeles was a description of a man woefully gazing at a gutted drycleaning establishment to which he had entrusted seven pairs of trousers. The riots changed the attitude of some Americans toward the civil rights movement from sympathy to antipathy. And of course there is no sense to the idea—in the doubtful event that anyone seriously entertains it—that sporadic outbursts of frenzy and violence can solve complicated social problems.

However, to say that the riots were unplanned, undisciplined, unled, and incoherent is not to say that they expressed nothing and signified nothing. They expressed the general hostility many Negroes feel toward white people. They expressed the particular hostility many Negroes feel toward the police and toward ghetto merchants and businessmen. They expressed the outrage many Negroes feel at the conditions in which they must live. They expressed the increasing refusal by Negroes to accept further delay in being granted full participation in the social, economic, and political development of the Nation. They expressed the increasing conviction of Negroes that legal methods of protest have not accomplished enough fast enough. They signified that the ghettos of American cities are a threat to the peace and safety of all of America. They sig-

From The Task Force Report, *Crime and Its Impact—An Assessment,* 1967, Chapter 9, pp. 116-22.

nified that the need to abolish ghettos is urgent, and that the time is short.

Unmistakably, then, the riots were social protest of a sort—a criminal sort. Thousands of acts of assault, of arson, of theft, of vandalism are what a riot is. Putting an end to a riot is a police problem. Almost every riot was touched off by an encounter between the police and a Negro. The majority of those encounters were essentially commonplace or even trivial; in many of them the police were responding to a complaint by a Negro; in most of them the police acted, at least to begin with, with prudence and propriety. In short, an integral element in every riot was strain between the police and members of the Negro community. Finally, it cannot be a coincidence that riots take place in just those neighborhoods where there is the greatest amount of everyday crime. This is not to say, of course, that rioters and everyday criminals are the same people—though in some instances they may be. The point is that anger, violence, despair, and cynicism prevail in the Negro ghettos of America and these conditions contribute both to everyday crime and to protest riots. . . .

Violent racial conflict is not a new phenomenon in America. Perhaps the most atrocious riots that ever occurred in this country were the 1863 draft riots in New York. For about 4 days white mobs controlled much of the city, during which they looted stores, burned Negro dwellings, and beat or lynched those Negroes they got their hands upon. Before the State militia restored order there were about 2,000 casualties. The draft riots are notable for more than their extreme savagery. They were the archetype of most of the racial clashes that took place before the summer of 1964. They occurred during a time of national tension and anxiety, the Civil War. They occurred at a time when Negroes appeared to be on the verge of making a major social advance, emancipation. They were a response by predominantly working class white citizens to a requirement that they assist this Negro advance by making personal sacrifices and by serving in the Army. They consisted of offensive action by white mobs against the persons of Negroes, and defensive action by Negro mobs and individuals against the persons of whites, with looting and property destruction as by-products of those actions. They were not confined to any one part of the city, but involved raids and incursions, attacks and counterattacks. They lasted longer than they might have because of the reluctance of officials to invoke full military or police force against them promptly, and because of the more or less open sympathy of many members of the military or the police with the rioters. They were, in sum, actions by members of the majority against the presumably threatening minority.

All the bloodiest riots of the 20th century, until Watts, conformed to this pattern. The very bloodiest took place in East St. Louis, Ill., on July 3 and 4, 1916, during the First World War, slightly a week after the first American troops landed in France; 39 Negroes and 9 whites were killed, hundreds of people were injured or wounded, and 244 buildings, mostly Negro homes, and 44 railroad cars were destroyed by fire. This riot was the culmination of a long period of racial tension provoked by a massive influx of southern Negroes into East St. Louis, and their subsequent use as strikebreakers in some of the city's aluminum and steel plants. . . .

Between the early evening of June 20, 1943 . . . and the early morning of June 22, 24 Negroes and 9 whites were killed, and 933 people were injured in a riot in Detroit. Once again, the general background was wartime. Large numbers of Negroes had come to the city to work in the defense plants, with the resulting pressure on housing. Federal regulations prescribed equal employment standards in defense industries, and so Negroes were being upgraded in their jobs. The tension was so obvious that a year earlier Life magazine had published a feature article about it, entitled "Detroit is Dynamite." Characteristically enough, the riot started at the Belle Isle Amusement Park with a fight whose precise nature never was discovered. Within an hour, rioting was taking place in many parts of the city. Negroes began looting white-owned stores in the Paradise Valley ghetto. Whites attacked Negroes emerging from all-night movie theaters in the downtown district. The next evening the pattern of raids, ambushes, and sniping began to take shape. The Detroit police were unable to handle the situation; several well-documented accounts indicate that they were unwilling to because of their pro-white sympathies. The Governor had been reluctant to call in the National Guard, but by midnight Monday he was compelled to, and order was quickly restored.

Those three riots were the most violent of a dozen or more that followed similar courses during the first half of this century. While many factors contributed, they seemed to be the outcome of white resistance to social and economic progress by Negroes, and Negro response to that resistance. It is accurate to call them race riots. Their basic design was the infliction of personal injury by whites on Negroes and by Negroes on whites. People and homes were the important targets. However, there were two major riots during this period, the 1935 and 1943 riots in America's oldest, most famous Negro ghetto, Harlem in New York City, whose design was considerably different. They foreshadowed the ghetto riots of 1964, 1965, and 1966.

Neither of the Harlem riots was precipitated by an interracial clash on some piece of neutral ground, or by a white attack on Negroes. Both were set off by law enforcement incidents in the ghetto itself. On the afternoon of March 19, 1935, near the bottom of the great depression, a Negro boy was caught shoplifting in a five-and-ten-cents store. He was taken by store employees to the back of the store for questioning and to await the arrival of the police, but when he became hysterical he was released through a back door into an alley. However, the shoppers in the store believed that he was being beaten, and their anger and alarm were heightened by the grim coincidence that a hearse happened to be parked in the alley. Within a half hour there was a large and vociferous picket line in front of the store. A crowd assembled to watch. A policeman arrested a picketer, and the crowd began throwing rocks and bottles at the police. By early evening, several thousand Negroes were roaming around Harlem breaking store windows. Looting began after dark, and continued until the police restored order late the next day. Food stores were a particular target of the looters. There was much hunger in Harlem at the time; 70 percent of the population was on relief. In addition there was much resentment over the unwillingness of white merchants to employ Negroes. . . .

WATTS

The 5-day riot that began on Wednesday, August 11, 1965, in the South Central Los Angeles ghetto (the area of which the Watts neighborhood is a small part) has probably been more carefully examined than any riot that has ever occurred. The McCone Commission, appointed by the Governor of California to make a general report on the riot, held 60 formal hearings during which it received sworn testimony from 80 witnesses, it interviewed 90 of those arrested during the riot; and it opened an office in the riot area so that members of its staff could interview local residents. The Bureau of Criminal Statistics of the California Department of Justice made a detailed statistical study of the 3,927 people arrested during the riot. The California National Guard prepared a systematic account of its activities during the riot. Two members of the staff of the Los Angeles Times, which won a Pulitzer Prize for its reporting of the riot, wrote the book, *"Burn, Baby, Burn,"* describing the neighborhood, the events of the riot, and a number of the participants in it. Under a grant from the Office of Economic Opportunity, the Institute of Government and Public Affairs of the University of California, Los Angeles, has surveyed the extent of Negro participation in the riot, and Negro and white opinion of the riot and of its causes. Though the Institute's report has not yet been completed, the Commission's staff has had the opportunity to read those chapters that have been drafted.

The Watts riot was, of course, different from the other riots of the last three summers in several ways; no two riots are exactly alike. The most striking difference was its extreme violence and destructiveness. Thirty-four people were killed and 1,032 injured. Two hundred buildings were burned to the ground and 720 more looted or damaged; the total property loss was estimated at $40 million. The resources of the Los Angeles Police Department, the Los Angeles Fire Department, the Los Angeles County Sheriff's Department, and the California Highway Patrol were so overtaxed that 13,400 troops of the California National Guard were finally committed to controlling the riot.

However, there is no evidence that Watts lasted so long and caused so much damage because the Los Angeles ghetto is unique. What was unique in Los Angeles was a conjunction of topographical, organizational, jurisdictional, and operational circumstances that made controlling the riot exceptionally difficult. The area in which rioting occurred is big (46.3 square miles) and flat, and so preventing the riot from spreading required a large number of men. The Los Angeles Police Department had only about 5,000 officers to police a city that is the country's largest in area and second largest in population. Three-quarters of the riot area is in the city of Los Angeles and the rest is in Los Angeles County, which is under the jurisdiction of the county sheriff, and the two departments had done an insufficient amount of joint planning to meet a major emergency. . . .

South Central Los Angeles does not look any more like Harlem than the Sunset Strip looks like Times Square, but in that the conditions of life there compare unfavorably in all essential respects with those in the rest of the city, it is a typical ghetto. The density of population is greater. The unemployment rate is higher. The average income is lower. The housing is in worse repair. The average educational achievement is less. The crime rate is higher. The hostility toward the police is greater. And, perhaps the crux of the matter, those residents who have the means and the desire to move to better neighborhoods have only limited opportunities to do so, a fact of which they must be acutely aware; in 1964 the voters of California overwhelmingly repealed by referendum a State fair housing law. It is not too fanciful to compare a district like South Central Los Angeles to a heap of inflammable material that has been carelessly left, out of sight and mind, in an obscure corner of a cellar or an attic; the feeblest, most random spark can ignite it, and sometimes does.

Certainly the spark that ignited Watts was feeble and random. At about 7 p.m. on August 11, a day on which the temperature reached 94°, a Negro driving a pickup truck in a portion of South Central Los Angeles that is outside the city limits called the attention of a white California highway patrolman to the reckless way in which an old gray Buick was being driven north (toward the city limits) on Avalon Boulevard. The patrolman followed the Buick on his motorcycle and determined that it was going 50 miles an hour in a 35-mile-an-hour zone. He turned on his red light and siren, pulled alongside the car and ordered the driver to the curb. The driver, a 21-year-old Negro named Marquette Frye, obeyed at once and without demur. He was evidently drunk and he did not have a driver's license. The patrolman told him he was under arrest and radioed for his backup officer and a transport car to come and help him place Frye in custody. Both arrived promptly. Meanwhile 20 or 30 passersby and residents of nearby buildings had gathered to watch the scene, apparently purely for entertainment. There was no sign of trouble. The patrolman was friendly and polite. Frye was good humored, even jocular.

Suddenly the situation changed. Vociferously and belligerently Frye refused to get into the transport car. The officers attempted to handcuff him. He resisted. The spectators became sullen and hostile. The officers radioed for more help. Frye's stepbrother, who had been riding in the car, and his mother, who owned the car and who had hastened to the scene when a neighbor told her what was happening, came to Frye's assistance. More highway patrolmen and members of the Los Angeles Police Department arrived. The size of the crowd increased. Frye was forcibly subdued, and put in the car. The spectators who by then numbered several hundred, hurled abuse at the police, who by then numbered about 50. Finally the police, with the three Fryes as prisoners, managed to disengage themselves from the crowd and leave the scene, under a shower of rocks and bricks and bottles. In the course of doing so they made another arrest, of a young woman who, according to the police, was spitting and cursing at them and, according to herself, was doing nothing more than talking and giggling. She was a barber and was wearing her professional smock, which gave rise to an impression that the police had manhandled a pregnant woman; a report of this instance of "police brutality" spread through the ghetto area, and as it spread it became a rumor that the police had beaten and kicked Frye's pregnant mother. The crowd did not disperse after the police left. On the contrary, it stayed on Avalon Boulevard, which is a main thoroughfare through South Central Los Angeles, and bombarded passing motorists with whatever missiles were available. Meanwhile angry groups began assembling in other parts of the ghetto. The riot was on.

What is most suggestive—and alarming—about the events that began the Watts riot is the chain of accident and chance. The highway patrolman, responding to a complaint by a Negro citizen, had more than sufficient cause to arrest Frye, and he went about his business with efficiency and propriety. The act for which Frye was arrested, driving drunkenly and recklessly on a main city thoroughfare, could not possibly be interpreted as either a harmless lapse or as a gesture of protest, conscious or unconscious, against white oppression. Frye was not an agitator or a militant; there is not even reason to believe that he was an especially aggrieved young man. The people who first gathered to watch the scene were not looking for trouble, but for amusement. The particular police force against which there was the most antagonism in South Central Los Angeles was not the California Highway Patrol but the Los Angeles Police Department. If the highway patrolmen doing what they did could precipitate a catastrophe like Watts, it is surely safe to say that almost anything might have precipitated it. South Central Los Angeles was ready and willing—and perhaps even eager—to run amok.

WHO RIOTED?

That the Watts riot was a general outbreak in which all kinds of people took part—not just agitators or adolescents or criminals or new arrivals in town or the unemployed or "riff-raff"—is indicated by all the available information about the participants. The California Department of Justice's statistical analysis of those arrested in connection with the riot makes this case strongly. Of the 3,927 people arrested by the Los Angeles Police Department, the Los Angeles Sheriff's Office, the Compton and Long Beach Police Departments, and the California Highway Patrol the large majority, of course, were Negro men and boys; 3,609 were Negroes and 3,409 were males. But beyond these unsurprising figures there are some surprises. The rioters, to the extent that those arrested were a cross section of those who rioted, were not mostly adolescents or young adults. Only 556 were legally juveniles (under 18), while 2,111 were over 25; 602 were over 40. They were not predominantly people with serious criminal histories; 1,113 had no arrest records at all, and of the adults, 965 of those who had been arrested previously had not been convicted. At the other end of the spectrum, 363 adults had served prison terms on criminal convictions, and 52 juveniles had a record of institutional commitment. Considering the fact that a Negro male who grows up in a slum has something like a 75-percent chance of being arrested during his lifetime, these figures strongly suggest that the Watts rioters were drawn from all parts of the community. . . .

The results of the UCLA survey point in the same direction. They indicate that roughly 20 percent of the Negroes in the area actually did participate more or less actively in the riot, and that the general impression in the area was that many more people than that took part; more than 50 percent, by consensus. A more detailed breakdown of the circumstances of those who reported to interviewers that they were active fail to show significant differences between them and those who were inactive, in respect to place of origin, length of residence in Los

Angeles, degree of education, importance of religion in childhood, or self-classified social class. For example, 28.6 percent of those who said they were lower class were active; 20.4 percent of those who said they were working class; 23.5 percent of those who said they were middle class, and 15.7 percent of those who said they were upper class. Findings of this sort are not conclusive, of course. For one thing they are based on information volunteered after the riot and not on direct observation at the time of the riot; for another, precise questions about kinds of riot activity could not be asked because the interviewers could not guarantee the interviewees immunity from prosecution. They do not *prove* that the rioters were a fairly representative cross section of the males in the community, but they do suggest it.

A final indication that the riot was not the work of a tiny extremist or criminal minority is the reaction to the riot that the UCLA interviewers found among the Negroes in the area. More than half, 57.9 percent, said that its long-run effects would be favorable; 83.9 percent said that whites were now more aware of Negro problems; 64.4 percent said the victims of the riot deserved being attacked; 61.9 percent said the riot was a Negro protest; 9.9 percent even said that "everyone" in the area supported the riot. In sum, the riot was looked upon favorably by many people from every section of the community, an attitude that again suggests that participation in it was probably representative.

THE "LOGIC" BEHIND WATTS

It appears that the riot was associated with a general sense of grievance among the residents of South Central Los Angeles. What is difficult to establish is to what extent—if at all—it was associated with any specific grievance or grievances. In this connection both the events of the riot itself and the information accumulated by the UCLA survey are ambiguous. Take the relationship between the riot and police-community relations. The police were a principal target of the rioters. They were, from beginning to end, cursed, stoned, and sniped at. A sheriff's deputy was killed and 90 policemen were injured. The UCLA survey shows that there is an almost universal belief in the area that the police misbehave toward Negroes. . . . For example, in response to a question about whether the police use insulting language, some 90 percent answered that it happens in the area; more than half said that it had happened to people they knew; slightly less than half said they had seen it happen, and almost 30 percent said that it had happened to them. On the question of whether the police beat up people in custody, more than 90 percent, again, said it happens in the area; almost half said it had happened to people they knew; some 30 percent said they had seen it happen, and about 5 percent said that it had happened to them. This would imply widespread grievances against the police. . . .

However, there are other data that make this conclusion considerably less convincing. For one thing, although the UCLA surveyors found almost no one who believed that firemen performed their duties in a manner that discriminated against Negroes, firemen who tried to put out fires set by the rioters were also subjected to fierce stoning and sniping. Transparently innocent and harmless motorists—teenage couples and mothers with children—on their way through the riot area before effective roadblocks had been set up, were savagely assaulted. When the UCLA surveyors asked open-ended questions along the lines of "What is your biggest complaint about this neighborhood?", mistreatment by the police was seldom mentioned compared with poor physical conditions in the neighborhood, economic discrimination, inadequate schools, parks and transportation facilities, and a number of other matters. However, other questions such as "What caused the riot?" elicited a sizable (21 percent) citation of police mistreatment. . . .

In summary, the Watts riot appears to have been caused by no one set of people or conditions or grievances. It was a manifestation of a general sense of deep outrage, outrage at every aspect of the lives Negroes are forced to live, outrage at every element of the white community for forcing (or permitting) Negroes to live such lives. According to 56.1 percent of the Negroes interviewed in the course of the UCLA survey, the riot had a "purpose." This purpose, according to more than half of those who said there was one, was to express (in the survey's words) "hostility, resentment, revenge." As has already been noted almost two-thirds of the Negroes interviewed said the victims had deserved the attacks upon them. If the quality of life for so many Americans in Los Angeles, and undoubtedly in other cities as well, is such that they are filled with hostility, resentment, and a desire for revenge, there may be more cause for surprise over how few riots there have been than over how many. And in any case it is surely intolerable for hundreds of thousands, or millions, of Americans to have cause to feel that way, whether or not they riot.

Perhaps the most revealing finding of the UCLA survey was that another 41 percent of the Negroes who said the Watts riot had a purpose described that purpose as being (in the words of the survey again) to "gain attention, let them know," rather than simply to express hostility. In other words, the riot was not only an expression of hostility, but a cry for help. The implication is evident that many Negroes believe that if only the white community realized what the ghetto was like and how its residents felt, the ghetto would not be permitted to exist. Responding to this belief in the capacity of American institutions to be fair that accompanies the immense Negro resentment against the ways in which they have not been, is America's best hope, not merely of preventing riots, but of realizing its own ideals.

Doing such things as punishing police misconduct, providing decent housing and schooling, ending job discrimination and so forth are essential, but the problem goes deeper than that. The ghetto itself, with all the shameful economic, social, political, and psychological deprivation it causes, must be done away with once and for all. The riots have "let America know" that this is what must be done. Now America must do it.

LAWLESSNESS AND VIOLENCE IN AMERICA AND THEIR SPECIAL MANIFESTATIONS IN CHANGING NEGRO-WHITE RELATIONSHIPS
Allen D. Grimshaw

Ours has been a lawless and violent nation. Indeed, race riots and bombings, although they are particularly dramatic manifestations of conflict, have claimed fewer lives than many other varieties of violence, individual or social. There are more criminal homicides in some American metropolises every year than there have been deaths from all the urban race riots of the 20th Century combined. A few famous feuds, and some important labor disputes have rolled up casualty lists which compare in length with the most spectacular interracial disorders. Social violence, and lawlessness generally, have not been phenomena expressed only in interracial relations in this country. . . .

A. OUR LAWLESS HERITAGE

It is possible to make a rough classification of types of lawlessness and violence by reference to the areas of social interaction in which such lawlessness and violence occur. The two categories which emerge from such simple classification overlap, but are nonetheless distinguishable. The first category, that of ethnic violence includes, in addition to Negro-white social violence, conflict and violence focussed on religion and nativity. While the motivation behind much of this violence falls more accurately into the secular area of economic and political violence, the manifest reasons for "punishing" religious and nationality and racial groups have usually referred to religious, cultural and "racial" differences distinguishing these groups from "real Americans."

An anti-Catholic tradition, which has been expressed even in the 20th Century, was responsible for frequent eruptions in the last cen-

From *The Journal of Negro History,* Vol. XLIV, No. 1 (January 1959), 52-72. Reprinted by permission.

tury, particularly in the period before the Civil War. In the three decades immediately preceding that war, street fights were frequent; sometimes taking on the proportions of major riots, convents and other religious edifices were attacked and sometimes destroyed, and Catholics both within and without the Church hierarchy were subject to constant vilification and occasional physical assault. This anti-Catholicism, particularly as related to an expression of Native-Americanism and the "Know-Nothing" movement, was most frequently directed against Irish Catholics, perhaps because they were resistant to accepting a subservient accommodative status, and had significant economic and political overtones. Jews and Mormons, to mention only two other religious communities, have also been the focus of hostility and violence.

While the Irish Catholics may have received the brunt of the animus and overt violence in Native American riots, they were by no means the only ethnic group attacked. Almost all immigrant groups went through a period of unpopularity, an unpopularity inextricably tied up with their status as perceived economic and political threats to the "older" immigrant groups. Groups distinguishable from the larger population by virtue of physical characteristics were a particular focus of hostility. Assaults upon the indigenous Indian population, commonplace throughout the historical period, were certainly not always necessary for the protection of the white population. A growing resentment toward the Chinese, originally imported as laborers on the transcontinental railroads, culminated in anti-Chinese riots in the closing decades of the 19th Century. Treatment of Mexican-Americans in the American Southwest has been similar to treatment of Negro-Americans in the American South. And the decade of the 1940's saw attacks not only on the civil rights of, but also against the persons and property of Japanese-Americans and Mexican-Americans as well as against Negroes.

The second general category includes a variety of secular types of violence. Most important here are lawlessness and violence growing out of politics and the relations of the populace to the government and out of economic competition. . . .

Economic strife has erupted into violence countless times in the last one hundred years. No major industry accepted unionization without a struggle, but in some, such as the railroads and the mines, the struggle assumed the character of wars. "Bloody Harlan" and the "Herrin Massacre," the Haymarket riot and the Homestead strike, these names conjure up a pageant of lawlessness and violence continuing well into the present century. Assassination and terrorism have been used by both labor and management, and in the "Big Steel" strikes of the 'Thirties the steel companies spent thousands upon thousands of dollars on machine guns and tear gas. . . .

America has been, then, a land of lawlessness and violence, ranging from spontaneous brawls between servicemen of different branches and schoolboys from different schools, through the "blood feud" and gangster warfare, to the full-fledged military campaigns which have occurred in struggles between class and class and between adherents of different religious faiths. The tradition of lawlessness includes both a contempt of parking regulations and an admiration of gangster heroes and, on the other hand, an excess zeal in the administration of "vigilante justice," "lynch law," and "six-shooter law" on the frontier. Some areas, such as Harlan County in Kentucky and "Bloody" Williamson in Illinois, have run practically the full gamut of types of social violence suggested above. But there is practically no section of the United States which has not, at one time or another, been a center of lawlessness and violence. If there is less actual participation in violence today, and if Americans must sublimate their propensities to violence by watching television, the potentiality still remains.

The violence and bloodshed which has accompanied adjustments in the accommodative pattern between whites and Negroes in the United States is not unique to interracial relations. It is a thesis of the research on which this article is based that the violence which occurs in interracial relations is an inevitable product of assaults upon the accommodative pattern. Further research on the forms of violence which have been listed in this brief outline will, the writer believes, demonstrate that all social violence results from the interaction of conceptually similar forces in defining patterns of accommodation.

B. THE CHANGING CHARACTER OF NEGRO-WHITE RELATIONS

In this section a rough classification has been made of periods in race relations in this country, the social forces which defined them, and the types of social violence which characterized them. The periods covered are roughly as follows: the period of slave insurrections and resistance (1640-1861); Civil War and Reconstruction (1861-1877); the Second Reconstruction and the beginnings of the Great Migration (1878-1914); World War I and post-war boom and racial readjustment (1915-1929); interwar and Depression (1930-1941); World War II (1942-1945); and the period since World War II. The suggestion is made that in each of these periods the patterns of race relations and social racial violence were determined more by reaction of the dominant white community to attacks on the accommodative pattern by Negroes than by any conscious determination of policy by the white group. . . .

1. *The period of slave insurrections and resistance (1640-1861):* While the importation of Negro labor into this country began in 1619, the Negro's status as a member of a racial group was only gradually

defined. Frazier has pointed out that the distinction between slavery and servitude was not clear, and that during early years the status of the Negro was similar to that of the white indentured servant. It is only with a clarification of the Negro's status as being a racial one, rather than one of social class, that it becomes legitimate to speak of Negro-white relationships. This clarification was under way by the middle decades of the 17th Century. Even before the beginnings of what has been called the classic period of "ante-bellum slavery" race relations in this country had begun to emerge as a unique pattern of inter-group relations.

However, while there were slave insurrections and abortive rebellions in the 18th Century, interracial violence was interpreted less in racial terms than in class or social terms particularly in terms of the master-servant relationship. . . . There are reports of individual inter-racial assaults and homicides. There were slave plots of considerable scope, interestingly enough in New York, in 1712 and 1741. But while whites were killed in these plots and Negroes slain or transported in retaliation, they were interpreted as uprisings of a servant class or as political plots inspired by "foreign agents" rather than as uprisings of Negroes. . . .

With the firm establishment of slavery as an American institution, . . . the black man and his activities, and his racial status, took on a new character and significance. . . . A number of authors have shown the near obsession of many Southern whites over the possibilities of slave revolts and have further demonstrated that in many cases this concern and anxiety were well-founded. A number of factors contributed to the failure of slave rebellions. But the plans of Vesey, Gabriel and Turner, to mention only the most well-known insurrectionaries, came alarmingly close to fruition. And, these planned rebellions were not the protest merely of an economically down-trodden and subservient class. That they were racial in character is demonstrated by the fact that whites of all classes were to be exterminated, with the exception of those who had shown good-will toward Negroes. The characteristics of the rebels varied. Some were relatively new arrivals still imbued with the militance of their African tribal heritage, others were longer sojourners in this country who had become literate, acculturated and too familiar with ideas of equality which were meant only for their white masters. But all of them shared, in common with the white group, a conception of a society divided along racial, rather than simply social, lines. They differed from the whites in their refusal to accept the sanctity of the established accommodative pattern.

Other patterns of resistance to slave status are less clearly racial and more frequently individual in nature. There is documentation that suicide, infanticide and self-mutilation were widespread, not only in this country, but also on the boats which brought the slaves and even before that in the slave coffles of Africa itself. Other slaves took an easier pattern of resistance through what we now call the "slow-down" and various forms of "goldbricking". . . . It is true that much of this protest was not channeled into social racial protest. But the underlying substratum was one of protest against an accommodative pattern in which the Negro was in a permanently subordinate position. . . .

2. *Civil War and Reconstruction (1861-1877):* The period immediately prior to the Civil War was one in which the status of the Negro, and of his relationships to the dominant white group, became increasingly a matter of national concern. While almost all white Americans, from North or South, of Abolitionist or Slavery politics, were agreed on the innate inferiority of the Negro to the white man, there were those who felt that this inferiority did not justify holding the black man in slavery. The War of the Rebellion was an attempt to decide issues in the area of "State's Rights." But lying behind and around all other issues was that of slavery and, more broadly, the relationships between whites and Negroes in all parts of the country.

Even before the War had begun it was apparent that not all Northerners felt toward the Negro as did the abolitionists. . . . The domestic situation in the North during the War was marked by numerous civil disturbances. There was violent rioting in Cincinnati in 1862, apparently growing out of competition of Negro and Irish hands on the riverboats. There were lesser riots in Newark, New Jersey, and in Buffalo and Troy, New York. These latter riots, like other riots of the War period, combined as their basic causes hostility to the wartime draft and its inequities and a concomitant fear that Negroes would take over the jobs of white labor. The most spectacular of the so-called "Draft Riots," however, was that which took place in New York City in July of 1863.

The draft disturbances in New York remain the most sanguinary case of interracial violence in American history. Estimates of deaths of white rioters alone range as high as 1,500 and while the total number of Negroes slain is unknown, the population of Negroes in the city dropped by 20 per cent, from 12,472 to 9,945, between 1860 and 1865. . . . The Draft Riots in New York had at least two interacting causes, one direct and one indirect, which were related to the status of the Negro. The discriminatory nature of the draft legislation was felt particularly by working-class people who were unable to pay for substitutes. They were being forced to fight in a war about which they had no enthusiasm. In addition, they felt that they were being forced to fight to "free the niggers," whom they perceived as a threat as a source of cheap labor. In some of its aspects the New York riot was similar to earlier riots directed against various foreign-born groups, particularly the Irish themselves, who were considered as undermining the position of native-born white labor.

The Civil War also saw the first large-scale participation of Negroes in military activities in an American war. Negroes were utilized by both Union and Confederate forces, though in the South their participation was largely limited to work in labor battalions. In the Northern armies they fought in several major campaigns, occasionally distinguishing themselves to a minor degree. When captured by Southern troops they could expect no quarter and in at least one case were slaughtered wholesale. Relations with Northern white officers were frequently not much better, a unit of the Corps d'Afrique mutinied against its white officers and other incidents are recorded.

The situation of Negroes in the South during the war period was not uniform. In some cases white owners and other representatives of the dominant racial group thought it expedient to introduce even more rigid controls over their slaves. In other areas Negroes were given added responsibilities and loyal servants stayed at home and protected the "women folk." Even in areas characterized by the latter situation, however, there was a general air of tenseness and the number of slaves who attempted to gain their freedom in the confusion swelled to the point where they hindered the movements of the Northern military forces. The latter, at least in some cases showed their attitude by returning the runaway slaves to their masters. Some areas were swept with panic as rumors circulated of impending insurrection. The accommodative structure was disintegrating, but no new structure of social relationships was as yet appearing to take its place.

The bitterness of white Southerners at losing the war was hardly assuaged by events of the immediate post-War years. To the injury of shattered pride and economic ruination was added the insult of disfranchisement and "Black Republicanism." The oft-told activities and exploits of "carpetbaggers," "scalawags" and the members of the various "black government" need no re-telling. . . .

By the end of this period the relationship between whites and Negroes had been clearly defined as an interracial relationship and any inter-class aspects were clearly secondary. Henceforward, particularly in the South but with increasing frequency in the North, disputes between whites and Negroes were interpreted as interracial disputes no matter what may have been the initiating incident. . . .

3. *The Second Reconstruction and the beginnings of the Great Migration (1878-1914):* Although considerable hostility had been generated by events of the post-War period, the withdrawal of Federal troops from the South after the Compromise of 1877 was not followed

by an immediate wave of savage repression against the Negro in the South. Indeed, for a decade it seemed that the lines of struggle in the new South might be defined along class lines rather than along racial lines. For a brief period, that of the acme of Populist power, a tenuous alliance existed between the poor whites and the Negro populace. White and Negro alike united in a temporary and doomed attempt to overthrow the "Bourbon aristocracy." It was after the breakdown of this alliance . . . that the classic period of repression and lynching began.

. . . It was between the middle 'Eighties and the early 1900's that most of the increasingly discriminative and repressive legislation, the "Jim Crow" laws, was passed. During the same period these laws received support through the courts to the supreme judicial bench. The Negro was deprived effectively of the franchise, of equality in compulsory public education and of protection against discrimination in the use of public facilities. The Negro did not succumb to this attack on his rights without a struggle. The use of widespread repression and the high incidence of violence against the Negro populace was, at least in part, the manifest expression of white reaction to Negro resistance. If Negroes had "known their place" it would not have been necessary to lynch Negroes in order to remind them of that "place." There was considerable resistance, though usually unorganized, on the part of the Negro population. When that resistance failed, a trickle of northward migration began, a trickle which was to swell into a flood by the end of the First World War.

The manifest reason for much of the savage repression of this period was the protection of Southern white womanhood, still a major plank in the foundation of programs for maintaining white supremacy. However, while this may have been the public explanation for lynching, rape was not the most frequent alleged cause for the necessity of the primeval justice of lynching, even during the two big lynching decades, the last of the 19th and the first of the 20th Centuries. Failure to show the proper respect to a white man was equally important, and a cause which included a variety of offenses ranging from a demand for an explanation of financial transactions to the more heinous crime of engaging in political activity. Political activity was the underlying cause of the two most savage outbreaks of this period, riots in Wilmington, North Carolina, in 1896 and in Atlanta, Georgia, in 1906. In the latter case the alleged reason for the outbreak was a series of assaults on white women, but it is clear that the disturbance had as a latent function the exclusion of Negroes from political participation. . . .

4. *World War I and post-war boom and racial readjustment (1915-1929):* Events of this period made clear the fact that the Negro problem was no longer a regional one, but one shared by North and South alike.

Indeed, while lynching continued in the South, major outbreaks of interracial violence increasingly occurred in Northern urban areas with their growing concentrations of Negro population.

There are five patterns of interracial social violence in this period different enough in characteristics to be identifiable. They are (a) lynching, (b) mutiny and insurrection, (c) individual interracial assaults and homicides, racial arson and bombings, (d) "Southern style" race riots, and (e) "Northern style" race riots.

(a) *Lynching:* The first decade of the 20th Century was a peak decade for lynching in the South and during the same decade this pattern of interracial violence spread into Northern States. The most spectacular lynching of this century occurred immediately after World War I in Omaha, Nebraska. The immediate alleged cause was the assault of a Negro upon a white woman. The real cause, however, was at least in part a reflection of the nation-wide reaction of whites to the new militance of the Negro's assault upon the accommodative structure. This new militance was a result partly of the not unsubstantial gains of the Negro in moving north during the war and partly a result of the much publicized treatment of Negro soldiers overseas, particularly in France. Large numbers of whites shared in a determination to "put these uppity niggers back in their place," and violence occurred in widely scattered points throughout the country.

Lynchings continued to occur until the time of World War II and it is only since the war that the Bureau of Records and Research of Tuskegee has stopped publication of data on lynchings on the ground that their occurrence is no longer of major consequence. A common cause continued to be alleged Negro assault upon a white woman, but the actual pattern of precipitating causes remained as varied as it had been in earlier periods. It is probable that here, as in the case of other types of violence, there have been changes in etiology. Attempts, none very successful, have been made to demonstrate that lynchings, particularly during the Depression, were closely related to the fluctuation of various economic indices. While documentation for such relationships has proved insufficient, it is probably true that lynching in later years was founded less frequently on the myth of sexuality and more frequently was a direct expression of reaction against "felt" Negro aggression in the economic sphere.

(b) *Mutiny and insurrection:* Such aggression, in at least one instance, found expression in the renewal of a pattern which had not occurred since before the Civil War. In October, 1919, there occurred an insurrection of the Negro populace near Elaine, Arkansas. It was claimed that the inspiration for this rebellion came from "Bolshevik" agitation and there is some evidence that the "Progressive Farmer's Household

Union" was active in promoting the notion that Negroes were entitled to economic and social equality. Negroes of the area were well organized and were prepared, according to confessions made by several of their number, to follow up demands for fair payment for their cotton with an armed uprising. After a series of brief battles the Negroes were subdued and hunted down, given quick trials, and sentenced, several to death.

In addition to this uprising there were a number of mutinies in the military, the most famous of which developed into the Houston race riot of 1917. In this affair, Negro soldiers, enraged by the shooting of one of their comrades in an affray with the white police over alleged mistreatment of a Negro woman, mutinied against their officers, took weapons and proceeded to storm downtown Houston. Several people were killed, and as a result of the disturbance 65 Negro soldiers received sentences, several of them for life imprisonment.

It is interesting to note that the soldiers involved in the Houston race riot were largely from Northern States. The Elaine uprising and the several mutinies which occurred during the war make up the bulk of cases of direct assaults by Negroes upon the accommodative structure.

(c) *Individual interracial assaults and homicides, arson and bombings:* A third pattern of social violence consisted of individual interracial assaults and homicides and other attacks such as arson and bombing. Not all interracial homicides and assaults can be considered to be social violence. In any case where racial membership was important in the interactive pattern and the violence based ultimately on that membership, social violence may be said to have occurred. These manifestations of violence are a part of the riot cycle itself. During the period of increasing tension prior to major riots, during lulls within the riot, and in decreasing tempo after the riot has played itself out or has been quelled, such acts are indicators of the character of interracial relations. In those situations where adequate policing or firm governmental action prevent the actual eruption of hostility into full-fledged riots such behavior patterns may be the sole indication of the high degree of tension.

(d) *"Southern style" race riots:* The Atlanta riot of 1906 and the Springfield, Illinois, riot of 1908 are examples of Southern style race riots. During the period under discussion, the Washington, D. C., riot of 1919 and the Tulsa, Oklahoma, riot of 1921 can be taken as typical examples. In every such riot violence is largely one-sided and consists of attacks, of varying degrees of organization, by whites on Negroes and on the Negro community. In all such riots, whatever may have been the actual background of the riot, there are charges of Negro assaults upon white women.

(e) *"Northern style" race riots:* The Chicago riot of 1919 may be taken as the type-case of the Northern style urban race riot. Here the causation, both in background and in actual precipitating incident, is secular in nature and there is no focussing on the alleged violation of the sanctity of white womanhood. Rather there was a long period of constantly increasing tension in other areas, and a series of assaults upon the accommodative pattern by Negroes, indeed, a challenge to the very continued existence of that pattern. The assault was felt particularly in the areas of housing, labor competition and the use of public facilities, especially transportation. The actual precipitating incident was the death, perhaps accidental, of a Negro youth during a dispute over segregated swimming. The riot found organized and unorganized groups of both races engaged in occasional pitched battles and a widespread occurrence of attacks upon isolated individuals of one race by roaming gangs of the other race. While there were claims of police partiality and governmental inefficiency the role of the government was far more neutral than was the case in disturbances in the South, urban or rural.

5. *Inter-War and Depression (1930-1941):* In many ways this period is an extension of the immediately preceding one. It has been accorded separate treatment because of the sharp decline of reported violence of an interracial nature during the decade of the 'Thirties. While lynchings continued, particularly in the South, they decreased in number if not in barbarity. Only one major urban disturbance is recorded for the decade, the Harlem riot of 1935. The end of the period was characterized by an increasing incidence of individual interracial violence, presaging the major outbreaks of urban social violence which were to occur in the following period. The period was one in which there was a gradual building up of the strength of organizations on the extreme political left and the extreme political political right. These organizations played an as yet incompletely assessed role in the struggles which were coming.

6. *World War II (1942-1945):* The most dramatic racial outbreaks of the Second World War were the Detroit and Harlem disturbances of 1943. While there are some similarities between these two outbreaks, there are sharp differences both in background and in the actual course of events in the two cities. The Detroit race riot was, in background, in precipitating incident, and in chronology of violence a "Northern style" riot much like the 1919 Chicago riot. There was little actual interracial violence in the Harlem outbreak, but this lack of overt interracial conflict resulted from differences in ecology and in the application of police controls rather than from differences in general background factors in Detroit and Harlem or from any lower degree of strain in the accommodative relationship in Harlem.

The Harlem and Detroit riots of 1943 were only two of the more spectacular expressions of the resurgence of interracial conflict during World War II. There were riots in other urban centers, both North and

South. Nor were riots the only form of conflict and violence occurring during the war. There were difficulties involving Negro service personnel which in at least a few cases came close to ending in old-fashioned lynchings. There was a continuation of the pattern of individual assaults and homicides. Intimately related to all these patterns of actual violence was a much increased militance shown by the Negro press and by a number of Negro organizations. Perhaps most important in terms of long-range consequences was the burgeoning utilization of political, economic and legal coercion in the assault upon the pattern of interracial accommodation. Results of the interaction of all these factors have become obvious in the post-War period. . . .

With the exception of a brief period after the Civil War, the pattern of American Negro-white relationships, especially in the American South, has closely approximated the classic accommodative pattern of superordination-subordination, with the whites a continually dominant group. The most savage oppression, whether expressed in rural lynchings and pogroms or in urban race riots, has taken place when the Negro has refused to accept a subordinate status. The most intense conflict has resulted when the subordinate minority group has attempted to disrupt the accommodative pattern or when the superordinate group has defined the situation as one in which such an attempt is being made. Conflict in Negro-white relationships in the United States has been conflict generated by the breakdown of an essentially unstable accommodative pattern, essentially unstable because the subordinated group has refused to accept its status and has had sufficient power to challenge it.

THE FIRE THIS TIME

Time Magazine

. . . In the violent summer of 1967, Detroit became the scene of the bloodiest uprising in half a century and the costliest in terms of property damage in U.S. history. At week's end, there were 41 known dead, 347 injured, 3,800 arrested. Some 5,000 people were homeless (the vast majority Negro), while 1,300 buildings had been reduced to mounds of ashes and bricks and 2,700 businesses sacked. Damage estimates reached $500 million. The grim accounting surpassed that of the Watts riot in Los Angeles where 34 died two years ago and property losses ran to $40 million. More noteworthy, the riot surpassed those that had preceded it in the summers of 1964 and 1965 and 1966 in a more funda-

From *Time*, August 4, 1967, Vol. 90, No. 5, pp. 13-18. Reprinted by permission.

mental way. For here was the most sensational expression of an ugly mood of nihilism and anarchy that has ever gripped a small but significant segment of America's Negro minority.

Blind Pig. Typically enough, Detroit's upheaval started with a routine police action. Seven weeks ago, in the Virginia Park section of the West Side, a "blind pig" (afterhours club) opened for business on Twelfth Street, styling itself the "United Community League for Civic Action." Along with the afterhours booze that it offered to minors, the "League" served up black-power harangues and curses against Whitey's exploitation. It was at the blind pig, on a sleazy strip of pawnshops and bars, rats and pimps, junkies and gamblers, that the agony began.

Through an informant, police were kept advised of the League's activities. At 1:45 a.m. Sunday, the informant, a wino and ex-convict, passed the word (and was paid 50¢ for it): "It's getting ready to blow." Two hours later, 10th Precinct Sergeant Arthur Howison led a raid on the League, arresting 73 Negro customers and the bartender. In the next hour, while squad cars and a paddy wagon ferried the arrested to the police station, a crowd gathered, taunting the fuzz and "jiving" with friends who had been picked up. "Just as we were pulling away," Howison said, "a bottle smashed a squad-car window." Then it began.

Rocks and bottles flew. Looting, at first dared by only a few, became a mob delirium as big crowds now gathered, ranging through the West Side, then spilling across Woodward Avenue into the East Side. Arsonists lobbed Molotov cocktails at newly pillaged stores. Fires started in the shops, spread swiftly to homes and apartments. Snipers took up posts in windows and on rooftops. For four days and into the fifth, mobs stole, burned and killed as a force of some 15,000 city and state police, National Guardsmen and federal troops fought to smother the fire. The city was almost completely paralyzed.

It Can't Happen Here. For the last couple of years, city officials had been saying proudly: "That sort of thing can't happen here." It had seemed a reasonable enough prediction.

Fully 40% of the city's Negro family heads own their own homes. No city has waged a more massive and comprehensive war on poverty. Under Mayor Jerry Cavanagh, an imaginative liberal with a knack for landing Government grants, the city has grabbed off $42 million in federal funds for its poverty programs, budgeted $30 million for them this year alone. Because many of the city's 520,000 Negroes (out of a population of 1,600,000) are unequipped to qualify for other than manual labor, some $10 million will go toward special training and placement programs for the unskilled and the illiterate. A $4,000,000 medical program furnishes family-planning advice, out-patient clinics and the like. To cool any potential riot fever, the city had allotted an additional

$3,000,000 for this summer's Head Start and recreation programs. So well did the city seem to be handling its problems that Congress of Racial Equality Director Floyd McKissick excluded Detroit last winter when he drew up a list of twelve cities where racial trouble was likely to flare.

Anywhere. McKissick's list has proved to be woefully incomplete. So far this summer, some 70 cities—40 in the past week alone—have been hit. In the summer of 1967, "it" can happen anywhere, and sometimes seems to be happening everywhere. Detroit's outbreak was followed by a spate of eruptions in neighboring Michigan cities—Grand Rapids, Kalamazoo, Flint, Muskegon, West Michigan City and Pontiac, where a state assemblyman, protecting the local grocery that he had owned for years, shot a 17-year-old Negro looter to death. White and Negro vandals burned and looted in Louisville. Philadelphia's Mayor James Tate declared a state of limited emergency as rock-throwing Negro teen-agers pelted police prowl cars. A dozen youths looted a downtown Miami pawnshop and ran off with 20 rifles, leaving other merchandise untouched. Some 200 Negroes in Poughkeepsie, N. Y., smashed downtown store windows. In Arizona, 1,500 National Guard members were alerted when sniper fire and rock throwing broke out in Phoenix.

In New York's East Harlem, Puerto Ricans broke windows, looted and sniped from rooftops for three nights after a policeman fatally shot a man who had pulled a knife on him. At one point, the youths who led the rioting drew a chalk line across Third Avenue and tauntingly wrote: "Puerto Rican territory. Don't cross, flatfoot."

Ironically, New York—like Detroit—has launched a major summer entertainment program designed to cool the ghettos by keeping the kids off the streets. "We have done everything in this city to make sure we have a stable summer," said Mayor John Lindsay. But after one of those "stabilizing" events, a Central Park rock-'n'-roll concert featuring Smokey Robinson and the Miracles, a boisterous band of some 150 Negroes wandered down toward midtown Manhattan, heaved trash baskets through the windows of three Fifth Avenue clothing stores and helped themselves. The looters' favorite was a $56 Austrian alpaca sweater, which is a status symbol in Harlem. Among the 23 whom police were able to catch: four Harlem summer antipoverty workers who earn up to $90 a week from the city.

Black & White. All of these were tame enough alongside Detroit. The violence there last week was not a race riot in the pattern of the day-long 1943 battle between Negroes and whites that left 34 known dead. Last week poor whites in one section along Grand River Avenue joined teams of young Negroes in some integrated looting. When the rioters began stoning and sniping at firemen trying to fight the flames, many Negro residents armed themselves with rifles and deployed to protect the firemen. "They say they need protection," said one such Negro, "and we're damned well going to give it to them." Negro looters screamed at a well-dressed Negro psychiatrist: "We're going to get you rich niggers next."

Detroit has no single massive ghetto. Its Negroes, lower, middle and upper income, are scattered all over the city, close to or mixed in with white residents. But unemployment is high among Negroes (6% to 8% v. the over-all national level of 4%) and housing is often abominable. It is particularly ramshackle, crowded and expensive around the scabrous environs of Twelfth Street, once part of a prosperous Jewish section.

"They Won't Shoot." When the trouble began outside Twelfth Street's blind pig, the 10th precinct at that early hour could muster only 45 men. Detroit police regard the dawn hours of Sunday, when the action is heaviest in many slums, as a "light period." The precinct captain rushed containing squads to seal off the neighborhood for 16 square blocks. Police Commissioner Ray Girardin decided, because of his previous success with the method, to instruct his men to avoid using their guns against the looters. That may have been a mistake.

As police gave ground, the number of looters grew. "They won't shoot," an eleven-year-old Negro boy said coolly, as a pack of looters fled at the approach of a busload of police. "The mayor said they aren't supposed to."

At 6:30 a.m., the first fire was in a shoe store. When fire engines screamed to the scene, rocks flew. One fireman, caught squarely in the jaw, was knocked from a truck to the gutter. More and more rioters were drawn to the streets by the sound of the sirens and a sense of summer excitement.

"The noise of destruction adds to its satisfaction," Elias Canetti notes in *Crowds and Power*. "The banging of windows and smashing of glass are the robust sounds of fresh life, the cries of something newborn." In Detroit, they proved to be—with the rattling of gunfire—the sounds of death. Throughout the Detroit riot there was—as in Newark—a spectacularly perverse mood of gaiety and light-hearted abandon in the mob—a "carnival spirit," as a shocked Mayor Cavanagh called it, echoing the words used by New Jersey's Governor Richard Hughes after he toured stricken Newark three weeks ago.

"Sold Brother." Looters skipped gingerly over broken glass to rake in wrist-watches and clothing from shop windows. One group of hoods energetically dismantled a whole front porch and lobbed the bricks at police. Two small boys struggled down Twelfth Street with a load of milk cartons and a watermelon. Another staggered from a supermarket under the weight of a side of beef. One prosperous Negro used his Cadillac convertible to haul off a brand-new deep freeze.

Some of the looters were taking a methodical revenge upon the area's white merchants, whose comparatively high prices, often escalated to offset losses by theft and the cost of extra-high insurance premiums, irk the residents of slum neighborhoods. Most of the stores pillaged and destroyed were groceries, supermarkets and furniture stores; of Detroit's 630 liquor stores, 250 were looted. Many drunks careened down Twelfth Street consuming their swag. Negro merchants scrawled "Soul Brother"—and in one case, "Sold Brother"—on their windows to warn the mobs off. But many of their stores were ravaged nonetheless.

Into Next Year. The mobs cared nothing for "Negro leadership" either. When the riot was only a few hours old, John Conyers, one of Detroit's two Negro Congressmen, drove up Twelfth Street with Hubert Locke and Deputy School Superintendent Arthur Johnson. "Stay cool, we're with you!" Conyers shouted to the crowd. "Uncle Tom'" they shouted back. Someone heaved a bottle and the leaders beat a prompt retreat, not wanting to become "handkerchief heads" in the bandaged sense of the epithet. "You try to talk to these people," said Conyers unhappily, "and they'll knock you into the middle of next year."

Riots and looting spread through the afternoon over a 10.8-sq.-mi. area of the West Side almost as far north as the Northland Shopping Center. An entire mile of Twelfth Street was a corridor of flame; firemen answering the alarms were pelted with bricks, and at one point they abandoned their hoses in the streets and fled, only to be ordered back to the fire by Cavanagh.

Some 5,000 thieves and arsonists were ravaging the West Side. Williams Drug Store was a charred shell by dusk. More than one grocery collapsed as though made of Lincoln Logs. A paint shop erupted and took the next door apartment house with it. In many skeletal structures the sole sign of life was a wailing burglar alarm. Lou's Men's Wear expired in a ball of flame. Meantime, a mob of 3,000 took up the torch on the East Side several miles away. The Weather Bureau's tornado watch offered brief hope of rain to damp the fires, but it never came.

Spreading Fires. Rushing to Detroit at midday Sunday, Michigan's Governor George Romney called in 370 state troopers to beef up the defenses, then by late afternoon ordered 7,000 National Guardsmen mobilized.

Through the night the contagion spread. The small cities of Highland Park and Hamtramck, whose boundaries are encircled by Detroit, were under siege by looters. A four-mile section of Woodward Avenue was plundered. Twenty blocks of Grand River Avenue were in flames. Helicopters with floodlights chattered over the rooftops while police on board with machine guns squinted for the muzzle fire of snipers, who began shooting sporadically during the night.

Before dawn, Romney, Cavanagh and Negro Congressman Charles

Diggs began their day-long quest for the intervention of federal troops. Detroit's jails were jammed far past capacity, and police converted part of their cavernous garage at headquarters into a noisome, overflowing detention center.

Recorder's Court began marathon sessions to arraign hundreds of prisoners herded in from the riot areas. In twelve hours, Judge Robert J. Colombo heard more than 600 not-guilty pleas. To keep the arrested off the streets until the city stopped smoking, bonds were set at $25,000 for suspected looters, $200,000 for suspected snipers. Said the harrassed judge to one defendant: "You're nothing but a lousy, thieving looter. It's too bad they didn't shoot you."

Empty Streets. As Detroit's convulsion continued into the week, homes and shops covering a total area of 14 square miles were gutted by fire. While U.S. Army paratroopers skillfully quieted their assigned trouble area on the East Side, National Guardsmen, jittery and untrained in riot control, exacerbated the trouble where it all started, on Twelfth Street. Suspecting the presence of snipers in the Algiers Motel, Guardsmen laid down a brutal barrage of automatic-weapons fire. When they burst into a motel room, they found three dead Negro teen-age boys— and no weapon. The Guardsmen did have cause to be nervous about snipers. Helen Hall, a Connecticut woman staying at the Harlan House Motel just two blocks from Detroit's famed Fisher Building, on the fringe of the riots, walked to a hallway window Tuesday night to see what the shooting was about. She died with a sniper's bullet in her heart.

By Tuesday morning, Detroit was shrouded in acrid smoke. The Edsel Ford and John C. Lodge freeways were nearly deserted. Tens of thousands of office and factory workers stayed home. Downtown streets that are normally jammed were almost empty. Looters smashed the windows of a Saks Fifth Avenue branch near the General Motors office building, made off with furs and dresses. With many grocery stores wrecked and plundered throughout the city, food became scarce. Some profiteering merchants were charging as much as $1 for bread.

Well of Nihilism. George Romney had a terse evaluation of the chaos: "There were some civil rights overtones, but primarily this is a case of lawlessness and hoodlumism. Disobedience to the law cannot and will not be tolerated."

Some Negroes, to be sure, were among the most insistent in demanding that the police start shooting looters. But the eruption, if not a "civil rights" riot, was certainly a Negro riot. It was fed by a deep well of nihilism that many Negroes have begun to tap. They have despaired finally—some this summer, others much earlier—of hope in white America. . . .

LOOTING IN RECENT CIVIL DISORDERS: AN INDEX OF SOCIAL CHANGE

E. L. Quarantelli and Russell R. Dynes

Outbreaks of looting have increasingly become one of the core concerns of communities which have undergone large scale civil disorders in America within the past several years. Most current press reports of such outbreaks have as one of their central themes the occurrence of looting, and frequently depict looters in action. Even after-accounts of the civil disturbances or editorial polemics often emphasize stories of plunder to illustrate the "breakdown of law and order."

Part of the intensified popular attention to looting undoubtedly stems from actual increases of incidents. In one of the very first large scale disturbances, that in Harlem in 1964, 112 stores were looted. However, about 600 establishments were plundered or burned during the 1965 Watts outbreak. A peak was reached in Detroit in July, 1967, when, according to unofficial accounts, around 2,700 stores were raided by looters.

The explanation commonly given for such "anti-social" behavior is that, in periods of social stress, the thin veneer of civilization is stripped off the human animal revealing man's basest nature. Under more normal circumstances, these base tendencies are somehow held in check. However, under the pressure of crisis situations, man is revealed not as Rousseau's "noble savage," but as Hobbes' "creature," at war with all. Anticipating that certain kinds of large scale emergencies activate this depravity, community officials often request additional law enforcement officers. The National Guard is alerted or mobilized and a wide variety of supplementary security measures are undertaken.

Such steps are frequently initiated on first reports of the beginnings of a civil disturbance. Often expressions of concern that looting will occur and the steps being taken to prevent it are among the first stories circulated by radio and television after reporting the event itself. In the absence of any actual information about what is occurring, mass media outlets often report that which is expected to happen.

As a consequence of this common interpretation of looting as being a manifestation of man's irrationality in periods of social disorganiza-

From *American Behavioral Scientist,* Vol. 11, No. 4 (March-April 1968), 7-10.

tion, punitive control measures are most frequently advocated as befitting the situation. In addition, since at least current civil disturbances have a racial dimension, such behavior tends to reinforce both manifest and latent conceptions which many whites have of Negroes, i.e., looting is a manifestation of the bestial nature of the Negro or at least his inherent anti-social nature. Such views tend to reinforce calls for action which are repressive in nature.

While there is no doubt that much behavior in current urban civil disorders is illegal, we suggest that the spiraling outbreaks of looting are also indicative of the end of a particular era of accommodation between American Negroes and whites. In effect, the plundering and looting increasingly signal the end of a period of time when existing "rights" in a community will be automatically accepted as given by a significant proportion of Negroes therein. These signals, of course, can be read as an invitation to the institution of strong repressive measures, as they seemingly have been in most recent civil disturbances. (That the potential for highly repressive actions lies not far below the surface of American society is suggested by the herding of most Japanese-Americans into detention camps at the start of World War II.) However, looting can also be seen as a violent beginning to a new process of "collective bargaining" concerning rights and responsibilities of various groups in most American communities. The behavior, defined as anti-social by the larger community and unlawful according to legal norms, actually marks the end of one era and the beginning of a new one in racial intergroup relations in American society. In short, looting is an index of social change. (From another perspective it is also an *instrument* for societal change, but we will not develop that point in this article.)

The reasons for seeing looting as the end of one era and the start of another are perhaps not self evident. The same difficulty probably applies also to the meaning of looting and its implication. An understanding of both requires an analysis of existing definitions of property within a community.

As Kingsley Davis notes, "so ingrained in human thought is the fallacy of misplaced concreteness that property is often regarded as the thing owned rather than the rights which constitute the ownership." In popular parlance, property is generally equated with material goods or physical objects. Even the United States Supreme Court did not recognize that property refers to rights rather than a tangible object, until the end of the nineteenth century. Rights and obligations are not tangible in a physical sense nor is the tangibility or intangibility of what is owned of great consequence. What is important are the rights and obligations with respect to something scarce but valuable.

Property thus is a set of cultural norms that regulates the relations of persons to items with economic value. "It consists of the rights and duties of one person or group (the owner) as against all other persons and groups with respect to some scarce good. It is thus exclusive, for it sets off what is mine from thine; but it is also social, being rooted in custom and protected by law." In effect, property is a shared understanding about who can do what with the valued resources within a community.

The norms or rules, the legal ones in particular, specify the legitimate forms of use, control and disposal of economically valued objects. These norms, besides defining the rights and responsibilities of owners, also delineate social relationships among other individuals because the "right" of any person in relation to an object entails at the very least the "obligations" of others to respect that right. There is obviously considerable variation in what the norms specify in different time periods and different societies, but at any given point they are normally widely shared and accepted in a community.

In contrast, civil disturbances such as American communities have recently witnessed are *situations of temporary and localized re-definitions of property rights.* The urban disorders we are discussing represent conflict on community goals and manifest differences of opinion in the community regarding economically valued objects. In these situations, rights to the use of existing resources become problematical, and, in many instances, there are open challenges to prior ownership. If property is thought of as the shared understanding of who can do what with the valued resources within a community, in civil disorders there occurs a breakdown in this understanding. What was previously taken for granted now becomes a matter of open dispute expressed concretely in a redefinition of existing property rights.

The problematic nature of property in urban disorders can be seen by noting the pattern of looting in such situations. Two aspects of the pattern are particularly important. First, the looting is highly selective, focusing almost exclusively on certain kinds of goods or possessions. Second, instead of being negatively sanctioned, looters receive strong although localized social support for their actions.

The degree of selectivity can be seen in the fact that particular types of stores have been the prime focus of looting. In Detroit, 47 grocery stores were attacked, more than in any other category. Furniture, apparel and liquor stores are also frequent objects of looters, with more than a million dollars of stocks of each being plundered during the Newark disorder. In contrast, banks, schools, plants and private residences are generally ignored, although some of the latter have been inadvertently damaged as a result of being close to burned business establishments. Looting, contrary to many initial press reports of such situations, has not been indiscriminate; in fact, certain kinds of consumer goods have been the only fact of attention.

In addition to the selective pattern it assumes, looting at its peak is almost always if not exclusively engaged in by local residents who receive support from segments of their local community. This appearance of normative support can be seen in the almost spiraling pattern that occurs in situations of civil disorders and which reveal cumulative shifts in re-definitions of property rights. The pattern appears to proceed roughly through three stages. (1) A primarily symbolic looting stage where destruction rather than plunder appears to be the intent. It often seems initiated by alienated adolescents or ideologically motivated agitators in an area. (2) A stage of conscious and deliberate looting where the taking of goods is organized and systematic. It frequently appears spurred by the involvement of omnipresent delinquent gangs and theft groups operating on pragmatic rather than ideological considerations. (3) A stage of widespread and non-systematic seizing and taking of goods. At this point, plundering becomes the normative, the socially supported thing to do. Property rights become so re-defined that it becomes permissive if not mandatory to transfer to different private ownership the possession of certain material goods. The legal right does not change, but the group consensus supporting the prerogative to do what with valued resources in the community does shift among a segment of the population.

In the first phase, little looting, if by that is meant the taking of goods, occurs. Instead, destructive attacks are most often directed at objects symbolic of the underlying sources of conflict. Police cars and stores operated by white merchants are attacked. These attacks signal the start of the re-definitions of property rights. Illegal use is made of possessions normally and generally accepted as being under the control of formal community representatives (e.g., police and fire department equipment) or "extra-community" agents (e.g., stores in urban black ghetto areas owned by whites). In truth, many outbreaks of civil disorders up to the present have not progressed beyond this initial phase of window breaking, car burning, tossing of isolated fire bombs and the like.

In the second stage, there is a definite change. Looting of goods rather than destruction of equipment or facilities becomes the mode. White merchants dealing with consumer goods particularly become the object of attack. However, that the white merchants have goods which are readily moved probably makes them the focus of looters as much as the fact that the owners are white. Negro-owned stores of the same general type are not always spared by the marauding bands operating during this time period. There are some indications that a "soul brother" designation has become less and less of a protecting device as the disturbances have increased in intensity over the last several years. The racial dimension, while not absent, appears to be secondary to the economic factor in the behavior of the looters.

In the third stage there is a full re-definition of certain property rights. The "carnival spirit" particularly commented upon in the Newark and Detroit disturbances does not represent anarchy. It is, instead, an overt manifestation of widespread localized social support for the new definition of the situation. The new consensus that emerges in such situations is suggested by the almost total absence of competition or conflict by looters over plundered goods. In fact, in contrast to looting in other situations such as disasters, such behavior in civil disorders is quite open and often collective. Goods are openly taken, not by stealth. Looting is often undertaken by people working together in pairs, as family units or small groups; seldom is it carried out by solitary individuals. The availability of potential loot is frequently called to the attention of bystanders, and in some cases, strangers are handed goods by looters coming out of stores.

Not only is most looting in large scale civil disorders by "insiders," (i.e., local community members) and not outsiders, but there is evidence suggesting participants are from all segments of the population. Looters do not come only from the lowest socio-economic levels or from neighborhood delinquent gangs. Arrested looters are typically employed persons and roughly similar to persons generally participating in the disturbances. There is definite evidence the latter are from all segments of the community. Thus, a statistically random sample found that all participants in the Detroit outbreak were in about the same proportion across all income brackets. A UCLA survey in Watts discovered that those active in the disorders there—perhaps a fourth of the residents—along certain dimensions, represented a cross section of the younger male population in that ghetto area.

This type of phenomena is not new in history. Rude has analyzed nineteenth century demonstrating mobs in England and France. He found that they were typically composed of local residents, respectable and employed persons rather than the pauperized, the unemployed or the "rabble" of the slums. As in the instance of current disturbances, the more privileged classes of those times defined these popular agitations as criminal, i.e., as fundamentally and unconditionally illegitimate.

Certainly most contemporary community authorities see looting as essentially a legal problem and consequently as a matter largely of law enforcement. Many segments of American society, particularly middle class persons with their almost sacred conception of private property also tend to define the problem in the same way. Legislators in response to pressures generated by such perceptions move to strengthen "anti-riot" laws and other repressive measures.

There is, of course, no question that looting is criminal behavior, violating in various ways numerous statutes and ordinances. Viewed primarily in this context, looting, as well as the civil disorder, can be seen as stated in FBI and other reports as "meaningless" behavior. However, such a view obscures something more fundamental.

The laws themselves are based on certain dominant conceptions of property rights. The legal framework is the residue of the past consensus regarding the distribution of property. It reflects an accommodation arrived at sometime before the present.

We suggest that the current civil disorders in American cities are communicating a message about the society. A time of social change, particularly with regard to the distribution of valued resources in communities, is at hand. The old accommodative order defining certain limits to property rights of American Negroes is being directly challenged to the point of collapse, although this seems presently more recognized by the subordinate rather than the superordinate group involved.

Perhaps the current situation has many parallels to the situation in the United States over 100 years ago. The Civil War symbolized a period of time of disagreement about the property of human beings and the rights of their owners. The reluctance to re-define in a peaceful manner the legal structure which supported these property rights resulted in tremendous social costs to the society. Some of these costs were immediate, while others are still being collected today.

Viewed in this context, the attack against existing property rights is neither "irrational" nor "senseless." This is particularly so if it leads to a more institutionalized system of articulating demands and responses in which the rights and obligations of the contending parties becomes a matter of general community consensus. If this is the case, the current looting will mark the initial steps in the evolvement of a social system in which certain heretofore urban segments of the society can nonviolently express their views and in which the more favored groups and the elites will listen.

If more responsive and representative institutions cannot be established, certain groups in American urban communities will continue to engage in disorder and violence or, in our earlier terminology, to indicate their racial discontent and economic aspirations in periodic and increasingly costly re-definitions of property rights. There have been incidents of looting in earlier outbreaks in urban ghettos, some as long as two decades ago, as in Harlem in 1943. However, the scope and intensity of current attacks indicate that increasingly larger numbers of persons no longer share the consensus about property rights held by the larger community. If property is seen not just as physical goods, but as a shared understanding about the allocation of valued resources within a society, a growing lack of consensus will progressively manifest itself in open conflict.

In actual fact, a point of no return may already have been reached. Lambert, in his study of communal violence in India, found that a breakdown in the formal means of social control accompanied broad changes in the social organization of Indian society in the decades immediately preceding independence. Police officers there came to be viewed, not as impartial arbiters of social disputes and as operating within a system of legal redress for grivances; rather they were seen as armed representatives of their socio-ethnic groups. This interpretation of the policeman's roles was accepted by members of the opposing groups, their own groups, and increasingly, by the police officers themselves. "When this occurred the usefulness of the police in social control was sharply reduced and, in some cases, police activities contributed to further disruption of social organization."

Much of this reads as if it were written of local police actions in American ghettos. A typical popular interpretation is to see all of this as a breakdown of "law and order." In one sense it is that. However, in another more fundamental sense, as in Indian society, the failure or inability of the police in a community to prevent looting (apart from those instances where their own actions may initiate such behavior) can be seen as marking the end of an era. The psychological controls which really are the bases of police control in a community no longer suffice. The sheer power of National Guard or regular military units, when disorders reach a peak, is the only formal control left to communities.

Given any foreseeable combination of circumstances, military forces will prevail. However, it would seem that American society, if it wishes to insure domestic tranquility, should move to institutionalize non-violent means for re-distributing certain property rights. Looting can only be a temporary and localized re-definition of property rights. But if no other solution is found, the pattern itself may become routine across more and more American communities. If that is the case, instead of being an index of social change, the looting that has increasingly appeared in recent civil disorders may establish itself as a major structural device for change in the American social system.

Similar patterns of behavior have so established themselves in the past. Rude, in the analysis mentioned earlier, notes that the disorderly demonstrations became a means of protest that in time enabled a segment of the urban population to communicate to the elite. Hobsbawn, in his similar analysis of the pre-industrial "city mob" states the point even more strongly. He observes that the mobs did not just riot to protest, but because they expected to achieve something by their disorder. They assumed that the local authorities would be sensitive to the disturbances and make attempts to deal with the implicit demands of the mobs. According to Hobsbawn, "this mechanism was perfectly understood by both sides."

A similar situation could develop in American communities. Some militant Negro ghetto leaders have almost been explicit about such a possibility. However, the cost to the society would be high and would not really settle the underlying bases of the conflict.

Furthermore, an even greater threat to the society may develop in such a direction. Signs of it have already appeared. The participation of poor, white looters in the Detroit outbreak hints at the possibility that the broader middle class-lower class consensus about property rights may also become subject to attack if the more immediate problem is not solved. The development of such an open class conflict would make the current racial conflict a highly desirable alternative state of affairs.

Thus, a failure to see looting in current disorders as something more than "meaningless" or "criminal" behavior may eventually fragment the social consensus far more than it has been up to the present. This perspective upon looting as an index of social change may suggest alternative ways of dealing with property rights. In fact, if non-violent ways are to be found, there may be no choice in how to think about the current disturbances sweeping American cities.

5 DELINQUENCY

Juvenile delinquency is so much of a world-wide problem that nearly every language has a word or phrase—always negative—to describe and stereotype young people who violate the law. Compared with the terms used to designate the delinquents in other countries, our term, juvenile delinquent, is neutral and benign. There are "mods" and "rockers" in England, "taiyozuku" in Japan, *Halbstarken* in Germany, and *stiliagyi* in Russia.

Allowing for cultural differences, juvenile delinquency most frequently involves theft, vandalism and physical damage to property, sex offenses (mostly girls), truancy, running away from home, incorrigibility, gambling, drinking, vagrancy, and related offenses. By law, delinquency includes all those deviant acts which, if committed by adults, would be criminal. Delinquency also includes a variety of other acts which are exclusive to the minor, such as running away from home, violations of curfew, disrespect for parents, incorrigibility, use of alcohol, and school truancy.

The delinquency problem is serious. Absurd as it may seem, the largest number of arrests in the United States are of boys aged 15, 16, and 17. Arrests for the major felony crimes such as auto theft and burglary are predominantly of juveniles. Finally, and tragically, current estimates indicate that one boy in five, and 8 per cent of all girls, will have become involved with the police and courts by age 18. In a child-oriented society like ours, delinquency rates of this order point to failures in the socialization process, to a social structure which provides no meaningful status or roles for the young, to laws and concepts that are inadequate and archaic, and to the existence of a delinquency subculture.

The readings in this chapter do not cover all the possible aspects of the field. Such a compendium would require far more space. The intent is to present some of the more important concerns and problems. These include the vast amount of hidden delinquencies, the social-class concomitants of juvenile deviations, urban juvenile gangs, the middle-class gang, adaptive and maladaptive types of delinquents, and research on delinquency.

The "Incidence of Hidden Delinquency" by Murphy, Shirley, and Witmer is one of the earliest attempts to arrive at some estimate of the actual as opposed to the reported and processed cases of delinquency. Since 1946, when this study was first published, a whole new field of research has developed which seeks to obtain information about self-reported delinquencies. This research has cast serious doubt on the relationship between social-class position and delinquent conduct. Several studies have also concluded that within the same social class, delinquent *and* nondelinquent teenagers are involved in delinquent acts to about the same degree.

In this classic investigation, Murphy, Shirley, and Witmer compare the delinquent involvement of 61 "unofficial" with 40 official delinquents. The delinquencies studied were of three kinds: city ordinance violations, minor offenses, and serious crimes. Reports of violations were obtained from case-workers. In all, information was gathered on 114 boys, only 13 of whom had no violations to the caseworkers' knowledge.

Professor Walter Miller in "Lower Class Culture as a Generating Milieu of Gang Delinquency" focuses principally on the law-violating behavior of lower-class "street corner" boys, although there is reason to believe that his analysis can be generalized to other types of delinquents as well. The theme of the article is that the "focal concerns" in lower-class culture promote delinquency. The latter—delinquency—is an integral part of the cultural style in slum areas. In simple terms, adhering to the cultural practices of lower-class life automatically involves the violation of legal codes and norms.

In this brilliant analysis, Professor Miller persuasively states one of the two major theories of the development of the lower-class gang. The other thesis is that lower-class boys become gang members because the gang represents a solution to their status problems. Unable to achieve socially acceptable goals, many lower-class boys find an answer to their frustrations in the special values of the delinquent group. These values are the deliberate and exact opposite of those accepted in middle-class life.

In the 1950's the aggressive gang, in the absence of inner city riots, was a major concern of crime prevention and control agencies. Well armed and defending their "turf" or making incursions into other neighborhoods, these conflict gangs aroused considerable fear and demands for action. The New York City Youth Board put a number of detached workers on the streets to work with and, if possible, to redirect the gang members into other and less violent leisure pursuits. The effect of these workers in the streets was to reduce the violence in the aggressive gangs. There was a shift from an emphasis on conflict to one of defense. This change, deliberately and externally imposed, was testimony to the fact that change can be achieved and that, given determination, society is far from powerless to alter some aspects of social life. In "The Emergence of the Defensive Gang," Father Gannon presents a before-and-after picture of the effect of street worker intervention. The implications for delinquency control are especially interesting.

Professor Lewis Yablonsky spent a number of years studying delinquent gangs in New York City. Two of these—the Balkans and the Egyptian Dragons—were the focus of his attention. The Dragons were the perpetrators of one of the most heinous murders in memory—a crime which received national publicity in the mass media. In "The Delinquent Gang as a Near-Group," Professor Yablonsky contends that the violent gang, in its organization, fits somewhere between a mob, on the one hand, and an organized group, on the other. The article deals with a dozen characteristics unique to the near-group.

Almost all sociological studies have focused on the behavior of lower-class youth. For one thing, very few middle-class adolescents ever get to the juvenile court. Hidden behind a mask of respectability, middle-class deviants are usually funneled into private schools and psychiatric treatment and, if necessary, are sent out of the country to "study." They are shielded from public approbation in all possible ways, with the result that little is known of how they function in their normal environments. For this reason, the participant observation study by the Myerhoffs of what they loosely call middle-class "gangs" is suggestive if not definitive. The article also supports the view of the gang as a near-group. The deviant activities of middle-class adolescents, unlike those of lower-class youth, are characterized by "discretion, judgment, and self-possession." These same qualities are major virtues in nondeviant activities, as well. "The Field Observations of Middle Class 'Gangs' " offers an interesting contrast to the traditional delinquent seen in our courts. It also indicates the nature of deviancy spawned in affluence rather than poverty.

In a short but insightful article, "Adaptive and Maladaptive Delinquency," Dr. Richard Jenkins, a psychiatrist, tries to differentiate types of deviation. Maladaptive delinquency is that which generally falls into the bailiwick of psychiatry. Maladaptive delinquents are more frustrated (sick) than criminal, and their deviancy is sometimes explosive in nature. Adaptive delinquents are socially processed. Dr. Jenkins not only outlines these and other distinctions but offers some general recommendations for the management of each type.

As noted earlier, many youngsters are processed by our juvenile courts for acts which would not be crimes if committed by adults. Nevertheless, these "delinquents," estimated to number about one-fourth of all juvenile cases, are treated as ordinary delinquents. Their noncriminal but delinquent acts—truancy, ungovernability, running away from home—often lead to a correctional institution. William Sheridan is concerned about "Juveniles Who Commit Noncriminal Acts" and their handling in the courts. A number of choices are offered by him to remedy deficiencies in the current system of management of these noncriminal delinquents.

THE INCIDENCE
OF HIDDEN DELINQUENCY

Fred J. Murphy, Mary M. Shirley,
and Helen L. Witmer

Mental hygienists have always been concerned, on the one hand, that many a youthful violator of the law goes unprosecuted and even undetected until a delinquent pattern becomes deeply ingrained; and on the other, that many a lad receives a juvenile court record for a relatively innocent misdemeanor. Students of juvenile delinquency have long suspected that juvenile court statistics do not reflect adequately the extent of youthful misconduct and that a considerable number of violations and violators never find their way into official court records. Hitherto, research workers have been baffled as to how to get at this pool of hidden delinquency. The Cambridge-Sommerville Youth Study, which has maintained an intimate contact with a large group of boys throughout their adolescent years, has afforded a unique opportunity to arrive at some measure of the amount of juvenile law-breaking that is hidden from public view. From our case records, it is possible to make a minimum estimate of how frequently the group of boys under study committed acts that *could* have brought them into court if someone in the community had wanted to register a court complaint.

This program of character building and delinquency prevention sponsored by the late Dr. Richard Cabot directed its efforts chiefly toward underprivileged boys who lived amidst the congestion and squalor of high delinquency areas. The plan of treatment involved close contact with the subjects and their parents by case workers who became trusted friends and were consequently afforded the boys' confidences. In the course of work the case workers acquired a great deal of information concerning misdeeds that had never become a matter of official court complaint. . . .

From *The American Journal of Orthopsychiatry,* Vol. 16, No. 4 (October 1946), 686-96. Reprinted by permission.

Because the length of a period of probation or the term of institutional commitment for juvenile offenses does not serve as an adequate measure of the seriousness of an act, three groupings by nature of offenses were formulated with the assistance of the aforementioned authority. The three categories as developed in the order of seriousness were:

1. *Violations of city ordinances,* such as shining shoes or vending without a license, street ball playing, hopping street cars, swimming and/or fishing in forbidden places, and curfew laws.

2. *Minor offenses,* of the nature of truancy, petty stealing (5 and 10¢ stores), trespassing, running away, stubborn child, sneaking into movies.

3. *More serious offenses,* involving such acts as breaking and entering, larceny, assault, drunkenness, sex offenses.

The comprehensive list of approximately 50 offenses was drawn up on individual work sheets which provided space for identifying material on the boy and columns for tabulating his law violations.

A group consultation with the case workers, later to be interviewed individually, was held. This was done to avoid confusion and to assure consistency in the workers' understanding the procedure. The project was thoroughly explained and their advice sought particularly in reference to the tabulation of the frequency of unofficial acts wherein it did not always make for accurate enumeration. Case workers often knew that a boy had repeatedly committed a certain infraction during a given period, but they would have been at a loss to enumerate the individual occurrences. Hence, it was decided to use—*rarely, occasionally,* and *frequently*—giving to each a range of numerical value which would represent the number of violations in a given year of a boy's life. *Rarely* denoted a frequency span of from one to three offenses per year; *occasionally,* from four to nine, and *frequently,* ten and over. By this method it was obvious that we would have to be satisfied in most instances with a numerical approximation of a youth's unofficial offenses. This was termed a "score" of law infractions.

In the process of tabulating a boy's offenses, the case worker and I (F.J.M.) jointly reviewed each page of the case record. Any uncertainty as to whether an offense had been committed, either because the record was vague or because it seemed possible that the boy was entertaining his case worker with a story of fantasied misdeeds, always resulted in his being given the benefit of the doubt, and no tally was recorded. Likewise, in totaling the number of misdemeanors of a boy in a given year, we conservatively employed the lowest weighting; i.e., *rarely* was given a weight of 1, *occasionally,* 4, and *frequently,* 10. . . .

In order to obtain uniformity in the delinquency scores, it was necessary to select an age span that could be consistent for all cases. From a survey of the entire case load, it was found that the majority had received service throughout the age span from 11 to 16 years. A total of 114 boys had been given service throughout this five-year period, and the present study is based upon their analyses.

Table 1

COMPARISON OF VIOLATIONS FOR UNOFFICIAL AND OFFICIAL DELINQUENTS
(Based on records of 114 boys, ages 11-15) *

Violation	Unofficial delinquents	Official delinquents	Both
	N=61	N=40	N=101
City ordinance	739	655	1394
Minor offenses	1913	2493	4406
Serious offenses	174	442	616
Total	2826	3590	6416

* Of 114 boys, 13 had no violations to the case workers' knowledge.

To the workers' knowledge, only 13 of the boys had never committed an offense for which a complaint might have been made in court. The rest had all been more or less serious juvenile offenders; 40 designated as official delinquents because complaints were registered in court, and 61 as unofficial delinquents because they "got by" without court complaint.

The numerical scores hereafter referred to as "number of violations" represent the minimum number of law infractions committed by these boys between their eleventh and sixteenth years. At our conservative estimate, these boys had committed a minimum of 6,416 infractions of the law during the five-year period; while only 95 of their violations had become a matter of official complaint. In other words, authorities took official action in less than 1½ per cent of the infractions. Approximately 1,400 of these infractions were violations of city ordinances, none of which became a matter of court complaint. Of 4,400 minor offenses, only 27 (.60%) were prosecuted. Of 616 serious offenses, 68 (11%) were prosecuted.

Lest the small proportion of infractions resulting in court complaints should lead to the inference that law enforcement was lax in these communities, it must be explained that during the period covered by this study there was a policy of handling a large proportion of juvenile offenders informally. Hence, many of our boys were apprehended and warned by police but no complaint was registered in court. Furthermore, lest it be thought that CSYS case workers were protecting the boys from court involvement, it must be mentioned that in many instances the boys revealed their delinquencies months or even years after they had occurred. In reminiscing on their activities, they often owned up to earlier law violations hitherto unsuspected.

Analysis of the type of infractions for which court complaints were registered indicated that larceny and breaking and entering were the charges of highest frequency. Truancy and school offenses were a matter of official court complaint only rarely in comparison to the frequency with which these were committed. This suggests that school authorities manifest a considerable degree of tolerance of such juvenile offenses and tend to handle them by their own methods rather than to call upon the help of the court.

In the main, the transgressions of the official offenders were more frequent and more serious than those of the unofficial group. The total scores of violations for the officials ranged from 5 to 323 with a median of 79; whereas the unofficials ranged from 0 to 266 with a median of 30. Furthermore, the median official delinquent over the five-year period scored 10 city ordinance infractions, 53 minor acts, and 6 more serious offenses; whereas the median unofficial delinquent had scored 0 on city ordinance violations, only 20 on minor offenses, and 0 on serious offenses. There were, however, a number of exceptions because 5 boys having official records had total scores less than 30, the median of the unofficials; and 13 unofficials equaled or exceeded in minor and more serious offenses the median score of the official delinquents. . . .

Relevant to the bearing that intelligence might have as a differentiating factor between the two groups, we at first speculated that perhaps higher mental endowments enabled the unofficial delinquents to remain out of court. However, upon compiling the figures, it was found that there was no appreciable difference. . . .

We were interested further in ascertaining what the case records revealed concerning the personalities of these boys, especially insofar as these enabled us to judge whether the delinquencies seemed to spring from a neurotic basis or whether they resulted largely from the boys' acquiescence to the prevailing juvenile pattern of their communities. It was also hoped that the records might throw light on why some relatively law-abiding boys had court records and why some of the chronic offenders escaped court action. We therefore studied the case records of the five official delinquents who had low scores and the 13 unofficial delinquents with high scores. It appeared that three of the five official delinquents were dull, passive boys, who had considerable security within their own families and were not particularly troublesome in the community. For these three, court involvement seemed to be a piece of ill luck. Two were perhaps the victims of police vigilance directed toward their entire families. . . .

Of greater interest are the personalities of the 13 who avoided court records in spite of having committed a larger number of minor or serious infractions than the median official delinquent. These likewise could be grouped in a general way into two categories—gregarious, fairly well-adjusted boys whose delinquencies seemed free from a neurotic component; and emotionally disturbed boys whose asocial behavior seemed primarily the outgrowth of tension or friction within the home. There were five boys in the first group; eight in the second.

The four most frequent and most serious of these offenders gave no evidence of being poorly adjusted, in that their behavior reflected the mores of their particular group. . . .

The chief contribution of this study is that we have been able to arrive at a minimal estimate of the amount of unofficial delinquency that takes place among a sizable group of underprivileged boys. Both official and unofficial delinquents commit numerous infractions of juvenile laws which do not become a matter of official record. Although both groups differ somewhat in the frequency and seriousness of offenses, there is much overlapping between the two.

While it has not been within the scope of this paper to make a comprehensive analysis of factors which may perhaps differentiate the official and unofficial delinquents, some marked similarities between the two groups have been found. Both have a wide range in intelligence as measured by standard tests and show no difference in this respect. Both groups contain boys who are socially well adjusted to the pattern of life within their particular subcultures and whose asocial acts could not be considered as springing from emotional conflict or turmoil within themselves. These boys seem to commit most of the violations of property rights, such as larceny, breaking and entering, and destruction of property. Both groups also contain boys whose offenses seem to arise out of deep neurotic disturbance within themselves. These boys, with a neurotic component in their delinquencies, tend to commit aggressions directed toward the home or school in greater frequency than they commit violations against property rights. This observation is consistent with the findings of other students of delinquency and is what one would be led to expect from psychological theory. It is hoped that further analysis of the material will reveal factors that differentiate between the groups of official and unofficial delinquents.

LOWER CLASS CULTURE AS A GENERATING MILIEU OF GANG DELINQUENCY

Walter B. Miller

The etiology of delinquency has long been a controversial issue and is particularly so at present. As new frames of reference for explaining human behavior have been added to traditional theories, some authors have adopted the practice of citing the major postulates of each school of thought as they pertain to delinquency, and of going on to state that causality must be conceived in terms of the dynamic interaction of a complex combination of variables on many levels. The major sets of etiological factors currently adduced to explain delinquency are, in simplified terms, the physiological (delinquency results from organic pathology), the psychodynamic (delinquency is a "behavioral disorder" resulting primarily from emotional disturbance generated by a defective mother-child relationship), and the environmental (delinquency is the product of disruptive forces, "disorganization," in the actor's physical or social environment).

This paper selects one particular kind of "delinquency"—law-violating acts committed by members of adolescent street corner groups in lower class communities—and attempts to show that the dominant component of motivation underlying these acts consists in a directed attempt by the actor to adhere to forms of behavior, and to achieve standards of value, as they are defined within that community. It takes as a premise that the motivation of behavior in this situation can be approached most productively by attempting to understand the nature of cultural forces impinging on the acting individuals as they are perceived *by the actor himself*—although by no means only that segment of these forces of which the actor is consciously aware—rather than as they are perceived and evaluated from the reference position of another cultural system. In the case of "gang" delinquency, the cultural system which exerts the most direct influence on behavior is that of the lower class community itself—a long-established, distinctively patterned tradition with an integrity of its own—rather than a so-called "delinquent subculture" which has arisen through conflict with middle class culture and is oriented to the deliberate violation of middle class norms.

From *The Journal of Social Issues*, Vol. 14, No. 3 (1958), 5-19. Reprinted by permission.

The bulk of the substantive data on which the following material is based was collected in connection with a service-research project in the control of gang delinquency. During the service aspect of the project, which lasted for three years, seven trained social workers maintained contact with twenty-one corner group units in a "slum" district of a large eastern city for periods of time ranging from ten to thirty months. Groups were Negro and white, male and female, and in early, middle, and late adolescence. Over eight thousand pages of direct observational data on behavior patterns of group members and other community residents were collected; almost daily contact was maintained for a total time period of about thirteen worker years. Data include workers contact reports, participant observation reports by the writer—a cultural anthropologist—and direct tape recordings of group activities and discussions.

FOCAL CONCERNS OF LOWER CLASS CULTURE

There is a substantial segment of present-day American society whose way of life, values, and characteristic patterns of behavior are the product of a distinctive cultural system which may be termed "lower class." Evidence indicates that this cultural system is becoming increasingly distinctive, and that the size of the group which shares this tradition is increasing. The lower class way of life, in common with that of all distinctive cultural groups, is characterized by a set of focal concerns—areas or issues which command widespread and persistent attention and a high degree of emotional involvement. The specific concerns cited here, while by no means confined to the American lower classes, constitute a distinctive *patterning* of concerns which differs significantly, both in rank order and weighting, from that of American middle class culture. Chart 1 presents a highly schematic and simplified listing of six of the major concerns of lower class culture. Each is conceived as a "dimension" within which a fairly wide and varied range of alternative behavior patterns may be followed by different individuals under different situations. They are listed roughly in order of the degree of *explicit* attention accorded each and, in this sense, represent a weighted ranking of concerns. The "perceived alternatives" represent polar positions which define certain parameters within each dimension. As will be explained in more detail, it is necessary in relating the influence of these "concerns" to the motivation of delinquent behavior to specify *which* of its aspects is oriented to, whether orientation is *overt* or *covert, positive* (conforming to or seeking the aspect) or *negative* (rejecting or seeking to avoid the aspect).

The concept "focal concern" is used here in preference to the concept "value" for several interrelated reasons: (1) It is more readily derivable from direct field observation. (2) It is descriptively neutral—permitting independent consideration of positive and negative valences as varying under different conditions, whereas "value" carries a built-in positive valence. (3) It makes possible more refined analysis of subcultural differences, since it reflects actual behavior, whereas "value" tends to wash out intracultural differences since it is colored by notions of the "official" ideal.

Chart 1

Focal Concerns of Lower Class Culture

Area	Perceived alternatives (state, quality, condition)	
1. Trouble:	law-abiding behavior	law-violating behavior
2. Toughness:	physical prowess, skill; "masculinity"; fearlessness, bravery, daring	weakness, ineptitude; effeminacy; timidity, cowardice, caution
3. Smartness:	ability to outsmart, dupe, "con"; gaining money by "wits"; shrewdness, adroitness in repartee	gullibility, "con-ability"; gaining money by hard work; slowness, dull-wittedness, verbal maladroitness
4. Excitement:	thrill; risk, danger; change, activity	boredom; "deadness," safeness; sameness, passivity
5. Fate:	favored by fortune, being "lucky"	ill-omened, being "unlucky"
6. Autonomy:	freedom from external constraint; freedom from superordinate authority; independence	presence of external constraint; presence of strong authority; dependency, being "cared for"

Trouble. Concern over "trouble" is a dominant feature of lower class culture. The concept has various shades of meaning; "trouble" in one of its aspects represents a situation or a kind of behavior which results in unwelcome or complicating involvement with official authorities or agencies of middle class society. "Getting into trouble" and "staying out of trouble" represent major issues for male and female, adults and children. For men, "trouble" frequently involves fighting or sexual adventures while drinking; for women, sexual involvement with disadvantageous consequences. Expressed desire to avoid behavior which violates moral or legal norms is often based less on an explicit commitment to "official" moral or legal standards than on a desire to avoid "getting into trouble," e.g., the complicating consequences of the action.

The dominant concern over "trouble" involves a distinction of critical importance for the lower class community—that between "law-abiding" and "non-law-abiding" behavior. There is a high degree of sensitivity as to where each person stands in relation to these two classes of activity. Whereas in the middle class community a major dimension for evaluating a person's status is "achievement" and its external symbols, in the lower class personal status is very frequently gauged along the law-abiding–non-law-abiding dimension. A mother will evaluate the suitability of her daughter's boyfriend less on the basis of his achievement potential than on the basis of his innate "trouble" potential. This sensitive awareness of the opposition of "trouble-producing" and "non-trouble-producing" behavior represents both a major basis for deriving status distinctions and an internalized conflict potential for the individual.

As in the case of other focal concerns, which of two perceived alternatives—"law-abiding" or "non-law-abiding"—is valued varies according to the individual and the circumstances; in many instances there is an overt commitment to the "law-abiding" alternative, but a covert commitment to the "non-law-abiding." In certain situations, "getting into trouble" is overtly recognized as prestige-conferring; for example, membership in certain adult and adolescent primary groupings ("gangs") is contingent on having demonstrated an explicit commitment to the law-violating alternative. It is most important to note that the choice between "law-abiding" and "non-law-abiding" behavior is still a choice *within* lower class culture; the distinction between the policeman and the criminal, the outlaw and the sheriff, involves primarily this one dimension; in other respects they have a high community of interests. Not infrequently brothers raised in an identical cultural milieu will become police and criminals respectively.

For a substantial segment of the lower class population "getting into trouble" is not in itself overtly defined as prestige-conferring, but is implicitly recognized as a means to other valued ends, e.g., the covertly valued desire to be "cared for" and subject to external constraint, or the overtly valued state of excitement or risk. Very frequently "getting into trouble" is multi-functional and achieves several sets of valued ends.

Toughness. The concept of "toughness" in lower class culture represents a compound combination of qualities or states. Among its most important components are physical prowess, evidenced both by demonstrated possession of strength and endurance and by athletic skill; "masculinity," symbolized by a distinctive complex of acts and avoidances (bodily tatooing, absence of sentimentality, non-concern with "art," "literature," conceptualization of women as conquest objects, etc.); and bravery in the face of physical threat. The model for the "tough guy"— hard, fearless, undemonstrative, skilled in physical combat—is represented by the movie gangster of the thirties, the "private eye," and the movie cowboy.

The genesis of the intense concern over "toughness" in lower class culture is probably related to the fact that a significant proportion of lower class males are reared in a predominantly female household and lack a consistently present male figure with whom to identify and from whom to learn essential components of a "male" role. Since women serve as a primary object of identification during pre-adolescent years, the almost obsessive lower class concern with "masculinity" probably resembles a type of compulsive reaction-formation. A concern over homosexuality runs like a persistent thread through lower class culture. This is manifested by the institutionalized practice of baiting "queers," often accompanied by violent physical attacks, an expressed contempt for "softness" or frills, and the use of the local term for "homosexual" as a generalized pejorative epithet (e.g., higher class individuals or upwardly mobile peers are frequently characterized as "fags" or "queers"). The distinction between "overt" and "covert" orientation to aspects of an area of concern is especially important in regard to "toughness." A positive overt evaluation of behavior defined as "effeminate" would be out of the question for a lower class male; however, built into lower class culture is a range of devices which permit men to adopt behaviors and concerns which in other cultural milieux fall within the province of women, and at the same time to be defined as "tough" and manly. For example, lower class men can be professional short-order cooks in a diner and still be regarded as "tough." The highly intimate circumstances of the street corner gang involve the recurrent expression of strongly affectionate feelings towards other men. Such expressions, however, are disguised as their opposite, taking the form of ostensibly aggressive verbal and physical interaction (kidding, "ranking," roughhousing, etc.).

Smartness. "Smartness," as conceptualized in lower class culture, involves the capacity to outsmart, outfox, outwit, dupe, "take," "con" another or others and the concomitant capacity to avoid being outwitted, "taken," or duped onself. In its essence, smartness involves the capacity to achieve a valued entity—material goods, personal status—through a maximum use of mental agility and a minimum use of physical effort. This capacity has an extremely long tradition in lower class culture and is highly valued. Lower class culture can be characterized as "non-intellectual" only if intellectualism is defined specifically in terms of control over a particular body of formally learned knowledge involving "culture" (art, literature, "good" music, etc.), a generalized perspective on the past and present conditions of our own and other societies, and other areas of knowledge imparted by formal educational institutions. This particular type of mental attainment is, in general, overtly disvalued and frequently associated with effeminacy; "smartness" in the lower class sense, however, is highly valued.

The lower class child learns and practices the use of this skill in the street corner situation. Individuals continually practice duping and outwitting one another through recurrent card games and other forms of gambling, mutual exchanges of insults, and "testing" for mutual "con-ability." Those who demonstrate competence in this skill are accorded considerable prestige. Leadership roles in the corner group are frequently allocated according to demonstrated capacity in the two areas of "smartness" and "toughness"; the ideal leader combines both, but the "smart" leader is often accorded more prestige than the "tough" one—reflecting a general lower class respect for "brains" in the "smartness" sense.

The model of the "smart" person is represented in popular media by the card shark, the professional gambler, the "con" artist, the promoter. A conceptual distinction is made between two kinds of people: "suckers," easy marks, "lushes," dupes, who work for their money and are legitimate targets of exploitation; and sharp operators, the "brainy" ones, who live by their wits and "getting" from the suckers by mental adroitness.

Involved in the syndrome of capacities related to "smartness" is a dominant emphasis in lower class culture on ingenious aggressive repartee. This skill, learned and practiced in the context of the corner group, ranges in form from the widely prevalent semi-ritualized teasing, kidding, razzing, "ranking," so characteristic of male peer group interaction, to the highly ritualized type of mutual insult interchange known as "the dirty dozens," "the dozens," "playing house," and other terms. This highly patterned cultural form is practiced on its most advanced level in adult male Negro society, but less polished variants are found throughout lower class culture—practiced, for example, by white children, male and female, as young as four or five. In essence, "doin' the dozens" involves two antagonists who vie with each other in the exchange of increasingly inflammatory insults, with incestuous and perverted sexual relations with the mother a dominant theme. In this form of insult interchange, as well as on other less ritualized occasions for joking, semi-serious, and serious mutual invective, a very high premium is placed on ingenuity, hair-trigger responsiveness, inventiveness, and the acute exercise of mental faculties.

Excitement. For many lower class individuals the rhythm of life fluctuates between periods of relatively routine or repetitive activity and sought situations of great emotional stimulation. Many of the most characteristic features of lower class life are related to the search for excitement or "thrill." Involved here are the highly prevalent use of alcohol by both sexes and the widespread use of gambling of all kinds—playing the numbers, betting on horse races, dice, cards. The quest for excitement finds what is perhaps its most vivid expression in the highly patterned practice of the recurrent "night on the town." This practice, designated by various terms in different areas ("honky-tonkin' "; "goin' out on the town"; "bar hoppin' "), involves a patterned set of activities in which alcohol, music, and sexual adventuring are major components. A group or individual sets out to "make the rounds" of various bars or night clubs. Drinking continues progressively throughout the evening. Men. seek to "pick up" women, and women play the risky game of entertaining sexual advances. Fights between men involving women, gambling, and claims of physical prowess, in various combinations, are frequent consequences of a night of making the rounds. The explosive potential of this type of adventuring with sex and aggression, frequently leading to "trouble," is semi-explicitly sought by the individual. Since there is always a good likelihood that being out on the town will eventuate in fights, etc., the practice involves elements of sought risk and desired danger.

Counterbalancing the "flirting with danger" aspect of the "excitement" concern is the prevalence in lower class culture of other well-established patterns of activity which involve long periods of relative inaction or passivity. The term "hanging out" in lower class culture refers to extended periods of standing around, often with peer mates, doing what is defined as "nothing," "shooting the breeze," etc. A definite periodicity exists in the pattern of activity relating to the two aspects of the "excitement" dimension. For many lower class individuals the venture into the high risk world of alcohol, sex, and fighting occurs regularly once a week, with interim periods devoted to accommodating to possible consequences of these periods, along with recurrent resolves not to become so involved again.

Fate. Related to the quest for excitement is the concern with fate, fortune, or luck. Here also a distinction is made between two states— being "lucky" or "in luck" and being unlucky or jinxed. Many lower class individuals feel that their lives are subject to a set of forces over which they have relatively little control. These are not directly equated with the supernatural forces of formally organized religion, but relate more to a concept of "destiny," or man as a pawn of magical powers. Not infrequently this often implicit world view is associated with a conception of the ultimate futility of directed effort towards a goal: if the cards are right, or the dice good to you, or if your lucky number comes up, things will go your way; if luck is against you, it's not worth trying. The concept of performing semi-magical rituals so that one's "luck will change" is prevalent; one hopes as a result to move from the state of being "unlucky" to that of being "lucky." The element of fantasy plays an important part in this area. Related to and complementing the notion that "only suckers work" (Smartness) is the idea that once things start going your way, relatively independent of your own effort, all good things will come to you. Achieving great material rewards (big cars, big houses, a roll of cash to flash in a fancy night club), valued in lower class as well as in other parts of American culture, is a recurrent theme in lower class fantasy and folk lore; the cocaine dreams of Willie the Weeper or Minnie the Moocher present the components of this fantasy in vivid detail.

The prevalence in the lower class community of many forms of gambling mentioned in connection with the "excitement" dimension, is also relevant here. Through cards and pool which involve skill, and thus both "toughness" and "smartness"; or through race horse betting, involving "smartness"; or through playing the numbers, involving predominantly "luck," one may make a big killing with a minimum of directed and persistent effort within conventional occupational channels. Gambling in its many forms illustrates the fact that many of the persistent features of lower class culture are multi-functional—serving a range of desired ends at the same time. Describing some of the incentives behind gambling has involved mention of all of the focal concerns cited so far —Toughness, Smartness, and Excitement, in addition to Fate.

Autonomy. The extent and nature of control over the behavior of the individual—an important concern in most cultures—has a special significance and is distinctively patterned in lower class culture. The discrepancy between what is overtly valued and what is covertly sought is particularly striking in this area. On the overt level there is a strong and frequently expressed resentment of the idea of external controls, restrictions on behavior, and unjust or coercive authority. "No one's gonna push *me* around," or "I'm gonna tell him he can take the job and shove it . . ." are commonly expressed sentiments. Similar explicit attitudes are maintained to systems of behavior-restricting rules, insofar as these are perceived as representing the injunctions and bearing the sanctions of superordinate authority. In addition, in lower class culture a close conceptual connection is made between "authority" and "nurturance." To be restrictively or firmly controlled is to be cared for. Thus the overtly negative evaluation of superordinate authority frequently extends as well to nurturance, care, or protection. The desire for personal independence is often expressed in such terms as "I don't need *nobody* to take care of me. I can take care of myself!" Actual patterns of behavior, however, reveal a marked discrepancy between expressed sentiment and what is covertly valued. Many lower class people appear to seek out highly restrictive social environments wherein stringent external controls are maintained over their behavior. Such institutions as the armed forces, the mental hospital, the disciplinary school, the prison or correctional institution, provide environments which incorporate a strict and detailed set of rules, defining and limiting behavior and enforced by an authority system which controls and applies coercive sanctions for deviance from these rules. While under the jurisdiction of such systems, the lower class person generally expresses to his peers continual resentment of the coercive, unjust, and arbitrary exercise of authority. Having been released, or having escaped from these milieux, however, he will often act in such a way as to insure recommitment, or choose recommitment voluntarily after a temporary period of "freedom."

Lower class patients in mental hospitals will exercise considerable ingenuity to insure continued commitment while voicing the desire to get out; delinquent boys will frequently "run" from a correctional institution to activate efforts to return them; to be caught and returned means that one is cared for. Since "being controlled" is equated with "being cared for," attempts are frequently made to "test" the severity or strictness of superordinate authority to see if it remains firm. If intended or executed rebellion produces swift and firm punitive sanctions, the individual is reassured, at the same time that he is complaining bitterly at the injustice of being caught and punished. Some environmental milieux, having been tested in this fashion for the "firmness" of their coercive sanctions, are rejected, ostensibly for being too strict, actually for not being strict enough. This is frequently so in the case of "problematic" behavior by lower class youngsters in the public schools, which generally cannot command the coercive controls implicitly sought by the individual. . . .

FOCAL CONCERNS OF THE LOWER CLASS
ADOLESCENT STREET CORNER GROUP

The one-sex peer group is a highly prevalent and significant structural form in the lower class community. There is a strong probability that the prevalence and stability of this type of unit is directly related to the prevalence of a stabilized type of lower class child-rearing unit—the "female-based" household. This is a nuclear kin unit in which a male parent is either absent from the household, present only sporadically, or, when present, only minimally or inconsistently involved in the support and rearing of children. This unit usually consists of one or more females of child-bearing age and their offspring. The females are frequently related to one another by blood or marriage ties, and the unit often includes two or more generations of women, e.g., the mother and/ or aunt of the principal child-bearing female.

The nature of social groupings in the lower class community may be clarified if we make the assumption that it is the *one-sex peer unit* rather than the two-parent family unit which represents the most significant relational unit for both sexes in lower class communities. Lower class society may be pictured as comprising a set of age-graded one-sex groups which constitute the major psychic focus and reference group for those over twelve or thirteen. Men and women of mating age leave these groups periodically to form temporary marital alliances, but these lack stability, and after varying periods of "trying out" the two-sex family arrangement, they gravitate back to the more "comfortable" one-sex grouping, whose members exert strong pressure on the individual *not* to disrupt the group by adopting a two-sex household pattern of life. Membership in a stable and solidary peer unit is vital to the lower class individual precisely to the extent to which a range of essential functions —psychological, educational, and others—are not provided by the "family" unit.

The adolescent street corner group represents the adolescent variant of this lower class structural form. What has been called the "delinquent gang" is one subtype of this form, defined on the basis of frequency of participation in law-violating activity; this subtype should not be considered a legitimate unit of study per se, but rather as one particular variant of the adolescent street corner group. The "hanging" peer group is a unit of particular importance for the adolescent male. In many cases it is the most stable and solidary primary group he has ever belonged to; for boys reared in female-based households the corner group provides the first real opportunity to learn essential aspects of the male role in the context of peers facing similar problems of sex-role identification.

The form and functions of the adolescent corner group operate as a selective mechanism in recruiting members. The activity patterns of the group require a high level of intragroup solidarity; individual members must possess a good capacity for subordinating individual desires to general group interests as well as the capacity for intimate and persisting interaction. Thus highly "disturbed" individuals, or those who cannot tolerate consistently imposed sanctions on "deviant" behavior cannot remain accepted members; the group itself will extrude those whose behavior exceeds limits defined as "normal." This selective process produces a type of group whose members possess to an unusually high degree both the *capacity* and *motivation* to conform to perceived cultural norms, so that the nature of the system of norms and values oriented to is a particularly influential component of motivation.

Focal concerns of the male adolescent corner group are those of the general cultural milieu in which it functions. As would be expected, the relative weighting and importance of these concerns pattern somewhat differently for adolescents than for adults. The nature of this patterning centers around two additional "concerns" of particular importance to this group—concern with "belonging," and with "status." These may be conceptualized as being on a higher level of abstraction than concerns previously cited, since "status" and "belonging" are achieved *via* cited concern areas of Toughness, etc.

Belonging. Since the corner group fulfills essential functions for the individual, being a member in good standing of the group is of vital importance for its members. A continuing concern over who is "in" and who is not involves the citation and detailed discussion of highly refined criteria for "in-group" membership. The phrase "he hangs with us" means "he is accepted as a member in good standing by current consensus"; conversely, "he don't hang with us" means he is not so accepted. One achieves "belonging" primarily by demonstrating knowledge of and determination to adhere to the system of standards and valued qualities defined by the group. One maintains membership by acting in conformity with valued aspects of Toughness, Smartness, Autonomy, etc. In those instances where conforming to norms of this reference group at the same time violates norms of other reference groups (e.g., middle class adults, institutional "officials"), immediate reference group norms are much more compelling since violation risks invoking the group's most powerful sanction: exclusion.

Status. In common with most adolescents in American society, the lower class corner group manifests a dominant concern with "status." What differentiates this type of group from others, however, is the particular set of criteria and weighting thereof by which "status" is defined. In general, status is achieved and maintained by demonstrated possession of the valued qualities of lower class culture—Toughness, Smartness, expressed resistance to authority, daring, etc. It is important to stress once more that the individual orients to these concerns *as they are defined within lower class society;* e.g., the status-conferring potential of "smartness" in the sense of scholastic achievement generally ranges from negligible to negative.

The concern with "status" is manifested in a variety of ways. Intragroup status is a continued concern and is derived and tested constantly by means of a set of status-ranking activities; the intragroup "pecking order" is constantly at issue. One gains status within the group by demonstrated superiority in Toughness (physical prowess, bravery, skill in athletics and games such as pool and cards), Smartness (skill in repartee, capacity to "dupe" fellow group members), and the like. The term "ranking," used to refer to the pattern of intragroup aggressive repartee, indicates awareness of the fact that this is one device for establishing the intragroup status hierarchy.

The concern over status in the adolescent corner group involves in particular the component of "adultness," the intense desire to be seen as "grown up," and a corresponding aversion to "kid stuff." "Adult" status is defined less in terms of the assumption of "adult" responsibility than in terms of certain external symbols of adult status—a car, ready cash, and, in particular, a perceived "freedom" to drink, smoke, and gamble as one wishes and to come and go without external restrictions. The desire to be seen as "adult" is often a more significant component of much involvement in illegal drinking, gambling, and automobile driving than the explicit enjoyment of these acts as such.

The intensity of the corner group member's desire to be seen as "adult" is sufficiently great that he feels called upon to demonstrate qualities associated with adultness (Toughness, Smartness, Autonomy) to a much greater degree than a lower class adult. This means that he will seek out and utilize those avenues to these qualities which he perceives as available with greater intensity than an adult and less regard for their "legitimacy." In this sense the adolescent variant of lower class culture represents a maximization or an intensified manifestation of many of its most characteristic features.

Concern over status is also manifested in reference to other street corner groups. The term "rep" used in this regard is especially significant and has broad connotations. In its most frequent and explicit connotation, "rep" refers to the "toughness" of the corner group as a whole relative to that of other groups; a "pecking order" also exists among the several corner groups in a given interactional area, and there is a common perception that the safety or security of the group and all its members depends on maintaining a solid "rep" for toughness vis-a-vis other groups. This motive is most frequently advanced as a reason for involvement in gang fights: "We *can't* chicken out on this fight; our rep would be shot!"; this implies that the group would be relegated to the bottom of the status ladder and become a helpless and recurrent target of external attack.

On the other hand, there is implicit in the concept of "rep" the recognition that "rep" has or may have a dual basis—corresponding to the two aspects of the "trouble" dimension. It is recognized that group as well as individual status can be based on both "law-abiding" and "law-violating" behavior. The situational resolution of the persisting conflict between the "law-abiding" and "law-violating" bases of status comprises a vital set of dynamics in determining whether a "delinquent" mode of behavior will be adopted by a group, under what circumstances, and how persistently. The determinants of this choice are evidently highly complex and fluid, and rest on a range of factors including the presence and perceptual immediacy of different community reference-group loci (e.g., professional criminals, police, clergy, teachers, settlement house workers), the personality structures and "needs" of group members, the presence in the community of social work, recreation, or educational programs which can facilitate untilization of the "law-abiding" basis of status, and so on. . . .

LOWER CLASS CULTURE AND THE MOTIVATION OF DELINQUENT BEHAVIOR

The customary set of activities of the adolescent street corner group includes activities which are in violation of laws and ordinances of the legal code. Most of these center around assault and theft of various types (the gang fight; auto theft; assault on an individual; petty pilfering and shoplifting; "mugging"; pocketbook theft). Members of street corner gangs are well aware of the law-violating nature of these acts; they are not psychopaths, or physically or mentally "defective"; in fact, since the corner group supports and enforces a rigorous set of standards which demand a high degree of fitness and personal competence, it tends to recruit from the most "able" members of the community.

Why, then, is the commission of crimes a customary feature of gang activity? The most general answer is that the commission of crimes by members of adolescent street corner groups is motivated primarily by the attempt to achieve ends, states, or conditions which are valued and to avoid those that are disvalued within their most meaningful cultural milieu, through those culturally available avenues which appear as the most feasible means of attaining those ends.

The operation of these influences is well illustrated by the gang fight —a prevalent and characteristic type of corner group delinquency. This type of activity comprises a highly stylized and culturally patterned set of sequences. Although details vary under different circumstances, the following events are generally included. A member or several members of group A "trespass" on the claimed territory of group B. While there they commit an act or acts which group B defines as a violation of their rightful privileges, an affront to their honor, or a challenge to their "rep." Frequently this act involves advances to a girl associated with group B; it may occur at a dance or party; sometimes the mere act of "trespass" is seen as deliberate provocation. Members of group B then assault members of group A, if they are caught while still in B's territory. Assaulted members of group A return to their "home" territory and recount to members of their group details of the incident, stressing the insufficient nature of the provocation ("I just *looked* at her! Hardly even said anything!"), and the unfair circumstances of the assault ("About *twenty* guys jumped just the *two* of us!"). The highly colored account is acutely inflammatory; group A, perceiving its honor violated and its "rep" threatened, feels obligated to retaliate in force. Sessions of detailed planning now occur; allies are recruited if the size of group A and its potential allies appears to necessitate larger numbers; strategy is plotted, and messengers dispatched. Since the prospect of a gang fight is frightening to even the "toughest" group members, a constant rehearsal of the provocative incident or incidents and declamations of the essentially evil nature of the opponents accompany the planning process to bolster possibly weakening motivation to fight. The excursion into "enemy" territory sometimes results in a full scale fight; more often group B cannot be found, or the police appear and stop the fight, "tipped off" by an anonymous informant. When this occurs, group members express disgust and disappointment; secretly there is much relief; their honor has been avenged without incurring injury; often the anonymous tipster is a member of one of the involved groups. . . .

It would be possible to develop in considerable detail the processes by which the commission of a range of illegal acts is either explicitly supported by, implicitly demanded by, or not materially inhibited by factors relating to the focal concerns of lower class culture. In place of such a development, the following three statements condense in general terms the operation of these processes:

1. Following cultural practices which comprise essential elements of the total life pattern of lower class culture automatically violates certain legal norms.

2. In instances where alternate avenues to similar objectives are available, the non-law-abiding avenue frequently provides a relatively greater and more immediate return for a relatively smaller investment of energy.

3. The "demanded" response to certain situations recurrently engendered within lower class culture involves the commission of illegal acts.

The primary thesis of this paper is that the dominant component of the motivation of "delinquent" behavior engaged in by members of lower class corner groups involves a positive effort to achieve states, conditions, or qualities valued within the actor's most significant cultural milieu. If "conformity to immediate reference group values" is the major component of motivation of "delinquent" behavior by gang members, why is such behavior frequently referred to as negativistic, malicious, or rebellious? Albert Cohen, for example, in *Delinquent Boys* (Glencoe, Ill.: Free Press, 1955) describes behavior which violates school rules as comprising of "active spite and malice, contempt and ridicule, challenge and defiance." He ascribes to the gang "keen delight in terrorizing 'good' children, and in general making themselves obnoxious to the virtuous." A recent national conference on social work with "hard-to-reach" groups characterized lower class corner groups as "youth groups in conflict with the culture of their (sic) communities." Such characterizations are obviously the result of taking the middle class community and its institutions as an implicit point of reference.

A large body of systematically interrelated attitudes, practices, behaviors, and values characteristic of lower class culture are designed to support and maintain the basic features of the lower class way of life. In areas where these differ from features of middle class culture, action oriented to the achievement and maintenance of the lower class system may violate norms of middle class culture and be perceived as deliberately non-conforming or malicious by an observer strongly cathected to middle class norms. This does not mean, however, that violation of the middle class norm is the dominant component of motivation; it is a by-product of action primarily oriented to the lower class system. The standards of lower class culture cannot be seen merely as a reverse function of middle class culture—as middle class standards "turned upside down"; lower class culture is a distinctive tradition many centuries old with an integrity of its own. . . .

EMERGENCE OF THE "DEFENSIVE" GANG

Thomas M. Gannon

In light of the continually shifting nature of delinquent gang activity, it is time again to reconsider our profile of the teenage gang. Recent research into the types of groups serviced by the street club workers of the New York City Youth Board clearly points to the beginnings of a more sophisticated type of delinquent group, the "defensive" gang. The structure of these groups has been taking shape almost imperceptibly over the past several years in New York City, and deserves explicit recognition and closer observation from those concerned with problems of youth and their prevention. The folowing analysis is based on actual observation of the groups in their natural habitat, discussions with the boys themselves and with the street workers attached to them, as well as on questionnaires submitted to the street club staff as part of a research project at the Youth Board during the summer of 1965.

From *Federal Probation,* Vol. 30, No. 4 (December 1966), 44-47. Reprinted by permission.

A TYPOLOGY OF THE DELINQUENT GANG

Before going further, it would be helpful to delineate the various types of New York gangs. Traditionally, the Youth Board has distinguished four types of adolescent groups with whom it has come in contact.

(1) The *corner group* which develops from a particular spot, usually grows up together, and continues to hang around as a group, talking or engaging in some joint activity. Together they normally display little antisocial behavior.

(2) The *social club* almost always organizes around some common interest (e.g., baseball, basketball, jazz) and, like the corner group, is seldom involved in any serious group delinquency.

(3) The *conflict group* might begin either as a corner or social group, but has become involved in serious conflict with other groups. This conflict may result from the need for protection or be due to the desire for aggression; as a rule the group has weapons and an organizational structure designed to carry out its conflict orientation.

(4) The *thoroughly delinquent and pathological group* totally committed to continuous violent and often criminal activity. This last category closely resembles what Short has called the "hustling" group organized for the purpose of economic gain through nonlegitimate means, or Cloward and Ohlin's "criminal" gang whose primary activities are centered around rational, systematic, economically motivated criminal activity.

Most of the Youth Board's concern since the initiation of the street club project in 1950 has understandably focused on the conflict group. But fighting potential varies not only in degree from one gang to another, but also in the form of conflict itself. Thus the Youth Board came to distinguish between the fighting gang, strictly so called, and the *defensive group* as subtypes of the more general conflict group.

A fighting gang is involved in considerable aggressive conflict with rival gangs, in reputation and status-seeking, in protection of its own "turf," in initiating violence. It often boasts of arsenals that include tire irons, knives, guns, dynamite, and acid. The group is tightly organized with a clearly defined leadership structure (president, war counselors, etc.).

A *defensive* group, on the other hand, seeks to maintain its identity without initiating such conflict. It will usually prefer settling provocations through peaceful means, employing violent retaliation only for the most severe situations. Even this retaliation will frequently be carried out without weapons and may be followed by increased self-isolation from other gangs in the community.

This distinction between fighting gangs and defensive groups has become increasingly important. At the present time, over half of the Youth Board's street workers (53.8 percent) now describe their groups as defensive, less than one-sixth (15.0 percent) as fighting gangs, and almost one-third (31.2 percent) as corner or social groups. These findings collected in 1965 substantiate the results of a similar 1964 survey of the Street Club Project which found that, in the worker's judgment, over three-fourths of the approximately 300 groups now serviced by the Youth Board are organized and structured to meet needs other than aggression. Of course, all aggressive behavior is not excluded from the defensive, corner, and social groups; but fighting does not constitute their main activity.

CHARACTERISTICS OF THE DEFENSIVE GROUP

Generally, these defensive groups contain about 35 members, 10 of whom can be classified as "hard core." The group ranges in age from 13 to 19 years old, is either Puerto Rican or Negro, displays a rather loosely knit structure, informal leadership, and some relationship to an older or allied group.

The key to understanding the defensive group, however, is to grasp the shift in its patterns of aggression. In the traditional fighting gang, aggression generally falls into three categories. The first is a planned battle, often called "bopping" by the boys, a "rumble" by the press. In this kind of warfare the decision to fight is made by the rival clubs, and the time and place for battle is set in advance. Here some kind of weapons often will be used, especially when one or both groups come with the idea that the rival group will be well armed. Before fighting actually begins the opposing war counselors meet with their supporting forces drawn up behind them. When negotiations break down (e.g., when one counselor fails to give in after the other has recounted the "reps" of the various "warriors" present), conflict results.

A second type of gang fighting might be called "wolf packing," or "rat packing." Wolf packing generally consists of raids into enemy or neutral territory with the object of ambushing enemy forces. As a variation, the group may beat up any person they encounter on the street, just for the fun of it. As one of the boys told me, "Sure, we've done *some* of those things—beating people up, stealing, tearing up a house. But not night after night! Them other cats—they make a business out of it. That's a *rat pack*. They *mean* to be ornery. They're looking for trouble. My group's not like that. Guys don't go out, man, and just look for a fight. If they've been drinking, if they run into trouble, sure, they'll fight. But, man, they don't beg for it."

Finally, many gang fights result from the accidental confrontation of groups from rival clubs. Most of the boys refer to all kinds of fights as "jitterbugging" or "bopping." Usually this means deliberate raiding of another group. "Japping" refers to deliberate raiding of several members of one group by a small band from a rival club. Accidental fighting in this third category has no special designation. It often occurs as an accumulation of previous events and is frequently carried out along ethnic lines.

The defensive group seldom seems to engage in any of these kinds of conflict. Almost three-fourths of the street workers reported that their groups were involved in an average of four or five serious incidents over the past year, a decrease of almost 40 percent in the past 4 years. In comparison with the fighting gangs, the defensive groups encountered half as many serious incidents with rival groups and one-fourth less incidents with other people not involved with a gang. Actually, the corner and social groups tend to become involved in more conflicts with non-gang youths than either intragroup or intergroup conflicts.

The most common form of conflict for the defensive group includes individual skirmishes, spontaneous fighting, and japping. Planned "rumbles" rank fifth as one of the least common forms of group violence. In this connection, the Sherifs found in their studies of adolescent deviance, "A major concern of every group studied which engaged in violence against other groups and their members was avoidance of conflict." The New York defensive groups provide unmistakable evidence of this concern.

This shift in fighting patterns raises an interesting question as to the function conflict plays within the status system of the group. Matza has pointed out that the distinctive feature of the "spirit" of delinquency is the celebration of prowess. Prowess can add considerably to the adventurous element of life as well as to the success of one's reputation in the group. In this sense aggression is closely linked with the idea of prowess. The code of the "warrior" calls for an aggressive manliness, a reluctance to accept slight on one's honor. Such a code is reflected in the delinquent's esteem for "heart" (the ratio between bravery and fighting ability).

In the defensive group, fighting skills continue to run high as a status symbol. But with the decrease in gang warfare, a member's reputation tends to rest on his fighting *potential* rather than on his proved victories. Also, with more of the boys interested in getting jobs, staying in school, and "getting ahead," status begins to be measured in terms of a boy's job, weekly salary, future plans, and his involvement with the larger society. Given the fact that all these boys come from the lower class culture where toughness is virtually connatural with social prestige, aggression, and a certain amount of violence will continue to be a motivating factor. What is more surprising is the emergence of the desire to get ahead, to have a stake in society; this trend, which is reflected in all our data of the defensive group, runs a bit counter to the fatalism and lack of concern with legitimate achievement predicated of the lower class boy.

The emergence of the defensive group poses many questions to those interested in understanding the teenage gang. Three stand out in this writer's mind. Why has fighting declined in importance for these groups? What prognosis follows from our analysis of the defensive gang? And what are the implications of this phenomenon for social workers, police, and parole officers? As yet there have been no satisfactory answers to these questions. It is possible, however, to indicate certain factors and find some clues that shed some light on the problem.

THE DECREASE IN CONFLICT

In discussing the roots of the gang, Thrasher observed that "the gang represents the spontaneous effort of boys to create a society for themselves where none adequate to their needs exists." Indirectly Thrasher took the position that the various agencies responsible for the socialization of the child (the family, church, and school) failed in fulfilling the needs of these youngsters; hence their involvement in their own associations. "The gang functions with reference to these conditions in two ways; it offers a substitute for what society fails to give; and it provides a relief from suppression and distasteful behavior. It fills a gap and affords an escape."

Recent research like the Flint Youth Study and Short and Strodtbeck's investigations into 16 Chicago gangs suggests that disadvantaged youngsters do not become alienated; that even if the gang ethic is not one of reaction-formation *against* widely shared values in society, nevertheless peer groups in the lower class often come to serve important *status functions* for youngsters who are unable to "make it" according to the success criteria of the larger society. But there is also evidence that the gang offers far less solidarity and satisfaction to its members than might be imagined. Thus it would seem that the lack of "social assurance" which Whyte attributed to his "corner boys" is just as true for all delinquent gangs.

Given this status function of the gang, plus the precariousness of gang life and the lack of social asurance and social abilities among these youngsters, violence clearly functions as a significant status symbol precisely when these boys have no real stake in society or any hope in their own possibilities for success. Random violence, and certainly systematic violence, are consistently discouraged among middle-class youngsters because these boys are taught that their present decisions and behavior are inextricably linked with long-run consequences and their future well-being. But for most gang boys, the absence of these values and realistic achievement opportunities leaves a kind of vacuum which becomes occupied with other time-filling expenditures of energy centered around success and satisfaction in the gang.

Public concern over the violence of the fighting gang has increased, almost 150 street workers are attached to gangs in New York City where ten years ago there were 40, and methods of police enforcement and intervention have become more adept at meeting the needs of the fighting gangs and their victims. Federal and civic programs have crashed the scene (e.g., OEO, Mobilization for Youth, Haryou-Act, the Youth Board, and others). Today's gang boys have witnessed many older delinquents in their neighborhood killed or jailed as a result of their fighting involvement. All of these factors together and separately influence these youngsters to hesitate before they become similarly involved in serious, systematic gang warfare.

As these youngsters are given a hope for succeeding in society, as their stake in the adult work appears more tangible, fighting loses its appeal. With due account taken of cultural differences, the emerging defensive groups often seem to resemble their middle-class counterparts who also will fight to protect themselves or take retaliation against those who threaten their reputations or opportunities, even if in less violent fashion.

WHAT IS THE PROGNOSIS?

Short has suggested that "the gang's failure to deal satisfactorily with the very real concerns and problems of its members (i.e., status insecurity and social disability) contributes to the instability of most gangs. It also contributes to the fact that the direct influence of gang norms on gang boys' behavior appears to be limited to situations directly involving other gang boys." Thus, to the extent that a group is characterized by social disabilities, it will also be characterized by attempts to create symbols and situations that will allow the expression of the members' dependency needs and the achievement of interpersonal gratifications. In the defensive group, violence still serves as such a symbol, but to a lesser extent than it once did. If this trend is to continue, the larger society must become ever more concerned to provide these youths with real opportunities for gratification and success outside the limits of the gang. As the present research indicates, once the youngsters are given some access to legitimate social gain and a stake in the future, there is every reason to expect that they will perceive their gang experiences less as the source of stability and continuity and more in terms of short-run satisfaction. But only the larger society can finally ring down the curtain on the West Side Story.

IMPLICATIONS FOR DELINQUENCY CONTROL

This prognosis is closely tied to the implications of the emerging gangs for society's agencies of delinquency prevention and control. For the Youth Board the most profound ramifications of its study were felt in the street club project. In the past, the street worker was an individual, often with some social work orientation, who was assigned to one or more fighting gangs. His aim was to redirect their behavior especially by averting gang conflict. As the fighting began to decline, the worker has been called upon to serve more as liaison between the boys and the larger community. This involves much more than establishing personal relationships or mediating warfare. It demands contact with the institutional structure of the community. In the Youth Board's opinion, its street work will continue to be effective only if the workers can create clear-cut channels to training for increased skills and provide legitimate job opportunities, direct the youngsters to them, and provide followup guidance along the way. . . .

If the Youth Board findings about the defensive gang have relevance for street workers, they also have importance for the police. To treat all delinquent groups as if they were fighting gangs, is simply to misread the situation, and to run the risk of needlessly heightening antipolice feelings. One can no longer assume that breaking up the cohesiveness of the group by splitting apart the hard core members from the rest is an unqualified good. Yablonsky has observed that there is little hope of helping the group until this core has been broken away and dealt with severely. Few would question this approach to the traditional fighting gang. If the group's cohesiveness naturally decreases, is it fair to assume that the remaining structure must be split in order to maintain control and reduce violence? As delinquent groups turn further away from systematic aggression, is there not added reason for planning and cooperation between social agencies and police intervention policies? These and similar questions need not remain the subject of speculation or untested assumptions. They can be answered with data. Once responsible enforcement and social agencies consider together the shifting styles of the delinquent groups under their surveillance, greater strides can be made in developing empirically based programs for handling these boys.

CONCLUSION

We have reported some of the New York City Youth Board's research findings about the patterns of the youth groups it was serving at the time of this survey. Presumably, other large cities are beginning to experience a similar phenomenon.

When the Youth Board's street club project began in 1950, it directed its services to the highly structured, dangerously aggressive fighting gangs. These incidents of organized warfare reached their height in the middle and late fifties. With the intensified efforts of the workers, and other related social agencies, the police and the community, much of the violence declined. The gangs currently serviced by the Youth Board, display more defensive than aggressive patterns, appear less tightly structured, less cohesive, and less formally organized. In some instances this has led to a widening of the group's tolerance of deviance (e.g., the increase in drug use among members). More often it has led to increased social ability and occupational aspirations. . . .

THE DELINQUENT GANG AS A NEAR-GROUP

Lewis Yablonsky

This paper is based on four years of research and direct work with some 30 delinquent gangs in New York City. During this period I directed a crime prevention program on the upper West Side of Manhattan for Morningside Heights, Inc., a community social agency sponsored by 14 major institutions including Columbia University, Barnard, Teacher's College, Union Theological Seminary, and Riverside Church.

Approaches used in data gathering included field study methods, participant observation, role-playing, group interaction analysis, and sociometry. The data were obtained through close daily interaction with gang boys over the four-year period during which I was the director of the project.

Although data were obtained on 30 gangs, the study focused on two, the Balkans and the Egyptian Kings. It was the latter which committed the brutal killing of a polio victim, Michael Farmer, in an upper West Side park of New York City. The trial lasted over three months and received nation-wide attention. These two groups were intensively interviewed and contributed heavily to the formulation of a theory of near-groups. In addition to the analysis of the gang's structure, a number of delinquent gang war events produced vital case material.

There is a paucity of available theory based on empirical evidence about the structure of delinquent gangs. Two landmarks in the field are Thrasher's *The Gang* and Whyte's *Street Corner Society*. Some recent publications and controversy focus on the emergence of gangs and their function for gang members. Professor Cohen deals with gangs as sub-

From *Social Problems*, Vol. 7, No. 2 (Fall 1959), 108-17. Reprinted by permission.

cultures organized by working-class boys as a reaction to middle-class values. In a recent publication Bloch and Niederhoffer discuss gangs as organizations designed to satisfy the adolescent's striving for the attainment of adult status.

Although partial group structuring has been extensively discussed in sociological literature on "groups," "crowds," and "mobs," my gang research revealed that these collectivity constructs did not seem to adequately describe and properly abstract the underlying structural characteristics of the delinquent gang. Consequently, I have attempted here to construct a formulation which would draw together various described social dimensions of the gang under one conceptual scheme. I call this formulation Near-Group Theory.

NEAR-GROUP THEORY

One way of viewing human collectivities is on a continuum of organization characteristics. At one extreme, we have a highly organized, cohesive, functioning collection of individuals as members of a sociological group. At the other extreme, we have a mob of individuals characterized by anonymity, disturbed leadership, motivated by emotion, and in some cases representing a destructive collectivity within the inclusive social system. When these structures are observed in extreme, their form is apparent to the observer. However, in viewing these social structures on a continuum, those formations which tend to be neither quite a cohesive integrated group nor a disturbed malfunctioning mob or crowd are often distorted by observers in one or the other direction.

A central thesis of this paper is that mid-way on the group–mob continuum are collectivities which are neither groups nor mobs. These are structures prevalent enough in a social system to command attention in their own right as constructs for sociological analysis. Near-groups are characterized by some of the following factors: (1) diffuse role definition, (2) limited cohesion, (3) impermanence, (4) minimal consensus of norms, (5) shifting membership, (6) disturbed leadership, and (7) limited definition of membership expectations. These factors characterize the near-group's "normal" structure.

True groups may manifest near-group structure under stress, in transition, or when temporarily disorganized; however, at these times they are moving toward or away from their normative, permanent structure. The near-group manifests its homeostasis in accord with the factors indicated. It never fully becomes a *group* or a *mob*.

THE GANG AS A NEAR-GROUP PATTERN

Some recent sociological theory and discourse on gangs suffers from distortions of gang structure to fit a group rather than a near-group conception. Most gang theorizing begins with an automatic assumption that gangs are defined sociological groups. Many of these misconceived theories about gangs in sociological treatises are derived from the popular and traditional image of gangs held by the general public as reported in the press, rather than as based upon empirical scientific investigation. The following case material reveals the disparities between popular reports of gang war behavior and their organization as revealed by more systematic study.

The official report of a gang fight, which made headlines in New York papers as the biggest in the city's history, detailed a gang war between six gangs over a territorial dispute. The police, social workers, the press, and the public accepted a defined version of groups meeting in battle over territory. Research into this gang war incident, utilizing a near-group concept of gangs, indicates another picture of the situation.

N. Y. DAILY NEWS

NIP 200–PUNK FIGHT NEAR COLUMBIA CAMPUS
by Grover Ryder and Jack Smee

A flying squad of 25 cops, alerted by a civilian's tip, broke up the makings of one of the biggest gang rumbles in the city's turbulent teen history last night at the edge of Columbia University campus on Morningside Heights.

N. Y. HERALD TRIBUNE

POLICE SEIZE 38, AVERT GANG BATTLE–RIVERSIDE PARK RULE WAS GOAL

Police broke up what they said might have been "a very serious" battle between two juvenile factions last night as they intercepted thirty-eight youths.

N. Y. TIMES

GANG WAR OVER PARK BROKEN BY POLICE

The West Side police broke up an impending gang fight near Columbia University last night as 200 teen-agers were massing for battle over exclusive rights to the use of Riverside Park.

N. Y. JOURNAL-AMERICAN

6-GANG BATTLE FOR PARK AVERTED NEAR GRANT'S TOMB COPS PATROL TROUBLE SPOT

Police reinforcements today patrolled Morningside Heights to prevent a teen-aged gang war for "control" of Riverside Park.

WORLD-TELEGRAM AND SUN

HOODLUM WAR AVERTED AS COPS ACT FAST
38 to 200 Seized near Columbia
by Richard Graf

Fast police action averted what threatened to be one of the biggest street gang fights in the city's history as some 200 hoodlums massed last night on the upper West Side to battle over "exclusive rights" to Riverside Park.

Depth interviews with 40 gang boys, most of whom had been arrested at the scene of the gang fight, revealed a variety of reasons for attendance at the battle. There were also varied perceptions of the event and the gangs involved reported simply in the press as "gangs battling over territory." Some of the following recurring themes were revealed in the gang boys' responses.

Estimates of number of gang boys present varied from 80 to 5,000.

Gang boys interviewed explained their presence at the "battle" as follows:

I didn't have anything to do that night and wanted to see what was going to happen.

Those guys called me a Spic and I was going to get even. [He made this comment even though the "rival" gangs were mostly Puerto Ricans.]

They always picked on us. [The "they" is usually a vague reference.]

I always like a fight; it keeps up my rep.

My father threw me out of the house; I wanted to get somebody and heard about the fight.

The youth who was responsible for "calling on" the gang war—the reputed Balkan Gang leader—presented this version of the event:

That night I was out walkin' my dog about 7:30. Then I saw all these guys coming from different directions. I couldn't figure out what was happening. Then I saw some of the guys I know and I remembered we had called it on for that night.

I never really figured the Politicians [a supposed "brother Gang" he had called] would show.

Another boy added another dimension to "gang war organization":

How did we get our name? Well, when we were in the police station, the cops kept askin' us who we were. Jay was studying history in school—so he said how about The Balkans. Let's call ourselves Balkans. So we told the cops—we're the Balkans—and that was it.

Extensive data revealed this was not a case of two organized groups meeting in battle. The press, public, police, social workers, and others projected group conceptions onto a near-group activity. Most of the youths at the scene of the gang war were, in fact, participating in a kind of mob action. Most had no real concept of belonging to any gang or group; however, they were interested in a situation which might be exciting and possibly a channel for expressing some of their aggressions and hostilities. Although it was not necessarily a defined war, the possibilities of a stabbing or even a killing were high—with a few hundred disturbed and fearful youths milling around in the undefined situation. The gang war was not a social situation of two structured teen-aged armies meeting on a battlefield to act out a defined situation; it was a case of two near-groups in action.

Another boy's participation in this gang war further reveals its structure. The evening of the fight he had nothing to do, heard about this event, and decided that he would wander up to see what was going to happen. On his way to the scene of the rumored gang fight he thought it might be a good idea to invite a few friends "just to be on the safe side." This swelled the final number of youths arriving at the scene of the gang fight, since other boys did the same. He denied (and I had no reason to disbelieve him) belonging to either of the gangs, and the same applied to his friends. He was arrested at the scene of "battle" for disorderly conduct and weapon-carrying.

I asked him why he had carried a knife and a zip gun on his person when he went to the gang fight if he did not belong to either of the reputed gangs and intended to be merely a "peaceful observer." His response: "Man, I'm not going to a rumble without packin.'" The boy took along weapons for self-defense in the event he was attacked. The possibilities of his being attacked in an hysterical situation involving hundreds of youths who had no clear idea of what they were doing at the scene of a gang fight was, of course, great. Therefore, he was correct (within his social framework) in taking along a weapon for self-protection.

These characteristic responses to the situation when multiplied by the numbers of others present characterizes the problem. What may be a confused situation involving many aggressive youths (belonging to near-groups) is often defined as a case of two highly mechanized and organized gang groups battling each other with definition to their activities.

In another "gang war case" which made headlines, a psychotic youth acted out his syndrome by stabbing another youth. When arrested and questioned about committing the offense, the youth stated that he was a member of a gang carrying out retaliation against another gang which was out to get him. He attributed his assault to gang affiliation.

The psychotic youth used the malleable near-group, the gang, *as his psychotic* syndrome. Napoleon, God, Christ, and other psychotic syndromes, so popular over the years, may have been replaced on city streets by gang membership. Not only is it a convenient syndrome, but some disturbed youths find their behavior as rational, accepted, and even aggrandized by many representatives of society. Officials such as police officers and social workers, in their interpretation of the incident, often amplify this individual behavior by a youth into a group gang war condition because it is a seemingly more logical explanation of a senseless act.

In the case of the Balkans, the societal response of viewing them as a group rather than a near-group solidified their structure. After the incident, as one leader stated it, "lots more kids wanted to join."

Another gang war event further reveals the near-group structure of the gang. On the night of July 30, 1957, a polio victim named Michael Farmer was beaten and stabbed to death by a gang varyingly known as the Egyptian Kings and the Dragons. The boys who participated in this homicide came from the upper West Side of Manhattan. I had contact with many of these boys prior to the event and was known to others through the community program I directed. Because of this prior relationship the boys cooperated and responded openly when I interviewed them in the institutions where they were being held in custody.

Responses to my interviews indicated the near-group nature of the gang. Some of the pertinent responses which reveal this characteristic of the Egyptian King gang structure are somewhat demonstrated by the following comments made by five of the participants in the killing. (These are representative comments selected from over ten hours of recorded interviews.)

> I was walking uptown with a couple of friends and we ran into Magician [one of the Egyptian King gang leaders] and them there. They asked us if we wanted to go to a fight, and we said yes. When he asked me if I wanted to go to a fight, I couldn't say no. I mean, I could say no, but for old time's sake, I said yes.
>
> Everyone was pushin' and I pulled out my knife. I saw this face—I never seen it before, so I stabbed it.
>
> He was laying on the ground lookin' up at us. Everyone was kicking, punching, stabbing. I kicked him on the jaw or someplace; then I kicked him in the stomach. That was the least I could do was kick 'im.
>
> They have guys watching you and if you don't stab or hit somebody, they get you later. I hit him over the head with a bat. [Gang youths are unable to articulate specific individuals of the vague "they" who watch over them.]
>
> I don't know how many guys are in the gang. They tell me maybe a hundred or a thousand. I don't know them all. [Each boy interviewed had a different image of the gang.]

These comments and others revealed the gang youths' somewhat different perceptions and rationale of gang war activity. There is a limited consensus of participants as to the nature of gang war situations because the gang structure—the collectivity which defines gang war behavior—is amorphous, diffuse, and malleable.

Despite the fact of gang phonomena taking a diffuse form, theoreticians, social workers, the police, the press, and the public autistically distort gangs and gang behavior toward a gestalt of clarity. The rigid frame of perceiving gangs as groups should shift to the fact of gangs as near-groups. This basic redefinition is necessary if progress is to be made in sociological diagnosis as a foundation for delinquent gang prevention and correction.

THE DETACHED GANG WORKER

The detached-worker approach to dealing with gangs on the action level is increasingly employed in large cities and urban areas throughout the country. Simply stated, a professional, usually a social worker, contacts a gang in their milieu on the street corner and attempts to redirect their delinquent patterns into constructive behavior.

Because of the absence of an adequate perceptual framework, such as the near-group concept, detached gang workers deal with gang collectivities as if they were organized like other groups and social organizations. The following principle stated in a New York City Youth Board manual on the detached gang worker approach reveals this point of view:

> Participation in a street gang or club, like participation in any natural group, is a part of the growing-up process of adolescence. Such primary group associations possess potentialities for positive growth and development. Through such a group, the individual can gain security and develop positive ways of living with other individuals. Within the structure of his group the individual can develop such characteristics as loyalty, leadership, and community responsibility.

This basic misconception not only produces inaccurate reports and theories about gang structure but causes ineffectual work with gangs on the action level. This problem of projecting group structure onto gangs may be further illuminated by a cursory examination of detached gang-worker projects.

Approaching the gang as a group, when it is not, tends to project onto it a structure which formerly did not exist. The gang worker's usual set of notions about gangs as groups includes some of the following distortions: (1) the gang has a measurable number of members, (2) membership is defined, (3) the role of members is specified, (4) there is a consensus of understood gang norms among gang members, and (5) gang leadership is clear and entails a flow of authority and direction of action.

These expectations often result in a group-fulfilling prophecy. A group may form as a consequence of the gang worker's view. In one case a gang worker approached two reputed gang leaders and told them he would have a bus to take their gang on a trip to the country. This gang had limited organization; however, by travel-time there were 32 gang members ready to go on the trip. The near-group became more organized as a result of the gang worker's misconception.

This gang from a near-group point of view was in reality comprised of a few disturbed youths with rich delusional systems who had need to view themselves as leaders controlling hordes of other gang boys in their fantasy. Other youths reinforce this ill-defined collectivity for a variety of personal reasons and needs. The gang, in fact, had a shifting membership, no clarity as to what membership entailed, and individualized member images of gang size and function.

The detached worker, as an agent of the formal social system, may thus move in on a gang and give a formerly amorphous collectivity structure and purpose through the projection of group structure onto a near-group.

NEAR GROUP STRUCTURE

Research into the structure of 30 groups revealed three characteristic levels of membership organization. In the center of the gang, on the first level, are the most psychologically disturbed members—the leaders. It is these youths who require and need the gang most of all. This core of disturbed youths provides the gang's most cohesive force. In a gang of some 30 boys there may be five or six who are central or core members because they desperately need the gang in order to deal with their personal problems of inadequacy. These are youths always working to keep the gang together and in action, always drafting, plotting, and talking gang warfare. They are the center of the near-group activity.

At a second level of near-group organization in the gang, we have youths who claim affiliation to the gang but only participate in it according to their emotional needs at given times. For example, one of the Egyptian Kings reported that if his father had not given him a "bad time" and kicked him out of the house the night of the homicide, he would not have gone to the corner and become involved in the Michael Farmer killing. This second-level gang member's participation in the gang killing was a function of his disturbance on that particular evening. This temporal gang need is a usual occurrence.

At a third level of gang participation, we have peripheral members who will join in with gang activity on occasion, although they seldom identify themselves as members of the gang at times. This type of gang member is illustrated by the youth who went along with the Egyptian

Kings on the night of the Farmer killing, as he put it, "for old time's sake." He just happened to be around on that particular evening and went along due to a situational condition. He never really "belonged" to the gang nor was he defined by himself or others as a gang member.

The size of gangs is determined in great measure by the emotional needs of its members at any given point. It is not a measure of actual and live membership. Many of the members exist only on the thought level. In the gang, if the boys feel particularly hemmed in (for paranoid reasons), they will expand the number of their near-group. On the other hand, at other times when they feel secure, the gang's size is reduced to include only those youths known on a face-to-face basis. The research revealed that, unlike an actual group, no member of a near-group can accurately determine the number of its membership at a particular point in time.

For example, most any university department member will tell you the number of other individuals who comprise the faculty of their department. It is apparent that if there are eight members in a department of psychology, each member will know each other member, his role, and the total number of members of the department. In contrast, in examining the size of gangs or near-group participation, the size increases in almost direct relationship to the lack of membership clarity. That is, the second- and third-level members are modified numerically with greater ease than the central members. Third-level members are distorted at times to an almost infinite number.

In one interview, a gang leader distorted the size and affiliations of the gang as his emotional state shifted. In an hour interview, the size of his gang varied from 100 members to 4,000, from five brother gangs or alliances to 60, from about ten square blocks of territorial control to include jurisdiction over the five boroughs of New York City, New Jersey, and part of Philadelphia.

Another characteristic of the gang is its lack of role definition. Gang boys exhibit considerable difficulty and contradiction in their roles in the gang. They may say that the gang is organized for protection and that one role of a gang is to fight. How, when, whom, and for what reason he is to fight are seldom clear. The right duties and obligations associated with the gang member's role in the gang vary from gang boy to gang boy.

One gang boy may define himself as a protector of the younger boys in the neighborhood. Another defines his role in the gang as "We are going to get all those guys who call us Spics." Still other gang boys define their participation in the gang as involuntarily forced upon them, through their being "drafted." Moreover, few gang members maintain a consistent function or role within the gang organization.

Definition of membership is vague and indefinite. A youth will say he belongs one day and will quit the next without necessarily telling any other gang member. I would ask one gang boy who came into my office daily whether he was a Balkan. This was comparable to asking him, "How do you feel today?"

Because of limited social ability to assume rights, duties, and obligations in constructive solidified groups, the gang boy attaches himself to a structure which requires limited social ability and can itself be modified to fit his monetary needs. This malleability factor is characteristic of the near-group membership. As roles are building blocks of a group, diffuse role definitions fit in adequately to the near-group which itself has diverse and diffuse objectives and goals. The near-group, unlike a true group, has norms, roles, functions, cohesion, size, and goals which are shaped by the emotional needs of its members.

GANG LEADERSHIP CHARACTERISTICS

Another aspect of near-groups is the factor of self-appointed leadership, usually of a dictatorial, authoritarian type. In interviewing hundreds of gang members, one finds that many of them give themselves some role of leadership. For example, in the Egyptian Kings, approximately five boys defined themselves as "war counselors." It is equally apparent that, except on specific occasions, no one will argue with this self-defined role. Consequently, leadership in the gang may be assumed by practically any member of the gang if he so determines and emotionally needs the power of being a leader at the time. It is not necessary to have his leadership role ratified by his constituents.

Another aspect of leadership in the gang is the procedure of "drafting" or enlisting new members. In many instances, this pattern of coercion to get another youth to join or belong to the gang becomes an end in itself, rather than a means to an end. In short, the process of inducing, coercing, and threatening violence upon another youth, under the guise of getting him to join, is an important gang leader activity. The gang boy is not truly concerned with acquiring another gang member, since the meaning of membership is vague at best; however, acting the power role of a leader forcing another youth to do something against his will becomes meaningful to the "drafter."

GANG FUNCTIONS

In most groups some function is performed or believed to be performed. The function which it performs may be a constructive one, as in an industrial organization, a P.T.A. group, or a political party. On the other hand, it may be a socially destructive group, such as a drug syndicate, a group of bookies, or a subversive political party. There is usually a consensus of objectives and goals shared by the membership, and their behavior tends to be essentially organized group action.

The structure of a near-group is such that not only do its functions vary greatly and shift considerably from time to time, but its primary function is unclear. The gang may on one occasion be organized to protect the neighborhood; on another occasion, to take over a particular territory; and on still another, it may be organized in response to or for the purpose of racial discrimination.

The function of near-groups, moreover, is not one which is clearly understood, known, and communicated among all of its members. There is no consensus in this near-group of goals, objectives, or functions of the collectivity—much near-group behavior is individualistic and flows from emotional disturbance.

A prime function of the gang is to provide a channel to act out hostility and aggression to satisfy the continuing and momentary emotional needs of its members. The gang is a convenient and malleable structure quickly adaptable to the needs of emotionally disturbed youths, who are unable to fulfill the responsibility and demands required for participation in constructive groups. A boy belongs to the gang because he lacks the social ability to relate to others and to assume responsibility for the relationship, not because the gang gives him a "feeling of belonging."

Because of the gang youth's limited "social ability," he constructs a social organization which enables him to relate and to function at his limited level of performance. In this structure norms are adjusted so that the gang youth can function and achieve despite his limited ability to relate to others.

An example of this is the function of violence in the near-group of the gang. Violence in the gang is highly valued as a means for the achievement of reputation or "rep." This inversion of societal norms is a means for quick upward social mobility in the gang. He can acquire and maintain a position in the gang through establishing a violent reputation.

The following comments by members of the Egyptian Kings illustrate the point:

> If I would of got the knife, I would have stabbed him. That would have gave me more of a build-up. People would have respected me for what I've done and things like that. They would say, "There goes a cold killer."
>
> It makes you feel like a big shot. You know some guys think they're big shots and all that. They think, you know, they got the power to do everything they feel like doing.
>
> They say, like, "I wanna stab a guy," and the other guy says, "Oh, I wouldn't dare to do that." You know, he thinks I'm acting like a big shot. That's the way he feels. He probably thinks in his mind. "Oh, he probably

won't do that." Then, when we go to a fight, you know, he finds out what I do.

Momentarily, I started to thinking about it inside: den I have my mind made up I'm not going to be in no gang. Then I go on inside. Something comes up den here come all my friends coming to me. Like I said before, I'm intelligent and so forth. They be coming to me—then they talk to me about what they gonna do. Like, "Man, we'll go out here and kill this guy." I say, "Yeah." They kept on talkin' and talkin'. I said, "Man, I just gotta go with you." Myself, I don't want to go, but when they start talkin' about what they gonna do, I say, "So, he isn't gonna take over my rep. I ain't gonna let him be known more than me." And I go ahead just for selfishness.

The near-group of the gang, with its diffuse and malleable structure, can function as a convenient vehicle for the acting out of varied individual needs and problems. For the gang leader it can be a super-powered organization through which (in his phantasy) he dominates and controls "divisions" of thousands of members. For gang members, unable to achieve in more demanding social organizations, swift and sudden violence is a means for quick upward social mobility and the achievement of a reputation. For less disturbed youths, the gang may function as a convenient temporary escape from the dull and rigid requirements of a difficult and demanding society. These are only some of the functions the near-group of the gang performs for its membership.

NEAR-GROUP THEORY AND SOCIAL PROBLEMS

The concept of the near-group may be of importance in the analysis of other collectivities which reflect and produce social problems. The analysis of other social structures may reveal similar distortions of their organization. To operate on an assumption of individuals in interaction with each other, around some function with some shared mutual expectation, in a particular normative system as always being a group formation is to project a degree of distortion onto certain types of collectivities. Groups are social structures at one end of a continuum; mobs are social structures at another end; and at the center are near-groups which have some of the characteristics of both, and yet are characterized by factors not found fully in either.

In summary, these factors may include the following:

1. Individualized role definition to fit momentary needs.

2. Diffuse and differential definitions of membership.

3. Emotion-motivated behavior.

4. A decrease of cohesiveness as one moves from the center of the collectivity to the periphery.

5. Limited responsibility and sociability required for membership and belonging.

6. Self-appointed and disturbed leadership.

7. A limited consensus among participants of the collectivities' functions or goals.

8. A shifting and personalized stratification system.

9. Shifting membership.

10. The inclusion in size of phantasy membership.

11. Limited consensus of normative expectations.

12. Norms in conflict with the inclusive social system's prescriptions.

Although the gang was the primary type of near-group appraised in this analysis, there are perhaps other collectivities whose structure is distorted by autistic observers. Their organization might become clearer if subjected to this conceptual scheme. Specifically, in the area of criminal behavior, these might very well include adult gangs varyingly called the "Mafia," the "National Crime Syndicate," and so-called International Crime Cartels. There are indications that these social organizations are comparable in organization to the delinquent gang. They might fit the near-group category if closely analyzed in this context, rather than aggrandized and distorted by mass media and even Senate Committees.

Other more institutionalized collectivities might fit the near-group pattern. As a possible example, "the family in transition" may not be in transition at all. The family, as a social institution, may be suffering from near-groupism. Moreover, such standardized escape hatches as alcoholism, psychoses, and addictions may be too prosaic for the sophisticated intellectual to utilize in escape from himself. For him, the creation and perpetuation of near-groups requiring limited responsibility and personal commitment may be a more attractive contemporary form for expressing social and personal pathology. The measure of organization or disorganization of an inclusive social system may possibly be assessed by the prevalence of near-group collectivities in its midst. The delinquent gang may be only one type of near-group in American society.

FIELD OBSERVATIONS OF
MIDDLE CLASS "GANGS"

Howard L. Myerhoff and Barbara G. Myerhoff

. . . The field observations presented here are based on the experiences of a participant-observer who spent two weeks among several groups of deviant and non-deviant middle class youths in a suburb of Los Angeles. These observations are particularly pertinent to the pre-

From *Social Forces*, Vol. 42 (March 1964), 328-36. Reprinted by permission.

vailing conflicting interpretations of the extent of gang structure. The middle class youngsters described here were located through lists of "hangouts" provided by local police, school authorities, and probation officers. The observer "hung around" these places and when asked who he was, which was seldom, explained that he was a writer doing a series of articles on teenagers. The youngsters talked freely in front of and to the observer, and after a short time included him in many of their activities, such as house and beach parties, drag races, car club meetings, bull sessions, and bowling. Altogether, about eighty youngsters ranging in age between fifteen and eighteen were observed. All were Caucasian, most in high school, Protestant, and in appearance and manner readily distinguishable from the lower class boys and girls who occasionally mixed with them.

Impressions, activities, and conversations were recorded by the observer in a daily journal and roughly classified into the following categories: values and peer interactions, deviant activities, and group organization. It should be kept in mind that these comments are observations, not findings. Many authors have lamented the dearth of speculation about as well as empirical observations of gangs, in both the middle and lower classes. Cohen and Short recently said about middle class delinquent subcultures: "The saddest commentary, however, is that we are faced with a poverty of speculation, without which there can be no meaningful research, without which, in turn, there can be no conclusions that are more than speculation." These observations and comments lead to some of the speculation which must precede meaningful empirical research, and their greatest value may prove to be heuristic.

VALUES AND PEER INTERACTIONS

The youngsters observed, like most groups of teenagers, were rather uniform in dress and demeanor. Their self-possession and poise, along with elaborate grooming and expensive, well-tended clothes combined to give an impression of urbanity and sophistication beyond what would normally be expected of this age group. For most events, the girls wore tight capris, blouses or cashmere sweaters, silver fingernail and toenail polish, towering intricate coiffeurs, brush-applied iridescent lipstick, and heavy eye make-up. The boys, like the girls, were uniformly clean, and like them preferred their pants as tight as possible; levis were rarely seen. Usually an Ivy League shirt was worn outside the pants and over this a nylon windbreaker. At beaches both boys and girls wore bikinis, and apparently no one without a deep and even tan ever dared appear. The over-all impression fostered was one of careful, elegant casualness sustained in manner as well as appearance. The complete absence of the social and physical awkwardness usually associated with adolescence was indeed striking.

The content of conversation among these groups did not differ appreciably from what one would expect to find among most teenagers; it concerned clothes, dates, sex, school classes and activities, bridge, sports, and so forth. But no subject dominated the conversation as much as the car, which seemed an object of undying, one might say morbid, fascination. The majority of girls and boys owned their own cars and virtually all had access to a car, usually a late model American or foreign sports car. "Custom jobs" were not rare and cars were often "shaved," "chopped," "channeled," and "pin-striped." All were scrupulously clean and highly polished. The argot concerning the car was as elaborate and subtle as one might expect in view of its importance; such matters as "dual quads," "turning seven grand," "slicks," "3:7 trans ratio" were frequently discussed with great intensity. Driving skill and mechanical expertise were prized far above mere ownership of a desirable car.

The car, in fact, permeated every aspect of these youngsters' social life. The size of groups which gathered was usually limited by the number a single car could hold, and when several cars congregated, at drive-ins for example, youngsters demonstrated a distinct unwillingness to leave the car. Radios in cars were never off and all activities took place against a background of popular music. The car also affected the places frequented, with drive-in movies and restaurants preferred. After school and on weekends, many of these youngsters could be seen slowly cruising in their cars, up and down the neighborhood streets, greeting acquaintances, chatting, taking friends for short rides, all with an air of easy sociability. These cruises in manner and purpose were reminiscent of the Spanish late afternoon *Paseo,* in which young people stroll casually up and down streets closed off for that purpose. The cars were the location for nearly all social events engaged in by these youngsters. They were the site of bull sessions, drinking bouts, and necking parties. In all, the car provided a mobile parlor, clubhouse, dining room, and bedroom; it was at once the setting and symbol of much of adolescent deviant and non-deviant sociability and sexuality. . . .

In view of the importance of the car, it was not surprising to find that the only formal social organizations to which many of these youngsters belonged were car clubs, whose membership often transcended the class and age affiliations typical of the more informal gatherings. These clubs usually consist of about fifteen members and are devoted to the building and legal and illegal racing of cars. In order to be admitted, youngsters' cars must undergo rigorous police safety inspections and members may be expelled or excluded for too many traffic tickets. In marked contrast to the informal groups, these clubs are highly structured. Meetings are regular and frequent, membership is stable, leaders are elected for specified terms, and the clubs have names, plaques, and jackets. The meetings are conducted strictly according to Roberts' Rules of Order, fines are levied for infractions of rules, dues are collected, and events are planned in detail and in advance. A well-developed pattern of mutual aid and extensive cooperation has been established, and it is not unusual for members to pool money, skills, and time to build a car which is entered in races and rallies by the entire group. It is obviously no accident that the only object around which spontaneous, unsupervised yet structured groups form is the car.

DEVIANT ACTIVITIES

The deviant behavior of the groups observed varied greatly in seriousness. Some of their activities may be considered deviant only because technically illegal, such as curfew violation and beer drinking, while more serious infractions such as theft and narcotics are less common. The more serious deviant activities seemed to involve the least number of people at one time; youngsters were alone or with a friend or two on these occasions. The less serious infractions were not usually the purpose of a gathering but were rather incidental to another activity. These included spontaneous drag racing, drinking, and much sexual activity.

Of the more serious violations, theft was certainly the most common. Many boys spoke of frequent and regular stealing, often from employers. Ready access rather than need or desire seemed to determine the choice of stolen objects. These items were seldom traded or converted into cash. Great pride was evidenced in the cleverness with which the thefts were executed and a good performance seemed more important than the acquisition of goods. Several boys boasted about never having been caught although they had been engaging in this activity for years. The stolen goods were by no means small, inexpensive, or easily portable, but included such items as tires, car radios, phonographs, tape recorders, and television sets. Great care was taken in order to ensure that stolen goods were not missed. Thefts were timed so as to coincide with events such as inventories, and the filling of orders.

It is not possible on the basis of these observations to estimate the frequency of these thefts, but one can say with certainty that they were by no means uncommon. This phenomenon appears to be very similar to "white collar crime" and as such raises questions as to the generalizability of theories of delinquency causation based solely on socio-economic variables. As Wattenberg and Balistrieri have pointed out: "The point of impact of the concept of [white collar crime] lies in its assumption that the form of anti-social or illegal conduct rather than its frequency varies from . . . class to class in our society." It may well be that the "white collar delinquent" engages in as many anti-social activities as do lower class youngsters, but a combination of factors, particularly the form of delinquency, interact to prevent these activities from coming to the attention of the authorities, or if apprehended, prevent the middle class youngsters from being officially handled and recorded. Indeed, there is already much evidence to suggest this is the case.

The same discretion, judgment, and self-possession which characterized thefts was observed in the homosexual, and to a lesser degree, the heterosexual gatherings. These events were held in private homes and occasionally included slightly older boys from nearby colleges. They were not events which were likely to attract the attention of police or even parents. The homosexual youngsters often met one another at small cabarets, coffee houses, and bars in which few lower class teenagers or adults were to be seen. They also met in several private clubs whose members were primarily upper and middle class teenage homosexuals. These youngsters were typically inconspicuous and did not indulge in egregious displays of homosexuality either in dress or manner. While in the clubs, many were openly solicitous and flirtatious, but upon leaving, their more conventional manners were resumed. The same caution was apparent among those who purchased and used narcotics, usually marijuana. It was smoked at small, quiet parties, rarely while driving or in public places. It was not unusual to hear these poised, well-dressed youngsters speak of stealing, using narcotics, and the advantages and disadvantages of their respective college choices in the same tone of voice and conversation.

The middle class group anti-social activities which *do* come to the attention of the authorities are of a rather different nature than those just described. Several examples of these were provided by a local probation officer assigned to the neighborhood. On one occasion, he recalled, a group of about ten boys went back and forth across a busy intersection between 5:30 and 6:30 in the evening effectively bringing traffic to a complete standstill until dispersed by the police. Another time, a car full of boys drove slowly down a main shopping street spraying the well dressed shoppers with the contents of a fire extinguisher. One incident involved a group of boys who stole an old car and took it to a vacant lot and while one boy drove the car around in circles, the others threw stones at it, until it was nothing but a battered corpse.

There is a mischievous, often amusing overtone to all these incidents; they are not the kind likely to be thought malicious or violent. Rather, they are spontaneous and gratuitous, proving nothing but providing "kicks." This behavior is not the kind which is likely to seriously alarm parents or police. It has none of the grim overtones usually associated, correctly or not, with the activities of lower class gangs. In general, the non-violent nature of the deviant activities of these youngsters is salient, and personal aggression rare. The anti-social activities observed among these groups rarely took the form of open defiance of authority; manipulation rather than rebellion appeared to be the preferred technique for handling trouble with authorities. Cohen and Short have postulated just such a difference between lower and middle class delinquency:

> . . . we are persuaded that further research will reveal subtle but important differences between working class and middle class patterns of delinquency. It seems probable that the qualities of malice, bellicosity, and violence will be underplayed in the middle class subcultures and that these subcultures will emphasize more the deliberate courting of danger . . . and a sophisticated, irresponsible, "playboy" approach to activities symbolic in our culture, of adult roles and centering largely around sex, liquor, and automobiles.

How closely that description fits the middle class groups observed is readily apparent.

Interestingly enough, even while engaging in flagrant, frequent infractions of the law, these youngsters sustained the opinion that their activities would in no way interfere with their future plans. They did not define themselves as delinquents or even trouble makers and did not expect others to do so. More likely than not, upon graduating from high school and entering college, as most planned to do, these youngsters will leave their deviant activities behind without a trace in the form of official records, self-definition, or residues of unpleasant experiences with authorities. The police seemed to share this expectation. An incident was observed in which a boy was picked up for drinking and curfew violation. In the patrol car he expressed his concern lest the occasion jeopardize his chances for entering college. The officer, who had until that point been rather surly, hastened to reassure the boy that such a possibility was quite unlikely, and implied that nothing would come of the visit to the station.

The same expectations were shared by the people who worked at the places where these youngsters congregated—waitresses, life guards, theater managers—who did not feel that even as a group they constituted a serious nuisance. Their tolerance is no doubt increased by middle class youngsters' liberal spending habits which make it worth their while to put up with an occasional annoyance. But in addition their attitudes are affected by the usually pleasant relations they have with these boys and girls, whose interpersonal experiences with adults and peers are more harmonious and extensive than those observed among the more socially inadequate lower class gangs observed by Yablonsky and the supervisor of the detached worker program in Los Angeles. This difference in social ability is hardly surprising in view of the middle classes' traditional specialization in entrepreneurial activities. The techniques of smooth social relations are the bread and butter of the middle classes, and middle class teenagers, deviant and non-deviant alike, demonstrate remarkable agility in the manipulation of social situations. Their interpersonal skills enable them to control their social environment to a much greater degree than possible for lower class teenagers who have not had the opportunity to acquire and perfect these techniques.

GROUP ORGANIZATION

. . .

The adolescent in our culture, it is suggested, may be viewed as an aristocrat, a gentleman of leisure who, for a time, is not required to work but is allowed to play, explore, test limits, indulge his pleasures, and little else besides. This description of the delinquent as a kind of aristocrat closely resembles Finestone's characterization of the Negro teenage narcotic addict. The "cat" is an individual who has developed an elaborate repertoire of manipulative techniques for dealing with the world, eschewing violence in favor of persuasion and charm. "He seeks through a harmonious combination of charm, ingratiating speech, dress, music, the proper dedication to his 'kick' and unrestrained generosity to make of his day to day life itself a gracious work of art." The similarity between this depiction of the "cat" and the youngsters described here is indeed remarkable, especially in light of the differences between them in race, class, and circumstance.

There is, then, much reason to think that Matza and Sykes are justified in urging that delinquency might be better understood as an extension of the adult conforming world rather than as discontinuous with it. One advantage of this interpretation is that it allows for a single explanation of lower and middle class delinquency and thus avoids the inconsistency inherent in theories which specify the influence of socioeconomic factors in the etiology of lower class delinquency and psychological factors in the etiology of middle class delinquency. It is likely that much may be gained by exploring the similarity between the delinquent and the rest of society rather than his deviance from it. Certainly these observations suggest that middle class deviants may differ from lower class delinquents not in the frequency of their anti-social activities, but only in the form which they take and the sophistication, social intelligence, judgment, and skill with which they are executed.

SUMMARY

These observations have raised several important issues concerning the structure and values of delinquent groups. It may be that the extent of gang structure is frequently exaggerated and that such groups may not be as cohesive, structured, and stable as they are commonly depicted. The groups described here manifested all but one of the characteristics (disturbed leadership) described by Yablonsky as those of a near-group. There is a coincidence of opinion based on three sets of observations (Yablonsky's, the supervisor of a detached worker program in Los Angeles, and those reported in this paper) suggesting that the common conception of the gang as a highly organized primary group is not always accurate and may be the result of the gross exaggerations made possible by the dearth of empirical observations of gangs. Exaggeration may also have taken place in the extent of the differences between delinquent values and those of the dominant society. The observations reported in this paper are in accord with the suggestions of Matza and Sykes that the delinquent subculture is an extension of values held by most members of the society but indulged in less openly and less often. Certainly the behavior and beliefs of the middle class youngsters observed are not dramatically different from those of most conventional teenagers or adults.

In view of these three sets of observations, the following questions may be asked: (1) How often and to what extent are gangs primary groups with elaborate delinquent subcultures, and how prevalent are such groups when compared with the loosely structured, secondary, impermanent collectivities with little or no delinquent subculture such as those described here? (2) In view of the conflicting characterizations of the extent of gang structure and the nature of gang values, would not there be more scientific value in describing gangs in terms of at least these two variables rather than primarily on the basis of the content of their deviant activities? (3) To what extent, if any, does adult recognition, particularly in the form of the assignment of detached workers to gangs, legitimize and formalize these groups, lending them a cohesion and solidarity which they previously might not have had? (4) Has the emphasis on the deviant activities of these groups obscured their similarity to conventional teenagers and adults, thereby exaggerating the differences between delinquents and non-delinquents? And (5) would it not be more fruitful to examine the extent and nature of the similarities rather than differences between deviant and non-deviant teenagers and adults?

The action implications of these questions are far-reaching. If, as Yablonsky suggests, the gang meets different needs for different members, a uniform approach on a gang basis is inappropriate. More suitable would be an attempt to help individual members develop the interpersonal skills which would enable them to participate in structured, socially accepted groups. Or, by deliberately applying techniques such as Yablonsky's "group-fulfilling prophecy," gangs might be made into non-deviant clubs. And, if delinquent values are but a continuation of one aspect of the accepted value system subscribed to by most law abiding people, a program designed to integrate these values into a more appropriate place in deviant youngsters' lives (for example, by providing socially acceptable means of expressing aggression and seeking adventure) would be more honest and effective than attempts to eliminate them altogether. . . .

ADAPTIVE AND MALADAPTIVE DELINQUENCY

Richard L. Jenkins

Much of the confusion relating to current discussions of delinquency relates to a tendency to treat delinquency as though it were an entity resident within the personality of the delinquent. This is related to a failure to recognize that the patterns of behavior which the law lumps together under the title *delinquency,* have little universally in common except their illegality. Broadly speaking, delinquency represents a kind of a rebellion against the laws of society. In such instances of rebellion we can distinguish *delinquency as an adaptation* from *delinquency as a maladaptation.* This distinction has profound implications for treatment.

Norman Maier, working with rats, was able to distinguish two types of behavior which are discontinuous. What he calls *motivation behavior* is goal-directed, variable, plastic, educable and typically zestful. On the other hand, what he calls *frustration behavior,* which results from repeated frustration beyond the tolerance of the individual, is stereotyped and rigid to a degree not shown by motivation behavior, and punishment only serves more rigidly to establish its fixed character. The apparent complexity of the maladjustive pattern sometimes blinds us to the stereotypy and rigidity which are essential properties. Frustration leads to de-differentiation and tends to be associated with resignation, rather than the zestful behavior of motivation.

We see in delinquency examples which are unmistakably adaptive motivation behavior, and other examples which seem clearly to result from frustration and which fall within the rigid, non-adaptive stereotyped pattern which Maier designates as frustration behavior.

DELINQUENCY AS ADAPTATION

Delinquency as an adaptation differs from other behavior, which we praise, or at least condone, only in its illegality. It is goal-oriented, and

From *The Nervous Child,* Vol. 11, No. 1 (1955), 9-11. Reprinted by permission.

at its highest level combines careful planning with skillful, calculated, resolute action. Delinquency as adaptation has its elaborated counterpart in the adult criminal career. The motivation of the bootlegging gangs of prohibition days, of the gambling syndicates of the present day, or of the confidence game in its historic development appears to be at least in substantial part financial or acquisitional. That this is the same motivation our culture sanctions as the force which keeps our competitive economic system ticking sometimes makes treatment very difficult.

Probably the acme of successfully adaptive crime has been evolved in the highly developed art of the confidence game, in which the victims own desire to profit by illegally taking advantage of others is exploited as a means to his own undoing, and also utilized as a means of protection against the law. When we reflect that amounts of as much as $345,000 are known to have been taken in a single "touch"—and typically from hard, aggressive enterprising leaders of the business world —we must recognize that crime can be a highly evolved adaptation.

It is natural for the young child to take what he wants. Ideas of ownership are not innate but are acquired gradually. The young child shouting, "Mine! Mine!" while clutching an intriguing object he has seen for the first time may be merely failing to distinguish between desire and ownership. Nor are rights of ownership always observed when they are learned. It is indeed often hard to determine what apparently well adjusted adults have actually been taught about the "rights" of ownership. Most children steal at some time as a means of getting what they desire. That is, they take what they want when they want it with the clear realization that their act is objectionable, wil be considered "bad" and that they will be punished if caught. Most children give up the practice either partially or completely before reaching adult years. The exceptions occur chiefly in those who experience the encouragement and active social sanction of others in their delinquent careers or who are deeply frustrated in their primary desires. In the one instance we may see the evolution of delinquency as a skill, and in the other as a stereotyped maladaptation.

The successful criminal career is an adaptive one. It begins most often in the areas of social disorganization and maximum criminal activity, the deteriorated areas of our large cities. It typically follows a natural process of growth and criminal sophistication, learned socially, often in an atmosphere of the "secrets of the trade." A criminal career in our culture is evolved much as any other career is evolved, even though actual initiation into the technique of delinquency is not as a rule through formal instruction or formal apprenticeship, nor is it commonly passed directly from parent to child.

Its typical antecedents include physical vigor, an aggressive attitude toward life, a good musculature, an experience of having received maternal care adequate to have developed a social responsiveness to others, and either the absence of paternal guidance or conflict with the father in pre-adolescence and adolescence. Typically the home is cramped, disorderly, unattractive and overcrowded and a natural result is that the youngster "lives" with his street companions rather than with his parents. These associates become the important people in his life and their values and their approval become his goals. Prestige in the delinquent group becomes typically much more important than material gain, but prestige is established and maintained by daring and successful delinquencies.

The group code regards the informer as anathema, and one sees the evolution of an underworld society with its own set of moral values and social sanctions. To gain and maintain prestige in this atmosphere demands a kind of adaptive skill different from but not less than that which is needful to succeed in the upper-world.

The socialized delinquent does not differ conspicuously from the nondelinquent except in his associates, his code and his delinquency itself. While these are an expression of rebellion against the law, yet he is striving toward goals sanctioned by our competitive and acquisitive society, although striving by methods legally proscribed.

DELINQUENCY AS MALADAPTATION

There is another kind of delinquency which implies a grosser deviation in personality and in adjustment. It represents not an adaptation, but a maladaptation, not the selection and pursuit of a goal, so much as the renunciation of any real goal, and a minor disorganization punctuated by violence. Bitter frustration leads to explosions of blind destructiveness in which the delinquent utterly loses control of himself. It is not violence that makes the distinction, for violence can be planful, calculated and adaptive. It is the *maladaptive* (and often explosive) character of the response which differentiates it.

This often takes the pattern of uncontrolled violent attack which is cruel or destructive in its outcome. It is self-defeating in that the child worsens his own situation and draws punishment upon himself, Typically he reacts to the punishment with increased hostility, bitterness and reduced capacity for either adjustment or self-control.

We see then the vicious circle of impulsive hostility leading to punishment which in turn leads to more impulsive hostility. If untempered by understanding or other moderating influence it leads to that worsening spiral familiar in the history of any training school and sometimes informally referred to as the "institutional crackup." This phenomenon reaches the level of disorganization of an incipient psychosis, and may progress beyond it.

The background of this type of personality is one of gross frustration of primary needs. This delinquent was typically unwanted by both parents, but particularly by his mother, and he was rarely if ever in doubt about her fundamental rejection of him. The picture is one of rather gross poverty of the personality and poor personality organization coupled with a pattern of vengefulness, inability to get along with other children, sullenness, negativism, and suspicion. In those who have a good musculature and a high level of native vigor, such behavior may evolve in the direction of adaptation through the development of a pattern of meeting the world by directed aggressive attack. In those weaker and less well equipped for such behavior, it may result in an alternation of screaming loss of control with a hostile, resentful overdependence. It is the latter group who are more likely to progress toward a psychotic disorganization. In the really tough, well-muscled youngsters the pattern of constant aggressive attack, maladaptive as it is in essence, may engender enough by-products of intimidation, tribute, and respect partially to stabilize itself somewhere between true adaptation and the progressive maladaptation we call schizophrenia and give us the pattern of the eternally aggressive psychopath.

IMPLICATIONS FOR TREATMENT

There are essential implications for treatment in the distinction between adaptive and maladaptive delinquency. With adaptive delinquency the first emphasis must be upon *thwarting the delinquent activities*. With maladaptive delinquency it must be upon *reducing the frustration responsible for the maladaptation*.

The adolescent who has just begun to stray into delinquent activities may be easily influenced by the adults about him, but once he has become confirmed in a pattern of adaptive delinquency he is unlikely to change as long as his techniques of delinquency are succeeding. He has learned to meet the challenge of society to his behavior by denial, evasion and awaiting a favorable opportunity for a renewal of his delinquent activity. Group influences are powerful and ordinarily offset any adult influences on individual members of the group. The practical alternatives are the diversion of the entire group to non-delinquent activities, or the separation of the individual member with a combination of thwarting his delinquent activities while offering him opportunities for the use of acceptable techniques for satisfying human wants. Any use of acceptable techniques must be rewarded and encouraged, but their superficial mastery is not enough. There must also be an emotional reorientation with enlargement to the delinquents loyalty group to include socialized adults he does not want to let down. To effect this reorientation, the emotional exchange with the delinquent must be real and sincere. From it the delinquent may gradually modify his own inner standards. Hopefully these steps may be accomplished in the controlled environment of a good training school. The problem is particularly one of maintaining these gains when the delinquent returns to the influence of past associates in his own neighborhood.

With the maladaptive delinquent, the accent is upon reducing frustration, and this means an accent upon accepting warm interpersonal relations which must be maintained despite unacceptable behavior and low frustration tolerance. The reduction of frustration level must be accompanied by simple social training. The maintenance of an accepting attitude while unacceptable behavior is being limited will try the patience of the best, but is needful for the frustration and resultant emotional immaturity of the maladaptive delinquent are profound. The failure on the part of the parent to distinguish between the adaptive and maladaptive delinquency and the injudicious and frequently hostile use of punishment in the effort to check frustration behavior has typically been a central factor in the consolidation of delinquency.

In some circles much has been made of delinquency as a "neurotic symptom," by which what is generally meant is that it is a result of conflict within the personality and that the delinquent act is an unconsciously motivated expression of some unrecognized drive. A frequent explanation is that the delinquent is overwhelmed with a reaction of guilt, either conscious or unconscious, and that the delinquent act is motivated by an intense though unrecognized need of the delinquent to draw punishment upon himself for the relief of this sense of guilt.

That delinquents as well as non-delinquents have at best, imperfect knowledge of their own motivations is undoubtedly true. That individual cases can be cited in which delinquent actions may be understood as neurotic symptoms is also true. However, the assertion that all or a major fraction of delinquency can be accounted for as neurotic behavior neither rings true nor makes sense.

Inner conflict and neuroticism are typically associated with a high level of inhibition, sense of duty, introjected standards and superego controls. The typical delinquent, on the other hand is characterized by a personality and way of life relatively free from the dominance, let alone the tyranny, of such inner tendencies. In this regard he is quite likely to be freer than the rest of us. Usually he has a certain earthy realism and is less, rather than more inclined to be neurotic than is the nondelinquent. For these reasons, while there are clearly a good many delinquents who are capable of benefiting from an uncovering type of psychotherapy, just as there are an even greater proportion of nondelinquents capable of so benefiting, yet psychotherapy in its traditional forms does not offer a major contribution toward the solution to the problems of delinquency as such, in either their adaptive or their maladaptive forms.

SUMMARY

Delinquency is largely separable into adaptive and maladaptive forms. The former is goal-oriented, and involves adaptation and learning by experience. The latter is a result of frustration and is stereotyped. Its rigidity is typically increased by punishment.

Treatment of adaptive delinquency commonly requires thwarting the delinquent activities, teaching acceptable techniques for satisfying personality needs, and bringing about the addition of socialized adults to the individuals loyalty group with ultimate incorporation of some of their standards into his.

Treatment of maladaptive delinquency involves reducing frustration and a process of socialization at a much more primitive level.

JUVENILES WHO COMMIT NONCRIMINAL ACTS: WHY TREAT IN A CORRECTIONAL SYSTEM?

William H. Sheridan

Shortly after the release in the spring of 1966 of the U.S. Children's Bureau publication, Standards for Juvenile and Family Courts, I was asked by *Federal Probation* to discuss some of the standards set forth in the new document. Standards, however, are dynamic; they need to keep pace with new knowledge and experience. Also, standard-setting documents, jointly developed, reflect a consensus and do not always depict the specific view of the principal author. Therefore, a number of the concepts expressed in this article will depart from some of those set forth in the new Children's Bureau monograph.

Because of the interdependency of precourt processing, court adjudication and disposition, and implementation of the court order, and because changes or defects in the operation of one will have an impact on the others, I shall discuss in this, the first of a series of three articles, my proposed changes as they affect the entire system for handling juvenile offenders from apprehension to final discharge, or what I refer to in this article as the correctional process.

THE PROBLEM

Rising concern about the increasing rate of juvenile delinquency has stimulated activity by many professional groups. One of these, the legal profession, has been most lethargic about the courts and the law in this

From *Federal Probation*, Vol. 31, No. 5 (March 1967), 26-30. Reprinted by permission.

field, but nevertheless has criticized the courts for nonconformance with the requirements of due process of law. Other groups have accused them of both molly-coddling and being punitive. Still others charge the courts with being autocratic, of empire building, and of operating independently outside the community's social service structure. Much of this criticism was well founded so far as many courts were concerned. This was particularly true of those courts which interpreted their role to the public as being the primary preventive and correctional agency in the community. . . .

THE CHILDREN

Generally speaking, children coming under the jurisdiction of juvenile courts for delinquent conduct may be classified into two categories. First, there are those who have committed acts which would be crimes if committed by adults; and secondly, there are those who have not committed such offenses. The latter group may be further divided into two subcategories composed of youngsters who have violated specific ordinances only applicable to children, such as curfew, truancy, alcohol or tobacco ordinances, and those who have broken no law but who are designated as "beyond control," "ungovernable," "incorrigible," "runaway," "minors in need of supervision" (MINS), or "persons in need of supervision" (PINS). With few exceptions the same dispositions are permitted in the case of these children as are authorized for youngsters who have committed acts which would be crimes if committed by an adult. In other words, children who have not indulged in criminal conduct find themselves drawn into the correctional system.

The number of children in the second group coming before the courts is considerable. A conservative estimate indicates that this group comprises about 26 percent (approximately 184,000) of the total number of children's cases coming before the courts.

For example, a summary review of between 15 and 20 correctional institutions for delinquent children shows that about 30 percent of their inmates were children convicted of conduct which would not have been judged criminal had they been adults. Secondly, a review of 10 studies made by the Children's Bureau on state and local detention programs showed that 48 percent of the 9,500 children studied had not committed adult criminal acts. Of the 1,300 children in this study who were actually in jail pending hearings, about 40 percent fell into the noncriminal category. Of the remainder of the children, who were in detention homes, 50 percent were in this category. One state even reported that in 1965, 39 percent of the children appearing before its juvenile courts were there for noncriminal conduct—truancy, incorrigibility, and running away.

Finally, looking at the populations of public and private institutions for delinquent children in 1960, I found that in the United States there were 476 children under 10 years of age; one in every six of these was under 7!

There is evidence that a somewhat different practice applies in girls' cases. The Children's Bureau has found that more girls than boys fall into the category of children who have been tried for acts which would not have been criminal for adults. Fifty-two percent of all girls' delinquency cases were in the second category outlined above. This figure for boys was only 21 percent. This situation can be partially explained by the common practice of filing a petition for "incorrigibility" or "beyond control" for girls, when in fact their conduct would fall into the "criminal" category if committed by adults. This practice probably results from either a tendency to protect girls or the inability to prove a criminal act. It may also reflect the fact that we have permitted freer conduct for boys than for girls.

NEGATIVE IMPACTS

There is a considerable body of opinion which holds that the label of "delinquent" sets a youngster apart from his peers—in his own estimation and by the community in general. Through forced association with others similarly labelled, this feeling is reenforced. He begins to think of himself as a delinquent and acts accordingly.

Placing of such children in correctional institutions exposes them to association with more sophisticated delinquents who have committed serious offenses and developed a pattern of delinquent conduct. Even more to be condemned is the fact that they come in contact with hardened adult criminals in jail detention and in adult penal institutions to which some are committed or transferred as being incorrigible.

Juvenile correctional institutions are constantly plagued with the problem of overpopulation. The paucity of adequate staff in correctional programs, both in terms of training and temperament, is also common knowledge. Despite all measures, statutory or otherwise, to protect from stigma the youngster who is a product of the correctional system, it is well known that such stigma exists to almost as great a degree as in the adult field. It may act as a bar to employment or enlistment in the armed services. It may even continue to be a handicap for years. There is, for example, the case of the family whose application for public housing was turned down partly on the basis that the husband committed minor offenses as a juvenile.

In the light of the present inadequacy of our correctional systems and of their negative impact on youthful offenders, placement in the system should be used only as a last resort. Furthermore, it should not be used for children who have indulged in conduct which would not be a crime if committed by an adult. No doubt many children in this category are in need of better supervision, care, and treatment, even including removal from home, but their needs should not be met by subjecting them to a correctional process designed for persons involved in criminal conduct.

ONE SOLUTION

As a means of preventing this subjection of children to the correctional process, the suggestion has been made that the jurisdiction of the court in delinquency cases be limited to children who have broken laws which are applicable to all ages and that children alleged to be delinquent for other reasons be referred to public and private social agencies, clinics, and schools. Although this proposal has promise, it also may be an over-simplification of the problem.

Even in stable families there is a certain amount of child–parent conflict, particularly in relation to the older adolescent group. This conflict is a normal part of growing up, and generally a painful period for the adolescent. Many parents will readily agree that it is an equally difficult experience for themselves. Fortunately in all but a small percentage of families the storm is weathered through the use of common sense and skilled handling or through the gradual process of maturation, which appears to be a major curative factor even in serious cases of delinquency.

In a number of families, because of physical, emotional, or other social or cultural pressures, conflict reaches a point where the parents are unable to cope with it. A situation can develop where a 16- or 17-year-old adolescent decides to leave home and go out on his own without any supervision whatsoever. Is society willing to permit this kind of a situation? Probably not. To do so would appear to be unfair to the adolescent as well as to the parents who still may be held responsible for his care, supervision, and conduct. It is also unfair to the community since in such situations the adolescent's conduct may indicate a drift toward criminal acts. Furthermore, in such conflict situations experience has shown that it cannot be assumed that parents are always acting in the best interest of the child. The parents may be equally arbitrary and unreasonable in their demands. In these situations the courts have recognized that the youngster is entitled to an advocate in his own right.

Where parent–child relations reach an impasse, there must be some constituted authority which can intervene in the child–parent relationship with or without the consent of the parties. Such intervention obviously involves some curtailment of basic personal rights and should conform to due process of law. In this country we have traditionally looked to the courts to determine when, under what conditions, and to what extent the state may intervene in the private lives of its citizens.

For these reasons, I believe that a court should continue to have jurisdiction over these types of situations. But other remedies are worthy of exploration.

OTHER REMEDIES

1. *Intervening service between complainant and court.* In the first place, every possible step should be taken to reduce the need for intervention by the courts. This means that help must be available in the community to which police and court-intake staff can refer cases. In many communities, the only agencies which might provide such services are the welfare department and the school. Often they are not equipped to do so. Even in larger communities where a variety of public and private agencies have been established, corrections personnel have generally had little success in securing services: Rigid intake policies and already established waiting lists have effectively screened out the delinquent and his family; and established agencies have been extremely reluctant to accept referrals from police or court particularly where these involve troublesome and rebellious adolescents.

For this reason, we need a new program which would operate as an intervening service between complainants and the court by taking responsibility for working with community agencies to secure services for youngsters referred to it. Where these services are not available, it should be equipped to provide the service or care directly. There have been a few demonstration programs of a somewhat similar nature. For one reason or another, some have been terminated and to date we have no effective evaluations.

It would receive referrals from a variety of sources: police, juvenile courts, schools, public and private social agencies, and the parents of runaways or incorrigibles.

The new program should be required to accept all referrals from police and courts since this would represent a particularly vulnerable group. The same should apply to complaints of parents as to runaways or incorrigibles. A fixed but not unduly lengthy period, perhaps 30 days, would be permitted for evaluation. The case might then be closed as not needing further service, or an agreement might be concluded between the agency and family for continuing service or care. If the need for care was indicated and the family refused, then the situation would be referred back to the originating source for referral to court on the original complaint. Or where the original referral was the family and resolution is not possible without official action, the agency would refer the matter directly to court. But the family would always have freedom of choice, and could have the matter brought to the court.

Whether information secured through this process should be admissible in court and the adjudication hearing needs careful consideration. It should not be used where the original complaint involved an act which would be an adult crime, or a specific offense applicable to children only, such as a curfew violation. In cases such as incorrigibility and running away, a liberal use of such information may well be necessary.

Often children will be referred to court who are in need of counseling but not court action. The establishment of such service would provide police and court with an instrument of correction for all children not needing official action. Similarly, schools could avail themselves of the services pending establishment of such a program within their own area.

The above procedure would, of course, require some change in the process of court referral. Many statutes, as well as the Standard Family Court Act and the Standard Juvenile Court Act now provide that any person may file a petition if the court deems such action necessary to protect the child or the community.

I recommend that the filing of petitions alleging "incorrigibility," "beyond control," "runaway," or "truancy" be restricted to school officials or representatives of public or private agencies providing services for children and families. This would deny access to court to police, parents, and relatives, who now account for most of these types of referrals. And there should be an absolute bar to anyone to file a delinquency petition on any child under 7.

2. *Juvenile court intake.* Another checkpoint in the gateway to the correctional system is uvenile court intake. This process is essentially a screening device to determine whether court action is needed in the interests of the child or the community. Effective operating intake, of course, is necessary to curtail the number of youngsters being drawn into the correctional system. Some evidence indicates, however, that in many courts the process is either nonexistent or operates to speed up the flow of cases into the court rather than act as a screening mechanism. Since this is a specialized procedure, it should be discharged in larger courts by a separate unit, and in smaller courts by an individual. . . .

Determining the interests of the public or the child in requiring further action is probably one of the most crucial decisions in the entire correctional process. Since, in effect, it is "case control," it has an impact on court operations as well as on programs of other agencies which receive the individual for care after court disposition.

Although some common criteria are used in intake decision-making, great diversity exists in practice. Also, there has been little research to assess their reliability or the weight to be given each. In a sense, the nature of the decisions depends upon the philosophy or orientation of those responsible for them. These, in turn, are influenced by other factors affecting personal bias, such as professional background, training, experience, concepts of the role and function of the court, and community attitudes. And although studies show a large percentage of probation officers to be college graduates, only a small number of these specialized in social sciences. Smaller still was the group which had any graduate training. Also, inservice training programs are lacking and salaries are low.

Decision-making at intake is complicated by the rather broad (and often imprecise) nature of the jurisdiction conferred upon juvenile courts. Unless proved criteria, uniform policy, and proper staffing and organization are established, children will still be drawn into the correctional system on a haphazard basis—the highly subjective value judgments of a variety of individuals. For children who have not committed adult crimes, certain limitations need to be imposed upon court dispositions and agency action. Decisions of judges and of other personnel responsible for the care and treatment of children in the correctional and child welfare fields are presumably based on the traditional concept of "the best interests of the child." However, we all know this calls for almost unlimited freedom in decision-making. This achievement would be possible only under ideal conditions, e.g., envisioning all that needs to be known about human behavior is known; having all the necessary facilities and services of high caliber staff available; and possessing infallibility in decisions from the judge down to the custodial supervisor.

3. *Limitation on placements.* Obviously such conditions are not attainable. Therefore, certain limitations must be imposed on both judicial and executive decision-making to minimize error and insure protection against abuse.

Two such limitations are discussed here since they have particular reference to the group of children under discussion, viz, those children who have committed acts which would not be criminal if committed by an adult.

In order to keep these children out of the correctional system, disposition in these cases should be limited to placement in a noncorrectional setting. Vesting such legal custody in agencies or in institutions designed for children who have committed crimes should be prohibited. Some of those children may have committed minor violations even though they were brought to court as being "incorrigible" or "beyond control," and a tendency might arise to file more petitions alleging criminal conduct merely to get them placed in institutions. To counteract this, the court should be required to make not only jurisdictional findings but also additional findings as to the specific charges in the petition.

I further recommend that when legal custody of such children is vested in an agency, the agency should be prohibited from transferring them to a facility designed primarily for children who have committed criminal acts. The present Standard Family and Juvenile Court Acts prohibit the placement of neglected and incorrigible children in such institutions. They do not limit, however, the placement of children who have violated laws applicable only to children.

These limitations are admittedly stringent; however, if we are in earnest about reducing crime and delinquency and we believe in differential treatment, these steps are necessary. These limitations, furthermore, demand greater efforts by public and private social agencies. Their services will have to be strengthened to provide counseling and a variety of facilities if the needs of this particularly vulnerable group of children are to be met.

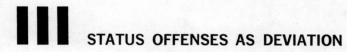

III STATUS OFFENSES AS DEVIATION

6 DRUNKENNESS AND ALCOHOLISM

Drunkenness and alcoholism are *status offenses*. As we discussed in Chapter 1, a *status offense* is a form of deviation in which harm is not necessarily done to any victims; status offenses lack the essential criminal ingredient of willfulness, being involuntary in character. One is a deviant because he is an alcoholic and not necessarily because he has victimized or may victimize others. The deviation is inherent in the chronic state of intoxication.

Status deviations are now undergoing marked transformation in social and legal definition. As the United States Court of Appeals for the Fourth Circuit said, in part, with regard to alcoholism:

> This addiction—chronic alcoholism—is now almost universally accepted medically as a disease. The symptoms, as already noted, may appear as a "disorder of behavior." Obviously, this includes appearances in public, as here, unwilled and ungovernable by the victim. When that is the conduct for which he is criminally accused, there can be no judgment of criminal conviction passed upon him. To do so would affront the Eighth Amendment, as cruel and unusual punishment in branding him a criminal, irrespective of consequent detention or fine.
>
> Although his misdoing objectively comprises the physical elements of a crime, nevertheless no crime has been perpetrated because the conduct was neither activated by an evil intent nor accompanied with a consciousness of wrongdoing, indispensable ingredients of a crime. . . .

It may yet come to pass, then, that status offenses will assume the character of medical problems and thus fall outside the purview of law. Even if they do, there will remain many associated aspects that will continue to be problematic, such as disorderly conduct, driving while drunk, and other crimes committed under the influence of alcohol.

This chapter is concerned not only with drunkenness and alcoholism but also with the institution of drinking and the role of alcohol in complex society. One selection deals with the public drinking establishment as a social setting for the consumption of alcohol.

In the lead-in article, Professor Selden Bacon of the Rutgers School of Alcohol Studies attempts to show that social complexity has fundamentally altered the role and use of alcohol. Gone are the traditional bases of alcohol consumption—as a medicine of sorts, as a food, and for its religious-ecstasy value. Instead, there is the use of alcohol in facilitating social interaction and lowering the barriers between people. Complex society also creates greater stress and anxiety in its members thereby enhancing the use of intoxicants. But complexity also requires heightened judgment and control of one's faculties since the potential for doing damage to self and others is much increased (as in driving under the influence). Finally, complex society has reduced the power of agencies of social control in prescribing and circumscribing the use of alcohol.

The subject matter of the second article is the public-centered drinking institution—the tavern, pub, or bar. Professor Marshall Clinard's "The Public Drinking House and Society" is the most complete work on the subject. The article describes the characteristics of a public drinking house, the regulations concerning its operation imposed by the various states, the types of drinking establishments, and the various social functions of the tavern in addition to its function as a place to drink. The last part of the article is devoted to a discussion of the tavern as a problem institution—its relation to alcoholism and the extent of juvenile participation. There is the implication in this article that the tavern, or at least certain of its types, may well function as an agent of social control over drinking.

"Drunkenness Offenses" is the summary statement of the President's Commission of Law Enforcement and the Administration of Justice. In this very brief review of the problem and recommendations for action, the President's Commission discusses the extent of the problem of drunkenness, the existing laws on the subject, the characteristics of the offenders, and their handling and disposition in the criminal justice system. Some of the hard facts in these areas are startling. For example, one third of all U.S. arrests—two million in all each year—are made for the "crime" of public drunkenness. Some of those arrested are part of the "revolving door" problem—arrest, thirty-day sentence in a jail or workhouse, release, and re-arrest. The President's Commission makes four recommendations designed to improve the situation. Of these, one concerns the redefinition of the problem, two involve new treatment approaches, and the last deals with the need for research.

In "Phases of Alcohol Addiction," the late Professor E. M. Jellinek, in his lifetime undoubtedly the foremost authority on alcoholism, is concerned with the nature of alcoholism as a disease. The most significant section of the paper deals with the stages or phases in alcohol addiction. The four phases—pre-alcoholic symptomatic, prodomal, crucial, and chronic—are described. The various symptoms in each stage are enumerated and their frequency noted. From beginning to end of the progression from occasional drinking to alcoholism some forty-three steps are involved. There is also an interesting digression into that most elusive and much sought for "alcoholic personality" and a short section on the nonaddictive alcoholic as a special type.

"Alcoholics Anonymous" by Chafetz and Demone describes the origins, the twelve steps, and the twelve traditions of AA, the most successful and useful approach to date in the treatment of alcoholism. As important as is their description of this highly imitated group, the questions they pose about its future and the answers they offer to these questions are even more significant.

In 1951, fifty local groups of nonalcoholic relatives, spouses, grown children, parents, and siblings joined together to form Al-Anon Family Groups. The purpose of these groups is to help nonalcoholic relatives understand and cope with an alcoholic family member. The number of groups increased dramatically. There are now approximately fifteen hundred. The program of Al-Anon and its organization and operation are the focal points in this article by Chafetz and Demone.

ALCOHOL AND COMPLEX SOCIETY

Selden D. Bacon

. . . Alcohol has certain effects on the individual and certain effects on the over-all group of individuals. Some of these effects seem to have value for the individual and for society, a conclusion buttressed by the observed fact that, as a custom, the drinking of alcoholic beverages has spread to almost all groups of men ever known, and has enjoyed a long life in almost every society of which we have knowledge. It is equally clear that some of the effects of alcohol on individuals and on groups have been disadvantageous.

Let me mention very briefly some of the outstanding effects. For the individual, alcohol can reduce tension, guilt, anxiety, and frustration; it also can reduce operational efficiency below the minimum necessary for social existence, or even for existence at all. In relation to the total society, alcohol can make possible association and interpersonal activity which may ordinarily be barred; it can permit variations in ideas and

From *Society, Culture and Drinking Patterns* (edited by David J. Pittman and Charles R. Snyder), New York: John Wiley and Sons, 1962, pp. 78-93. Reprinted by permission.

activities also, although this is a minor point; and it can allow an escape valve for socially frustrated individuals, an escape which can be relatively safe. Alcohol can also break down individual participation in associations, thus weakening them. It can impair the exactitude and rhythm of behavior patterns and socially valuable ideas, and it can impair foresight and the results of previous foresight. . . .

SIMPLICITY AND COMPLEXITY IN SOCIAL STRUCTURE

Simplicity and complexity as characteristics of a society are generally related not to end goals or final purposes but to the means of attaining those goals, the numbers and divisions of society and their interrelations. The end goals of the Trobriand Islanders are not basically different from those of the Manhattan Islanders. All these individuals want food, shelter, and clothing; they al want protection from enemies within and without their groups and from the unknown which is potentially dangerous; they all want pleasurable interaction with others—love, affection, prestige; they all want a certain degree of control over themselves and over their situation, both current and future. The way in which these wishes are concretely expressed or attained will vary, of course, in different societies, although there will be for all a minimum core of similarity determined by the biological similarity of all mankind.

The needs of the societies are: (a) a minimum satisfaction of the individual needs; (b) perpetuation of the species; (c) internal unity and order; and (d) protection from outside groups. The achievement of these ends can be relatively simple or relatively complex. For example, a group of fifty families, comprising perhaps three hundred people, can maintain itself by what we could call simple social processes. The members of each family could serve as a unit for production and consumption, grow their own crops, store them, prepare them, and eat them; they could build their own dwellings and make their own clothes, utensils, and weapons. They would worship their ancestral spirits through avoidance, sacrifice, prayer, and other ritual at their home.

Division of labor could be based on sex, age, and talent, but the latter would be only occasional; that is, on a hunt or in constructing a dwelling, one function might invariably be activated by a given individual, but the others would be capable of doing it. Except for age and sex differences, almost any member of the group could fulfill almost any of the activities of the group. Property ownership would vary with talent, application, and luck, but would not vary in as great a degree as in our society, since the possibility of exchange, the range of types of production, and the quantity of durable goods would be limited. Defense of one's physical self and of one's social prestige would be largely a familial and individual matter.

In contrast to this picture, consider the industrial, commercial, service, or professional worker in the large contemporary city. He does not produce his own food, shelter, clothing, or utensils. He does not distribute or store them. He may, in the case of food, do something about final or immediate preparation. Yet he must obtain food, clothing, and shelter, and he does so, but by totally different life activities. The steps by which this social revolution occurred are highly complex and cannot be detailed here. In the main, however, specialization had the result of allowing more and a greater variety of production and finer output—a result of great value for group survival. Its incidence continued to increase—in the areas of both the production of goods and the rendering of services— to an extent, in contemporary society, that almost defies description. Specialization has occurred, moreover, not only in the realm of mechanical acts but also in the realms of foresight and imagination, organization, responsibility, and the giving of orders. There are all manner of gradations and specialties along these lines within the specialized economic categories.

Not that specialization is limited to the economic sphere. Recreation, education, medication, religious activities, and protection from personal attack, from disease, from poverty in old age, and from fire, to mention the most obvious, have, to a very large extent, been taken over by specialists. Once these functions were activated in the home by a member of the family or by the person involved. Now we have professions, businesses, industries, services, and institutions to do these things for us. The same values of specialization apply here as in the economic sphere. Variety, quality, quantity, and speed are mightily enhanced. This specialization process has been speeded, refined, and enlarged by the development of a machine technology. . . .

Specialization has resulted in the greatest production of goods and services yet attained by any society. It had also the following effects, although it alone may not have been responsible: (a) horizontal stratification; (b) vertical stratification; (c) less and less knowledge of the whole society, its ways, subgroups, and ideas; (d) extreme mutual dependence of subgroups and individuals; (e) a utilization of money which allowed impersonal contact between individuals and resulted in a new life orientation of all individuals, but which defied human control and resulted at times in the inability of masses of people to avail themselves even of the extraordinary amount of goods and services at hand; and (f) a great increase in the social potentiality of the individual and a decrease both in the unity of the society as a whole and in the enduring strength of any of its subgroups.

SOCIAL COMPLEXITY AND ALCOHOL

Donald Horton, in his description of primitive societies, has pointed out certain individual needs which are answered, more or less, by alcohol.

One of these is the satisfaction of hunger and thirst, a very minor factor, another is a medicinal need, also very minor. Let us consider the effect of our complex societies on these two needs. In the society where increased complexity is dominated by the economic institution, beverage alcohol is not used for these needs. Goods and services have become so refined, have been so tested in competition, and are so plentiful, that such a second-rate food and fourth-rate medicine as beverage alcohol will tend in these regards to die out or be limited to those rare instances where alcohol has some special value. There will be a lag in ideas, however. Old ideas of the nutritional and medicinal values of alcohol will persist long after the best knowledge and experience will have shown them to be mistaken.

Another function of alcohol mentioned by Horton was its use in attaining religious ecstasy. Here alcohol must compete with fasting, purposefully induced exhaustion, self-laceration, drugs, and autohypnosis. Religious ectasy, however, must be a generally approved and prestigeful affair before any of these techniques will be utilized. In our highly specialized economic life there is small place for religious ectasy. Moreover, the mental state achieved by alcohol intake has been considered for many generations as ludicrous or disgusting rather than mysterious. Catalepsy, automatic writing, and conversion hysteria may still inspire some awe in the more superstitious, but even the most confirmed crystal gazers are scornful of alcohol-induced spiritual experiences. In this complex society, these functions of alcohol may safely be forgotten.

Another function of alcohol has been its use in social jollification. Although the distinction between the needs of the society as separate from those of the individual is occasionally difficult to perceive, in this instance a fairly clear discrimination can be made. The maintenance of order and of unity within the society is imperative for the survival of the society. The feeling that the individuals are a "we-group" as opposed to "others," the feeling that it is pleasurable to be one of "us," the restatement of the fundamental mutuality of the members—these values are attained by meetings of pleasurable purpose. In any society there will be stresses and strains which tend to break the unity; certain individuals will be unsatisfied, will be more ambitious than achieving; certain groups will be antagonistic. Meetings in which such ambitions, frustrations, and resentments are irrelevant, in which purely rewarding pursuits are at hand, will help restore or enhance the integrating principles.

As we have seen, one of the concomitants of complexity is stratification, another is ignorance of other subgroups, a third is the increased aggression allowed by the widespread utilization of money, a fourth is increased individualism. The need for integrating mechanisms in a more and more complex society is a phenomenon whose existence can hardly be challenged. The difficulty of effecting such mechanisms is apparent.

One of the best ways, aside from great external danger, is through amusements. They present an activity or interest which can be neutral to conflicting interests and personalities; they can be stimulating, they can be rewarding, and they hold small threat of punishment.

Theoretically we would expect an increase of pleasure meetings in a complex, competitive, individualistic civilization, and in our society this theoretical expectancy is fully met. There has been a development of both commercialized and non-commercialized pleasure rituals which would seem extraordinary to the members of the simpler society. From organized spectacles which operate 8 to 16 hours a day every day to the informal tea, cocktail, and card-game gatherings, the members of our society are almost surfeited with recreational association. As would be expected, activities connected with occupational specialty are generally held taboo at these meetings. Specialization and specialists, however, have infiltrated this area of behavior as they have almost all others.

With this extension and elaboration of recreation, alcohol's part in jollification or in pleasure association has become enhanced. Note the role of alcohol in these situations. We have, on the one hand, a society whose individuals are often (a) more self-contained and independent, (b) more ignorant of each other's interests and activities, (c) more separate from each other, and (d) more prone to aggressive and competitive relationships; on the other hand, there is a need for unsuspicious, pleasant, relatively effortless joint activity. How can one put these together? One way is to transfer the ordinary, diverse, specialized attentions of the individuals to one neutral object interesting to all—a spectacle, for example, or a chess game. The trouble with this adjustment is that it does not allow much interpersonal activity.

Another way is to relax all the people. All of us here have undoubtedly experienced meetings intended to be recreational and found them stiff, uncertain, and tense. Intermixture does not take place. Despite the need to spread interaction, individuals remain aloof, or little groups of previous acquaintance maintain their own safe little cliques. The organizers have to break down the hostilities, the indifference, the ignorance, and the suspicions. To do this they try to get the individuals to relax. Alcohol is a quick, easy, fairly sure means of accomplishing this end. It may have other, less desirable effects; at the moment, that is irrelevant.

The conclusion on this point, whether reached by deduction from principles or by observation of our own society, is that the stratification, individualism, intergroup ignorance, and internal competitive tradition—all engendered by the complexity of society—enhance the function of alcohol. Complexity results in a need for greater integrative functioning; lessening of tension, uncertainty, and suspicion is necessary for this function; alcohol has been found useful in its accomplishment.

In addition to the need of the society for greater integration, there is also the need of the individual to make contacts, both occupational and recreational. In a mobile, multistratified world, this is more difficult than in a stable, less-stratified world. In a specialized, competitive world, recreational devices for the individual seem more essential. Yet the factors just discussed make difficult the attainment of that easy, trustworthy, non-competitive friendship situation which is requisite for interpersonal relaxation. Alcohol is obviously functional for achieving the lessening of suspicion, of competitive tension, of the barriers usually present between strangers in our society.

In contrast, then, to the effect of a complex society on the medical, food, and religious-exaltation functions of alcohol is the effect of the complex society on alcohol's function of promoting recreational and other association. This function is definitely enhanced.

ALCOHOL AND TENSION

We now approach the more important, perhaps the fundamental, function of alcohol for individuals. As you are all aware, alcohol is a depressant. It allows, through its depressing function, a relaxation of tension, of inhibition, of anxiety, of guilt. There is no need to define narrowly the meanings incorporated in these words. I will consider, however, the areas of behavior and attitude which are most commonly colored with these emotional characteristics. The listing I shall present is quite arbitrary. Around what personal problems of adjustment do anxiety, tension, guilt, and the like arise?

I would suggest the following: (a) the individual's opinion of himself; (b) gaining and holding the respect and the affections of others; (c) conflicting with others, through self-assertion, through criticism, through out-and-out aggressions; (d) over-all security in ownership, prestige, and personal safety, as they are tied up with money; (e) responsibilities accepted in the achievement of specific goals; and (f) sexual matters.

This is a purely descriptive listing. It may seem to imply that these six are totally separate matters. They are not! The list is merely a convenient set of handles by which one can pick up and examine the package labeled "one human being." The handles alone are meaningless.

In a complex society these areas of behavior and attitude are more greatly challenged, are more difficult to live through or adjust to, than they are in a simpler society. For a very simple example, take the matter of self-assertion or the exhibition of aggression. In a world of extraordinary dependence on others, aggression is very dangerous. In a complex, specialized, stratified society we are continually in situations where we are dependent on others, and the others do not seem to care much about us. Elevator operators, waiters, salespeople, clients, partners—all of them have it in their power to frustrate us. By the very nature of the system they must frustrate us somewhat, since they serve fifty or five hundred other people in addition to us, and we must take our turn; that is ineradicable in association. So we get angry. But we cover it up. The complexity of society increases the incidence of aggression-provoking situations. The complexity of society renders the expression of aggression ever more dangerous.

Consider the matter of prestige, or recognition from others. In a society in which there is great homogeneity of activity, where most people do about the same things in the same way, the range of prestige is smaller. You are a good, a mediocre, or a bad workman. Furthermore, in a simple society the tangible marks of success, such as conspicuous consumption or ownership, are also limited in variety and quantity. In a complex society, however, the situation is dramatically different. There is an extraordinarily refined hierarchy of prestige. Much of the prestige goes with the position rather than with the individual's talent or exertion of effort or pleasing personality.

Furthermore, recognition and prestige depend more and more on obvious, often tangible, symbols. In the simple society, it is easy to tell who is an efficient, pleasant person. In the stratified, specialized society, it is not easy. People are more and more inclined to give recognition according to conspicuousness and wealth. There is not the time, there is not the knowledge, there is not the personal interaction on a variety of levels of experience, for people to judge. Yet, despite this weakness, the need to get good persons for specialized positions is pressing, and the goal of gaining prestige is enhanced. The result, of course, is increased apprehension, increased sensitivity, increased tension.

In a complex society where personal relationships are more and more specialized, impersonal, and competitive, and where various specialties are not understood by others, recognition, respect, and prestige are more intensely desired, are more difficult to attain, and are, perhaps, more suspect, than in simpler societies. This results in frustration, envy, aggression, and anxiety which do not appear in such marked form from this source in simpler societies.

The increased complexity of our social existence has increased social responsibilities. One of the outstanding characteristics of high position in any of our ways of life is increase in responsibilities. For many hierarchies we may say that the assumption of higher office is matched by an increase in the anxieties a person carries. One of the earmarks of the executive is his ability to assume anxiety with understanding and with poise. The person in the lowest rank carries very little anxiety about the function of the organization. At 5 P.M. he quits work and forgets about it, although he still carries personal anxieties. The high-ranking man carries his anxiety concerning the whole organization all the time. The one has little or no prestige and little or no anxiety on this account; the other has much prestige and much anxiety.

The general over-all security represented by money in a complex society has already been discussed. The increased anxiety from this source reflects through all of the significant emotional areas that were listed, in addition to possessing a ranking of its own. Although it weighs most obviously on the people in the lowest economic ranks or in marginal positions, it can be equally oppressive to people who, while not threatened with starvation, are threatened as to their social position and prestige.

Time forbids dealing with the other emotional areas. It is, or should be, sufficiently clear that interpersonal relationships and personal satisfactions are more difficult, are more anxiety provoking, are more exhausting, in a complex society.

The advantages of a complex society are manifest, but there is a price to pay. That price is intangible, difficult to measure or define. It can roughly be labeled as emotional insecurity for the individual. Since alcohol can reduce the impact, can allow escape from the tensions, fears, sensitivities, and feelings of frustration which constitute this insecurity, its role will be more highly valued.

I shall mention one more view of the enhanced importance or power of the alcohol-drinking custom that results from social complexity. The most obvious aspect of complexity has been described as specialization. Specialization occurred in the activation of this custom as in all the others. Specialized crops, specialized industries, specialized distribution, advertising, and financing, specialized retailing, all occur in the realm of alcoholic beverages just as in that of railroading, of dairy products, of education, or of men's clothing. Just as the function of clothing is extraordinarily expanded and enmeshed in other social organizations, beliefs, and activities because of specialized institutionalization, so is that of alcohol production, distribution, and consumption. For example, when one makes one's own clothes or one's own wine or whisky, there is a great deal of pressure, of anxiety, about not using the product unless it is really needed. Under conditions of specialized production, where there is competition, a monetary basis, and impersonal relations between producer, distributor, retailer, and consumer, this pressure is completely reversed. The more consumption, the more success. This process is heavily reinforced by the fact that unit costs tend to go down as the number of units produced goes up.

The effect of this concomitant of social complexity is to equip the whole constellation of alcoholic beverage activities, ideas, material objects, and organizations with motives, mechanisms, and functions which are utterly disconnected with the physiological and psychological functions of alcohol. The same distinction, of course, is true for all other specialized institutions.

DYSFUNCTIONAL ASPECTS

Now we come to the effects of societal complexity on what might be called the socially and individually dysfunctional aspects of alcohol. The potentialities of alcoholic beverage consumption remain the same but are to be viewed in a different light. We could speak of dynamite in the same way; its properties do not change, but its effects on human beings can be of a tremendously constructive or tremendously destructive nature.

The complex society presents great rewards to individuals; two factors balance these rewards and are a sort of fixed charge: (1) breakdown of any part is far more dangerous than in the simple society; (2) there must be a more exact fulfillment of function than was previously necessary on the part of every subgroup and every individual. To put this in a more general way: the need for imagination and perception, for control over responses, for timing and balance, is greatly increased by the complex culture; just to get things done is a more delicate task, and the penalty for not getting things done has far greater social implications than in the simpler society. Do not illustrate this in your minds solely by the picture of a person driving a car or tending a machine. One tendency of our material culture has been to dominate our thinking in just such a narrow way. Think rather of relations between groups of people, employer and employee, principal and agent, people of different social classes; think rather of the foresight necessary in a production schedule, in bringing up children, in establishing governmental procedures. These activities in a complex society demand greater sensitivity, greater efficiency in action, greater imagination, and greater caution than in a simpler society.

Alcohol lowers sensitivity, efficiency, and caution. It deteriorates balance and timing. Personal aggression and irresponsibility are far more dangerous in a complex society, and, as an adjustment to this, child-training in complex society lays heavy emphasis on self-control—on inhibitions and repressions of aggression and irresponsibility; alcohol releases these inhibitions. Regularity of behavior is as essential in a complex society as in a complex machine. Alcohol can wreck regularity of behavior. I need not expand on this point; the conclusion is apparent. The need of the society for regularity, precision, individual responsibility, and integration, through self-control and cooperation, is increased by complexity. The achievement of these values is directly threatened by alcohol in proportion to its depressant action.

A further societal complication is to be seen in the means of control.

It has been pointed out that specialized and formal groups have become more powerful and have extended their functions while all-purpose and intimate groups have been weakened. If the drinking of alcohol and its effects were limited to the area of one of these specialized groups, sanctions could be efficient; or if the society were simpler, more homogeneous, more dominated by some all-purpose, personally intimate and significant association, sanctions could be significant. The drinking of alcohol and its effects, however, infiltrate all manner of acts, associations, and ideas. The attempt to exert sanctions over this wide, loosely organized area will be met with opposition, argument, and relatively unabashed violation. The sanctioning authority will not be recognized. The ideology behind the attempt will be challenged. Social classes, minority groups, religious groups, locality groups, and other categories will not have the identity of purpose, understanding, and experience which would allow such action to proceed smoothly. The complexity of society is of manifest significance with regard to this point. Furthermore, the question of control can itself create further disorganization in the society. This, of course, is quite irrelevant to the physical and psychological properties of alcohol.

In a society already impersonal, competitive, individualistic, and stratified, the effect of excessive drinking on the individual is dramatic. I would only draw attention to the fact that the complexity of the society, and the concomitants of that complexity as here described, exaggerate and speed the deterioration process in the maladjusted person.

SUMMARY

Now let us recapitulate the particular sociological viewpoint on alcohol here presented: Social complexity, in the case of Western civilization dominated by economic specialization, has enormously increased the number and variety of goods and services, has improved quality beyond measurement, and can produce with unparalleled speed. This is as true of alcoholic goods and services as of others. Complexity has also resulted in horizontal and vertical stratification, in mutual ignorance and disinterest of societal subgroups, in extreme interdependence of subgroups and of individuals, in the emergence of money as a controlling factor in human life, and in an individualism marked by the increased power of each person and the decreased power of such all-purpose, intimate groups as the family and the small neighborhood.

In relation to alcohol, these concomitants of social complexity have had the following seven effects:

1. They have practically eliminated three functions of alcohol which were of minor importance in primitive society, namely, food value, medicinal value, and religious-ecstasy value.

2. They have enhanced the need for integrative mechanisms in the society which are personally significant. The pleasure group is important here, but other meetings are not excluded. The function of alcohol in depressing certain inhibitions, anxieties, aggressions, and tensions, thus allowing relaxation, has increasing significance, since it can help in this process.

3. These concomitants of complex society have increased, compared with simpler societies, the weight of the anxieties of most individuals, and have added new anxieties. The depressant function of alcohol thus becomes more significant, especially since these anxieties are directly related to the most basic human drives.

4. The very nature of the specialization process has created a network of relationships, activities, wealth, social position, and so on, which revolve around the business of alcohol, thus bringing into existence a set of factors not present in the simpler society, a set of factors unrelated to the physiological or psychological properties of alcohol.

5. The complexity of society increases the need, if the society is to exist, for sharp discrimination, caution, accurate responses, timing, cooperation, and the acceptance of responsibilities. Alcohol, taken excessively, can deteriorate all of these.

6. The nature of the complex society makes social control over behavior that is not strictly compartmentalized into one or another institution an extremely difficult task. The drinking of alcohol and its effects are not present in only one institution or pattern of behavior but infiltrate throughout; the drinking itself is largely in the loosely organized area of individual recreation. Control of drinking behavior in the complex society is therefore a more difficult problem than in the simpler society.

7. The individual in the complex society has a far more formidable task in integrating himself to groups and ideas in a satisfying way, is equipped with more personal choice, and belongs to looser, more specialized, less personally satisfying associations. The excessive use of alcohol can more rapidly and thoroughly destroy such participation in complex societies than it can in the simpler, more general, more intimate groups of primitive societies. The power of alcohol to deteriorate personality is thus enhanced in complex society.

It can be seen, thus, that the complexity of society is a significant factor in the relations of alcohol and man. It obviously enhances the uses of alcohol for man. It obviously increases the dangers of alcohol for man. Social complexity has added new forces and motivations for the production and distribution of alcohol. It has diminished the power of agencies of control which could once be efficiently used.

THE PUBLIC DRINKING HOUSE AND SOCIETY

Marshall B. Clinard

Since time immemorial, man has enjoyed the use of alcoholic beverages, and for centuries society has argued, fought, and sought to control its use and misuse. The conflict over the use of alcohol has been directed at not only those who consume it but also those who dispense it. As the institutionalized public drinking house became the focal point of the drink, the drinker, and the dispenser, values and conflicts over this institution developed. . . .

Although public drinking houses are known by a variety of names, such as taverns, bars, pubs, bistros, wine houses, and beer halls, we shall largely use the term "tavern." For purposes of definition, one might simply say that public drinking houses are establishments whose business consists mainly of selling and serving beer, wine, or other intoxicating liquors for consumption on the premises. Actually this definition is inadequate, for it does not emphasize several important institutional features of a public drinking house.

A more complete definition would include these characteristics: (*a*) The serving of alcoholic beverages is an indispensable feature and an important source of revenue even if food is served. Because they do not serve alcoholic beverages, such places as soda fountains or milk bars, coffee houses of Greece and the Middle East, or tea houses of the Orient are not public drinking houses as the term is used here. (*b*) As a drinking establishment it is commercial and public in the sense that theoretically the opportunity to purchase a drink is open to all, whereas the bar of a private club or fraternal organization is restricted to members and their guests. (*c*) The drinking of alcoholic beverages is *group drinking* in the sense that it is done in the company of others in a public place. (*d*) It must have a functionary—a tavernkeeper, bartender, or, as in Europe, a barmaid. This person, in addition to serving alcoholic beverages, also acts as a sort of receptionist. (*e*) Finally, it has a physical structure and a set of norms. Patrons are served at a bar, tables, or booths, in specially decorated surroundings, with entertainment or rec-

From *Society, Culture and Drinking Patterns* (edited by David J. Pittman and Charles R. Snyder), New York: John Wiley & Sons, 1962, pp. 270-92. Reprinted by permission.

reational facilities like cards, darts, and shuffleboard available, thus distinguishing it in some way from the customary activities of other similar establishments. Certain norms are also well established, including certain hours of drinking and appropriate drinking behavior.

TAVERN PARTICIPATION AND REGULATION

The number of taverns in the United States is not known, but a conservative estimate would be at best 200,000. Wisconsin has about 14,000 public drinking establishments, New York City has over 11,000, and Chicago has about 9,000. A Chicago survey, some 20 years ago, reported that the annual patronage of the city's taverns was more than 30,000,000, while the motion-picture theaters of the city had an attendance of 20,000,000, and baseball and football alone at least 5,000,000. On this basis the report concluded that taverns at least have more patronage than all other forms of commercial recreation combined. A survey of an English industrial community found that more people spent more time in public drinking houses than in any other buildings except private homes and places of employment. In this city of 180,000 people about 20,000 pub-goers made approximately 140,000 visits to pubs a week. Furthermore, "the pub has more buildings, holds more people, takes more of their time and money, than church, cinema, dance-hall, and political organizations put together." From the survey of this community, and other data, it was concluded that about one-twelfth or more of the population of England is consuming alcohol in pubs on Saturday evening and more still at home.

A random sample of 1,441 persons in Dane County, Wisconsin, was surveyed as to the extent they used the tavern. Three categories were used, non-patrons, irregular patrons (less than once a month), and regular (more than once a month). Of the 872 men in the survey, one-fourth were non-patrons, one-fourth irregular, and a half regular patrons. One out of ten went to a tavern nine or more times a month. Tavern patronage of the men did not materially differ by farm, village, or urban residence. Among the 569 women, three-fifths were non-patrons, a little over one-fourth were irregular patrons, and only 15 per cent were regular. Urban women appeared to be more frequent patrons than either village or rural women.

As the public drinking house, regardless of its name, has become a firmly entrenched institution in Western society, open conflicts have developed between wets and drys over it and its growing patronage. Extensive propaganda has been disseminated both for and against it, especially in the United States, and the controversy has been intensified and heightened by religious exhortations and heated legislative hearings. The situation in England has differed little from that in this country. In this continuing controversy the wets have generally referred to the tavern as a poor man's club which affords him the same enjoyment and communality as the exclusive country club provides the socially elite. The drys, on the other hand, contend that the tavern constitutes a serious threat to the home and family, leads to crime and delinquency, and weakens the moral standards of society. Largely as a result of these accusations, taverns, especially in the United States, have been more and more strictly regulated. These regulations indicate some of the values believed to be associated with public drinking houses. Those states which permit the sale of alcoholic beverages for consumption on the premises have two types of regulations, one relating to persons who own and operate taverns, and the other setting standards under which ownership and operation are valid. In other words tavern regulations are concerned with the who, where, and when of drinking.

1. *Regulations controlling licensing and qualifications of tavernkeepers and bartenders*

The most important instruments of tavern control are state licensing and taxation statutes, and they set forth the various reasons for the necessity to control alcoholic beverages. The statutes of fifteen states mention the general welfare, sixteen cite health, twelve maintenance of peace, twelve the upholding of morals, and four the prohibition of the open saloon. Eight statutes indicate that the purpose of control is to promote temperance. It would appear that only one-sixth of the states are interested in regulating retailers in the promotion of moderate drinking. However, when one turns to the specific regulations, the picture changes quickly.

Among the requirements which a prospective tavern owner must meet, the one most commonly agreed upon, by forty-one states, is United States citizenship. Thirty-six states insist that no one previously convicted of violating any federal or state liquor laws, or who has had a liquor license revoked, shall be eligible for licensing. Thirty-four states refuse to grant a license to any person who has a criminal record although five of them provide for licensing if the record is not a recent one. In thirty-two states the applicant must be of "good moral character," and the same number require bona fide state residence, the time limit stretching to as long as 10 years in Kansas.

Twenty-seven states insist on legal maturity, from 21 years of age in most states to 30 in Delaware. Four of these states require the applicant to be a qualified voter. Twenty-one states prohibit interlocking vertical ties between the tavernkeeper and other persons and companies in the liquor trade, an aftermath of saloon days. Seventeen states insist that the applicant be a legitimate party in the place to be licensed. Thirteen states will not license any licensing or enforcement official. In twelve states tavern owners must demonstrate ability to read and write. In six states the applicant must be financially responsible, whereas only four refuse to approve applicants who use alcoholic beverages to excess. In most states many of these provisions can, of course, be evaded by having the license issued to a relative or some other person.

Standards for bartenders are far less rigid than those for tavern owners. The most general rule is that the employee be over 18 or 21 years of age, depending upon the jurisdiction in which he seeks employment. Seventeen states have "anti-barmaid" laws. In most cases these rules do not apply to women who work on the premises as waitresses, but only to those who operate behind the bar itself. Exceptions to the latter rule are made in some states where the woman is the wife of the tavern owner.

In many states tavernkeepers are subject to a special type of liability. A tavernkeeper must post a bond which supposedly guarantees payment of damages to any person for injuries suffered as the result of drinking in a tavern. In Illinois this is called the "Dram Act" and because the law has been sometimes used to collect damages unfairly, a subsequent bill was passed setting the limit of $20,000 in damages for injuries or death resulting from intoxication and setting a time limit of 1 instead of 2 years for the filing of a suit against a tavernkeeper.

2. *Regulations concerning drinkers*

Tavern licenses can be revoked or suspended if liquor is sold, either by the drink or package, to the following major classes of persons:

(*a*) Forty-six states forbid the sale of alcoholic beverages to visibly intoxicated persons.

(*b*) Thirty-two states do not permit the serving of drinks to known alcoholics, habitual drunkards, or persons of intemperate habits.

(*c*) Forty-six states prohibit the sale of intoxicating beverages to minors. In nearly all states the minimum age is 21, although in a few it is 18. Frequently the legal age for entering taverns selling distilled spirits is 21, while it is 18 for those serving only beer. Almost without exception the retailer is solely responsible for serving minors, but in a few instances the minor is subject to penalty if he knowingly misrepresents his age in order to procure liquor. It is the seller's responsibility to secure positive proof of a patron's age before any transactions take place.

(*d*) Twenty states forbid the sale of alcoholic beverages to "interdicted" persons. By interdicted is meant any individual whose family, the courts, welfare agencies, mental institutions, public and private officials have specifically notified the licensee that such persons may not be sold intoxicating beverages. These persons are usually persons on public relief, parolees and probationers, and persons judged insane.

(e) Four states specifically prohibit prostitutes and keepers of houses of ill repute from patronizing taverns.

3. *Time of drinking*

Regulations regarding time of drinking vary considerably from state to state. The hours for sale of liquor are fixed by state law, local ordinances, or by rules of the state liquor commissions. Most states call for an 8-hour halt to business, generally from midnight to 8 A.M. The two extremes are South Carolina, which fixes the closing hour at sundown, and Maine, which permits taverns to operate except for one hour daily, from 8 A.M. to 9 A.M. Every state except Wyoming prohibits taverns from operating on election day either or at least while the polls are open, and five states require taverns to close on Christmas Day. In most other states there is considerable informal pressure on taverns, however, to have them close early on Christmas Eve. Three states require the closing of all taverns on Thanksgiving Day, and two of these make this rule apply to Armistice Day as well. Twent-five states prohibited taverns from operating at any time on Sundays. Six others set specified times on Sundays during which taverns must remain closed. Many of the remaining states leave this decision to local authorities. . . .

TYPES OF TAVERNS

The tavern is often stereotyped by persons not personally acquainted with it. These stereotyped attitudes appear to be based on a combination of "hearsay," half-truths, misinformation, ignorance, prejudice, propaganda, and biased on inadequate data. The stereotyped conception of the tavern is also based on stories of saloon days, newspaper reports, observations of the worst taverns, and the belief that the drinking of alcoholic beverages is its only function. Some people believe tavern patronage is one of the chief causes of alcoholism, broken homes, neglected children, highway accidents, juvenile delinquency, and even crime.

A significant factor in this stereotyped conception of a tavern is the general lack of familiarity with this institution. Actual investigations have shown that the majority of the taverns do not fit the stereotype but are of different types. Four criteria may be used in describing types of patronage and the functions it performs. A tentative classification is the Skid-Row tavern, the downtown bar and cocktail lounge, the drink and dine tavern, the night club, and the neighborhood tavern.

1. *Skid-Row taverns*

These taverns are usually located in the deteriorated Skid-Row areas close to the central business district. Many establishments are simply "holes in the wall" with only a bar and stools, while others may have tables and poorly lighted booths. The patronage is largely single and homeless men, migrant laborers, and alcoholics. Although their primary function is to provide a place for cheap drinking, they are often the site of gambling and soliciting for prostitution. There are frequent violations of state and municipal laws relating to taverns, as well as drunk and disorderly conduct and gambling. In this type of tavern, violations of regulations which are strictly enforced in other places are often permitted; for example, closing hours are widely disobeyed, and many establishments virtually operate on a 24-hour basis. While taverns somewhat similar to this description may be found in nearly all cities, the most typical ones are found on New York's Bowery or Chicago's West Madison Street. The reputation of this type of tavern has contributed much toward the development of the stereotype of all taverns.

2. *The downtown bar and cocktail lounge*

These drinking places are located in business and shopping areas of cities. They usually have long bars, booths, and attractive decorations, and are predominantly patronized by men of the white-collar and business class. Besides drinking, visiting, and talking about business problems the patrons can often watch television or a professional performer, or listen to juke box music. Occasionally a sport like shuffleboard or bowling is available. The downtown cocktail lounge serves primarily mixed drinks and attracts some unaccompanied women. It is open for business chiefly in the early afternoon and caters to afternoon and late evening patrons. Most customers of the bars and cocktail lounges are transient. Because of the location and type of patrons there is much less emphasis on the social and recreational activities than in the neighborhood taverns.

3. *Drink-and-dine taverns*

These taverns are located either in business districts or near the city limits along main highways. The bar is not the center of attraction but is frequently part of a spacious, well-appointed dining room. Patrons are most frequently businessmen, but many women patronize this type of drinking establishment. While serving alcoholic beverages is an important source of income, the primary drawing card is the service of fine foods, and often there is music. Many business deals are transacted over cocktails and steaks. There is little interaction between patrons as they tend to come in small individual groups. Although the frequency of attendance is much less than at a downtown bar, the length of stay is generally longer.

4. Night clubs and roadhouses

Located generally in city amusement centers or along main highways outside of but near the city limits, the night club or roadhouse is usually large and impressive, with neon lights and illuminated billboards attracting the traveler's attention. The bar is usually located adjacent to the dining room whose seating arrangement centers around a stage and dance floor. Although the night club or roadhouse is situated out from the city center, its patronage is predominantly urban couples who come chiefly on weekends. While drinking is encouraged and there is some visiting, the primary functions are dancing, the enjoyment of fine foods, listening to the orchestra, and watching the floor show. Most persons who attend are spectators and there is little social interaction among the patrons.

5. Neighborhood taverns

Of all taverns the most numerous and apparently the most important type functionally is the neighborhood tavern. . . . This type can be divided primarily by location and secondarily by patronage into four subtypes: rural, village, suburban, and city. Neighborhood taverns are more than places for people to drink, visit, exchange ideas, discuss politics and problems, joke, play cards or other games, watch television, and listen to their favorite records on the juke box. Generally speaking, these establishments tend to cater to a local clientele; the bulk of the patrons are "regulars" who are often on intimate speaking terms with one another and with the owner and bartenders. In addition, these taverns do most of their business in the evenings and on weekends and holidays.

Rural neighborhood taverns are located either in the open country along a highway, usually at a crossroad, or in some small unincorporated village. Besides the bar stools they usually have tables and booths, and on weekends may serve fish and chicken dinners. Practically all have juke boxes, many have radio or television, and some have pianos; playing cards are also available. . . . An important function is providing a meeting place for friends and neighbors where they may share like interests and problems, or relax and enjoy visiting together.

Village neighborhood taverns are located in an incorporated village usually at or near the center of the small business district. Structurally and functionally it is about the same as the rural neighborhood tavern. As is the case with all neighborhood taverns, one of the most important functions is to provide a meeting place and social center for patrons and friends.

The city neighborhood tavern is located in a more densely populated area often at or near street intersections, and the suburban neighborhood tavern is located near the city limits, often on highways leading to the city. Structurally they are similar, with a bar, tables, and chairs, although the suburban tavern is usually more modern in appearance with larger and more attractive signs to attract the attention of highway patronage. . . .

Almost all neighborhood taverns have television, juke boxes, card games, and other games. As with the rural and village taverns, both suburban and city neighborhood taverns provide a meeting place for people to talk and relax from the monotony of work.

A British neighborhood pub often represents a combination of several types of taverns. Most English pubs have three rooms: the vault, the taproom and the lounge. The essential difference between them is in the relationship among the people themselves and with the people who run the tavern. The vault has a bar or counter where an exclusively male patronage drink standing. Most men come singly, and some are total strangers. In the taproom, drinking is a male group affair, and they are seated around plain wooden tables and benches. It is like a clubroom and strangers are not welcome. While games are played in both the vault and the taproom, most are in the latter. The lounge, or "best room," is well decorated and comfortably furnished with tables, chairs, and a piano; it attracts women and couples. There are no games, the demeanor is more homelike, and it attracts mostly middle-class patrons.

THE SOCIAL FUNCTIONS OF PUBLIC DRINKING HOUSES

Most taverns in the United States or the pubs of England are of the neighborhood type. While the consumption of alcohol plays a predominant but not exclusive part in taverns of the Skid-Row type, as well as in downtown bars and cocktail lounges, alcoholic drinking in neighborhood taverns or pubs plays a secondary role. People go to the tavern to drink, but they also go there for other reasons. In fact to "have a drink in a tavern" actually often means "let's talk" or "play a game or two," in much the same way that "let's play bridge" often means "let us get together and visit." The British pub has been characterized not only as a center of social activities but as the principal locale of the pub-goers' social life.

> Worktown working people rarely meet in each other's homes for social activities in the way middle classes do. For some there is the social activity of politics, football or cricket clubs. But participators in these activities are a small minority. The place where most Worktowners meet their friends and acquaintances is the pub. Men can meet and talk of the way of their womenfolk.
>
> A drink is the only price of admission into this society. And so, for the pubgoers, drink becomes inseparably connected with social activity, relaxation, and pleasure. And the picnic, the outling, the angling competition,

the bowls match, the savings club, games of cards and darts, betting—all these forms of non-pub social activity become connected with the pub, and thus are "incomplete" without drink.

The forms taken by pub social activity bear on the conclusions that we have drawn from the behavior of drunks. Here, too, the social and the alcoholic motive cannot be disentangled. The alcoholic motive itself is primarily social, if it is given a long term definition; it is a motive that seeks the breaking down of barriers between men, the release from the strain of everyday life in the feeling of identification with a group. And the rituals of the Buffs and the clubs, the merging of groups in singing, all in different ways are part of this process.

Other than drinking there appear to be three chief functions of the tavern: (a) as a meeting place where social relationships with other persons can be established, (b) as a place for recreation such as games, and, (c) as a place to talk over personal problems with the tavernkeeper or others.

1. *The public drinking house as a meeting place*

The primary purpose of most taverns appears to be that of serving as a place where people can meet, become acquainted, and enjoy social relationships. In one survey a considerable proportion of more than five hundred Wisconsin regular tavern-goers said they felt the tavern played an important social role in their lives and those of others. About three-fourths felt that the tavern was a social club, two-thirds thought that the tavern provided a place for friends to meet, and one-half felt that meeting friends is an even more important function of the tavern than drinking. In fact, 43 per cent felt that the tavern was as important as the church to many patrons. Persons attending a church, the theater, or various athletic events are usually spectators. Instead of being the audience, tavern patrons are participating actively; instead of having their thoughts and actions patterned for them, they are free to act and think and talk as they wish. To the extent that these needs are met, the tavern acts as an integrating force in the lives of its patrons.

The anonymous opinions of tavernkeepers, while possibly revealing some vested interests, may also be considered valid insomuch as tavern-keepers, both as observers and as tavern functionaries, participate daily in tavern life. Some 150 Wisconson tavernkeepers indicated that an hour with friends is the most important reason for tavern patronage, followed in order by drinking, talking over problems, and recreation in the form of cards or other games. Over nine-tenths of all responding tavernkeepers said that their taverns were social centers. Over half of the tavernkeepers commented on their patrons' meeting and visiting together regularly; three-tenths made remarks about patrons discussing work, business, family, social, and political problems; about one-fifth mentioned playing either cards or other games; and about 15 per cent gave as a reason enjoying drinks together. The common thread running through all of these responses is the word or the implication of the word "together."

Chandler has pointed out the importance of the tavern in the social organization of persons living in rooming-house areas. Taverns serve as meeting places for people who have no way of meeting other persons living in rooming-house areas. In the tavern the individual finds a sense of belonging and a place in the community. In the tavern group the individual seeks friendship and prestige, during his leisure hours. At night it becomes the working man's club. The social life of the rooming-house tavern-goer is confined either to a single tavern or to a type of tavern, and the average tavern has a remarkably stable and regular group of patrons. "The tavern-goer could be counted on to appear at a certain place at a certain time. When others wanted to seek him out they knew exactly where to find him. The tavern-goer met his friends at the bar in the same way that the corner boy met them on his corner. This regular patterned participation involved close interpersonal relations."

The extensive participation in British pubs also cannot be explained as merely the desire to consume ale, beer, and other alcoholic beverages. People seldom go to pubs exclusively to drink or get drunk; rather, they go primarily for sociability and recreation. One study has definitely stated:

> No pub can simply be regarded as a drinking shop. It may be lacking in facilities for games and music, present no organized forms of social activity, and its actual accommodation be of the crudest; but none the less the activities of the drinkers are not confined to drinking. . . . The pub is a centre of social activities—for the ordinary pubgoer the main scene of social life.

2. Recreational activities

Recreation in the form of games, music, and other activities is a leading function of the tavern. Most communities provide, except for bowling or billiards, few opportunities for the average person to play games or enjoy other recreational outlets in small groups outside of the home. Some of the games regularly played inside British pubs, for example, are darts, dominoes, cards, and raffles. There is also much singing. It is possible that these activities reduce the amount of actual drinking in a tavern or pub.

When asked why they went to taverns, a large number of Wisconsin patrons also replied that they went for various recreational activities. Consequently, as one might expect, a survey of 150 Wisconsin taverns indicated that among the recreational outlets offered, 44 per cent provided card games, 41 per cent shuffleboard, and others pinball machines and various mechanical games. Other forms of recreation included the 90 per cent who had juke boxes for their patrons' enjoyment, while others had television, radio, dancing, singing, and bowling. Many provided not one but various forms of recreation. Some of the comments of the tavernkeepers were:

> All know each other and gather to play cards for relaxation. Quite a few of them are retired and card games seem to be the only pleasure they have left at a low cost. [City neighborhood tavern, 250–300 patrons a day.]
>
> I believe my tavern is a social center because most of my patrons are the type that enjoy an evening of friendly companionship. They enjoy visiting and singing, and where you have singing you never have arguing. I believe in keeping my customers happy and willing to come back again and enjoy themselves. [Village neighborhood tavern, 100–150 patrons per day.]

3. *Talking over problems*

Neighborhood taverns often serve as places where one can talk over personal problems. This "talking over" may serve simply as a release for tensions while in other instances the person may actively be able to get "help" from the tavernkeeper or others. In one survey, responses from regular patrons indicated that the tavern had played an important role in offering a place for discussing personal problems.

When Wisconsin tavernkeepers were asked about why people went to one tavern rather than another and what they considered to be the important qualifications of a "good bartender," they obviously mentioned serving good drinks and keeping an orderly place, but they also mentioned, as more significant, being friendly, being attentive, understanding the patron's problems, keeping confidences, sharing the good fortunes and sympathizing with the misfortunes of the patrons, and giving advice to a patron in a "jam." Some of the patrons' difficulties may involve family problems and problems in personal adjustment and on the job. One bartender stated:

> We try to be cheerful. Customers never want to hear your troubles, only to tell us theirs without fear of them being repeated. We are honest and try to show our appreciation of patronage. We try to show interest in their work, crops and family. We greet all by their names and interest ourselves in local things—ball games, legion affairs, etc. [Village neighborhood tavern.]

TAVERN DRINKING NORMS

Certain norms and values often develop in those taverns which have a large proportion of regular patrons. These norms and values control the behavior of the customer to a large extent. Customers are largely known to each other by first names and the bartender is familiar not only with the person's name but with his drinking and other habits as well. In fact one of the ways in which a "regular" tavern patron can be identified is by the degree of familiarity with the staff. In a British pub, for example, a whole system of social norms involve not only the various pub-goers but also the staff. Pub regulars "tend to sit or stand in the same places every night; and this is particularly noticeable with regular groups who stand at the bar; they always retain the same relative positions to one another, and if the room is crowded or they find their usual space in front of the bar partly occupied, though the shape of the group will have to change, their positions relative to one another tend to remain the same."

Group drinking whether in a tavern or pub involves other social factors. The tavern-goer never sits without a drink, he adapts his drinking pace to the group, and the person who pays for the round of drinks sets the pace for the others. Each person must pay in his turn, and if he misses there is danger of social stigma. If a man knocks another man's glass over, it often means that he must buy him another drink. Often games are played for rounds of drinks.

Regular tavern patrons not only regulate the behavior of other regular patrons but can identify and often will reject the newcomer. Even the extent of drinking and drunkenness which is permitted is subject to social control in taverns where there is a good deal of close social interaction. In some taverns old timers may be allowed more freedom than others. On the other hand the customers of certain taverns may not permit any drunkenness or boisterousness and may ostracize offenders. One neighborhood bartender commented:

> Every once in a while one of the fellows will overdo it . . . too much drinking. . . . The others don't go for it, and they tell him. . . . We've got one guy that still comes in here . . . used to be a pretty steady drinker. Then he started drinking heavy. . . . The fellows liked him, and we all tried to get him to cut down. . . . It was no use. . . . After awhile the fellows started to complain so we asked the guy not to come. . . . Well, he still comes in, but they've got nothing to do with him. . . . I guess he's found a new place by now.

THE TAVERN AND ALCOHOLISM

In 1953 it was estimated that sixty-eight million adults in the United States used alcoholic beverages either regularly or sporadically and that of these some five million persons were estimated to be alcoholics. Since millions of drinkers go to taverns and do not become alcoholics, this would indicate that the tavern does not have a direct relationship to alcoholism. On the other hand patronage of taverns in many cases probably speeds up progression in alcoholism. This was the conclusion of a study of 197 members of Alcoholics Anonymous in Wisconsin where an attempt was made to determine the relation of the tavern to each of the three drinking phases of alcoholism, namely the social, the excessive, and the alcoholic. As a control group estimates of the patronage of regular tavern patrons were secured from 106 tavernkeepers. The alcoholics most frequently cited social rather than drinking reasons for their visits in the social drinking phase, and on most of the variables examined the alcoholics could not be differentiated from regular tavern patrons as social drinkers. As they progressed from social drinkers to excessive drinkers, and finally to alcoholics, however, there was a statistically significant increase in their tavern participation as measured by chi-square tests and coefficients of contingency. In all phases, taverns were more important than package stores as sources of supply of alcoholic beverages.

1. *The social drinking phase*

In the social drinking phase, the tavern was the principal source of alcoholic beverages, two-thirds procuring and consuming most of their intoxicating drinks in the tavern. For the alcoholic subjects and for the regular customers, however, the tavern did not necessarily serve as the place in which to get drunk. A minority of only about one-third did most of their "serious" drinking, that is, indulgence for the direct purpose of intoxication, in the tavern, and this was approximately the same figure given by tavern proprietors for their regular patrons.

The mean attendance of taverns by alcoholics at this stage was slightly over once a week. About one in eleven frequented the tavern at least five times a week, although about one in twenty did not patronize taverns at all. According to the estimates of tavernkeepers, regular patrons visit taverns on an average of four times weekly.

It is difficult to see how the tavern during this drinking phase would have significantly affected the drinking patterns of most of these subjects since only a limited amount of time was spent in taverns. About three-fourths of the alcoholics estimated that at this time they spent less than 10 per cent of their leisure time in taverns, and about the same per cent stated that an average visit was an hour or less in duration.

As social drinkers, alcoholics tended to frequent taverns at the same time of day or week as other patrons. The chief times of patronage for the alcoholics, like regular patrons, were weekends, evenings, holidays, and after work. In both groups, however, about 10 per cent of the individuals patronized taverns in the mornings, during lunch hours, and during the working day. The chief places of patronage for the subjects were downtown bars, followed in order of preference by neighborhood taverns near their homes and places of work.

Nine out of ten alcoholics and an estimated three out of four regular patrons drank in the company of others. Some two-thirds of the alcoholics thought that the social contacts in the taverns were more important than the drinking at this stage. Slightly over one-half of the tavern proprietors felt that this was also true for their regular customers. Among the social reasons most often given by both the alcoholic and the regular group were the meeting of friends, the spending of free time, the lack of anything else to do, the playing of cards, and celebrating.

2. Excessive and alcoholic phases

Between the social and excessive drinking phases and between the excessive and alcoholic phases there was a statistically significant increase in the frequency of tavern patronage, the estimated percentage of leisure time spent in taverns, and the amount of time spent per average visit. Significantly more of them did their "serious" drinking in the tavern in the excessive phase.

The amount of morning and daytime patronage of taverns, as well as visitation at other times, significantly increased between the social and excessive and the excessive and alcoholic phases. On the other hand, there was a statistically significant shift of patronage from certain downtown bars and neighborhood taverns to the places nearest the subjects when they wanted a drink.

During the excessive and alcoholic phases, the reasons for patronizing the tavern changed significantly. For most of the subjects social factors became subsidiary, as they most often went to the tavern to drink, get drunk, and forget their problems. There was a decreasing interest in games and friends and a marked increased interest in drinking. This shift was also indicated by the fact that more of the subjects came alone to the tavern and fewer preferred the company of others while drinking, although even as alcoholics about half the subjects still were accompanied by other persons.

3. Tavern practices and alcoholism

Charges are often made that tavern patronage contributes to excessive drinking and alcoholism through encouraging excessive drinking, extension of credit, cashing pay checks, and gambling, and by serving persons already intoxicated. Slightly over half of the alcoholic subjects believed that they were encouraged, at least once, to continue drinking until they were drunk. On at least one occasion, one-third of the alcoholics drank more than they cared to because of friendship with the bartender. Though the extension of credit is generally illegal, 85 per cent were able to buy drinks on credit on at least one occasion, but of those who received credit in taverns fewer than one in three found this to be a reason for drinking more. Only about one-third was able to procure liquor from package stores on credit. Approximately four out of five at some time in their drinking histories cashed their pay checks in taverns. Of those who did so, fewer than one out of three, however, felt that this led to greater indulgence.

In general, gambling in taverns appears to have a negligible influence on excessive drinking. Almost two out of five alcoholics never gambled in taverns for drinks as social drinkers. An additional one-fourth gambled for the pleasure of doing so and were not concerned with winning drinks. Of those persons who had gambled for drinks, one-half did so less frequently after becoming excessive drinkers while the other half did so more often than before. Almost all the alcoholics were served drinks on at least one occasion in spite of the fact that they were intoxicated, as compared with about two-thirds who were able to procure liquor in package stores while intoxicated.

In summary, as the alcoholics progressed through the various phases in their drinking histories, their tavern patronage tended not only to increase quantitatively but to become subjectively more meaningful. The general social functions of the tavern became of subsidiary importance to the alcoholic, but the tavern did provide a comfortable environment for drinking and this seemed, in part, to account for the added tavern patronage.

TAVERN PARTICIPATION AND JUVENILE DELINQUENCY

It has been stated that often delinquent acts are committed under the influence of alcohlic beverages, largely obtained from taverns. Likewise, taverns and tavernkeepers are often regarded as a leading source of immoral influence for delinquency and crime among youth. There is little evidence to support such beliefs. In the first place, delinquent or criminal acts seldom appear to be committed under the influence of alcohol. When drunkenness does occur among juveniles it is an unwarranted assumption to maintain that the tavern was necessarily the source. Undoubtedly one major source of delinquency, however, is the arrest of those under 18 years of age for drinking.

In one of the few specific studies it was found that the tavern was not an important factor in producing delinquency. Taverns which sell to minors, however, are a source of trouble among teenagers. Two types of taverns are frequented by teenagers. One type makes an effort to prevent teenage drinking by checking ages, refusing to serve to known minors, and in general upholding the laws concerning minor drinking and tavern participation. This type, classified as the "good" tavern, is in the majority. The second type caters to teenage trade, seldom checks ages, often provides lewd entertainment, and is even sometimes a source of drugs. This "bad" type was generally frequented by delinquents, whereas the control group frequented the "good" type.

The delinquents frequented taverns more often than non-delinquents, and those who did generally had a previous official record of antisocial acts, in high school and among neighbors. The used the tavern more frequently for admittedly antisocial acts, drunkenness, and for the prestige gained through illegal drinking. Their behavior in the tavern was more often loud and boisterous, and invited trouble such as fights and brawls. The delinquents tended to frequent taverns which catered to minors, and because such taverns are checked more frequently by the police, the delinquents' preference for this type of tavern increased their chances of being apprehended and committed to an institution.

In general, taverns did not play as important a part as often assumed among teenagers. There were many teenagers in both groups who did not go to taverns. The chief source of alcoholic beverages for teenagers was the home, and drunkenness tended to occur in the home of friends. Many illegal methods were used by teenagers in both groups to obtain alcoholic beverages, a common method involved adults buying them.

In spite of laws prohibiting a minor from entering taverns, many tavernkeepers are of the opinion that the illegal patronage of minors is their gravest problem. In a Wisconsin survey tavernkeepers generally approved of the Age Certificate Law which provides penalties for minors who misrepresent their age and permits the tavernkeeper to ask for proof of age, but their was noticeable lack of agreement as to its workability and effectiveness. About one-sixth of them were in favor of permitting minors 18 years of age or over to drink intoxicating liquor in taverns, while approximately half were in favor of raising the age limit to 21 for beer drinking. Some were of the opinion that both the law and a considerable proportion of the public consider teenage business detrimental to the best interests of society and that there exists a lack of cooperation on the part of some public leaders in working with tavernkeepers in attempting to solve the problem of minors drinking in taverns. About one-seventh indicated that minors should be punished more severely for entering taverns unlawfully, for falsifying their ages, and for drunken driving. . . .

DRUNKENNESS OFFENSES

The President's Commission on Law Enforcement
and the Administration of Justice

Two million arrests in 1965—one of every three arrests in America— were for the offense of public drunkenness. The great volume of these

From The Task Force Report, *Drunkenness*, 1967, pp. 1-6.

arrests places an extremely heavy load on the operations of the criminal justice system. It burdens police, clogs lower criminal courts, and crowds penal institutions throughout the United States. . . .

THE EXISTING SYSTEM

DRUNKENNESS LAWS

Drunkenness is punishable under a variety of laws, generally describing the offense as being "drunk in a public place," often without providing a precise definition of drunkenness itself. Some laws include as a condition that the offender is "unable to care for his own safety."

In some jurisdictions there are no laws prohibiting drunkenness, but any drunkenness that causes a breach of the peace is punishable. In Georgia and Alabama, for example, drunkenness that is manifested by boisterous or indecent conduct, or loud and profane discourse, is a crime. Other jurisdictions apply disorderly conduct statutes to those who are drunk in public. In Chicago, for example, the police, having no drunkenness law to enforce use a disorderly conduct statute to arrest nondisorderly inebriates. Some jurisdictions permit police to make public drunkenness arrests under both State laws and local ordinances.

The laws provide maximum jail sentences ranging from 5 days to 6 months; the most common maximum sentence is 30 days. In some States an offender convicted of "habitual drunkenness" may be punished by a 2-year sentence of imprisonment.

THE OFFENDERS

The 2 million arrests for drunkenness each year involve both sporadic and regular drinkers. Among the number are a wide variety of offenders —the rowdy college boy; the weekend inebriate; the homeless, often unemployed single man. How many offenders fall into these and other categories is not known. Neither is it known how many of the offenders are alcoholics in the medical sense of being dependent on alcohol. There is strong evidence, however, that a large number of those who are arrested have a lengthy history of prior drunkenness arrests, and that a disproportionate number involve poor persons who live in slums. In 1964 in the city of Los Angeles about one-fifth of all persons arrested for drunkenness accounted for two-thirds of the total number of arrests for that offense. Some of the repeaters were arrested as many as 18 times in that year. . . .

The great majority of repeaters live on "skid row"—a dilapidated area found in most large and medium-size cities in the United States. On skid row substandard hotels and roominghouses are intermingled with numerous taverns, pawn shops, cheap cafeterias, employment agencies that specialize in jobs for the unskilled, and religious missions that provide free meals after a service. Many of the residents—including the chronic drunkenness offenders—are homeless, penniless, and beset with acute personal problems.

The police do not arrest everyone who is under the influence of alcohol. Sometimes they will help an inebriate home. It is when he appears to have no home or family ties that he is most likely to be arrested and taken to the local jail.

One policeman assigned to a skid row precinct in a large eastern city recently described how he decided whom to arrest:

> I see a guy who's been hanging around; a guy who's been picked up before or been making trouble. I stop him. Sometimes he can convince me he's got a job today or got something to do. He'll show me a slip showing he's supposed to go to the blood bank, or to work. I let him go. But if it seems to me that he's got nothing to do but drink, then I bring him in.

Drunkenness arrest practices vary from place to place. Some police departments strictly enforce drunkenness statutes, while other departments are known to be more tolerant. In fact, the number of arrests in a city may be related less to the amount of public drunkenness than to police policy. . . .

In some large and medium-size cities, police departments have "bum squads" that cruise skid rows and border areas to apprehend inebriates who appear unable to care for their own safety, or who are likely to annoy others. Such wholesale arrests sometimes include homeless people who are not intoxicated.

OPERATION OF THE CRIMINAL SYSTEM AFTER ARREST

Following arrest, the drunk is usually placed in a barren cell called a "tank," where he is detained for at least a few hours. The tanks in some cities can hold as many as 200 people, while others hold only 1 or 2. One report described the conditions found in a tank in this way:

> Although he may have been picked up for his own protection, the offender is placed in a cell, which may frequently hold as many as 40–50 men where there is no room to sit or lie down, where sanitary facilities and ventilation are inadequate and a stench of vomit and urine is prevalent.
>
> The drunken behavior of some of the inmates is an added hazard. It is questionable whether greater safety is achieved for the individual who is arrested for his safe keeping.

The chronic alcoholic offender generally suffers from a variety of ailments and is often in danger of serious medical complications, but medical care is rarely provided in the tank; and it is difficult to detect or to diagnose serious illness since it often resembles intoxication. Occasionally, chronic offenders become ill during pretrial detention and die without having received adequate medical attention. . . .

If the offender can afford bail, he usually obtains release after he sobers up. In many jurisdictions an offender is permitted to forfeit bail routinely by not appearing in court. Thus, if the arrested person has the few dollars required, he can avoid prosecution; if he has no money, as is usually the case, he must appear in court.

Drunkenness offenders are generally brought before a judge the morning after their arrest, sometimes appearing in groups of 15 or 20. Rarely are the normal procedural or due process safeguards applied to these cases. Usually defendants are processed through the court system with haste and either released or sentenced to several days or weeks in jail. In some cities only those offenders who request it are jailed. In others chronic offenders, who are likely to be alcoholics, are generally sent to jail.

When a defendant serves a short sentence, he is fed, sheltered, and given access to available recreational facilities. In most institutions there is such a lack of facilities and financial resources that it is not possible to do more. Austin MacCormick, a former New York City commissioner of corrections, noted recently:

> The appallingly poor quality of most of the county jails in the United States is so well known that it is probably not necessary to discuss this point at any great length. The fact that the majority of all convicted alcoholics go to these institutions, however, makes it imperative that the public, and particularly those thoughtful citizens who are interested in the treatment of alcoholics, never be allowed to forget that our county jails are a disgrace to the country . . . and that they have a destructive rather than a beneficial effect not only on alcoholics who are committed to them but also on those others who are convicted of the most petty offenses.

After serving a brief sentence, the chronic offender is released, more likely than not to return to his former haunts on skid row, with no money, no job, and no plans. Often he is rearrested within a matter of days or hours. . . .

EVALUATION OF THE EXISTING SYSTEM

EFFECT ON THE OFFENDER

The criminal justice system appears ineffective to deter drunkenness or to meet the problems of the chronic alcoholic offender. What the system usually does accomplish is to remove the drunk from public view, detoxify him, and provide him with food, shelter, emergency medical service, and a brief period of forced sobriety. As presently constituted, the system is not in a position to meet his underlying medical and social problems.

EFFECT ON THE SYSTEM OF CRIMINAL JUSTICE

Including drunkenness within the system of criminal justice seriously burdens and distorts its operations. Because the police often do not arrest the intoxicated person who has a home, there is in arrest practices an inherent discrimination against the homeless and the poor. Due process safeguards are often considered unnecessary or futile. The defendant may not be warned of his rights or permitted to make a telephone call. And although coordination, breath, or blood tests to determine intoxication are common practice in "driving-while-intoxicated" cases, they are virtually nonexistent in common drunk cases. Yet, without the use of such chemical tests, it is often difficult to determine whether the individual is intoxicated or suffering from a serious illness that has symptoms similar to intoxication.

The handling of drunkenness cases in court hardly reflects the standards of fairness that are the basis of our system of criminal justice. One major reason is that counsel is rarely present. Drunkenness cases often involve complex factual and medical issues. Cross-examination could be conducted on "observations" of the arresting officer such as "bloodshot" and "glassy" eyes, "staggering gait," "odor" of alcohol on the defendant's breath. The testimony of an expert medical witness on behalf of the defendant could be elicited.

The extent of police time allotted to handling drunkenness offenders varies from city to city and from precinct to precinct. In most cities a great deal of time is spent. The inebriate must be taken into custody, transported to jail, booked, detained, clothed, fed, sheltered, and transported to court. In some jurisdictions, police officers must wait, often for hours, to testify in court.

There is a commensurate burden on the urban courts. Notwithstanding the fact that an overwhelming caseload often leads judges to dispose of scores of drunkenness cases in minutes, they represent a significant drain on court time which is needed for felony and serious misdemeanor cases. More subtly, drunkenness cases impair the dignity of the criminal process in lower courts, which are forced to handle defendants so casually and to apply criminal sanctions with so little apparent effect.

In correctional systems, too, resources are diverted from serious offenders. After court appearance, some offenders are sent to short-term penal institutions, many of which are already overcrowded. Correctional authorities estimate that one-half the entire misdemeanant population is comprised of drunkenness offenders. In one city it was reported that 95 percent of short-term prisoners were drunkenness offenders.

LINES FOR ACTION

The sheer size of the drunkenness problem in relation to the very limited knowledge about causes and treatment makes it impossible to speak in terms of "solutions." There are, however, some important and promising lines that the Commission believes should be explored.

TREATING DRUNKENNESS AS NONCRIMINAL

The Commission seriously doubts that drunkenness alone (as distinguished from disorderly conduct) should continue to be treated as a crime. Most of the experts with whom the Commission discussed this matter, including many in law enforcement, thought that it should not be a crime. The application of disorderly conduct statutes would be sufficient to protect the public against criminal behavior stemming from intoxication. This was the view of the President's Commission on Crime in the District of Columbia, which recommended that the District of Columbia drunkenness law "be amended to require specific kinds of offensive conduct in addition to drunkenness."

Perhaps the strongest barrier to making such a change is that there presently are no clear alternatives for taking into custody and treating those who are now arrested as drunks. The Commission believes that current efforts to find such alternatives to treatment within the criminal system should be expanded. For example, if adequate public health facilities for detoxification are developed, civil legislation could be enacted authorizing the police to pick up those drunks who refuse to or are unable to cooperate—if, indeed, such specific authorization is necessary. Such legislation could expressly sanction a period of detention and allow the individual to be released from a public health facility only when he is sober.

The Commission recommends:

Drunkenness should not in itself be a criminal offense. Disorderly and other criminal conduct accompanied by drunkenness should remain punishable as separate crimes. The implementation of this recommendation requires the development of adequate civil detoxification procedures.

Among those seeking alternatives to processing drunkenness cases through the criminal system are the Vera Institute of Justice in New York City and the South End Center for Alcoholics and Unattached Persons in Boston. The Vera Institute has recently undertaken a project to explore the feasibility of using personnel other than the police to pick up drunks. Included in the study is an attempt to determine what percentage of drunks will come to a treatment facility voluntarily. The Vera program would circumvent the criminal process by establishing a system within a public health framework to care for the immediate and long-range needs of the skid row inebriate.

The Boston program, which has received funds from the Office of Economic Opportunity, provides an alternative to the police-correctional handling of the homeless alcoholic. Staff personnel of the Boston South End Center have approached homeless inebriates in skid row and offered them assistance. An official of the program estimates that 80 percent of the people approached in this way responded willingly. The center screens and evaluates the cases and refers homeless alcoholics to appropriate community facilities. In the past year it has handled the cases of over 900 homeless alcoholics. . . .

DETOXIFICATION CENTERS

An alternate approach to present methods of handling drunkenness offenders after arrest and a prerequisite to taking drunkenness out of the criminal system is the establishment of civil detoxification centers. The detoxification center would replace the police station as an initial detention unit for inebriates. Under the authority of civil legislation, the inebriate would be brought to this public health facility by the police and detained there until sober. Thereafter, the decision to continue treatment should be left to the individual. Experience in New York and Boston indicates that some alcoholics may be willing to accept treatment beyond the initial "sobering up" period. . . .

The Commission recommends:

Communities should establish detoxification units as part of comprehensive treatment programs.

The Department of Justice has recently provided funds to establish detoxification centers as demonstration projects in St. Louis and Washington, D.C. The St. Louis center is already in full operation; plans for the Washington center are underway. Both units have sufficient facilities to house for a period of a few days those who are in need of "drying out." They also have "inpatient programs," in which patients are given high protein meals with vitamin and mineral supplements and appropriate medication to alleviate alcohol withdrawal symptoms. Bath and laundry facilities are available, as are basic clothing and limited recreational facilities. Regularly scheduled Alcoholics Anonymous meetings, film showings, work projects, group therapy, and lectures are part of the program. During their stay patients are counseled by social workers and other staff members.

The police might also bring to such a center intoxicated persons charged with a variety of petty offenses apart from drunkenness, with violations of administrative codes, and with such felony offenses as driving while intoxicated, assault, and larceny. If the police planned to prosecute the case, a summons could be left with the offender to appear in court at a later date. If an intoxicated defendant was charged with committing a felony, the police could make an individual determination as to the most appropriate detention facility. If he seemed likely to appear in court he might be taken to the detoxification facility. Otherwise, he would presumably be taken to the local jail, unless there were adequate detention facilities on the premises of the detoxification center.

AFTERCARE PROGRAMS

There is little reason to believe that the chronic offender will change a life pattern of drinking after a few days of sobriety and care at a public health unit. The detoxification unit should therefore be supplemented by a network of coordinated "aftercare" facilities. Such a program might well begin with the mobilization of existing community resources. Alcoholics Anonymous programs, locally based missions, hospitals, mental health agencies, outpatient centers, employment counseling, and other social service programs should be coordinated and used by the staff of the detoxification center for referral purposes. It is well recognized among authorities that homeless alcoholics cannot be treated without supportive residential housing, which can be used as a base from which to reintegrate them into society. Therefore, the network of aftercare facilities should be expanded to include halfway houses, community shelters, and other forms of public housing.

The Commission recommends:

Communities should coordinate and extend aftercare resources, including supportive residential housing.

The success of aftercare facilities will depend upon the ability of the detoxification unit to diagnose problems adequately and to make appropriate referrals. A diagnostic unit attached to, or used by, the detoxification unit could formulate treatment plans by conducting a thorough medical and social evaluation of every patient. Diagnostic work should include assistance to the patient and his family in obtaining counseling for economic, marital, or employment problems. . . .

RESEARCH

With over 5 million alcoholics in the country, alcoholism is the Nation's fourth largest health problem. Research aimed at developing new methods and facilities for treating alcoholics should be given the priority called for by the scope of the need.

The Commission recommends:

Research by private and governmental agencies into alcoholism, the problems of alcoholics, and methods of treatment, should be expanded.

The application of funds for research purposes appears to be an appropriate supplement to the proposed detoxification and treatment units. Consideration should be given to providing further legislation on the Federal level for the promotion of the necessary coordinated treatment programs. Only through such a joint commitment will the burdens of the present system, which fall on both the criminal system and the drunkenness offender, be alleviated.

PHASES OF ALCOHOL ADDICTION

E. M. Jellinek

Only certain forms of excessive drinking—those which in the present report are designated as alcoholism—are accessible to medical-psychiatric treatment. The other forms of excessive drinking, too, present more or less serious problems, but they can be managed only on the level of applied sociology, including law enforcement. Nevertheless, the medical profession may have an advisory role in the handling of these latter problems and must take an interest in them from the viewpoint of preventive medicine.

The conditions which have been briefly defined by the Alcoholism Subcommittee of the World Health Organization as alcoholism are described in the following pages in greater detail, in order to delimit more definitely those excessive drinkers whose rehabilitation primarily requires medical-psychiatric treatment. Furthermore, such detailed description may serve to forestall a certain potential danger which attaches to the disease conception of alcoholism, or, more precisely, of addictive drinking. . . .

THE DISEASE CONCEPTION OF ALCOHOL ADDICTION

The Subcommittee has distinguished two categories of alcoholics, namely, "alcohol addicts" and "habitual symptomatic excessive drinkers." For

Alcoholism Subcommittee of the World Health Organization, Second Report, Annex 2, World Health Organization Technical Report Series No. 48, August 1952. Reprinted by permission.

brevity's sake the latter will be referred to as non-addictive alcoholics. Strictly speaking, the disease conception attaches to the alcohol addicts only, but not to the habitual symptomatic excessive drinkers.

In both groups the excessive drinking is symptomatic of underlying psychological or social pathology, but in one group after several years of excessive drinking "loss of control" over the alcohol intake occurs, while in the other group this phenomenon never develops. The group with the loss of control is designated as "alcohol addicts." (There are other differences between these two groups and these will be seen in the course of the description of the "phases.")

The disease conception of alcohol addiction does not apply to the excessive drinking, but solely to the loss of control which occurs in only one group of alcoholics and then only after many years of excessive drinking. There is no intention to deny that the non-addictive alcoholic is a sick person; but his ailment is not the excessive drinking, but rather the psychological or social difficulties from which alcohol intoxication gives temporary surcease.

The loss of control is a disease condition per se which results from a process that superimposes itself upon those abnormal psychological conditions of which excessive drinking is a symptom. The fact that many excessive drinkers drink as much as or more than the addict for 30 or 40 years without developing loss of control indicates that in the group of alcohol addicts a superimposed process must occur.

Whether this superimposed process is of a psychopathological nature or whether some physical pathology is involved cannot be stated as yet with any degree of assurance, the claims of various investigators notwithstanding. Nor is it possible to go beyond conjecture concerning the question whether the loss of control originates in a predisposing factor (psychological or physical), or whether it is a factor acquired in the course of prolonged excessive drinking.

The fact that this loss of control does not occur in a large group of excessive drinkers would point towards a predisposing X factor in the addictive alcoholics. On the other hand this explanation is not indispensable, as the difference between addictive and non-addictive alcoholics could be a matter of acquired modes of living—for instance, a difference in acquired nutritional habits.

THE MEANING OF SYMPTOMATIC DRINKING

The use of alcoholic beverages by society has primarily a symbolic meaning, and secondarily it achieves "function." Cultures which accept this custom differ in the nature and degree of the "functions," which they regard as legitimate. The differences in these functions are determined by the general pattern of the culture—for example, the need for the release and for the special control of aggression, the need and the ways and means of achieving identification, and the nature and intensity of anxieties and the modus for their relief. The more the original symbolic character of the custom is preserved, the less room will be granted by the culture to the functions of drinking.

Any drinking within the accepted ways is symptomatic of the culture of which the drinker is a member. Within that frame of cultural symptomatology there may be in addition individual symptoms expressed in the act of drinking. The fact that a given individual drinks a glass of beer with his meal may be the symptom of the culture which accepts such a use as a refreshment, or as a "nutritional supplement." That this individual drinks at this given moment may be a symptom of his fatigue, his elation, or some other mood, and thus an individual symptom, but, if his culture accepts the use for these purposes, it is at the same time a cultural symptom. In this sense even the small or moderate use of alcoholic beverages is symptomatic, and it may be said that all drinkers are culturally symptomatic drinkers or, at least, started as such.

The vast majority of the users of alcoholic beverages stay within the limits of the culturally accepted drinking behaviors and drink predominantly as an expression of their culture. While an individual expression may be present in these behaviors its role remains insignificant.

For the purpose of the present discussion the expression "symptomatic drinking" will be limited to the predominant use of alcoholic beverages for the relief of major individual stresses.

A certain unknown proportion of these users of alcoholic beverages, perhaps 20 per cent, are occasionally inclined to take advantage of the functions of alcohol which they have experienced in the course of its "cultural use." At least at times, the individual motivation becomes predominant and on those occasions alcohol loses its character as an ingredient of a beverage and is used as a drug.

The "occasional symptomatic excessive drinker" tends to take care of the stresses and strains of living in socially accepted—that is, "normal"— ways, and his drinking is most of the time within the cultural pattern. After a long accumulation of stresses, however, or because of some particularly heavy stress, his tolerance for tension is lowered and he takes recourse to heroic relief of his symptoms through alcoholic intoxication. Under these circumstances the "relief" may take on an explosive character, and thus the occasional symptomatic excessive drinker may create serious problems. No psychological abnormality can be claimed for this type of drinker, although he does not represent a well-integrated personality.

Nevertheless, within the group of apparent occasional symptomatic excessive drinkers, there is a certain proportion of definitely deviating personalities who after a shorter or longer period of occasional sympto-matic relief take recourse to a constant alcoholic relief, and drinking be-comes with them a "mode of living." These are the "alcoholics" of whom again a certain proportion suffer loss of control—that is, become ad-dictive alcoholics.

The proportion of alcoholics (addictive and non-addictive) varies from country to country, but does not seem to exceed in any country 5 per cent or 6 per cent of all users of alcoholic beverages. The ratio of addictive to non-addictive alcoholics is unknown.

THE CHART OF ALCOHOL ADDICTION

The course of alcohol addiction is represented graphically in Figure 1. The diagram is based on an analysis of more than two thousand drink-ing histories of male alcohol addicts. Not all symptoms shown in the diagram occur necessarily in all alcohol addicts, nor do they occur in every addict in the same sequence. The "phases" and the sequences of symptoms within the phases are characteristic, however, of the great majority of alcohol addicts and represent what may be called the average trend.

For alcoholic women the phases are not as clear cut as in men, and the development is frequently more rapid.

The phases vary in their duration according to individual character-istics and environmental factors. The "lengths" of the different phases on the diagram do not indicate differences in duration but are determined by the number of symptoms which have to be shown in any given phase.

The chart of the phases of alcohol addiction serves as the basis of description, and the differences between addictive and non-addictive alcoholics are indicated in the text.

1. THE PREALCOHOLIC SYMPTOMATIC PHASE

The very beginning of the use of alcoholic beverages is always socially motivated in the prospective addictive and non-addictive alcoholic. In contrast to the average social drinker, however, the prospective alcoholic (together with the occasional symptomatic excessive drinker) soon ex-periences a rewarding relief in the drinking situation. The relief is strongly marked in his case because either his tensions are much greater than in other members of his social circle, or he has not learned to handle those tensions as others do.

Initially this drinker ascribes his relief to the situation rather than to the drinking and he seeks therefore those situations in which incidental drinking will occur. Sooner or later, of course, he becomes aware of the contingency between relief and drinking.

In the beginning he seeks this relief occasionally only, but in the

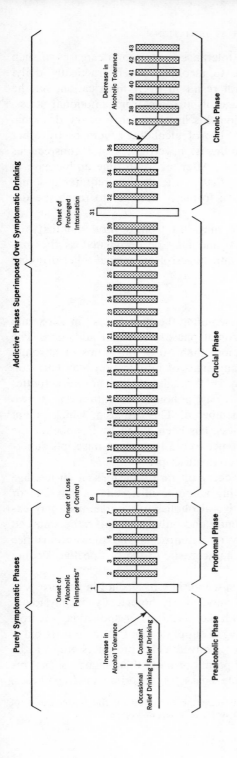

Figure 1. The phases of alcohol addiction. The large bars denote the onset of major symptoms that initiate phases. The short bars denote the onset of symptoms within phases. Reference to the numbering of the symptoms is made in the text, where the numbers appear in boldface type in parentheses.

course of 6 months to 2 years his tolerance for tension decreases to such a degree that he takes recourse to alcoholic relief practically daily. Nevertheless his drinking does not result in overt intoxication, but he reaches toward the evening a stage of surcease from emotional stress. Even in the absence of intoxication this involves fairly heavy drinking, particularly in comparison to the use of alcoholic beverages by other members of his circle. The drinking is, nevertheless, not conspicuous either to his associates or to himself. After a certain time an increase in alcohol tolerance may be noticed; that is, the drinker requires a somewhat larger amount of alcohol than formerly in order to reach the desired stage of sedation.

This type of drinking behavior may last from several months to 2 years, according to circumstances, and may be designated as the prealcoholic phase, which is divided into stages of occasional relief drinking and constant relief drinking.

2. THE PRODROMAL PHASE

The sudden onset of a behavior resembling the "blackouts" in anoxemia marks the beginning of the prodromal phase of alcohol addiction. The drinker who may have had not more than 50 or 60 grams of absolute alcohol and who is not showing any signs of intoxication may carry on a reasonable conversation or may go through quite elaborate activities without a trace of memory the next day, although sometimes one or two minor details may be hazily remembered. This amnesia, which is not connected with loss of consciousness, has been called by Bonhoeffer the "alcoholic palimpsests," with reference to old Roman manuscripts superimposed over an incompletely erased manuscript.

Alcohol palimpsests (1)* may occur on rare occasions in an average drinker when he drinks intoxicating amounts in a state of physical or emotional exhaustion. Non-addictive alcoholics, of course, also may experience palimpsests, but infrequently and only following rather marked intoxication. Thus, the frequency of palimpsests and their occurrence after medium alcohol intake are characteristic of the prospective alcohol addict.

This would suggest heightened susceptibility to alcohol in the prospective addict. Such a susceptibility may be psychologically or physiologically determined. The analogy with the blackouts of anoxemia is tempting. Of course, an insufficient oxygen supply cannot be assumed, but a malutilization of oxygen may be involved. The present status of the knowledge of alcoholism does not permit of more than vague conjectures which, nevertheless, may constitute bases for experimental hypotheses.

---

* The numerals in boldface type in parentheses following the designations of the individual symptoms represent their order as given in Figure 1.

The onset of alcoholic palimpsests is followed (in some instances preceded) by the onset of drinking behaviors which indicate that, for this drinker, beer, wine, and spirits have practically ceased to be beverages and have become sources of a drug which he "needs." Some of these behaviors imply that this drinker has some vague realization that he drinks differently from others.

Surreptitious drinking (2) is one of these behaviors. At social gatherings the drinker seeks occasions for having a few drinks unknown to others, as he fears that if it were known that he drinks more than the others he would be misjudged. Those to whom drinking is only a custom or a small pleasure would not understand that because he is different from them alcohol is for him a necessity, although he is not a drunkard.

Preoccupation with alcohol (3) is further evidence of this need. When he prepares to go to a social gathering his first thought is whether there will be sufficient alcohol for his requirements, and he has several drinks in anticipation of a possible shortage. Because of this increasing dependence upon alcohol, the onset of *avid drinking* (4) (gulping of the first or first two drinks) occurs at this time.

As the drinker realizes, at least vaguely, that his drinking is outside of the ordinary, he develops *guilt feelings about his drinking behavior* (5), and because of this he begins to *avoid reference to alcohol* (6) in conversation.

These behaviors, together with an *increasing frequency of alcoholic palimpsests* (7), foreshadow the development of alcohol addiction, they are premonitory signs. This period may be called the prodromal phase of alcohol addiction.

The consumption of alcoholic beverages in the prodromal phase is "heavy," but not conspicuous, as it does not lead to marked, overt intoxications. The effect is that the prospective addict reaches towards evening a state which may be designated as emotional anesthesia. Nevertheless, this condition requires drinking well beyond the ordinary usage. The drinking is on a level which may begin to interfere with metabolic and nervous processes as evidenced by the frequent alcoholic palimpsests.

The "covering-up" which is shown by the drinker in this stage is the first sign that his drinking might separate him from society, although initially the drinking may have served as a technique to overcome some lack of social integration.

As in the prodromal phase rationalizations of the drinking behavior are not strong and there is some insight as well as fear of possible consequences, it is feasible to intercept incipient alcohol addiction at this stage. In the United States of America, the publicity given to the prodromal symptoms begins to bring prospective alcoholics to clinics as well as to groups of Alcoholics Anonymous. It goes without saying that even at this stage the only possible modus for this type of drinker is total abstinence.

The prodromal period may last anywhere from 6 months to 4 or 5 years according to the physical and psychological makeup of the drinker, his family ties, vocational relations, general interests, and so forth. The prodromal phase ends and the crucial or acute phase begins with the onset of loss of control, which is the critical symptom of alcohol addiction.

3. THE CRUCIAL PHASE

Loss of control (8) means that any drinking of alcohol starts a chain reaction which is felt by the drinker as a physical demand for alcohol. This state, possibly a conversion phenomenon, may take hours or weeks for its full development; it lasts until the drinker is too intoxicated or too sick to ingest more alcohol. The physical discomfort following this drinking behavior is contrary to the object of the drinker, which is merely to feel "different." As a matter of fact, the bout may not even be started by any individual need of the moment, but by a "social drink."

After recovery from the intoxication, it is not the loss of control—that is, the physical demand, apparent or real—which leads to a new bout after several days or several weeks. The renewal of drinking is set off by the original psychological conflicts or by a simple social situation which involves drinking.

The loss of control is effective after the individual has started drinking, but it does not give rise to the beginning of a new drinking bout. The drinker has lost the ability to control the quantity once he has started, but he still can control whether he will drink on any given occasion or not. This is evidenced in the fact that after the onset of loss of control the drinker can go through a period of voluntary abstinence ("going on the water wagon").

The question of why the drinker returns to drinking after repeated disastrous experiences is often raised. Although he will not admit it, the alcohol addict believes that he has lost his will power and that he can and must regain it. He is not aware that he has undergone a process which makes it impossible for him to control his alcohol intake. To "master his will" becomes a matter of the greatest importance to him. When tensions rise, "a drink" is the natural remedy for him and he is convinced that this time it will be one or two drinks only.

Practically simultaneously with the onset of loss of control the alcohol addict begins to *rationalize his drinking behavior* (9): he produces the well-known alcoholic *"alibis."* He finds explanations which convince him that he did not lose control, but that he had a good reason to get intoxicated and that in the absence of such reasons he is able to handle alcohol as well as anybody else. These rationalizations are needed primarily for himself and only secondarily for his family and associates. The rationalizations make it possible for him to continue with his drinking, and this is of the greatest importance to him as he knows no alternative for handling his problems.

This is the beginning of an entire "system of rationalizations" which progressively spreads to every aspect of his life. While this system largely originates in inner needs, it also serves to counter *social pressures* (10) which arise at the time of the loss of control. At this time, of course, the drinking behavior becomes conspicuous, and the parents, wife, friends, and employer may begin to reprove and warn the drinker.

In spite of all the rationalizations there is a marked loss of self-esteem, and this of course demands compensations which in a certain sense are also rationalizations. One way of compensation is the *grandiose behavior* (11) which the addict begins to display at this time. Extravagant expenditures and grandiloquence convince him that he is not as bad as he had thought at times.

The rationalization system gives rise to another system, namely the "system of isolation." The rationalizations quite naturally lead to the idea that the fault lies not within himself but in others, and this results in a progressive withdrawal from the social environment. The first sign of this attitude is a *marked aggressive behavior* (12).

Inevitably, this latter behavior generates guilt. While even in the prodromal period remorse about the drinking arose from time to time, now *persistent remorse* (13) arises, and this added tension is a further source of drinking.

In compliance with social pressures the addict now goes on *periods of total abstinence* (14). There is, however, another modus of control of drinking which arises out of the rationalizations of the addict. He believes that his trouble arises from his not drinking the right kind of beverages or not in the right way. He now attempts to control his troubles by *changing the pattern on his drinking* (15), by setting up rules about not drinking before a certain hour of the day, in certain places only, and so forth.

The strain of the struggle increases his hostility towards his environment and he begins to *drop friends* (16) and *quit jobs* (17). It goes without saying that some associates drop him and that he loses some jobs, but more frequently he takes the initiative as an anticipatory defense.

The isolation becomes more pronounced as his entire *behavior becomes alcohol centered* (18); that is, he begins to be concerned about how activities might interfere with his drinking instead of how his drinking may affect his activities. This, of course, involves a more marked egocentric outlook which leads to more rationalizations and more isolation. There ensues a *loss of outside interests* (19) and a *reinterpretation of interpersonal relations* (20) coupled with *marked self-pity* (21). The isolation and rationalizations have increased by this time in intensity and find their expression either in contemplated or actual *geographic escape* (22).

Under the impact of these events, a *change in family habits* (23) occurs. The wife and children, who may have had good social activities, may withdraw for fear of embarrassment or, quite contrarily, they may suddenly begin intensive outside activities in order to escape from the home environment. This and other events lead to the onset of *unreasonable resentments* (24) in the alcohol addict.

The predominance of concern with alcohol induces the addict to *protect his supply* (25)—that is, to lay in a large stock of alcoholic beverages, hidden in the most unthought-of places. A fear of being deprived of the most necessary substance for his living is expressed in this behavior.

Neglect of proper nutrition (26) aggravates the beginnings of the effects of heavy drinking on the organism, and frequently the *first hospitalization* (27) for some alcoholic complaint occurs at this time.

One of the frequent organic effects is a *decrease of the sexual drive* (28) which increases hostility towards the wife and is rationalized into her extramarital sex activities, which gives rise to the well-known *alcoholic jealousy* (29).

By this time remorse, resentment, struggle between alcoholic needs and duties, loss of self-esteem, and doubts and false reassurance have so disorganized the addict that he cannot start the day without steadying himself with alcohol immediately after arising or even before getting out of bed. This is the beginning of *regular matutinal drinking* (30), which previously had occurred on rare occasions only.

This behavior terminates the crucial phase and foreshadows the beginnings of the chronic phase.

During the crucial phase intoxication is the rule, but it is limited to the evening hours. For the most part of this phase drinking begins sometime in the afternoon and by the evening intoxication is reached. It should be noted that the "physical demand" involved in the loss of control results in continual rather than continuous drinking. Particularly the "matutinal drink" which occurs toward the end of the crucial phase shows the continual pattern. The first drink at rising, let us say at 7 A.M., is followed by another drink at 10 or 11 A.M., and another drink around 1 P.M., while the more intensive drinking hardly starts before 5 P.M.

Throughout, the crucial phase presents a great struggle of the addict against the complete loss of social footing. Occasionally the aftereffects of the evening's intoxication cause some loss of time, but generally the addict succeeds in looking after his job, although he neglects his family. He makes a particularly strong effort to avoid intoxication during the day. Progressively, however, his social motivations weaken more and more, and the "morning drink" jeopardizes his effort to comply with his vocational duties as this effort involves a conscious resistance against the apparent or real physical demand for alcohol.

The onset of the loss of control is the beginning of the "disease process" of alcohol addiction which is superimposed over the excessive symptomatic drinking. Progressively, this disease process undermines the morale and the physical resistance of the addict.

4. THE CHRONIC PHASE

The increasingly dominating role of alcohol, and the struggle against the demand set up by matutinal drinking, at last break down the resistance of the addict and he finds himself for the first time intoxicated in the daytime and on a weekday and continues in that state for several days until he is entirely incapacitated. This is the onset of *prolonged intoxications* (31), referred to in the vernacular as "benders."

This latter drinking behavior meets with such unanimous social rejection that it involves a grave social risk. Only an originally psychopathic personality or a person who has later in life undergone a psychopathological process would expose himself to that risk.

These long-drawn-out bouts commonly bring about *marked ethical deterioration* (32) and *impairment of thinking* (33), which, however, are not irreversible. True *alcoholic psychoses* (34) may occur at this time, but in not more than 10 per cent of all alcoholics.

The loss of morale is so heightened that the addict *drinks with persons far below his social level* (35) in preference to his usual associates—perhaps as an opportunity to appear superior—and, if nothing else is available, he will *take recourse to "technical products"* (36) such as bay rum or rubbing alcohol.

A *loss of alcohol tolerance* (37) is commonly noted at this time. Half of the previously required amount of alcohol may be sufficient to bring about a stuporous state.

Indefinable fears (38) and *tremors* (39) become persistent. Sporadically these symptoms occur also during the crucial phase, but in the chronic phase they are present as soon as alcohol disappears from the organism. In consequence, the addict "controls" the symptoms through alcohol. The same is true of *psychomotor inhibition* (40), the inability to initiate a simple mechanical act—such as winding a watch—in the absence of alcohol.

The need to control these symptoms of drinking exceeds the need of relieving the original underlying symptoms of the personality conflict, and the *drinking takes on an obsessive character* (41).

In many addicts, approximately 60 per cent, some *vague religious desires develop* (42) as the rationalization becomes weaker. Finally, in the course of the frequently prolonged intoxications, the rationalizations become so frequently and so mercilessly tested against reality that the entire *rationalization system fails* (43) and the addict admits defeat. He now becomes spontaneously accessible to treatment. Nevertheless, his obsessive drinking continues as he does not see a way out.

Formerly it was thought that the addict must reach this stage of utter defeat in order to be treated successfully. Clinical experience has shown, however, that this "defeat" can be induced long before it would occur of itself and that even incipient alcoholism can be intercepted. Since the incipient alcoholic can be easily recognized, it is possible to tackle the problem from the preventive angle.

5. THE "ALCOHOLIC PERSONALITY"

The aggressions, feelings of guilt, remorse, resentments, withdrawal, etc., which develop in the phases of alcohol addiction, are largely consequences of the excessive drinking. At the same time, however, they constitute sources of more excessive drinking.

In addition to relieving, through alcohol, symptoms of an underlying personality conflict, the addict now tends to relieve, through further drinking, the stresses created by his drinking behavior.

By and large, these reactions to excessive drinking—which have quite a neurotic appearance—give the impression of an "alcoholic personality," although they are secondary behaviors superimposed over a large variety of personality types which have a few traits in common, in particular a low capacity for coping with tensions. There does not emerge, however, any specific personality trait or physical characteristic which inevitably would lead to excessive symptomatic drinking. Apart from psychological and possibly physical liabilities, there must be a constellation of social and economic factors which facilitate the development of addictive and non-addictive alcoholism in a susceptible terrain.

THE NON-ADDICTIVE ALCOHOLIC

Some differences between the non-addictive alcoholic and the alcohol addict have previously been stated in this chapter. These differences may be recapitulated and elaborated, and additional differential features may be considered.

The main difference may be readily visualized by erasing the large bars of the diagram in Figure 1. This results in a diagram which suggests a progressive exacerbation of the use of alcohol for symptom relief and of the social and health consequences incumbent upon such use, but without any clear-cut phases.

The prealcoholic phase is the same for the non-addictive alcoholic as for the alcohol addict. That is to say, he progresses from occasional to constant relief of individual symptoms through alcohol.

The behaviors which denote that alcohol has become a drug rather than an ingredient of a beverage—symptoms (2) to (6)—occur also in the non-addictive drinker, but, as mentioned before, the alcoholic palimpsests occur rarely and only after overt intoxication.

Loss of control is not experienced by the non-addictive alcoholic, and this is the main differentiating criterion between the two categories of alcoholics. Initially, of course, it could not be said whether the drinker had yet reached the crucial phase. However, after 10 or 12 years of heavy drinking without loss of control, while symptoms (2) to (6) were persistent and palimpsests were rare and did not occur after a medium intake of alcohol, the differential diagnosis is rather safe.

The absence of loss of control has many involvements. First of all, as there is no inability to stop drinking within a given situation there is no need to rationalize the inability. Nevertheless, rationalizations are developed for justifying the excessive use of alcohol and some neglect of the family attendant upon such use. Likewise, there is no need to change the pattern of drinking, which in the addict is an attempt to overcome the loss of control. Periods of total abstinence, however, occur as responses to social pressure.

On the other hand, there is the same tendency toward isolation as in the addict, but the social repercussions are much less marked, as the non-addictive alcoholic can avoid drunken behavior whenever the social situation requires it.

The effects of prolonged heavy drinking on the organism may occur in the non-addictive alcoholic too; even delirium tremens may develop. The libido may be diminished and "alcoholic jealousy" may result.

Generally, there is a tendency toward a progressive dominance of alcohol resulting in greater psychological and bodily effects. In the absence of any grave underlying psychopathies a deteriorative process is speeded up by habitual alcoholic excess, and such a non-addictive drinker may slide to the bottom of society.

ALCOHOLICS ANONYMOUS

Morris E. Chafetz and Harold W. Demone, Jr.

Alcoholics Anonymous was founded by a doctor, Dr. Bob, and a stockbroker, Bill W., at a chance meeting in Akron, Ohio, on June 10, 1935. Bill W. had, through a mystical experience, stopped drinking and he wanted to share his sobriety. Significantly, both founders had extensive contact with the Oxford Group Movement, participating actively in their respective homes of New York and Akron. The strong influence of the Oxonians survives and can be seen within the twelve steps of AA. Bill W. wrote, "the early Alcoholics Anonymous got its ideas of self-examination, acknowledgement of character defects, restitution for harm done, and working with others straight from the Oxford groups."

During the earliest days of AA the co-founders were able to maintain allegiance to both their own group and to the Oxford Group Movement. The separation from the older movement began in 1937, In New York, and a bit later in Akron. This was inevitable because their fundamental goals were sufficiently different to make success as a joint endeavor impossible. The Oxonians were broader in aim, attempting essentially to include all mankind. At the same time, the Oxford Group Movement used a "rather aggressive evangelism," and would not and could not "accept the principle of team guidance" for their personal lives. The need of the Oxonians to reach for the absolutes of purity, honesty, unselfishness, and love was too much to expect of the alcoholic waging his overwhelming battle with alcohol. Sobriety was a possibility. But to include the highest goals of the Christian ethic for personalities which had suffered from and had been subjected to some of the most detrimental forces of society seemed unrealistic. The final conflict between both groups involved the principle of anonymity. The alcoholic felt safe, secure, and comfortable surrounded anonymously by his similarly afflicted brothers, while the Oxonians thrived on the use of the names of prominent members. . . .

In the beginning, the growth of AA was extremely slow. Under Dr. Bob's influence, however, the Akron group solidified, and Bill W.'s efforts brought the same accomplishment in New York. Slowly the march began. From June 1935, through November 1937, sobriety had been

From *Alcoholism and Society* by Morris E. Chafetz and Harold W. Demone, Jr. Copyright © 1962 by Oxford University Press, Inc. Pp. 146-65. Reprinted by permission.

achieved by 40 alcoholics. By April 1939 the number had jumped to 100 and within a year, in early 1940, to 800. By the end of 1941, 8000 had found the respectable state of sobriety. With increasing strength the figures rolled in: by 1952 there were 150,000 and in 1960 the estimate had reached "more than 200,000."

AA is based upon Twelve Steps and Twelve Traditions. The intense, possibly overdramatized importance attributed to the Twelve Steps is described by co-founder Bill W. as follows: Unless each AA member follows to the best of his ability our suggested Twelve Steps of recovery, he almost certainly signs his own death warrant . . . we must obey certain principles, or we die." In spite of the strength of these words, Bill W. maintained that these steps were merely suggestions and that absolute belief in them was not a prerequisite for membership. They are as follows:

STEP ONE: "We admitted we were powerless ovèr alcohol—that our lives had become unmanageable."

· · ·

STEP TWO: "Came to believe that a Power greater than ourselves could restore us to sanity."

· · ·

STEP THREE: "Made a decision to turn our will and our lives over to the care of God as we understood Him."

· · ·

STEP FOUR: "Made a searching and fearless moral inventory of ourselves."

· · ·

STEP FIVE: "Admitted to God, to ourselves, and to another human being, the exact nature of our wrongs."

· · ·

STEP SIX: "Were entirely ready to have God remove all these defects of character."

· · ·

STEP SEVEN: "Humbly asked Him to remove our short-comings."

· · ·

STEP EIGHT: "Make a list of all persons we had harmed, and become willing to make amends to them all."

· · ·

STEP NINE: "Made direct amends to such people whenever possible, except when to do so would injure them or others."

· · ·

STEP TEN: "Continued to take personal inventory and when we were wrong promptly admitted it."

• • •

STEP ELEVEN: "Sought through prayer and meditation to improve our conscious contact with God as we understood Him, praying only for knowledge of His will for us and the power to carry that out."

• • •

STEP TWELVE: "Having had a spiritual awakening as the result of these steps, we tried to carry this message to alcoholics, and to practice these principles in all our affairs."

• • •

Now that we have viewed the steps the AA member must take to achieve sobriety, let us look at the AA traditions which provide continuity.

TRADITION ONE: "Our common welfare should come first; personal recovery depends on AA unity."

• • •

TRADITION TWO: "For our group purpose there is but one ultimate authority—a loving God as He may express Himself in our group conscience. Our leaders are but trusted servants; they do not govern."

• • •

TRADITION THREE: "The only requirement for AA membership is a desire to stop drinking."

• • •

TRADITION FOUR: "Each group should be autonomous except in matters affecting other groups or AA as a whole."

• • •

TRADITION FIVE: "Each group has but one primary purpose—to carry its message to the alcoholic who still suffers."

• • •

TRADITION SIX: "An AA group ought never endorse, finance, or lend the AA name to any related facility or outside enterprise lest problems of money, property, and prestige divert us from our primary purpose."

• • •

TRADITION SEVEN: "Every AA group ought to be fully self-supporting, declining outside contributions."

• • •

TRADITION EIGHT: "Alcoholics Anonymous should remain forever nonprofessional, but our service centers may employ special workers." . . .

. . .

TRADITION NINE: "AA, as such, ought never to be organized; but we may create service boards or committees directly responsible to those they serve."

. . .

TRADITION TEN: "Alcoholics Anonymous has no opinion on outside issues; hence the AA name ought never be drawn into public controversy."

. . .

TRADITION ELEVEN: "Our public relations policy is based on attraction rather than promotion; we need always maintain personal anonymity at the level of press, radio, and films."

. . .

TRADITION TWELVE: "Anonymity is the spiritual foundation of our traditions, ever reminding us to place principles before personalities."

. . .

While the Twelve Steps and Twelve Traditions are the backbone of AA, the reader will wonder if such a large evangelical movement can have no institutional structure at all. Its leaders are "servants" without governing power. Yet AA is not an anarchy or the utopian, communistic order in which only the masses rule. They have their General Service Board made up of nonalcoholics (in the majority) and AA members. The Board assumes the responsibility for the integrity and service standards of AA's General Service Headquarters. In addition, there is the General Service Conference Charter. The Conference is not incorporated, nor is the Charter a legal instrument. Rather the Conference meets periodically to elect delegates from United States and Canadian groups and to perpetuate and guide AA in its world service. In New York, where the General Headquarters of AA is located, the linkage to the various groups throughout the world is maintained. Besides maintaining domestic and foreign group relations, General Headquarters fulfills various other duties.

AA speaks through its General Service Conference, General Service Board, Headquarters, and most effectively through its publications printed by the Alcoholics Anonymous Publishing Company. Besides books . . . the company publishes *AA Grapevine,* a monthly journal of a circulation of approximately 50,000. The *AA Grapevine,* well edited and well written, is a systematic and continuous effort on the part of AA to improve communication among its members and groups. In fact this perusal of Alcoholics Anonymous was developed directly from AA material and sources.

Now that we have looked at AA, what can we learn and understand of its significance and meaning? Seldon Bacon, a sociologist, suggests that AA may be a resocialization process weaning the individual back into society. As Bacon interprets AA, it permits its members to go through a maturing process. This process begins when the member first comes into the program and is dependent on a sponsor. In time, with continued sobriety, he assumes more and more responsibility, and ultimately he himself becomes a sponsor. Finally, with more continuous AA involvement and activity with other alcoholics, the member may mature sufficiently to assume the responsibility of a leadership role in the group.

Trice views AA's effectiveness as a result of the new self-concept it gives its members. This new self-concept evolves, according to Trice, when new members recognize that they have been sick and not necessarily bad, while at the same time they are developing new feelings of belonging. Feeling for the group is strengthened as the sharing of obligations, aims, and emotional problems progresses. To Trice, the more outgoing, sociable individuals, who can share emotionally with others, are most likely to be attracted to and succeed in AA. Trice points out that Step One "relieves the alcoholic of the need to demonstrate that he can drink like others"; Steps Two and Three "enable the alcoholic to realize that . . . he needs help from outside himself"; Step Five reduces anxiety by sharing and Step Eight helps to reduce guilt through restitution. He further contends that successful AA members are motivated toward social acceptance and are anxious concerning rejection and separation.

Hanfmann suggests briefly that successful AA members may be "those in whose life, for one reason or another, belongingness with a group of peers has been, from childhood on a significant or even the most significant relationship."

Lemert also had some comments on Alcoholics Anonymous, based on his studies of West Coast Indians. He observed that non-reservation Indian members of AA were usually more acculturated and better educated than the reservation Indians, the latter interpreting AA as a further restraint on their drinking. Inability to accept AA was observed in those Indians who were hostile to whites. In addition, many Indians were unable to subordinate themselves to a power higher than themselves. Thus, cultural influences may affect acceptance of AA.

The very size of AA is socially significant. It is a reflection of the ostracism that always has plagued alcoholics. Morally shunned, punitively treated, the alcoholic's only hope for help lay in one person helping another. It is a sad commentary that even to this day the sick must lead the sick because of ignorance and bias. What we are suggesting is that because we failed the alcoholic, AA came into being. An invention does not occur when there is no necessity. We have stated before that AA has been the most effective mass approach to date. Their accomplishment is the result of a number of social and psychological mechanisms:

1. The focus on the symptom rather than the underlying problems which resulted in alcoholism. This focus fits rather well with the psychodynamic formulations of addictive drinking . . . namely, that alcoholism involves, among other things, object loss, especially of a mother figure during the earliest stage of psychosexual development. The symbolic and physiological replacement of this object loss is dealt with by substituting alcohol. AA in its uncritical accepting role, by its action on doing-for-the-other-alcoholic approach and especially by its heavy emphasis on spiritual conversion, produces a gratifying maternal reunion symbol like that formerly played by alcohol. As alcohol lubricates social intercourse, reducing cultural differences and personal inadequacies, so does AA. With alcohol it is the few drinks which fortify, with AA it is the suffering of a common calamity which creates the bond of equality. Physician, businessman, ditchdigger, the beautiful and the ugly, the rich and the poor, all are sufferers. This equality, besides satisfying the need to belong, alleviates the possibility of judgment or recrimination. For many, the surroundings of the anonymous mass are comforting and secure.

2. The mechanism of compulsion. We see this reflected in the strength of the AA member's compulsive, almost vengeful attention to the AA way of life, in his nightly attendance at meetings, and in the fervor of his proselytizing. Here we see AA attempting to use this compulsion constructively to fulfill needs formerly met by alcohol.

3. The pointing of the road back to our middle-class way of life. We think that perhaps this is the essence of AA derived as it is from our dominant "Protestant Ethic" (emotional control, cleanliness, strength, and godliness). Drinking to loss of control is by these standards a sin, symbolizing failure and the basic weakness of the individual. Thus, the alcoholic must continue to drink or be confronted by the reality of the culturally defined Puritan image. AA on the other hand, offers redemption, permitting the wayward to admit his feelings and ultimately to turn his life over to God. We might expect to find that AA is not popular where cultural values are different, and in France this is true. Here, AA has had only limited acceptance.

4. We are struck by the sect or cult-like aspects of AA. This is true in terms of its history, structure, and the charisma surrounding its

leader, Bill W. There is even a bible; the old testament of AA is the "Big Book." . . . Its new testament is *The Twelve Steps and Twelve Traditions*. Its Jehovah is Bill W., for it was he who developed the steps and traditions, wrote his own history; he is the main motivating force of AA. Bill W. aided others whose histories also comprise the "Big Book." We are not theologians and it is with some hesitance that we offer comments about the spiritual meaning of AA. Yet because the spiritual element is so critical in the dynamics of the organization, we suggest the following possible interpretations of AA. AA, as a social organization attempting to cope with a psychological problem, uses a unique combination of the sociological, the psychological, and the spiritual. The relationship with God is viewed as a living, dynamic one. God can be reached personally and will give help. The emphasis is on what God does. This view of God does not appear to be a highly intellectual understanding of spiritual means but a more fundamental or emotional relationship. Thus as with many components of AA, the religion seems somewhat simple, but nevertheless it is appropriately developed in terms of the members' own emotional needs.

Before leaving this perusal of Alcoholics Anonymous, we wish to raise certain questions:

1. How accurate are the figures of AA's phenomenal growth? We know that each year the secretary of each individual AA group compiles the figures and forwards them, not the names, to the New York office. Since the secretaries are asked to include only regular members in their figures, the assumption is made that individuals are counted only once. But there can be many groups in just one city, and, with the mobility of AA members from group to group there may be a significant overestimate in the total of up to 20 per cent. Such a possible overlap in the figures does not, of course, negate prodigious growth.

Aside from numbers, one may seriously object to the criterion used—sobriety—as the sole measure of success. What about employment and marital status, or interaction with others? Have they improved or deteriorated further? Or, when is sobriety, sobriety? If a member has been dry for eleven months and drinks the week before the census, is he counted as recovered?

2. Will AA continue to grow? Most likely yes, but at a greatly reduced rate. We make this assumption because, as noted above, many alcoholics best served by AA are already involved. Also, AA's successes have promoted the interest of professionals in the alcoholic, thereby decreasing the number of candidates.

3. Why does it work with some patients and not with others? . . . We believe AA works for patients whose social and psychological needs it can meet. However, the conscious turning toward God or emotional

giving to others requires a certain sense of being a person, which many alcoholics do not possess. Therefore, alcoholics who fail in AA should not feel that they are beyond the pale. They have just been asked to give when they had nothing to give.

4. Should AA change its procedures to bring in previous failures? The thought of change of method raises the specter of the Washingtonian Movement and its eventual failure.

5. If adaptation of procedures occurred, would this affect the group with whom AA is now so successful? In an interesting address to the 11th Annual Meeting of the North American Association of Alcoholism Programs in 1960, Bill W. noted the need for flexibility in AA. He pointed out that AA was "beset with fears of survival" for many years, and that with developing maturity the AA "family was about to be weaned." Bill W. envisioned a much closer relationship in the future for AA with the professional community. We are uncertain as to whether this can be accomplished without diluting the necessary identity of the organization, which new AA members need so strongly. But if a closer relation can be effected and the identity sustained, then in this there would be great promise for the future.

6. Why AA's hostility toward other forms of rehabilitation? We believe this hostility exists to maintain AA's separate identity. Also, for the new member the suggestion of other approaches might undermine his tenuous faith in the spirituality of AA.

7. What will happen when the motivating force of Bill W. is no longer around? Is AA prepared to make the transition? The smooth transition of authority from a charismatic leader to an organization depends upon careful advance preparation. Bill W., an astute and wise man, recognizes the seriousness of this problem. He is attempting to plan for the future, and preserve AA by reducing his influence, permitting an orderly transfer of leadership to take place.

8. Is AA's focus alcoholism, alcoholics, or Alcoholics Anonymous? This important question reveals much by its answer. AA is not interested in alcoholism as a medical problem. If it did have such an interest, it would be interested in etiology, research, and prevention. AA is not. On the other hand if it did have such an interest, AA might lose its therapeutic effectiveness.

The members maintain that they prefer to be involved with present-day, suffering alcoholics who are potential members than with theoretical formulations. In our opinion, AA is really not interested in alcoholics in general, but only as they relate to AA itself. By action and by rules, AA expresses more interest in strengthening and perpetuating Alcoholics Anonymous than in helping alcoholics. Many alcoholics cannot make the AA program for one reason or another. AA, if it were interested in alcoholics, would attempt to help these failures seek out other rehabilitative resources. In most cases they do not. At the same time, if AA were interested in alcoholics and not itself alone, it would not criticize AA members who use other treatment facilities. The pietism of AA may be necessary to many, but it strikes us as primarily a means of strengthening the group.

In conclusion, we feel that the major contribution of Alcoholics Anonymous has been not only in the rehabilitation of alcoholics, but also in the dramatization that alcoholics can be helped. By their efforts they have shown further that no one but the alcoholic himself was interested in dealing with his problem and that the community let him down. By virtue of their interest, they have made work with alcoholics legitimate.

AL-ANON FAMILY GROUPS

Morris E. Chafetz and Harold W. Lemone, Jr.

Contrary to widespread belief, alcoholics do indeed have families, and whether or not the alcoholic lives alone, these families may influence the course of his alcoholism. All alcoholics do not live on Skid Row, friendless and forgotten. Most alcoholics seen in alcoholism clinics are married and live with their wife and children, and in general their marriage rate is not strikingly different from that of the general population for the same age range. Alcoholics, however, have a higher incidence of marriage break-up than the rest of the general population. This indicates that alcoholism does have an impact on the family life and interpersonal relationships. Spouses, parents, children, and relatives are affected by the pathological drinker; naturally, the more intimate the relationship the more severe the effect. The recognition that the alcoholic himself is not the only one who needs help is manifested in the Al-Anon Movement. Al-Anon evolved to meet the needs of the affected individuals.

Al-Anon is composed primarily of the spouses of alcoholics. Parents, relatives, children over twenty-one, and interested friends at times have also become members.

The idea of family groups is almost as old as that of Alcoholics Anonymous and began when the wives of early AA members realized that they too had problems. These wives tried to deal with this need by attending AA meetings, by seeking church aid, or by turning to social agencies. Although these "usual" sources gave some help, a gap nevertheless remained. As a consequence, nonalcoholics began to meet at the same time that AA held its meetings. There was no established formal program. Yet the informal groups continued to grow.

This growth was not without opposition. Some AA members "frowned on the idea, feeling Family Groups could become gossip clubs or divert AA from its main purpose." Similar opposition continues to exist among certain AA members and it is not difficult to imagine some spouses using the group as a means for controlling and punishing their alcoholic mates. Nevertheless the core idea was sound. Basic and mutual problems did exist among members of the alcoholic's family and as a consequence more groups sprang up around North America (in Chicago, Toronto, San Pedro, and Richmond).

By 1949 AA's General Headquarters were receiving an increasing number of inquiries from nonalcoholics. Fifty groups (called Family Groups) requested listing in the AA Directory. Since AA felt this would be branching afield and might endanger their own organization, they refused. Consequently, in New York husbands and wives of AA members formed a committee which eventually became the Al-Anon Family Group Clearing House and in time was incorporated as the Al-Anon Family Group Headquarters, Inc. There is no formal relationship with AA.

The movement grew rapidly. Fifty groups in 1951 expanded to 700 in 1955 and to 1308 in 1960. We suggest that in another ten years, Al-Anon Groups and membership may easily outnumber Alcoholics Anonymous.

Despite the lack of formal ties with AA, Al-Anon has strong informal and spiritual ties to AA. Similarly, from small donations of its members it finances itself, and like AA has steps and traditions.

Al-Anon asks its members these pertinent questions:

1. Are you the wife, husband, relative or friend of a problem drinker who still *refuses* help?
2. Are you concerned with a member of AA who is still having trouble with alcohol?
3. Though the alcoholic member of your family may now be sober, do you still feel that your home life is insecure or difficult?
4. Do you understand fully how alcoholism and its consequences may have warped your own thinking and your own personality?
5. Do you know that you can find understanding, friendship and help in the Al-Anon Family Groups (a) regardless of whether the alcoholic member of your family has sobered up, or (b)

whether he has made good in his business affairs, or (c) whether normal family relationships have been restored?

6. Do you know that your own ability to face every life problem serenely and with constructive attitudes can be a most important factor in helping your alcoholic partner to achieve a full and happy recovery from problem drinking?

To answer these questions, certain responses and behavior are stated. First, the essential plea for unity; that "our common welfare should come first"; and from unity, personal progress for the greatest number can be accomplished. Second, that the single authority for group purposes is "a loving God as He may express Himself in our group conscience." The point is re-emphasized as in AA, that leaders are but trusted servants who do not govern.

For membership, the requirement is broad: a relative or friend with the problem of alcoholism. When the relatives and friends of alcoholics gather together for mutual aid, they may call themselves an Al-Anon Family Group provided that the group has no other affiliations. The groups are autonomous, except as they affect other Al-Anon Groups or AA.

The singular purpose of Al-Anon Groups is to help families of alcoholics. This is achieved by the members themselves practicing the Twelve Steps of AA, by encouraging and understanding their afflicted alcoholic relatives, and by aiding the families of other alcoholics.

Like AA, Al-Anon will not lend itself to any outside enterprise or purpose. Although it maintains its identity, Al-Anon co-operates with Alcoholics Anonymous. Like AA, Al-Anon is self-supporting, declining outside help; Twelfth Step work (helping nonalcoholics who need help) is nonprofessional; groups are never organized except as service boards; Al-Anon has no opinion on outside issues and cannot be drawn into public controversy. Public relations are accomplished via attraction rather than promotion; the anonymity principle is a reminder to place principles above personalities. The reader can readily see in AA and Al-Anon the same tradition of focusing primary concern on understanding the alcoholic, which is extended in the case of Al-Anon to the alcoholic's family also.

In understanding the alcoholic, it is considered essential to understand that alcoholism is an illness and the alcoholic a sick person, that alcoholics can be helped and that pleas to will power, threats, and accusations are useless. The alcoholic's lack of drinking control is considered an obsession. The causes of alcoholism are seen to lie deep. Al-Anon writes, "Very often basic personality flaws can be traced back to the alcoholic's childhood," and therefore it is advised that the spouse or alcoholic is not to blame. Alcoholics as described by Al-Anon are "different," "perfectionistic," and "often lack emotional stability to face life's problems in a realistic manner."

Al-Anon goes into further detail to understand the alcoholic. The alcoholic is described as an attractive and intelligent person who, when drinking, subordinates everything to his "craving for alcohol"; who lacks insight as to his disorder; who frequently does not want to recover; whose thinking is "warped and distorted"; and who, despite the facts, rejects the reality of his drinking. Al-Anon goes on to iterate that few alcoholics are beyond hope; they must admit that they cannot cope alone with the problem after they eventually "hit bottom" (mentally, emotionally, or physically).

After considering the means of understanding the alcoholic, Al-Anon offers guidelines for understanding the indirectly afflicted, i.e. themselves. Some guidelines involve the understanding of their own emotional reaction to the alcoholic spouse, the possibility of self-righteousness and even retaliation. They recognize that the response to the alcoholic mate may be literally or figuratively getting "drunk ourselves," or looking for help for themselves. They confront the recognition that alcoholism "made us sick, too"; that their "emotional sobriety" is essential; that their thinking has become "twisted and warped"; cynical, negative, without faith in life, and without belief in the possibility of change in the spouse. As a consequence of the behavior of the alcoholic, family members can become arrogant and assume the alcoholic is always wrong and the nonalcoholic always right. The alcoholic submerges himself in self-pity and his positive features are ignored. Gradually, because the alcoholic is unpredictable, the mate must assume more and more responsibilities. With the alcoholic's recovery, it becomes difficult for the nonalcoholic to let the reins go. Al-Anon wisely advises that life, even after sobriety, does "not stay rosy," and that AA's Twelve Steps should be practiced by both the nonalcoholic and alcoholic. Al-Anon attempts to show the intertwined relations between alcoholic and family. It also raises the possibility that the nonalcoholic partner may resent time spent at AA meetings and the fact that AA has been able to help the alcoholic where the spouse has failed.

Al-Anon has taken a broader view than AA about problems it cannot deal with. They have no qualms about suggesting other modes of help. They recognize that sex and marital problems will require assistance. "Affiliation with the Family Groups certainly offers no cure-all for the complex problems of marriage and sex as they are affected by alcoholism; and in severe cases, it is, of course, wise to seek the advice also of doctor, minister or marriage counsellor."

The concern of Al-Anon with the effect of alcoholism on the children of alcoholics has been paramount. The manner of explaining AA and the reality that the parent is an alcoholic have led to the development around the country of a movement called Al-Ateen. This will, hopefully, provide information and aid to children of alcoholics.

In summary, Al-Anon follows AA's structure but focuses on the partner of the alcoholic. The movement is a spiritually oriented effort to gain uncritical understanding of the alcoholic, and Al-Anon uses the "AA Prayer" at meetings. Their focus, like that of AA, is on helping themselves through helping others. It is striking that the number of Al-Anon members whose spouses have not yet begun to seek help is growing. Since most alcoholics have not yet sought help, this leads us to predict a more rapid growth of Al-Anon than AA. It is hoped that in time the influence of the nonalcoholics will cause more alcoholics to seek treatment. Al-Anon's influence will also grow because of the apparent diminishing of hostility toward Al-Anon by AA members and the gradual and increased support of Al-Anon by the members of AA and the organized social and health agencies of the community.

7 DRUG ABUSE AND ADDICTION

It is one of those peculiar aspects of our culture that the far greater problems associated with alcohol—drunkenness, driving while intoxicated, vagrancy, "Blue Mondays," and alcoholism—evoke less concern than the numerically and medically less important problem of dangerous drug use. Public fascination with the use and abuse of narcotics and the hallucinogens is a phenomenon worthy of study in itself. The simplest explanation for this paradox is that alcohol "fits" better into complex society because of its tension reduction properties and facilitation of interpersonal relationships. Drugs, on the other hand, tend to turn the person inward—back on the self. In a competitive, impersonal, urban society, turning in on the self (retreatism) and privatizing one's life are incomprehensible to many. (Some of our fear of schizophrenics and other psychotics is based on the inability of such persons to communicate and relate). In other parts of the world, given a different value-orientation and greater emphasis on the contemplative life, it is drugs which are tried and used, while alcohol is the more feared.

Whereas the narcotic and hallucinogenic drugs are of paramount concern, other kinds of mind-altering drugs are used in many perfectly legally and socially acceptable ways. For example, amphetamines are widely prescribed by physicians for weight reduction, in controlling fatigue, and in overcoming "blues" and minor depressions. Students, truckers, and other night persons frequently resort to "pep" pills. Barbiturate usage is, if anything, even more acceptable then amphetamine use. Millions of insomniacs depend on the sedative effect of "goof balls." And who is unaware of the tremendous revolution occasioned by the tranquilizers? Thus, it is not the use, and abuse, of all psychotropic and psychoactive drugs which are deviant. Only the use of certain classes of dangerous drugs—the narcotics, hallucinogens, and marihuana—are considered deviant. Because such use is labeled deviant, criminal, and outside legitimate medical practice, users develop a life style quite far removed from that of straight society. The roles, statuses, functioning, and self-concepts of the users are derived from this subculture. Quite apart from the effects of the drugs, it is this involvement and participation in a deviant subculture which nullifies most treatment efforts and leads to the high rates of return to drug use after treatment.

The first contribution is a calm description by the President's Commission on Law Enforcement and the Administration of Justice of the state of current knowledge about marihuana and the hallucinogens. This summary examines the extent of the use of these substances in the United States and the characteristics of the users. The reported risks of such use are contrasted with the verified risks. The latter, naturally, are far less extreme. There is also a discussion of the effectiveness of legal controls, and some tentative recommendations are offered. There is one extremely interesting recommendation regarding marihuana. It is that marihuana acquisition and possession be reduced from a felony to a misdemeanor. Although very unlikely to occur, the implementation of this recommendation would certainly alter the status of the problem and reduce the "speakeasy" aspects of present use. The report also suggests that states which have or are in the process of making the possession of hallucinogens unlawful may be acting precipitously. The result of such laws may lead to the repetition of the problems presently encountered with heroin and other "hard" drugs.

Professor Howard Becker in his classic "Becoming a Marihuana User" describes the process of socialization to drug use. This socialization process consists of internalizing the language, beliefs, practices, and patterns associated with marihuana use. The culmination of the process results in the definition of self as marihuana user. Professor Becker insists that there are three prerequisites to becoming a user: learning how to smoke marihuana "correctly," learning how to get high, and learning to enjoy the effects of the marihuana. Far from being inherently pleasurable, the use of marihuana is tied in with the social elements of the smoking setting and must be learned.

The Report on the Treatment of Drug Addiction was prepared for the President's Commission on Law Enforcement and the Administration of Justice. In it Dr. Jonathan Cole, former chief of the Psychopharmacology Research Branch of the National Institute of Mental Health, spells out the various treatment options in addiction. The article discusses involuntary, voluntary, and ancillary treatment programs as well as the results of treatment. Several treatment modalities are described, including the methods at Daytop Lodge in New York and at the California Rehabilitation Center in Corona. Of very special interest are the drug therapies, including methadone maintenance and the use of an opiate antagonist called cyclazocine. The report concludes with a listing and brief description of seven possible new approaches to treatment.

One of the oldest and best-known opiate treatment settings is the

United States Public Health Service Hospital at Lexington, Kentucky. Dr. John O'Donnell describes this program in some detail. Capable of treating one thousand patients at a time, the hospital serves both legally committed and voluntary patients. The minimum length of stay is about five months, except for voluntary patients who may leave "against medical advice" at any time. The program consists of four phases: withdrawal, orientation and evaluation, treatment, and aftercare. The basic elements in each phase are discussed. The article closes with some illustrative case outcome material and a discussion of the problem of relapse.

The last selection is "The Anticriminal Society: Synanon." Somewhat akin to Alcoholics Anonymous, Synanon is a fascinating organization which in working with the addict employs a variant of group therapy called "attack therapy." Professor Yablonsky who has intensively studied the Synanon approach presents a straightforward account of the formation, growth and development, fundamental principles, and future prospects of Synanon.

Charles Dederick, a sober alcoholic and charismatic leader, founded Synanon—a name which stuck even though it was a mispronunciation by a confused addict of the word "seminar." Unlike Alcoholics Anonymous in several respects (there is no carrying of the message to others or twelve-step work, and the nature of the group sessions is different) Synanon is more a colony than a group. Addicts live under one roof and the model of organization is the family. In living with and confronting one another continuously, addicts have the opportunity to see themselves as others do. There is no need for "playing a role" since, in intimate face-to-face contact, conventional masks are dropped. The addict is compelled to search for the self and for self-understanding. The process, if successful, results in the development of a different self—a new personality.

Nevertheless, the self-selection of the addicts who join Synanon and the lack of outcome research data make it premature to judge the effectiveness of Synanon as a treatment modality in addiction. Its great success has been the transformation in the public image of the addict. Just as Alcoholics Anonymous succeeded in enlisting public sympathy and understanding for the problems of alcoholism, so Synanon may have the same general effect in heroin addiction. This alone would make Synanon a landmark in the road to the development of rational and effective approaches to the understanding and management of drug addiction.

MIND-ALTERING DRUGS
AND DANGEROUS BEHAVIOR

Richard H. Blum

. . .

Mind-altering drug use is common to mankind. Such drugs have been employed for millennia in almost all cultures. In our own work we have been able to identify only a few societies in the world today where no mind-altering drugs are used; these are small and isolated cultures. Our own society puts great stress on mind-altering drugs as desirable products which are used in many acceptable ways (under medical supervision, as part of family home remedies, in self-medication, in social use [alcohol, tea parties, coffee klatches, etc.] and in private use [cigarettes, etc.]). In terms of drug use the rarest or most abnormal form of behavior is not to take any mind-altering drugs at all. Most adult Americans are users of drugs, many are frequent users of a wide variety of them. If one is to use the term "drug user" is applies to nearly all of us. Given this fact, the frequently expressed concern about drug "use" might better be put in terms of drug "abuse." "Abuse" of course is also ill defined. Presumably judgments of abuse rest on such questions as (a) How much of the drug, or drug combinations, is taken and how is intake distributed? (b) Does the person take disapproved drugs? (for example, heroin instead of alcohol, marihuana instead of tranquilizers), (c) Does he take drugs in unapproved settings? (an adolescent drinking wine with a gang rather than at the family dinner table, an adult taking amphetamines without medical approval), (d) Does his behavior under drugs offer some real risk to himself or to others? (Our primary concern here: Crime, accidents, suicide, but also dependency, medical danger, etc.) There are, no doubt, other factors that would be revealed should one do a study of how people come to judge that drug "abuse" is occurring. The critical point for us is the realization that "use," "abuse," and "risk" are emotionally charged terms that may be based on hidden determinants or open assumptions that cannot be shown to have a factual basis.

To offer one conclusion at the outset, it is that current evaluations of drug use by the public, by the mass media, and by some officials, are often emotional. The programs, laws, and recommendations that arise

From *Narcotics and Drug Abuse,* The Task Force Report, The President's Commission on Law Enforcement and the Administration of Justice, 1967, pp. 23-29.

from these emotional responses may well be inappropriate if the steps taken do not match drug use realities. What those "realities" might be is most uncertain, for at the present time we know little about the extent of the use of any of the mind-altering drugs, about the characteristics of those using one or another "dangerous drug" (excluding alcohol and opiates), or about the kinds and frequencies of risks as a function of dosage, frequency, setting, and kinds of persons using any of these drugs. Consequently, we do not presently have enough knowledge at hand about persons, about conduct, about drugs per se, or about the effects of one or another programs of control or cure to make any recommendations for prevention, control, or cure where there can be certainty about the results even if those recommendations were to be fully implemented. . . .

MARIHUANA

DISTRIBUTION

Nearly worldwide in both production and use.

EXTENT OF USE IN THE UNITED STATES

Only limited epidemiological data available. A few sociological studies of special using groups (musicians, professional people, slum Negroes, students.) Police statistics are an inadequate source of data because of apparent concentration of arrests in lower class groups and because marihuana arrests may be combined statistically with heroin and opium arrests. There is no current way of assessing the relationship of cases known to the authorities to actual prevalence of use in the population. Furthermore, fashions in drug use appear to be changing rapidly so that earlier data is likely to be inaccurate. One recent pilot study . . . in two west coast metropolitan communities, the sample size too small to allow any assumption of accuracy of estimate, reported 9 percent of the adult population had tried marihuana and 2 percent were using it either occasionally or regularly. In one west coast university, a university health officer . . . estimated 20 percent of the students were using marihuana; the police department . . . estimated only 1 percent use. Another unpublished student study . . . reported 11 percent experienced but none as regular users. . . . Great Britain . . . reports sixfold increase in hashish smuggling from 1963 to 1964 and other British reports suggest, as do impressionistic United States reports, a continuing increase in use.

CHARACTERISTICS OF USERS

There are no epidemiological or "drug census" studies for the Nation as a whole. Descriptions made in the 1930's and 1940's found use was predominantly among minority group members and economically depressed urban youth, especially those judged as having inadequate personalities. Studies in Asia and Africa . . . suggest use is concentrated among the young, urban poor and is associated with dissatisfaction, deprivation, and mobility. In India upper class and "respectable" use occurs. . . . In the United States the impression, not supported by adequate studies, is that use ranges from young urban poor, including minorities, to disaffected "beatniks" through artistic and university communities to younger professional persons in metropolitan centers. Use appears to be concentrated in the 18 to 30 age group but reports of both downward . . . and upward (over 30) diffusion are appearing. The best estimate is that experimentation is far more common than regular use and that heavy use (as occurs in Africa and Asia) is quite rare.

REPORTED RISKS

Some law enforcement officials and Federal Bureau of Narcotics personnel have held that marihuana leads to (a) criminal acts associated with impulsivity, recklessness, and violence, (b) distasteful behavior associated with disregard for cleanliness, unrestrained sexuality, rebelliousness, unpredictable relations with others, (c) risk of later heroin dependency because marihuana use creates interest in having drugs experiences which marihuana cannot produce and because it is obtained through illicit channels which also provide opportunities for access to heroin (and cocaine). . . .

VERIFIED RISKS

Studies in India . . . and North Africa . . . show that cannabis phychoses occur in association with heavy use of potent forms of cannabis. Dependency is also described, as is apathy, reduced work, and social effectiveness, etc. These effects may be due, in some measure, to the vulnerability of the using population (already hopeless, sick, hungry, etc.). In the United States neither cannabis phychosis nor cannabis dependency has been described, although marihuana may be one of a variety of drugs used in the multihabituation . . . pattern, where a person takes many different drugs and appears dependent, but not on any one of them. Case history material suggests that many identified heroin users have had earlier experiences with marihuana, but their "natural history" is also likely to include even earlier illicit use of cigarettes and alcohol. The evidence from our college students . . . and news articles is clear that many persons not in heroin-risk neighborhoods who experiment with marihuana do not "progress" to "hard" narcotics.

With regard to crime, other than the violation of law occurring by virtue of acquiring and possessing marihuana, there is no reliable evidence that marihuana "causes" crime. One Brazilian study . . . observed 120 marihuana-using criminals and concluded their criminal actions were not a result of their drug use. A Nigerian study . . . suggests that those who are at risk of hashish use are also at risk of criminality because of their primary social and psychological characteristics (being members of frustrated underprivileged groups living in urban areas with opportunities for committing crimes). In Nigerian hospitals with patients with histories of cannabis psychosis or use, there was no relationship of use to crime. In Indian studies . . . a negative relationship has been suggested, for with heavy cannabis use stupor occurs during which the commission of crimes is unlikely. Among populations of students, artists, and other more "privileged" pot smokers in the United States there is no recent evidence of associated criminality; similarly in the famous "La Guardia Report" . . . in New York City marihuana was not found to be either criminogenic nor associated with criminal subgroups. With regard to traffic accidents, data is lacking. One study . . . using a cannabis-like compound suggested that motor performance was not impaired but that the ability to shift attention was reduced. Effects are no doubt related to dosage but no studies on varied dosage using driving tasks have been done.

LEGAL CONTROLS AND THEIR EFFECTIVENESS

Except for very limited research purposes, marihuana is not legally available. Its acquisition and/or possession are punishable by law in the United States. Both felony and misdemeanor charges may be levelled; we are not aware of any studies of actual charges and dispositions. In spite of legal controls marihuana is said to be obtainable in most metropolitan centers in the United States. It is not, however, readily available in the sense that a naive person has an easy opportunity to obtain it. Acquisition is dependent upon being a member of, or having access to, some social group where it is used. The penalty has clearly not prevented all marihuana use nor the reported recent upsurge in use. To what extent controls on availability and the penalty risks have reduced use cannot be said. If one were to argue by analogy, taking alcohol which is available without penalty as a comparison, then one would suggest that legal controls have worked to suppress if not to prevent marihuana use. Some users interviewed recently argue that they have chosen to smoke "pot" because the laws are so patently inappropriate and they wish to signify their disapproval through direct disobedience. In California, a movement called LEMAR (legalize marihuana) is now collecting signatures for a referendum asking the voters to make the drug legally available. There is in addition sentiment among scholars and some liberal legislators not to legalize use but drastically to reduce the penalties now written in the law. . . .

COMMENT

We have suggested that educational and legal efforts should reflect a rational policy about marihuana. We have further suggested that policy itself should be based on the facts. The inadequate data available today indicate that risk of crime, accidents, and suicide (and of undesirable physiological side effects) are not likely to be greater than those associated with alcohol (and may be less). If the equivalence between alcohol and marihuana is to be accepted as an operating assumption until more facts are at hand—and we think that is a prudent position to take—it then follows that a public debate is in order with regard to the best regulation of marihuana.

It must be acknowledged that there are other "facts" besides those of risk which will enter into policymaking. Perhaps the most significant of these is the widespread law enforcement and public belief that marihuana is as dangerous as heroin in terms of dependency-producing potential and that its use is associated with criminality. These beliefs, even if incorrect, are facts to which policy must address itself. Since there is no strong evidence . . . of the medical value of marihuana, there cannot be said to be any urgent reason to make it available, except for research purposes. Similarly if there is a parallel in kinds of outcomes between it and alcohol, there is clearly a risk of unknown proportion that increased marihuana availability, as for example with its legalization, might lead to increased dependency and dangerous outcomes of the sort associated with alcohol itself, the latter unquestionably being a "dangerous" drug in the social rather than legal sense. The recent experience of Asian and African countries is compatible with such a fear.

In the meantime there appears to be good reason to encourage research on marihuana which in turn requires increased ease of obtaining it and permission to employ it on human subjects for bona fide experiments. There also appears to be good reason to moderate present punitive legislation so that penalties are more in keeping with what is now known about risks; that is, they are not great. A revision of penal codes so that marihuana acquisition and possession becomes a misdemeanor only would not seem inappropriate. In addition, since the significance of marihuana use may well be for some persons that of rebellion or disrespect for law or tentative explorations in criminality, or it may portend developing dependency proneness on drugs as such, it would appear worthwhile for apprehended persons to undergo social and psychological (psychiatric) evaluations. If destructive tendencies (toward self or others) are found the person can then become the subject of nonpunitive rehabilitative or preventive efforts by welfare, medical, probation, or community psychiatric agencies.

In point of fact we do not know if such preventive or therapeutic efforts are of value; the hope is that they will be. We may at least expect them not to be harmful.

TENTATIVE RECOMMENDATION

In consultation with police, legal, and health personnel and with participation of research workers and interested citizen groups to formulate procedures (a) allowing for increased access to and human experimentation with marihuana by bona fide research workers, (b) to encourage funds for epidemiological research on drug use aimed at defining the characteristics of users and non-users, their interests, conduct, health, etc., (c) to revise present penal codes so that marihuana acquisition and possession becomes a misdemeanor rather than a felony, (d) to support research and practical experiments in education, in schools and among parents and peers, focusing on conveying information about drugs which encourages nondamaging conduct, (e) to assume a policy stance of flexibility and objectivity which will not only allow for but anticipate that changes in legislative, health, and educational programs will occur as new facts about drug use arise and as new public problems or benefits become apparent.

In addition to the immediate steps set forth above, there are several areas in which long-term endeavors may be envisioned. We conceive of these to involve planning and consultative efforts with law enforcement agencies, with health and behavioral scientists, and with legislators. Work with the public both in terms of assessment of views on drug use and on the determinants of those views and educational efforts designed to alter incorrect opinions might also be appropriate. It is premature to set forth in this paper the details of these several efforts.

In general, the goal would be to provide a common base among informed and interested persons and institutions for planning—in concert —revisions in the law, in police procedures, and perhaps in public health and other medical-psychiatric practice so that marihuana and related drug use—and we must stress here that marihuana is frequently but one of a number of drugs being interchangeably used—can be handled with minimum cost to the taxpayer, minimum damage to the offender, with minimum strain on the police, and without creating anxiety among the public which in turn expresses itself as pressure on legislators for inappropriate laws. These goals, while sounding utopian, may very well be capable of at least partial achievement for of all the drugs considered in this report, marihuana is the one where there is the greatest discrepancy between public beliefs and probable drug effects, and between present versus reasonable legislation. The development of a moderate and consistent policy will much improve the present state of affairs.

HALLUCINOGENS

A group of drugs whose effects often include imagery and changes in felt sensory intensity—less often hallucinations as such—including lysergic acid diethylamide LSD-25, dimethyltriptamine DMT, mescaline, peyote, and others.

DISTRIRUTION

Naturally occurring in many plants (mushrooms, cactus, tree barks, flower seeds, seaweed, etc.) and capable of being synthesized in laboratories, hallucinogens are widely distributed over the world.

EXTENT OF USE

Hallucinogen use has been restricted to relatively isolated nonliterate societies. Certain South and North American Indian groups and Siberian tribes have employed the hallucinogen historically. Within the last century the use of peyote by American Indians has spread widely and within the last decade the use of LSD, DMT, mescaline, and other products has been adopted in metropolitan areas of the Western countries, primarily in the United States.

USE IN THE UNITED STATES

No reliable epidemiological or "drug" census data exist. Use appears to be concentrated in young adults age 20 to 35 but there are signs of rather rapid diffusion to high school age levels and less rapidly to middle and older age adults. Employed in medical research, LSD has been given to small numbers of psychiatric patients, alcoholics, schizophrenic children and has been tested on terminal (dying) patients as a means of easing their distress. Employed in pharmacological and behavioral research, it has been given to volunteers, for the most part students. Employed by religious and philosophical seekers it has been given in institutions and centers, and other settings. These institutional uses account for only a fraction of current use; impressionistic but probably trustworthy reports indicate expanding social and private use of the drug derived from black market sources. Ease of transport and of synthesis make LSD distribution easy. The use of other hallucinogens, peyote for example . . . has been fairly well confined to traditional (Indian) groups, but their use, too, is expanding to young urban people.

   As has been the history with many mind-altering drugs, the pattern of LSD diffusion has been overtime from older prestigeful persons downward to younger less prestigeful ones, also from institutionalized medical and religious (or pseudoreligious) settings to more secular use. . . . With secular use, a drug becomes "social," use is subject to less constraint, and greater variability in outcomes can be expected as a greater variety of personalities, settings, and expectations are involved. At the present time, it would be unwise to venture any estimate of the number of Americans who have tried one or another hallucinogen; any numerical estimates must be suspect. One may presume that given a condition of continued easy availability of the drug plus wide publicity about its favorable effects, use would expand rapidly; historically the epidemic spread of tobacco smoking, opium use, and distilled alcoholic beverages provide illustrations. What effect current legislation to control manufacture, distribution, sale—and in some States, possession—will have on LSD use cannot be said at this time. It has generally been the case that interest in drugs can be channeled but not repressed; so it is that the choice of available drugs may be limited, but not the practice of using one or another drug. Historical examples showing shifts are those of opium to heroin, hashish to alcohol, and more generally from naturally occurring milder drugs to synthetic stronger ones.

CHARACTERISTICS OF USERS

In the United States—as has been indicated—peyote use is concentrated among American Indians, but does not occur among all tribes. LSD, DMT, etc., were first confined to physicians and other research workers and then spread to their subjects, patients, families, and friends. Until a few years ago, LSD remained limited to an "elite" group of successful professionals, artists, and communications industry personnel, their families and friends. These same groups still appear to be using hallucinogens, but the concentration of use appears to have shifted to younger persons. Among teenagers, motorcycle club members, delinquents, urban poor and minorities, etc., there are reports . . . of spreading interest, suggesting the expected diffusion down the socioeconomic scale. No common psychological or sociological features may be expected among the users of any secular and social drug; different people take drugs for different reasons. Within groups sharing common sociological characteristics it is sometimes possible to differentiate drug-interested persons, regular users, heavy users, etc., on the basis of psychological or background factors. For example, among graduate students one study reports that LSD-interested persons are more introverted and at the same time more excitement seeking than disinterested persons. . . . Similar studies comparing psychological and background characteristics have identified certain differences among those trying (and not trying), continuing (and discontinuing) to use, and becoming dependent (and not becoming dependent upon) other drugs, for example, tobacco, heroin, alcohol. . . .

REPORTED RISKS

Risks reported in popular articles include, especially for LSD, psychosis, suicide, continuing undesirable personality changes, release of sexual and aggressive impulses (leading to murder, rape, homosexual episodes, etc.), habitation, hallucinatory redintegration (return of the LSD state unasked and without taking the drug), development of interests in illicit drugs (marihuana, "goof balls," etc.), development of "cult" interests, and consequent warping of ordinary social outlooks, reduced work and social effectiveness, risk of divorce, increased accident risks when driving under drug influence, etc. Its exploitative use (control, seduction, purposeful production of psychoses) has also been reported.

VERIFIED RISKS

Psychosis following LSD is verified. . . . there is no adequate estimate of the frequency of psychosis as a function of incidence of use. Mescaline psychoses are also verified. Some psychotic reactions are temporary, many are now "treated" at home by the subject's friends; counteracting tranquilizers (e.g., thorazine) are now sold on the black market as part of the LSD "trip" equipment. Other psychotic reactions require long-term hospitalization. The most recent study available to us . . . studied 70 post-LSD psychiatric admissions during a 6-month period in a Los Angeles medical center, these patients representing 12 percent of all admissions during that period. One-third of the LSD patients were psychotic on admission; two-thirds of the patients required more than 1 month of hospitalization. Recently reported in California . . . is teenage use of jimsonweed (datura stramonium) a substance employed by Luiseno and Chumash Indians to achieve visions. Deaths among these Indians occurred following overdose . . . and overdose among contemporary youth may also be expected to lead to illness or death. Suicide attempts are hard to distinguish from bizarre behavior occurring under LSD, for example jumping from windows because "I can fly," so it is that although suicidal feelings are reported and clinical workers describe attempts, there is no sound data on the probability of suicide attempts as a function of dosage, setting, personality, incidence of use, etc.

Crime associated with hallucinogen use appears to have been minimal. Police reports before a California legislative committee emphasized disturbances of the peace . . . rather than felonies. Occasional accounts of homicide . . . violence, resisting arrest, etc., have not been subject to followup case studies. It would appear that insofar as decent citizens take hallucinogens their behavior will remain lawful. We may expect that with the expansion of halucinogen use to delinquent groups—and perhaps because it is now unlawful in some States, so that its use becomes criminal—a greater frequency of crime will be reported. A tangential remark is offered here. It is the person, not the drug, which is "responsible" for criminal acts. When an already delinquent youth takes LSD and commits yet another delinquent act, it may well be that the timing or expression of the delinquency is shaped by the drug-induced state of mind, but—as an example—aggression will not be a drug phenomenon. Generally speaking, one would expect (although the scientific evidence is far from adequate) that well-integrated people under heavy drug doses will not do things contrary to their ordinary conduct. Less mature, more neurotic or otherwise less well integrated persons would seem to be more vulnerable to the acting-out of impulses, the temporary expression of conflicts or of being persuaded by others to misbehave. Consequently, one's review of crimes reportedly committed under drug influence must attend to the prior criminal and sociopsychological history of the offender. It is also necessary to have regard for the role of clouded judgment or reduced muscular coordination in producing behavior (e.g., a traffic accident leading to manslaughter) that is criminal. There can also be long-run changes associated with drug use, as for example, the clouding of judgment associated with habituation and drug stupor or in psychotic personality change, where criminal acts may conceivably occur (e.g., smuggling marihuana, perjury, theft) as part of a poor judgment syndrome.

With regard to vehicle accidents and hallucinogens, there have been no studies and no verified reports in spite of some remarkable "I was there" accounts. Experimental work showing slowed responses and reduced information processing make it highly likely that accidents will occur when under hallucinogen influence. This expectation should be tested in laboratory studies.

With regard to the other claims about hallucinogens—dependency, social and work decrement, divorce, etc.—the scientific sources are reliable but samples are small and insufficient followup studies exist.

COMMENT

It is particularly difficult to assess either the significance or the social effects of the hallucinogens during the present period when there is such a widespread change in the pattern of use. The present LSD "epidemic" generates interest and alarm as well as social research; unfortunately, the research results take a while to be generated—by which time they may no longer be applicable. As a best estimate one may suggest that any powerful drug produces dangerous side effects and that any powerful mind-altering drug is likely to alter judgment and conduct, some of which alteration is likely to make trouble for someone. But the problem of trouble over frequency of drug use remains a critical one and until the facts are at hand any extreme programs—either for the use of the drug or for punishment of use—would appear precipitous. Indeed, the present spate of publicity, whether crying alarm or claiming untold delights, is likely to be highly undesirable in itself; creating interest in the use of potent substances among a number of young people or disturbed personalities who are clearly ill-equipped to handle an intense drug experience. Similarly, this same publicity creates fear in the public and generates pressures on legislators to pass premature punitive legislation. We agree with the present plans of the National Institutes of Health . . . to conduct epidemiological research on expanding American drug use and to finance further research on the hallucinogens. We also agree with the present policy of the Food and Drug Administration setting up controls over the manufacture and distribution of LSD but not making possession a law violation.

Precipitously, several States (California and Nevada) have made possession unlawful. Peace officers have pressed for such laws partly because of the difficulty they have in proving intent to sell in cases where persons possess drugs at the time of arrest, but where no long preparation of a case has taken place, so that a sale is witnessed by officers. The dilemma of the law enforcement people is genuine and arises out of pressures on them to "crack down" on sales alone, since the (mostly undercover) effort in such cases consumes an immense amount of time. The arrest and conviction of those possessing drugs is much easier. Since much police experience with narcotics suggests that those possessing and those selling will be one and the same (except at upper echelons of organization), the popular desire to "bear down heaviest" on drug sellers results in fact in bearing down on user-possessors. Whether or not the narcotics seller-user pattern will be repeated with LSD and the other "soft" drugs is not yet known. It remains likely that some of the best organized production and distribution will be by persons not users; whether or not they can be controlled by local police using ordinary procedures is a question beyond the scope of this report. In any event, it must be recognized that if the law does outlaw sale, but does not allow arrest for possession, whether this be for LSD, marihuana, or any other drug, the work of the police will be long and hard and the public must not expect large numbers of arrests. As a corollary it is quite possible that such a policy would, as many law enforcement persons might fear, result in less suppression of illicit drug traffic and subsequent greater use.

Should this prove to be the case—and an evaluative effort is most strongly recommended to find out—there are several alternatives. One is to accept some illicit use as a fact of modern life and to concentrate on its control through educational and social rather than legal means. Another is to retain the nonpunitive aspects of the law, but nevertheless to require mandatory examination of all illicit and dangerous drug user-possessors by health, psychiatric, and possibly welfare (or other socio-criminological) authorities. Any found to be ill, disturbed, or otherwise maladapted might be referred to outpatient clinics for care or, failing their appearance for treatment, be subject to hospitalization under public health rather than criminal codes. These suggestions are only tentative and can be seen to follow present developments in the treatment of alcoholics and narcotic users. They also introduce serious problems of civil rights in terms of deprivation of liberty by health officers without due process. . . .

RECOMMENDATIONS

It is recommended that Federal agencies be encouraged to support clinical and experimental research on the hallucinogens and epidemiological studies of population drug use. It is recommended that current FDA codes on hallucinogens be accepted as adequate, at least until more is known, and that individual States be discouraged from making hallucinogen possession a felony. It is recommended that the difficulty of the police task in controlling illicit drug traffic be acknowledged, especially when arrest for possession is not possible. In consultation with persons and staff groups interested in the prevention of drug dependency and in rehabilitation it is further recommended that various plans and programs for nonpunitive handling of the user of illicit drugs be evaluated. . . .

As a final recommendation we would request of the mass media an emphasis on less sensational reporting and feature writing in regard to LSD and other drugs, would invite the public to give their legislators a moratorium during which time knowledge can be evaluated and reasonable approaches proposed, and would generally suggest as a matter of school and public health education that an effort be made to admit to uncertainty and to restrain emotion in the consideration of drug effects and the changing pattern of drug use. . . .

BECOMING A MARIHUANA USER

Howard S. Becker

I

The novice does not ordinarily get high the first time he smokes marihuana, and several attempts are usually necessary to induce this state.

From *American Journal of Sociology,* 59: 236-42, November 1953. Reprinted by permission.

One explanation of this may be that the drug is not smoked "properly," that is, in a way that insures sufficient dosage to produce real symptoms of intoxication. Most users agree that it cannot be smoked like tobacco if one is to get high:

> Take in a lot of air, you know, and . . . I don't know how to describe it, you don't smoke it like a cigarette, you draw in a lot of air and get it deep down in your system and then keep it there. Keep it there as long as you can.

Without the use of some such technique the drug will produce no effects, and the user will be unable to get high:

> The trouble with people like that [who are not able to get high] is that they're just not smoking it right, that's all there is to it. Either they're not holding it down long enough, or they're getting too much air and not enough smoke, or the other way around or something like that. A lot of people just don't smoke it right, so naturally nothing's gonna happen.

If nothing happens, it is manifestly impossible for the user to develop a conception of the drug as an object which can be used for pleasure, and use will therefore not continue. The first step in the sequence of events that must occur if the person is to become a user is that he must learn to use the proper smoking technique in order that his use of the drug will produce some effects in terms of which his conception of it can change.

Such a change is, as might be expected, a result of the individual's participation in groups in which marihuana is used. In them the individual learns the proper way to smoke the drug. This may occur through direct teaching:

> I was smoking like I did an ordinary cigarette. He said, "No, don't do it like that." He said, "Suck it, you know, draw in and hold it in your lungs till you . . . for a period of time."
> I said, "Is there any limit of time to hold it?"
> He said, "No, just till you feel that you want to let it out, let it out." So I did that three or four times.

Many new users are ashamed to admit ignorance and, pretending to know already, must learn through the more indirect means of observation and imitation:

> I came on like I had turned on [smoked marihuana] many times before, you know. I didn't want to seem like a punk to this cat. See, like I didn't know the first thing about it—how to smoke it, or what was going to happen, or what. I just watched him like a hawk—I didn't take my eyes off him for a second, because I wanted to do everything just as he did it. I watched how he held it, how he smoked it, and everything. Then when he gave it

to me I just came on cool, as though I knew exactly what the score was. I held it like he did and took a poke just the way he did.

No person continued marihuana use for pleasure without learning a technique that supplied sufficient dosage for the effects of the drug to appear. Only when this was learned was it possible for a conception of the drug as an object which could be used for pleasure to emerge. Without such a conception marihuana use was considered meaningless and did not continue.

II

Even after he learns the proper smoking technique, the new user may not get high and thus not form a conception of the drug as something which can be used for pleasure. A remark made by a user suggested the reason for this difficulty in getting high and pointed to the next necessary step on the road to being a user:

> I was told during an interview, "As a matter of fact, I've seen a guy who was high out of his mind and didn't know it."
> I expressed disbelief: "How can that be, man?"
> The interviewee said, "Well, it's pretty strange, I'll grant you that, but I've seen it. This guy got on with me, claiming that he'd never got high, one of those guys, and he got completely stoned. And he kept insisting that he wasn't high. So I had to prove to him that he was."

What does this mean? It suggests that being high consists of two elements: the presence of symptoms caused by marihuana use and the recognition of these symptoms and their connection by the user with his use of the drug. It is not enough, that is, that the effects be present; they alone do not automatically provide the experience of being high. The user must be able to point them out to himself and consciously connect them with his having smoked marihuana before he can have this experience. Otherwise, regardless of the actual effects produced, he considers that the drug has had no effect on him: "I figured it either had no effect on me or other people were exaggerating its effect on them, you know. I thought it was probably psychological, see." Such persons believe that the whole thing is an illusion and that the wish to be high leads the user to deceive himself into believing that something is happening when, in fact, nothing is. They do not continue marihuana use, feeling that "it does nothing" for them.

Typically, however, the novice has faith (developed from his observation of users who do get high) that the drug actually will produce some new experience and continues to experiment with it until it does. His failure to get high worries him, and he is likely to ask more experienced users or provoke comments from them about it. In such conversations he is made aware of specific details of his experience which he may not have noticed or may have noticed but failed to identify as symptoms of being high:

I didn't get high the first time. . . . I don't think I held it in long enough. I probably let it out, you know, you're a little afraid. The second time I wasn't sure, and he [smoking companion] told me, like I asked him for some of the symptoms or something, how would I know, you know. . . . So he told me to sit on a stool. I sat on—I think I sat on a bar stool— and he said, "Let your feet hang," and then when I got down my feet were real cold, you know.

And I started feeling it, you know. That was the first time. And then about a week after that, sometime pretty close to it, I really got on. That was the first time I got on a big laughing kick, you know. Then I really knew I was on.

One symptom of being high is an intense hunger. In the next case the novice becomes aware of this and gets high for the first time:

They were just laughing the hell out of me because like I was eating so much. I just scoffed [ate] so much food, and they were just laughing at me, you know. Sometimes I'd be looking at them, you know, wondering why they're laughing, you know, not knowing what I was doing. [Well, did they tell you why they were laughing eventually?] Yeah, yeah, I come back, "Hey, man, what's happening?" Like, you know, like I'd ask, "What's happening?" and all of a sudden I feel weird, you know. "Man, you're on, you know. You're on pot [high on marihuana]." I said, "No, am I?" Like I don't know what's happening.

The learning may occur in more indirect ways:

I heard little remarks that were made by other people. Somebody said, "My legs are rubbery," and I can't remember all the remarks that were made because I was very attentively listening for all these cues for what I was supposed to feel like.

The novice, then, eager to have this feeling, picks up from other users some concrete referents of the term "high" and applies these notions to his own experience. The new concepts make it possible for him to locate these symptoms among his own sensations and to point out to himself a "something different" in his experience that he connects with drug use. It is only when he can do this that he is high. In the next case, the contrast between two successive experiences of a user makes clear the crucial importance of the awareness of the symptoms in being high and re-emphasizes the important role of interaction with other users in acquiring the concepts that make this awareness possible:

[Did you get high the first time you turned on?] Yeah, sure. Although, come to think of it, I guess I really didn't. I mean, like that first time it was more or less of a mild drunk. I was happy, I guess, you know what I mean. But I didn't really know I was high, you know what I mean. It was only after the second time I got high that I realized I was high the first time. Then I knew that something different was happening.

[How did you know that?] How did I know? If what happened to me that night would of happened to you, you would've known, believe me. We played the first tune for almost two hours—one tune! Imagine, man! We got on the stand and played this one tune, we started at nine o'clock. When we got finished I looked at my watch, it's a quarter to eleven. Almost two hours on one tune. And it didn't seem like anything.

I mean, you know, it does that to you. It's like you have much more time or something. Anyway, when I saw that, man, it was too much. I knew I must really be high or something if anything like that could happen. See, and then they explained to me that that's what it did to you. You had a different sense of time and everything. So I realized that that's what it was. I knew then. Like the first time, I probably felt that way, you know, but I didn't know what's happening.

It is only when the novice becomes able to get high in this sense that he will continue to use marihuana for pleasure. In every case in which use continued, the user had acquired the necessary concepts with which to express to himself the fact that he was experiencing new sensations caused by the drug. That is, for use to continue, it is necessary not only to use the drug so as to produce effects but also to learn to perceive these effects when they occur. In this way marihuana acquires meaning for the user as an object which can be used for pleasure.

With increasing experience the user develops a greater appreciation of the drug's effects; he continues to learn to get high. He examines succeeding experiences closely, looking for new effects, making sure the old ones are still there. Out of this there grows a stable set of categories for experiencing the drug's effects whose presence enables the user to get high with ease.

The ability to perceive the drug's effects must be maintained if use is to continue; if it is lost, marihuana use ceases. Two kinds of evidence support this statement. First, people who become heavy users of alcohol, barbiturates, or opiates do not continue to smoke marihuana, largely because they lose the ability to distinguish between its effects and those of the other drugs. They no longer know whether the marihuana gets them high. Second, in those few cases in which an individual uses marihuana in such quantities that he is always high, he is apt to get this same feeling that the drug has no effect on him, since the essential element of a noticable difference between feeling high and feeling normal is missing. In such a situation, use is likely to be given up completely, but temporarily, in order that the user may once again be able to perceive the difference.

III

One more step is necessary if the user who has now learned to get high is to continue use. He must learn to enjoy the effects he has just learned to experience. Marihuana-produced sensations are not automatically or necessarily pleasurable. The taste for such experience is a socially acquired one, not different in kind from acquired tastes for oysters or dry martinis. The user feels dizzy, thirsty; his scalp tingles; he misjudges time and distances; and so on. Are these things pleasurable? He isn't sure. If he is to continue marihuana use, he must decide that they are. Otherwise, getting high, while a real enough experience, will be an unpleasant one he would rather avoid.

The effects of the drug, when first perceived, may be physically unpleasant or at least ambiguous:

> It started taking effect, and I didn't know what was happening, you know, what it was, and I was very sick. I walked around the room, walking around the room trying to get off, you know; it just scared me at first, you know. I wasn't used to that kind of feeling.

In addition, the novice's naïve interpretation of what is happening to him may further confuse and frighten him, particularly if he decides, as many do, that he is going insane:

> I felt I was insane, you know. Everything people done to me just wigged me. I couldn't hold a conversation, and my mind would be wandering, and I was always thinking, oh, I don't know, weird things, like hearing music different. . . . I get the feeling that I can't talk to anyone. I'll goof completely.

Given these typically frightening and unpleasant first experiences, the beginner will not continue use unless he learns to redefine the sensations as pleasurable:

> It was offered to me, and I tried it. I'll tell you one thing. I never did enjoy it at all. I mean it was just nothing that I could enjoy. [Well, did you get high when you turned on?] Oh, yeah, I got definite feelings from it. But I didn't enjoy them. I mean I got plenty of reactions, but they were mostly reactions of fear. [You were frightened?] Yes. I didn't enjoy it. I couldn't seem to relax with it, you know. If you can't relax with a thing, you can't enjoy it, I don't think.

In other cases the first experiences were also definitely unpleasant, but the person did become a marihuana user. This occurred, however, only after a later experience enabled him to redefine the sensations as pleasurable:

[This man's first experience was extremely unpleasant, involving distortion of spatial relationships and sounds, violent thirst, and panic produced by these symptoms.] After the first time I didn't turn on for about, I'd say, ten months to a year. . . . It wasn't a moral thing; it was because I'd gotten so frightened, bein' so high. An' I didn't want to go through that again, I mean, my reaction was, "Well, if this is what they call bein' high, I don't dig [like] it." . . . So I didn't turn on for a year almost, accounta that. . . .

Well, my friends started, an' consequently I started again. But I didn't have any more, I didn't have that same initial reaction, after I started turning on again.

[In interaction with his friends he became able to find pleasure in the effects of the drug and eventually became a regular user.]

In no case will use continue without such a redefinition of the effects as enjoyable.

This redefinition occurs, typically, in interaction with more experienced users who, in a number of ways, teach the novice to find pleasure in this experience which is at first so frightening. They may reassure him as to the temporary character of the unpleasant sensations and minimize their seriousness, at the same time calling attention to the more enjoyable aspects. An experienced user describes how he handles newcomers to marihuana use:

Well, they get pretty high sometimes. The average person isn't ready for that, and it is a little frightening to them sometimes. I mean, they've been high on lush [alcohol], and they get higher that way than they've ever been before, and they don't know what's happening to them. Because they think you're going to keep going up, up, up till they lose their minds or begin doing weird things or something. You have to like reassure them, explain to them that they're not really flipping or anything, that they're gonna be all right. You have to just talk them out of being afraid. Keep talking to them, reassuring, teling them it's all right. And come on with your own story, you know: "The same thing happened to me. You'll get to like that after awhile." Keep coming on like that; pretty soon you talk them out of being scared. And besides they see you doing it and nothing horrible is happening to you, so that gives them more confidence.

The more experienced user may also teach the novice to regulate the amount he smokes more carefully, so as to avoid any severely uncomfortable symptoms while retaining the pleasant ones. Finally, he teaches the new user that he can "get to like it after awhile." He teaches him to regard those ambiguous experiences formerly defined as unpleasant as enjoyable. The older user in the following incident is a person whose tastes have shifted in this way, and his remarks have the effect of helping others to make a similar redefinition:

A new user had her first experience of the effects of marihuana and became frightened and hysterical. She "felt like she was half in and half out
of the room" and experienced a number of alarming physical symptoms.
One of the more experienced users present said, "She's dragged because
she's high like that. I'd give anything to get that high myself. I haven't
been that high in years."

In short, what was once frightening and distasteful becomes, after a
taste for it is built up, pleasant, desired, and sought after. Enjoyment is
introduced by the favorable definition of the experience that one acquires
from others. Without this, use will not continue, for marihuana will not
be for the user an object he can use for pleasure.

In addition to being a necessary step in becoming a user, this represents an important condition for continued use. It is quite common for
experienced users suddenly to have an unpleasant or frightening experience, which they cannot define as pleasurable, either because they
have used a larger amount of marihuana than usual or because it turns
out to be a higher-quality marihuana than they expected. The user has
sensations which go beyond any conception he has of what being high
is and is in much the same situation as the novice, uncomfortable and
frightened. He may blame it on an overdose and simply be more careful
in the future. But he may make this the occasion for a rethinking of his
attitude toward the drug and decide that it no longer can give him
pleasure. When this occurs and is not followed by a redefinition of the
drug as capable of producing pleasure, use will cease.

The likelihood of such a redefinition occurring depends on the degree
of the individual's participation with other users. Where this participation is intensive, the individual is quickly talked out of his feeling
against marihuana use. In the next case, on the other hand, the experience was very disturbing, and the aftermath of the incident cut the
person's participation with other users to almost zero. Use stopped for
three years and began again only when a combination of circumstances,
important among which was a resumption of ties with users, made possible a redefinition of the nature of the drug:

> It was too much, like I only made about four pokes, and I couldn't even
> get it out of my mouth, I was so high, and I got real flipped. In the base-
> ment, you know, I just couldn't stay in there anymore. My heart was
> pounding real hard, you know, and I was going out of my mind; I thought
> I was losing my mind completely. So I cut out of this basement, and this
> other guy, he's out of his mind, told me, "Don't, don't leave me, man.
> Stay here." And I couldn't.
>
> I walked outside, and it was five below zero, and I thought I was dying,
> and I had my coat open; I was sweating, I was perspiring. My whole in-
> sides were all . . . , and I walked about two blocks away, and I fainted

behind a bush. I don't know how long I laid there. I woke up, and I was feeling the worst, I can't describe it at all, so I made it to a bowling alley, man, and I was trying to act normal, I was trying to shoot pool, you know, trying to act real normal, and I couldn't lay and I couldn't stand up and I couldn't sit down, and I went up and laid down where some guys that spot pins lay down and that didn't help me, and I went to a doctor's office. I was going to go in there and tell the doctor to put me out of my misery . . . because my heart was pounding so hard, you know. . . . So then all week end I started flipping, seeing things there and going through hell, you know, all kinds of abnormal things. . . . I just quit for a long time then.

[He went to a doctor who defined the symptoms for him as those of a nervous breakdown caused by "nerves" and "worries." Although he was no longer using marihuana, he had some recurrences of the symptoms which led him to suspect that "it was all his nerves."] So I just stopped worrying, you know; so it was about thirty-six months later I started making it again. I'd just take a few pokes, you know. [He first resumed use in the company of the same user-friend with whom he had been involved in the original incident.]

A person, then, cannot begin to use marihuana for pleasure, or continue its use for pleasure, unless he learns to define its effects as enjoyable, unless it becomes and remains an object which he conceives of as capable of producing pleasure. . . .

REPORT ON THE TREATMENT OF DRUG ADDICTION

Jonathan O. Cole

CONTROL AND TREATMENT METHODS

What, then, are the available treatment methods which need to be considered? These need to be crudely grouped into voluntary and involuntary approaches. This poses some problem since voluntary commitment is often only relatively voluntary, being chosen by the addict in lieu of imprisonment or being deserted by his wife or other less desirable consequence.

From *Narcotics and Drug Abuse*, The Task Force Report, The President's Commission on Law Enforcement and the Administration of Justice, 1967, Appendix C, pp. 135-42.

INVOLUNTARY TREATMENTS

1. *Imprisonment.*   Being placed in jail or prison for a short or long period is a frequent result of heroin addiction. Available followup studies . . . do not suggest that this treatment, per se, has any particular benefit to the individual, although it may be good for society. It is possible that the addition of more intensive treatment and rehabilitation programs to conventional incarceration might be worthwhile, but this has not been demonstrated to be effective and is only being tried in a few locations. . . . Prisoners have been treated at the U.S. Public Health Service hospitals at Lexington and Fort Worth for many years. It may, of course, be that repeated imprisonment is one of the factors leading to the probable aging out whereby older addicts gradually give up their drug use.

2. *Imprisonment Plus Parole.*   There is evidence . . . that intensive parole supervision is more effective than minimal parole in keeping addicts drug free and out of criminal activities. There is also a followup study . . . which suggests that conventional parole, per se, may be useful in keeping addicts off drugs.

Diskind and Klonsky of the New York State division of parole have reported on three followup studies. The longest followup study looked at 673 offenders referred between November 1, 1956, and December 31, 1961. Their adjustment as of December 1962 was noted. Twenty-seven percent made a fully satisfactory recovery (abstinent and without further criminal record) while 36 percent were at least abstinent. The median length of supervision for the successful cases was 16 months (range 2 months to 2 years) compared with 8 months for unsuccessful cases.

The authors point to the fact that unsupervised patients in the community have been shown (in 90 percent of cases) to relapse in 6 months, whereas their group showed only 69 percent relapse in this time period. . . .

3. *Probation.*   Assuming that the patient's addiction can be medically handled in a hospital, or in jail before trial, there is no a priori reason for believing that probation might not be as effective as parole.

4. *Involuntary Commitment.*   The major difference between this modality and those noted above lies in the facilities and personnel being used. Psychiatric hospitals and psychiatrically run aftercare clinics would be employed with imprisonment lurking in the background as a threat to induce compliance.

5. *Voluntary Commitment.*   If this is accepted in a setting of threat of trial and imprisonment for noncompliance, the differences for the

individual addict may be more apparent than real. However, involuntary commitment usually follows criminal conviction while voluntary commitment may precede any trial or conviction. The individual addict may be less stigmatized by the latter approach. It seems unlikely that these factors per se would have any major impact on treatment outcome, though they may indicate precommitment differences in the kinds of addicts getting into either system.

All of the above methods can be viewed as devices for forcing addicts to expose themselves to surveillance and treatment. If only the formal legal procedures exist without staff or facilities, there may be little difference in outcome between approaches.

VOLUNTARY TREATMENTS

Four major voluntary treatment settings exist:

1. *Medical-psychiatric.* A number of hospitals will admit heroin addicts on a voluntary basis for detoxification with or without other treatment modalities being applied. These may be utilized by addicts under legal pressure to avoid trial and imprisonment and, thus, resemble voluntary commitment but without quite as much pressure for cooperation in long-term treatment. Addicts may seek hospitalization to reduce the size and cost of their habit without any motivation for a real cure. They may also be used by addicts really wanting help. The efficacy of such programs may be quite different for each of the three groups of patients.

2. *Synanon-type Programs.* Several primarily nonmedical programs exist which utilize ex-addict personnel and group pressures and therapeutic community and interpersonal confrontation techniques to help addicts face their problems and change their behavior.

3. *Addicts Anonymous.* This voluntary group program modeled after Alcoholics Anonymous provides group meetings and interpersonal support.

4. *Religious Program.* These rely on religion as a major motivation for abstinence.

ANCILLARY TREATMENTS AIMED PRIMARILY AT ENSURING ABSTINENCE

1. *Nalline Testing.* California and a few other programs utilize periodic injections of Nalline, a narcotic antagonist to test patients for evidence of readdiction. Addicted patients show pupillary dilation; nonaddicted patients show pupillary constriction.

2. *Urine Testing.* Thin-layer chromotography and, potentially, other methods, can be used to examine the urines of addicts under treatment for the presence of opiates.

3. *Cyclazocine.*   This long-acting Nalline-like drug, if taken daily in large (4 mg. or larger) doses can, apparently, successfully prevent even relatively large doses of heroin from having any effect. Readdiction is therefore impossible.

4. *Methadone.*   This long-acting opiate, if taken daily in a relatively large dose, provides a substitute addiction which also makes heroin-taking ineffective.

All four methods are designed to prevent readdiction to heroin. The Nalline and urine methods both discourage readdiction and insure that relapses will be picked up. The rapidity and reliability with which this is done depends on the frequency of testing. Both methods pose a secondary problem. Should occasional brief returns to heroin use result in return to an institution—penal or medical—or should they be used as a focus of discussion in outpatient treatment? If the latter, how much heroin use is too much?

All four methods depend on the patient's daily or periodic compliance, but can be used in either voluntary or involuntary programs. They all provide forms of external control over the addict's behavior.

ANCILLARY TREATMENTS AIMED AT REHABILITATION

1. *Individual Psychotherapy.*   Work with an individual addict by a single treater has been frequently attempted. The types of therapists have included psychiatrists, social workers, psychologists, ministers, parole officers, and even ex-addicts. The kinds of treatment used have included everything from psychoanalytically oriented psychotherapy to intensive reality-oriented supportive psychotherapy to less structured irregular contacts. It is often difficult to define this modality and the approach used may vary widely even with different patients seen by the same therapist. A single study . . . has demonstrated that LSD, a psychotomimetic drug, given with hypnotherapy, can produce a significant short-term favorable change in the attitudes of addicts toward themselves and toward the future. This approach needs further evaluation with followup of treated addicts into the community. LSD in this context is chiefly a way of intensifying the impact of short-term psychotherapy.

2. *Group Psychotherapy.*   Again the level and nature of this treatment of addicts in groups varies greatly and can include everything from formal psychoanalytically oriented group psychotherapy to psychodrama to Synanon and Addicts Anonymous.

3. *Mileu Treatment.*   Here structured settings are used as a treatment modality. At the Synanon end this can resemble chronic 24-hour group psychotherapy. At the minimal end it can consist chiefly of a drug-free environment which provides reasonable rules and regulations and some activities to keep patients occupied.

4. *Special Living Arrangements.*   Here again Synanon houses, half-way houses or, potentially, placement of addicts to live with normal families can be used to give the addict a stable place to live in the community while attempting to build a better life adjustment for himself back in the community. Patient clubs providing recreation and social contacts during evening and weekend hours can also be included here.

5. *Vocational Rehabilitation.*   Since many addicts have never achieved any stable work role, training ex-addicts may be necessary to make them employable or to enable them to hold jobs which will be satisfying and offer hope of a better future. Such training can, of course, take place in institutions or on an outpatient basis. Job placement for addicts who have skills is also a necessary service.

6. *Family and Social Services.*   Work with the addict's family may be useful in correcting old and harmful interpersonal attitudes and behaviors and in helping the family support and assist the patient. For patients without families, assistance may be needed to find reasonable places to live and to develop recreational and other leisure-time activities. Ex-addicts may also need help with a variety of medical, social, or legal problems which may not be directly related to their past addiction.

The above lists cover most of the currently possible techniques and approaches to the treatment of heroin addicts. At present, there is little basis for identifying any particular constellation of approaches, facilities, and services as being most effective. . . .

TREATMENT OUTCOME

There is overwhelming consensus, based on a good deal of evidence, on a few statements about the outcome of treatments of heroin addicts.

1. Methadone treatment during the acute withdrawal phase is safe, sound, and reasonable and is superior to the use of nonopiate tranquilizers and sedatives.

2. The relapse rate following simple institutionalization (medical or penal) and release without aftercare or rehabilitation is very high.

3. Three classes of opiate addicts may show a somewhat better prognosis for abstinence independent of treatment:

    (a) Medical addicts—patients becoming addicted in the course of treatment by physicians for real or functional physical complaints

    (b) Physicians or other professional addicts

    (c) Older heroin addicts

4. Enforced parole or aftercare leads to less readdiction or reimprisonment than minimal or no aftercare treatment.

5. Most heroin addicts do not cooperate well in formal interview-type dynamic psychotherapy or casework of the sort ordinarily provided to middle-class psychoneurotics.

6. Most heroin addicts have a large array of needs and inadequacies over and above their use of narcotics—no money, no place to live, no readily marketable job skills, low frustration tolerance, low interest in or experience with the usual activities and pressures of the "square" world, plus, usually, difficult family situations, plus low motivation to solve any of these problems and little trust in professional therapists.

Given the above as a reasonably probable set of facts, it is interesting to note that programs claiming substantial (if often undefined) success may be superficially very different (e.g., Synanon, Daytop Lodge, the California Rehabilitation Center, New York City's intensive parole, methadone, cyclazocine, frequent urine testing) but all have several elements in common:

1. Considerable outside pressure to stay off drugs—provided in Synanon by group pressure and in more penal programs by a real threat of return to an institution.

2. Reasonably frequent supportive contact with the treatment agency.

3. Some assistance or encouragement to get a job and find a suitable place to live.

Given all the above, a number of areas of disagreement exist as to the best treatment approach.

1. *Voluntary vs. Involuntary Treatment.*   This is, in part, an ethical philosophic issue relating to one's attitude to force vs. free will. Although voluntary programs like Synanon may, as they claim, do very well (this program refuses to give any data at all on its failure rate or allow controlled evaluation), at the moment it seems unlikely that most addicts will seek voluntary treatment spontaneously. The parallel question concerns the long-term efficacy of various approaches. Do Synanon graduates living in the ordinary world do better than addicts who have stayed off drugs and adjusted reasonably well during a prolonged obligatory parole or aftercare program and are then left without controls? We know of no data pertinent to answer this question.

2. *The Optimal Period of In-Patient Treatment.* Again, although it would appear reasonable that intensive psychotherapy, sociotherapy and vocational rehabilitation in an inpatient or prison setting should enable the addict to do better when he is returned to the community, we know of no positive evidence that this is the case. Although there is some evidence in addicts that some physiological alterations (slightly elevated body temperature, elevated blood sedimentation rate, increased cold-pressor test response) may persist for 5 or 6 months after withdrawal from opiates, the relation of such abnormalities to psychological craving for heroin or to actual return to heoin use is unknown. This latter problem needs systematic study, since hospitalization is expensive and may be unnecessarily prolonged for no valid reason.

3. *Treatment Setting.*   Are medical settings really superior to penal ones? Does treating addicts in settings devoted solely to the treatment of addicts help or hurt? It has been claimed that such settings teach naive addicts how to become professional and competent addicts. Are addicts really too troublesome to be treated on ordinary psychiatric or medical services? Are ex-addict personnel necessary or particularly effective? Or is their use partially justified because it creates jobs for ex-addicts? . . .

DESCRIPTIONS OF A REPRESENTATIVE SPECTRUM OF
TREATMENT PROGRAMS IN THE UNITED STATES

Daytop Lodge.   An open, voluntary treatment program serving drug addicts placed on probation by the local courts in Brooklyn, N. Y. This is, technically, a halfway house but has a much more active treatment program headed by a Synanon-trained ex-addict and staffed chiefly by ex-addicts. The major features are:

1. The newly referred addict is made to fight his way into the program.

2. Rigid high standards for behavior in all areas are expected and enforced by all patients.

3. The new addict is treated as a helpless child at first but gradually moves from menial to responsible jobs at the lodge and finally to work outside.

4. Vigorous, aggressive, "gut-level" group sessions are held frequently.

5. More intellectual, philosophic seminar sessions are also held.

The similarity to Synanon descriptions is striking, the major differences being that Synanon is a purely voluntary private organization, while Daytop Lodge (capacity 25) is supported by a National Institute of Mental Health grant and is under court sponsorship. Very recently, the Daytop Lodge program has been moved to a larger 130-bed facility which receives support from the city of New York and now also accepts voluntary admissions and patients from sources other than the Brooklyn courts.

Puerto Rico.   Dr. Ramirez, now in charge of the New York City narcotics addict program, has developed an elaborately phased program in which addicts first get involved either while still addicted or in prison, attend group sessions, and gradually work their way through phases of increasing responsibility and increasing involvement in the contacting and treating of other addicts. As of February 1966, it appeared that the few full graduates of this program were all employed by the program as helpers for new patients.

California Rehabilitation Center, Corona, Calif.   This treatment program, under the corrections system of the State, has been running for 4 years. All patients, even volunteers, are committed, volunteers for 2½ years, while patients committed following a criminal conviction have a 7-year commitment.

The inpatient treatment program is modeled on Maxwell Jones' "therapeutic community" concept, with 60-man living groups comprising the treatment unit. Daily group discussion meetings are held at which both current living problems and deeper matters are discussed. Emphasis is also given to increasing assumption of responsibility by the patients. Work therapy, school, and vocational training are provided. The period in the institution is relatively long, at least 6 months being required by law. Actual inpatient time is averaging 15 months for men and 11 months for women. The timing of release to the community is based on staff evaluation of each patient's evidence of growth and strength and ability to assume responsibility for his own behavior.

On return to the community, patients are intensively supervised by caseworkers with special training and low (30) caseloads, including weekly group meetings and individual contacts with each patient, at home or on the job. Nalline tests are given, both on a regular and surprise basis five times a month for at least the first 6 months.

Urinalysis is now being studied as an alternative monitoring technique. Patients showing signs of relapse—either a return to drugs or heavy drinking or inability to hold jobs or other delinquent activity—are returned to Corona for further treatment. A halfway house program is being developed.

In December 1965, there were 1,672 males and 268 females in the center. Also 2,578 men and 665 women had been released to the community. Almost half had been returned to the center for further treatment. Only about 33 percent of released patients last a year in the community free of drugs, but only half of those returned for further treatment had actually returned to heroin abuse. . . .

Fort Worth and Lexington U.S.P.H.S. Hospitals.   These programs include detoxification, a stable controlled environment, some access to individual and group psychotherapy, educational and vocational rehabilitation programs, industrial and recreational therapy. The results of this program in either voluntary addict admissions who are supposed to stay 5 months, but average about 6 weeks, or for prisoner patients, are relatively poor. About 10 percent stay drug-free for the first year after release. . . .

Methadone Maintenance Treatment.   This approach has been recommended by Drs. Dole and Nyswander but has also been used by Dr. Jaffe at Einstein and by Canadian groups. It consists of two variants:
   1. Gradual outpatient withdrawal with methadone being administered

in slowly decreasing doses for several months but leading reasonably directly to total abstinence.

2. Prolonged maintenance on relatively high dosages of methadone (up to 80–100 mgs. per day) in a single supervised daily dose of liquid medication. At this level, self-administration of relatively large amounts of illicit heroin has little effect. The patient is thus "protected" against illicit heroin abuse.

As managed by Dole and Nyswander, their program has a certain missionary zeal and esprit de corps which may be partially responsible for their claims of almost universal success. Of 108 patients started in their program prior to February 1, 1966, 101 were still under their care. Of the 48 patients under treatment for 8 to 25 months, more than half were employed or in school and were self-supporting.

This program is currently being extended to a new parallel unit at Harlem Hospital.

It should be noted that the methadone is accompanied by a good deal of supportive contact and pressure toward rehabilitation. It will be interesting to see whether other units not run by this dynamic duo will have similar success. Urinary monitoring for abuse of heroin or other drugs is employed. Dr. Dole does not deny that his patients may abuse some nonopiate drugs, but claims that they take no drugs which they had not taken prior to treatment. . . .

Cyclazocine Treatment.   This long-acting opiate antagonist (similar to Nalline) . . . has now been tried as a treatment in addicts on a pilot basis by Jaffe and by Freedman in New York.

If an addict is gradually built up to a daily dose of 4 to 6 mgs. of cyclazocine a day (too rapid increase causes feelings of unreality and hallucinations), the effects of illicit heroin will be essentially completely blocked as long as he keeps taking the drug. . . . The drug is well-tolerated as a treatment procedure in addicts. The treatment is monitored by frequent urinalysis.

Philadelphia Board of Parole.   Here prisoners with a history of addiction are begun on group therapy sessions in prison several months before release. They continue with the same therapist after release and rceive relatively intensive parole supervision and casework from specially trained parole officers with small caseloads. Some urine testing is done. A 60-percent success rate for the first year after release is reported.

Baltimore Drug Addiction Clinic.   Here, addicts are contacted in prison concerning interest in a daily urine testing program. If they volunteer for the program and can obtain a job, they are followed daily in a clinic in downtown Baltimore with active parole supervision and some group psychotherapy. Positive urine tests are initially used as a basis for intensive discussion of the patient's dynamics and problems. Continued drug taking leads to return to prison. About a 30-percent abstinence rate for the first year appears to be achieved.

TREATMENT FOR PERSONS USING NONOPIATE DRUGS OF ABUSE

There are no special treatment facilities specifically designed to serve individuals dependent on nonopiate drugs and most programs are restricted to opiate addicts.

Withdrawal detoxification of patients heavily dependent on barbiturates or most other sedatives and some tranquilizers (e.g., meprobamate or chlordiazepoxide), can pose serious difficulties requiring more intensive medical supervision than does opiate withdrawal. If dependence is undetected and convulsions and delirium occur, administration of barbiturates can sometimes fail to reverse the process. Deaths can occur.

Although adequate data are lacking, abusers of barbituates and amphetamines probably include more medical (doctor-dependent) abusers and fewer street users than is true for opiate abusers. It seems likely that some combination of intensive supervision and treatment plus regular urine monitoring to detect relapse might be useful, but more study of this group or groups of drug abusers is needed urgently as a basis for clearer recommendations.

Abusers of LSD or other hallucinogens who develop psychiatric symptoms (schizophrenic-like or panic reactions) can probably be adequately handled in conventional psychiatric settings.

POSSIBLE NEW METHODS OF TREATMENT

1. A cyclazocine-like drug with a much longer duration of action (3 days to 2 weeks) would be useful since the patients would have to come to the clinic less frequently.

2. Formal conditioning theory . . . suggests that cyclazocine or similar treatments could be made more effective if the addict tried heroin or a similar drug several times and got no effect, thus extinguishing his earlier conditioned positive response to the drug.

3. Behavior therapy—a form of conditioning treatment developed chiefly by Wolpe in this country has been applied successfully to one physician addict. This work could be extended.

4. Preliminary reports from Iran claim that an antidepressant phenothiazine combination (amitriptyline-perphenazine) is effective in Persian addicts in preventing relapse.

5. Obviously addicts are a heterogeneous group of people and if further research could tell us which patients do better on which kind of treatment, a substantial advance would have been made.

6. As with alcoholism, it is likely that addicts might benefit from better

integration and coordination of the various medical, social rehabilitation, and welfare services available in most large cities.

7. It is possible that the treatment of heroin addicts in nonaddict settings—general hospitals, psychiatric clinics, a doctor's private office— might aid his separation from the addict culture. This possibility should be explored. . . .

THE LEXINGTON PROGRAM
FOR NARCOTIC ADDICTS
John A. O'Donnell

. . .

Located about 5 miles from Lexington, Kentucky, the USPHS hospital for narcotic addicts was opened in 1935. The present functional capacity of the hospital is about 1,050 patients. This represents a reduction in capacity of about 150 patients [between 1957 and 1962]. . . . This reduction in capacity was the result of converting some dormitory space to additional or expanded treatment facilities. About 240 of these beds are in medical, surgical, intensive psychiatric, and withdrawal units. The rest of the beds are in continued treatment units; 440 of the beds are in single rooms, another 220 beds are in double rooms, and the remainder in multiple rooms none of which has more than six beds.

Since its opening the hospital has handled about 70,000 admissions. Roughly 60 percent of these have been first admissions, and a large part of the readmissions are accounted for by a relatively small number of persons. In recent years, the average number of addict admissions has been about 3,500 per year. This figure is about twice as high as it was in the first 10 years the hospital was open, but is much less than it was in the early 1950's. Slightly over 10 percent of admissions are accounted for by federal prisoners, and 50 to 60 admissions a year are accounted for by federal probationers. To the extent that beds are available after eligible prisoners and probationers have been admitted, voluntary patients are admitted at their own request. They account for almost 90 percent of all addict admissions.

The essential eligibility requirement for admission is that the patient has been addicted to narcotic drugs as defined in the federal law. These include: Cocaine, Coca Leaves, Codeine, Dihydrocodeinone (Dicodid, Hycodan), Dihydromorphinone (Dilaudid), Heroin, Indian Hemp (mar-

From *Federal Probation,* Vol. 26, No. 1 (March 1962), 55-59. Reprinted by permission.

ihuana), Laudanum, Meperidine (Demerol, Isonipecaine), Methadon (Dolophine), Metopon, Morphine, Opium, Pantopon, Paregoric, Peyote (mescaline), and NU-2206 (3-Hydroxy-N-Methyl-Morphinan). Persons addicted to barbiturates, alcohol, or other drugs not listed above are not eligible for admission unless they are also addicted to a narcotic drug.

While federal prisoners represent only about 10 percent of admissions, they account for about half of the patients in the hospital on any given date because they remain longer. These prisoners are not necessarily persons who have violated one of the federal laws concerning drugs. Many, for example, were sentenced for stealing from the mails, transporting cars across state lines, etc. They are sent to the hospital rather than one of the Bureau of Prisons institutions because they happen to be addicts and require treatment. Those selected for commitment to Lexington actually form only a small percentage of federal addict prisoners, many of whom are committed to reformatories and penitentiaries because they have marked antisocial records prior to addiction, are escape risks, or for other reasons are unsuitable for the treatment program at Lexington.

Federal probationers are committed to the hospital as a condition of their probation and would normally be regarded as violating probation if they demanded release and left the hospital before the staff felt they had completed the period of treatment indicated for them.

The voluntary patient applies for admission and may leave the hospital against medical advice at any time. Many of these patients come to the hospital under a great deal of pressure, perhaps from their families or physicians. Quite frequently the voluntary patient is on probation from a county or city court. There are two chief differences between such a patient and the federal probationer. One is that the hospital is not required to accept him as a patient. He must go through the usual admission procedures for voluntary patients, sometimes including a fairly long waiting period. Another difference is that if a person on probation from a nonfederal court demands his release, the hospital cannot notify his probation officer or anyone else without the patients consent.

Voluntary patients are required to pay for the cost of hospitalization if they can afford to do so. This cost has varied over the years. At the present time it is $9.50 per day. The determination as to ability to pay is made by the medical officer in charge of the hospital and is based on information the applicant furnishes on his application. In practice, few voluntary patients can afford to pay the cost of hospitalization.

LENGTH OF HOSPITALIZATION

A prisoner can be kept under treatment for the full length of his sentence, or may be transferred to a penal institution after whatever treatment period seems adequate to the medical staff. For probationers and voluntary patients there is no fixed length of hospitalization, though normally a period of about 5 months is considered the minimum. Treatment considerations may require extending the period of hospitalization to a year or even more, and in unusual cases a shorter period may be considered sufficient.

ADMISSION POLICIES

The admission policies and procedures are simple. Federal prisoners and probationers must be admitted. Voluntary patients will be admitted when beds are available for their treatment. A person desiring to be admitted as a voluntary patient may obtain an application form from the hospital, complete it, and mail it directly to the hospital. He will be notified by letter that he is to report to the hospital by a certain date, that his name is being placed on a waiting list and that he will be notified when a bed is available, or that he is not eligible for treatment.

Admissions are authorized in the order in which the applications are received, though the hospital reserves the right, during periods when a waiting list is established, to give priority to applicants who have not been treated before. The Lexington hospital accepts women from any state and men from east of the Mississippi River. Men from west of the Mississippi usually are treated at the United States Public Health Service Hospital at Fort Worth, Texas. There are minor exceptions to this rule. Others may be made when waiting lists exist.

TREATMENT PROGRAM

The treatment program consists of four phases. For voluntary patients, the first phase is usually the withdrawal of narcotics. Methadone is substituted for the various narcotics used by patients and reduced gradually but rapidly in amount. If a patient is also addicted to barbiturates, a similar but slower gradual reduction is carried on simultaneously. The average time for withdrawal is about a week, but may range from a day or two to 3 or 4 weeks. The withdrawal procedure varies from individual to individual, the time required depending on many factors, most important of these being the drug used, the quantity used, and the physical condition of the patient. Prisoners and probationers have usually been withdrawn from drugs before they arrive at the hospital.

The second phase begins when withdrawal has been completed, or when it has been determined that withdrawal is not necessary. The patient is transferred to an Orientation and Evaluation Unit. The time spent in this ward will vary from about 2 weeks to 1 month. During this time patients are seen, in groups and individually, by a psychiatrist, a psychologist, a social worker, a vocation and education officer, and a psychiatric aide. As the name of the unit implies, these contacts have two purposes: The patient is familiarized with the hospital program in terms of what is expected from him and of what kinds of treatment facilities are available. Simultaneously, the professional personnel of the hospital are engaged in the study of the patient, each focusing on the area of his specialization. The purpose of this study is to evaluate the nature of the psychiatric disorder and the patient's readiness for the different kinds of treatment available. When pre-sentence investigation reports are available, they are extremely valuable in the study of the patient.

When the study is completed the staff members meet, discuss the case, and agree on a hospital program for the individual patient.

The third phase of treatment begins with the patient's transfer from the Orientation and Evaluation Unit to a Continued Treatment Unit. Normally he is first assigned to a ward where supervision is quite close, with the understanding that he can be transferred later to medium or minimum supervision wards as he demonstrates his ability to function with less supervision.

The psychiatric staff of the hospital consists of eight staff psychiatrists and 10 to 12 psychiatric residents in the first or second year of their training. While these numbers seem high to those who are familiar with the staffing of correctional institutions, they are low for the number of annual admissions and the number of patients who are potential candidates for psychotherapy. During 1960, a total of 263 addict patients were carried in psychotherapy, 156 in individual psychotherapy, and 117 in group psychotherapy. (These figures total more than 263 because some patients were in both individual and group psychotherapy.) In 1960 a total of almost 8,000 hours was spent by these patients in psychotherapy.

In most cases of individual psychotherapy the patient is seen a minimum of 1 hour per week on a regular basis. Some are seen more frequently. In 1960 two were being seen five times a week. The usual pattern of group psychotherapy is one 90-minute session per week, but several groups meet twice a week. Group therapy is normally conducted by a therapist-observer team.

Whether or not a patient is assigned to formal psychotherapy, he continues under psychiatric supervision throughout his hospital stay. To each continued treatment area, of approximately 200 patients, there are assigned one or more psychiatric residents, a staff psychiatrist, and a social worker. Together with the psychiatric aides in these areas they are responsible for the clinical management of the patients.

The hospital emphasizes the vocational assignment of patients as one of its major treatment methods. . . . As examples of the jobs for which formal training programs are available, the agricultural industry trains patients in the fields of dairying, meat packing, equipment operation and maintenance, greenhouse operation, truck gardening, landscaping, office record management, and others. The needletrades industry has six training units aimed at developing specific vocational skills required in the garment industry. The printing and woodcrafts industries similarly prepare patients for specific skills in these industries. Patients can be assigned as helpers to the skilled tradesmen represented in the maintenance and housekeeping areas for job training in these specialties. These job assignments are by no means a complete listing.

Some of these assignments are also used for women patients who, in addition, can receive training in a microfilm unit as chairside dental assistants and as office personnel.

While this vocational training can obviously be of value in itself, the skills learned often are conceived as a secondary goal. The primary aim is therapeutic and arises from the relationship between the patient and the work supervisor. Many of the patients admitted to Lexington are not good candidates for any form of psychotherapy because this type of relationship has no meaning for them. A relationship with a work supervisor, however, has usually been part of their background and quite frequently is a troublesome relationship for them. With the training and consultation he receives from the psychiatric staff, the work supervisor can frequently establish a relationship with a patient which is potentially more therapeutic than would be a relationship with a therapist. This is true to the extent that frequently the work assignments are made not so much on the basis of the skill which the patient may be able to learn, as the personal characteristics and abilities of a given work supervisor who may have demonstrated that he works unusually well with patients of a certain type.

In some cases, of course, patients show little motivation for vocational advancement. Training in work habits may be the highest goal that can be set. Such patients are usually assigned to jobs which must be done to keep the hospital operating, for example, kitchen work, cleaning, and messenger service. In no case, however, is a patient given a meaningless task simply to keep him busy. He can always feel that he is doing something useful and constructive. . . .

In summary, this third phase of the treatment program is not a single program, alike for all patients. Rather, there is an indefinite number of possible programs, ranging from those in which only physical and custodial care in a drug-free environment are of significance, to those where intensive treatment, perhaps along several different lines, is provided. The determination of which program a patient will follow depends partly on his needs, and partly on his desire to participate in treatment. The patient himself determines to a large extent whether his period of hospitalization is to be a matter of "doing time" in an institution, or of active treatment. When a patient complains, as some do, that the hospital is really not a hospital but a prison, it is made because the patient makes it so.

Whatever the specific program, the hospital tries to establish a therapeutic environment in which the patient's attitudes and personality can be modified. As one example, many addict patients see authority as an irrational, unpredictable, and hostile force to be placated, to be seduced, and to be out-maneuvered by those who are clever enough to find its weak spots. To the extent that the hospital succeeds in being firm and consistent, but kind and reasonable in its handling of patients, it presents the patient with a new situation, and forces him to find new ways of relating to authority.

The fourth phase of treatment, in some respects the most important, is unfortunately the least well developed. This is the followup help a patient can use from agencies in his home community. Treatment of addiction which does not include this followup is inadequate, and in this sense few addicts receive adequate treatment. At the present time, this followup help is, in effect, available only for those prisoners and federal probationers who are discharged under the supervision of a federal probation officer, and in a few cases of voluntary patients, where community agencies exist and are willing to work with addict patients.

RESULTS OF TREATMENT

The most obvious criterion of success of treatment is the patient's abstinence or relapse to drug use after he leaves the hospital. There is no logical reason to expect a high rate of abstinence in patients who receive only the first three phases of treatment—those which are accomplished in the hospital. To date there have been no formal attempts to provide the fourth phase, for Lexington patients, and to evaluate the results. Suggestive material, however, may be found in the case records of Lexington patients released on parole.

> Diana was admitted to the hospital in February 1958, less than a month after her twenty-first birthday. A white, married woman, she was sentenced under the Youth Corrections Act for illegal importation of narcotics. She and her husband were apprehended in an attempt to bring heroin and amphetamine into this country from Mexico.
>
> This patient had been in difficulties since age thirteen, when she began running away from home. Use of marihuana, and quite quickly of heroin, dated from about age fifteen. She had a ninth grade education, and no employment history except for very brief periods as a waitress. She had been married twice and her second husband was an addict.
>
> In the hospital she adjusted well, and was given training in developing

X-ray films. She was an excellent worker, learned quickly, and her supervisor felt she had the ability to become an X-ray technician. She obviously had difficulty in getting along with other people, not in the sense of any overt misbehavior, but in letting herself feel close to them. She was seen in individual therapy weekly for a period of about 4 months. While in therapy she moved toward a decision that she would not reunite with her husband. During her hospitalization her parents moved to a different state, and the probation officer who interviewed them felt that they were sincerely interested in helping her make a fresh start. She was released on parole in October 1959.

In April 1961 her probation officer reported a good adjustment under supervision. The plans for training as an X-ray technician had fallen through but she had completed training as a beauty operator and was employed at this work. The probation officer felt her adjustment warranted a recommendation that her supervision be terminated in November 1961. There was no indication of any relapse to drug use or of other offenses.

Robert was a 28-year-old Negro admitted to the hospital is December 1953 with a sentence of 40 months to 10 years for sale of narcotics. His drug use dated back 5 years, but prior to that he had had a fairly stable home environment, a period of satisfactory adjustment in the Army, and had completed high school and about half of a training course as a dental technician. He was married once, but separated from his wife and then had a series of "common law" relationships.

In the hospital the patient was not in psychotherapy, but was given a training assignment as a shipping clerk in the printing industry where he did quite well. Parole was granted in March 1957.

He returned to an eastern seaboard city where he lived with his sister. For the first several years he was out of the hospital he had a great deal of difficulty finding employment, and when he did succeed the jobs did not last long and were at menial work. With the support and encouragement of his probation officer, he managed to get through this period without getting into any difficulty and finally in January 1960 was able to get a job with the Federal Government as a messenger. Within a year after that he received two grade raises because of his fine work. He never reunited with his wife, but at the time of the last report in March 1961 was courting a girl of good character and reputation, her influence being one of the factors which the probation officer considered largely responsible for his "striking" improvement. Again, there was no hint of any further drug use or of any further difficulty with the law.

Any probation officer who has worked with a number of addicts can match these cases with others in which the person relapsed to drug use almost immediately after leaving the hospital or after a period of very marginal adjustment. What accounts for the success in these cases, and the failure in others? What proportion of cases could be classed with the cited ones as successful, and what proportion as failures in the sense of relapse to drug use?

No satisfactory answer can be given to these questions at the present time, because the research necessary to answer them has not yet been done. The early stage of a followup study of Kentucky addicts presently being conducted by the author of this paper suggests that the percentage who remain off drugs, at least in the area being studied, may be much higher than most people would have expected, perhaps in the range of 40 to 50 percent, even among persons with long histories of addiction and repeated relapses. Other studies, and clinical impressions, suggest that the relapse rate may well vary geographically, with higher rates of relapse in the metropolitan centers like New York and Chicago where the number of addicts is higher. Studies by Pescor and Diskind indicate that supervision, and particularly intensive supervision, produces lower relapse rates at least for the periods of supervision. . . .

Clinical impressions (still not corroborated by research) also suggest that, for at least some patients, success in abstaining from drugs is associated with a move away from the area in which the person was addicted. If this turns out to be correct, it will probably be explainable not as a simple function of availability of drugs, but rather as removal of the person from all of the cues and reminders of previous drug use. . . .

THE ANTICRIMINAL SOCIETY: SYNANON
Lewis Yablonsky

THE BACKGROUND OF SYNANON

The Synanon organization . . . has been in operation about 4 years. As a result of exposure to this unique social system approximately 100 persons, most with long criminal and addiction records, no longer find it necessary to use drugs or commit crimes. Some Synanon residents have been clean of these deviant patterns for periods of up to 4 years.

This anti-addiction society originated with Charles E. Dederich, a former business executive, who had worked through an alcoholic problem and was motivated to transmit the forces which had led to his own recovery. A strong personality with characteristics of a charismatic leader, Dederich attracted to his residence by the beach in Ocean Park a coterie of alcoholics and drug addicts who found stimulating and interesting the lengthy philosophical discussions which he led. Many of these persons had no roots and moved into Dederich's "pad." Within a short time a

From *Federal Probation*, Vol. 26, No. 3 (September 1962), pp. 50-57. Reprinted by permission.

small colony of about 15 addicts moved into the various apartments in the immediate area and emerged as the early core of the Synanon movement. At this point, about 6 months after its inception, there emerged an idealized assumption that no one was using drugs; although this fact was only true for about half the residents at the time.

Two incidents sharply changed the nature of this unusual collectivity and projected the evolution of a clean Synanon community. One was what later became known as the "big cop-out." This involved the open admission of occasional use by several key residents. Shortly after this episode the balance of power shifted over to a community with a majority of *clean addicts*. This new situation gave strength and credence to an antiaddiction, anticriminal ethos. To my knowledge, it was the first time anywhere that a group of nonprisoner ex-addicts could be found in one location.

By the summer of 1959 about 40 to 50 men and women, not using drugs, were living in a Synanon colony in one large building. The Synanon movement had become more established and aroused the interest of many significant professionals. . . .

Interestingly, the potential of this type of an anticriminal society for modifying difficult offenders had been forecast by Professor Cressey in an article published in 1955 in *The American Journal of Sociology*. His projection of the need for this treatment approach was based upon Sutherland's causal theory of criminal "differential association." Cressey logically speculated that, "if the behavior of an individual is an intrinsic part of the groups to which he belongs, attempts to change the behavior must be directed at groups."

Cressey utilizing "differential association" theory as a diagnostic base projected the necessity for an anticriminal society to modify deviant behavior.

> The differential association theory of criminal behavior presents implications for diagnosis and treatment consistent with the group-relations principle for changing behavior and could be advantageously utilized in correctional work. According to it, persons become criminals principally because they have been relatively isolated from groups whose behavior patterns (including attitudes, motives, and rationalizations) are anticriminal, or because their residence, employment, social position, native capacities, or something else has brought them into relatively frequent association with the behavior patterns of criminal groups. A diagnosis of criminality based on this theory would be directed at analysis of the criminal's attitudes, motives, and rationalizations regarding criminality and would recognize that those characteristics depend upon the groups to which the criminal belongs. Then if criminals are to be changed, either they must become members of anticriminal groups, or their present procriminal group relations must be changed.

Life in the Synanon anticriminal society revolves around a set of educational and apparently group therapeutic procedures developed by Dederich and the group of ex-addict leaders he had personally trained. Synanon by this time had many characteristics of an extended father-dominated family. As Dederich himself described it in an address before The Southern California Parole Officers Association:

> We have here a climate consisting of a family structure similar in some areas to a primitive tribal structure, which seems to affect individuals on a sub-conscious level. The structure also contains overtones of a 19th century family set-up of the type which produced inner-directed person-alities. It is the feeling of the Synanon Foundation that an undetermined percentage of narcotic addicts are potentially inner-directed people as dif-ferentiated from tradition-directed people. A more or less autocratic family structure appears to be necessary as a pre-conditioning environment to buy time for the recovering addict.
>   . . . The autocratic overtone of the family structure demands that the patients or members of the family perform tasks as part of the group. As a member is able to take direction in small tasks such as helping in the preparation of meals, housecleaning and so forth, regardless of his rebel-lion of being "told what to do," his activity seems to provide exercise of emotions of giving or creating which have lain dormant. As these muscles strengthen, it seems that the resistance to cooperating with the group tends to dissipate.

SYNANON GROUP THERAPY

The daily program for the Synanon resident includes some type of work, a noon educational seminar, the synanon (a form of leaderless group therapy in which all residents participate three times a week), and daily interaction and communication with hundreds of "squares" (nonaddicts) from all walks of life who visit the building regularly.

The synanon, a form of group interaction vital to the overall ap-proach, tends to be a unique form of aggressive leaderless nonprofes-sional group psychotherapy, directed by what Dederich has referred to as a Synanist. According to Dederich:

> The Synanist leans heavily on his own insight into his own problems of personality in trying to help others find themselves, and will use the weap-ons of ridicule, cross-examination, and hostile attack as it becomes neces-sary. Synanon sessions seem to provide an emotional catharsis and trigger an atmosphere of truth-seeking which is reflected in the social life of the family structure. The Synanist does not try to convey to another that he himself is a stable personality. In fact, it may very well be the destructive drives of the recovered or recovering addictive personality embodied in a Synanist which makes him a good therapeutic tool—fighting fire with fire.

This form of group therapy is ideally suited for the overall Synanon community. The group sessions do not have any official leader. They are autonomous; however, leaders emerge in each session in a natural fashion. The emergent leader tells much about himself in his questioning of another. Because he is intensely involved with the subject or the problem in the particular session he begins to direct, he is in a natural fashion the "most qualified" session leader for that time and place. In short, the expert of the moment may be emotionally crippled in many personal areas, but in the session where he is permitted by the group to take therapeutic command, he may be the most qualified therapeutic agent.

Synanon, as a side effect, trains persons to become a new brand of therapeutic agent in the correctional field. The system provides the opportunity for offenders to modify their own deviant behavior and then work with other offenders. In this context I view the phenomenon of Synanon at Terminal Island as a major break-through in the field of correction.

Although ex-offenders have been randomly used over the years in the processes of correction, Synanon provides a unique contribution. . . . Unlike most professional or ex-offender workers in the field the trained synanist has three levels of experience which uniquely qualify him for work with other offenders.

1. He has a lengthy history of criminal experience. He himself has made the "scene." He knows the crime problem in its many dimensions —at first hand.

2. At Synanon, this individual has deeply experienced the emotional upheaval of rejecting one way of life for another. He has "in his gut" gone through a resocialization process and knows something about the set of experiences and the pain involved in the transition.

3. He knows the Synanon social system. He has a subconscious conception of the processes at work for helping others and he is himself a functional part of this organization. He has been trained at "the Synanon College" for working with recalcitrant offenders.

This triad of experiences qualified the Synanist uniquely for the task at hand. . . . The Synanist is difficult to con or juggle out of position. The Synanist cannot easily be out-maneuvered from his zeal to point up a new direction in life to replace the roles of crime and addiction which he now views as wasteful and stupid behavior. This point of view of the Synanist seems to get across to the inmate seeking a noncriminal mode of existence.

Although the synanon form of group therapy is an important aspect of the method, the basic therapeutic force is the overall synanon social system. . . .

PRINCIPAL FORCES AT WORK IN THE SYNANON SOCIETY

Involvement.—Initially, Synanon society is able to involve and control the offender. This is accomplished through providing an interesting social setting comprised of associates who understand him and will not be outmaneuvered by his manipulative behavior.

An Achievable Status System.—Within the context of this system he can (perhaps, for the first time) see a realistic possibility for legitimate achievement and prestige. Synanon provides a rational and attainable opportunity structure for the success-oriented individual. He is no longer restricted to inmate status; since there is no inmate-staff division. All residents are staff.

New Social Role.—Synanon creates a new social role which can be temporarily or indefinitely occupied in the process of social growth and development. (Some residents have made the decision to make Synanon their life's work.) This new role is a legitimate one supported by the ex-offender's own community as well as the inclusive society. With the opening of new Synanons . . . Synanon trained persons are increasingly in demand. Since the Synanon organization is not a hospital or an institution, there is no compulsion to move out of this satisfying community.

Social Growth.—In the process of acquiring legitimate social status in Synanon the offender necessarily, as a side effect, develops the ability to relate, communicate and work with others. The values of truth, honesty, and industry become necessary means to this goal of status achievement. After a sufficient amount of practice and time, the individual socialized in this way in a natural fashion develops the capability for behaving adequately with reference to these values.

Social Control.—The control of deviance is a by-product of the individual's status-seeking. Conformity to the norms is necessary in order to achieve. Anomie, the dislocation of goals and means, becomes a minimal condition. The norms are valid and adhered to within this social system since means are available for legitimate goal attainment.

Another form of control is embodied in the threat of ostracism which becomes a binding force. After being initially involved in Synanon, the individual does not at the time feel adequate for participation in the larger society. After a sufficient residue of Synanon social living has been acquired the individual no longer fears banishment; however, at the same time he is then better prepared for life on the outside (if this is his choice). He no longer fears ostracism and may remain voluntarily because he feels Synanon is a valid way of life for him. In Synanon he has learned and acquired a gratifying social role which enables him as a "coordinator" or a "director" to help others who can benefit from Synanon treatment.

Other forms of immediate social control include ridicule ("hair-cuts," the "fireplace") and the synanon sessions. The individual is required to tell the truth in the synanon. This also regulates his behavior. Real life transgressions are often prevented by the knowledge that the individual's deviance will automatically, rapidly, and necessarily be brought to the attention of his community within the synanon session. He is living within a community where others know about and, most important, are concerned with his behavior.

Empathy and Self-Identity.—The constant self-assessment required in his daily life and in the synanon sessions fosters the consolidation of self-identity and empathy. His self-estimation is under constant assessment and attack by relevant others, who become sensitive to and concerned about him. The process provides the opportunity for the individual almost literally "to see himself as others do." He is also compelled as part of this process to develop the ability to identify with and understand others. A side consequence is the development of self-growth, social awareness, the ability to communicate and empathic effectiveness. When these socialization processes are at work and take hold the youth becomes reconnected with the legitimate society and no longer finds it necessary to use drugs or assume a deviant role.

SYNANON'S FUTURE

From its unusual beginnings the Synanon Foundation has emerged as a highly efficient organization. The Foundation has federal tax exempt status and is a corporate entity in the State of California. The State Legislature passed and the Governor signed into law The Petris Bill on June 15, 1961, officially sanctioning Synanon as a "Place" for rehabilitating drug addicts.

Synanon, over the past year, as a partial consequence of donations and the earning power of its residents, has rented four buildings with a total rental of over $1500 a month. Although its budgeting is tight, comparable to other nonprofit organizations, it has met all of its financial obligations as a result of community support. The organization over the past year has sustained approximately 85 residents in food and clothing, and has entertained approximately 19,000 guests (mostly professional visitors). In addition to the Terminal Island project a Synanon educational and addiction-prevention program has involved most of the 100 Synanon members in over 400 speaking engagements delivered to business, professional, religious, youth, and college and university groups. One evening a week about 40 nonaddicts from all segments of society participate in the so-called "Square Synanons." Here the variety of human problems are examined through utilization of the Synanon method involving Synanon residents mixed with "squares." This interaction and cross-fertilization of ideas and insights appear to be of benefit to all. As a social science research center Synanon is unique. In this open-door environment run by ex-offenders themselves, persons with long addiction and criminal background freely provide important data unavailable in the usual custodial setting. Synanon thus enables the systematic gathering of much useful information about crime, addiction, and the solution of these problems.

The Synanon approach which has emerged under the creative and capable leadership of Dederich and his uniquely trained staff of directors as an effective anticriminal and antiaddiction society, also involves an organization of distinguished citizens from all walks of life called "S.O.S." or Sponsors of Synanon. This supportive organization has a national membership of over 600 persons who donate money, goods, and services. They are currently launching a building program for an ideal Synanon community.

The organization is naturally committed to expansion. Synanon-trained personnel of the type carrying out the program at Terminal Island will no doubt shortly be utilized as the core staff for Synanon Houses planned for other communities. Each new establishment has the potential for "cleaning-up" another hundred offenders.

As viewed by its founder, Charles Dederich, Synanon is still in its infancy. The fact of 100 individuals with long addiction and criminal histories currently clean attests to its effectiveness. However, Synanon, as a social movement or community way of life, appears to have possibilities beyond exclusive application to the addiction problem. . . .

8 HOMOSEXUALITY

Even more than drunkenness, alcoholism, and drug addiction, homosexuality is a status rather than an offense. That is, the deviation lies in the stigmatization of the person by others and in the self-concept of the homosexual. It is also a *status offense* in that the participants are quite willing so that the relationship is voluntary in character rather than the type described by a victim-perpetrator model. Because of the willingness of the persons involved, law enforcement in this area is bound to be ineffective. Yet the disgust, fear, and ignorance that surround homosexuality have also prevented major alterations in public policy. It is doubtful that American public opinion would presently be willing to tolerate the decriminalization of homosexuality.

No one really knows very much about the prevalence of this form of deviation. There are at least two important reasons for this. First, homosexuality is not very clearly defined. Should an occasional episode categorize an individual as a homosexual, or does homosexuality mean the chronic, if not exclusive, desire to express one's sexuality in response to members of one's own sex. If the former, then Kinsey has suggested that over one-third of the male population has probably experienced such encounters. If the latter, then the prevalence may be as low as 3 or 4 per cent or as high as 15 per cent.

Second, the homosexual experience, like heterosexual intercourse, is not a public matter. Because it is masked or hidden, there is no good way to estimate its prevalence. Most estimates are derived from occasional research study like Kinsey's pioneering effort or from psychiatrists and other clinicians. And there are obvious problems connected with each of these sources of data. Since homosexuality carries great stigma and opens the person to all manner of exploitation, homosexuals are not very likely to present themselves for evaluation in any situation in which their deviation is likely to become a matter of public record. Just how hidden homosexuality really is can be surmised from interview data on 550 "hard core" male homosexuals gathered by Kinsey. Over 75 per cent had experienced no trouble with the police and were not officially known as homosexuals. An even higher percentage were free of trouble at work. Most surprising, of those who had been in the military, only 20 per cent reported having had any difficulties. It is clear, then, that much of even chronic homosexuality is unreported and unrecorded.

Still, whether known officially or not, homosexuality, like all other forms of deviancy, is a socially devalued status. On the personal level, such social devaluation results in alienation, despair, and self-hatred. Fear of exposure and depreciation of the self force the homosexual into relationships with others equally devalued. Out of this push and pull—push from legitimate society and pull from those with similar status and problems—arises the subculture. Like all subcultures, the homosexual community provides the individual homosexual with a shared set of norms and practices and a feeling of belonging.

The three contributions to this chapter are concerned with these various aspects of homosexuality, especially the subcultural. The first article deals only peripherally with the individual homosexual and centrally with his community. William A. Westley and Maurice Leznoff derived their data from interviews with a considerable number of homosexuals and indicate that there are a variety of homosexual groups in any community—some secret and some overt. These are tied together, however, by friendships and sexual contacts. The "community" consists of persons with knowledge of one another, common interests, and the need to co-operate, if only to protect themselves from legal punishment and social condemnation.

In 1967, the British Parliament by an overwhelming majority—on the order of seven to one—repealed the ancient statute that made homosexuality a criminal offense. The basis for this legalization of homosexuality is contained in a most characteristically British document—the Wolfenden Commission's report on homosexuality. In this closely reasoned paper, based on legal, medical, psychiatric, and other expert testimony, the following aspects of the problem are considered: the nature and definition of homosexuality, its frequency and distribution in England, the arguments concerning homosexuality as a disease, the issue of the limited responsibility of the homosexual, and related matters of critical concern. The report presents and discusses the arguments in favor of retaining the criminal offense status of homosexuality and its reasons for rejecting them. This heavily edited version of the report concludes with the commission's recommendation that homosexual behavior between consenting adults in private should no longer be a criminal offense.

In the last article, Professors Simon and Gagnon deal with what might be called the life cycle problems in homosexuality. Apart from the usual exigencies of everyday life, such as earning a living, which the homosexual shares with the heterosexual person, there are special and unique problems that the homosexual alone faces. Among them is the problem that occurs when the homosexual first begins to think of himself as a deviant and to make contacts in the homosexual community—a process called "coming out." A second critical life cycle crisis is that of aging. Tough as it is for a heterosexual male in a youth-oriented society to grow older, the problems of the homosexual are even greater. Aging not only increases the difficulty in finding suitable partners but raises questions about the self that are particularly troublesome. Nevertheless, most homosexuals, like most heterosexuals, weather these stages with ease, if not joy. The options and crises in the management of homosexual careers, then, is the subject matter of "Homosexuality: The Formulation of a Sociological Perspective."

THE HOMOSEXUAL COMMUNITY

Maurice Leznoff and William A. Westley

The significance of homosexuality in our society has been minimized and obscured by the force of social taboo. Yet there is evidence that homosexuals are distributed throughout all geographical areas and socio-economic strata. Furthermore, the subjection of homosexuals to legal punishments and social condemnation has produced a complex structure of concealed social relations which merit sociological investigation. The psychological isolation of the homosexual from society, his dependence upon other deviants for the satisfaction of sexual needs and self-expression, the crystallization of social roles and behavior patterns within the deviant group, the reciprocal obligations and demands within the homosexual community, and their significance for the larger society in which they occur, are but a few of the areas of theoretical interest to the sociologist.

In this paper we shall confine our discussion to the social organization of one homosexual community and its constituent social groups: their function, etiology, and interrelationships.

The report is based upon an intensive study of 60 homosexuals in a large Canadian city. The data consist of four-hour interviews with 40 homosexuals and briefer interviews with 20 others. In addition, the data include information based on the observation of many homosexual

From *Social Problems,* Vol. 3, No. 4 (April 1956), 257-63. Reprinted by permission.

parties and gatherings in bars and restaurants, and a series of 30 letters written by one homosexual to another.

FUNCTIONS OF HOMOSEXUAL GROUPS

The primary function of the homosexual group is psychological in that it provides a social context within which the homosexual can find acceptance as a homosexual and collective support for his deviant tendencies. Most homosexuals fear detection and are often insecure and anxious because of this. The following statement illustrates this:

> The thought that you are "gay" is always with you and you know it's there even when other people don't. You also think to yourself that certain of your mannerisms and your ways of expression are liable to give you away. That means that there is always a certain amount of strain. I don't say that it's a relief to get away from normal people, but there isn't the liberty that you feel in a gay crowd. When I associate with normal people I prefer very small groups of them. I don't like large groups and I think I try to avoid them when I can. You know, the only time when I really forget I'm gay is when I'm in a gay crowd.

To relieve this anxiety the deviant seeks collective support and social acceptance. Since the homosexual group provides the only social context in which homosexuality is normal, deviant practices moral, and homosexual responses rewarded, the homosexual develops a deep emotional involvement with his group, tending toward a ready acceptance of its norms and dictates, and subjection to its behavior patterns. The regularity with which he seeks the company of his group is a clear expression of this dependency.

A prohibition against sexual relationships within the group, in a manner suggestive of the incest taboo, indicates the extent to which the group culture is oriented to this function. The quotation which follows is indicative of this taboo:

> As far as I know, people who hang around with each other don't have affairs. The people who are friends don't sleep with each other. I can't tell you why that is, but they just don't. Unless you are married you have sex with strangers mostly. I think if you have sex with a friend it will destroy the friendship. I think that in the inner mind we all respect high moral standards, and none of us want to feel low in the eyes of anybody else. It's always easier to get along with your gay friends if there has been no sex. Mind you, you might have sex with somebody you just met and then he might become your friend. But you won't have sex with him any more as soon as he joins the same gang you hang around with.

Within these groups the narration of sexual experiences and gossip about the sexual exploits of others is a major form of recreation. The narration of sexual experiences functions to allocate prestige among the members because of the high evaluation placed upon physical attraction and sexual prowess. Yet it creates hostility and sexual rivalry. The intense involvement of homosexuals in the results of this sexual competition is illustrated in the following statement which was overhead in a restaurant:

> Who wouldn't blow up. That bitch is trying to get her clutches into Richard. She can't leave anybody alone. I wouldn't be surprised if she ended up with a knife in her back. I don't mean to say I'm threatening her. But she's not going to get away with that stuff forever . . . playing kneesies under the table all night long. I had to get her away from Richard. That lousy bitch. From now on she better keep away from me.

An additional function is the provision of a social situation in which the members can dramatize their adherence to homosexual values. Thus, the gossip about sex, the adoption and exaggeration of feminine behavior, and the affectation of speech, represent a way of affirming that homosexuality is frankly accepted and has the collective support of the group. . . .

ETIOLOGY: THE EVASION OF SOCIAL CONTROLS

In our society, homosexuality is defined both legally and socially as a criminal and depraved practice and the homosexual is threatened by powerful legal and social sanctions such as imprisonment, physical violence, social and occupational ostracism, and ridicule. Therefore, all homosexuals face the problem of evading social controls. They do this in two predominant ways.

Some pass for heterosexuals on the job and in most of their social relationships. They mix regularly with heterosexuals for business, entertainment, and other social activities. They avoid situations and persons publicly recognized as homosexual for they fear that discovery will threaten their career and expose them to sanctions. This is illustrated in the following statement of a lawyer:

> I know a few people who don't care. They are really pitiful. They are either people who are in very insignificant positions or they are in good positions but are independent. I know of one who is in the retail business. He doesn't care. A lot of the artists don't care. For that reason I have never cultivated the friendship of artists. I just don't get along with anybody who doesn't care. That's why I really can't give you information about those who don't. It's just that I can't afford to get to know them very well, and I try to avoid them. Sometimes personal friends become this way. Then there is a mutual rejection of the friendship. From my point of view I am just no longer interested when they adopt that kind of attitude. From

their point of view it means completely living outside of society and they are no longer interested in people who they consider hypocrites.

Others openly admit and practice homosexuality. They usually work in occupations where the homosexual is tolerated, withdraw from uncompromising heterosexual groups, and confine most of their social life to homosexual circles. . . .

While the problem of evasion is common to all homosexuals, the mechanisms of evasion present various alternatives. Most homosexuals find themselves compelled to conform outwardly to societal demands. They are conscious of their social position within society and seek such satisfactions as occupational mobility and prestige. They endeavor to retain intimate associations within the heterosexual community, and fear recognition as a status threat. Such homosexuals rely upon secrecy and the concealment of their deviant practices. They will therefore be referred to as "secret" homosexuals. A minority retreats from the demands of society and renounce societal goals. Such individuals will be referred to as "overt" homosexuals.

The mode of adaption is largely dependent upon the extent to which identification as a homosexual is a status threat. While economic status cannot be equated with social status, the individual's position within the work world represents the most significant single factor in the prestige scale. Therefore, the extent to which homosexuality is tolerated in various occupations determines to a great extent the mode of evasion chosen by the homosexual. Thus, there are many occupations, of which the professions are an obvious example, where homosexuals are not tolerated. In other areas, the particular occupation may have traditionally accepted homosexual linkages in the popular image or be of such low rank as to permit homosexuals to function on the job. The artist, the interior decorator, and the hairdresser exemplify the former type; such positions as counter man or bell-hop, the latter. Thus we find a rough relationship between form of evasion and occupation. The overt homosexual tends to fit into an occupation of low status rank; the secret homosexual into an occupation with a relatively high status rank. . . .

DISTINCTIONS BETWEEN THE SECRET AND OVERT GROUPS

The chief distinctions between homosexual groups correspond to the differences in the general modes of evading social controls which homosexuals have developed. Thus, secret and overt homosexuals form distinctive groups. . . .

The distinctions between these groups are maintained by the secret homosexuals who fear identification and refuse to associate with overt homosexuals. This statement by a secret homosexual is illustrative:

If someone who is gay wanted to be spiteful they could say something in the wrong quarter. Nobody who cared about himself would say anything. The trouble is that some don't care. I make it a rule to avoid anybody who is perfectly open about himself. It's easy not to become friendly with those people but it's hard to avoid them entirely. You certainly don't want to snub them because that might make them antagonistic. You just don't call them or see them at social gatherings. But you do meet them at bars and that's where you can be introduced to them. If they remember you and continue to say hello to you on the street, you have to acknowledge them or they might feel that you are trying to snub them.

As a result of this social distance a certain amount of reciprocal hostility has developed between the members of secret and overt groups. This hostility helps maintain the social distance and distinctions between these groups. . . .

This poses serious problems for the homosexual who is socially mobile. He is forced to change his primary group affiliations within the homosexual community.

The following statement by the manager of an appliance shop shows how the homosexual tends to change his orientation from "overt" to "secret" as he becomes upwardly mobile.

My promotions have made me more conscious of the gang I hang around with. You see, for the first time in my life I have a job that I would really like to keep and where I can have a pretty secure future. I realize that if word were to get around that I am gay I would probably lose my job. I don't see why that should be, because I know that I'm the same person gay or not. But still that's the way it works. I don't want to hang around with Robert* any more or any of the people who are like Robert. I don't mind seeing them once in a while at somebody's house, but I won't be seen with them on the street any more.

Both types of groups were identified and observed in the course of this research. Each group consisted of fourteen members. The descriptions which follow are based on the study of these groups.

SECRET GROUPS

The secret homosexuals form groups which consist of a loose amalgamation of small cliques. Interaction within the cliques is frequent, with members meeting at each other's homes and in bars and restaurants. The clique's structure is a product of the diverse interests and occupations and of the desire to limit homosexual contacts which characterize secret homosexuals. The clique unites its several members in common specialized interests apart from the larger group. . . .

* Robert is the leader of an overt group of which the respondent was a member at the time he was contacted.

A secret homosexual group is generally characterized by: (a) informal standards of admission; (b) discretion in the manner in which homosexuality is practiced; (c) an attempt at concealment; (d) partial rather than complete involvement in the homosexual world.

OVERT GROUPS

Overt homosexuals gather in cohesive social groups which become the dominant focus of their lives. These groups are openly homosexual in character. The members make little effort to conceal their deviation, spend almost all their free time with the group, and tend to regard their other activities as peripheral.

These groups generally draw their members from persons of low socio-economic status who have jobs where concealment is not a prerequisite. . . .

The members of the group met daily either at a bar, a restaurant, or at the house of the acknowledged leader or "queen." They spent their time in endless gossip about the sexual affairs of the members or other homosexuals known to them. Often they would go to bars and restaurants in the attempt to make a "pick-up," or spend the evening "cruising" individually or in groups of two's and three's.

The queen seems to characterize only "overt" groups. Functionally, the role of the queen is very important in the life of these groups. He provides a place where the group may gather and where its individual members may have their "affairs." He helps finance members in distress, functions as an intermediary in making sexual contacts, partially controls the entrance of new members, and warns the members of hoodlums who would prey upon them. Generally the queen is an older homosexual who has had wide experience in the homosexual world. . . .

Overt groups are characterized by: (a) no particular standards of admission; (b) unselfconscious and unrestrained practice of homosexuality; (c) little or no concealment; (d) high degree of social isolation with little involvement in heterosexual activities; (e) little concern with identification as a status threat or the sanctions of heterosexual society.

THE HOMOSEXUAL COMMUNITY

The diverse secret and overt homosexuals are linked together either through bonds of sex or of friendship. Within the primary group, the emphasis upon friendship rather than sex serves to eliminate excessive sexual competition and preserves group unity. However, this creates a sexual interdependency upon those outside the group with important social consequences.

In the first place, it forces the secret homosexual out into the open in an attempt to solicit sexual partners. He thus frequents the known homosexual meeting places within the city such as specific bars, hotel lobbies, street corners, and lavatories. These activities make him an increasingly familiar figure within the homosexual world.

Secondly, this solicitation leads to the interaction of secret and overt homosexuals on a sexual as opposed to a social basis. While these contacts occur in a spirit of anonymity, an approach to the other often requires an exchange of confidences.

Thirdly, this sexual interdependency increases the anxiety of secret homosexuals since it forces them to contact the overt ones whom they fear as a threat to their security.

Thus, it is the casual and promiscuous sexual contacts between the members of different categories of evasion (i. e. the secret and the overt) which weld the city's homosexuals into a community. . . .

THE WOLFENDEN REPORT ON HOMOSEXUALITY

The Wolfenden Commission

RECOMMENDATIONS CONCERNING HOMOSEXUAL OFFENSES

. . .

Homosexuality is a sexual propensity for persons of one's own sex. This definition of homosexuality involves the adoption of some criteria for its recognition. As in other psychological fields, an inference that the propensity exists may be derived from either subjective or objective data, that is, either from what is felt or from what is done by the persons concerned. Either method may lead to fallacious results. In the first place, introspection is neither exhaustive nor infallible; an individual may quite genuinely not be aware of either the existence or the strength of his motivations and propensities, and there is a natural reluctance to acknowledge, even to oneself, a preference which is socially condemned, or to admit to acts that are illegal and liable to a heavy penalty. Rationalization and self-deception can be carried to great lengths, and in certain circumstances lying is also to be expected. Secondly, some of those whose main sexual propensity is for persons of the opposite sex indulge, for a variety of reasons, in homosexual acts. It is known, for example, that some men who are placed in special circumstances that prohibit contact with the opposite sex (for instance, in prisoner-of-war camps or prisons) indulge

Report of the Committee on Homosexual Offences and Prostitution (The Wolfenden Report), London: Her Majesty's Printing Office, 1957, pp. 11-25 in 1962 edition. Reprinted by permission.

in homosexual acts; though they revert to heterosexual behavior when opportunity affords; and it is clear from our evidence that some men who are not predominantly homosexual lend themselves to homosexual practices for financial or other gain. Conversely, many homosexual persons have heterosexual intercourse with or without homosexual fantasies. Furthermore, a homosexual tendency may not be manifested exclusively, or even at all, in sexual fields of behavior.

There is the further problem how widely the description "homosexual" should be applied. According to the phychoanalytic school, a homosexual component (sometimes conscious, often not) exists in everybody; and if this is correct homosexuality in this sense is universal. Without going so far as to accept this view in toto, it is possible to realize that the issue of latent homosexuality is relevant to any assessment of the frequency of occurrence of the condition of homosexuality. However, in connection with our recommendations, we are strictly speaking concerned only with those who, for whatever reason, commit homosexual offenses.

In spite of difficulties, there is a general measure of agreement on two propositions: (i) that there exists in certain persons a homosexual propensity which varies quantitatively in different individuals and can also vary quantitatively in the same individual at different epochs of life; (ii) that this propensity can affect behavior in a variety of ways, some of which are not obviously sexual, although exactly how much and in what ways may be matters for disagreement and dispute.

The first of these propositions means that homosexuality as a propensity is not an "all or none" condition, and this view has been abundantly confirmed by the evidence submitted to us. All gradations can exist from apparently exclusive homosexuality without any conscious capacity for arousal by heterosexual stimuli to apparently exclusive heterosexuality, though in the latter case there may be transient and minor homosexual inclinations, for instance in adolescence. According to the psychoanalytic school, all individuals pass through a homosexual phase. Be this as it may, we would agree that a transient homosexual phase in development is very common and should usually cause neither surprise nor concern.

It is interesting that the late Dr. Kinsey, in his study entitled *The Sexual Behavior of the Human Male,* formulated this homosexual-heterosexual continuum on a 7-point scale, with a rating of 6 for sexual arousal and activity with other males only, 3 for arousals and acts equally with either sex, 0 for exclusive heterosexuality, and intermediate ratings accordingly. The recognition of the existence of this continuum is, in our opinion, important for two reasons. First, it leads to the conclusion that homosexuals cannot reasonably be regarded as quite separate from the rest of mankind. Secondly, it has some relevance in connection with claims made for the success of various forms of treatment.

As regards the second proposition, we have already pointed out that a distinction should be drawn between the condition of homosexuality (which relates to the direction of sexual preference) and the acts or behavior resulting from this preference. It is possible to draw a further distinction between behavior which is overtly sexual and behavior, not overtly sexual, from which a latent homosexuality can be inferred.

It must not be thought that the existence of the homosexual propensity necessarily leads to homosexual behavior of an overtly sexual kind. Even where it does, this behavior does not necessarily amount to a homosexual offense; for instance, solitary masturbation with homosexual fantasies is probably the most common homosexual act. Many persons, though they are aware of the existence within themselves of the propensity, and though they may be conscious of sexual arousal in the presence of homosexual stimuli, succesfully control their urges towards overtly homosexual acts with others, either because of their ethical standards or from fear of social or penal consequences, so that their homosexual condition never manifests itself in overtly sexual behavior. There are others who, though aware of the existence within themselves of the propensity, are helped by a happy family life, a satisfying vocation, or a well-balanced social life to live happily without any urge to indulge in homosexual acts. Our evidence suggests, however, that complete continence in the homosexual is relatively uncommon—as, indeed, it is in the heterosexual—and that even where the individual is by disposition continent, self-control may break down temporarily under the influence of factors like alcohol, emotional distress, or mental or physical disorder or disease.

Moreover, it is clear that homosexuals differ one from another in the extent to which they are aware of the existence within themselves of the propensity. Some are, indeed, quite unaware of it, and where this is so the homosexuality is technically described as latent, its existence being inferred from the individual's behavior in spheres not obviously sexual. Although there is room for dispute as to the extent and variety of behavior of this kind which may legitimately be included in the making of this inference, there is general agreement that the existence of a latent homosexuality is an inference validly to be drawn in certain cases. . . .

We believe that there would be a wide measure of agreement on the general account of homosexuality and its manifestations that we have given above. On the other hand, the general position which we have tried to summarize permits the drawing of many different inferences, not all of them in our opinion justified. Especially is this so in connection with the concept of "disease." There is a tendency, noticeably increasing in strength over recent years, to label homosexuality as a "disease" or "illness." This may be no more than a particular manifestation of a general tendency discernible in modern society, by which, as one leading sociologist puts it, "the concept of illness expands continually at the expense of the concept of moral failure." There are two important practical consequences which are often thought to follow from regarding homosexuality as an illness. The first is that those in whom the condition exists are sick persons and should therefore be regarded as medical problems and consequently as primarily a medical responsibility. The second is that sickness implies irresponsibility, or at least diminished responsibility. Hence it becomes important in this connection to examine the critera of "disease," and also to examine the claim that these consequences follow. . . .

The traditional view seems to be that for a condition to be recognized as a disease, three criteria must be satisfied, namely, (i) the presence of abnormal symptoms, which are caused by (ii) a demonstrable pathological condition, in turn caused by (iii) some factor called "the cause," each link in this causal chain being understood as something necessarily antecedent to the next. . . .

While we have found this traditional view a convenient basis for our consideration of the question whether or not homosexuality is a disease, it must be recognized that the three criteria, as formulated above, are oversimplified, and that each needs some modification. Moreover, there are conditions now recognized as diseases though they do not satisfy all three criteria. Our evidence suggests, however, that homosexuality does not satisfy any of them unless the terms in which they are defined are expanded beyond what could reasonably be regarded as legitimate. . . .

Besides the notion of homosexuality as a disease, there have been alternative hypotheses offered by others of our expert witnesses. Some have preferred to regard it as a state of arrested development. Some, particularly among the biologists, regard it as simply a natural deviation. Others, again, regard it as a universal potentiality which can develop in response to a variety of factors.

We do not consider ourselves qualified to pronounce on controversial and scientific problems of this kind, but we feel bound to say that the evidence put before us has not established to our satisfaction the proposition that homosexuality is a disease. . . .

Even if it could be established that homosexuality were a disease, it is clear that many individuals, however their state is reached, present social rather than medical problems and must be dealt with by social, including penological, methods. . . .

The claim that homosexuality is an illness carries the further implication that the sufferer cannot help it and therefore carries a diminished responsibility for his actions. Even if it were accepted that homosexuality could properly be described as a "disease," we should not accept this corollary. There are no prima facie grounds for supposing that because a particular person's sexual propensity happens to lie in the direction of persons of his or her own sex it is any less controllable than that of those whose propensity is for persons of the opposite sex. . . . The question which is important for us here is whether the individual suffers from a condition which causes diminished responsibility. This is a different question from the question whether he was responsible in the past for the causes or origins of his present condition. That is an interesting inquiry and may be of relevance in other connections; but our concern is with the behavior which flows from the individual's present condition and with the extent to which he is responsible for that behavior, whatever may have been the causes of the condition from which it springs. . . .

Some psychiatrists have made the point that homosexual behavior in some cases may be "compulsive," that is, irresistible; but there seems to be no good reason to suppose that at least in the majority of cases homosexual acts are any more or any less resistible than heterosexual acts, and other evidence would be required to sustain such a view in any individual case. Even if immunity from penal sanctions on such grounds were claimed or granted, nevertheless preventive measures would have to be taken for the sake of society at large, in much the same way as it is necessary to withhold a driving license from a person who is subject to epileptic fits. This is particularly true of the offender who is a very bad risk for recurrence, but is not certifiable either as insane or as a mental defective.

Homosexuality is not, in spite of widely held belief to the contrary, peculiar to members of particular professions or social classes; nor, as is sometimes supposed, is it peculiar to the intelligentsia. Our evidence shows that it exists among all callings and at all levels of society; and that among homosexuals will be found not only those possessing a high degree of intelligence, but also the dullest oafs.

Some homosexuals, it is true, choose to follow occupations which afford opportunities for contact with those of their own sex, and it is not unnatural that those who feel themselves to be "misfits" in society should gravitate towards occupations offering an atmosphere of tolerance or understanding, with the result that some occupations may appear to attract more homosexuals than do others. Again, the arrest of a prominent national or local figure has greater news value than the arrest of, say, a laborer for a similar offense, and in consequence the press naturally finds room for a report of the one where it might not find room for a report of the other. Factors such as these may well account to some extent for the prevalent misconceptions.

THE EXTENT OF THE PROBLEM

Our consideration of the problems we have had to face would have been made much easier if it had been possible to arrive at some reasonably firm estimate of the prevalence either of the condition of homosexuality or of the commission of homosexual acts. So far as we have been able to discover, there is no precise information about the number of men in Great Britain who either have a homosexual disposition or engage in homosexual behavior.

No inquiries have been made in this country comparable to those which the late Dr. Kinsey conducted in the United States of America. Dr. Kinsey concluded that in the United States, 4 per cent of adult white males are exclusively homosexual throughout their lives after the onset of adolescence. He also found evidence to suggest that 10 per cent of the white male population are more or less exclusively homosexual for at least three years between the ages of sixteen and sixty-five, and that 37 per cent of the total male population have at least some overt homosexual experience, to the point of orgasm, between adolescence and old age. Dr. Kinsey's findings have aroused opposition and skepticism. But it was noteworthy that some of our medical witnesses expressed the view that something very like these figures would be established in this country if similar inquiries were made. The majority, while stating quite frankly that they did not really know, indicated that their impression was that his figures would be on the high side for Great Britain.

A recent inquiry in Sweden suggested that 1 per cent of all men were exclusively homosexual and 4 per cent had both homosexual and heterosexual impulses, and we were interested to learn from official sources in Sweden that other information available seemed to indicate that these figures were too low. But here again, there is no evidence that similar inquiries in this country would yield similar results.

Such statistical information as we have been able to obtain about incidence in this country has been extracted almost entirely from criminal and medical records. It is obvious that only a minority of homosexuals, or, for that matter, of those who indulge in homosexual acts, fall into the hands of the police, and it is likely also that only a minority of such persons find their way to the doctor's consulting room. But it is impossible to determine what proportion of the persons concerned these minorities represent; still less, on this evidence, what proportion of the total population falls within the description "homosexual." These figures, therefore, cannot be relied on as an indication of the extent of homosexuality or homosexual behavior among the community as a whole. . . .

It is widely believed that the prevalence of homosexuality in this country has greatly increased during the past fifty years and that homosexual behavior is much more frequent than used to be the case. It is certainly true that the whole subject of homosexuality is much more freely discussed today than it was formerly; but this is not in itself evidence that homosexuality is today more prevalent, or homosexual behavior more widespread, than it was when mention of it was less common. Sexual matters in general are more openly talked about today than they were in the days of our parents and grandparents; and it is not surprising that homosexuality should take its place, among other sexual topics, in this wider range of permissible subjects of conversation. Public interest in the subject has undoubtedly increased, with the consequences that court cases are more frequently reported and that responsible papers and magazines give considerable space to its discussion. In general literature, too, there is a growing number of works dealing incidentally or entirely with the subject. All this has no doubt led to a much greater public awareness of the phenomenon and its manifestations. But it does not necessarily follow that the behavior which is so discussed is more widespread than it was before.

It is certainly true also that the number of homosexual offenses known to the police has increased considerably. It does not, however, necessarily follow from these figures that there has been an increase either in homosexuality or in homosexual behavior; still less can these figures be regarded as an infallible measure of any increase which may have occurred during that period. Unlike some offenses (e.g., housebreaking), which, by their nature, tend to be reported to the police as they occur, many sexual offenses, particularly those taking place between consenting parties, become "known to the police" only when they are detected by the police or happen to be reported to them. Any figures relating to homosexual offenses known to the police will therefore be conditioned to a large extent both by the efficiency of the police methods of detecting and rcording, and by the intensity of police activity. These factors vary from time to time and from place to place.

Clearly, the more efficient the police methods of detection, the higher the proportion of offenses detected. It was to be expected that the more intensive training given to police officers in recent years, particularly in methods of detection, would result in the discovery of a higher proportion of offenses; but this does not necessarily indicate that more offenses have occurred. We understand, too, that efforts have been made in recent years to improve the methods by which offenses known to the police are recorded, and these may have been reflected in higher figures without any necessary implication of a higher number of offenses. Lastly, the extent to which the police follow up suspicions of homosexual behavior varies considerably as between one police force and another according to the outlook of the senior officers; and sometimes even within a given police force the intensity of action varies from time to time along with the ups and downs of public indignation aroused, or public annoyance caused, by the behavior of the offenders.

In brief, therefore, it would be dangerous to argue from the police statistics alone either that there was an over-all increase or that homosexual behavior was most prevalent in those areas where the number of cases recorded as known to the police was the highest. Most of us think it improbable that the increase in the number of offenses recorded as known to the police can be explained entirely by greater police activity, though we all think it very unlikely that homosexual behavior has increased proportionately to the dramatic rise in the number of offenses recorded as known to the police.

Our medical evidence seems to show three things: first, that in general practice male homosexuals form a very small fraction of the doctor's patients; secondly, that in psychiatric practice male homosexuality is a primary problem in a very small proportion of the cases seen; and thirdly, that only a very small percentage of homosexuals consult doctors about their condition. It is almost impossible to compare the incidence of homosexual behavior with the incidence of other forms of sexual irregularity, most of which are outside the purview of the criminal law and are therefore not recorded in criminal statistics; our impression is that of the total amount of irregular sexual conduct, homosexual behavior provides only a very small proportion. It cannot, however, be ignored. The male population of Great Britain over the age of fifteen numbers nearly eighteen million, and even if the Swedish figures, which are the lowest figures relating to incidence that have come to our notice, are at all applicable to this country, the incidence of homosexuality and homosexual behavior must be large enough to present a serious problem.

Our conclusion is that homosexual behavior is practiced by a small minority of the population, and should be seen in proper perspective, neither ignored nor given a disproportionate amount of public attention. . . .

THE PRESENT LAW AND PRACTICE

It is against the foregoing background that we have reviewed the existing provisions of the law in relation to homosexual behavior between male persons. We have found that with the great majority of these provisions we are in complete agreement. We believe that it is part of the function of the law to safeguard those who need protection by reason of their youth or some mental defect, and we do not wish to see any change in the law that would weaken this protection. Men who commit offenses against such persons should be treated as criminal offenders. Whatever may be the causes of their disposition or the proper treatment for it, the law must assume that the responsibility for the overt acts remains theirs, except where there are circumstances which it accepts as exempting from accountability. Offenses of this kind are particularly reprehensible when the men who commit them are in positions of special responsibility or trust. We have been made aware that where a man is involved in an offense with a boy or youth the invitation to the commission of the act sometimes comes from him rather than from the man. But we believe that even when this is so that fact does not serve to exculpate the man.

It is also part of the function of the law to preserve public order and decency. We therefore hold that when homosexual behavior between males takes place in public it should continue to be dealt with by the criminal law.

There is a third class of offense to which we have had to give long and careful consideration. It is that of homosexual acts committed between adults in private. In England and Wales, during the three years ended March 1956, 307 men (300 in England and Wales and 7 in Scotland), guilty, as far as is known, only of offenses committed in private with consenting adult partners, were convicted by the courts.

On the basis of [general] considerations, we have reached the conclusion that legislation which covers acts in the third category we have mentioned goes beyond the proper sphere of the law's concern. We do not think that it is proper for the law to concern itself with what a man does in private, unless it can be shown to be so contrary to the public good that the law ought to intervene in its function as the guardian of that public good.

In considering whether homosexual acts between consenting adults in private should cease to be criminal offenses, we have examined the more serious arguments in favor of retaining them as such. We now set out these arguments and our reasons for disagreement with them. In favor of retaining the present law, it has been contended that homosexual behavior between adult males, in private no less than in public, is contrary to the public good on the grounds that—

(i)   it menaces the health of society;
(ii) it has damaging effects on family life;
(iii) a man who indulges in these practices with another man may turn his attention to boys.

As regards the first of these arguments, it is held that conduct of this kind is a cause of the demoralization and decay of civilization, and that therefore, unless we wish to see our nation degenerate and decay, such conduct must be stopped by every possible means. We have found no evidence to support this view, and we cannot feel it right to frame the laws which should govern this country in the present age by reference to hypothetical explanations of the history of other peoples in ages distant in time and different in circumstances from our own. In so far as the basis of this argument can be precisely formulated, it is often no more than the expression of revulsion against what is regarded as unnatural, sinful, or disgusting. Many people feel this revulsion, for one or more of these reasons. But moral conviction or instinctive feeling, however strong, is not a valid basis for overriding the individual's privacy and for bringing within the ambit of the criminal law private sexual behavior of this kind. It is held also that if such men are employed in certain professions or certain branches of the public service their private habits may render them liable to threats of blackmail or to other pressures which may make them "bad security risks." If this is true, it is true also of some other categories of person: for example, drunkards, gamblers, and those who become involved in compromising situations of a heterosexual kind; and while it may be a valid ground for excluding from certain forms of employment men who indulge in homosexual behavior, it does not, in our view, constitute a sufficient reason for making their private sexual behavior an offense in itself.

The second contention, that homosexual behavior between males has a damaging effect on family life, may well be true. Indeed, we have had evidence that it often is; cases in which homosexual behavior on the part of the husband has broken up a marriage are by no means rare, and there are also cases in which a man in whom the homosexual component is relatively weak nevertheless derives such satisfaction from homosexual outlets that he does not enter upon a marriage which might have been successfully and happily consummated. We deplore this damage to what we regard as the basic unit of society; but cases are also frequently encountered in which a marriage has been broken up by homosexual behavior on the part of the wife, and no doubt some women, too, derive sufficient satisfaction from homosexual outlets to prevent their marrying. We have had no reasons shown to us which would lead us to believe that homosexual behavior between males inflicts any greater damage on family life than adultery, fornication, or lesbian behavior. . . .

We have given anxious consideration to the third argument, that an adult male who has sought as his partner another adult male may turn from such a relationship and seek as his partner a boy or succession of boys. We should certainly not wish to countenance any proposal which might tend to increase offenses against minors. Indeed, if we thought that any recommendation for a change in the law would increase the danger to minors, we should not make it. But in this matter we have been much influenced by our expert witnesses. They are in no doubt that whatever may be the origins of the homosexual condition, there are two recognizably different categories among adult male homosexuals. There are those who seek as partners other adult males, and there are pedophiliacs, that is to say, men who seek as partners boys who have not reached puberty.

We are authoritatively informed that a man who has homosexual relations with an adult partner seldom turns to boys, and vice versa, though it is apparent from the police reports we have seen and from other evidence submitted to us that such cases do happen. But pedophiliacs, together with the comparatively few who are indiscriminate, will continue to be liable to the sanctions of criminal law, exactly as they are now. And the others would be very unlikely to change their practices and turn to boys simply because their present practices were made legal. . . . Our evidence, in short, indicates that the fear that the legalization of homosexual acts between adults will lead to similar acts with boys has not enough substance to justify the treatment of adult homosexual behavior in private as a criminal offense, and suggests that it would be more likely that such a change in the law would protect boys rather than endanger them.

In addition, an argument of a more general character in favor of retaining the present law has been put to us by some of our witnesses. It is that to change the law in such a way that homosexual acts between consenting adults in private ceased to be criminal offenses must suggest to the average citizen a degree of toleration by the legislature of homosexual behavior, and that such a change would "open the floodgates" and result in unbridled license. It is true that a change of this sort would amount to a limited degree of such toleration, but we do not share the fears of our witnesses that the change would have the effect they expect. This expectation seems to us to exaggerate the effect of the law on human behavior. It may well be true that the present law deters from homosexual acts some who would otherwise commit them, and to that extent an increase in homosexual behavior can be expected. But it is no less true that if the amount of homosexual behavior has, in fact, increased in recent years, then the law has failed to act as an effective deterrent. It seems to us that the law itself probably makes little difference to the amount of homosexual behavior which actually occurs; whatever the law may be, there will always be strong social forces opposed to homosexual behavior. It is highly improbable that the man to whom homosexual behavior is repugnant would find it any less repugnant because the law permitted it in certain circumstances; so that even if, as has been suggested to us, homosexuals tend to proselytize, there is no valid reason for supposing that any considerable number of conversions would follow the change in the law.

We recognize that a proposal to change a law which has operated for many years, so as to make legally permissible acts which were formerly unlawful, is open to criticisms which might not be made in relation to a proposal to omit from a code of laws being formulated de novo any provision making these acts illegal. To reverse a long-standing tradition is a serious matter and not to be suggested lightly. But the task entrusted to us, as we conceive it, is to state what we regard as a just and equitable law. We therefore do not think it appropriate that consideration of this question should be unduly influenced by a regard for the present law, much of which derives from traditions whose origins are obscure.

There remains one additional counter-argument which we believe to be decisive, namely, the importance which society and the law ought to give to individual freedom of choice and action in matters of private morality. Unless a deliberate attempt is to be made by society, acting through the agency of the law, to equate the sphere of crime with that of sin, there must remain a realm of private morality and immorality which is, in brief and crude terms, not the law's business. To say this is not to condone or encourage private immorality. On the contrary, to emphasize the personal and private nature of moral or immoral conduct is to emphasize the personal and private responsibility of the individual for his own actions, and that is a responsibility which a mature agent can properly be expected to carry for himself without the threat of punishment from the law.

We accordingly recommend that homosexual behavior between consenting adults in private should no longer be a criminal offense.

HOMOSEXUALITY: THE FORMULATION OF A SOCIOLOGICAL PERSPECTIVE

William Simon and John A. Gagnon

The study of homosexuality today, except for a few rare and relatively recent examples, suffers from two major defects: it is ruled by a simplistic and homogeneous view of the psychological and social contents of the category "homosexual," and at the same time it is nearly exclusively interested in the most difficult and least rewarding of all questions, that of etiology. While some small exceptions are allowed for adolescent homosexual experimentation, the person with a major to nearly exclusive sexual interest in persons of the same sex is perceived as belonging to a uniform category whose adult behavior is a necessary outcome and, in a sense, re-enactment of certain early and determining experiences. This is the prevailing image of the homosexual and the substantive concern of the literature in psychiatry and psychology today.

In addition to the fact that sexual contact with persons of the same sex, even if over the age of consent, is against the law in 49 of the 50 states, the homosexual labors under another burden that is commonly the lot of the deviant in any society. The process of labeling and stigmatizing behavior not only facilitates the work of legal agencies in creating a

From *Journal of Health and Social Behavior,* Vol. 8, No. 3 (September 1967), 177-85. Reprinted by permission.

bounded category of deviant actors such as the "normal burglar" and the "normal child molester" . . . but it also creates an image of large classes of deviant actors all operating from the same motivations and for the same etiological reasons. The homosexual, like most significantly labeled persons (whether the label be positive or negative), has *all* of his acts interpreted through the framework of his homosexuality. Thus the creative activity of the playwright or painter who happens to be homosexual is interpreted in terms of his homosexuality rather than in terms of the artistic rules and conventions of the particular art form in which he works. . . .

It is this nearly obsessive concern with the ultimate causes of adult conditions that has played a major role in structuring our concerns about beliefs and attitudes toward the homosexual. Whatever the specific elements that make up an etiological theory, the search for etiology has its own consequences for research methodology and the construction of theories about behavior. In the case of homosexuality, if one moves beyond those explanations of homosexual behavior that are rooted in constitutional or biological characteristics—that is, something in the genes or in the hormonal system—one is left with etiological explanations located in the structure of the family and its malfunctions. The most compelling of these theories are grounded ultimately in Freudian psychology, where the roots of this as well as the rest of human character structure is to be found in the pathological relationships between parents and their children.

As a consequence of our preliminary work and the work of others . . . we would like to propose some alternative considerations in terms of the complexity of the life cycle of the homosexual, the roles that mark various stages of this cycle, and the kinds of forces, both sexual and nonsexual, that impinge on this individual actor. It is our current feeling that the problem of finding out how people become homosexual requires an adequate theory of how they become heterosexual; that is, one cannot explain homosexuality in one way and leave heterosexuality as a large residual category labeled "all other." Indeed, the explanation of homosexuality in this sense may await the explanation of the larger and more modal category of adjustment.

Further, from a sociological point of view, what the original causes were may not even be very important for the patterns of homosexuality observed in a society. Much as the medical student who comes to medicine for many reasons, and for whom the homogenous character of professional behavior arises from the experiences of medical school rather than from the root causes of his occupational choice, the patterns of adult homosexuality are consequent upon the social structures and values that surround the homosexual after he becomes, or conceives of himself as, homosexual rather than upon original and ultimate causes.

What we are suggesting here is that we have allowed the homosexual's sexual object choice to dominate and control our imagery of him and have let this aspect of his total life experience appear to determine all his products, concerns, and activities. This prepossessing concern on the part of nonhomosexuals with the purely sexual aspect of the homosexual's life is something we would not allow to occur if we were interested in the heterosexual. However, the mere presence of sexual deviation seems to give the sexual content of life an overwhelming significance. Homosexuals, moreover, vary profoundly in the degree to which their homosexual commitment and its facilitation becomes the organizing principle of their lives. . . .

Obviously, the satisfaction of a homosexual commitment—like most forms of deviance—makes social adjustment more problematic than it might be for members of a conventional population. What is important to understand is that consequences of these sexual practices are not necessarily direct functions of the nature of such practices. It is necessary to move away from an obsessive concern with the sexuality of the individual, and attempt to see the homosexual in terms of the broader attachments that he must make to live in the world around him. Like the heterosexual, the homosexual must come to terms with the problems that are attendant upon being a member of society: he must find a place to work, learn to live with or without his family, be involved or apathetic in political life, find a group of friends to talk to and live with, fill his leisure time usefully or frivolously, handle all of the common and uncommon problems of impulse control and personal gratification, and in some manner socialize his sexual interests.

There is a seldom-noticed diversity to be found in the life cycle of the homosexual, both in terms of solving general human problems and in terms of the particular characteristics of the life cycle itself. Not only are there as many ways of being homosexual as there are of being heterosexual, but the individual homosexual, in the course of his every-day life, encounters as many choices and as many crises as the heterosexual. It is much too easy to allow the label, once applied, to suggest that the complexities of role transition and identity crises are easily attributable to, or are a crucial exemplification of, some previously existing etiological defect.

An example of this is in the phase of homosexuality called "coming out," which is that point in time when there is self-recognition by the individual of his identity as a homosexual and the first major exploration of the homosexual community. At this point in time the removal of inhibiting doubts frequently releases a great deal of sexual energy. Sexual contacts during this period are often pursued nearly indiscriminately and with greater vigor than caution. This is very close to that period in the life of the heterosexual called the "honeymoon," when coitus is legitimate and is pursued with a substantial amount of energy. This high rate of marital coitus, however, declines as demands are made on the young couple to take their place in the framework of the larger social system. In these same terms, during the homosexual "honeymoon" many individuals begin to learn ways of acting out a homosexual object choice that involve homosexual gratification, but that are not necessarily directly sexual and do not involve the genitalia.

It is during this period that many homosexuals go through a crisis of femininity; that is, they "act out" in relatively public places in a somewhat effeminate manner; and some, in a transitory fashion, wear female clothing, known in the homosexual argot as "going in drag." During this period one of the major confirming aspects of masculinity—that is, nonsexual reinforcement by females of masculine status—has been abandoned, and it is not surprising that the very core of masculine identity should not be seriously questioned. This crisis is partially structured by the already existing homosexual culture in which persons already in the crisis stage become models for those who are newer to their homosexual commitment. A few males retain this pseudo-feminine commitment, a few others emerge masquerading as female prostitutes to males, and still others pursue careers as female impersonators. This adjustment might be more widely adapted if feminine behavior by men—except in sharply delimited occupational roles—was not negatively sanctioned. Thus the tendency is for this kind of behavior to be a transitional experiment for most homosexuals, an experiment that leaves vestiges of "camp" behavior, but traces more often expressive of the character of the cultural life of the homosexual community than of some overriding need of individual homosexuals. Since this period of personal disorganization and identity problems is at the same time highly visible to the broader community, this femininity is enlisted as evidence for theories of homosexuality that see, as a central component in its etiology, the failure of sexual identification. The homosexual at this point of his life cycle is more likely to be in psychotherapy, and this is often construed as evidence for a theory which is supported by a missampling of the ways of being homosexual.

Another life cycle crisis that the homosexual shares with the heterosexual in this youth-oriented society is the crisis of aging. While American society places an inordinate positive emphasis on youth, the homosexual community, by and large, places a still greater emphasis on this fleeting characteristic. In general, the homosexual has fewer resources with which to meet this crisis. For the heterosexual there are his children whose careers assure a sense of the future and a wife whose sexual availability cushions the shock of declining sexual attractiveness. In addition, the crisis of aging comes later to the heterosexual, at an age when his sexual powers have declined and expectations concerning his sexuality are considerably lower. The management of aging by the homosexual is not well understood, but there are, at this point in his life, a series of behavioral manifestations (symptoms) attendant to this dramatic transition that are misread as global aspects of homosexuality. Here, as with "coming out," it is important to note that most homosexuals, even with fewer resources than their heterosexual counterparts, manage to weather the period with relative success.

A central concern underlying these options and the management of a homosexual career is the presence and complexity of a homosexual community, which serves most simply for some persons as a sexual market place, but for others as the locus of friendships, opportunities, recreation, and expansion of the base of social life. Such a community is filled with both formal and informal institutions for meeting others and for following, to the degree the individual wants, a homosexual life style. Minimally, the community provides a source of social support, for it is one of the few places where the homosexual may get positive validation of his own self-image. Though the community often provides more feminine or "camp" behavior than some individuals might desire, in a major sense "camp" behavior may well be an expression of aggregate community characteristics without an equal commitment to this behavior on the part of its members. Further, "camp" behavior may also be seen as a form of interpersonal communication characteristic of intracommunity behavior and significantly altered for most during interaction with the larger society. . . . Insofar as the community provides these relationships for the individual homosexual, it allows for the dilution of sexual drives by providing social gratification in ways that are not directly sexual. Consequently, the homosexual with access to the community is more protected from impulsive sexual "acting out" than the homosexual who has only his own fear and knowledge of the society's prohibitions to mediate his sexual impulses.

It should be pointed out that in contrast to ethnic and occupational subcultures the homosexual community, as well as other deviant subcommunities, has very limited content. This derives from the fact that the community members often have only their sexual commitment in common. Thus, while the community may reduce the problems of access to sexual partners and reduce guilt by providing a structure of shared values, often the shared value structure is far too narrow to transcend other areas of value disagreement. The college-trained professional and the bus boy, the WASP and the Negro slum dweller, may meet in sexual congress, but the similarity of their sexual interests does not eliminate larger social and cultural barriers. The important fact is that the homosexual community is in itself an impoverished cultural unit. This impoverishment, however, may be only partially limiting, since it constrains most members to participate in it on a limited basis, reducing their anxiety and conflicts in the sexual sphere and increasing the quality of their performance in other aspects of social life.

Earlier we briefly listed some of the general problems that the homosexual—in common with the heterosexual—must face; these included earning a living, maintaining a residence, relations with family, and so on. At this point we might consider some of these in greater detail.

First there is the most basic problem of all: earning a living. Initially, the variables that apply to all labor force participants generally apply to homosexuals also. In addition there are the special conditions imposed by the deviant definition of the homosexual commitment. What is important is that the occupational activity of homosexuals represents a fairly broad range. The differences in occupational activity can be conceptualized along a number of dimensions, some of which would be conventional concerns of occupational sociology, while others would reflect the special situation of the homosexual. For example, one element is the degree of occupational involvement, that is, the degree to which occupational activity, or activity ancillary to it, is defined as intrinsically gratifying. This would obviously vary from professional to ribbon clerk to factory laborer. A corollary to this is the degree to which the world of work penetrates other aspects of life. In terms of influence upon a homosexual career, occupational involvement very likely plays a constraining role during the acting-out phase associated with "coming out," as well as serving as an alternative source of investment during the "crisis of aging." Another aspect bears directly upon the issue of the consequences of having one's deviant commitment exposed. For some occupational roles disclosure would clearly be a disaster—the school teacher, the minister, and the politician, to mention just three. There are other occupations where the disclosure or assumption of homosexual interests is either of little consequence or—though relatively rare—has a positive consequence. . . .

A second series of questions could deal with the effects of a deviant sexual commitment upon occupational activity itself. In some cases the effect may be extremely negative, since the pursuit of homosexual interests may generate irresponsibility and irregularity. Some part of this might flow from what we associate with bachelorhood generally: detachment from conventional families and, in terms of sex, constant striving for what is essentially regularized in marriage. Illustrations of these behaviors include too many late nights out, too much drinking in too many taverns, and unevenness in emotional condition. On the other hand, several positive effects can be observed. Detachment from the demands of domestic life not only frees one for greater dedication to the pursuit of sexual goals, but also for greater dedication to work. Also, the ability of some jobs to facilitate homosexual activity—such as certain marginal, low-paying, white-collar jobs—serves as compensation for low pay or limited opportunity for advancement. There may be few simple or consistent patterns emerging from this type of consideration, yet the overdetermination of the sexual element in the study of the homosexual rests in our prior reluctance to consider these questions which are both complex and pedestrian.

Similarly, just as most homosexuals have to earn a living, so must they come to terms with their immediate families. There is no substantial evidence to suggest that the proportion of homosexuals for whom relatives are significant persons differs from that of heterosexuals. The important differences rest in the way the relationships are managed and, again, the consequences they have for other aspects of life. Here also one could expect considerable variation containing patterns of rejection, continuing involvement without knowledge, ritualistically suppressed knowledge, and knowledge and acceptance. This becomes more complex because several patterns may be operative at the same time with different members of one's family constellation. Here again it is not unreasonable to assume a considerable degree of variation in the course of managing a homosexual commitment as this kind of factor varies. Yet the literature is almost totally without reference to this relationship. Curiously, in the psychiatric literature—where mother and father play crucial roles in the formation of a homosexual commitment—they tend to be significant by their absence in considerations of how homosexual careers are managed.

This order of discussion could be extended into a large number of areas. Let us consider just one more: religion. As a variable, religion (as both an identification and a quality of religiosity) manifests no indication that it plays an important role in the generation of homosexual commitments. However, it clearly does, or can, play a significant role in the management of that commitment. Here, as in other spheres of life, we must be prepared to deal with complex, interactive relations rather than fixed, static ones. Crucial to the homosexual's ability to "accept himself" is his ability to bring his own homosexuality within a sense of the moral order as it is projected by the institutions surrounding him as well as his own vision of this order. It may be that the issue of including homosexuality within a religious definition is the way the question should be framed only part of the time, and for only part of a homosexual population. At other times and for other homosexuals, to frame the question in terms of bringing religiosity within the homosexual definition might be more appropriate. The need for damnation (that rare sense of being genuinely evil) and the need for redemption (a sense of potentially being returned to the community in good standing) can be expected to vary, given different stages of the life cycle, different styles of being homosexual, and varying environments for enactment of the homosexual commitment. And our sense of the relation suggests that, more than asking about the homosexual's religious orientation and how it expresses his homosexuality, we must also learn to ask how his homosexuality expresses his commitment to the religious.

The aims, then, of a sociological approach to homosexuality are to begin to define the factors—both individual and situational—that predispose a homosexual to follow one homosexual path as against others; to spell out the contingencies that will shape the career that has been embarked upon; and to trace out the patterns of living in both their pedestrian and their seemingly exotic aspects. Only then will we begin to understand the homosexual. This pursuit must inevitably bring us— though from a particular angle—to those complex matrices wherein most human behavior is fashioned.

IV VICTIMLESS ACTS AS DEVIATION

9 ABORTION

Abortion, prostitution, and illegal gambling are prime illustrations of the difficulty of enforcing laws that prohibit practices which are in fact desired by all of the parties involved. They are, in short, offenses and deviations without "victims." In all instances, the services are desired, indeed demanded, by the clients who themselves are law-abiding persons. In all instances it is the purveyor of the service and not the consumer who is the concern of law enforcement. The female seeking the abortion, the "trick" or the "John," and the gambler are almost wholly exempt from criminal taint and stigma. Under these circumstances, the historic American adage of "let the buyer beware" is translated into "let the seller take his risk as a law violator." Little wonder, then, that in this situation the consumer, devoid of risk, provides an endless market for these services and the seller, accepting all of the risk, simply tailors his organization and prices to fit.

Unlike the status offenses of drunkenness, drug addiction, and homosexuality, in which the deviant may lack the necessary intent in the eyes of the law, the victimless crimes involve no such "limited liability." One can hardly contend that the prospects or purveyors of these services are irresponsible and unable to control this aspect of their conduct. Indeed, the reverse is usually, though not always, the case. Hence the chief characteristic of these specific deviations is in the willingness and eagerness of all parties concerned to provide or to receive an unlawful service—for a price.

Abortion typifies the problem about as well as any other victimless crime. Many thousands, perhaps millions, of women each year seek to terminate unwanted pregnancies. Some, perhaps even the majority, attempt self-induced abortions. The remainder seek out men and women, skilled and unskilled to do the job. The great pressure for abortion has led to the development of the professional abortionist who works either solo or as a member of an abortion mill or ring. Some police authorities consider illegal abortion as one of the top five criminal enterprises, although the President's Commission on Law Enforcement and the Administration of Justice paid little attention to this kind of illegal activity in its task force reports.

There are four articles in this chapter on abortion as a victimless offense. The first is a *Time* essay "The Desperate Dilemma of Abortion," which outlines the legal, moral, medical, psychological, and social issues in abortion in a straightforward manner. In the second, Professor Edwin M. Schur is chiefly concerned with the emergence of the "professional" criminal abortionist as a predictable response to the thriving traffic in abortions. Two types of criminal-abortion practitioners are identified and described. There is some discussion of the variations in the skill of the abortionists, in their fees, and of the dangers to the women seeking the abortions. Much of the article is given over to a description of the illegal organization of the abortion business, particularly to the abortion mill and ring. The business aspect of abortion is described, not the medical or surgical aspects. Discussion of the opportunities for police corruption and the general and difficult problems of enforcing abortion laws concludes the article.

Father David Granfield in "Rethinking Abortion Legislation: Law and Morals" argues that "from the very moment of conception, a living, human organism comes into being." It follows, therefore, that abortion, no matter how early in the course of pregnancy, is a form of murder (infanticide) as well as sinful conduct. Professor Granfield also discusses, and dismisses, the major arguments in favor of liberalizing abortion laws. He suggests that it is perfectly reasonable both morally and legislatively to support laws that make sinful behavior unlawful. He also takes issue with the view that we should not have laws making illegal those acts which we cannot, in fact, prevent. Equally controversial is his argument that although the United States is a pluralistic society, this does not mean that our laws ought to be predicated on the lowest common moral denominator. In short, his thesis is based on the proposition that life occurs at conception. Those who dispute this will probably reject the rest of the argument.

In the fourth and last article, Robert E. Hall, a professor of Obstetrics and Gynecology, is concerned principally with "The Medico-Legal Aspects of Abortion." This medical-legal conflict has resulted in a situation which cannot be justified or rationalized much longer. He offers four alternatives to the present chaotic situation, all of them involving greater freedom for the medical group than is presently the case. Dr. Hall seems to imply that the solution to the medical-legal dilemma has been measurably hastened by what amounts to the *de facto* acceptance of mechanical and chemical techniques of birth control even among the majority of Catholics in America.

THE DESPERATE DILEMMA OF ABORTION

Time Magazine

For a century, state laws in the U.S. have generally made abortion a crime except where necessary to save a woman's life. The ban is enforced by religious beliefs, medical ethics, fear of social scandal. Yet it is flouted throughout the country—in the same pattern, though not in the same numbers, as Prohibition was decades ago. Written by men, anti-abortion laws cannot quell the desperation of women for whom a particular pregnancy is a hateful foreign object. At their time of despair, women agree with Author Marya Mannes, who reviles such laws as the work of "the inseminators, not the bearers."

How women react to unwanted pregnancy is the most crucial—and least acknowledged—issue in the current debate over U.S. abortion laws. Each year, an estimated 25 million legal abortions occur throughout the world (*v.* roughly 120 live births). The fact is that women have always practiced abortion, defying all laws or taboos against it, including the death penalty, which still exists in Pakistan. The inevitable Egyptian papyrus mentions it; Aristotle urged it in general terms, and so did Plato for every woman after 40; Roman husbands were entitled to order it. Anthropologist George Devereux has catalogued dozens of ancient methods—magical incantations, jumping from high places, applying hot coals to the abdomen. Hawaiian women fashioned stilettos representing Kupo, god of abortions, then thrust them into the uterus. Even now, Ceylonese girls brew an abortifacient by boiling a poisonous yam in cow urine or liquid dung, and then swallow the stuff for seven days.

It is a male theory (or unconscious demand) that women feel deep guilt after abortion. In fact, most women react with a feeling of great relief. None of this should obscure the biological fact that abortion is abnormal, a product of grave medical, economic and psychological pressures. Says a twice-aborted schoolteacher: "No one would go through it unless they *had* to."

PRACTICE v. POLICY

How many women have illegal abortions rather than suffer the far-reaching effects of unwanted pregnancy? Estimates range from 200,000 to 1,500,000 a year in the U.S. (*v.* 3,700,000 live births). No one re-

From *Time*, October 13, 1967. Reprinted by permission.

cords illegal abortions; all statistics are extrapolated from shaky sample studies going as far back as Germany in the 1920s. As for deaths resulting from abortions, which are better recorded, the annual toll is probably about 1,000. No one can accurately add up the number of U.S. women who go to Puerto Rico, Japan, and other places where abortions are easily, if expensively, obtained. The firmest figure is the number of legal abortions (10,000 a year) performed in hospitals—and they are decreasing. In the early 1940s, one pregnancy in 150 was aborted to save women with such diseases as diabetes, tuberculosis and hypertension. Now medical advances have helped to cut the ratio to one in 500.

Today, hospital abortions are usually quite safe, especially during the first trimester of pregnancy. Until the twelfth week, the standard technique is dilatation and curettage ("D and C"); a surgeon merely stretches the cervix with dilators, then removes the conceptus with a tiny, scoop-shaped instrument called a curette. After three months, one method is to inject a salt solution into the amniotic sac, thus starting labor contractions that expel the fetus. In Communist countries, where the right to abortion is given or withheld at the whim of the state, a small vibrodilator is inserted in the uterus for 45 seconds; a tiny vacuum then empties the contents. Widely used until the twelfth week, the method minimizes injury, takes only three minutes. In 1964, Czechoslovakia reported no deaths in 140,000 legal abortions, Hungary only two in 358,000.

Despite the safeness, abortion is an emotion-charged equation: a maternal life saved equals a fetal life destroyed. Out of deep concern for the fetus—as well as tribal survival—men disapproved of abortion even before the Hippocratic oath. The very first Christians called it infanticide; in A.D. 314, the church prescribed ten years' penance for it. Thereafter, theologians debated the point at which the fetus is "animated" with a rational soul and hence murderable. By the 12th century, abortion was generally not punished by excommunication when performed within 40 days of conception for a male fetus and 80 days for a female, though it was impossible then (as it is difficult now) to fix the time of conception, and no one ever explained how fetal sex could be predetermined. Pope Sixtus V (1585-90) made abortion an excommunicatory sin at any stage of development, but this order was reversed in the year after his death by Gregory XIV, who approved excommunication only after a fetus was 40 days old. In 1869, Pius IX reverted the Roman Catholic Church to the Sixtus position, which holds that ensoulment begins at conception.

Modern Catholic clerics increasingly rely on embryology rather than ensoulment to urge that a newly fertilized ovum is virtually a person because it contains all the cell-creating chromosomes that a human ever has. As they see it, the conceptus is a living continuum from the start, a life that dies only by outside interference. In 1930, Pius XI made it clear that abortion is forbidden, even to save a woman's life, because the fetus is "equally sacred." The church's stand is widely ignored in Catholic countries, which ban birth control and have high rates of abortion as a result. In France, illegal abortions roughly equal—and may well exceed—live births. In South America, induced abortion is the No. 1 cause of death for women of childbearing age. Similar patterns exist in no-abortion Moslem countries; an estimated one-third of Iran's pregnancies are aborted.

In medical eyes, a fetus is usually incapable of independent life before 20 weeks, thus presenting no murder issue in abortion. In contrast to Catholic doctrine, most other Western religions now view the mother's life as primary. Many Jews accept abortion because they regard a fetus as an organic part of the mother and not as a living soul until its birth. The National Council of Churches has approved hospital abortions "when the health or life of the mother is at stake," and many clergymen broadly define health to mean social as well as physical well-being. Last month the nation's Episcopal bishops approved limited legal abortion "with proper safeguards against abuse." The assembly of the Unitarian Universalist Association has decried abortion laws as "an affront to human life and dignity."

IN A LEGAL MAZE

The central problem of abortion in the U.S. is that it is governed by criminal law rather than medical knowledge. Following English common law, the early U.S. regarded abortion as no crime before the fetus quickens in the womb (about five months); a miscarriage before 20 weeks still generally requires no death certificate or interment. But starting in 1860, many states outlawed abortion before as well as after quickening. New Hampshire, for example, bans hospital abortion before quickening, even to save a dying woman. The legal maze is extraordinary. In 17 states, unjustified abortion is a felony that carries sentences ranging up to 21 years. In some states, the woman herself can be charged (but seldom is) for cooperating in the abortion.

Prosecution is rare: women do not testify. Yet doctors in most states can never forget that the sole defense is proven necessity to save the patient's life. Only seven states even consider her health or safety. Actually, most hospital abortions are performed for admittedly illegal reasons, notably mental illness and German measles (25% of the 1964 total). Unfortunately, fear of the consequences creates vast inequities. To fend off prosecution, special hospital boards often use quotas and render questionable moral judgments.

The inescapable result is that women able to pay fees of $300 to $600 frantically seek illegal abortionists, who seem remarkably available (one middle-class East Coast wife asked five friends, got five names). About 75% of abortionists are doctors, some of them genuine humanitarians. Until he retired a while ago, Dr. Robert Spencer of Ashland, Pa., was considered a saint by thousands of Eastern college girls. Even the police sent him their wives. One New Jersey general practitioner performs 250 abortions a year in his spotless, two-nurse clinic. "Every day I tell myself, 'This is the last,' " he says. "And every day someone else calls and sounds so frightened and alone. I just can't tell them no."

Florida currently has an influx of skilled Cuban refugee doctors who once made Havana an abortion mecca and are now doing the same for Miami, where some 30 abortion mills last year paid off assorted officials and took in an estimated $20 million. But all too many U.S. abortionists are dangerous defrocked doctors—alcoholics, drug addicts, sexual perverts—or worse, bungling amateurs who don't hesitate to finish a sloppy job by tossing clients off tenement roofs or dismembering those who die. Equally sobering are the slum women who cannot afford even amateurs and do it themselves with hatpins, coat hangers and putrid soap solutions, which are often followed by lethal infection. Most desolate of all, perhaps, are those who cannot and dare not abort. Among the poor, who still know little about contraceptives, one result is ever more unwanted children, the key carriers of delinquency, divorce and crime. In 20 years, illegitimate births in the U.S. have more than doubled, to 291,000 a year, rising to 26% of all nonwhite births, compared with 3.6% of whites.

TOWARD REFORM

All the polls show that Americans heavily favor reform. Of 40,089 U.S. physicians who answered a survey by *Modern Medicine* last spring, 87% favored liberalizing the abortion laws—including 49% of the Catholics. According to the National Opinion Research Center, 71% of Americans favor legal abortion if the woman's health is endangered, 56% in rape cases and 55% if there is a strong chance that the baby may have a serious defect. Conversely, 80% are against abortion for unwed girls and 83% against it for mothers who do not want more children—the main seekers of abortion.

As in other sex-law issues, the surveys suggest that Americans tend to disapprove publicly what they practice privately. Now the consensus is having political effects. Last spring Colorado became the first state to legalize hospital abortions on three principal medical grounds. Based on a model code drafted by the American Law Institute, the new statute authorizes abortion whenever a pregnancy 1) threatens grave damage to the woman's physical or mental health, 2) results from rape or incest, or 3) is likely to produce a child with a severe mental or physical defect. Even then, abortions require unanimous approval by a hospital panel of three doctors. North Carolina has followed suit, but does not require panels. California's new law is similar to Colorado's but bars abortion of potentially defective children. In varying degrees, the same formula is up for debate in at least ten other state legislatures.

The key question is whether limited legislation is any solution. In fact, the new laws merely codify what hospitals are already doing. They do embolden doctors, but in practice they may prove more restrictive—and even increase illegal abortions. So it seems in Sweden, which in 1938 enacted a law almost exactly like Colorado's. Far from being an abortion mecca (foreigners are rarely accepted), Sweden puts women through a multilayered screening that creates excruciating delays; 56% of Stockholm-area legal abortions occur after the 16th week of pregnancy. Bureaucratic paper shuffling often holds up legal operations until the 24th week—producing live babies that sometimes cry for hours before dying. To avoid *de facto* infanticide, Swedish women flock to Poland for early, efficient $60 abortions. Appalled, the Swedish government has concluded that the law must be broadened to allow more and faster abortions.

More complicated objections to limited legislation are now being raised by Catholic clerics, who regard Colorado-style laws as a blatant case of state-approved eugenics, never before established in U.S. law. To abort a rubella (German measles) victim, they say, is to rely on the purely statistical chance (average odds: 50-50) that her child may be defective—and to doom a possibly perfect baby in the process. To abort a fetus produced by rape or incest, they say, is to execute the most innocent party in the triangle purely for the mother's social convenience. Even the rapist is guaranteed a trial based on all of law's due-process standards. Why no due process for the fetus? Not only that: some states already grant an unborn child rights of inheritance and recovery for prenatal injuries. Since those rights are contingent on his being born alive, does he not also have a right to be born in order to exercise them?

CONSCIENCE & INTELLIGENCE

Beyond these profound moral questions, however, lies the stubborn reality that women denied legal abortions go on getting illegal ones—and that those unborn babies get even less due process than would a rape-fetus in Colorado. This leads to the argument that the real immorality is the retention or enactment of laws that drive women to illegal abortion. In empirical terms, the debaters are mired in side issues. Vital as fetal rights unquestionably are, the bedrock problem is not whether the fetus is inchoate and hence expendable, as law reformers claim, or whether it is human and inviolable, as opponents insist. The problem is unwanted pregnancy and how to treat it.

How? The reformers have solid answers: not by public indifference but by more birth control information and family support. Not by moral absolutes toward unwed pregnancy but by moral concern for each concrete situation. Not by punitive laws but by medical freedom to help panicky women make rational choices—and if need be, have safe, early, cheap abortions. For both mother and fetus the reform movement holds, such is the real due process required. Much of this might come about simply by more liberal interpretation of existing state laws. Court cases going back to 1929 give U.S. doctors almost the exclusive right to decide when abortion is necessary to save maternal life; several decisions hold that the danger need not be imminent or certain; in the future, even life-shortening unhappiness might be a legal ground. But few doctors are ready to rely on those decisions in the absence of a Supreme Court ruling.

That leaves state legislatures facing the most important question in the debate: Why not repeal all abortion laws? Last month that suggestion came from Jesuit Theologian-Lawyer Robert F. Drinan, dean of Boston College Law School and chairman of the American Bar Association's family-law section. In attacking the limited-abortion plan, Father Drinan argued that repeal has "at least the merit of not involving the law and society in the business of selecting those persons whose lives may be legally terminated."

Ultimately, of course, the issue may become academic. The rapid development of contraceptives suggests that women may some day become essentially infertile and thus free to decide precisely when they wish to become fertile. Such safe, do-it-yourself abortifacients as the morning-after and the once-a-month pill are also likely to make abortion entirely a private matter. Still, those pills are far from being perfected—and may well run afoul of anti-abortion laws. Meanwhile, even present contraceptives do not solve the abortion problem.

Along with poverty, ignorance and moral strictures against birth control, the unpredictability of human sexual practices makes unwanted pregnancy inevitable. The way to deal with the problem forthrightly is on terms that permit the individual, guided by conscience and intelligence, to make a choice unhampered by archaic and hypocritical concepts and statutes.

CRIMES WITHOUT VICTIMS: ABORTION

Edwin M. Schur

Abortion is the termination of pregnancy before the unborn child or fetus attains viability—i.e., capacity for life outside the womb. In this discussion the term abortion refers to induced or intentional abortion; it does not include miscarriage, which is technically designated spontaneous abortion.

According to an authoritative anthropological survey, it appears that abortion is a universal phenomenon, and that "it is impossible even to construct an imaginary social system in which no woman would even feel at least impelled to abort. There have always been women who became pregnant against their wills, and different cultures have chosen different ways of dealing with this problem. Abortion has been incurred for almost every conceivable reason, and through a vast array of techniques. Cross-cultural evidence also reveals tremendous variation in the acceptable grounds for abortion.

In the United States, legal norms regarding abortion are highly restrictive. A well-publicized illustration of this fact was provided in 1962 by the case of Mrs. Robert Finkbine, a thirty-year-old resident of Arizona and the mother of four children. Early in her pregnancy, Mrs. Finkbine had taken some tranquilizers containing thalidomide—a drug later revealed to lead to a high rate of birth deformities when taken by pregnant women. Believing that the birth of a deformed baby would impose an undue hardship on the other members of the family, Mrs. Finkbine and her husband sought medical advice. Although at first reluctant to have an abortion, they eventually decided that such a step would be best for all concerned. A panel of staff physicians at a local hospital agreed that the operation should be performed, and this decision was concurred in by examining psychiatrists. At the last minute, however, the doctors were overruled by the hospital administrator, who demanded clarification of the operation's legal status. Mrs. Finkbine then sought from the Arizona courts a declaratory judgment certifying that her abortion would fall within the statutory exception ("when necessary to preserve the mother's life"). She was unable to obtain it. As a result of this setback, Mrs. Finkbine decided "to seek help in a more

From *Crimes Without Victims: Deviant Behavior and Public Policy—Abortion, Homosexuality and Drug Addiction,* Englewood Cliffs, N.J.: Prentice-Hall, Inc. (Spectrum), 1965, pp. 11-40. Reprinted by permission.

favorable legal climate," and eventually obtained a legal abortion in Sweden, where the laws on this matter are much less restrictive. . . .

Although Mrs. Finkbine's specific problem was an unusual one, there is nothing very unusual about the demand for, and the obtaining of, abortions in this country. Summing up extensive research on a sample of over 5000 white nonprison females, the late Dr. Alfred Kinsey reported that, by the time they were forty-five years of age, 22 per cent of the married women had had one or more induced abortions. According to careful evaluation by an expert statistical committee established by the Planned Parenthood Federation's 1955 conference on abortion, the number of induced abortions in the United States each year is probably at least 200,000, and may be as high as 1.2 million. Available evidence indicates that the women seeking abortions are of all races, religions, and socioeconomic classes; many are married, and often already mothers. Under the laws of the various American states—which generally permit abortion only when medically necessary to save the mother's life—most of the abortions are illegal. . . .

THE ABORTIONIST

Society's unwillingness to provide social and legal sanction for abortion has led to the growth of a thriving illicit traffic in such operations, and to the emergence of the "professional" criminal abortionist. An early discussion nicely summarized the strength of the abortionist's position and the way a social need propelled the development of illegal abortion machinery:

> An endless circle was . . . set in motion. The ready willingness of women to visit an abortionist brought him immense profits. A fraction of these profits made it possible to cause an abortion with a greater degree of safety to the woman and a smaller chance of exposure of either the woman or the doctor. This led to a further appeal to women who wished to bring an abrupt termination to their pregnancies. And so the chain was complete.

There is little doubt that the abortionist's practice is extremely widespread in the United States today, although estimates on criminal abortion (which would include self-induced abortions as well as those performed by "professionals") are uncertain. One writer in 1951 estimated a minimum of 330,000 criminal abortions each year, of which at least 300,000 involved an abortionist. This figure was based on an assumed grand total of a million abortions, about two thirds spontaneous and one third induced. Yet, as the abortion conference estimate cited suggests, the total of induced abortions alone may be as high as a million; in that case the number of criminal abortions would be much higher than 330,000. It has been reported that police consider criminal abortion the third biggest illegal endeavor in the United States, surpassed only by gambling and narcotics, and experts claim that criminal abortions exist in almost every city (perhaps even every town) throughout the country.

Conflicting statements have been made concerning the training, skill, and motives of the professional abortionist. Some accounts insist that most illegal abortions are performed by persons who have no medical training, and refer to such persons as "butchers" or "mechanics." There is little doubt that some professional abortionists do fall into this category. On the other hand, there are abortionists who are fully trained physicians. It is well-known that the physician who for one reason or another has lost his license to practice medicine, and the foreign-trained doctor who experiences difficulty in being admitted to practice in this country, may be especially likely to turn to an illegal abortion practice. There are also trained physicians who drift into illegal abortion work gradually, usually beginning with the performance of abortions as favors to their legitimate patients. Some physicians simply enter the field because of the lure of easy money. It is sometimes suggested that there are special psychological reasons which propel a given physician into abortion practice, but the substantiation of such claims appears rather meager.

VARIATIONS IN SKILL

There is no way of accurately gauging the relative proportions of physician and nonphysician abortionists. In the Kinsey survey, women reporting illegal abortions indicated that about 85 per cent had been performed by physicians. Probably there were some instances in which women reported as physicians persons who were not actually licensed practitioners. Furthermore, Kinsey's general sample was biased toward those groups of women who would best be able to obtain competent abortion services. In addition, many of the illegal abortions reported in this study were performed without cost, or at least by doctors who had legitimate medical practices. As a result, the findings may exaggerate the actual participation by licensed physicians in regular abortion work. Nonetheless, the data from this study do suggest that some abortionists are well-trained, skilled medical men. On the basis of interviews with a limited number of professional abortion specialists, the Kinsey team reported being impressed with their technical ability and with the low number of reported deaths and other complications from their operations. They even cited the case of one specialist (with a fairly well-supported claim of having performed 30,000 abortions without a single death) who tried, unsuccessfully, to hire a psychiatric social worker to counsel prospective patients. More generally, these researchers emphasized that although the profit motive obviously may lead a doctor into an abortion practice, those they interviewed displayed a higher degree of medical qualifications than earlier accounts had led them to expect. . . .

Even if it is impossible to determine the extent of medical accreditation among abortionists, it is clear that at least the more skilled among them can claim an indirect link with legitimate medical practice—in that a considerable proportion of their patients have been referred to them by licensed physicians. This point was discussed at the Planned Parenthood Federation's 1955 conference on abortion by a once-licensed doctor who for some twenty years had carried on an illegal abortion practice in Baltimore. He asserted that there were 353 doctors in that community whom he had served for many years, and from many of whom he actually had signed letters of referral. He claimed further that when he had been brought to trial on abortion charges, he refrained from implicating any of these physicians. They, on the other hand, refused to support him in any way, and a few were actually instrumental in bringing about his conviction. If this story is true, and there is little reason to doubt it, it nicely points up the ambivalent attitude of the medical profession on the abortion issue.

This case also suggests the highly ambiguous professional status of the skilled abortionist. The non-medical abortionist, who clearly defines himself as an illicit practicioner and who is so defined by the public at large, may experience somewhat less role confusion than the one who is medically trained. The nonmedical abortionist is less concerned about being labeled a criminal, he has no formal medical credentials to lose, he makes no pretense to medical competence. He may associate with various disreputable individuals who serve to confirm and support his deviant self-image. The medical man who takes up an abortion practice, however, may often be torn between conflicting images of his professional and social self. He is more likely than his nonphysician counterparts to desire the esteem of, and contact with, legitimate practitioners. He still considers himself a doctor, and only with the greatest reluctance can he accept concern for the plight of his patients, and is anxious to exercise due care in their treatment—something he is not always able to do if he is at the same time to insure his own safety from detection and prosecution. Although he feels he performs a useful function both for his patients and for his legitimate professional colleagues, he knows that when the chips are down he will receive little open support.

DANGERS OF ILLEGAL ABORTION

It may be useful at this point to comment briefly on the question of the deaths that occur in illegal abortions. Early estimates placed the annual number of such deaths in this country at 8,000 or more. As late as 1951, one expert suggested there still might be 5,000-6,000 such deaths annually. The use of antibiotics and the exercise of increased care have clearly decreased the likelihood of death from criminal abortion. Statistics on known abortion deaths in New York City show a steady declining trend, from 144 deaths in 1921 to 15 in 1951. Commenting on these figures, the city's chief medical examiner stated: "I believe there are just as many abortions being done, but that they are being done under better conditions." He also noted some interesting breakdowns of these statistics: a disproportionate number of the women who died from abortions were Negroes, and although more of the women who underwent abortions were married, there were "more deaths from crudely done criminal abortion with very severe injury" among those who were single. These data indicate the relatively more desperate plight of the single woman. She is more likely than the married woman to expose herself to a crude abortionist, and if postabortal complications develop, she is apt to wait longer before seeking medical help.

There are cases in which the inept technique of an unskilled abortionist directly leads to death. But even the fairly conscientious abortionist works under imperfect conditions, and must for his own safety get the woman to leave his place of work as soon after the operation as possible. Hence the inadequacy of aftercare, the frequent lack of necessary medicines and emergency equipment, and the dangers inherent in the abortion itself (at least when the abortionist has not had the proper training) combine to make criminal abortion highly dangerous even today. The immediate dangers and primary causes of death are shock, hemorrhage, embolism, infection, and poisoning.

Certain illegal abortion techniques may pose special dangers. For instance, injection of potassium soap compounds into the uterus by pressure syringe may be extremely dangerous. These pastes have been available "on the open market, . . . being sold ostensibly for use as antiseptics and not as abortifacients . . . " despite federal prosecutions under misbranding provisions of the federal Food, Drug and Cosmetic Act.

Another popular abortion procedure has been the insertion into the uterus of a catheter—an elongated, tubular instrument often made of rubber or fiber. Left in the uterus, it acts as an irritant. This technique is sometimes used even in the late months of pregnancy. It has been widely used in New York City, often in such a way as to facilitate "getting around the law." The abortionist inserts a catheter and, knowing that bleeding may not start for some time, immediately sends the woman home with instructions to return when she begins to bleed. If by chance his office is raided during her return visit, the abortionist can claim that he was merely treating her for the bleeding. Usually the woman will uphold his story.

FEES

In the Kinsey sample most illegal abortions were reported to have been operative (i.e. dilatation and curettage) and, as already noted, performed by physicians. These factors would minimize the risk of death or serious complications, but the limitations of the sample make it impossible to infer that most criminal abortions are now being performed under these relatively favorable conditions. As suggested earlier, the woman's socioeconomic status will help to determine the legal and illegal treatment she receives. One commentator has suggested that the distinction between "therapeutic" and "illegal" abortion represents merely a financial artifact: "in many circumstances the difference between the one and the other is $300 and knowing the 'right' person." The opportunities for illegal treatment are also determined largely by finances. . . . While a five-dollar job (performed by an untrained operator) is quite likely to be bungled and to lead to serious complications or even death, the patient able to pay a large sum of money (say, a thousand dollars) can obtain the services of a skilled physician.

Not only does this ability-to-pay criterion lead to less competent and safe treatment for working-class women, but it also introduces the irony that the well-to-do woman with "connections" may be more likely to encounter the sympathetic practitioner who will charge only a reasonable (for her) fee. It is noteworthy that the Kinsey sample, which overrepresented the higher socioeconomic categories, contained quite a few cases of abortions performed free of charge—presumably as a favor by a family physician. The fees paid by these women do not appear excessive. Excluding all abortions secured without cost, the median amounts paid for illegal operative abortions were: $84 for single women, $77 for the married ones, and $98 for the previously married. The working-class or lower-middle-class woman, on the other hand, will often obtain the services of an unscrupulous operator who is really out to get all he can. Thus the clients' socioeconomic position (some of the Kinsey data indicate that this is the case), the relative deprivation may actually be greater in the lower strata.

The woman seeking an abortion is usually in no position to argue strongly about the fee:

Criminal abortionists charge as much as $2000—whatever the traffic will bear. Today the average fee in Chicago is $400 or $500. It is more in New York. In Los Angeles a midwife charges $25; a male nurse, $100; a chiropractor, $150 to $200; and a medical doctor or osteopath, at least

$500. The highest price known there in recent years is $1800, and $1000 is not uncommon. . . .

ILLEGAL ORGANIZATION

It is not at all surprising that an illegal business with such potentially high profits should, at least in part, be well organized. The modifying phrase at least in part is necessary to indicate that illicit abortion services are not controlled by a monolithic criminal organization and to take into account that different types of individuals perform these services under a wide variety of circumstances. Except for the legitimate practitioner who occasionally performs an abortion for a patient or friend, it should be evident that the nature of abortion practice invariably implies a certain amount of organization. To be successful, the abortionist requires adequate equipment, a place in which to work, and some technical or other assistance. Potential customers must learn of his existence and location, yet at the same time a certain amount of anonymity must be maintained. Some means of avoiding police interference must also be developed—whether it be the elaboration of an extremely convincing front, a continuous shifting of location, or a direct or indirect financial arrangement with the authorities.

Given these imperatives, highly elaborate behavior systems have developed in the abortion profession. One report noted the existence in New York City of two "fairly complex social structures," the abortion "mill" and the abortion "ring." The mill involved one or more abortionists permanently located and aborting about a dozen women daily. The ring consisted of "a number of interacting abortionists or mills working intermittently at several occasionally changing locations and aborting an even more considerable number of women daily. . . . Clients are accommodated at the various locations depending on the pressure of referrals, the availability of operators at the moment of need, and the ability of the client to pay. . . . " Although mill may not seem a properly nonmoralistic designation, this term, apparently adopted from enforcement parlance, does point up the organized nature and continually high rate of activity of even the smaller of the two types of enterprises. According to Bates, the physician whose abortion practice is large and well-organized enough to fall into the mill category is likely to employ a business staff as well as medical assistants. Besides a secretary-receptionist, there may often be a business agent or manager. The business agent handles dealings with the landlord, and the payment of salaries, bills, bribes, and split fees. He may also function as contact man between the abortionist and the various sources of referral. Some large mills have also been known to employ "runners" to bring sources of referral into contact with the business agent. Bates notes that because of the confidential nature of the job, the abortionist may employ as business manager a relative or closely trusted friend. In the cases he studied, the business agent invariably had either a degree in law or at least some legal training (probably to provide for future contingencies).

Bates lists the local druggist, the general practitioner, and previous patients as the primary sources of referral to a mill, and includes taxi-drivers and bellboys as secondary sources. The role of the legitimate physician in effecting referrals should not be underestimated; recall the case of the physician-abortionist who had "served" over 350 practitioners in his city. Individual patterns of referral are determined largely by the prospective client's economic and social situation. The woman of means obtains better illegal services partly because she gains the assistance of a reputable doctor who can often refer her to a competent physician-abortionist. The woman of lower socioeconomic status will usually have to rely on general word-of-mouth referrals in her neighborhood or on the secondary sources mentioned above, and is correspondingly more likely to be referred to a less competent abortionist.

Frequently some sort of respectable front is used to shield the illicit practice. The abortionist may adopt some seemingly proper designation to cover, yet also hint at, the real character of his activities. According to Rongy, office gynecology was once the "casually accepted medical term for the abortionist," recognized by every practitioner. Similarly, in a California case, a card on the door of the defendant's apartment indicated that he was engaged in "physiotherapy and spot reducing." At times the front becomes expanded, as in the case of an enterprise conducted by two women, one of whom was a Peruvian doctor, though neither had a license to practice medicine in New York:

> The Peruvian led a double life. She posed as a respectable director of the Inter-American Cultural School which she operated at her palatial private residence on Fifth Avenue. This fancy front was maintained with revenues derived from the performance of abortions at her co-defendant's home. The abortion clientele consisted almost entirely of poor, Spanish-speaking people, who looked up to the affluent Peruvian because she lived on Fifth Avenue and associated with leaders in the Latin-American Community.
>
> The conspirators had a complicated code system for telephone conversations. Patients were packages. Six pairs of nylons or eight pairs of nylons meant that the patient was six to eight weeks pregnant. Information concerning a patient's financial status was imparted by terms such as special delivery, which indicated ability to pay double the usual fee, or parcel post, meaning a moderate increase over the usual charge.

A code of this sort is but one of many precautionary measures utilized by abortionists. Equipment may be kept under cover—a portable folding operating table, a sterilizer ingeniously hidden somewhere in the office. This office may, as already mentioned, be shifted from place to place, and often the abortionist comes to his place of work only for scheduled operations. Anonymity is a pervasive concern, in the interest of which the patient may be blindfolded, various devices such as surgical masks or operating table screens may be used to shield the abortionist's identity, and direct conversations between the two will be avoided. Under the system recently described by a New York observer, a woman wanting an abortion calls one doctor, who arranges for another doctor (whom she does not know)—perhaps accompanied by a nurse—to come to her home by appointment and to perform the abortion there. This technique seems roughly analogous to the modus operandi of call girls. Although it may represent a relatively costly procedure for obtaining illicit services, a mobile and anonymous pattern of this sort certainly minimizes the risk of legal interference. Whatever the specific procedures adopted by a criminal abortionist, his behavior will always exhibit elements of what Bates calls "defensive social adaptation." As he notes: "Since attack from any legitimate or predatory source threatens the social and economic adjustment of mill functionaries, one is not surprised to find them taking energetic countermeasures both on a planned and emergent basis."

POLICE CORRUPTION

One type of countermeasure involves the payment of "protection" money to law enforcement officers. It seems reasonable to assume such payment on the part of abortionists who operate "undetected" for any length of time in a metropolitan location. On the other hand, the abortionist who is constantly on the move and who utilizes numerous intermediaries and elaborate codes probably has not purchased police protection—if he had, such measures would not be necessary. One commentator has stated that, on the whole, abortion is probably less protected than either gambling or prostitution. There is no way of knowing what proportion of abortionists fall into these categories. It may be that there has been an increase in the mobile system, which abortionists might find safer than reliance on regular police protection. However, according to another account, supposedly based on an abortionist's own experiences:

> One reason fees are high is because the patient must absorb the payoff to police and top officials. Abortionists tell of judges, lawyers, jailers, and police whom they pay for protection, some of whom have brought their wives, daughters, or mistresses to the abortionist. Graft is accepted by all abortionists as a necessary annoyance and added expense passed on to the patient.

Many law enforcement personnel share the widespread belief that the abortionist is in fact performing a useful service, and are also well aware of the public indifference to strong enforcement of this particular law. Under such conditions it is relatively easy, as an early analysis pointed out, "for officials to convince themselves that there is nothing morally reprehensible in accepting bribes or protection money from abortionists." Some law enforcement officials insist there is no longer widespread police corruption connected with abortion. But there is little doubt that the abortionist continues to present an inviting prospect for extortion by the police as well as by others. . . .

LAW ENFORCEMENT

It is widely recognized that the laws against abortion are highly unenforceable. Over the years, the annual number of prosecutions and convictions has been negligible. Along with his estimate of over 300,000 criminal abortions performed annually, Fisher held that the annual number of convictions might be less than 1000. He concluded: "It is doubtful if any other felonious act is as free from punishment as criminal abortion." Occasionally law enforcement authorities in a particular area will make a special effort to apprehend criminal abortionists. For example, during the years of 1946-53 the office of the District Attorney in New York County prosecuted 136 cases of abortion, a very high proportion of which resulted in conviction on one or more of the offenses charged in the indictment. However, as has been pointed out elsewhere, this figure must represent but a tiny fraction of the abortions occurring in the country during that period. Furthermore, in a high percentage of the cases, the defendants received suspended sentences.

Even such a concerted effort, then, can only be expected to scratch the surface of the illegal abortion problem. Most law enforcement officials recognize the determination of unwillingly pregnant women to obtain abortions, law or no law. As a result, law enforcement goals are —in practice—limited to the control of abortion rather than to its elimination. As has been shown, self-induced abortion is probably widespread. Yet the prosecutor ordinarily does not consider it a phenomenon with which he must be concerned. Likewise, although some states make it a crime for a woman to submit to an abortion, women have traditionally been immune from prosecution in abortion cases. There is no record of reported American cases involving conviction of a woman for submitting to an abortion. Hospitals, which contravene the abortion laws from time to time, also are—within broad limits—free from prosecution. Similarly, the legitimate medical practitioner may perform an occasional abortion without anticipating legal difficulties—provided the operation does not result in the woman's death or hospitalization. A large number of professional abortionists may also manage to avoid detection. The fact is that the extent of abortion practice is so great, and available police manpower is so far below the level needed even to try to curb it, that the urban prosecutor confines his efforts to building up a case against a few of the more notorious offenders. . . .

UNENFORCEABLE LAWS

Unsatisfactory experience with the laws against abortion points up some of the major consequences of attempting to legislate against the crimes without victims. As an English legal authority states, unsuccessful laws against abortion illustrate "the inherent unenforceability of a statute that attempts to prohibit a private practice where all parties concerned desire to avoid the restriction." It is evident that large numbers of persons, otherwise quite respectable, find themselves compelled—for a variety of reasons—to violate the proscription against abortion. Abortion is a private consensual transaction, a willing payment of money for (illicit) services rendered. Although some persons may view the aborted woman as the "victim" of the abortionist, the woman herself does not share this definition of the situation. Even where she has found the experience extremely distasteful or frightening—perhaps especially in such cases— she is most unlikely to wish to bring a complaint against the person who has performed the operation.

From a law enforcement standpoint, this lack of a complainant is crucial. The only possible law enforcement approach, particularly in view of the widespread reluctance to convict abortionists, is to concentrate on a small number of the more flagrant violators of the law, and to build up an airtight case in each instance. This involves . . . long-term surveillance of selected suspects—a questionable use of valuable law enforcement manpower. It may also involve compelling the testimony of former clients who had thought that an extremely unpleasant life experience was over and done with. In cases of overzealous investigation, there may be searches and seizures of evidence that border on infringement of the suspect's constitutional guarantees.

As noted also, such a situation holds a clear-cut invitation to police corruption and to illegal exploitation by others as well. Because there are no data indicating a decline in the over-all abortion rate, and because there is a known tendency to grant fewer and fewer legal abortions, the only possible conclusion is that the demand is being deflected into illicit channels. Under current hospital policy, even the sophisticated woman of means and influence, who might once have been able to secure a "therapeutic" abortion, is now driven to the illegal abortionist. Because she can afford to pay an especially high price for his services, the entire illegal process may be enriched and strengthened. It is difficult not to conclude that the thriving illicit market is largely a direct result of the current restrictions on legal abortion. The efforts to combat abortion and the protective measures adopted by the abortionist provide a clear example of what Sutherland termed "the competitive development of techniques of crime and of protection against crime." Repressive laws have nurtured the development of a well-organized criminal profession, which provides strongly demanded services at a high profit, using part of the profit to improve the services and to insulate itself from the negative reaction of official agencies. . . .

RETHINKING THE ABORTION PROBLEM: LAW AND MORALS
David Granfield

The problem of abortion has been a perennial one, medically, morally, and legally. In a pluralistic society, the difficulties are compounded, especially on the legal level, by conflicts between medical indications and moral precepts. This struggle is unavoidable since it is through its laws that society evaluates abortion as criminal or justifiable. Currently, there is a move to liberalize the abortion laws. This effort forces us to rethink the abortion problem: to study the empirical facts; to evaluate the moral principles; and, above all, to ponder the social and political implications.

What kind of abortion laws we have depends on our general value choices, on the kinds of public goals we have set for ourselves as a social organization. Laws cannot be made in a vacuum or applied in isolation. The legal process and the larger social processes constantly interact. There is not merely a collection of laws but a fairly consistent and well-integrated body of prescriptions both produced by and determinative of the public image. A change in the public image affects the political organization. The passing of legislation in conflict with the public image tends to undermine the basic societal form and may eventually force a change in its essential characteristics. American democracy is structured on a public image of human dignity and the fundamental equality of all men. Our greatness as a nation will ever be measured by the strength of our stand on human rights. All our laws, including our abortion laws, must be tested by this touchstone of democracy, for the American way of life is as strong or as frail as the public philosophy upon which it is grounded.

From *Criminologica*, Vol. 4, No. 4 (February 1967), 11-18. Reprinted by permission. .

THE EMPIRICAL CONTINUUM

To talk constructively about the morality or advisability of abortion laws demands some scientific understanding of that process of generation whose untimely interruption we call abortion. The life sciences have made astounding progress during the first two-thirds of the twentieth century in genetics and molecular biology. Though Mendel published his "laws of inheritance" in 1865, it was not until the turn of the century that his findings were acknowledged. O. T. Avery's discovery in 1944 of certain functions of RNA, ribonucleic acid, established molecular biology on a truly scientific basis and led recently to the deciphering of the genetic code. It was as late as 1957 before scientists concluded that human cells have forty-six, not forty-eight chromosomes, as hitherto believed.

Fortunately, in reappraising the abortion laws today, we work in the light of advanced scientific research affording us sound biological facts upon which to base our personal and our political decision-making.

Embryological fact-finding has two aspects. We can study the process of generation *phenotypically,* looking to appearances, to that system of qualities and characteristics which make up the organism—a graphic and effective approach but not completely satisfying. Or we can study the process of generation *genotypically,* that is in terms of the gene structure of an organism. This approach is more abstract, but intellectually more cogent, giving us a grasp of the underlying principles of embryological development.

Without pretending to scientific expertise, a legislator or an appraiser of legislation should make use of the conclusions of the experts. Let us first touch simply and briefly on some genotypical points of special significance. The smallest human cell, the sperm, unites with the largest human cell, the ovum, to form the first cell of the new human being, a cell of forty-six chromosomes. Each chromosome has some 3,000 genes which determine the mental and physical characteristics of the organism. From this one cell, through a process of division called mitosis, all the other cells of the body, fifty trillion of them, develop according to a strict time table with only forty-seven replications. Each cell contains identical chromosomes and genes despite the broad range of cell specialization. From the beginning, this living continuum nourishes itself from its environment and ever moves to maximize the very definite specifications of its genotypic inheritance.

From another point of view, the changing and growing *phenotype* substantiates visibly the existence of an embryological continuum. Without any unexplained leaps and without the addition of new and essential elements, as far as science can see, the fertilized ovum moves to birth, to maturity, and to death. Here are a few examples. When the embryo is only six weeks old and less than an inch long, its external features are already established. The proportions change but no new surface structures develop. Brain activity as shown by electric encephalograms, learning ability as demonstrated by conditioned reflexes, reflect the fact that before the child is born it has all the brain cells that it will ever have. In fact, before the child is born its brain cells have lost the ability to multiply as for example the cells of the skin continue to do.

The child lives within its mother, it depends on its mother, but it is not part of its mother. Its gene structure is different. All its cells are different. The fertilized ovum does implant itself in the womb and develops the placenta to enable it to live, but the placenta is an organ of the child, parasitic perhaps but not maternal. It enables the child to fulfil its needs of nutrition, respiration, and excretion. Mother and child have a separate blood supply, circulation and nervous system.

The child is spatially within its mother, but this fact does not exclude the possibility of test-tube babies. The child is dependent on its mother, yet scientific substitutes are at least conceivable. The distinction between viable and non-viable fetuses is still a real one, but the age of viability has been moved back through medical techniques and may continue to be so. The unborn child is undeniably human although admittedly somewhat less perfect than a newly born child, but not as different from a newly born child as the latter is from a mature adult.

To summarize: from the moment of conception, a living, human organism comes into being. The basic pattern of this one cell, its chromosome and gene structure, is repeated in the trillions of cells that will develop. Yet there is more than genotypic replication, for from the beginning the activity of the human being is ordered and goal-oriented. An inborn dynamism moving with scheduled efficiency produces an organism in some ways very different from its one-celled beginning, but this phenotype, through an orderly process of multiplication and specialization, has, however, merely actualized the already determined or fixed potentialities of the geotype. The changing features of this human being show a unity of design and purpose, in the continuing process of generation.

Science has lifted the veil and we see almost face to face. We recognize in the fetus, a fellow citizen, weak and imperfect, but equal to each one of us in his human dignity and in his right to life. The key is the living continuum. However we define life, whatever we mean by the soul, whether or not we believe in immortality, we learn from science that the fetus shares with us a common principle of vitality, activity and growth. Nor are we caught up in the interminable arguments of a prescientific past about the time of formation, animation, or quickening.

The vital principle that comes into being with the fertilization of the ovum by the sperm is scientifically adequate to explain the inner dynamism of growth from conception to maturity. There is no scientific evidence for an essential addition. If human beings have life or have a soul, they have it from the beginning.

THE PUBLIC INTEREST

Analysis of man's genetic and embryological development builds the groundwork for decisions about the morality and legality of abortion. No longer can we call abortion one of those "crimes without victims," to use a popular but misleading catch-phrase. For whether considered legally, justifiable, or clearly criminal, abortion, unfortunately, has its fetal victims. Sound scientific and empirical evidence leads to the conviction that abortion is morally wrong, that the direct killing of an innocent human being born or unborn, is a grave injustice. However, there is an additional problem: whether or not laws allowing abortion should be opposed. Many say no. Let us examine three of the reasons given.

1. Some say that we should not legislate against abortion since we should not legislate morals. This objection misses the point by oversimplifying the problem. In controlling crime, we necessarily legislate morality but we do not necessarily legislate against everything we consider morally bad. It is consistent with good morals and good law-making to oppose laws which would condemn evil behavior. For instance, we may classify deviate sexuality as immoral, yet consistently oppose the criminal punishment of such acts if they occur in private between consenting adults.

The moral component in decision-making cannot be overlooked, but it does not stand alone. We are concerned with the social implications, the effects and the enforceability of the law, and the alternate means of achieving the goal. Abortion legislation is not an automatic moral derivative, but must be the result of a study of physical facts, social and political conditions, as well as moral prescriptions. The real legal issue is not solely the immorality of the act, but its effect on the common good, on public order. We put restraints on personal freedom when the result of certain conduct is so detrimental to society as to warrant the intrusion.

The Anglican bishop of Woolwich, J. A. T. Robinson, believes that laws against abortion should be abolished. He would, however, leave the decision about abortion to the moral conscience of the individual. Yet, in a speech given in London, in October 1966, at the annual general meeting of the Abortion Reform Association, the bishop pointed out the great harm that is caused to society by abortions. From his own words, we can see that laws against abortion are not simply an attempt to legislate morals, for he lists the many effects which cause all of us grave concern and which prompt some of us to seek out at least partial help by restrictive legislation. He writes:

It may perhaps seem that I am permissive about abortion as to imply that I regard it quite neutrally, or even as a good thing. In fact, I regard it as an evil thing, as a scourge to be removed from any civilized society. For there is nothing creative about it at all. It is destructive of personal life, and, I see no point in arguing exactly when this may be said to begin. It is not in itself therapeutic, except of a purely gynaecological disorder. It is much more likely to bring on adverse physical or psychological consequences. Unlike contraception, it does not make for love. Indeed, as a widespread phenomenon it undermines the relationships as well as the health of a society. Countries that have dropped all barriers to it have on the whole not liked what they have seen, and have drawn back.

2. Another general objection, a more difficult one, is that we should not legislate against what we cannot successfully prevent. The extent to which the abortion laws are unenforced and unenforceable is indeed relevant, but this fact must be seen in perspective. Few laws, if any, are obeyed perfectly. Most laws merely hold down the number of violations. There are more thefts than abortions yet we would hesitate to justify misappropriation of property on the grounds of unenforceability. As a matter of fact, however, statistics from other countries indicate that when abortion laws are expanded, there is, as expected, a drastic increase in the number of legal abortions and, surprisingly enough, a proportionate increase in the number of illegal abortions. Even limited legal justification of abortion helps develop a climate of opinion favorable to its increase. So too a restraint on abortion, though not strictly enforced, does tend to limit the amount of proscribed behavior. Abortions laws cut down significantly on the number of fetal deaths, on the number of innocent lives that would otherwise be destroyed.

3. The third and last general objection to opposing a liberalization of abortion laws is that such opposition runs counter to the mores of contemporary life. Certainly in a pluralistic society, respect for the consciences and moral liberty of others is a paramount value. We are not comfortable in setting standards for another's personal behavior. Nonetheless, acceding to the lowest common moral denominator is neither the road to community excellence or social well-being, but rather subjection to the tyranny of the weak.

American criminal law gives testimony to the principle that all men are equal in human dignity by forbidding the direct killing of an innocent human being, even by the state itself, however useful the elimination of the chosen victim might be to all concerned. In fact, this consciousness of human dignity and the sacredness of life has prompted many to work for the abolition of the death penalty even when the convicted criminal has been found guilty of multiple first degree murders or of treasonous acts which have put in jeopardy the lives of all the members of the body politic.

Currently, there is a move to extend the permissive grounds for justifiable abortion. However, if we compare these legislative proposals with the generally accepted criminal process in other types of killing, we see clearly how radical an exception to the common principles of the public philosophy, the act of abortion really is, and how inconsistent it is with our commitment to equality before the law.

As a matter of fact, abortion in 90% of the states is drastically limited to cases in which it is necessary to preserve the life of the mother. The medical incidence of such need is, fortunately, very low. Only five states and the District of Columbia allow abortion to safeguard the health or safety of the mother. No state allows abortion for birth defects or when the pregnancy is the result of rape or incest. Consequently, although abortion is permissible in all the states, the narrow grounds justifying it indicate its exceptional character. A look at some of the salient aspects of criminal law substantiates this judgment that abortion is in conflict with the basic political premises of our society.

The principle of legality that there shall be no punishment without a crime no crime without a law is fundamental to criminal law. Our constitutional insistence that there shall be no deprivation of life, liberty, or property without due process of law is an application of this principle. Yet in abortion a severe deprivation is imposed, a death sentence, on one who has committed no crime, deserved no punishment. The condemned fetus is to forfeit his life through no fault of his own, simply for following his biological impulse to growth and development. Placed in a position of legal inequality, his innocent life can be sacrificed for the good of others, even for those who brought him into being by their own immoral or criminal actions.

In a criminal trial, the guilt of the accused must be proved beyond a reasonable doubt. The Model Penal Code would justify abortion if a licensed physician "believes that there is substantial risk . . . that the pregnancy resulted from rape, incest, or other felonious intercourse." Here, a non-professional is to make a technical legal decision—a matter of life or death—without any of the legal safeguards that a trial, a judge, a jury, and counsel guarantee, in an area, such as rape, of which Matthew Hale said, "It is an accusation easily to be made and hard to be proved and harder to be defended by the party to be accused though never so innocent." Would the medical profession agree to let a lawyer make as conclusive a diagnosis in as complex and crucial a medical case, even if another lawyer joins with him in certifying this belief?

Overlooking the incredible provisions that make the medical doctor, judge, jury, and executioner in complicated legal matters such as rape and incest, we are nonetheless shocked by the flimsy requirements of proof. Even when the issue is obliquely formulated as a benefit to the victim fetus out of fear "that the child would be born with grave physical or mental defect," the physician can decide to kill "if he believes that there is substantial risk." What this vague standard means in practice is clearly and openly indicated by doctors. For example, in a recent symposium on abortion, the statistical approach to abortion was largely acceptable. Dr. Kenneth Niswander, M.D., wrote:

> When one considers how severe the fetal abnormalities following maternal rubella can be, it would certainly seem more desirable from an economic, as well as a humanitarian viewpoint to have terminated pregnancy when the odds were so relatively high that the child would be abnormal. The actual risk of malformation is unknown, but a summary of the literature indicated a 21.4 per cent risk during the first four weeks of pregnancy, and a 21.3 per cent risk in the second month, and in the third month, a 10.4 per cent risk. After the twelfth week, there seemed to be no increased risk of congenital malformation.

The percentage of affected children from mothers with German measles is about one out of five. Dr. Niswander considers this a high risk, substantial enough to justify abortion, despite the fact that as Dr. Kenneth Ryan, M.D., in the same symposium pointed out, many of these abnormal children have correctable defects and that there is no higher incidence of mental retardation among such children than in the general population.

In a criminal trial, deprivation of life, liberty, or even property on such small statistical probabilities would be unthinkable. It would be like sentencing to death five suspects whose arrest was based on probable cause though only one of them could have committed the capital crime. Although infanticide is admittedly a barbarous practice repugnant to civilized minds, it has one advantage over this type of abortion: it would reduce the number of useless killings. Not vague probability but positive proof would determine the victim thus saving the healthy eighty per cent who would have died if the indications for justifiable abortion had been carried out.

Birth is a decisive biological fact, but it is not determinative of human dignity or personality. Both the born and the unborn are human persons with the right to life. Abortion weakens our sense of justice since it fosters a second-rate citizenship based on utilitarian expendibility, a monstrous exception to our public philosophy, to the charter of democracy.

CONCLUSION

What, then, must be our practical conclusion about the advisability of liberalizing abortion? In brief, we oppose abortion not simply because it is immoral but because the immoral conduct is harmful, primarily to the unborn child, but to others as well, the parents and society at large. We respect the consciences of all. We sympathize with the tragedies which blight so many lives. We understand the frantic appeal that this deadly shortcut which is abortion has for so many souls. But we cannot forget that the happy ending that is sought must be paid for with the blood of innocent children. If we lose sight of our human condition, if we forget that we are all members of the family of man, we exchange our birthright of democratic dignity for a ruthless alienation.

The American tradition of equality, the foundation of our public philosophy, would be radically undermined by liberalizing the abortion laws. Truth, of science, of genetics and embryology enlightens our minds as we seek in painful awareness of the sufferings of others, a better way to maximize their values. In the light of modern science, we see that abortion is an attempt to maximize the values of some by utterly minimizing the values of others. That living continuum which is human life, from conception to death, is of a piece. To destroy the unborn does more than kill an innocent human being, it delivers a mortal blow to the consensus that has made America great. It cuts away something from the common good of all citizens, because it puts a price on the head of everyone. All become theoretically expendable if their death proves useful enough. We are not pleading here simply for the unborn, but for the preservation of the heritage we have all been born to enjoy: the right to life, to a life of human dignity, in a community of political equals.

THE MEDICO-LEGAL ASPECTS OF ABORTION

Robert E. Hall

The laws governing abortion in the United States vary in the details of their phraseology, but basically the laws in 45 states permit abortion only if necessary to preserve the life of the mother and in 5 states and the District of Columbia to protect the health or safety of the mother. Most of these laws were written about one hundred years ago, when the

From *Criminologica,* Vol. 4, No. 4 (February 1967), 7-10. Reprinted by permission.

operation for abortion was hazardous and the science of psychiatry and the dangers of German measles (rubella) in pregnancy were unknown.

Twenty-five years ago such diseases as tuberculosis, diabetes, and hypertension imposed sufficient risk upon pregnant women that abortions could be performed for these reasons in compliance with the law. One pregnancy in 150 was interrupted in those days upon such purely medical grounds. Recent advances in medical knowledge now enable us to carry most of these complicated pregnancies safely to term and the abortion rate has correspondingly dropped to one in 500 pregnancies or about 10,000 per year.

But meanwhile the discovery of psychiatry and of the dangers of rubella have led both the medical profession and the laity to believe that abortions should be performed to protect the mental and physical health of the woman and to prevent the development of a seriously deformed fetus. Hence most hospital abortions are now done for these two admittedly unlawful reasons. Whereas the laws of many other countries have, in the past 30 years, been modified to permit such abortions, the original, 19th-century abortion laws still enshackle the practice of abortion in 20th-century America.

Further enshacklement of this practice has been provided in the past 15 years in the form of therapeutic abortion boards, which serve in theory to police and protect the medical profession but in practice serve as medico-legal tribunals rendering moral judgments. In the Sloane Hospital for Women the institution of such a committee resulted in an immediate two-thirds reduction in the incidence of therapeutic abortions.

The picture which has evolved from this conflict between medicine and the law is not pretty. For every abortion performed in hospitals today there are an estimated 100 abortions performed outside hospitals and therefore outside the law. And of the hospital abortions about 80% are performed on private patients. In New York City, in 1960-62, abortions in proprietary hospitals were 400 times more common than in municipal hospitals.

There can be little doubt that this situation is untenable. Until the recent change in the attitude toward birth control, however, and the generally enhanced view of individual human dignity, the abortion situation was also unmentionable. Now, at last, the abortion dilemma is being recognized and solutions to it are being actively sought.

The most seriously considered alternative solutions to this dilemma are as follows: 1. More liberal interpretations of the present state abortion laws. 2. Legalization of abortion by the abolition of these laws. 3. Nullification of these laws by the courts. 4. Liberalization of the laws. Let us deal with each of the alternatives in greater detail.

First, a more liberal interpretation of the existing state laws. A fairly good case can be made for the theoretical feasibility of doing this. No doctor has ever been successfully prosecuted for doing a hospital abortion in this country. The medical profession has been given the almost exclusive privilege of interpreting which abortions are necessary to preserve maternal life, and whenever this necessity has been juridically reviewed, as in California in the case of *People vs. Ballard,* the courts have held that the danger to maternal life need be neither imminent nor certain. If applied in its broadest sense, this view could be used to justify the termination of any unwanted pregnancy, for unhappiness interferes with mental health and any interference with health may ultimately abbreviate life. If this reasoning sounds far-fetched, let me remind you that it may be partially founded upon the World Health Organization's definition of health, to wit, "a state of complete physical, mental, and social well being and not merely the absence of disease or infirmity."

But there is a practical circumstance which prevents the conversion of this theory into fact and that is that the medical profession will not participate in such a game of medico-legal semantics. Doctors want their rights spelled out specifically by the law. No amount of reassurance will convince the average physician that a looser interpretation of the law will not lead to criminal prosecution in his individual case and this is a risk that he is unwilling to take, even with the protection of his therapeutic abortion board. Some doctors do, of course, work within the law more freely than others, but their action evokes professional criticism more often than praise.

A second alternative in dealing with the abortion dilemma would be the legalization of abortion altogether. Perhaps the best case can be made for this solution, for it is the only one which would eliminate the prevalent and malevolent practice of criminal abortion. Although hardly the ideal form of birth control, abortion will remain a corollary of contraception as long as the sexual practices of men and women remain unpredictable. And it is difficult to refute the contention that the decision to destroy a pregnancy more rightfully belongs to the pregnant woman than to her physician, her lawyer, or her clergyman. This contention has actually been translated into law by the Communist countries and Japan, where abortion has been legalized. In 100 years, when the population of the United States reaches one billion (as it surely will if it continues to increase at its present pace), abortion will be legalized here too. But now, in 20th-century America, with its proud if impractical Puritan heritage, its boundless faith in the perfection and prevalence of contraceptive measures, and its still plentiful supply of land and resources, unrestricted abortion is regarded as an unnecessary evil rather than an evil necessity.

So let us turn to the third possibility. It is often suggested that the abortion laws would be declared unconstitutional if reviewed by the United States Supreme Court or that they would be more broadly interpreted if tested further in the lower courts. Why, it is argued, cannot some courageous doctor openly perform an illegal abortion in a reputable hospital and force the district attorney to prosecute him? The answer is threefold: few doctors have such courage, few reputable hospitals would permit such action, and few district attorneys would prosecute under these circumstances. Furthermore, although this sort of test case was successfully carried out in England (*Rex vs. Bourne,* 1938), it wrought no significant change in the English practice of abortion.

So finally we come to the last of the four possible solutions to the abortion problem—the solution which in my opinion has the most merit —liberalization of our outdated State abortion laws. The laws of Sweden, Denmark, Norway, Finland, and Iceland have been liberalized to permit abortion for the protection of maternal health, for the prevention of fetal deformity, and even for such categories as "worn-out mothers" and "anticipated weaknesses." As a result, the therapeutic abortion rate in these countries is not a staggering 50%, as it is in Hungary and Japan, nor an infinitesimal 0.2%, as it is in the United States, but a perfectly respectable 5%. A similar law soon to be passed in England will go so far as to permit abortion when "the pregnant woman's capacity as a mother will be severely overstrained by the care of a child or another child." This bill was approved in its Second Reading before the House of Commons by a vote of 223 to 29.

Liberalization of our abortion laws was recommended in 1959 by the American Law Institute in its Model Penal Code, which would specifically permit abortion to protect the physical or mental health of the mother, to prevent fetal deformity, and to deal with cases of rape and incest. This proposal has been publicly endorsed by such prestigious groups as the New York Academy of Medicine, the New York County and State Medical Societies, the New York Obstetrical Society, the New York Bar Association, the New York Civil Liberties Union, the California Medical Association, and the Unitarian Universalist Church. A poll of the obstetricians of New York State reveals that 85% of them would prefer the American Law Institute's recommendation to the present State abortion law. Recent polls of the laity and even of professional politicians reveal similar sentiment. Bills embodying the American Law Institute's proposal have been introduced before the California and New York legislatures. There is reason to believe that they will be passed in the foreseeable future.

As I have pointed out above, liberal abortion laws will not solve the abortion problem, for criminal abortions will continue to abound; but liberal laws will at least legitimize the current medical practice of abortion. As it is, the majority of even the hospital abortions are, strictly speaking, illegal. In the 1964 rubella epidemic, for example, thousands of therapeutic abortions were performed—329 in New York City alone; yet none of them were necessary to preserve the mother's life. As a result of this medico-legal chaos, nine prominent California obstetricians have been charged by their State Board of Medical Examiners with unprofessional conduct for having performed rubella abortions and in New York a hospital is being sued for not having performed an abortion on a rubella victim who subsequently gave birth to a seriously deformed infant.

10 PROSTITUTION

Prostitution, simply defined, is the use of sexual stimulation to attain nonsexual ends. One of the most pervasive and universal forms of deviance, prostitution involves a socially devalued female and a "respectable" client in an economic arrangement concerning sexual activity. As in abortion, the victim is both law-abiding and willing, making enforcement largely impossible.

The business of prostitution has undergone considerable change in the last few decades. Largely gone are the brothels in which young women catered to patrons under the watchful supervision of a madam. Organized vice and red-light districts, once very apparent in the urban community, are no more, although vestiges of brothel prostitution may still be found in the inner city ghettos and near military posts and bases. The demise of organized prostitution may be attributed to a variety of social changes: freer relations between the sexes at all ages, changing conceptions of sex norms, easier divorce and remarriage, and legitimate economic opportunities for females. Like the saloon, the speakeasy, and the taxi-dance hall, the brothel is Americana of the past—of primary interest to antiquarians and historians.

The demise of organized prostitution has not, of course, meant that the economic exploitation of sex has ceased. Several new breeds of prostitute have emerged to serve as replacements for the brothel prostitute: the high-class call girl, the streetwalker (hustler or hooker), and the part-time amateur. Less visible in her occupation than her predecessors, each of these types is more seeker than sought. All are entrepreneurs. The call girl, of course, is the highest paid and the most professional; the streetwalker much less so, and the part-time amateur least so.

The three selections which follow deal with different yet overlapping aspects of prostitution as social and personal deviation. In the first article, "The Sociology of Prostitution," Professor Kingsley Davis presents an incisive analysis of the social structural basis of prostitution. His initial question: "Why is it that a practice so thoroughly disapproved, so widely outlawed in Western civilization, can yet flourish so universally?" results in a funtional analysis of prostitution. Prostitution, says Professor Davis, can be studied on three interrelated yet separate levels: (1) the causes of the existence of prostitution, (2) the causes of the amount of prostitution, and (3) the causes of why only a specific type of person enters into prostitution.

In an especially interesting digression, Professor Davis contends that prostitution and the family can co-exist and thrive at the same time. Ironically, the chief enemy of both is not the other, but the loosening of sex norms. One measure, therefore, of the solidity of the family is the extent of prostitution. The disruption of the family and its reorganization are accompanied by a corresponding decrease in prostitution. This is both an interesting and unusual thesis and is well worth pondering.

No matter how functional prostitution is as a safety valve to society, it is socially disvalued. The result, of course, is that prostitutes, pimps, and procurers develop correspondingly poor images (concepts) of themselves. Almost without exception, deviants, having learned the generalized norms of society, feel guilty and ashamed of their deviant status and evolve rationalizations to justify their behavior to themselves and others. Professors Jackman, O'Toole, and Geis discuss these matters in "The Self-Image of the Prostitute." The article is based on interviews with prostitutes—most of them in jail at the time of interview. The interview material centers on two questions. First, how are women recruited into prostitution? Second, how do prostitutes explain to themselves and others their violations of dominant social norms and taboos? The article suggests that prostitutes typically adjust to their lack of self-respect and esteem in at least three ways. Some accept the subcultural values of the underworld, some make prostitution but one phase of their lives, and some become wholly alienated from life and take refuge in drink and drugs. These adaptations to the stigmatization inherent in being a prostitute have consequences for the prostitute as well as implications for understanding and controlling such behavior.

Every profession has its successes and its also-rans. Prostitution as a profession is no exception. The call or party girl is the acknowledged success in her business. With earnings of $20,000 or more per year and a minimum of $20 per contact, she is usually well educated, sophisticated, personable, and winsome—hardly recognizable as a practicing member of her profession according to the prevailing stereotype. Very selective of her clientele and highly protective of their anonymity, foibles, and inadequacies, she is as necessary to a successful business or professional convention as the banquet meal and the roster of long-winded speakers.

Sutherland once described professional crime in terms of five criteria: skill, status, consensus, organization, and differential association. Dr.

Greenwald in "The Social and Professional Life of the Call Girl," which is a chapter in his book, *The Call Girl,* describes the life style of these high-class professionals in these same terms. All, of course, are skilled, particularly in the negotiations end of their business. This skill was acquired through apprenticeship and interaction (differential association) with other call girls. They develop a *modus operandi* and share a language, code of behavior, and the appropriate norms and rationalizations with others in their business (consensus). Working in a loose relationship with other call girls, pimps, and procurers (organization), they attain a certain level of recognition in the profession (status). Some are $20 girls and others are $100 girls or higher. These aspects plus other facets of their life style are presented and described by Dr. Greenwald, who gathered this material through interviews with his call-girl patients and their friends.

THE SOCIOLOGY OF PROSTITUTION
Kingsley Davis

. . . We cannot define human prostitution simply as the use of sexual responses for an ulterior purpose. This would include a great portion of all social behavior, especially that of women. It would include marriage, for example, wherein women trade their sexual favors for an economic and social status supplied by men. It would include the employment of pretty girls in stores, cafes, charity drives, advertisements. It would include all the feminine arts that women use in pursuing ends that require men as intermediaries, arts that permeate daily life, and, while not generally involving actual intercourse, contain and utilize erotic stimulation.

But looking at the subject in this way reveals one thing. The basic element in what we actually call prostitution—the employment of sex for non-sexual ends within a competitive-authoritative system—characterizes not simply prostitution itself but all of our institutions in which sex is involved, notably courtship and wedlock. Prostitution therefore resembles, from one point of view, behavior found in our most respectable institutions. It is one end of a long sequence or gradation of essentially similar phenomena that stretches at the other end to such approved patterns as engagement and marriage. What, then, is the difference between prostitution and these other institutions involving sex?

From *American Sociological Review,* Vol. 2 (October 1937), 746-55. Reprinted by permission.

The difference rests at bottom upon the functional relation between society and sexual institutions. It is through these institutions that erotic gratification is made dependent on, and subservient to, certain co-operative performances inherently necessary to societal continuity. The sexual institutions are distinguished by the fact that though they all provide gratification, they do not all tie it to the same social functions. This explains why they are differently evaluated in the eyes of the mores.

The institutional control of sex follows three correlative lines. First, it permits, encourages, or forces various degrees of sexual intimacy within specific customary relations, such as courtship, concubinage, and marriage. Second, to bolster this positive control, it discourages sexual intimacy in all other situations, e.g., when the persons are not potential mates or when they are already mated to other persons. Finally, in what is really a peculiar category of the negative rules, it absolutely prohibits sexual relations in certain specified situations. This last form of control refers almost exclusively to incest taboos, which reinforce the first-named (positive) control by banishing the disruptive forces of sexual competition from the family group.

These lines of control are present no matter what the specific kind of institutional system. There may be monogamy, polygyny, or concubinage; wife exchange or religious prostitution; premarital chastity or unchastity. The important point is not the particular kind of concrete institution, but the fact that without the positive and negative norms there could be no institutions at all. Since social functions can be performed only through institutional patterns, the controls are indispensable to the continuance of a given social system.

Of the numerous functions which sexual institutions subserve, the most vital relate to the physical and social reproduction of the next generation. If we ask, then, which sexual institutions in a society receive the greatest support from law and mores, we must point to those which facilitate the task of procreating and socializing the young. It follows that sanctioned sexual relations are generally those within these (or auxiliary) institutions, while unsanctioned relations are those outside them.

Marriage and its subsidiary patterns constitute the chief cultural arrangement through which erotic expression is held to reproduction. It is accordingly the most respectable sexual institution, with the others diminishing in respectability as they stand further away from wedlock. Even the secondary forms of erotic behavior—flirtation, coquetry, petting, etc.—have their legitimate and their illegitimate settings. Their legitimate aspects may be subsumed under courtship, leading to marriage; but if indulged in for themselves, with no intention of matrimony, they are devoid of the primary function and tend to be disapproved. If practised by persons married to others, they are inimical to reproductive relations already established and are more seriously condemned. If practised by close relatives within the primary family, they represent a threat to the very structure of the reproductive institution itself, and are stringently tabooed. These attitudes are much more rigid with regard to actual intercourse, not solely because coitus is the essence of the sexual but because it has come to symbolize the *gemeinschaft* type of relation present in the family. With this in mind we can add that when coitus is practised for money its social function is indeterminate, secondary, and extrinsic. The buyer clearly has pleasure and not reproduction in mind. The seller may use the money for any purpose. Hence unless the money is earmarked for some legitimate end (such as the support of a family, a church, or a state), the sexual relation between the buyer and seller is illegitimate, ephemeral, and condemned. It is pure commercial prostitution.

Of course many sexual institutions besides courtship and marriage receive, in various cultures and to varying degrees, the sanction of society. These generally range themselves between marriage and commercial prostitution in the scale of social approval. They include concubinage, wife exchange, and forms of sanctified prostitution. Religious prostitution, for example, not only differs from wedlock, but also from commercial prostitution; the money that passes is earmarked for the maintenance of the church, the woman is a religious ministrant, and the act of intercourse is sacred. Similar considerations apply to that type of prostitution in which the girl obtains a dowry for her subsequent marriage. Whenever the money earned by prostitution is spent for a sanctified purpose, prostitution is in higher esteem than when it is purely commercial. If, for instance, prostitution receives more approval in Japan than in America, it is significant that in the former country most of the *joro* enter the life because their family needs money; their conduct thereby subserves the most sacred of all Japanese sentiments—filial piety. The regulation of prostitution by governments and churches in such a way that at least some of the proceeds go towards their maintenance is control of sex behavior at a second remove. By earmarking a part of the money, the bought intercourse is made to serve a social function; but *this function is not intrinsically related to coitus in the same way as the procreative function of the family.*

In commercial prostitution both parties use sex for an end not socially functional, the one for pleasure, the other for money. To tie intercourse to sheer physical pleasure is to divorce it both from reproduction and from the sentimental primary type of relation which it symbolizes. To tie it to money, the most impersonal and atomistic type of reward possible, with no stipulation as to the use of this medium, does the same thing. Pure prostitution is promiscuous, impersonal. The sexual response of the prostitute does not hinge upon the personality of the other party, but upon the reward. The response of the customer likewise does not depend upon the particular identity of the prostitute, but upon the bodily gratification. On both sides the relationship is merely a means to a private end, a contractual rather than a personal association.

These features sharply distinguish prostitution from the procreative sexual institutions. Within a group organized for bearing and rearing children bonds tend to arise that are cemented by the condition of relative permanence and the sentiment of personal feeling, for the task requires long, close, and sympathetic association. Prostitution, in which the seller takes any buyer at the price, necessarily represents an opposite kind of erotic association. It is distinguished by the elements of hire, promiscuity, and emotional indifference—all of which are incompatible with primary or *gemeinschaft* association.

The sexual appetite, like every other, is tied to socially necessary functions. The function it most logically and naturally relates to is procreation. The nature of procreation and socialization is such that their performance requires institutionalized primary-group living. Hence the family receives the highest estimation of all sexual institutions in society, the others receiving lower esteem as they are remoter from its *gemeinschaft* character and reproductive purpose. Commercial prostitution stands at the lowest extreme; it shares with other sexual institutions a basic feature, namely the employment of sex for an ulterior end in a system of differential advantages, but it differs from them in being mercenary, promiscuous, and emotionally indifferent. From *both* these facts, however, it derives its remarkable vitality.

Since prostitution is a contractual relation in which services are traded (usually in terms of an exchange medium) and sex is placed in an economic context, it is strange that modern writers have made so much of the fact that the "social evil" has economic causes. One might as well say, with equal perspicacity, that retail merchandising has economic causes. Prostitution embraces an economic relation, and is naturally connected with the entire system of economic forces. But to jump from this truism to the conclusion that prostitution can be abolished by eliminating its economic causes is erroneous. Economic causes seldom act alone, and hence their removal is seldom a panacea.

The causal ramifications of commercial coitus extend beyond the economic sphere. At least three separable but related problems must be recognized: (1) the causes of the existence of prostitution; (2) the causes of the *rate* or *amount* of prostitution; and (3) the causes of *any particular individual's entrance into, or patronage of,* prostitution. The existence of prostitution seems related both to the physiological nature of man and to the inherent character of society, both of which include more than the sheer economic element. These basic factors, constantly operative, account for the ubiquity of prostitution, but not for the variations in its rate. This second problem must be dealt with in terms of the specific institutional configuration existing at the time, in which economic factors are highly but not exclusively important. Finally, any particular person's connection with prostitution is a result of his or her own unique life-history, into which an infinite variety of strands, some economic and some not economic, are woven. The factors in (1) and (2) are operative in the individual's life, but are never sufficient in themselves to explain his or her behavior. . . .

When outlawed, prostitution falls into one peculiar category of crime— a type exceedingly hard to deal with—in which one of the willful parties is the ordinary law-abiding citizen. This kind of crime, of which bootlegging is the archetype, is supported by the money and behavior of a sizeable portion of the citizenry, because in it the citizen receives a service. Though the service is illegitimate, the citizen cannot be held guilty, for it is both impossible and inadvisable to punish half the populace for a crime. Each citizen participates in vital institutional relationships— family, business, church, and state. To disrupt all of these by throwing him in jail for a mere vice would be, on a large scale, to disrupt society. But the eagerness of otherwise decent citizens to receive the illicit service attests powerful forces behind the demand element.

On the one hand, the demand is the result of a simple biological appetite. When all other sources of gratification fail, due to defects of person or circumstance, prostitution can be relied upon to furnish relief. None of the exacting requirements of sex attraction and courtship are necessary. All that is needed is the cash, and this can be obtained in a thousand ways. Prostitution is the most malleable, the most uninvolved form of physical release.

But in addition to the sheer desire for sexual satisfaction, there is the desire for satisfaction in a particular (often an unsanctioned) way.

> The common and ignorant assumption that prostitution exists to satisfy the gross sensuality of the young unmarried man, and that if he is taught to bridle gross sexual impulse or induced to marry early the prostitute must be idle, is altogether incorrect . . . The prostitute is something more than a channel to drain off superfluous sexual energy, and her attraction by no means ceases when men are married, for a large number of men who visit prostitutes, if not the majority, are married. And alike whether they are married or unmarried the motive is not one of uncomplicated lust.

The craving for variety, for perverse gratification, for mysterious and provocative surroundings, for intercourse free from entangling cares and civilized pretense, all play their part.

Prostitution, again by its very nature, is aptly suited to satisfy this second side of demand. The family, an institution of status rather than contract, limits the variety, amount, and nature of a person's satisfactions. But since with the prostitute the person is paying for the privilege, he is in a position to demand almost anything he wants. The sole limitation on his satisfactions is not morality or convention, but his ability to pay the price. This is an advantage which commercial recreation generally has over kinds handled by other institutional channels.

There is no reason to believe that a change in the economic system will eliminate either side of demand. In any system the effective demand as expressed by price will vary with current economic and moral forces, but the underlying desire both for sheer gratification and for gratification in particular ways will remain impregnable.

We can imagine a social system in which the motive for prostitution would be completely absent, but we cannot imagine that the system could ever come to pass. It would be a regime of absolute sexual freedom, wherein intercourse were practised solely for the pleasure of it, by both parties. This would entail at least two conditions: *First,* there could be no institutional control of sexual expression. Marriage, with its concomitants of engagement, jealousy, divorce, and legitimacy, could not exist. Such an institution builds upon and limits the sexual urge, making sex expression contingent upon non-sexual factors, and thereby paving the way for intercourse against one's physical inclination. *Second,* all sexual desire would have to be mutually complementary. One person could not be erotically attracted to a non-responsive person, because such a situation would inevitably involve frustration and give a motive for using force, fraud, authority, or money to induce the unwilling person to co-operate.

Neither of these conditions can in the nature of things come to pass. As we have seen, every society attempts to control, and for its own survival must control, the sexual impulse in the interest of social order, procreation, and socialization. Moreover, all men are not born handsome nor all women beautiful. Instead there is a perfect gradation from extremely attractive to extremely unattractive, with an unfavorable balance of the old and ugly. This being the case, the persons at the wrong end of the scale must, and inevitably will, use extraneous means to obtain gratification.

While neither the scale of attractiveness nor the institutionalization of sex are likely to disappear, it is possible that the *particular form of institutionalization* may change. The change may be in the direction of greater sex freedom. Such a change must inevitably affect prostitution, because the greater the proportion of free, mutually pleasurable intercourse, the lesser is the demand for prostitution. . . .

The conclusion that free intercourse for pleasure and friendship rather than for profit is the greatest enemy of prostitution emerges logically from our statement that a basic trait of prostitution is the use of sex for an ulterior purpose. Should one wish to abolish commercial coitus, one would have to eliminate this trait. This proposition however, is unacceptable to moralists, because, as we saw, the underlying trait of prostitution is also a fundamental feature of reputable sexual institutions, and intercourse for sheer pleasure is as inimical to our sacred institutions as it is to the profane one of mercenary love. Though Lecky's suggestion that harlotry sustains the family is perhaps indefensible, it seems true that prostitution is not so great a danger to the family as complete liberty.

Where the family is strong, there tends to be a well-defined system of prostitution and the social regime is one of status. Women are either part of the family system, or they are definitely not a part of it. In the latter case they are prostitutes, members of a caste set apart. There are few intermediate groups, and there is little mobility. This enables the two opposite types of institutions to function side by side without confusion; they are each staffed by a different personnel, humanly as well as functionally distinct. But where familial controls are weak, the system of prostitution tends to be poorly defined. Not only is it more nearly permissible to satisfy one's desire outside the family, but also it is easier to find a respectable member of society willing to act as partner. This is why a decline of the family and a decline of prostitution are both associated with a rise of sex freedom. Women, released from close family supervision, are freer to seek gratification outside it. The more such women, the easier it is for men to find in intimate relations with them the satisfactions formerly supplied by harlots. This is why the unrestricted indulgence in sex for the fun of it by both sexes is the greatest enemy, not only of the family, but also of prostitution. . . .

But even if present trends continue, there is no likelihood that sex freedom will ever displace prostitution. Not only will there always be a set of reproductive institutions which place a check upon sexual liberty, a system of social dominance which gives a motive for selling sexual favors, and a scale of attractiveness which creates the need for buying these favors, but prostitution is, in the last analysis, economical. Enabling a small number of women to take care of the needs of a large number of men, it is the most convenient sexual outlet for an army, and for the legions of strangers, perverts, and physically repulsive in our midst. It performs a function, apparently, which no other institution fully performs.

THE SELF-IMAGE OF THE PROSTITUTE

Norman R. Jackman, Richard O'Toole, and Gilbert Geis

Sexual behavior represents one of the most sensitive areas in American life. Within this sphere, professional promiscuity on the part of females stands as a striking deviation from what a large segment of the society declares to be acceptable sexual performance. Prostitutes are undoubtedly well aware of the prevailing social attitudes toward their behavior. It would seem, therefore, that these women develop a set of beliefs which counteract the social anathema attached to their way of life. This set of beliefs allows them to continue their behavior and to face and retaliate against persons who share the dominant and negative social values toward them. . . .

Two questions appear to be central to the problem of the prostitute's self-identity. First, since most Americans scorn prostitutes and these dominant social values travel throughout the society, how are women recruited to prostitution? Second, since a high degree of conformity to the dominant, middle-class American society is considered necessary for the maintenance of self-esteem, how do prostitutes rationalize their violation of a dominant social norm?

INTERVIEW PHASE

Fifteen prostitutes were interviewed for periods averaging two hours each. Thirteen interviews were obtained while these women were held in the city jail awaiting the results of clinical tests. Two other women were interviewed in night clubs.

Open-ended questions were employed for interviewing. The questions were used only to get the respondents to talk: everything they said was recorded and subsequently coded. Standard profile questions were asked (name, age, education, marital status, number, sex, and age of children, religion, etc.) followed by a series of questions organized around certain principal topics. These were (a) account of career, (b) self-conception, (c) group identifications, and (d) role expectations. Specific but unformalized questions were asked in each of these major areas, such as childhood experiences, recruitment to prostitution, attitudes toward clients, police, neighbors, etc., relationships with parents, husbands,

From *Sociological Quarterly*, Vol. 4, No. 2 (Spring 1963), 150-61. Reprinted by permission.

children, relatives, other prostitutes, etc., attitudes toward work, future hopes, fears and plans, moods, fantasies, daydreams, and recreation.

ANALYSIS OF THE DATA

The three following propositions concerning the formation and the structure of the self-image of the prostitute emerged from the data.

1. *The more isolated girl in urban society comes to define as acceptable patterns of behavior condemned by general social values more readily than does the less isolated individual.* Evidence indicated that the respondents were alienated from their parents following a break with the father toward whom they all expressed extreme hostility. After their introduction to prostitution, many of them became reconciled with their mothers, though they all maintained that they had kept knowledge of their activities from the mother:

> I would go through hell for my mother, but my father is a bastard. Every time my mother got pregnant [respondent has five siblings] my father went out with other women.
> My parents were divorced when I was eight. I lived with relatives and in an orphan home until I was thirteen and then I went to live with my mother. . . . My father was cruel to me. . . . I hated my father and stepfather. . . . I was glad when my father died. . . .
> My father was a carpenter and a gambler. . . . He always treated me like I was strictly from age two. But I got along good with my mother.

Alienation during the period of entrance into prostitution was indicated by the respondents' statements that they associated with people who meant little to them, or that they had no friends at all. In every case they felt that they stood alone against a hostile or indifferent world, though some of them were introduced to semi-criminal groups with which in time they came to identify themselves.

> I ran around with a girl who started and so I started, too. She had a lot of friends. . . . I got to know a lot of people in the hustling racket.
> I just been runnin' around with rum-dums all my life, I guess. . . . There was a fellow once in San Antone—I came in off a box-car, believe it or not, and I met him in a honky-tonk.
> I was hanging 'round bars in Tulsa just looking for kicks. I had no place to go, like. It was strictly from hunger, man.
> I figgered it was easy money—prostitution. . . . Nobody cared what I did anyway, and I knew a fellow who would set it up for me.

2. *The general social values, nevertheless, have some impact on the isolated individual. Therefore, the violation of these values must be rationalized by the individual.* The violation of sexual values is justified in two ways: (*a*) Everyone is rotten. Hence, prostitutes are no worse

than other people, and they are less hypocritical. (b) Society doesn't really scorn prostitutes. Every prostitute interviewed expressed some degree of guilt feeling about her activity. This attitude ranged from mild expressions of guilt to statements like the following.

> I will rot in hell for what I am doing. If you don't know what you are doing is sinful, then it is not so bad. But it is an unpardonable sin if you know what you are doing is sinful and keep on sinning.
>
> My father told me two things: "Don't ever become a prostitute and don't marry a nigger."

Several respondents reflected in their defensive attitudes their imputation of middle-class disapproval on the part of the interviewers. These responses took the form of an attack on men or women, the world in general, or they reflected the attitude that prostitution did not mean a person was bad.

> Men are . . . shrimps. Show me the man that's worth killing and I'll do the job.
>
> Little chippies in bars give it away for a couple of beers.
>
> This business doesn't keep you from having good children. Religion is right. It's a good thing. What we do doesn't affect religious feeling—being a wife, mother, housewife.
>
> Other people look down on you. Deep down inside it hurts, but you ignore it . . . biggest majority are nice people. Several of the vice squad men hold the squad car door open for me [when they arrest her].

3. *The rationalization by prostitutes violating social taboos against commercial sex behavior takes the form of exaggerating other values, particularly those of financial success, and for some the unselfish assumption of the financial burden of people dependent upon them.* Support for these justifications is found through reference groups, real or fictional, whose values the prostitute internalizes and thus is able to act in a consistent and "normal" manner. The behavior of prostitutes is not abnormal given the norms of those groups with which they identify themselves.

We identified two principal types of reference group orientations: one we labeled the *criminal world contraculture* and the other *dual worlds,* the world of prostitution and the middle-class world of American society.

The criminal world contraculture. The principal characteristic of this type of prostitute is a strong identification with criminals and with those on the edge of the criminal world—Hobohemians. Yinger argues for the use of the concept *contraculture* for this type of group identification:

> . . . I suggest the use of the term contraculture wherever the normative system of a group contains, as a primary element, a theme of conflict with the values of the total society where personality variables are directly in-

volved in the development and maintenance of the group's values, and wherever its norms can be understood only by reference to the relationships of the group to a surrounding dominant culture.

This group had the greatest contempt for middle-class, "proper" people, whom they felt to be dull, frightened, and hypocritical. On the other hand, they made some attempt to justify their behavior by appealing to such dominant social values as financial success, their ability to move in "big business" circles, and being good mothers.

One respondent in this group said that prostitution was a means to secure money for her husband and herself so that they could lead an exciting life. Her husband is her procurer, and the group with which they associate is composed of people connected with prostitution. They are heavy drinkers, and many of them are addicts. They appear to be carefree and irresponsible, deciding at a moment's notice to go off on trips together. . . .

Another respondent stated that she liked the easy money. She had gotten tired of working twelve to fourteen hours a day as a waitress.

Another respondent displayed a great deal of satisfaction from claiming to be a big spender, wearing good clothes, and going to expensive restaurants and night clubs. She also associated with a semi-criminal group. She bragged about X,

> . . . a very wealthy businessman who pays me twenty-five to thirty dollars an evening just for my company. He takes me to the best places in town for dinner and dancing, and buys me expensive gifts. And I've never been in bed with the man! He told me that I mingled well with the finest people. He said once, "You act like a lady." She also mentioned a boy friend who was in trouble with the Kansas City police.

This respondent, the only one in the criminal subculture who had children, stated that she was "a good mother" who visited her children regularly. However, her account of the break-up of her first marriage indicated that this self-evaluation, as well as the characterization that she acted like a lady, might be questioned.

> My husband started running around. I wanted to make him leave so I could keep the children. I cut him off, cursed him, and cut him with a knife, but I couldn't make him go.

Her children lived with her first husband and his second wife. When she visited her children once, she told her ex-husband that his present wife, "had better be good to my kids or I'll stomp her in a mudhole."

The final respondent in this group also stressed the luxurious life she leads as a prostitute and aligned herself with a criminal group. Like the second respondent she stressed her claim to association with the "best" people in the city and her attendance at social functions where such people gather. A vice squad officer said that she had been arrested while they were investigating a tip that she was harboring a criminal who was a known drug peddler.

These four respondents were generally friendly in their findings toward their clients and middle-class society in general. As indicated above, they maintained with considerable pride that they associated with the best people. Toward their clients they expressed some ambivalence:

> Most of my clients are nice guys. . . . Most of them are married. . . . I like older men because younger men look down on you.
>
> Some men take it out on you because they feel guilty about cheating on their wives. . . . I don't hold it against married men for going to prostitutes. Actually, it teaches them the values of affection because prostitutes are so cold. . . .All in all they are pretty nice.

Dual worlds. The five cases which fell into this category were characterized by a strong identification with their families and a rejection of the world of prostitutes which they were in, but not of. Two of the respondents claimed to be supporting their husbands and children, while the other two lived alone and claimed to be supporting children in other states whom they visited occasionally. The two married prostitutes said that their husbands acted as procurers for them, but for no other women. This group strongly and consistently expressed middle-class values. Unlike those in the criminal subculture, they never swore or used obscene words. They sought constantly to assure the interviewers that they were excellent mothers who made great sacrifices for their husbands, children, and relatives. They professed religious beliefs, and the two married respondents claimed that their associates (with the exception of their husbands) were not prostitutes or criminals. The two single prostitutes said that they associated with no one except their families whom they visited occasionally in another town. They resisted questions about their clients and other aspects of the business of prostitution. In short, they have seemingly dichotomized their world successfully by depersonalizing their prostitute roles and living almost entirely in the dominant world of American middle-class values.

Sherif and Cantril have noted that the ego can be dissociated from the self under certain extreme situations, and they illustrated this concept with a reference to the autobiography of a London prostitute who wrote, "I have moments when I realize that I am a person to no one . . . The act of sex I could go through because *I hardly seemed to be taking part in it . . . Indeed, it was scarcely happening even to me: It was happening to something lying on a bed that had a vague connection with me. . . .*"

All of the respondents reported a certain amount of dissociation in their initial commercial experience. What would seem to distinguish the *dual worlds* groups from other groups was that this initial dissociation was continued and strengthened. The other two groups reported varying degrees of dissociation or none at all, some respondents claiming that they occasionally participated emotionally in the sex act and enjoyed it. Because of their middle-class moral values most of the *dual worlds* group avoided the topic of sex completely. The members of this group had successfully repressed their prostitute role and justified it as a self-sacrificing necessity to support those who were helpless and dependent upon them.

One of the married prostitutes in this group said that when she became pregnant her husband left her. She became a prostitute to support herself and her child. Her present husband is an unemployed tile-setter. She apologized for her husband by saying that there isn't too much demand for tile-setters. She claimed that she was supporting six persons and herself.

> They don't know what I do for a living, except my husband. I see my little girl often. About once a week. I don't work weekends so I can go see her.
> . . . My sister just got a job, but she's not on her feet yet. She has a tiny baby. Her husband is in the penitentiary. [Embarrassed laugh.]

The other married prostitute also claimed to be supporting an unemployed husband, two children, and her mother. Her mother takes care of her children and none of them knows that she is a prostitute:

> I think that I am a good mother who takes care of her children. I love my family very much. I have a normal family life other than being a prostitute. I hope that my husband can find a job and gets to working steadily again so I can be an ordinary housewife.

Of the single prostitutes in this group, one had five children by a previous marriage and the other had never been married. The first strongly identified herself with her children, while the second strongly identified herself with her parents. Neither of them associated intimately with other people. Both claimed they had become prostitutes in order to care for their children or their parents.

> I am very proud of my family. Even though the mother is a prostitute it doesn't reflect on her family—this business doesn't keep you from having good children. I keep my children in the best private schools and colleges in Texas. One of them married very well. They don't know what I do.

The respondent who identified herself with her parents maintained that her father had given her the best of everything as a child, but she had failed to live up to his expectations because she was too much like him. Nevertheless, she helped both parents financially:

My parents are the most wonderful people alive. I like 'em both but my mother is easier to get along with. Dad and I fight like cats and dogs. Both alike. He thinks I'm two years old. He said, "I knew the day you was born you'd be just like me." He's got suspicious of my work, but not my mother. She had an operation—cancer of the brain. I gave him [father] four hundred dollars and three hundred more after I came back from Chicago. He said, "Myra, I know what you're doing, but for God's sake don't let your mother know."

All four respondents in the *dual worlds* category expressed middle-class values:

I have some friends, some are married women, and some work.

My husband and I run around with other couples where the wife isn't a prostitute.

I got lots of friends not even connected with hustling. Went with a Kansas City dick for a long time.

I don't associate with hustling people. Half their husbands are in McAlester [state penitentiary] or the county jail.

Alienation. The six respondents who fell into this group were characterized by feelings of normlessness, apathy, lack of direction or future goal orientation. They identified themselves with no one and felt their lives to be empty and meaningless. Two of them were young: one an eighteen-year-old who was new to the profession, and the other a nineteen-year-old who had been a prostitute for one year. It is possible that the newest recruit's sense of alienation will become modified as she becomes less a stranger to her environment. The third respondent had been a prostitute for ten years. The length of time in prostitution is evidently not a factor in alienation, however, since the second youngest respondent in this group had been a prostitute for one year, and the prostitute with the longest record (eleven years) seemed to be well integrated in a criminal subculture. As noted above, all of this group dissociated themselves from the sex act.

Their conditions of alienation may be summarized by the following selected quotations:

I been in this racket ten years, I guess it's too late to get out. . . . I got no future; I been married four times and that's enough. . . . I don't care. I spent a hundred and fifty dollars over the weekend on drinking and gambling. I can't save. But I kicked the habit cold turkey. [Another respondent in the *dual worlds* category, who knew this prostitute, said: "Hustling's got the best of Jerry. She's drunk all the time. Girls like that are weak. They got no will power."] I got no friends; everybody's rotten, anymore.

Women are as bad as men. Women ain't worth a damn. I'm usually too drunk to know what's going on [sex act].

I live by myself and have no friends. I just sleep and hustle at the night club. No, TV shows and books just bore me. Daydreams? Why daydream when you can't be out doing the things you daydream about? . . . Just before you came in, I was out standing in the rain watching the world cry because it's been so screwed up by all the bastards in it. [This respondent was interviewed in a night club.]

I was drunk when I was arrested—had been drinking for several days. I was too drunk to care. I don't live with anybody. I don't know anyone in this town, except the porter [procurer]. My parents don't care about me, they put me in an Indian boarding school and I ran away from it. Drinking is very bad. I've been so bad I decided I might as well go all the way. I used to walk around town late at night and once a porter from one of the hotels stopped me and tried to get me to start working. He asked me twice. I felt it didn't matter. I was sober when I started, but I had to get drunk to finish it. . . .

THE SOCIAL AND PROFESSIONAL LIFE OF THE CALL GIRL

Harold Greenwald

Little is known generally of the life of the call girl. How does she earn her living? How much does she earn? Where does she get her clients? What does she have to do in order to be good at her job? Does she have a code of behavior like, let us say, that of the lawyer or doctor? What is her social life like? With whom does she associate and what is the nature of such associations? . . .

INCOME

The call girls I interviewed earned in the neighborhood of twenty thousand dollars a year. Since they live outside the law, all of this was untaxed. The girls charged from twenty to a hundred dollars for each session and on a few occasions were able to charge even more. The higher figures were paid either by extremely affluent people or by those who had special tastes for which the girls wanted extra pay. A man might require an entire night of a girl's time, perhaps taking her out to a night club to pretend that it wasn't purely a commercial transaction but a

From *The Call Girl: A Social and Psychoanalytic Study,* New York: Ballantine Books, 1958, pp. 8-23. Reprinted by permission.

semi-social occasion. In such cases the girls usually expected to be compensated accordingly.

EXPENSES

The income of twenty thousand dollars is a gross figure from which a large number of expenses must be deducted. First and foremost in the life of the call girl is the telephone; without it she could not practice her special form of prostitution. Call girls make almost all of their appointments by phone. However, in some instances the girls are so apprehensive about the possibility of arrest or of being traced that they do not use personal telephones but receive their calls from an answering service or a telephone exchange. This is a number which the girl gives to her clients; she herself is never at the number but calls it several times a day and then phones the various callers who have left messages. The cost of telephone and answering service is about forty-five dollars a month.

With few exceptions, the girls live at addresses where they can on occasion entertain clients. Although most of them prefer to go to the client's home or, more often, his hotel room or suite, there are some clients, usually local married men, who do not provide a place of their own; therefore the girls have to have their own apartments—the fee is usually the same. Call girls' apartments are generally in expensive neighborhoods. . . . Not only is the rent high, but the girl often has special expenses because the landlord or superintendent is aware of her occupation and therefore boosts the rent even higher, or she has to compensate the landlord or his representative or the superintendent or manager with extra large monthly bonuses. Rents average about three hundred dollars a month.

It would be difficult to estimate clothing expenses. In the circle in which they move the girls have to make a good appearance. They must, for example, be able to walk in and out of the finest hotels without attracting undue attention because of dressing either too poorly or too garishly. It is difficult, however, to say how much of the clothing expenditure is a necessity. Like many women, a call girl, when depressed or annoyed, may go on a shopping spree and spend a great deal of money on clothes. Some of the clothes are bought from conventional sources: department stores, specialty shops and others. However, there are other sources. Because of their contacts with underworld figures, many of the girls are able to buy their clothes at substantial discounts. In New York, the center of the garment industry, there is organized stealing of high-quality clothes, from trucks and from factories. These clothes are sold through a series of small dealers or fences, and the girls often have contact with such sources and so are able to buy expensive clothing at low prices. In many cases, when clients are themselves owners or executives of apparel firms, the girls may receive gifts, or their services are performed on a barter basis with payment being made in clothes rather than in cash.

In addition to outer wear, the girls understandably spend a great deal of money on their undergarments. Here, too, these garments are obtained from both conventional and unconventional sources. A number of former and some still occasionally practicing call girls have gone into the lingerie business, and call girls frequently patronize such places. There are also dealers who specialize in selling lingerie, negligees and perfumes to the call girls and such dealers frequently visit them at their homes. These dealers are recommended by other call girls.

One special item of expense, particularly for a girl who uses her own apartment a great deal, is the laundry bill. Fastidious clients require a change of sheets and pillow cases before each visit. Large numbers of towels are used. The laundry bill thus frequently runs much higher than any conventional householder's.

A great deal of money is also spent on cosmetics, perfumes and beauty shop expenses. All of the girls try to keep their hair in good condition and spend a large amount of time on their personal appearance. There are a number of all-night beauty shops in cities like New York and Chicago which the girls find convenient. Again, like many of their more respectable sisters, call girls frequently, when depressed, will take themselves off to the beauty parlor for a facial, a hair-do, a wash, a rinse, a dye, and others of the complicated rituals of the beauty parlor.

Their medical expenses also tend to be higher than average. For one thing they usually patronize physicians who have large call-girl clienteles and who often charge them higher fees than their more respectable clients. Many of the girls go for monthly check-ups to ascertain whether they have venereal disease, and some go to the length of getting prophylactic doses of antibiotics to prevent the possibility of contracting a venereal disease. However, venereal disease in this group does not seem to be a serious problem. With the spread of antibiotic drugs it has lessened in all society and particularly at the socioeconomic level at which these girls operate.

Abortions—occasionally necessary—are highly expensive for those call girls who want them. Although the professional call girl is well versed in the facts of contraception, many of them forget to use or dislike using female devices and most of their clients refuse to employ any devices to prevent pregnancy. Also many of the girls believe that they are unlikely to become pregnant as long as they are so active sexually. Their theory is that the different strains of semen destroy each other. Several of the girls reported that they had not used any method of contraception for long periods of time and did not become pregnant. However, when they do conceive they usually know doctors who are willing to perform abortions, the fee for which may be as high as three thousand dollars.

One item of expense which cannot be calculated is the amount of money that has to be spent for direct and indirect protection from arrest. Some of the girls secrete sums of money in their apartments which may run as high as two thousand dollars, or leave sums of money in the hands of friends who can be reached at any hour in case of difficulties with the police. When such difficulties arise, the girls frequently attempt to bribe their way out of them, and such bribery is usually not conducted on a credit basis. Therefore it is important to have money readily available for such emergencies.

There are many other extra expenses. For example, if the girl lives in an apartment house with elevator operators, the operators have to be tipped liberally and frequently, and the doorman as well, if there is one. In general most of the girls tend to be quite liberal tippers in any situation.

The largest drain on a call girl's income arises out of her relationship with a pimp. In most such relationships the call girl will turn over practically her entire income to the pimp, who will then dole out whatever money he feels she needs for expenses. However, the money given to the pimp cannot be considered a normal living expense. . . . Her reasons for giving this money are intimately connected with her psychology. . . .

SOURCES OF CLIENTS

One of the girls, Stella, wrote especially for my use a description of the relationship of the professional call girl to her clients:

> The first prerequisite is a telephone in good working order, with an answering service connected so that business can continue even when the proprietor is out on a call—away from home. Usually as soon as "business has been completed," the girl will call her answering service for messages, thus enabling her to hop from one address to another without wasting expensive time. If there has been a call at her residence while the present job is in progress, and the phoned-in customer has left a message or number with the girl's answering service, it is not unusual for the amenities of the current business to be completed quickly (the passage of fee from "John" [client] to girl) and a hasty departure for the next destination made by the busy young lady. For example:
>
> Jim Jones calls Terry Toon. He says: "I'm a friend of Bill Brown; he gave me your number."
>
> She says: "Oh yes, Bill Brown. Where are you staying?" (Most calls seem to come from out-of-towers—the local chaps are less active, although when in Chicago a New Yorker acts like a Chicagoan in New York.)
>
> He says: "Blank Hotel." (This is rarely more than a twenty-five or

thirty-dollar call—usually a "quick twenty"—about forty-five minutes to one hour.) Some girls pride themselves on giving less or more time according to their tastes and styles, but all do so with the attitude of having a successful, effective approach to conducting their business. It is of considerable pride whether they do a twenty-minute "twenty" or an hour "twenty." But time and money usuallly determine each other in this income bracket. The fifty- or hundred-dollar John has a more elastic schedule granted him; also a clever girl will not phone into the "office" for messages too frequently while on duty with a fifty- or hundred-dollar man. It is bad taste, as it reminds the buyer that his purchase is not exclusive. A man spending this amount of money expects deception and romance, as well as the orgasm. The girls often prefer to do several quick twenties rather than one slow, long-drawn-out job for a hundred dollars.

Back to Jim Jones and Terry Toon. He identifies himself and the source of his information regarding her, and if the name he uses as introduction is a valid customer, the girl will accept business thus recommended. If the name of the original customer, however, recalls any problems sexually, a demanding tough John or financial hazards (arguments about amount or rubber checks, et cetera), the girl will frequently refuse the new applicant, considering him not a good risk if his friend has created a bad impression before him.

However, if everything is in order, and there is no doubt in the girl's mind that this is a legitimate John, not a cop playing her for trouble (as some arrests have been planned and effected this way), she will make a note of his hotel and room number and set an appointment. Usually the John says, "Come over in a hurry, I have to leave soon." This also reassures the girl that it will be a "quick one."

This type is one classification; a cut-and-dried affair in which there is no illusion of romance or subterfuge. The girl arrives and the man often is already disrobed totally or partially, and he answers the door furtively, removing her coat and exchanging amenities on the way to the bedroom (if it's a suite). The preliminaries in this case are dispensed with quickly and the physical action begins. The John expresses his sexual preference or in some cases inquires as to the girl's preference. One type of girl considers this stupid, figuring that he is paying, why ask her her preference; another girl would find this an act of consideration, but the finer functionings of these affairs are full of contradictions. (There I go analyzing!)

This is an example of word-of-mouth advertising which is the basis for increasing a clientele. A call girl's business should constantly increase as Johns distribute her number to their friends. One John can recommend as many as four others and sometimes more, depending on his number of contacts.

Another source of enlarging clientele is fellow call girls who exchange "numbers" and "dates." A "number" is a man who is on the John list. In this maneuver the positions are reversed. The girl calls the man and says that her girl friend told her to call him. A date is arranged and these cases usually are local business men who come to the girl's place.

Location and style are important here. The fee of the girl often depends on the address and furnishings of her place of business, as much as her attractiveness of physique and manner.

It will be seen from Stella's description, which seems quite accurate on the basis of the information I was given by other girls, that most of the clients are not obtained by direct solicitation. Usually they acquire clients from each other or by recommendation from previously satisfied clients. Occasionally, however, when business is slack, the call girl will initiate calls. She doesn't solicit in the usual sense of streetwalking, but she will call a number of men in an effort to drum up trade.

There are other sources of clientele, too. In breaking into the profession, girls usually work first through some type of procurer or madam. Some of these procurers are themselves practicing call girls who, for a percentage, will pass on excess business to other girls. This percentage varies from as high as two-thirds of the total fee in cases of the raw beginners who are breaking into the field, to as low as twenty per cent. In the twenty-per-cent bracket there is a special twist. The standard minimum fee for a call girl in most of the large cities is twenty dollars. Sometimes madams add an extra five dollars, making the fee twenty-five dollars, and this five dollars is deducted by the madam, although such a small percentage is rare. It usually runs to at least fifty per cent.

In addition to madams who are practicing or former call girls, another source of outside business is a male procurer. There is a distinction between the procurer and the pimp. The pimp as such, . . . performs no economic function. The procurer performs the function of getting clients for the girl. Call-girl pimps are rarely procurers.

Another source of clients is the voluntary procurer, the businessman who entertains male acquaintances by providing them with call girls. The girls are used in the entertainment of out-of-town buyers, lucrative customers, and sometimes even important personnel who may be taken out on the town by their employer, included in which evening will be the treat of visiting a call girl.

There are a number of cocktail lounges and restaurants which are known haunts of call girls, but the solicitation here is usually not direct. In these places the management encourages the trade of call girls. They usually sit at the bars, drinking by themselves; occasionally introduction is made by the bartender or manager where the potential client is not very adventurous and asks aid. The more adventurous clients will approach the girl themselves, in which case the encounter frequently takes on the appearance of an ordinary barroom conversation. It is then important for the call girl to display her skill in negotiation so that she can obtain the promise of a fee without being too crudely commercial in her negotiations, as many men find such an attitude dampening to their ardor.

In addition to the exchange of telephone numbers, customer lists are also sold. One way in which this is done is through the sale of the "black book." A girl planning to leave the city or planning to retire from the profession will sell her black book of addresses to another girl. Black books of good clients have been known to sell for as much as five thousand dollars. Sometimes a pimp will advance this money, secure in the knowledge that the girl for whom he buys the book will soon earn it back.

WORKING HOURS

Because of the nature of their work the girls usually are late sleepers, rising at one or two o'clock in the afternoon, which is the time that the telephone first starts to ring. Quite a few men seem to be interested in the services of a call girl in the afternoon. For the next few hours the girl is usually busy tidying up her apartment, making herself up and in general preparing for the evening's activities, at the same time receiving telephone calls. Her active work usually starts at about four o'clock, with business men who stop in on their way home from the office, and usually continues until two or three in the morning. At that time, girls will often gather in restaurants, go to late movies, one of the all-night beauty parlors, or to an after-hours spot. The after-hours spots are restaurants, often in the guise of private clubs, which operate after the legal curfew. Many of these are frequented by call girls and pimps.

LANGUAGE

As Sutherland described it, in the case of the professional thief, so call girls too have ways of recognizing each other by the use of special slang. Not all of this slang is peculiar only to the call girl; many of the words are also part of the vernacular of various groups in and around the underworld, and many are taken from the slang of jazz musicians. Words like "bread" for money, "stoned" for drunk, "dig" for understand, "pad" for a place to sleep are just as common with the call girl as they are with jazz musicians and their fans. Of special interest is the way the girls describe fellow-professionals. They speak of them as being "in the racket," as being "in the life," as "a regular girl," or "one of the girls," with particular emphasis given to the word "girl." This emphasis is extremely important in their discussions. Frequently when they use ordinary words, the inflection or the emphasis or the accompanying winks give them special meaning. Numbers, for example, are never given in their original form. If a client wants to discuss a fee, the call girl will never say, "Twenty dollars"; she may say, "It will be twenty blocks away." If a girl is giving the telephone number of another girl, usually she will not give it as a telephone number, but perhaps as a price. Thus Spring 7-3100 might be given as: "The spring price is seven for thirty-one hundred dollars." In special circumstances when call girls need to communicate with each other while working together on a job, they may use "carny" talk, a complicated form of pig latin which supposedly originated among carnival employees, but which is very popular among people having connections in and around the underworld.

CODE

The professional call girl has a code regulating her relations with the client. For example, it is customary for a call girl never to show any signs of recognizing a customer when she meets him in public, unless he greets her first. If their clients are prominent people the girls will not readily identify them or name them in conversation even with each other. Also a girl with an established clientele will not steal from her customers nor permit them to overpay her if she feels they are doing so because they are drunk. A professional call girl will make every effort to satisfy a client even if he has difficulties. When working with groups of men she will not reveal the inadequacies of one of the men to the others in the group, but will praise him.

Their code also regulates their relations with each other. If one girl sends a client to another she expects reciprocity. Similarly if one girl takes another girl along on a job with her she expects the other to return the favor at the earliest opportunity.

STATUS

The call girl gives a great deal of attention to her status. She is particularly anxious to distinguish herself from the ordinary streetwalker or house girl—Karen, in discussing an example of mistreatment, said of a man: "He acted as if I was a street girl."

Her status is based on her attractiveness, financial standing, political connections, dress, apartment, manners and the state in which she keeps her "old man" or pimp. Call girls have more scorn for the streetwalker than does the most puritanical reformer. They will avoid bars and restaurants that are patronized by girls who, they feel, have inferior status as professionals or whom they consider amateurs just "chippying around," girls who occasionally "turn a trick" (accept men for a fee) even though they have other means of earning a living. They want nothing to do with girls who in their opinion are not truly professional in their approach.

While there is no common agreement as to the gradations within the general profession of prostitute, Stella divided them into three broad categories:

The "party girl" (who is often also a model, actress, or a chorus "broad").

The "hustler," or "hooker."

The prostitute, or whore.

By the "party girl," Stella meant the girl who goes out on no more than one date per evening and where the question of fee is not made explicit. That is, the girl never discusses fee with clients, but it is understood, usually by arrangement with the person making the introduction, that at the end of the evening the man will unobtrusively slip her an envelope containing anywhere from a hundred dollars up for "taxi fare." Also, most girls in the "party girl" category will occasionally refuse their favors to a man who does not appeal to them. "Party girls" are very careful to keep this prerogative of refusal as a means of denying that they are engaged in prostitution.

The "hustler," or "hooker," is the call girl who operates on an appointment basis, maintaining her own residence, which may or may not serve as a place for entertaining clients. It is interesting to note that Stella applied the term "prostitute" only to the streetwalker in order to avoid using the term for her own group, which included the call girl and the party girl, because she had been both.

In addition to the categories that Stella mentioned, there are others. The "house girl" operates within a house of prostitution. Except for special sections of New York where there is much poverty, like Harlem or some of the Puerto Rican neighborhoods, there seem to be very few houses of prostitution in operation at the present time. Occasionally two girls will share an apartment, but not in the organized way that houses of prostitution flourished in New York in pre-World War II days, as described by Polly Adler. The "kept woman" is another category that Stella omitted. The kept woman usually gives her favors to only one man at a time in return for financial security during the time that the arrangement is in effect. Kept women differ from a girl who is living with a man without benefit of marriage in that they frequently move on from one lover to another, and when not being kept they are usually looking for someone to attach themselves to in order to secure a livelihood. What distinguishes the kept woman further is that her relationship with the man is solely and frankly an economic one, in which she may pretend affection, but where her own subjective feelings are that he is a John or "sucker." Occasionally one of the girls in the other categories will move into the kept woman class for a short period of time. However, the typical call girl is not interested in this arrangement and usually finds such a life much too boring and dull to be able to tolerate it for long.

The clothes the call girl wears are very important to her status, both in her eyes and in the eyes of her clients. Etta, for example, usually bought a new mink coat every season, trading in last season's coat, in very much the same way many people trade in their cars. She told how a regular customer of hers in describing her to a friend of his said: "Wait till you see what a gorgeous mink coat this kid has."

The amount of money a girl charges as her customary fee is obviously important to her status. For example, as previously mentioned, none of the girls included in this study would dream of charging less than twenty dollars. To do so would make them feel like "common prostitutes." Girls who charge above this minimum consider themselves on a higher status and one assured me during our interview that she was "strictly a fifty-dollar girl."

The dress and standard of living of the pimp (paid lover) supported by the girl—if she has one—are important to her status. One of the reasons why many of the girls are willing to part with large sums of money to keep their pimps well dressed and riding around in Cadillac convertibles is that this enhances their status in the profession.

The type of clientele to which a girl caters is another factor in establishing her status. Girls will often boast that they see only "the nicest type of men," business men, professionals and people from the theatrical world. Many of the girls during their interviews managed to mention casually that they had had business relations with leading television or movie stars at one time or another but usually remained true to their code by not mentioning names.

It is important for the girl to have her status as a professional recognized by others in the group. Trading of telephone numbers will be done only with other professionals who are considered of equal status. Thus a girl who is on the fifty-dollar level will not be likely to trade names with a twenty-dollar girl. Also, a girl will not trade names with another one who she thinks will injure her reputation with a client because of not knowing how to handle herself properly in the situation. When several girls work together at an occasion where a number of men are present, such as during conventions or arrangement of big business or political deals, a girl will be very careful as to which girls she works with. On such occasions a girl who is liable to lose self-control or mistreat clients may become dangerous. Since such parties are usually accompanied by heavy drinking, one girl who behaves in such a way as to arouse the anger of some of the inebriated clients may cause all of the girls to lose their fees, receive beatings, or even in some cases to risk arrest.

ASSOCIATION

Call girls prefer to associate with people like themselves, who are in the racket or who know what they are doing.

Chief among their associates are the members of that special sub-culture which is described later as the "gray world," drug addicts, bookmakers, promoters of worthless stock and others who live in the gray area between respectability and outright criminality.

Since the girls recognize that society at large considers them outcasts, they are very apprehensive when with strangers that somebody will discover their profession. This worry about what other people would think of them if their profession became known is a chief reason for restricting their contacts with respectable society. Their awareness of society's attitude toward them is a great obstacle in the path of many of the girls who would like to choose a more respectable way of life. Stella, for example, was worried, when she became interested in a theatrical career, that she might be recognized on television by former clients. Frequently their associates who are not in and around the racket are creative people —artists, musicians, writers—who tend to be more tolerant of them.

All of the girls I interviewed were working at the time in New York City. However, several of them had worked at various times as call girls in Chicago, Los Angeles, Miami Beach and Las Vegas. While call girls may be numerous in other cities, these were the cities and locations that were mentioned most frequently. The conditions of work in these places are almost identical to those in New York. The only ascertainable difference seems to be that the police in other cities were accused by the girls of being more graft-hungry than the New York police. In Miami Beach, they stated that the cupidity of the personnel of the large hotels was so great that they found that they were working for the elevator operators, bell hops, room clerks and chambermaids—in the words of one of them: "I found that I was working to support all these parasites and making hardly anything for myself." In Chicago, the girls reported that there were organized mobs who had to be paid off with regular contributions.

AMUSEMENTS

The amusements of the call girl are not much different from those of other girls of the same educational level. They like the movies and television. They tend to read a great deal and their tastes in reading material vary with their education and background. I have frequently been in respectable homes where no books were in evidence. I have never been in a call girl's home where there were not at least some books to be seen and, in many cases, large numbers of books. Marie, for example, had one wall completely covered with filled bookshelves. Large numbers of these books were paperback romantic novels, but there was a good selection of serious plays and of novels, chiefly of the best-seller variety. Their preference in reading matter would seem to be, first, periodical literature, tabloid newspapers, the exposé type of magazines, and other mass circulation magazines, including a variety of woman's magazines. After that come romantic novels. Books about prostitutes are quite popular if the prostitute is a romantic figure. Even though they were derisively aware of the inaccuracy and distortion of some of the fictional portraits, many of the girls stated they enjoyed such books. Most of them were avid television fans, especially of programs on which their clients appeared.

There was very little evidence that the girls had any great interest in gambling. While many of them would go to race tracks in the company of male friends or habitual customers—who would sometimes even pay them for their time either because they felt they brought them good luck or because they liked their company—the girls rarely bet with their own money. Sometimes they would bet with their companions' money. Gambling did not seem to be an important activity with them.

The movies, particularly those movie houses that are open in the early hours of the morning, were a great attraction for the girls. A number of the girls were theatre enthusiasts and went to the hit plays, frequently in the company of good customers. Since many of them knew men who were interested in sports, they frequently went to important prize-fighting events, in addition to the horse races mentioned previously. Their work took many of them into night clubs, but they usually found the night-club shows boring.

V ALIENATION AS DEVIATION

11 FORMS OF ALIENATIVE BEHAVIOR

If there is a "sickness unto death" in modern industrial existence, it is quite likely that this sickness is alienation. Under one label or another —detached, estranged, isolated, apathetic, anomic, powerless, retreatist —the concept of alienation intrudes into all of the social sciences and into the consciousness of many of us. And, indeed, in the reorganization of the traditional family system and the community there is reason enough for the concern with alienation. Modern technology detached many from control over their work destinies. Urbanization and mass society detached them from their institutional ties. Primary group breakdown detached them from themselves. Material affluence seems to have detached some from all that was left.

This chapter is concerned only with deviant modes of coping with alienation and not with the condition itself. There are other and nondeviant responses to conditions of anomie in society and its personal equivalent of alienation. Contrast the hippie movements, for example, with the activism of students in recent protest and political movements that are neither deviant nor retreatist. It is only those responses that are purely escapist and passive, and wholly reject the social order, without seeking to modify or improve it in any sense, which concern us in this section. These deviant methods of coping with alienation range from bohemianism (beatniks), especially its most recent hippie variant, political "turncoatism," to the retreat to skid row, and to the ultimate of suicide. There are numerous other retreatist variants, such as doomsday and other religious cults, which will not be treated here, which represent equally good illustrations of the problem of alienation and deviant behavior.

The hippie movement, which some of its ideologues and spokesmen publicly buried in a three-day ceremony in San Francisco in the autumn of 1967, is the subject matter of the first selection. The hippie movement has been widely dissected by the mass media, but June Bingham's "The Intelligent Square's Guide to Hippieland" is an especially incisive analysis of some of the major underlying values and assumptions. As everyone knows, middle-class rebels—with or without cause—tend to "act in" while lower-class rebellion more frequently involves "acting out." The hippie "acts in." He seeks to privatize his life, to expand his inner world, to accept passively and hence dominate reality, and to be spontaneous and genuine. Nonviolent, nonaggressive, nonmaterially oriented, he rejects just about every major middle-class virtue. Little wonder that the hippie movement and the "do your own thing" philosophy has aroused such passionate concern and ambivalence. The passive rejection and withdrawal from reality are antithetical to our dominant "progress" and competitive value orientation, and as such are viewed with alarm, distrust, and fear. By his use of LSD and marihuana, the hippie does little to lower the societal intolerance shown the movement and its participants.

It is one thing to reject material values and blatant hypocrisies and another to renounce life in the United States for life in an "enemy" nation. "Turncoatism" is probably the most serious form of alienation in secular society—roughly equivalent to apostasy in religious life. The war in Viet Nam—a conflict with perhaps even less public support than the Korean war—has led to renewed interest in matters of conscience, loyalty and alienation.

On January 23, 1954, twenty-one American youths, all but one brought up in small towns and rural communities, educated in American schools, all trained in the United States Army, turned their backs on their families, friends, and country to accept the way of life of the Chinese Communists who had held them in Korean prison camps for three years or more. While the country has had its Benedict Arnolds, never before had a group of American prisoners of war chosen to remain with their captors. This collective heresy became an important element in a continuing discussion about the nature of patriotism and the steps requisite for the protection of American ideologies. "Brainwashing" and "turncoat" came into the language.

The Korean war was, in many respects, a curious war. Officially it was not a war, but a police action. While it was a war that ended in a stalemate, it was one that for much of its duration proceeded simultaneously with truce negotiations. Much of the negotiations centered on the question of prisoners of war and their repatriation. In July 1953 an armistice was signed and, in August and September—3629 American prisoners were repatriated—but twenty-three announced they would stay. There was a final period of 120 days when such prisoners had an opportunity to change their minds. Two did come back, but when the final deadline came there were still twenty-one American prisoners of war who decided to stay with the Communists.

Many of those who returned had spent almost three years in imprisonment. During this extended period, the American press focused a great deal of attention on these prisoners. Besides stories of atrocities and brainwashing, there were reports of misconduct and collaboration among American prisoners.

In particular, misconduct and collaboration were underscored by widely publicized trials which led to the conviction of eleven former prisoners. Since many of the accusations concerning prisoner misconduct were made prior to repatriation, the army set up interrogation teams to seek information from returning prisoners. There was rather strong evidence that the twenty-one who chose to remain behind in China did so because they feared that punishment awaited them if they were repatriated. All of those who refused to be repatriated had been accused by other prisoners of collaborating in some way with the enemy.

Those who chose to stay were given the label of "turncoats" and there were many attempts to try to understand what was to many the greatest heresy of all: voluntarily rejecting one's country and its ideology. The article "Twenty-One G.I.'s Who Chose Tyranny" presents a social profile of the defectors and probes the reasons why these twenty-one remained. While fear of punishment may have been an important factor, almost all of the twenty-one were "outsiders" in their backgrounds, marginal to the dominant themes of American culture. As such, alienation is a descriptive concept for the experiences of these men throughout their lives.

There is a footnote which should be added. In the ensuing years, nineteen of the twenty-one have returned to the United States. Otho Bell, mentioned in the article, was one of the first to return. Since the returnees are now civilians, they could not be prosecuted under military law. And the Department of Justice has felt that civilian trial is impractical since the years have dimmed the memory of prospective witnesses concerning events about which they would be called upon to testify. The punishment for their heresy has been the years of exile, based on fear.

In an excellent contribution "Careers on Skid Row," Professor Samuel Wallace is concerned with what might best be termed the culture and social organization of skid row. Like other communities, skid row has a status hierarchy. Men are socialized to live in this deviant subculture, to accept its norms, and to understand its nuances. Living on skid row, as Professor Wallace so nicely puts it, is the culmination of "working one's way downhill." In addition to the drunk and the alcoholic, skid row sub-types include the hobo, tramp, and bum, the professional beggar, the physically handicapped, the tour directors, and the mission stiffs. The American hobohemias, though to some extent victims of technological progress and urban renewal, remain a fascinating backwater of marginal and homeless men all of whom, in common, live for their drinking. The inhabitants of skid row well illustrate the alcohol abuse problem. They also illustrate the fifth type of deviancy, alienation, or the rejection of the norms of the larger society.

Suicide is on the extreme end of the alienation continuum. There is here a finality and irreversibility which are unique. For these and other reasons, suicide has been an area of continuing interest and concern to sociologists. Durkheim, whose ideas constitute the basic theoretical framework, viewed suicide in relation to social integration and cohesion. He identified three specific types of suicide—altruistic, egoistic, and anomic. The first two are by-products of too much and too little integration. The third—anomic—is associated with sudden shifts in the social structure and the consequent breakdown in the regulatory mechanisms in society. Menninger, reflecting a psychiatric orientation, speaks of suicide as a symbolic act involving the wish to kill, to be killed, and to die. Regardless of theoretical persuasion, nearly all who deal with attempted suicide are aware that feelings of despair and isolation and futility are common in persons attempting and completing suicide.

In the final article in this section, "A Phenomenological Study of Suicide Notes," Professor Jacobs presents an interesting analysis of suicide in the Los Angeles area, based on 112 suicide notes. Suicide is seen from the point of view of the actor, and a reconstruction presented on how he must have felt and how he succeeded in overcoming the social restraints to suicide. The focus is on the process of becoming a suicide. Several different types of notes are examined, ranging from what the author calls "first form" notes to those of a residual nature. These notes can hardly fail to move the reader. There are few better illustrations of alienation than the closing suicide note in this selection. Hung on the dashboard of a car was this two-sentence conclusion to a life: "Please do not disturb. Someone sleeping."

THE INTELLIGENT SQUARE'S GUIDE
TO HIPPIELAND
June Bingham

No generation, it is said, can predict the weapons that the next one will use against it. Surely few Americans who grew up during the Depression and struggled to win middle- or upper-middle-class privileges for their family would have dreamed that, by 1967, some of their most gifted sons and daughters would purposely be hurrying from riches to rags.

From *The New York Times Magazine*, September 24, 1967, pp. 25, 68-84.
Copyright © 1967 by The New York Times Company. Reprinted by permission.

Today, these visible, audible and sometimes smellable young rebels are loosely called hippies. Constituting a tiny minority, they are mostly white, carefully nurtured and educated beyond the average; some were former leaders of their class in school. Their young Negro counterpart is trying to achieve, rather than "drop out" of, higher education and professional status; or, if he is trapped in the slums, he may turn to addictive drugs, such as heroin, which are scorned by the hippies, or to violence, which is abhorred by them.

Within the hippie subculture—mostly urban—not all are intelligent and promising. Some are mentally ill or not very bright; some are merely unformed and seduced by the gross simplifications and absolute certainties that seem to result from even a rare use of LSD or a heavy use of marihuana. Mental hospitals throughout the United States report a startling drop in admissions of the two kinds of schizophrenics whose symptoms are similar to those of someone on an LSD trip: the young inappropriately laughing hebephrenics and frozenly posturing catatonics have gone to live among the hippies who tolerate them, thus discouraging their seeking psychiatric treatment.

But partly because many hippies are imaginative, articulate and artistic, their world-view has spread to the far larger number of their well-shod and well-shorn contemporaries, especially to those appalled by the American involvement in Vietnam. Hippiedom, in one sense, is part of the Vietnam fallout.

But this is not all that it is. For there are hippies in England and Canada, Denmark and France, countries not involved in Vietnam or in the credibility gap.

The hippies are in rebellion also against nuclear fission, automation, and bigness in industry, labor and government—in sum, against everything that diminishes the importance of the individual. Their slogan is, "I am a human being: Do not fold, spindle or mutilate." And their value system is the mirror-opposite of the middle-class or square system (while the hippie terms himself a "human being," he terms the square "subhuman" or "humanoid").

If one imagines the questions that a suburban father would ask of a future son-in-law, about family background and religious affiliation, academic degrees and career prospects, previous record and future plans, the hippies would say that None of These Matter (they always seem to talk in capital letters). What matters, they say, is not what a person *does* but what he is, not outer forms or "games," but "Being At One With Yourself."

The hippie phenomenon, once thought to be only a passing phase, is probably more dangerous to its conforming nonconformists than to society as a whole. For the hippie minority, though revolutionary, is neither subversive nor violent. There has been a recent divorce between the hippies and the New Left. While the hippies reject the capitalist emphasis on "mine," whether my house, my money, my gadgets, my child or my work of art, they also reject the Communist practice of job assignment and restriction of the arts and individual freedom. The love-ins, while sometimes unattractive, are an improvement over the deafening silence of the "cool" young of the McCarthy period, or the destructiveness of some beatniks, beats and hipsters, those immediate predecessors of the hippies. There is no hippie leader like Norman Mailer, who tried to link the hipster to Black Power.

The squares who wish to alert a hippie—or demihippie—to the hidden dangers to which he is exposed will find disgust less helpful than an attempt to understand the hippie "transvaluation of values." Though the hippies' positive program comprises little that is new or practical, their negative strictures may well be a judgment upon the squares' value system.

There is nothing new, for instance, in the hippies' privatism (the solipsists long ago took it to the end of the line), nor in their hedonism (ancient Greece coined the word for it), nor in the reversion to the Natural (Rousseau promoted the "Noble Savage" whether with hair on his face, like the hippie boys, or under the arms, like the hippie girls). Similarly, there is nothing new in the hippies' passivity and pipe dreaming (hashish—a stronger variety of pot—has been used for millennia).

The following hippie judgments, however, are worth square consideration:

> At a time when sexual excitement by way of the media has reached laughable, if not obscene, proportions, these boys and girls in identical tight pants and shoulder-length hair are signaling that the male and female secondary sexual characteristics are not that important; their form of address for one another is "Man."

> At a time when racial antagonisms erupt on the street, these boys and girls appear relaxedly integrated. The problems of poverty and the ghetto—together with those of leisure—are no problems to the hippies who embrace all three. In their own sections of cities there is little serious crime and no prostitution.

> At a time when national and ideological rivalry may lead to nuclear apocalypse, the hippies preach, "Make love, not war," and refuse to offer themselves for service to their country if this means that they may have to kill or be killed.

> At a time when Organization Man and his wife have been clutching material possessions not only for health and comfort but for prestige and a kind of security, the hippies share their food, their pad, their guitars, and such cash as they earn or are given. They would agree with Joseph Wood

Krutch that true security depends upon how much one can do *without*, and they are proud of their own instantaneous mobility. Some move onto the land in small rural kibbutzlike settlements reminiscent of Brook Farm and other 19th-century idealistic experiments. Their guru, Allen Ginsberg, notes that the only technologically complicated item they wish to own is a stereo phonograph.

At a time when some churches have been exposed as slumlords and some church membership stems from other than religious reasons, the hippies stretch for spiritual meaning beyond the Judeo-Christian tradition. This has led some to study Hinduism and Buddhism, ancient philosophies too long spurned by the West.

At a time when planning—by government, by business, by individuals—is still highly touted, the hippies do not bother to turn the leaves of the calendar, or look at their watches (if they own any), or read or listen to the news. They wish to live by whim, by spontaneity, by the non-rules of Now. They are not interested in what someone else has said is right or has planned for them. If they feel in the mood they will neglect all appointments to marvel at the sight of an onion: intricacy and beauty enclosing the purity of the Void. In reacting against pressures of home and school that may have started in kindergarten, many are taking what Erik Erikson has called a "psychological moratorium." Said a male 26-year-old demi-hippie: "We don't know what we'll be when we're 40; we'll have to wait and see."

At a time when Hidden Persuaders, when politics and advertising are frankly based on image-making, on fooling as many of the people as much of the time as possible, the hippies cry, "Hypocrisy!" As for the politeness and self-restraint that grease the social, as well as business and political, wheels, the hippies prefer discussion of Birth and Death, Creation and Destruction, to small talk. Say the Diggers, a leading subgroup in San Francisco's Haight-Asbury section, " 'Normal' citizens with store-dummy smiles stand apart from each other like cotton-packed capsules in bottles."

At a time when the American divorce rate is one out of four marriages (in California, one out of two), the hippies point to square hypocrisy in the sphere of sex. Many adults who have preached virginity before marriage and fidelity after it have practiced neither, the hippies say, and many who have practiced these have done so out of fear rather than love—out of, if you will, a form of biological capitalism.

Says a girl hippie: "What's the big deal when a girl hoards a bit of skin just so she can exchange it for a gold ring or a ranch house in the suburbs?"

Says a boy: "In the days before the Pill, people made a virtue of necessity and praised virginity; well the necessity is gone."

A physical factor in this new equation, in addition to the Pill, is that the average age for the onset of menstruation is 12, whereas a hundred years ago it was 17; while our female forebears—who usually married young—had only a year or two between menstruation and marriage, a girl today may have, because of the length and expense of education, more than a decade.

At a time when the "nuclear family," just two parents and their children, often must, because of the father's job, move away from grandparents, uncles and aunts and cousins, the hippies have established a form of the "extended family" in their pads. Unwittingly they may dilute the intensity of Oedipal conflicts that once were lessened by buffers such as relatives and, you should excuse the expression, servants. This would be "unwittingly," because most hippies, in their sentimental or drug-flattened view of human nature, deny that there is such a thing as primal aggression and possessiveness. They choose to think of the child as born "beautiful" and they blame any subsequent destructive behavior on the society or the parents that warped him (this view includes Hitler).

Their intention, therefore, cannot be to dilute what they deny exists, a denial that persists despite the rather stunning evidence to the contrary provided by the Bible and Sophocles, Shakespeare and Freud, by the ethologists who have added "territoriality" as a newly observed category of the power drive, and by lovingly nurtured 2-year-olds themselves.

At a time when many squares assume that there has been no historic mutation, that nuclear warheads differ merely in quantity, but not in quality, from the fire raids of World War II, the hippies insist on historic discontinuity. They believe both in the infinite plasticity of human nature and also in themselves as "a new kind of human being."

In a limited sense perhaps they are right, since theirs is the first post-nuclear generation: their impressionable earliest years were spent with parents who, for the first time, had to face the fact that the future of human civilization and of all life on earth had been thrown into question.

Underneath the hippie refusal to sacrifice the present on the altar of the future is often a black despair which is sometimes relieved and sometimes accentuated by the drugs they take. Basically they seem to be saying that only what they have already enjoyed cannot be taken from them. Perhaps, indeed, a hippie who faces up to the depth of his despair is more realistic than the square who blocks it out, who meticulously plans his life as if his personal future and that of mankind were any longer more than a good bet. In a time of rapid change, the radical may turn out to be more solidly grounded than the stand-patter.

The hippies are hipped on the value of the individual and the disvalue of the state. Thoreau is one of their gods. They speak, therefore, less about some crazy state in the future causing the annihilation of the world than of the crazy individual who caused the annihilation of one man, a President in his prime (it was less Kennedy's program than his style that appealed to them).

Their philosophy of "eat, drink and be merry, for tomorrow we die" is not irrational if, in fact, tomorrow we all do die. It is uncreative, however, if we and they do not die—if, in fact, as seems to be the prospect, we live even beyond the age when we can contribute to our society or enjoy ourselves.

The questions raised by the hippies are thus often profound ones; but their solutions, being neither well-thought-out nor realistic, are of value mostly when they raise other questions. Their greatest contribution may turn out to be "set-breaking," the "put-on," which, though initiated by the "mind-expanding" drugs, can be followed without these. Primarily this involves an exploding of old mental associations, such as, "Love leads to marriage; marriage lead to children." Why? What if they don't? Certainly in some hippie pads—though not in all—sex has been broken out from the old privacy, the old heterosexual one-to-one, the old erogenous zones.

What will the hippie experimentation lead to? No one, psychiatrist or layman, can say for sure. The old and middle-aged take the dimmest of views. Often the demisquare young, like the psychiatrists, say let's wait and see; neither wishes to be caught voicing an automatic disapproval of something yet unproved.

The chief—and by now fairly well-proved—danger to the hippies comes from LSD. The person who takes it as rarely as once or twice, in moderate dosages, may have suffered a chromosome "breakage" comparable to that caused by radiation and perhaps equally inexpungeable. In the East Village, New York City's "Hashbury," there has been for sale, among other psychedelia, a campaign button with a one-word slogan, "Mutate." If the mutated babies of today's acidheads, babies reminiscent of the deformed creatures produced in Hiroshima and Nagasaki after 1945, begin appearing in sizable numbers, the irony will be almost unbearable: that the very people who most fear and hate the nuclear bomb should be the ones to perpetuate one of its direct by-products.

Many a hippie, as a result of learning about the chromosomes breakage, has renounced LSD. But some continue taking large doses of marihuana, which has been found to reactivate the effects of LSD previously ingested. LSD, like malaria, can remain in the bloodstream or the brain (no one yet knows where) and after a week or a month (the longest period on record is two years)—with or without pot—can cause a freakout. This may happen without warning, as when a person is driving a car, and in parts of the U.S. acidheads are having their driver's licenses revoked. Dr. Dana Farnsworth of Harvard suggests that no one make any major decision for three months after an LSD trip.

Another danger from LSD or heavy use of pot is that its host may become a psychological Typhoid Mary, spreading infection through word and example to the tender young. Says Dr. Woodrow W. Burgess, a psychiatrist at the University of California at Davis, these hippies "are untreatable because they are so subjectively convinced of a better way of living."

Their subjective conviction is so unshakable ("I know more about me than those doctors do") that some of them, consciously or unconsciously are self-appointed missionaries for their "better way" of living. Their negative bait to the adolescent is "Don't be chicken," their positive bait is, "LSD is the only way really to find yourself."

An adult who, for better or worse, has "found himself" sufficiently to know the areas wherein he is, and is not, chicken, may not be seriously tempted. But the adventurous young person naturally is tempted. No one, particularly when young, enjoys missing out on something good, even though, or especially because, it involves a mild amount of danger. The psychedelic "pusher"—not motivated by money like the narcotics pusher, but still "a clear and present danger" to those younger than himself—must be kept from long unchaperoned periods with baby-sittees or smaller siblings, lest he do them the "favor" of starting them at least on pot (hard-core hippies, such as Timothy Leary, give their own children LSD).

Certainly, to "find oneself" is a lofty—and ancient—goal. Unfortunately, however, it seems to involve arduous effort over an extended period of time. It can be done, but not on an "add water and mix" basis. The Lord Buddha, who left his affluent home 2,500 years ago to wander barefoot and long-haired in search of the answer to human suffering, spent 14 years in rigorous meditation before attaining the state of mind-expansion he called Nirvana and that others have termed "the peace that passeth understanding."

The Lord Buddha, also in contrast to the hippie, was tolerant of all kinds of people, princes as well as paupers, old as well as young, from every caste and no-caste; he did not consider the squares as untouchable, nor did he recline all day watching colorama behind his eyelids; he constantly checked his ideas against reality ("The chief advantage of the uninterrupted daydream," says Dr. Fritz Redlich, dean of the Yale Medical School, "is its absence of risk.")

While LSD can shake people loose from old rigidities, and has some value as a psychotherapeutic tool, the "instant psychoanalysis" that some hippies claim for it appears to be mainly a reduction of physical aggression. Unfortunately there is no comparable reduction of verbal aggression (Leary's speeches are rife with it). The hippie who claims to have "found himself" has thus found only a part of himself, a part he wishes to find. While the hippie validly condemns some conscious hypocrisies of the squares, he often expresses unconscious hypocrisies or rationalizations that are damaging to other people—and ultimately to himself.

These rationalizations of the hippie may derive from carrying over into consciousness the both-and (as against either-or) thinking that is typical of the unconscious. In dreams we can all be both child and adult simultaneously, but in reality *either* we must prepare ourselves in youth for a career *or* we find ourselves unprepared in middle age. (The hippie answer: "It does not matter if an artist never produces a work of art, as long as he sees with the eyes of an artist." The hippie thus spares himself the need to choose one art form and master it.)

These rationalizations of his may derive from his preference for subjective feeling as against objective evidence ("There is no such a thing as objective truth"). Science, of course, is disparaged ("The truth has never been found under the microscope"), and so is cause-and-effect reasoning when inconvenient (a hippie may reject the advice of a doctor who himself has not taken LSD, but accept, in time of pregnancy, the advice of a male obstetrician, who has obviously not given birth).

These rationalizations of the hippie may derive from his paucity of mental furniture. Though bright, he is likely to be a drop-out who has studied little, and that little confined mostly to the recent past.

Society, moreover, is a subject he knows even less about than he does about the individual. For example, more than 30 years ago Reinhold Niebuhr showed that, while the individual can hold self-sacrificial love, *agape,* as his highest goal (and may indeed sacrifice himself for a national aim such as democracy), a state, because of its internal dynamics and the built-in responsibilities of its leaders, cannot. Sometimes, indeed, the very idealism and selflessness with which the citizen devotes himself to his society becomes a power factor in the injustice perpetrated by this society on other societies. The highest goal for international affairs, therefore, cannot be love, but justice, and the idealists who refuse to face the difference between "Moral Man and Immoral Society" may muddy the issues and thus perhaps abet the forces of ruthlessness.

Admittedly terrible as are some aspects of the current American scene, the anthill society of China is no improvement. And when even a small section of America's greatest natural resource—namely, her young people—absent themselves from social responsibility, one is reminded that ancient Rome fell less because of the hammering outside the gate than of the listlessness within.

The hippie, however, cares little for history or for Santayana's dictum that those who do not study history are doomed to repeat it. "Who cares what those old writers had to say?" He refuses to admit that patterns may exist in history, just as he refuses to admit that patterns may exist in hippie behavior. He views himself as freely choosing each step he takes, while to the outsider he appears to be riding an escalator in a clump with his peer group. A hippie on a "high" will paint a picture he is certain is original; a psychiatrist can spot it at once as drug-influenced: It has no integral unity, merely repetitive motifs embellished with tiny— and often merry—detail.

All in all, the hippie, despite his high potential, often ends up with less self-knowledge than his square contemporary. Trying directly to "find oneself" seems paradoxically less effective than first becoming the kind of person upon whom others can rely and then learning existentially from this revealing experience.

The hippie honestly believes that he is practicing Love, but if you shut your eyes while he discusses suburbanites, you would think he was a bigoted white talking about Negroes.

The hippie honestly believes that he is achieving Freedom, but in fact he is slamming doors on himself, now as in the future. Because he operates on whim ("if it feels good, I'll do it,") he cannot be relied on in momentous times such as birth or death, family celebrations or crises. While dropping out he may have made himself worth dropping, by the very people who are nearest, if not dearest, to him.

The hippie honestly believes that he is honest. *He* has nothing to hide —nothing, that is, except the curved knife that he refuses to admit generically rests in the human hand. When the person the hippie cuts by way of his "honesty" cries out in pain, the hippie's first reaction is genuine surprise. His second is, "Well, that's your problem." Since, as he believes, there was, in his own purity, no wish to hurt, then the victim must surely be at fault, must have some hidden weakness that he would do well to explore.

And if the victim, in his freedom, has no wish thus to explore? Then the hippie may turn visibly hostile: "You are jealous, you wish you could live the way I do." If the older person responds that his concern is not about his own life at the moment but about the hippie's, the pat answer is that older people often use their worry as a means of subjugating the young. For the hippie, therefore, to avoid hurting his elders would be an unthinkable caving-in to pressure, a loss of his own integrity.

A clear difference between the hippies of today and their parents-when-young is that the parents handled their not so uncolorful rebellion discreetly and in the fear, if not of God, then of their parents. The hippies, on the other hand, through their ambivalent behavior—pregnancies out of wedlock, diaries left open to shocking pages—or their unambivalent appearance, trumpet their rebellion and thus challenge their parents, if not God, to smite them down.

A clear difference between the parents of today and their parents is the reluctance to smite the young down. Rarely is the cry "Never darken my doorstep" heard in the land; infrequently are the old expletives "impertinence" or "insolence" dusted off.

Instead, many concerned squares, either to keep open the paths of communication, or to help their almost-grown child, under whose truculence they think they hear a muted cry for help, or simply in the generic American willingness to admit that oneself may have goofed, are making the supreme effort to dissolve their own crystallized hierarchy of values into liquidity again. Is it possible, these parents ask themselves (or their spouse), that their dismay at their hippie is, in part, based on their own fear of loss of job, or of respect by their neighbors, or of approval by relatives?

In any event, some men and women in their 40's and 50's are putting themselves through, for a second time, the anxieties, even the agonies, of what is now called the "identity crisis"—it used to be called "growing pains." (One frantic parent in an attempt to save a hard-core hippie's marriage took LSD with the couple; the marriage did not survive, and the parent barely so.)

While the lucky parents can dissolve their value-system and re-establish one that does not make their whole past life seem futile, the unlucky ones may look back on the various crossroads of life and think, too late, that they took the wrong turn. The young person, through his unintentionally cruel questioning, may be toppling Humpty Dumpty at a time in life when all the king's horses and all the psychiatrists cannot put Humpty Dumpty together again.

Those now over 40 were often burdened by their late-Victorian and pre-Freudian parents with a harsh conscience, a tendency to overblame themselves. They are sandwiched between a generation that questioned too little and a generation that questions too much. They themselves never had the white meat of the turkey. When they were children, the best parts were saved, as a matter of course, for the adults; by the time they grew up, the best parts were being saved, as a matter of course, for the children.

Having been children in an adult-centered world, they are now adults in a child-centered world. And how do they react to finding themselves in this historic tide rip of values? By feeling guilty. . . .

TWENTY-ONE G.I.'S WHO CHOSE TYRANNY: WHY THEY LEFT US FOR COMMUNISM

Harold Lavine

There were twenty-one who stayed behind, twenty-one GI's, captives of the Reds, who chose to remain with the Reds rather than come home. They were only a handful compared with the 3,746 who did return; and no doubt many Americans have already washed their minds of them, saying "Good riddance." Others, however, cannot forget them so readily. In the American doxology, this is "God's country" and the best way of life is "the American way of life." What made the twenty-one desert Mom's apple pie and the right to heckle the umpire, for Communist slavery? What made them prefer the regimentation and poverty of the Communist state to the blessings of General Motors and democracy? . . .

Nearly all the twenty-one were captured very early in the war. They had spent about three years in prison when the cease-fire finally was declared. Since they had, therefore, been subjected to a great deal more Communist propaganda over many more months than most of the other PW's, could the reason they chose tyranny be that new, horrendous word, "brainwashing"? Even if the answer were yes, it wouldn't mean much. For scores of the PW's who never hesitated a moment when offered the opportunity to return home were far more deeply indoctrinated with Communism than any of the twenty-one. The army believes that at least 200 who returned are "Progs," just like the twenty-one, and that a few may even be Communists. One of the worst "Progs" in the prison camps, in fact, was Corporal Claude Batchelor, who had at first decided to stay with the Communists and then changed his mind at the urging of his Japanese wife, the army says. He now faces a court-martial.

After the Defense Department released the names, home towns, and next of kin of the twenty-one, the rumors and the speculation started: they were homosexuals, drunks, dope-addicts; they had committed such terrible crimes in civilian life that they were afraid to come home; they had committed equally terrible crimes in the PW camps. Some commentators blamed the American educational system for their decision: the twenty-one were the inevitable product of a school system rotten with left-wing ideology, these commentators said. Others were certain that if

From *Commentary*, Vol. XVIII (July 1954), 41-46. Reprinted by permission.

the twenty-one had been subjected to religious training, they never would have succumbed to Communist propaganda; Christianity would have insulated them against Communism.

There is some supporting evidence for the rumors—but not much. There is absolutely no evidence that any of the twenty-one was a homosexual before his capture; but the Indians who guarded the prison compounds do say that at least three, and possibly more, appear to have become overt homosexuals in captivity. One did have a record of juvenile delinquency in civilian life, but he never had been considered a criminal. Several were listed as "Rats" by other PW's, but scores of the PW's who rejected Communism had far worse records in the prison camps. Only one of the twenty-one seems to have come across any left-wing propaganda in civilian life. And the vast majority not only had had religious teaching, they were practicing Protestants and Catholics; a few had seemed exceptionally devout to all who knew them; and one remained devout even after embracing Communism.

Were the twenty-one just sports, each completely different from the other? Or did they have some characteristics in common? Is there an identifiable type of American who not only can be captured by Communist propaganda but who can be persuaded to renounce his country and himself?

To repeat, the questions aren't easy to answer; the facile answers do not fit the facts, and what is more, we still don't know all the facts and probably never will. However, we now do have some interesting clues.

Perhaps the most striking statistical fact about the twenty-one is that eighteen of them were Regular Army men. The overwhelming majority of those who fought in Korea were Selective Service soldiers and Reservists. Yet the overwhelming majority of the men who stayed behind were men who looked on the army as a career. Most were fairly young when they joined up—seventeen or eighteen; several enlisted at sixteen, when they were legally under age. Their average age when they rejected democracy for Communism was twenty-three.

Nearly all came from families that by American standards were poor. Fourteen came from broken homes; their parents were dead, divorced, or separated. Two had attended college; ten had attended high school, but only three of these had graduated.

Three were married. None was engaged.

These are the bare statistics and in some ways they are revealing enough. The fact that eighteen of the twenty-one were Regular Army, for example, cannot be without significance; nor can the fact that fourteen of the twenty-one came from broken homes. However, we have other clues. In the months since the twenty-one renounced home and country, we have learned something about their lives.

Most of what we know about Sergeant Andrew Fortuna, twenty-seven, of Detroit, we learned from his half-brother Donald, twenty-two, a four-time loser, now in jail for "assault with intent to rob while armed." Don obviously loves and admires Andy; he considers Andy's fate far worse than his own. "When I heard about Andy wanting to stay over there, it was just like a wall had fallen on me," says Don.

"Andy and I had a rough life; from my very first memory, we had a hard way to go, but he's the guy who overcame it. He was a normal kid, well-liked, a hard worker and capable. He tried to hold our family together. He was more mature than most kids, and he was a good soldier. He isn't like me at all."

Andy is illegitimate. His mother was a Kentucky farm girl who brought him to Detroit in 1929; there she married an Italian auto worker. His stepfather gave Andy his name. Mrs. Fortuna subsequently had two children by her husband, Don and a daughter, Viola.

The 30's were tough years in Detroit. The elder Fortuna frequently was unemployed. Mrs. Fortuna became an alcoholic, who "wandered away for weeks or months at a time." The last time Don saw her she was sitting in a Michigan Avenue skid-row saloon. "When she was home Mom never was mean to us," Don says. "She never beat us or anything." The elder Fortuna finally got sick and tired of his wife and divorced her.

Don adds: "Andy was about four years older than me. He used to make Viola and me sandwiches and take care of us until Dad came home from work."

Andy received good grades in school, Don recalls, "and he was very popular. If I got run out by a bunch of kids, Andy would take care of it. He wasn't a tough kid, but he could take care of himself. We never had much money, and Andy would figure out ways of getting the things we wanted, such as a new pair of pants or a cap gun. We'd collect pop bottles and do odd jobs."

Andy quit school in the eighth grade and got a job as a grocery clerk. Later, he went to work with a construction crew. In 1943 he joined the army. He fought in the European campaign, re-enlisted after V-E Day, and was discharged in 1947. He went to work operating a bulldozer, making between $80 and $85 a week. He shared his money with his stepfather and every week he took Viola shopping and bought her "a dress or something."

In 1948, he rejoined the army and went to Japan, where he married a Japanese girl. They had a child, who died of polio.

While overseas, Andy wrote Don that he was thinking of quitting the army when he finished his new hitch; he wanted to start a small contracting business. Early in the war he wrote: "We're going to push the Communists back where they belong." The first indication Don had that his attitudes had changed was in March 1953, when he wrote from a PW camp: "There are American people who don't understand what the Korean war is all about." Don is baffled. Andy was such a swell guy, and a good Catholic too.

Andy's story isn't typical. No one's story is ever quite like anyone else's. And yet, there are elements in Andy's story that we find, say, in Corporal Aaron Phillip Wilson's.

Aaron Wilson is twenty-one. He comes from the sawmill town of Urania, deep in the piney woods of north-central Louisiana. Urania is little more than a large clearing in the forest, a rude, unprepossessing settlement of tin-roofed shacks.

The Wilsons are devout members of the Pine Hill Baptist Church. The walls of their home are covered with religious symbols, and Aaron's mother, Mrs. Henry Wilson, still proudly recalls that he never missed a Sunday at church. "He liked to dress up in his Sunday best and go to prayer meeting," she says wistfully.

Mrs. Wilson also says that Aaron was a "tender-hearted, humble boy, who never did give nobody no trouble." Aaron's boyhood chums and neighbors say he was a docile, easily led youngster "who would take a lot of lip without getting his dander up."

Says his sister Myrtle, who is passionately devoted to him: "Bud [her nickname for Aaron] was a big hand to play. He liked nothing better than to beat on the old git-tar, and he listened to phonograph records right smart. Bud never had a care in the world. He never was troublesome or got out of hand. He was always one to tag along with the crowd. I guess you might say he was a born follower."

The Wilsons were indulgent parents. Mrs. Wilson, who refers to Aaron as "Sonny," declares: "We never punished him. Fact is, we never laid a hand on him since he was twelve." And Henry Wilson, a simple, direct man of fifty, with a gaunt face and thinning hair, neatly combed, adds: "I wanted him to have it easy. Sometimes he washed and polished cars on Saturdays so he could have some pin money. That's about all the work he did. I never objected to his piddlin' around, hoping he would get an education and then amount to something. I only went to the Fifth Reader myself, and I knowed what a powerful drawback that can be."

Aaron wasn't much of a student, however. He advanced in school so slowly that pretty soon Myrtle, though two years younger, was in the same class. Myrtle became his protector. "I always took up for him because he'd never take up for himself," she says. "Once, when the teacher scolded him for reading the blackboard too slow, I jumped out of my seat and told off the teacher. She sent me home for it, but she never fussed at him again."

Myrtle says that Aaron had only a lukewarm interest in girls. "He'd break a lot of dates on any old pretense. He'd never go steady with a girl for more than a few weeks; he'd lose interest."

Aaron quit school in the eighth grade to join the army. He was then just seventeen. He was reported killed in action in Korea in January 1951, but two months later the Wilsons received a letter from him in a Chinese PW camp. His first few letters obviously were written with a Chinese propagandist sitting beside him. In his later letters he spoke with affection of the Communists.

Henry Wilson says: "If I thought my boy didn't come back account of anything I'd done, I'd take a gun and blow my brains out."

Let's take a look now at the story of Private First Class Otho Bell. Otho is twenty-three. He comes from Hillsboro, Mississippi. His mother died in giving birth to him, and Otho has always thought of himself as a murderer. He believes he killed his mother. She was twenty-three when she died, and shortly before he went overseas Otho told his wife that he, too, would die at twenty-three.

Seven months after Otho was born, his father remarried. There are now six other children in the Bell family.

The Bells had a hard life. During the 30's they were sharecroppers. Later they became tenant farmers. They now own their own farm and in the past three years they have been making a little money. However, Otho doesn't know about that. He was already a prisoner of the Reds when the Bells had their first good year.

Otho's father and stepmother are church-going people, but Otho never attended church. He just wasn't interested, and his father didn't believe in forcing him to attend.

Otho was an indifferent student. He wasn't stupid, his teachers say, but he just couldn't learn from books. His teachers liked him. "Nobody could ever get mad at Otho," says his father.

There's one thing his father and stepmother always emphasize when they're discussing Otho: he was easily led. "He was never a leader, but he was a very good follower. If you told him to do something he'd do it."

Otho was in the eighth grade when he quit school to join the army. He was in for three months when he decided that he didn't like it. His father got him discharged as under age.

When he was eighteen he joined up again. While he was stationed at Ft. Lewis, Washington, he married Jewell Olson, the daughter of a farmer and logger. They have a child, a girl, whom Otho has never seen. He was fighting in Korea when she was born.

Jewell remembers this about Otho: she could never make him strike her. One night she made an all-out attempt to provoke him. She taunted him. She said things she doesn't want to repeat. Otho shook. He shook and cried and cried. Then he toppled over. Jewell remembers that.

Jewell says that while Otho was in Korea he wrote her that he was attending chapel regularly, and that he wanted to attend church when he returned. He never wrote about combat, she says; he didn't want to worry her. He never discussed Communism.

"He didn't know what Communism is. If you'd have asked him what he was doing in Korea, he wouldn't have known what to say."

Jewell thinks Otho became a Communist because he likes everybody. Though born a Mississippi sharecropper, she points out, he never had any prejudice against Negroes.

Otho's father thinks he went Communist because the Reds promised him "better food and easier living." Also, he repeats, Otho was "easily influenced."

Each of the twenty-one is quite different from the others. And yet, with only two notable exceptions—Corporal John Roedel Dunn, twenty-five, of Baltimore, and Corporal Larence V. Sullivan, twenty-three, of Omaha, a Negro—they all seem to fit into a pattern.

Private First Class Arlie Pate is twenty-two. He was born in the small coal-mining town of Weaver, Illinois. He comes from a long line of Baptist ministers, although his father isn't one.

His father, Howard Pate, has been an epileptic since Arlie was an infant. The family was on relief before Arlie started grade school. Howard Pate still draws a disabled father's pension from the state and Mrs. Pate gets dependent children's aid for the five youngsters still at home.

Mrs. Pate says that Arlie seemed well liked by most of his classmates but that some of the older boys picked on him because "his clothes were ragged and patched." He never defended himself when they did, because "I always told them [the children] not to kick up any fuss around the house and I guess they never did fight unless they were just pushed into it." In high school Arlie made good grades when he wanted to. However, he wasn't happy in high school, according to his sister Beulah, because "someone always seemed to have it in for him." His attendance became less and less frequent. One day someone broke into his locker and stole a pair of pants and $2. At that, he quit school.

He was sixteen then. He got a job driving a truck in East St. Louis. According to Beulah, he usually came straight home from work and stayed home, "reading or working with some hobby, like building shelves." He didn't care much for girls or for sports, though he did follow the baseball results in the papers.

One of Arlie's fondest memories was a trip he made at fourteen to visit his grandmother and his uncle in Carbondale, Illinois. He enjoyed walking through the rugged, hilly Ozark country and hunting rabbits and squirrels. He liked it because he could walk for hours without meeting a human being. Mrs. Pate says: "He was always begging for us to get a farm down there."

"He was always a good boy and never caused nobody no trouble,"

Mrs. Pate declares. "He was helpful around the house. He never had much to say but was an attentive listener, especially when his uncles were telling war stories. He never raised his voice when he was angry or upset. He just walked out of the house without a word and took a long walk."

Arlie enlisted in the army at seventeen. Six months later he was in Korea. . . .

Corporal John Dunn's father, William, says: "I'm bewildered." And he might well be. It's quite possible to understand why someone like Arlie Pate should prefer Communism to democracy. The same isn't true of Dunn.

The Dunns are the kind of family advertising men dream about. William Dunn is personnel manager for the American Smelting and Refining Company. Mrs. Dunn is office manager of the Quality Products Company, a wholesale grocery firm for which her son John worked, too, before he was drafted. A daughter, Barbara, who is pretty, blue-eyed, blond, and unmarried, lives with them. Their only other child, William Jr., a veteran of the Marine Corps, is unmarried and owns his own home. The Dunns buy a new car every year.

Corporal Dunn was educated in the public schools of Baltimore and at Baltimore City College. He was graduated in the top third of his class in 1948.

Jack, as his family calls him, spent little time in sports. He preferred reading, particularly adventure stories and history. His major outside activity was the Episcopal Church of the Resurrection. He was assistant superintendent of the church school and he took part in other church work.

"He was one of the finest boys I've ever known," says the Reverend Elmer P. Baker. "Most of his life hovered around the church. I wish I had about twenty more like him."

As a child, according to his father, Jack Dunn was happy and obedient. He displayed a strong sense of responsibility toward his younger brother and sister. "Jack always made me and Bill toe the line," says Barbara.

Although Jack was a tractable child, he also displayed strong qualities of leadership, his father declares. He wasn't easily influenced by his associates; he couldn't be pushed around.

"I don't know what happened to him, but I don't believe he's staying with the Communists of his own accord."

Dunn's story is notable precisely because it's so different from those of all the others except Larence Sullivan, who also comes from a stable middle-class family. The rest of the nineteen have so much in common that it's possible to build up a composite portrait of the kind of PW who stayed behind.

His parents are divorced or separated, or else his father is dead. His home, by American standards, was a poor one. He wasn't much of a student in school and hasn't much education. He was "a good boy." He was quiet, tractable, he did what he was told, he conformed.

He was a follower, not a leader. When he got into trouble it was usually because someone with a stronger personality had led him into it. He was like Corporal Lowell D. Skinner, twenty-two, of Akron, Ohio, whose mother says: "He was quiet and old for his years. He always went along with what the others wanted to do. He never caused me worry. I used to lean on him for help with the younger children, because he was so sensible and seemed so grown up."

He didn't particularly like sports. He preferred reading, listening to music, playing an instrument, hiking, hunting, and fishing. (One of the twenty-one went in for spear-fishing.)

His favorite amusements, in other words, were those he could pursue by himself. For he didn't particularly like to mix with other boys. Not that he was shy or anti-social. He just never felt part of a group.

He didn't care much about girls. He dated one every now and then, but only because everyone else was doing it.

He came into the army a child—and a child more ignorant than most. After two or three years in the army and three years in prison camps, home, which had been an unpleasant place at best, became a dim and distant one as well. There was no wife to return to, no child, no girl, and, for him, not really much of a life. He couldn't argue with the Communists; they had all the answers, and he, none at all. Neither school nor society had given him any.

All the twenty-one don't fit exactly into this pattern; Dunn and Sullivan hardly fit at all. Yet nineteen of the twenty-one fit fairly closely. It's no accident that eighteen of the twenty-one were Regular Army and that most of them joined the moment they could, and some even when they were only sixteen. Nor was it only poverty that had driven them into the army. There were many more important things lacking in their lives than money—security, companionship, the feeling of being part of something, a purpose in life. In the GI phrase, they joined the army "to find a home." Most of them did "find a home in the army." Faced with the prospect of going back to the life they had known in the States, they chose Communism, which seemed to offer them the kind of home not unlike the army.

Perhaps we can draw no larger moral from the cases of these twenty-one youths than the familiar one that there are people for whom tyranny meets needs that freedom does not. Some of us will consider it cause for self-congratulation that the number was so few, others will find in these boys a reminder that our society needs to be vigilant lest too many adolescents and young people feel themselves homeless.

SKID ROW

Samuel E. Wallace

Whether or not a man has had a successful career depends upon the standards by which he is judged and who is doing the judging. Commonly, society sets the standards, and a man's career is judged by a community of his peers. This is as true of skid row as it is of any other community. The skid rower is judged by other skid rowers and evaluated according to skid row standards.

It is not easy to become a model skid rower. Nor is every skid rower able or willing to become totally committed to skid row society. For those who stop short of total commitment, skid row society offers alternatives, and the degree to which a skid rower becomes committed to his society is reflected by the particular skid row career which he follows. While one career may carry more status than another when judged by skid row standards, each career is an accepted feature of the skid row way of life.

Skid row is like other communities in that it has a status hierarchy. Unlike other communities, however, the skid row status hierarchy is an inverted one. Since no one wants to claim membership in skid row, "progress" in one's career, quite logically, is a matter of working one's way downhill—departing further and further from what is considered acceptable behavior in the wider community.

En route to homelessness the skid rower becomes socialized, and the more successfully he learns his lessons the more fully he becomes committed to a skid row career. He is partially committed when he goes beyond casual or random involvement with the skid row way of life. At this stage he either has already moved to skid row or developed a regular pattern of contact with it. His habits, the routine of his life, include one or more features of skid row. He may go to mission services. He may frequent skid row bars. He may eat in a favorite skid row hash house. He may hang around certain skid row street corners. His meeting with the skid row subculture can, in other words, no longer be considered minimal, haphazard, or accidental. Nevertheless, at this stage of partial commitment, he will continue to claim to the outside world, to fellow skid rowers, and to himself, that he is a member of a status group recognized in the society at large.

From *Skid Row as a Way of Life* by Samuel E. Wallace, The Bedminster Press, New Jersey, 1965. Reprinted by permission.

If his initial contact with skid row came about while he was a member of the casual labor force, for instance, he will still lay claim to membership in that occupational group. No matter how long it may have been since he was employed, he will still call himself a seaman, migrant worker, harvest hand, fruit picker, or lumberjack. If he first made contact with skid row through a welfare agency, he will continue to describe himself as being retired and will still claim the status of a pensioner. . . . Each one of these self-determined statuses carries with it the important inference that one still belongs, by whatever slim degree, to the world of respectability.

At the point of contact with skid row a man does have a legitimate status in the outside community. At the point of partial commitment he still lays claim to his old status but this is not objectively supported. In the final phase he accepts a status which is totally and completely a part of the subculture and all claim to membership in the outside world is forsaken. At this turning point in the natural history of the skid rower, the scale is tipped in favor of skid row, and the standards by which one is judged are now determined by the members of this deviant community.

To be completely acculturated in skid row subculture is to be a drunk —since skid rowers place strong emphasis on group drinking and the acculturated person is by definition a conformist. The drunk has rejected every single one of society's established values and wholly conformed to the basic values of skid row subculture. Food, shelter, employment, appearance, health, and all other considerations are subordinated by the drunk to the group's need for alcohol. This group constitutes the drunk's total social world and it in turn bestows upon him any status, acceptance, or security he may possess.

It is the conformity to group norms rather than individual pathological cravings which marks the distinction between the skid row drunk and the alcoholic. This distinction, found in several places in the literature, is supported by the relation between drinking patterns and socialization into skid row subculture. A study of 444 men using the shelter facility of New York's Bowery concludes:

> Although pathological drinking is characteristic of a majority of the so-called homeless man population, a substantial portion of these men could not be classified as addictive drinkers . . .
>
> Data in the present report point to an impressive number of homeless men whose routine of living is dominated by the use of alcohol but who show no outward manifestation of addictive traits.

In his article on chronic drunkenness offenders, Earl Rubington of the Center for Alcohol Studies, after discussing the drinking patterns of skid rowers, has this to say:

The pattern of sharing money and drink is perhaps the most conclusive proof that this is not a way of life based upon the personality traits of alcoholics, although confirmed addicts can participate. Respectable alcoholics are more likely to drink alone; chronic offenders drink, for the most part, in a group. . . .

Those transplanted from a former way of life into the isolated all-male society of first the mobile occupations, and then skid row, undoubtedly experience some degree of deprivation and anxiety. Since alcohol is generally acknowledged to be useful in reducing anxiety, a pattern of habitual and ultimately heavy drinking is predictable for the skid rower. Then, too, in the absence of negative sanctions which ordinarily come from family, neighbors, and work associates, there is nothing to prevent heavy drinking from becoming socially acceptable, even desirable, in skid row terms. Neither of these two factors play the same part in the life history of an alcoholic as they do in the making of a skid row drunk.

That heavy drinking is a product of group behavior patterns rather than the result of individual cravings for alcohol has been substantiated in a number of other ways. Practically all drinking on skid row takes place in groups; few men drink alone. One such group, the bottlegang, typically congregates on the street or in hotel lobbies rather than in bars.

During the next half hour the winos drank two more bottles of wine. One commented that they were a good bunch to drink with because they just took normal slugs. They didn't act like they weren't going to get any and hog it all down.

One said that since John bought three bottles, now he was going to buy one. He said he only had a dollar, but he would "reciprocate" the good friendship. He sent Leo off for more. When Leo returned, John said: "What the hell did you get, white wine?"

"What do you care what color it is, it all tastes alike. Wine is wine."

Later, when the drinking slowed down, John said: "Let's move this bottle. No use waiting around."

Charley announced he had taken two friends to the hospital yesterday. He said they had wanted to go to the hospital since they had been drunk for three weeks. So he took them.

"Hey, Joe," another began, "you want to save Stubby's life? He just said on the street a while ago if he didn't have a drink, he'd die."

"Let him die. We won't miss him. You goin' to help him?"

"I gave him a dime for an ale."

The winos systematically killed the fifth of wine. Each would take a swallow and hold it until someone held out a hand for it. They argued about a policeman's salary. While they disagreed with each other, there was no anger.

When the bottle was empty, John said, "Leo, I got some money. I'm gonna git a bottle; here, go git it." They all praised John. He said he had to sober up tomorrow, though, because he had to go to work; he added, "Dammit, Leo, why didn't you work today so we'd have some money? I've spent $100 this week on us." Leo pointed out that he had been too drunk from drinking John's wine to work. John said, "This is the second bottle I bought today. But when I'm with friends I don't care. I'll give you guys the shirt off my back." Leo staggered off and soon returned with another bottle.

The way in which winos organize themselves illustrates the group control over drinking and the pattern of mutual sharing characteristic of skid row subculture.

A bottlegang may be formally organized by a number of individuals who decide to "go in on a bottle." According to James Rooney, currently a Philadelphia skid row researcher, the bottlegang "is similar to a corporate group in that a number of individuals pool their capital for a common goal." The initiator and therefore leader embarks on this venture with at least a dime of his own, asking others on the street if they want to go in on a bottle. The contributors, again to borrow Rooney's phraseology, become stockholders. After sufficient funds have been secured, the leader makes the purchase and the group moves out of sight of the police to begin drinking.

A fairly complex system of norms is built up regarding what is considered appropriate behavior, and punishment is meted out to those who do not "treat" others when they have funds or who attempt to drink more than their share. The time and place of meeting, the amount of alcohol consumed, and the conduct of the drinkers are all controlled by the group. This is the pattern of drinking typically a feature of the subculture. . . .

As the only fully acculturated member of skid row subculture, the drunk—including the various sub-types such as the wino, the lush, and the rubbydub—lives his life totally within the deviant community. He sacrifices everything to the drinking practices and needs of the group. The push of community condemnation and the pull of drinking companions, plus a habituated desire for drinking have combined to structure his life around alcohol—the point at which he has now arrived. In his own eyes as well as in the eyes of others, skid rowers and non-skid rowers alike, he has become a totally committed member of a deviant group. It has taken much more than a physiological craving, a personality type, an occupational history, destitution, and isolation to produce him—the skid row derelict. It has taken years of socialization en route to homelessness and a complex process of career commitment to produce this totally deviant individual. Small wonder that it may take more than conversations with a social worker to reverse the pattern.

If the status of drunk is the essential core of skid row subculture, the small proportion of alcoholics stands just to one side of the center. The life of the alcoholic touches that of the drunk at a number of points: both are arrested, jailed, and incarcerated together; both spend a large amount of time in bars; both must occasionally resort to panhandling to secure drink; and both sacrifice all other needs to those of alcohol.

At several critical points, however, the alcoholic parts company from the drunk. The alcoholic, for one thing, prefers to drink alone. Rarely is he willing to share either his scarce funds or his bottle. Whereas the drunk's aim is to regulate his drinking so that he may maintain a fairly constant level of intoxication at all times—with as few dry spells as possible—the alcoholic seeks to achieve maximum intoxication as quickly as he can. Once he has had his bout, he is willing to rest on his laurels, as it were, content with little or no alcohol for at least a short intermission before starting the cycle all over again.

A further difference already existed between alcoholic and drunk before they came to skid row. The drunk's route to homelessness came about through his world of work. The alcoholic, on the other hand, is more apt to have been drawn from the ranks of the aficionado. This suggests that his former social status was probably higher than the drunk's, that he is likely to have had more education, made or had more money, and enjoyed more of respectable society's advantages, possibly even marriage.

What it all adds up to in terms of comparative skid row status is that the alcoholic loses prestige with the inner circle of drunks by not sharing, and is consequently treated with some contempt by its members. On the other hand, high man on the totem pole though the drunk may be in the skid row hierarchy, the alcoholic because of his superior background is disinclined to identify himself with "the common drunk." The ramifications of the status system appear to be quite as subtle on skid row as anywhere else.

The hobo and his various fraternity brothers occupy the next rung of the status order on today's skid row. Formerly a real distinction existed between the hobo, the tramp, and the bum. "The hobo works and wanders, the tramp dreams and wanders, and the bum drinks and wanders." Today the status of hobo, tramp, or bum has little meaning on skid row as their prototypes have practically disappeared from the scene. Certain types of agricultural workers such as the "fruit-tramp" still exist along the West Coast, but these are exceptions to the general rule. Today's skid rower is not a traveling man of either the worker or nonworker variety. Even in the summer when he sometimes leaves the city for short-term jobs in resort areas, he frequently has to be "encouraged" to go by welfare department personnel who are reluctant to give relief if jobs are available. When the hobo was strong in number, skid row was sometimes called by a name derived from him—hobohemia. Today both the hobo and the term hobohemia have been practically forgotten. . . .

Professional beggars are a distinct and fascinating type within the skid row community. Beggars are indeed professionals, complete with a long history and tradition. In a small book edited by Martin Luther and published in 1528, some thirty different classes of beggars and their typical backgrounds are described. Advice to the reader varies from the admonition to "give them all thou canst," to "give them a kick on their hind parts if thou canst, for they are nought but cheats."

It is interesting to note that not only are beggars still with us but so is the four hundred year old controversy regarding their "take home pay." That begging was once apparently both popular and lucrative is suggested by the fact that beggars used to be organized into gangs and syndicates who bribed the police for the privilege of operating in certain preferred areas. In her recent publication, Sara Harris argues that there are some who collect two to three hundred dollars a week. This observer admits he is more impressed with the longevity of the argument than he is with the data on income offered in any of the studies.

The beggar thrives on a complex relationship with the public, one perhaps best summed up by this perceptive social worker.

> The vagrant accepts a donation with the conviction that he has brightened the day for his benefactor. He knows that he sells merit to masquerading philanthropy and ideas to the funny man, the marginal utility to each individual purchaser being greater than from a like expenditure in gum, cigars or vaudeville.

Often the beggar fakes a physical disability. The truly handicapped were once so common on skid row that a wide variety of nicknames grew up to designate each specific disability. Because of the hazards involved both in the skid rower's work and in his way of life, every skid row had its assortment of "lefties, shorties, blinkies, and stumps." Today the National Safety Council still rates agriculture the third most hazardous industry. In past days the skid rowers' other usual occupations—logging, river levee and dam construction, railroading, ice cutting—must have been equally hazardous if not more so. . . .

While most handicapped persons on skid row are beggars, not all beggars are handicapped, even in disguise. Nor are beggars rated by skid row standards according to the degree of their handicap whether real or assumed, or even by their need. Beggars are rated by the nature of their demand. A further refinement, also by skid row standards, draws a distinction between begging and panhandling. It is all right for a skid rower to panhandle from anyone. The panhandler's request, it is understood, rests upon the stated or unstated need for alcohol—universally recognized among skid rowers. No self-respecting skid rower, however, will panhandle another skid rower for food or lodging. This would constitute begging, and insiders simply do not beg from each other. The very word beg implies a disparity in social and economic status between the one who asks and the one who gives. Clearly they belong to separate social worlds. The supplicant has no legitimate claim over the donor, the donor no responsibility for the beggar. Note finally that whereas begging is a profession, panhandling is the last resort of the penniless and thirsty amateur.

Beggars are classified by skid row standards from those of top status who beg for money on the streets, down to the scavengers who pick through refuse for rags, bottles, and other re-salable goods. The successful beggar combines the ability of tactician, psychologist, and actor. . . . Orwell's classic comments on the subject can scarcely be bettered.

> It is worth saying something about the social position of beggars, for when one has consorted with them, and found that they are ordinary human beings, one cannot help being struck by the curious attitude that society takes toward them. People seem to feel that there is some essential difference between beggars and ordinary "working" men. They are a race apart—outcasts, like criminals and prostitutes. Working men "work," beggars do not "work," they are parasites, worthless in their very nature. It is taken for granted that a beggar does not "earn" his living, as a bricklayer or a literary critic "earns" his. He is a mere social excrescence, tolerated because we live in a humane age, but essentially despicable.
>
> Yet if one looks closely one sees that there is no essential difference between a beggar's livelihood and that of numberless respectable people. Beggars do not work, it is said; but, then, what is work? A navvy works by swinging a pick. An accountant works by adding up figures. A beggar works by standing out of doors in all weather and getting varicose veins, chronic bronchitis, etc. It is a trade like any other; quite useless, of course —but, then, many reputable trades are quite useless. And as a social type a beggar compares well with scores of others. He is honest compared with the sellers of most patent medicines, highminded compared with a Sunday newspaper proprietor, amiable compared with a hire-purchase tout—in short, a parasite, but a fairly harmless parasite. He seldom extracts more than a bare living from the community, and what should justify him according to our ethical ideas, he pays for it over and over in suffering. I do not think there is anything about a beggar that sets him in a different class from other people, or gives most modern men the right to despise him.

An unusual and uniquely skid row status is that of tour director. The position held by the "t.d." is nowhere explicitly recognized in the skid row literature owing perhaps to the lengths tour directors go to disguise their operations. Although few in number, the tour directors—incognito of course—have won the confidence (sic) of many a journalist and given rise to many of the myths and fables about skid row. Meet one:

> . . . the first Skid Rower I met who was conscious of the difference between drunks and other Skid Rowers (was) Dr. Mark Keller, Ph.D., Phi Beta Kappa, onetime professor of English in a Midwestern university, and Bowery habitue for the past nine years.

The tour directors are the wanderers, the dreamers, the disenchanted, the self-styled artists who have landed on skid row for a variety of personal reasons.

> His name was Gordon. He told me he takes a job with the railroads during the summer, and spends the rest of the time writing fiction. He doesn't ever intend to get married because "I'm going to stick to my ideal and keep writing even if it or the drink kills me." He showed me some of his poetry. His eyes were very bleary and he said ever since he got on skid row his nerves had been shot.

The tour directors have taken on the entertainment of tourists, newspaper reporters, and researchers, as their particular responsibility on skid row. They are likely to be intelligent and to have read enough to know what their listeners want to hear. The tragic personal life histories they have worked up are almost certain to earn them at least a few drinks, if not some cash besides. The tour directors are often the first persons that the skid row visitors meet, and probably more than one book on skid row has been based on tales dreamed up by these grassroots, skid row folklorists.

There is one final genuine skid row status and those who hold it are traditionally held in disrepute. These are the mission stiffs and reliefers, one depending for support upon the mission, the other upon the public agency. The fact that these men are looked down upon points once more to the in-group nature of the skid row community, which considers them collaborators with the hostile outside world. In listening to the preacher damning the souls of the skid rower, in accepting even though momentarily the outsider's view of the skid rower, in submitting to religious conversion, and in accepting assistance which is therefore based on betrayal, the mission stiff threatens the boundaries of the group, and consequently brings havoc down upon his head.

The fact that mission stiffs and reliefers are considered collaborators compels them to loudly proclaim their condemnation of welfare agencies and officials—hoping thus to testify to their loyalty to the in-group. No skid rower will readily communicate with a social worker, since to do so threatens his standing within his own community. The moment the skid rower leaves the mission or social worker, he must disavow the same person whom he perhaps otherwise respects and trusts.

Drunk, alcoholic, hobo, beggar, tour director, and mission stiff—these are the six primary statuses on skid row today—from the most to the least acculturated. . . .

Although the drunk is the most valued member of the community, it is difficult to say that all skid rowers aspire toward becoming drunks since no one wants to claim membership in any part of skid row. However neither do all aspire to be mission stiffs, the least acculturated in the skid row way of life, since their very position between inside and outside worlds exposes them to the condemnation of both, and earns them the support of neither. A man's career on skid row, as is in the outside world, is determined by his individual characteristics as well as by the nature of the society to which he belongs.

A PHENOMENOLOGICAL STUDY
OF SUICIDE NOTES

Jerry Jacobs

. . . Suicide notes offer an invaluable source of data for gaining some insight into what it was that brought the individual to adopt this form of behavior. Their importance is based upon the assumption made by this and other authors that they contain an unsolicited account of the victim's thoughts and emotions regarding his intended act and, often, what he felt was responsible for it. . . .

The author believes that an explanation of suicide can be empirically derived from the notes themselves without the necessity of referring to a synthetic outside system. There is no need to proceed in the traditional fashion of either imputing meaning to the notes or, since there are essentially an infinite number of categorical distinctions to be made, categorizing them on whatever common sense grounds strike the analyst as being either potentially "fruitful" or expedient, e.g., demographic, environmental, physical, or psychological categories. A description of suicidal motivation and the experiences and thought processes involved in acquiring it are not likely to be arrived at without some broader theoretical perspective which in turn is given to some empirical validation by the notes themselves. . . .

The data and insights upon which this formulation is based come from

From *Social Problems,* Vol. 15, No. 1 (Summer 1967), 62-72. Reprinted by permission.

two main sources: 112 suicide notes of adults and adolescents who succeeded in suicide in the Los Angeles area, and insights gained by the author through his participation in a study of adolescent suicide attempters for 2½ years.

Whereas participation in this study has provided me with many valuable insights used in the formulation, the data on which it is based are taken from the 112 suicide notes previously mentioned. The paper will offer a sampling of notes from the various categories identified by the author. These will be analyzed and discussed within the framework of a theoretical perspective which is designed to account for the conscious deliberations that take place before the individual is able to consider and execute the act of suicide. This is seen within the broader context of what the individual must experience in order to become capable of these verbalizations. The notes provide the basis for the formulation and, at the same time, offer the reader a means of verifying it. It is the author's belief that such verification is not contingent upon these notes in particular, but that any set of notes collected from within the same cultural environment would do as well.

The key to this formulation, i.e., the concept of trust violation, and how the individual accomplishes it while remaining convinced that he is a trusted person, is taken from Donald Cressey's work on embezzlement, *Other People's Money*. The final form of the evolved hypothesis reads:

> Trusted persons become trust violators when they conceive of themselves as having a financial problem which is non-shareable, are aware that this problem can be secretly resolved by violation of the position of financial trust, and are able to apply to their own conduct in that situation verbalizations which enable them to adjust their conceptions of themselves as users of the entrusted funds or property.

This conception of trust violation is extended to the act of suicide, i.e., the individual's violation of the sacred trust of life, and to the verbalizations he must entertain in order to reconcile the image of himself as a trusted person with his act of trust violation—suicide. It followed from these considerations that an excellent source of data for this undertaking would be the transcribed accounts of these verbalizations found in suicide notes. Here the similarity with Cressey's work ends, since the method of the author in studying the above is not one of analytic induction.

Both suicides and suicide attempters are considered in this paper. The events and processes leading them to these acts are held to be equatable within the following definitions of these terms, i.e., the suicide attempt is considered as a suicide attempt only if death was intended but did not result. Persons "attempting suicide" with the intent of not dying but only of using the "attempt" as an "attention-getting device," a "manipulative technique," etc., were not considered by the author as suicide attempters within the limits of this paper. The intentions of persons "attempting suicide" as an attention-getting device may miscarry and result in death. Persons actually attempting suicide may, through some misinformation or fortuitous circumstance, continue to live. This in no way alters their intent or the experiences which led them to entertain the verbalizations necessary for establishing this intent. It is in this sense that suicide and suicide attempts are considered by the author to be synonymous.

These three categories of persons were distinguished from one another in the following way. The authors of the 112 notes to be discussed in this paper were all considered to be suicides based upon a designation assigned to them by the Los Angeles County Coroner's Office upon investigating the circumstances of their death. The distinction between suicide attempters and "attention-getters" was based upon the adolescent's account of his intentions at the time of his act. All adolescent suicide attempters in the above-mentioned study were seen within 48 hours of the attempt. Their intentions were related to three separate persons during their voluntary commitment at the hospital—to the attending physician who treated them in the emergency room, to the psychiatrist during a psychiatric interview, and to the author or his assistant in an interview which lasted about two hours. The designation by the author of suicide attempter was based upon a comparison and assessment of these three accounts. The three adolescent suicide attempters referred to later in this paper in a section dealing with the "next world" all intended at the time of the attempt to take their own lives.

INTRODUCTION TO THE FORMULATION

Nearly all of the suicide notes studied were found to fall within one of six general categories, i.e., "first form notes," "sorry illness notes," "not sorry illness notes," "direct accusation notes," "will and testament notes" and "notes of instruction." The sum total of all six categories of suicide notes and the explanations given for the notes taking the form they do, constitute "The Formulation"—a systematic explanation for all but ten notes, i.e., 102 out of 112 notes studied by the author. The exceptions are noted later. The ten point process to be discussed is characteristic of "first form notes." Thirty-five of the 112 notes took this form. In addition, "sorry illness notes" also contained all or most of the characteristics found in "first form notes," depending upon their length. The reader is cautioned not to view the other four forms of notes as exceptions which tend to negate the process associated with "first form" and "sorry illness notes." These four forms and the explanations accompanying them are not exceptions but qualified additions that supplement the scope of the original ten points. . . .

THE FORMULATION

Trusted persons appear to become trust violators when they conceive of themselves as having a problem, the nature of which is a view of the past plagued by troubles, a troubled present, and the expectation of future troubles erupting unpredictably in the course of their lives. Paradoxically, these unpredictable troubles occur with absolute predictability in that it is held that they are sure to come—as sure as they are here now, unexpectedly, as sure as they arose unexpectedly in the past, and as sure as one's future existence to arise unexpectedly in the future. The problem is thus seen to be as absolute as life and must be resolved by something no less absolute than death. Since it is impossible to dispose of the problem of change, where change is viewed as unanticipated, inevitable, and inevitably for the worse, and since one sees it necessary to resolve this problem in order to live, i.e., to fulfill one's trust, and since the absolute nature of the problem makes it amenable only to absolute solutions, and since there is only one absolute solution, one finds it necessary to resolve the problem of living by dying, or—to put it another way—one appears to betray one's most sacred public trust by the private act of suicide.

Implicit or explicit in most of the suicide notes is the notion that "they didn't want it this way . . . but . . . " From this perspective, they are now in a position to view themselves as blameless, i.e., trusted persons, while at the same time knowing that you will view them as trust violators because you have not experienced what they have and therefore cannot see the moral and reasonable nature of the act. With this in mind, they beg your indulgence and ask your forgiveness, for, in short, they know what they're doing, but they also know that you cannot know.

Life's problems, which one is morally obligated to resolve by way of not violating the sacred trust to live, can only be resolved by death, a not-too-pretty paradox, but from the perspective of the potential suicide, a necessary and consequently reasonable and moral view. From the absence of choice, i.e., no freedom, emerges the greatest freedom—"the recognition of necessity"—stemming from the apparent lack of choice. Thus it is that the suicidal person sees in the act of suicide at long last the potential for the freedom he has sought in life. This can be seen in the notes themselves. The note writers are rarely "depressed" or "hostile." The notes are by and large very even, as though at the time of writing the suffering no longer existed and a resolution to the problem had been reached. Tuckman states that 51% of the notes he studied expressed "positive affect without hostility" and another 25% expressed "neutral affect." This is further supported by the finding of Farberow *et al.* that the period of highest risk was not during the depression or "illness" but just after it when the patient seemed much improved.

FIRST FORM NOTES

The outline presented below describes the formal aspects of a process that the individual must first experience in order to be able to seriously entertain suicide and then actually attempt it. The extent to which this process is operative will be illustrated through an analysis of "first form" notes. The extent to which the other five forms of notes deviate from the characteristics found in "first form notes" will be discussed in the explanations accompanying each of the five remaining forms. The sum total of all six forms of notes and their accompanying explanations constitute "The Formulation," i.e., a systematic rational explanation of suicide based upon the suicide's own accounts at the time of the act.

Durkheim went to great lengths to show that private acts contrary to the public trust are irrational and/or immoral and constrained by public sanctions from ever occurring. In order to overcome these constraints and appear to others as a trust violator, the private individual must 1) be faced with an unexpected, intolerable, and unsolvable problem; 2) view this not as an isolated unpleasant incident, but within the context of a long biography of such troubled situations, and the expectation of future ones; 3) believe that death is the only absolute answer to this apparent absolute dilemma of life; 4) come to this point of view (a) by way of an increasing social isolation whereby he is unable to share his problem with the person or persons who must share it if it is to be resolved, or (b) being isolated from the cure of some incurable illness which in turn isolates him from health and the community, thereby doubly insuring the insolubility of the problem; 5) overcome the social constraints, i.e., the social norms he had internalized whereby he views suicide as irrational and/or immoral; 6) succeed in this because he feels himself less an integral part of the society than the others and therefore is held less firmly by its bonds; 7) succeed in accomplishing step 6 by applying to his intended suicide a verbalization which enables him to adjust his conception of himself as a trusted person with his conception of himself as a trust violator; 8) succeed in doing this by defining the situation such that the problem is (a) not of his own making (b) unresolved, but not from any lack of personal effort, and (c) not given to any resolution known to him except death (he doesn't want it this way, but . . . it's "the only way out"); 9) in short, define death as necessary by the above process and in so doing remove all choice and with it sin and immorality; and finally, 10) make some provision for insuring against the recurrence of these problems in the afterlife.

Thirty-five out of 112 notes were "first form notes" and expressed all or most of the above aspects, depending on their length. All "first form" notes are characterized by the author's begging of forgiveness or request for indulgence. The following will serve to illustrate the general tenor.

It is hard to say why you don't want to live. I have only one real reason. The three people I have in the world which I love don't want me.

Tom, I love you so dearly but you have told me you don't want me and don't love me. I never thought you would let me go this far, but I am now at the end which is the best thing for you. You have so many problems and I am sorry I added to them.

Daddy, I hurt you so much and I guess I really hurt myself. You only wanted the very best for me and you must believe this is it.

Mommy, you tried so hard to make me happy and to make things right for all of us. I love you too so very much. You did not fail, I did.

I had no place to go so I am back where I always seem to find peace. I have failed in everything I have done and I hope I do not fail in this.

I love you all dearly and am sorry this is the way I have to say goodbye. Please forgive me and be happy.

Your wife and your daughter.

First, the problem is not of their own making. At first glance the suicide seems to be saying just the opposite. "You did not fail, I did," "I have failed in everything." However, having acknowledged this, she states: "Tom, I love you so dearly but you have told me you don't want me and don't love me. *I never thought you would let me go this far.*" Then, of course, she loves them. It is they who do not love her, and this is "the problem."

Second, a long-standing history of problems. "Mommy, you tried so hard to make me happy and to make things right for all of us. I love you too so very much. You did not fail, I did," or "Tom . . . you have so many problems and I am sorry I added to them," etc. It seems from this that she has created a long-standing history of problems. She was, nevertheless, subject to them as well. "Daddy, I hurt you so much and I guess I *really hurt myself.*"

Third, the escalation of problems of late beyond human endurance. "It is hard to say why you don't want to live. I have only one real reason. The three people I have in the world which I love don't want me," or "Tom, I love you so dearly but you have told me you don't want me and don't love me."

These particular problems are clearly of recent origin and of greater magnitude than any she had previously experienced. By her own account, had she experienced problems of this order before, she would have taken her life before, since they led to her losing what had previously constituted sufficient reason for her to go on living.

Fourth, death must be seen as necessary. "It is hard to say why you don't want to live. I have only one real reason. The three people I have in the world which I love don't want me," or " . . . but now I'm at the end . . . ," and finally, "I love you all dearly and am sorry this is the way *I have to* say goodbye."

Fifth, beg your indulgence. "I love you all dearly and am *sorry* this is the way I have to say goodbye."

Sixth, they know what they're doing but know you cannot know. "Daddy . . . You only wanted the very best for me and *you must believe this is it.*"

It is the author's opinion that the suicide's message in point (3) is the same as that given by nearly all the others who attempt or succeed in suicide, insofar as this is a particular case of the general condition of "a progressive social isolation from meaningful relationships." Ellen West, whose case history is perhaps the most famous, wrote in her diary less than a year before taking her life:

> . . . by this fearful illness I am withdrawing more and more from people. I feel myself excluded from all real life. I am quite isolated. I sit in a glass ball. I see people through a glass wall, their voices come to me muffled. I have an unutterable longing to get to them, I scream, but they do not hear me. I stretch out my arms toward them; but my hands merely beat against the walls of my glass ball.

All of the remaining "first form" notes have all or most of the above characteristics in common. *All of the notes in this class, without exception, beg forgiveness or indulgence on the part of the survivors.*

ILLNESS NOTES

Requests for forgiveness or indulgence may be omitted when the writer feels that the public *may have* made exceptions to its general indignation at suicide, exceptions which should be known to all, e.g., in the case of persons suffering from an incurable disease, suffering great pain, etc. In such cases, the suicide may feel that no apologies are necessary, and requests for forgiveness may be included or excluded, due to the ambiguity surrounding the degree of public acceptance of the above view.

Thirty-four notes were included in the "illness" category. Twenty-two of these omitted requests for forgiveness; twelve included them. This category of notes has most of the same general characteristics as those of the "first form." How many conditions of the "first form" notes are met by those of the "illness" category depends primarily on their length. The two formal distinguishing features of these two sets of notes are that the "illness" set may or may not beg forgiveness for the reasons stated above, and, secondly, the source of the problem is generally better defined and restricted to the area of illness, pain, etc., and its social and personal implications to the individual. Some examples of illness notes follow.

SORRY ILLNESS NOTES:

Dearly Beloved Children: For the last three weeks I have lost my blood circulation in my feet and in my hands. I can hardly hold a spoon in my hand. Before I get a stroke on top of my other troubles of my legs I decided that this would be the easier for me. I have always loved you all dearly. Think of me kindly sometimes. Please forgive me. I cannot endure any more pains. Lovingly, mother.

NOT SORRY ILLNESS NOTES:

If you receive this letter you will know that I have emptied my bottle of sleeping pills.

And a second note by the same author addressed to the same person included the line: *"Surely there must be a justifiable mercy death."* Another reads:

Dear Jane: You are ruining your health and your life just for me, and I cannot let you do it. The pains in my face seem worse every day and there is a limit to what a man can take. I love you dear.

Bill

NOTES OF DIRECT ACCUSATION

None of the notes in this class beg forgiveness or offer an apology. The suicide feels that not only is the problem not of his making, but he knows who is responsible for his having to commit suicide. As a result, he feels righteously indignant and omits requests for indulgence, especially when the note is directed to the guilty party. "Direct accusation notes" are generally very brief, rarely more than a few lines long. Ten of the 112 notes studied were of the "direct accusation" type. For example:

You Bob and Jane caused this—this all.

Goodbye Jane. I couldn't take no more from you. Bob.

Mary, I hope you're satisfied. Bill.

If you had read page 150 of Red Ribbons this wouldn't have happened.

LAST WILL AND TESTAMENTS AND NOTES OF INSTRUCTIONS

None of these notes contained requests for forgiveness or indulgence either. This omission, as in the above case, results from the form of the notes themselves. These notes usually concern themselves exclusively with the manner in which the suicide's property is to be apportioned. They give no mention of the circumstances of the suicide and, as a result, there is no need for the notewriter to admit of guilt or request forgiveness. None of them do so.

LAST WILL AND TESTAMENTS:

> I hereby bequeath all my worldly goods and holdings to Bill Smith. $1 to Chris Baker, $1 to Ann Barnes. Signed in sober consideration.
>
> Mary Smith

NOTES OF INSTRUCTIONS

The following are some examples of notes of instructions. They are almost always very brief and the above comments regarding "last will and testaments" apply here as well.

> Call Jane. S. Street, Apt. 2. Thank Officer No. 10.

> I have gone down to the ocean. Pick out the cheapest coffin Jones Bros. has. I don't remember the cost. I'll put my purse in the trunk of the car.

PRECAUTIONS TAKEN TO EXCLUDE THIS WORLD'S PROBLEMS FROM THE NEXT WORLD

To guard against the eventuality of a similar set of troubles erupting in the afterlife, the very thing one is dying to overcome, one of six possible courses of action are formulated and internalized. These forms first came to the attention of the author while studying suicidal adolescents; the suicide notes tend to bear them out.

(1) The potential suicide who was in the past quite religious and a diligent church-goer rather abruptly stops attending church and starts considering himself a non-religious person. He thereby disposes of heaven and hell, makes death absolute, and secures for himself all the benefits of the non-believer with respect to the act of suicide.

(2) The person who attended church irregularly but had enough religious training to make him ambivalent about an afterlife, suddenly begins to make inquiries of very religious persons as to whether "God forgives suicides" or "Will God forgive anything?" And those to whom the question is put, believing that He does, or pleased that it was asked, or anxious for the convert, or for whatever reason, say "Yes, of course, if you really believe, God will forgive anything," at which point the suicidal person suddenly "gets religion" and tries very hard to "believe," thus securing a place in heaven free from future troubles.

The following is an abstract of a note written by a 16-year-old female suicide attempter. Both the adolescent and her mother reported that the girl's preoccupation with religion began unexpectedly within the last few months. The note is illustrative of the adolescent's attempt to resolve the anticipated problems of the hereafter through the process described in (2) above.

Please forgive me, God. . . . In my heart I know there is a Christ everywhere in the world that is being with everyone. Every second of every day and he represents God in every way. I know that in my brain (mind) I think evil things about different situations and sometimes I think that Christ never existed. But my heart always is strong and that when I think that Christ never lived I know that in my heart He did. . . . *Mother thinks that there is no hell and no heaven (I guess) and I know there is a hell and heaven. I don't want to go to the devil, God, so please forgive me to what I have just done. John L. said that if I believe in and accept Jesus that I would go to heaven. Some people say that if you ask forgiveness to God for things you do to yourself or others, that he would forgive you (if you believe in Jesus and love him) . . .*

. . . Heaven is so peaceful and the earth is very troublesome and terrifying.

(3) The religious person, believing that suicide is an absolute, irreversible, and damnable sin, will make an attempt to resolve this by asking a mother or some other authority, "Will God forgive anything?," knowing full well that suicide is the exception, and will be answered, "If you believe." The Pope's pronouncement to the contrary notwithstanding, the suicidal person will accept this and act as though it were true.

(4) The religious person, believing that he is unable to secure a place in heaven or insure an absolute death, or any other resolution to his present problem, will fly in the face of God, e.g., "Even if I go to hell, at least I won't have those headaches and worry about the baby and that will be one thing anyway." At least you don't have to violate a trust in hell, for no one on earth has ever told you how to act in hell, and you are left to your own resources without the problem of becoming a trust violator. Its very ambiguity allows for a happy ending, or beginning.

Parts of a lengthy note written by a man to his wife and family serve to illustrate the uncertainty of the hereafter.

My Dearest Ones:
When you get this it will all be over for me on earth *but just the beginning of my punishment for what I have done to you all.* . . . I have given what I am about to do lots of thought and each time I have thought about it there seems no other way . . . *I don't know what's on the other side perhaps it will be worse than here.*

It is interesting to see that the author of the note begins by stating that his punishment in the hereafter is just beginning. It is a very positive statement; the punishment seems a certainty. However, the letter ends on this note: "I don't know what's on the other side *perhaps* it will be worse than here." The "perhaps" nature of this statement provides for the possibility that "perhaps" it will be better. In the hope of tipping the scales in the right direction, the suicide concludes his note with . . .

I love you all *May God help me and forgive for what I am about to do.*
Again good-bye.

Jack and Daddy

(5) Another group concerned with the prospect of hell will request
in a suicide note that others "pray for my soul" or "God forgive me" and
—having taken this precaution—hope for the best.

(6) Reincarnation is the last form of possible salvation: "Maybe it
will be better the next time around; it couldn't be worse." This resolution to life's problems and the hope of preventing future ones was discovered through interviews with adolescent suicide attempters. One 15-
year-old Jewish boy, who until a year ago when the family moved from
New York had been attending the synagogue regularly, suddenly stopped
attending services and recently became preoccupied with the prospect of
reincarnation. A 14-year-old Negro Baptist girl, who until about a year
ago had been a steady church-goer, also stopped attending church and
became interested in reincarnation. It is perhaps unnecessary to point out
how peculiar it is for a Jew and a Baptist to undergo a conversion to the
expectations of reincarnation, especially since there seem to be no external indoctrinating influence. Both adolescents also recognized its peculiarity to the outsider and although they mentioned its existence, refused to discuss it in detail.

In brief, religious convictions do not appear to be ultimately binding
upon the individual as a constraint against suicide, since one tends to
interpret religious dogma as one has a need to interpret it.

It is true that Durkheim dealt at length with this notion by establishing the degree of social integration within various religions as the constraining factor against suicide, rather than the religious dogma *per se.*
However, what has not been discussed is the way in which religious
dogma, specifically intended to prevent suicide, can, with the proper
"rationalization," serve to encourage suicide. The preceding discussion
dealt with why and how this is actually accomplished by the potential
suicide.

The author acknowledges that some exceptions occurred within the
above categories. But among the 112 suicide notes studied, the paucity
of cases falling into a "residual category" is heartening. There were ten
of these in all, four of which contained the only elements of humor found
in all of the notes. For example:

Please do not disturb. Someone sleeping. (Hung on the dashboard of his
car.) . . .

VI PATHOLOGY AS DEVIATION

12 MENTAL ILLNESS

Throughout history the mentally ill have been considered deviant and have aroused fear, revulsion, and disgust. One of the earliest interpretations was that they were possessed by demons, and part of our lingering antipathy is surely attributable to this demonological explanation of the cause of their affliction. Later, and until relatively recent times in fact, the more severely disturbed were considered to be almost non-human and proper subjects to be burned, stoned, beaten, and persecuted. Those whose problems and aberrations were somewhat more tolerable remained the responsibility of family and community. Every community had its share of disturbed persons as well as mental defectives and other chronically deviant members.

Although the mental hospital dates back to the first known house for lunatics in Byzantium in the fourth century of the Christian era, mental hospitals were still relatively rare until the end of the eighteenth century. Those that existed were uniformly foul, prison-like establishments hardly fit for human beings. In the United States, for example, as late as 1840 there were only fourteen public asylums housing about twenty-five hundred persons. As long as the society remained largely rural, the mentally ill either wandered from place to place or somehow survived in their local communities. The cumulative effects of industrialization—for example urbanization, increasing community complexity, and the weakening of family and community ties—led to the development of the large custodial asylum in England, France, and the United States. The urban industrial community simply could no longer feed, clothe, shelter, tolerate, or maintain deviant persons. The asylum served to remove the disturbed and disturbing members of a community—on a long-term and often permanent basis. The mentally ill were already considered to be moral lepers, but the asylum added official stigma and indescribably brutal living conditions. Not even the simplest amenities were provided the inmates in many of the institutions. So horrible were the circumstances in these asylums that it was a toss-up whether the tender mercies of the hospital were superior to the pariah status in the community.

Until very recently, the status of the mentally ill, while improved over that of an earlier day, was still very poor. Lately, however, a member of revolutionary changes have begun to occur. The conception of mental aberration has changed. Although there is still fear and misunderstanding of the disturbed, attitude change has occurred. Changes in treatment are also most evident. The widespread use of psychoactive drugs has proved revolutionary; more and more patients are being treated in the community, in outpatient centers, and in general hospitals. The mental hospital itself, although far from transformed, has also been improving in the quality of its care. It is fair to say that more change—in definition, societal reaction, and treatment—has occurred since 1955 than in all previous periods combined. We are in the midst of a profound revolution—one which promises to reshape the idea of *conception* and management of the deviant who is "sick."

Just how far we are from these goals, however, is most evident in the first two selections in this chapter. Both are taken from the Message from the President of the United States, the late John F. Kennedy, to the 88th Congress on February 5, 1963. In this message, President Kennedy spelled out the status of the problems of mental illness and mental retardation. The message indicates the dimensions of the problem, the costs, and the extent of accumulated lag in treatment and other aspects. Each section—mental illness and mental retardation—contains the late President's recommendations for improving the situation. It should be noted that most of these recommendations have been enacted by the Congress and that many have already been translated into operating programs.

The concluding remarks of the late President may well serve as an introduction to both the mental illness and mental retardation sections. He said:

> We as a Nation have long neglected the mentally ill and the mentally retarded. This neglect must end, if our Nation is to live up to its own standards of compassion and dignity and achieve the maximum use of its manpower.
>
> This tradition of neglect must be replaced by forceful and far-reaching programs carried out at all levels of government, by private individuals and by State and local agencies in every part of the Union.
>
> We must act—
>   to bestow the full benefits of our society on those who suffer from mental disabilities;
>   to prevent the occurrence of mental illness and mental retardation wherever and whenever possible;
>   to provide for early diagnosis and continuous and comprehensive care, in the community, of those suffering from these disorders;

to stimulate improvements in the level of care given the mentally disabled in our State and private institutions, and to reorient those programs to a community-centered approach;

to reduce, over a number of years, and by hundreds of thousands, the persons confined to these institutions;

to retain in and return to the community the mentally ill and mentally retarded, and there to restore and revitalize their lives through better health programs and strengthened educational and rehabilitation services; and

to reinforce the will and capacity of our communities to meet these problems, in order that the communities, in turn, can reinforce the will and capacity of individuals and individual families.

We must promote—to the best of our ability and by all possible and appropriate means—the mental and physical health of all our citizens.

In an unusually provocative essay, Professor Erving Goffman describes and analyzes a class of institutions—the total institutions—and their effects on the inmates. Total institutions—mental hospitals, prisons —have certain important elements in common: the removal of barriers ordinarily separating various spheres of life, a single authority system, lack of privacy, regimentation, explicit formal rules that take in all manner of restrictions, and an unbridgable gulf between the managed groups (inmates) and the managers (the staff). The total institution must strip the inmate of his "presenting culture" and corresponding self and endow him with a modified culture and self. This stripping is called the process of mortification. The essay describes this process of mortification in some detail. After reading this selection one wonders at the naïveté of thinking that total institutions can be rehabilitative or correctional.

The fourth selection has had a profound influence on the professions of psychiatry, psychology, sociology, and related disciplines. In a very controversial essay which has been most favorably received outside of psychiatry itself, Dr. Thomas S. Szasz categorically rejects the concept of mental illness. Speaking of the "Myth of Mental Illness," Szasz believes that the term "mental illness" is broadly used to describe certain personality and social disabilities that have nothing to do with health or illness but instead refer to deviations from psychosocial, ethical, and moral norms. Mental illness is not, strictly speaking, medical in any acceptable sense of that term. Mental illness, instead, is a name or cover for a multitude of problems of living. The myth of mental illness is a social tranquilizer. It leads us, implicitly, to believe that human interaction and existence would be more secure, harmonious, and satisfying if it were not for the negative and disruptive influences of psychopathology. To achieve a better life and a more tranquil world, Dr. Szasz urges that we forgo the notion of mental illness and concentrate our attention on the real problems of living, "whether," as he says, "these be biologic, economic, political or sociopsychological."

These views have not gone uncontested. Any number of clinicians and experimental scientists have responded to Szasz's "heresy." Nevertheless, in addition to provoking extensive controversy, "The Myth of Mental Illness" and related essays by Szasz have raised value issues which cannot in themselves be resolved in the scientific sphere.

These value issues and ethical and moral concerns are pursued in depth by Lady Barbara Wootton in an essay which she originally presented at the annual meeting of the American Psychopathological Association in 1967. In her paper, "Social Psychiatry and Psychopathology," Lady Wootton engagingly describes the broadening of the involvement of psychiatry; perhaps "encroachment" would be closer to the sense of her meaning, into such institutional areas as government, education, and industry. This encroachment has occurred and is occurring because the definition of mental illness has been tied to certain cultural values and psychiatry has been enlisted in behalf of these values. The first order of business, then, is to see to it that the concept of mental health is emptied of ethical content. Mental illness need not include "problems of living." It is enough to define mental illness in terms of impairment of function.

Further, the present all-inclusive nature of the definition of mental illness has tended to involve modern psychiatrists in activities that extend far beyond the legitimate one of restoring the patient's impaired functions. Especially perplexing, says Lady Wootton, are the problems raised by the incursion of psychiatry into the legal and penal fields and the questions raised about criminal and legal responsibility. Lady Wootton is also concerned about the ethical questions raised by psychiatrists who work for the state (for example, those in state penal and mental institutions). Finally, there is the matter of the use of various therapies and techniques in dealing with institutionalized persons. For Lady Wootton, the use of such therapies cannot be reconciled with the ethics of the medical profession. This article, whatever one's evaluation of the specific arguments, is a first-rate introduction to the dilemmas and conflicts that beset psychiatry in the wake of the drug and related revolutions of the 1950's.

In all of the dispute about the nature of mental illness and its characteristics, the focus is nearly always on the symptomatic behavior of the patient. Depending on his symptoms and signs, he is given a diagnosis that ranges from some form of organic impairment, such as acute or chronic brain syndrome, through the functional psychoses, such as schizophrenia or manic-depressive psychosis, to the psychoneuroses and character disorders. The point is that this diagnosis and evaluation are the outcome of the process of becoming mentally ill. Professor Thomas Scheff in "The Role of the Mentally Ill and the Dynamics of Mental Disorder: A Research Framework" is interested in the dynamics of becoming labeled "mentally ill." He emphasizes the societal reaction to the initial deviance of the patient and the process through which the patient comes to think of himself as mentally ill and to act out the illness role. Since a process, in its very nature, is continuous, Dr. Scheff attempts to make it discrete by positing a series of nine hypotheses which deal with the various time slices of the process. Scheff prefers to speak of mental illness as residual deviance—conduct that, it "goes without saying," is unthinkable for most persons. This selection concludes that whatever its name—mental illness or residual deviance—labeling is the most important element in the process.

The final selection is an overview and interpretation of an experimental study which attempted to evaluate the desirability of a home-care treatment program for schizophrenic patients. The article is taken from the last chapter of a volume, *Schizophrenics in the Community,* which was awarded the Hofheimer Research Prize for Research by the American Psychiatric Association in 1967.

Schizophrenia is the most common, most serious and most chronic of the functional mental disorders. Fully one-fourth of all state hospital admissions are diagnosed as schizophrenic and, because of its resistance to treatment, about a half of all persons in public institutions at any one time are schizophrenic. Hence any treatment program that would be effective in schizophrenia would measurably reduce the population census in state hospitals, to say nothing of bringing relief and comfort to these unfortunate patients and their families.

In the past a diagnosis of schizophrenia as often as not meant a prolonged and indefinite period of confinement and little or no hope for the future. With the advent of the psychoactive drugs, however, the picture was radically altered for the better. Because of these drugs and other treatment modalities, the number of hospitalized has decreased, the length of hospital stay shortened, and the prognosis very much improved.

One of the elements hampering recovery is the official label, mentally ill, conferred on the person when he is institutionalized. If such stigma could be avoided, the recovery process might be facilitated. This being the case, a controlled study was designed to determine whether even initial hospitalization was wholly necessary. In this study, schizophrenic patients were randomly assigned to either home care or hospitalization. Of those on home care, some received drug treatment and the others an inert drug (placebo). All home-care patients were visited regularly by a public health nurse. The results of this experimental program were remarkable. A description of the program and the findings are presented in the article.

MENTAL ILLNESS
AND MENTAL RETARDATION I
John F. Kennedy

To the Congress of the United States:

. . . [Yet] mental illness and mental retardation are among our most critical health problems. They occur more frequently, affect more people, require more prolonged treatment, cause more suffering by the families of the afflicted, waste more of our human resources, and constitute more financial drain upon both the Public Treasury and the personal finances of the individual families than any other single condition.

There are now about 800,000 such patients in this Nation's institutions—600,000 for mental illness and over 200,000 for mental retardation. Every year nearly 1,500,000 people receive treatment in institutions for the mentally ill and mentally retarded. Most of them are confined and compressed within an antiquated, vastly overcrowded, chain of custodial State institutions. The average amount expended on their care is only $4 a day—too little to do much good for the individual, but too much is measured in terms of efficient use of our mental health dollars. In some States the average is less than $2 a day.

The total cost to the taxpayers is over $2.4 billion a year in direct public outlays for services—about $1.8 billion for mental illness and $600 million for mental retardation. Indirect public outlays, in welfare costs and in the waste of human resources, are even higher. But the anguish suffered both by those afflicted and by their families transcends financial statistics—particularly in view of the fact that both mental illness and mental retardation strike so often in childhood, leading in most cases to a lifetime of disablement for the patient and a lifetime of hardship for his family.

This situation has been tolerated far too long. It has troubled our national conscience—but only as a problem unpleasant to mention, easy to postpone, and despairing of solution. The Federal Government, despite the nationwide impact of the problem, has largely left the solutions

Message to the 88th Congress, 1st Session, House of Representatives, Document No. 58. February 5, 1963.

up to the States. The States have depended on custodial hospitals and homes. Many such hospitals and homes have been shamefully under-staffed, overcrowded, unpleasant institutions from which death too often provided the only firm hope of release.

The time has come for a bold new approach. New medical, scientific, and social tools and insights are now available. A series of comprehensive studies initiated by the Congress, the executive branch, and interested private groups have been completed and all point in the same direction.

Governments at every level—Federal, State, and local—private foundations and individual citizens must all face up to their responsibilities in this area. Our attack must be focused on three major objectives:

First, we must seek out the causes of mental illness and of mental retardation and eradicate them. Here, more than in any other area, "an ounce of prevention is worth more than a pound of cure." For prevention is far more desirable for all concerned. It is far more economical and it is far more likely to be successful. Prevention will require both selected specific programs directed especially at known causes, and the general strengthening of our fundamental community, social welfare, and educational programs which can do much to eliminate or correct the harsh environmental conditions which often are associated with mental retardation and mental illness. . . .

Second, we must strengthen the underlying resources of knowledge and, above all, of skilled manpower which are necessary to mount and sustain our attack on mental disability for many years to come. Personnel from many of the same professions serve both the mentally ill and the mentally retarded. We must increase our existing training programs and launch new ones, for our efforts cannot succeed unless we increase by severalfold in the next decade the number of professional and sub-professional personnel who work in these fields. . . . We must also expand our research efforts if we are to learn more about how to prevent and treat the crippling or malfunction of the mind.

Third, we must strengthen and improve the programs and facilities serving the mentally ill and the mentally retarded. The emphasis should be upon timely and intensive diagnosis, treatment, training, and rehabilitation so that the mentally afflicted can be cured or their functions restored to the extent possible. Services to both the mentally ill and to the mentally retarded must be community based and provide a range of services to meet community needs.

It is with these objectives in mind that I am proposing a new approach to mental illness and to mental retardation. This approach is designed, in large measure, to use Federal resources to stimulate State, local, and private action. When carried out, reliance on the cold mercy of custodial isolation will be supplanted by the open warmth of community concern and capability. Emphasis on prevention, treatment, and rehabilitation will be substituted for a desultory interest in confining patients in an institution to wither away. . . .

I. A NATIONAL PROGRAM FOR MENTAL HEALTH

I propose a national mental health program to assist in the inauguration of a wholly new emphasis and approach to care for the mentally ill. This approach relies primarily upon the new knowledge and new drugs acquired and developed in recent years which make it possible for most of the mentally ill to be successfully and quickly treated in their own communities and returned to a useful place in society.

These breakthroughs have rendered obsolete the traditional methods of treatment which imposed upon the mentally ill a social quarantine, a prolonged or permanent confinement in huge, unhappy mental hospitals where they were out of sight and forgotten. I am not unappreciative of the efforts undertaken by many States to improve conditions in these hospitals, or the dedicated work of many hospital staff members. But their task has been staggering and the results too often dismal, as the comprehensive study by the Joint Commission on Mental Illness and Health pointed out in 1961. Some States have at times been forced to crowd five, ten, or even fifteen thousand people into one large understaffed institution. Imposed largely for reasons of economy, such practices were costly in human terms, as well as in a real economic sense. The following statistics are illustrative:

> Nearly one-fifth of the 279 State mental institutions are fire and health hazards; three-fourths of them were opened prior to World War I.
>
> Nearly half of the 530,000 patients in our State mental hospitals are in institutions with over 3,000 patients, where individual care and consideration are almost impossible.
>
> Many of these institutions have less than half the professional staff required—with less than 1 psychiatrist for every 360 patients.
>
> Forty-five percent of their inmates have been hospitalized continuously for 10 years or more.

But there are hopeful signs. In recent years the increasing trend toward higher and higher concentrations in these institutions has been reversed—by the use of new drugs, by the increasing public awareness of the nature of mental illness, and by a trend toward the provision of community facilities, including psychiatric beds in general hospitals, day care centers, and outpatient psychiatric clinics. Community general hospitals in 1961 treated and discharged as cured more than 200,000 psychiatric patients.

I am convinced that, if we apply our medical knowledge and social insights fully, all but a small portion of the mentally ill can eventually achieve a wholesome and constructive social adjustment. It has been demonstrated that two out of three schizophrenics—our largest category of mentally ill—can be treated and released within 6 months, but under the conditions that prevail today the average stay for schizophrenia is 11 years. In 11 States, by the use of modern techniques, 7 out of every 10 schizophrenia patients admitted were discharged within 9 months. In one instance, where a State hospital deliberately sought an alternative to hospitalization in those patients about to be admitted, it was able to treat successfully in the community 50 percent of them. It is clear that a concerted national attack on mental disorders is now both possible and practical.

If we launch a broad new mental health program now, it will be possible within a decade or two to reduce the number of patients now under custodial care by 50 percent or more. Many more mentally ill can be helped to remain in their own homes without hardship to themselves or their families. Those who are hospitalized can be helped to return to their own communities. All but a small proportion can be restored to useful life. We can spare them and their families much of the misery which mental illness now entails. We can save public funds and we can conserve our manpower resources.

1. COMPREHENSIVE COMMUNITY MENTAL HEALTH CENTERS

Central to a new mental health program is comprehensive community care. Merely pouring Federal funds into a continuation of the outmoded type of institutional care which now prevails would make little difference. We need a new type of health facility, one which will return mental health care to the main stream of American medicine, and at the same time upgrade mental health services. I recommend, therefore, that the Congress authorize grants to the States for the construction of comprehensive community mental health centers, beginning in fiscal year 1965. . . .

While the essential concept of the comprehensive community mental health center is new, the separate elements which would be combined in it are presently found in many communities: diagnostic and evaluation services, emergency psychiatric units, outpatient services, inpatient services, day and night care, foster home care, rehabilitation, consultative services to other community agencies, and mental health information and education.

These centers will focus community resources and provide better community facilities for all aspects of mental health care. Prevention as well as treatment will be a major activity. Located in the patient's own enrivonment and community, the center would make possible a better understanding of his needs, a more cordial atmosphere for his recovery, and a continuum of treatment. As his needs change, the patient could move without delay or difficulty to different services—from diagnosis, to cure, to rehabilitation—without need to transfer to different institutions located in different communities.

A comprehensive community mental health center in receipt of Federal aid may be sponsored through a variety of local organizational arrangements. Construction can follow the successful Hill-Burton pattern, under which the Federal Government matches public or voluntary nonprofit funds. Ideally, the center could be located at an appropriate community general hospital, many of which already have psychiatric units. In such instances, additional services and facilities could be added —either all at once or in several stages—to fill out the comprehensive program. In some instances an existing outpatient psychiatric clinic might form the nucleus of such a center, its work expanded and integrated with other services in the community. Centers could also function effectively under a variety of other auspices: as affiliates of State mental hospitals, under State or local governments, or under voluntary nonprofit sponsorship.

Private physicians, including general practitioners, psychiatrists, and other medical specialists, would all be able to participate directly and cooperatively in the work of the center. For the first time, a large proportion of our private practitioners will have the opportunity to treat their patients in a mental health facility served by an auxiliary professional staff that is directly and quickly available for outpatient and inpatient care.

While these centers will be primarily designed to serve the mental health needs of the community, the mentally retarded should not be excluded from these centers if emotional problems exist. They should also offer the services of special therapists and consultation services to parents, school systems, health departments, and other public and private agencies concerned with mental retardation. . . .

These comprehensive community mental health centers should become operational at the earliest feasible date. I recommend that we make a major demonstration effort in the early years of the program to be expanded to all major communities as the necessary manpower and facilities become available. . . .

2. IMPROVED CARE IN STATE MENTAL INSTITUTIONS

Until the community mental health center program develops fully, it is imperative that the quality of care in existing State mental institutions be improved. By strengthening their therapeutic services, by becoming open institutions serving their local communities, many such institutions can perform a valuable transitional role. The Federal Government can assist materially by encouraging State mental institutions to undertake intensive demonstration and pilot projects, to improve the quality of care, and to provide inservice training for personnel manning these institutions. . . .

3. RESEARCH AND MANPOWER

Although we embark on a major national action program for mental health, there is still much more we need to know. We must not relax our effort to push back the frontiers of knowledge in basic and applied research into the mental processes, in therapy, and in other phases of research with a bearing upon mental illness. More needs to be done also to translate research findings into improved practices. I recommend an expansion of clinical, laboratory, and field research in mental illness and mental health.

Availability of trained manpower is a major factor in the determination of how fast we can expand our research and expand our new action program in the mental health field. At present manpower shortages exist in virtually all of the key professional and auxiliary personnel categories —psychiatrists, clinical psychologists, social workers, and psychiatric nurses. To achieve success, the current supply of professional manpower in these fields must be sharply increased—from about 45,000 in 1960 to approximately 85,000 by 1970. . . .

MENTAL ILLNESS
AND MENTAL RETARDATION II

II. A NATIONAL PROGRAM TO COMBAT MENTAL RETARDATION

Mental retardation stems from many causes. It can result from mongolism, birth injury or infection, or any of a host of conditions that cause a faulty or arrested development of intelligence to such an extent that the individual's ability to learn and to adapt to the demands of society is impaired. Once the damage is done, lifetime incapacity is likely. With early detection, suitable care and training, however, a significant improvement in social ability and in personal adjustment and achievement can be achieved.

The care and treatment of mental retardation, and research into its causes and cure, have—as in the case of mental illness—been too long neglected. Mental retardation ranks as a major national health, social and economic problem. It strikes our most precious asset—our children. It disables 10 times as many people as diabetes, 20 times as many as tuberculosis, 25 times as many as muscular dystrophy, and 600 times as many as infantile paralysis. About 400,000 children are so retarded they require constant care or supervision; more than 200,000 of these are in residential institutions. There are between 5 and 6 million mentally retarded children and adults—an estimated 3 percent of the population. . . .

Mental retardation strikes children without regard for class, creed, or economic level. Each year sees an estimated 126,000 new cases. But it hits more often—and harder—at the underprivileged and the poor; and most often of all—and most severely—in city tenements and rural slums where there are heavy concentrations of families with poor education and low income.

There are very significant variations in the impact of the incidence of mental retardation. Draft rejections for mental deficiency during World War II were 14 times as heavy in States with low incomes as in others. In some slum areas 10 to 30 percent of the school-age children are mentally retarded, while in the very same cities more prosperous neighborhoods have only 1 or 2 percent retarded.

There is every reason to believe that we stand on the threshold of major advances in this field. Medical knowledge can now identify precise causes of retardation in 15 to 25 percent of the cases. This itself is a major advance. Those identified are usually cases in which there are severe organic injuries or gross brain damage from disease. Severe cases of mental retardation of this type are naturally more evenly spread throughout the population than mild retardation; but even here poor families suffer disproportionately. In most of the mild cases, although specific physical and neurological defects are usually not diagnosable with present biomedical techniques, research is rapidly adding to our knowledge of specific causes: German measles during the first 3 months of pregnancy, Rh blood factor incompatibility in newborn infants, lead poisoning of infants, faulty body chemistry in such diseases as phenylketonuria and galactosemia, and many others.

Many of the specific causes of mental retardation are still obscure. Socioeconomic and medical evidence gathered by a panel which I appointed in 1961, however, shows a major causative role for adverse social, economic, and cultural factors. Families who are deprived of the basic necessities of life, opportunity, and motivation have a high proportion of the Nation's retarded children. Unfavorable health factors clearly play a major role. Lack of prenatal and postnatal health care, in particular, leads to the birth of brain-damaged children or to an inadequate physical and neurological development. Areas of high infant mortality are often the same areas with a high incidence of mental retardation. Studies have shown that women lacking prenatal care have a much higher likelihood of having mentally retarded children. Deprivation of a child's opportunities for learning slows development in slum and distressed areas. Genetic, hereditary, and other biomedical factors also play a major part in the causes of mental retardation.

The American people, acting through their Government where necessary, have an obligation to prevent mental retardation, whenever possible, and to ameliorate it when it is present. I am, therefore, recommending action on a comprehensive program to attack this affliction. The only feasible program with a hope for success must not only aim at the specific causes and the control of mental retardation but seek solutions to the broader problems of our society with which mental retardation is so intimately related.

The panel which I appointed reported that, with present knowledge, at least half and hopefully more than half, of all mental retardation cases can be prevented through this kind of "broad spectrum" attack—aimed at both the specific causes which medical science has identified, and at the broader adverse social, economic, and cultural conditions with which incidence of mental retardation is so heavily correlated. At the same time research must go ahead in all these categories, calling upon the best efforts of many types of scientists, from the geneticist to the sociologist.

The fact that mental retardation ordinarily exists from birth or early childhood, the highly specialized medical, psychological, and educational evaluations which are required, and the complex and unique social, educational, and vocational lifetime needs of the retarded individual, all require that there be developed a comprehensive approach to this specific problem.

1. PREVENTION

Prevention should be given the highest priority in this effort. Our general health, education, welfare, and urban renewal programs will make a major contribution in overcoming adverse social and economic conditions. More adequate medical care, nutrition, housing, and educational opportunities can reduce mental retardation to the low incidence which has been achieved in some other nations. The recommendations for strengthening American education which I have made to the Congress in my message on education will contribute toward this objective as will the proposals contained in my forthcoming health message.

New programs for comprehensive maternity and infant care and for the improvement of our educational services are also needed. Particular attention should be directed toward the development of such services for slum and distressed areas. Among expectant mothers who do not receive prenatal care, more than 20 percent of all births are premature —two or three times the rate of prematurity among those who do receive adequate care. Premature infants have two or three times as many physical defects and 50 percent more illnesses than full-term infants. The smallest premature babies are 10 times more likely to be mentally retarded.

All of these statistics point to the direct relationship between lack of prenatal care and mental retardation. Poverty and medical indigency are at the root of most of this problem. An estimated 35 percent of the mothers in cities over 100,000 population are medically indigent. In 138 large cities of the country an estimated 455,000 women each year lack resources to pay for adequate health care during pregnancy and following birth. Between 20 and 60 percent of the mothers receiving care in public hospitals in some large cities receive inadequate or no prenatal care—and mental retardation is more prevalent in these areas.

Our existing State and Federal child health programs, though playing a useful and necessary role, do not provide the needed comprehensive care for this high-risk group. . . .

Cultural and educational deprivation resulting in mental retardation can also be prevented. Studies have demonstrated that large numbers of children in urban and rural slums, including preschool children, lack the stimulus necessary for proper development in their intelligence. Even when there is no organic impairment, prolonged neglect and a lack of stimulus and opportunity for learning can result in the failure of young minds to develop. Other studies have shown that, if proper opportunities for learning are provided early enough, many of these deprived children can and will learn and achieve as much as children from more favored neighborhoods. This self-perpetuating intellectual blight should not be allowed to continue. . . .

2. COMMUNITY SERVICES

As in the case of mental illnesses, there is also a desperate need for community facilities and services for the mentally retarded. We must move from the outmoded use of distant custodial institutions to the concept of community-centered agencies that will provide a coordinated range of timely diagnostic, health, educational, training, rehabilitation, employment, welfare, and legal protection services. For those retarded children or adults who cannot be maintained at home by their own families, a new pattern of institutional services is needed.

The key to the development of this comprehensive new approach toward services for the mentally retarded is twofold. First, there must be public understanding and community planning to meet all problems. Second, there must be made available a continuum of services covering the entire range of needs. States and communities need to appraise their needs and resources, review current programs, and undertake preliminary actions leading to comprehensive State and community approaches to these objectives. To stimulate public awareness and the development of comprehensive plans, I recommend legislation to establish a program of special project grants to the States for financing State reviews of needs and programs in the field of mental retardation. . . .

To assist the States and local communities to construct the facilities which these surveys justify and plan, I recommend that the Congress authorize matching grants for the construction of public and other nonprofit facilities, including centers for the comprehensive treatment, training, and care of the mentally retarded. Every community should be encouraged to include provision for meeting the health requirements of retarded individuals in planning its broader health services and facilities. . . .

A full-scale attack on mental retardation also requires an expansion of special education, training, and rehabilitation services. Largely due to the lack of qualified teachers, college instructors, directors, and supervisors, only about one-fourth of the 1,250,000 retarded children of school age now have access to special education. During the past 4 years, with Federal support, there has been some improvement in the training of leadership personnel. However, teachers of handicapped children, including the mentally retarded, are still woefully insufficient in number and training. . . .

Vocational training, youth employment, and vocational rehabilitation programs can all help release the untapped potentialities of mentally retarded individuals. This requires expansion and improvement of our vocational education programs, as already recommended; and, in a subsequent message, I will present proposals for needed youth employment programs. . . .

State institutions for the mentally retarded are badly underfinanced, understaffed, and overcrowded. The standard of care is in most instances so grossly deficient as to shock the conscience of all who see them. . . .

3. RESEARCH

Our single greatest challenge in this area is still the discovery of the causes and treatment of mental retardation. To do this we must expand our resources for the pursuit and application of scientific knowledge related to this problem. This will require the training of medical, behavioral, and other professional specialists to staff a growing effort.

CHARACTERISTICS OF TOTAL INSTITUTIONS

Erving Goffman

INTRODUCTION

Total Institutions. Every institution captures something of the time and interest of its members and provides something of a world for them; in brief, every institution has encompassing tendencies. When we review the different institutions in our Western society we find a class of them which seems to be encompassing to a degree discontinuously greater than the ones next in line. Their encompassing or total character is symbolized by the barrier to social intercourse with the outside that is often built right into the physical plant: locked doors, high walls, barbed wire, cliffs and water, open terrain, and so forth. These I am calling total institutions, and it is their general characteristics I want to explore. This exploration will be phrased as if securely based on findings but will in fact be speculative.

The total institutions of our society can be listed for convenience in five rough groupings. *First,* there are institutions established to care for persons thought to be both incapable and harmless; these are the homes for the blind, the aged, the orphaned, and the indigent. *Second,* there are places established to care for persons thought to be at once incapable of looking after themselves and a threat to the community, albeit an unintended one: TB sanitoriums, mental hospitals, and leprosoriums. *Third,* another type of total institution is organized to protect the community against what are thought to be intentional dangers to it; here the welfare of the persons thus sequestered is not the immediate issue. Examples are: Jails, penitentiaries, POW camps, and concentration camps. *Fourth,* we find institutions purportedly established the better to pursue some technical task and justifying themselves only on these instrumental grounds: Army barracks, ships, boarding schools, work camps, colonial compounds, large mansions from the point of view of those who live in the servants' quarters, and so forth. *Finally,* there are those establishments designed as retreats from the world or as training stations for the religious: Abbeys, monasteries, convents, and other cloisters. This sublisting of total institutions is neither neat nor exhaustive, but the listing itself provides an empirical starting point for a purely

From *Symposium on Preventive and Social Psychiatry,* Walter Reed Army Institute of Research, Washington, D.C., April 15-17, 1967, pp. 43-84. Reprinted by permission.

denotative definition of the category. By anchoring the initial definition of total institutions in this way, I hope to be able to discuss the general characteristics of the type without becoming tautological.

Before attempting to extract a general profile from this list of establishments, one conceptual peculiarity must be mentioned. None of the elements I will extract seems entirely exclusive to total institutions, and none seems shared by every one of them. What is shared and unique about total institutions is that each exhibits many items in this family of attributes to an intense degree. In speaking of "common characteristics," than, I will be using this phrase in a weakened, but I think logically defensible, way.

Totalistic Features. A basic social arrangement in modern society is that we tend to sleep, play and work in different places, in each case with a different set of coparticipants, under a different authority, and without an overall rational plan. The central feature of total institutions can be described as a breakdown of the kinds of barriers ordinarily separating these three spheres of life. *First,* all aspects of life are conducted in the same place and under the same single authority. *Second,* each phase of the member's daily activity will be carried out in the immediate company of a large batch of others, all of whom are treated alike and required to do the same thing together. *Third,* all phases of the day's activities are tightly scheduled, with one activity leading at a prearranged time into the next, the whole circle of activities being imposed from above through a system of explicit formal rulings and a body of officials. *Finally,* the contents of the various enforced activities are brought together as parts of a single overall rational plan purportedly designed to fulfill the official aims of the institution.

Individually, these totalistic features are found, of course, in places other than total institutions. Increasingly, for example, our large commercial, industrial and educational establishments provide cafeterias, minor services and off-hour recreation for their members. But while this is a tendency in the direction of total institutions, these extended facilities remain voluntary in many particulars of their use, and special care is taken to see that the ordinary line of authority does not extend to these situations. Similarly, housewives or farm families can find all their major spheres of life within the same fenced-in area, but these persons are not collectively regimented and do not march through the day's steps in the immediate company of a batch of similar others.

The handling of many human needs by the bureaucratic organization of whole blocks of people—whether or not this is a necessary or effective means of social organization in the circumstances—can be taken, then, as the key fact of total institutions. From this, certain important implications can be drawn.

Given the fact that blocks of people are caused to move in time, it becomes possible to use a relatively small number of supervisory personnel where the central relationship is not guidance or periodic checking, as in many employer-employee relations, but rather surveillance—a seeing to it that everyone does what he has been clearly told is required of him, and this under conditions where one person's infraction is likely to stand out in relief against the visible, constantly examined, compliance of the others. . . .

In total institutions . . . there is a basic split between a large class of individuals who live in and who have restricted contact with the world outside the walls, conveniently called *inmates,* and the small class that supervises them, conveniently called *staff,* who often operate on an 8-hour day and are socially integrated into the outside world. Each grouping tends to conceive of members of the other in terms of narrow hostile stereotypes, staff often seeing inmates as bitter, secretive and untrustworthy, while inmates often see staff as condescending, highhanded and mean. Staff tends to feel superior and righteous; inmates tend, in some ways at least, to feel inferior, weak, blameworthy and guilty. Social mobility between the two strata is grossly restricted; social distance is typically great and often formally prescribed; even talk across the boundaries may be conducted in a special tone of voice. These restrictions on contact presumably help to maintain the antagonistic stereotypes. In any case, two different social and cultural worlds develop, tending to jog along beside each other, with points of official contact but little mutual penetration. It is important to add that the institutional plan and name comes to be identified by both staff and inmates as somehow belonging to staff, so that when either grouping refers to the views or interests of "the institution," by implication they are referring (as I shall also) to the views and concerns of the staff.

The staff-inmate split is one major implication of the central features of total institutions; a second one pertains to work. In the ordinary arrangements of living in our society, the authority of the workplace stops with the worker's receipt of a money payment; the spending of this in a domestic and recreational setting is at the discretion of the worker and is the mechanism through which the authority of the workplace is kept within strict bounds. However, to say that inmates in total institutions have their full day scheduled for them is to say that some version of all basic needs will have to be planned for, too. In other words, total institutions take over "responsibility" for the inmate and must guarantee to have everything that is defined as essential "layed on." It follows, then, that whatever incentive is given for work, this will not have the structural significance it has on the outside. Different attitudes and incentives regarding this central feature of our life will have to prevail.

Here, then, is one basic adjustment required of those who work in total institutions and of those who must induce these people to work. In some cases, no work or little is required, and inmates, untrained often in leisurely ways of life, suffer extremes of boredom. In other cases, some work is required but is carried on at an extremely slow pace, being geared into a system of minor, often ceremonial payments, as in the case of weekly tobacco ration and annual Christmas presents, which cause some mental patients to stay on their job. In some total institutions, such as logging camps and merchant ships, something of the usual relation to the world that money can buy is obtained through the practice of "forced saving"; all needs are organized by the institution, and payment is given only after a work season is over and the men leave the premises. And in some total institutions, of course, more than a full day's work is required and is induced not by reward, but by threat of dire punishment. In all such cases, the work-oriented individual may tend to become somewhat demoralized by the system.

In addition to the fact that total institutions are incompatible with the basic work-payment structure of our society, it must be seen that these establishments are also incompatible with another crucial element of our society, the family. The family is sometimes contrasted to solitary living, but in fact the more pertinent contrast to family life might be with batch [block] living. For it seems that those who eat and sleep at work, with a group of fellow workers, can hardly sustain a meaningful domestic existence. Correspondingly, the extent to which a staff retains its integration in the outside community and escapes the encompassing tendencies of total institutions is often linked up with the maintenance of a family off the grounds.

Whether a particular total institution acts as a good or bad force in civil society, force it may well have, and this will depend on the suppression of a whole circle of actual or potential households. Conversely, the formation of households provides a structural guarantee that total institutions will not arise. The incompatibility between these two forms of social organization should tell us, then, something about the wider social functions of them both.

Total institutions, then, are social hybrids, part residential community, part formal organization, and therein lies their special sociological interest. There are other reasons, alas, for being interested in them, too. These establishments are the forcing houses for changing persons in our society. Each is a natural experiment, typically harsh, on what can be done to the self.

Having suggested some of the key features of total institutions, we can move on now to consider them from the special perspectives that seem natural to take. I will consider the inmate world, then the staff world, and then something about contacts between the two.

THE INMATE WORLD

Mortification Processes. It is characteristic of inmates that they come to the institution as members, already full-fledged, of a *home world,* that is, a way of life and a round of activities taken for granted up to the point of admission to the institution. It is useful to look at this culture that the recruit brings with him to the institution's door—his *presenting culture,* to modify a psychiatric phrase—in terms especially designed to highlight what it is the total institution will do to him. Whatever the stability of his personal organization, we can assume it was part of a wider supporting framework lodged in his current social environment, a round of experience that somewhat confirms a conception of self that is somewhat acceptable to him and a set of defensive maneuvers exercisable at his own discretion as a means of coping with conflicts, discreditings and failures.

Now it appears that total institutions do not substitute their own unique culture for something already formed. We do not deal with acculturation or assimilation but with something more restricted than these. In a sense, total institutions do not look for cultural victory. They effectively create and sustain a particular kind of tension between the home world and the institutional world and use this persistent tension as strategic leverage in the management of men. The full meaning for the inmate of being "in" or "on the inside" does not exist apart from the special meaning to him of "getting out" or "getting on the outside."

The recruit comes into the institution with a self and with attachments to supports which had allowed this self to survive. Upon entrance, he is immediately stripped of his wonted supports, and his self is systematically, if often unintentionally, mortified. In the accurate language of some of our oldest total institutions, he is led into a series of abasements, degradations, humiliations, and profanations of self. He begins, in other words, some radical shifts in his *moral career,* a career laying out the progressive changes that occur in the beliefs that he has concerning himself and significant others.

The *stripping processes* through which *mortification of the self* occurs are fairly standard in our total institutions. Personal identity equipment is removed, as well as other possessions with which the inmate may have identified himself, there typically being a system of nonaccessible storage from which the inmate can only reobtain his effects should he leave the institution. As a substitute for what has been taken away, institutional issue is provided, but this will be the same for large categories of inmates and will be regularly repossessed by the institution. In brief, standardized defacement will occur. . . . Family, occupational, and educational career lines are chopped off, and a stigmatized status is submitted. Sources of fantasy materials which had meant momentary releases from stress in the home world are denied. Areas of autonomous decision are eliminated through the process of collective scheduling of daily activity. Many channels of communication with the outside are restricted or closed off completely. Verbal discreditings occur in many forms as a matter of course. Expressive signs of respect for the staff are coercively and continuously demanded. And the effect of each of these conditions is multipled by having to witness the mortification of one's fellow inmates. . . .

In the background of the sociological stripping process, we find a characteristic authority system with three distinctive elements, each basic to total institutions.

First, to a degree, authority is of the *echelon* kind. Any member of the staff class has certain rights to discipline any member of the inmate class. . . . In our society, the adult himself, however, is typically under the authority of a *single* immediate superior in connection with his work or under authority of one spouse in connection with domestic duties. The only echelon authority he must face—the police—typically are neither constantly nor relevantly present, except perhaps in the case of traffic-law enforcement.

Second, the authority of corrective sanctions is directed to a great multitude of items of conduct of the kind that are constantly occurring and constantly coming up for judgment; in brief, authority is directed to matters of dress, deportment, social intercourse, manners and the like. . . .

The third feature of authority in total institutions is that misbehaviors in one sphere of life are held against one's standing in other spheres. Thus, an individual who fails to participate with proper enthusiasm in sports may be brought to the attention of the person who determines where he will sleep and what kind of work task will be accorded to him.

When we combine these three aspects of authority in total institutions, we see that the inmate cannot easily escape from the press of judgmental officials and from the enveloping tissue of constraint. The system of authority undermines the basis for control that adults in our society expect to exert over their interpersonal environment and may produce the terror of feeling that one is being radically demoted in the age-grading system. On the outside, rules are sufficiently lax and the individual sufficiently agreeable to required self-discipline to insure that others will rarely have cause for pouncing on him. He need not constantly look over his shoulder to see if criticism and other sanctions are coming. On the inside, however, rulings are abundant, novel, and closely enforced so that, quite characteristically, inmates live with chronic anxiety about breaking the rules and chronic worry about the consequences of breaking them. The desire to "stay out of trouble" in a total institution is likely to require persistent conscious effort and may lead the inmate to abjure certain levels of sociability with his fellows in order to avoid the incidents that may occur in these circumstances.

It should be noted finally that the mortifications to be suffered by the inmate may be purposely brought home to him in an exaggerated way during the first few days after entrance, in a form of initiation that has been called *the welcome*. Both staff and fellow inmates may go out of their way to give the neophyte a clear notion of where he stands. As part of this *rite de passage,* he may find himself called by a term such as "fish," "swab," etc., through which older inmates tell him that he is not only merely an inmate but that even within this lowly group he has a low status.

Privilege System. While the process of mortification is in progress, the inmate begins to receive formal and informal instruction in what will here be called the *privilege system.* Insofar as the inmate's self has been unsettled a little by the stripping action of the institution, it is largely around this framework that pressures are exerted, making for a reorganization of self. Three basic elements of the system may be mentioned.

First, there are the *house rules,* a relatively explicit and formal set of prescriptions and proscriptions which lay out the main requirements of inmate conduct. These regulations spell out the austere round of life in which the inmate will operate. Thus, the admission procedures through which the recruit is initially stripped of his self-supporting context can be seen as the institution's way of getting him in the position to start living by the house rules.

Second, against the stark background, a small number of clearly defined *rewards or privileges* are held out in exchange for obedience to staff in action and spirit. It is important to see that these potential gratifications are not unique to the institution but rather are ones carved out of the flow of support that the inmate previously had quite taken for granted. On the outside, for example, the inmate was likely to be able to unthinkingly exercise autonomy by deciding how much sugar and milk he wanted in his coffee, if any, or when to light up a cigarette; on the inside, this right may become quite problematic and a matter of a great deal of conscious concern. Held up to the inmate as possibilities, these few recapturings seem to have a reintegrative effect, re-establishing relationships with the whole lost world and assuaging withdrawal symptoms from it and from one's lost self.

The inmate's run of attention, then, especially at first, comes to be fixated on these supplies and obsessed with them. In the most fanatic way, he can spend the day in devoted thoughts concerning the possibility of acquiring these gratifications or the approach of the hour at which they are scheduled to be granted. The building of a world around these minor privileges is perhaps the most important feature of inmate culture and yet is something that cannot easily be appreciated by an outsider, even one who has lived through the experience himself. This situation sometimes leads to generous sharing and almost always to a willingness to beg for things such as cigarettes, candy and newspapers. It will be understandable, then, that a constant feature of inmate discussion is the *release binge fantasy,* namely, recitals of what one will do during leave or upon release from the institution.

House rules and privileges provide the functional requirements of the third element in the privilege system: *punishments.* These are designated as the consequence of breaking the rules. One set of these punishments consists of the temporary or permanent withdrawal of privileges or abrogation of the right to try to earn them. In general, the punishments meted out in total institutions are of an order more severe than anything encountered by the inmate in his home world. An institutional arrangement which causes a small number of easily controlled privileges to have a massive significance is the same arrangement which lends a terrible significance to their withdrawal.

There are some special features of the privilege system which should be noted.

First, punishments and privileges are themselves modes of organization peculiar to total institutions. . . . And privileges, it should be emphasized, are not the same as prerequisites, indulgences or values, but merely the absence of deprivations one ordinarily expects one would not have to sustain. The very notions, then, of punishments and privileges are not ones that are cut from civilian cloth.

Second, it is important to see that the question of release from the total institution is elaborated into the privilege system. Some acts will become known as ones that mean an increase or no decrease in length of stay, while others become known as means for lessening the sentence.

Third, we should also note that punishments and privileges come to be geared into a residential work system. Places to work and places to sleep become clearly defined as places where certain kinds and levels of privilege obtain, and inmates are shifted very rapidly and visibly from one place to another as the mechanisms for giving them the punishment or privilege their cooperativeness has warranted. The inmates are moved, the system is not. . . .

Immediately associated with the privilege system we find some standard social processes important in the life of total institutions.

We find that an *institutional lingo* develops through which inmates express the events that are crucial in their particular world. Staff too, especially its lower levels, will know this language, using it when talking to inmates, while reverting to more standardized speech when talking to superiors and outsiders. Related to this special argot, inmates will possess knowledge of the various ranks and officials, an accumulation of lore about the establishment, and some comparative information about life in other similar total institutions.

Also found among staff and inmates will be a clear awareness of the phenomenon of *messing up,* so called in mental hospitals, prisons, and barracks. This involves a complex process of engaging in forbidden activity, getting caught doing so, and receiving something like the full punishment accorded this. An alteration in privilege status is usually implied and is categorized by a phrase such as "getting busted." Typical infractions which can eventuate in messing up are: fights, drunkenness, attempted suicide, failure at examinations, gambling, insubordination, homosexuality, improper taking of leave, and participation in collective riots. While these punished infractions are typically ascribed to the offender's cussedness, villainy, or "sickness," they do in fact constitute a vocabulary of institutionalized actions, limited in such a way that the same messing up may occur for quite different reasons. Informally, inmates and staff may understand, for example, that a given messing up is a way for inmates to show resentment against a current situation felt to be unjust in terms of the informal agreements between staff and inmates, or a way of postponing release without having to admit to one's fellow inmates that one really does not want to go.

In total institutions there will also be a system of what might be called *secondary adjustments,* namely, technics which do not directly challenge staff management but which allow inmates to obtain disallowed satisfactions or allowed ones by disallowed means. These practices are variously referred to as: the angles, knowing the ropes, conniving, gimmicks, deals, ins, etc. Such adaptations apparently reach their finest flower in prisons, but of course other total institutions are overrun with them too. It seems apparent that an important aspect of secondary adjustments is that they provide the inmate with some evidence that he is still, as it were, his own man and still has some protective distance, under his own control, between himself and the institution. . . .

The occurrence of secondary adjustments correctly allows us to assume that the inmate group will have some kind of a *code* and some means of informal social control evolved to prevent one inmate from informing staff about the secondary adjustments of another. On the same grounds we can expect that one dimension of social typing among inmates will turn upon this question of security, leading to persons defined as "squealers," "finks," or "stoolies" on one hand, and persons defined as "right guys" on the other. It should be added that where new inmates can play a role in the system of secondary adjustments, as in providing new faction members or new sexual objects, then their "welcome" may indeed be a sequence of initial indulgences and enticements, instead of exaggerated deprivations. Because of secondary adjustments we also find *kitchen strata,* namely, a kind of rudimentary, largely informal, stratification of inmates on the basis of each one's differential access to disposable illicit commodities; so also we find social typing to designate the powerful persons in the informal market system.

While the privilege system provides the chief framework within which reassembly of the self takes place, other factors characteristically lead by different routes in the same general direction. Relief from economic and social responsibilities—much touted as part of the therapy in mental hospitals—is one, although in many cases it would seem that the disorganizing effect of this moratorium is more significant than its organizing effect. More important as a reorganizing influence is the *fraternalization process,* namely, the process through which socially distant persons find themselves developing mutual support and common *counter-mores* in opposition to a system that has forced them into intimacy and into a single, equalitarian community of fate. It seems that the new recruit frequently starts out with something like the staff's popular misconceptions of the character of the inmates and then comes to find that most of his fellows have all the properties of ordinary decent human beings and that the stereotypes associated with their condition or offense are not a reasonable ground for judgment of inmates. . . .

Adaptation Alignments. The mortifying processes that have been discussed and the privilege system represent the conditions that the inmate must adapt to in some way, but however pressing, these conditions allow for different ways of meeting them. We find, in fact, that the same inmate will employ different lines of adaptation or tacks at different phases in his moral career and may even fluctuate between different tacks at the same time.

First, there is the process of *situational withdrawal.* The inmate withdraws apparent attention from everything except events immediately around his body and sees these in a perspective not employed by others present. This drastic curtailment of involvement in interactional events is best known, of course, in mental hospitals, under the title of "regression." . . . I do not think it is known whether this line of adaptation forms a single continuum of varying degrees of withdrawal or whether there are standard discontinuous plateaus of disinvolvement. It does seem to be the case, however, that, given the pressures apparently required to dislodge an inmate from this status, as well as the currently limited facilities for doing so, we frequently find here, effectively speaking, an irreversible line of adaptation.

Second, there is the *rebellious line.* The inmate intentionally challenges the institution by flagrantly refusing to cooperate with staff in almost any way. The result is a constantly communicated intransigency and sometimes high rebel-morale. Most large mental hospitals, for example, seem to have wards where this spirit strongly prevails. Interestingly enough, there are many circumstances in which sustained rejection of a total institution requires sustained orientation to its formal organization and hence, paradoxically, a deep kind of commitment to the establishment. . . .

Third, another standard alignment in the institutional world takes the form of a kind of *colonization.* The sampling of the outside world provided by the establishment is taken by the inmate as the whole, and a stable, relatively contended existence is built up out of the maximum satisfactions procurable within the institution. Experience of the outside world is used as a point of reference to demonstrate the desirability of life on the inside; and the usual tension between the two worlds collapses, thwarting the social arrangements based upon this felt discrepancy. Characteristically, the individual who too obviously takes this line may be accused by his fellow inmates of "having found a home" or of "never having had it so good." Staff itself may become vaguely embarrassed by this use that is being made of the institution, sensing that the benign possibilities in the situation are somehow being misused. Colonizers themselves may feel obliged to deny their satisfaction with the institution, if only in the interest of sustaining the counter-mores supporting inmate solidarity. They may find it necessary to mess up just prior to their slated discharge, thereby allowing themselves to present involuntary reasons for continued incarceration. It should be incidentally noted that any humanistic effort to make life in total institutions more bearable must face the possibility that doing so may increase the attractiveness and likelihood of colonization.

Fourth, one mode of adaptation to the setting of a total institution is that of *conversion.* The inmate appears to take over completely the official or staff view of himself and tries to act out the role of the perfect inmate. While the colonized inmate builds as much of a free community as possible for himself by using the limited facilities available, the convert takes a more disciplined, moralistic, monochromatic line, presenting himself as someone whose institutional enthusiasm is always at the disposal of the staff. . . . Some mental hospitals have the distinction of providing two quite different conversion possibilities—one for the new admission who can see the light after an appropriate struggle and adapt the psychiatric view of himself, and another for the chronic ward patient who adopts the manner and dress of attendants while helping them to manage the other ward patients with a stringency excelling that of the attendants themselves. . . .

While the alignments that have been mentioned represent coherent courses to pursue, few inmates, it seems, carry these pursuits very far. In most total institutions, what we seem to find is that most inmates take the tack of what they call *playing it cool*. This involves a somewhat opportunistic combination of secondary adjustments, conversion, colonization and loyalty to the inmate group, so that in the particular circumstances the inmate will have a maximum chance of eventually getting out physically and psychically undamaged. Typically, the inmate will support the counter-mores when with fellow inmates and be silent to them on how tractably he acts when alone in the presence of staff. Inmates taking this line tend to subordinate contacts with their fellows to the higher claim of "keeping out of trouble." They tend to volunteer for nothing, and they may even learn to cut their ties to the outside world sufficiently to give cultural reality to the world inside but not enough to lead to colonization. . . .

Culture Themes. A note should be added here concerning some of the more dominant themes of inmate culture.

First, in the inmate group of many total institutions there is a strong feeling that time spent in the establishment is time wasted or destroyed or taken from one's life; it is time that must be written off. It is something that must be "done" or "marked" or "put in" or "built" or "pulled." . . . As such, this time is something that its doers have bracketed off for constant conscious consideration in a way not quite found on the outside. And as a result, the inmate tends to feel that for the duration of his required stay—his sentence—he has been totally exiled from living. It is in this context that we can appreciate something of the demoralizing influence of an indefinite sentence or a very long one. We should also note that however hard the conditions of life may become in total institutions, harshness alone cannot account for this quality of life wasted. Rather we must look to the social disconnections caused by entrance and to the usual failure to acquire within the institution gains that can be transferred to outside life—gains such as money earned, or marital relations formed, or certified training received.

Second, it seems that in many total institutions a peculiar kind and level of self-concern is engendered. The low position of inmates relative to their station on the outside, as established initially through the mortifying processes, seems to make for a milieu of personal failure and a round of life in which one's fall from grace is continuously pressed home. In response, the inmate tends to develop a story, a line, a sad tale —a kind of lamentation and apologia—which he constantly tells to his fellows as a means of creditably accounting for his present low estate. While staff constantly discredit these lines, inmate audiences tend to employ tact, suppressing at least some of the disbelief and boredom engendered by these recitations. In consequence, the inmate's own self may become even more of a focus for his conversation than it does on the outside.

Perhaps the high level of ruminative self-concern found among inmates in total institutions is a way of handling the sense of wasted time that prevails in these places. If so, then perhaps another interesting aspect of inmate culture can be related to the same factor. I refer here to the fact that in total institutions we characteristically find a premium placed on what might be called *removal activities,* namely, voluntary unserious pursuits which are sufficiently engrossing and exciting to lift the participant out of himself, making [him] oblivious for the time to his actual situation. If the ordinary activities in total institutions can be said to torture time, these activities mercifully kill it.

Some removal activities are collective, such as ball games, woodwork, lectures, choral singing and card playing; some are individual but rely on public materials, as in the case of reading, solitary TV watching, etc. No doubt, private fantasy ought to be included too. Some of these activities may be officially sponsored by staff; and some, not officially sponsored, may constitute secondary adjustments. In any case, there seems to be no total institution which cannot be seen as a kind of Dead Sea in which appear little islands of vivid, enrapturing activity.

Consequences. In this discussion of the inmate world, I have commented on the mortification process, the reorganizing influences, the lines of response taken by inmates under these circumstances, and the cultural mileu that develops. A concluding word must be added about the long-range consequences of membership.

Total institutions frequently claim to be concerned with rehabilitation, that is, with resetting the inmate's self-regulatory mechanisms so that he will maintain the standards of the establishment of his own accord after he leaves the setting. In fact, it seems this claim is seldom realized and even when permanent alteration occurs, these changes are often not of the kind intended by the staff. With the possible exception presented by the great resocialization efficiency of religious institutions, neither the stripping processes nor the reorganizing ones seem to have a lasting effect. No doubt the availability of secondary adjustments helps to account for this, as do the presence of counter-mores and the tendency for inmates to combine all strategies and "play it cool." In any case, it seems that shortly after release, the ex-inmate will have forgotten a great deal of what life was like on the inside and will have once again begun to take for granted the privileges around which life in the institution was organized. The sense of injustice, bitterness and alienation, so typically engendered by the inmate's experience and so definitely marking a stage in his moral career, seems to weaken upon graduation, even in those cases where a permanent stigma has resulted.

But what the ex-inmate does retain of his institutional experience tells us important things about total institutions. Often entrance will mean for the recruit that he has taken on what might be called a *proactive status*. Not only is his relative social position within the walls radically different from what it was on the outside, but, as he comes to learn, if and when he gets out, his social position on the outside will never again be quite what it was prior to entrance. . . . When the proactive status is unfavorable, as it is for those in prisons or mental hospitals, we popularly employ the term "stigmatization" and expect that the ex-inmate may make an effort to conceal his past and try to "pass."

THE MYTH OF MENTAL ILLNESS
Thomas S. Szasz

My aim in this essay is to raise the question "Is there such a thing as mental illness?" and to argue that there is not. Since the notion of mental illness is extremely widely used nowadays, inquiry into the ways in which this term is employed would seem to be especially indicated. Mental illness, of course, is not literally a "thing"—or physical object—and hence it can "exist" only in the same sort of way in which other theoretical concepts exist. Yet, familiar theories are in the habit of posing, sooner or later—at least to those who come to believe in them—as "objective truths" (or "facts"). During certain historical periods, explanatory conceptions such as deities, witches, and microorganisms appeared not only as theories but as self-evident *causes* of a vast number of events. I submit that today mental illness is widely regarded in a somewhat similar fashion, that is, as the cause of innumerable diverse happenings. As an antidote to the complacent use of the notion of mental illness—whether as a self-evident phenomenon, theory, or cause—let us ask this question: What is meant when it is asserted that someone is mentally ill?

In what follows I shall describe briefly the main uses to which the concept of mental illness has been put. I shall argue that this notion has outlived whatever usefulness it might have had and that it now functions merely as a convenient myth.

MENTAL ILLNESS AS A SIGN OF BRAIN DISEASE

The notion of mental illness derives its main support from such phenomena as syphilis of the brain or delirious conditions—intoxications, for

From *American Psychologist*, Vol. 15 (February 1960), 113-18. Reprinted by permission.

instance—in which persons are known to manifest various peculiarities or disorders of thinking and behavior. Correctly speaking, however, these are diseases of the brain, not of the mind. According to one school of thought, *all* so-called mental illness is of this type. The assumption is made that some neurological defect, perhaps a very subtle one, will ultimately be found for all the disorders of thinking and behavior. Many contemporary psychiatrists, physicians, and other scientists hold this view. This position implies that people *cannot* have troubles—expressed in what are *now called* "mental illnesses"—because of differences in personal needs, opinions, social aspirations, values, and so on. *All problems in living* are attributed to physicochemical processes which in due time will be discovered by medical research.

"Mental illnesses" are thus regarded as basically no different than all other diseases (that is, of the body). The only difference, in this view, between mental and bodily diseases is that the former, affecting the brain, manifest themselves by means of mental symptoms; whereas the latter, affecting other organ systems (for example, the skin, liver, etc.), manifest themselves by means of symptoms referable to those parts of the body. This view rests on and expresses what are, in my opinion, two fundamental errors.

In the first place, what central nervous system symptoms would correspond to a skin eruption or a fracture? It would *not* be some emotion or complex bit of behavior. Rather, it would be blindness or a paralysis of some part of the body. The crux of the matter is that a disease of the brain, analogous to a disease of the skin or bone, is a neurological defect, and not a problem in living. For example, a *defect* in a person's visual field may be satisfactorily explained by correlating it with certain definite lesions in the nervous system. On the other hand, a person's *belief*—whether this be a belief in Christianity, in Communism, or in the idea that his internal organs are "rotting" and that his body is, in fact, already "dead"—cannot be explained by a defect or disease of the nervous system. Explanations of this sort of occurrence—assuming that one is interested in the belief itself and does not regard it simply as a "symptom" or expression of something else that is *more interesting*—must be sought along different lines.

The second error in regarding complex psychosocial behavior, consisting of communications about ourselves and the world about us, as mere symptoms of neurological functioning is *epistemological*. In other words, it is an error pertaining not to any mistakes in observation or reasoning, as such, but rather to the way in which we organize and express our knowledge. In the present case, the error lies in making a symmetrical dualism between mental and physical (or bodily) symptoms, a dualism which is merely a habit of speech and to which no known observations can be found to correspond. Let us see if this is so. In medical practice, when we speak of physical disturbances, we mean either signs (for example, a fever) or symptoms (for example, pain). We speak of mental symptoms, on the other hand, when we refer to a patient's *communications about himself, others, and the world about him.* He might state that he is Napoleon or that he is being persecuted by the Communists. These would be considered mental symptoms *only* if the observer believed that the patient was *not* Napoleon or that he was *not* being persecuted by the Communists. This makes it apparent that the statement that *"X is a mental symptom"* involves rendering a judgment. The judgment entails, moreover, a covert comparison or matching of the patient's ideas, concepts, or beliefs with those of the observer and the society in which they live. The notion of mental symptom is therefore inextricably tied to the *social* (including *ethical*) *context* in which it is made in much the same way as the notion of bodily symptom is tied to an *anatomical* and *genetic context.*

To sum up what has been said thus far: I have tried to show that for those who regard mental symptoms as signs of brain disease, the concept of mental illness is unnecessary and misleading. For what they mean is that people so labeled suffer from diseases of the brain; and, if that is what they mean, it would seem better for the sake of clarity to say that and not something else.

MENTAL ILLNESS AS A NAME FOR PROBLEMS IN LIVING

The term "mental illness" is widely used to describe something which is very different than a disease of the brain. Many people today take it for granted that living is an arduous process. Its hardship for modern man, moreover, derives not so much from a struggle for biological survival as from the stresses and strains inherent in the social intercourse of complex human personalities. In this context, the notion of mental illness is used to identify or describe some feature of an individual's so-called personality. Mental illness—as a deformity of the personality, so to speak—is then regarded as the *cause* of the human disharmony. It is implicit in this view that social intercourse between people is regarded as something *inherently harmonious,* its disturbance being due solely to the presence of "mental illness" in many people. This is obviously fallacious reasoning, for it makes the abstraction "mental illness" into a *cause,* even though this abstraction was created in the first place to serve only as a shorthand expression for certain types of human behavior. It now becomes necessary to ask: "What kinds of behavior are regarded as indicative of mental illness, and by whom?"

The concept of illness, whether bodily or mental, implies *deviation from some clearly defined norm.* In the case of physical illness, the norm is the structural and functional integrity of the human body. Thus, although the desirability of physical health, as such, is an ethical value, what health *is* can be stated in anatomical and physiological terms. What is the norm deviation from which is regarded as mental illness? This question cannot be easily answered. But whatever this norm might be, we can be certain of only one thing: namely, that it is a norm that must be stated in terms of *psychosocial, ethical,* and *legal* concepts. For example, notions such as "excessive repression" or "acting out an unconscious impulse" illustrate the use of psychological concepts for judging (so-called) mental health and illness. The idea that chronic hostility, vengefulness, or divorce are indicative of mental illness would be illustrations of the use of ethical norms (that is, the desirability of love, kindness, and a stable marriage relationship). Finally, the widespread psychiatric opinion that only a mentally ill person would commit homicide illustrates the use of a legal concept as a norm of mental health. The norm from which deviation is measured whenever one speaks of a mental illness is a *psychosocial and ethical one.* Yet, the remedy is sought in terms of *medical* measures which—it is hoped and assumed— are free from wide differences of ethical value. The definition of the disorder and the terms in which its remedy are sought are therefore at serious odds with one another. The practical significance of this covert conflict between the alleged nature of the defect and the remedy can hardly be exaggerated.

Having identified the norms used to measure deviations in cases of mental illness, we will now turn to the question: "Who defines the norms and hence the deviation?" Two basic answers may be offered: (*a*) It may be the person himself (that is, the patient) who decides that he deviates from a norm. For example, an artist may believe that he suffers from a work inhibition; and he may implement this conclusion by seeking help *for* himself from a psychotherapist. (*b*) It may be someone other than the patient who decides that the latter is deviant (for example, relatives, physicians, legal authorities, society generally, etc.). In such a case a psychiatrist may be hired by others to do something *to* the patient in order to correct the deviation.

These considerations underscore the importance of asking the question "Whose agent is the psychiatrist?" and of giving a candid answer to it. The psychiatrist (psychologist or nonmedical psychotherapist), it now develops, may be the agent of the patient, of the relatives, of the school, of the military services, of a business organization, of a court of law, and so forth. In speaking of the psychiatrist as the agent of these persons or organizations, it is not implied that his values concerning norms, or his ideas and aims concerning the proper nature of remedial action, need to coincide exactly with those of his employer. For example, a patient in individual psychotherapy may believe that his salvation lies in a new marriage; his psychotherapist need not share this hypothesis. As the patient's agent, however, he must abstain from bringing social or legal force to bear on the patient which would prevent him from putting his beliefs into action. If his *contract* is with the patient, the psychiatrist (psychotherapist) may disagree with him or stop his treatment; but he cannot engage others to obstruct the patient's aspirations. Similarly, if a psychiatrist is engaged by a court to determine the sanity of a criminal, he need not fully share the legal authorities' values and intentions in regard to the criminal and the means available for dealing with him. But the psychiatrist is expressly barred from stating, for example, that it is not the criminal who is "insane" but the men who wrote the law on the basis of which the very actions that are being judged are regarded as "criminal." Such an opinion could be voiced, of course, but not in a courtroom, and not by a psychiatrist who makes it his practice to assist the court in performing its daily work.

To recapitulate: In actual contemporary social usage, the finding of a mental illness is made by establishing a deviance in behavior from certain psychosocial, ethical, or legal norms. The judgment may be made, as in medicine, by the patient, the physician (psychiatrist), or others. Remedial action, finally, tends to be sought in a therapeutic—or covertly medical—framework, thus creating a situation in which *psychosocial, ethical,* and/or *legal deviations* are claimed to be correctible by (so-called) *medical action.* Since medical action is designed to correct only medical deviations, it seems logically absurd to expect that it will help solve problems whose very existence had been defined and established on nonmedical grounds. I think that these considerations may be fruitfully applied to the present use of tranquilizers and, more generally, to what might be expected of drugs of whatever type in regard to the amelioration or solution of problems in human living.

THE ROLE OF ETHICS IN PSYCHIATRY

Anything that people *do*—in contrast to things that *happen* to them—takes place in a context of value. In this broad sense, no human activity is devoid of ethical implications. When the values underlying certain activities are widely shared, those who participate in their pursuit may lose sight of them altogether. The discipline of medicine, both as a pure science (for example, research) and as a technology (for example, therapy), contains many ethical considerations and judgments. Unfortunately, these are often denied, minimized, or merely kept out of focus; for the ideal of the medical profession as well as of the people whom it serves seems to be having a system of medicine (allegedly) free of ethical value. This sentimental notion is expressed by such things as the doctor's willingness to treat and help patients irrespective of their religious or political beliefs, whether they are rich or poor, etc. While there may be some grounds for this belief—albeit it is a view that is not impressively true even in these regards—the fact remains that ethical considerations encompass a vast range of human affairs. By making the practice of medicine neutral in regard to some specific issues of value need not, and cannot, mean that it can be kept free from all such values. The practice of medicine is intimately tied to ethics; and the first thing that we must do, it seems to me, is to try to make this clear and explicit. I shall let this matter rest here, for it does not concern us specifically in this essay. Lest there be any vagueness, however, about how or where ethics and medicine meet, let me remind the reader of such issus as birth control, abortion, suicide, and euthanasia as only a few of the major areas of current ethicomedical controversy.

Psychiatry, I submit, is very much more intimately tied to problems of ethics than is medicine. I use the word "psychiatry" here to refer to that contemporary discipline which is concerned with *problems in living* (and not with diseases of the brain, which are problems for neurology). Problems in human relations can be analyzed, interpreted, and given meaning only within given social and ethical contexts. Accordingly, it *does* make a difference—arguments to the contrary notwithstanding— what the psychiatrist's socioethical orientations happen to be; for these will influence his ideas on what is wrong with the patient, what deserves comment or interpretation, in what possible directions change might be desirable, and so forth. Even in medicine proper, these factors play a role, as for instance, in the divergent orientations which physicians, de- pending on their religious affiliations, have toward such things as birth control and therapeutic abortion. Can anyone really believe that a psy- chotherapist's ideas concerning religious belief, slavery, or other similar issues play no role in his practical work? If they do make a difference, what are we to infer from it? Does it not seem reasonable that we ought to have different psychiatric therapies—each expressly recognized for the ethical positions which they embody—for, say, Catholics and Jews, re- ligious persons and agnostics, democrats and communists, white suprem- acists and Negroes, and so on? Indeed, if we look at how psychiatry is actually practiced today (especially in the United States), we find that people do seek psychiatric help in accordance with their social status and ethical beliefs. This should really not surprise us more than being told that practicing Catholics rarely frequent birth control clinics.

The foregoing position which holds that contemporary psychother- apists deal with problems in living, rather than with mental illnesses and their curses, stands in opposition to a currently prevalent claim, accord- ing to which mental illness is just as "real" and "objective" as bodily illness. This is a confusing claim since it is never known exactly what is meant by such words as "real" and "objective." I suspect, however, that what is intended by the proponents of this view is to create the idea in the popular mind that mental illness is some sort of disease entity, like an infection or a malignancy. If this were true, one could *catch* or *get* a "mental illness," one might *have* or *harbor* it, one might *transmit* it to others, and finally one could get *rid* of it. In my opinion, there is not a shred of evidence to support this idea. To the contrary, all the evidence is the other way and supports the view that what people now call mental illnesses are for the most part *communications* expressing unacceptable ideas, often framed, moreover, in an unusual idiom. . . .

This is not the place to consider in detail the similarities and differences between bodily and mental illnesses. It shall suffice for us here to emphasize only one important difference between them: namely, that whereas bodily disease refers to public, physiocochemical occurrences, the notion of mental illness is used to codify relatively more private, sociopsychological happenings of which the observer (diagnostician) forms a part. In other words, the psychiatrist does not stand *apart* from what he observes, but is, in Harry Stack Sullivan's apt words, a "participant observer." This means that he is *committed* to some picture of what he considers reality—and to what he thinks society considers reality—and he observes and judges the patient's behavior in the light of these considerations. This touches on our earlier observation that the notion of mental symptom itself implies a comparison between observer and observed, psychiatrist and patient. This is so obvious that I may be charged with belaboring trivialities. Let me therefore say once more that my aim in presenting this argument was expressly to criticize and counter a prevailing contemporary tendency to deny the moral aspects of psychiatry (and psychotherapy) and to substitute for them allegedly value-free medical considerations. Psychotherapy, for example, is being widely practiced as though it entailed nothing other than restoring the patient from a state of mental sickness to one of mental health. While it is generally accepted that mental illness has something to do with man's social (or interpersonal) relations, it is paradoxically maintained that problems of values (that is, of ethics) do not arise in this process. Yet, in one sense, much of psychotherapy may revolve around nothing other than the elucidation and weighing of goals and values—many of which may be mutually contradictory—and the means whereby they might best be harmonized, realized, or relinquished.

The diversity of human values and the methods by means of which they may be realized is so vast, and many of them remain so unacknowledged, that they cannot fail but lead to conflicts in human relations. Indeed, to say that human relations at all levels—from mother to child, through husband and wife, to nation and nation—are fraught with stress, strain, and disharmony is, once again, making the obvious explicit. Yet, what may be obvious may be also poorly understood. This I think is the case here. For it seems to me that—at least in our scientific theories of behavior—we have failed to *accept* the simple fact that human relations are inherently fraught with difficulties and that to make them even relatively harmonious requires much patience and hard work. I submit that the idea of mental illness is now being put to work to obscure certain difficulties which at present may be inherent—not that they need be unmodifiable—in the social intercourse of persons. If this is true, the concept functions as a disguise; for instead of calling attention to conflicting human needs, aspirations, and values, the notion of mental illness provides an amoral and impersonal "thing" (an "illness") as an explanation for *problems in living.* We may recall in this connection that not so long ago it was devils and witches who were held responsible for men's problems in social living. The belief in mental illness, as something other than man's trouble in getting along with his fellow man, is the proper heir to the belief in demonology and witchcraft. Mental illness exists or is "real" in exactly the same sense in which witches existed or were "real."

CHOICE, RESPONSIBILITY, AND PSYCHIATRY

While I have argued that mental illnesses do not exist, I obviously did not imply that the social and psychological occurrences to which this label is currently being attached also do not exist. Like the personal and social troubles which people had in the Middle Ages, they are real enough. It is the labels we give them that concerns us and, having labelled them, what we do about them. While I cannot go into the ramified implications of this problem here, it is worth noting that a demonologic conception of problems in living gave rise to therapy along theological lines. Today, a belief in mental illness implies—nay, requires—therapy along medical or psychotherapeutic lines.

What is implied in the line of thought set forth here is something quite different. I do not intend to offer a new conception of "psychiatric illness" nor a new form of "therapy." My aim is more modest and yet also more ambitious. It is to suggest that the phenomena now called mental illnesses be looked at afresh and more simply, that they be removed from the category of illnesses, and that they be regarded as the expressions of man's struggle with the problem of *how* he should live. The last mentioned problem is obviously a vast one, its enormity reflecting not only man's inability to cope with his environment, but even more his increasing self-reflectiveness.

By problems in living, then, I refer to that truly explosive chain reaction which began with man's fall from divine grace by partaking of the fruit of the tree of knowledge. Man's awareness of himself and of the world about him seems to be a steadily expanding one, bringing in its wake an ever larger *burden of understanding. This burden,* then, *is to be expected and must not be misinterpreted.* Our only *rational* means for lightening it is *more understanding,* and appropriate *action* based on such understanding. The main alternative lies in acting as though the burden were not what in fact we perceive it to be and taking refuge in an outmoded theological view on man. In the latter view, man does not fashion his life and much of his world about him, but merely lives out his fate in a world created by superior beings. This may logically lead to pleading nonresponsibility in the face of seemingly unfathomable problems and difficulties. Yet, if man fails to take increasing responsibility for his actions, individually as well as collectively, it seems unlikely that some higher power on being would assume this task and carry this burden for him. Moreover, this seems hardly the proper time in human history for obscuring the issue of man's responsibility for his actions by hiding it behind the skirt of an all-explaining conception of mental illness.

CONCLUSIONS

I have tried to show that the notion of mental illness has outlived whatever usefulness it might have had and that it now functions merely as a convenient myth. As such, it is a true heir to religious myths in general, and to the belief in witchcraft in particular; the role of all these belief-systems was to act as *social tranquilizers,* thus encouraging the hope that mastery of certain specific problems may be achieved by means of substitutive (symbolic-magical) operations. The notion of mental illness thus serves mainly to obscure the everday fact that life for most people is a continuous struggle, not for biological survival, but for a "place in the sun," "peace of mind," or some other human value. For man aware of himself and of the world about him, once the needs for preserving the body (and perhaps the race) are more or less satisfied, the problem arises as to what he should do with himself. Sustained adherence to the myth of mental illness allows people to avoid facing this problem, believing that mental health, conceived as the absence of mental illness, automatically insures the making of right and safe choices in one's conduct of life. But the facts are all the other way. It is the making of good choices in life that others regard, retrospectively, as good mental health!

The myth of mental illness encourages us, moreover, to believe in its logical corollary: that social intercourse would be harmonious, satisfying, and the secure basis of a "good life" were it not for the disrupting influences of mental illness or "psychopathology." The potentiality for universal human happiness, in this form at least, seems to me but another example of the I-wish-it-were-true type of fantasy. I do believe that human happiness or well-being on a hitherto unimaginable large scale, and not just for a select few, is possible. This goal could be achieved, however, only at the cost of many men, and not just a few being willing and able to tackle their personal, social, and ethical conflicts. This means having the courage and integrity to forgo waging battles on false fronts, finding solutions for substitute problems—for instance, fighting the battle of stomach acid and chronic fatigue instead of facing up to a marital conflict.

Our adversaries are not demons, witches, fate, or mental illness. We have no enemy whom we can fight, exorcise, or dispel by "cure." What we do have are *problems in living*—whether these be biological, economic, political, or sociopsychological. In this essay I was concerned only with problems belonging in the last mentioned category, and within this group mainly with those pertaining to moral values. The field to which modern psychiatry addresses itself is vast, and I made no effort to encompass it all. My argument was limited to the proposition that mental illness is a myth, whose function it is to disguise and thus render more palatable the bitter pill of moral conflicts in human relations.

SOCIAL PSYCHIATRY AND PSYCHOPATHOLOGY: A LAYMAN'S COMMENTS ON CONTEMPORARY DEVELOPMENTS

Barbara Wootton

. . . In the past decade or so it has become increasingly fashionable to attach the adjective "social" to "psychiatry," and to suggest that practically every field of human activity falls within the province of the social psychiatrist. Thus in the United States, Dr. Alexander H. Leighton has written enthusiastically of the possible contribution of social psychiatry in the spheres of law, the armed forces, education, industry, and government; while at the Madrid Congress of the World Psychiatric Association it is reported that papers were presented dealing with subjects as diverse as drug addiction, criminology, mental disturbance and art, architecture and psychiatry, problems of sleep and dreaming, the bio-

Samuel W. Hamilton Award Lecture to the 57th Annual Meeting of the American Psychopathological Association, February 18, 1967. Reprinted by permission.

chemistry of the mind, the application of electronics to psychiatry, and the theory of sexual perversion. Some of this, one suspects, is simple empire building or an attempt to cash in on what has become a laudatory adjective—akin to the practice of euphemistic re-naming which is to-day so popular in my own country, where unemployment has become "redeployment," deflation "disinflation," and a hobo a "person without a settled way of living." But in more sober mood, the time is ripe for critical evaluation of the circumstances in which psychiatry, which can only be literally construed as the healing of the individual psyche, can justifiably call itself "social."

Current usage covers a variety of different meanings. Thus group therapy is sometimes said to be social; but this I would regard as a misnomer since group therapy is not in fact directed towards the group as such: rather is it a technique for using the interactions of the group members as a means of resolving their personal troubles. It is, therefore, fundamentally individual in purpose.

Secondly, there are those who seek to apply psychiatric diagnoses to a society or to a pattern of culture, as when reference is made to the "sick society" or when "the community" is said to be the patient, and techniques are suggested for "treating the collectivity" or for "treatment at the collective level." Such expressions, though much in vogue at the moment, are meaningless if literally interpreted. For, realistically speaking, criteria of health or sickness can only be applied to creatures which are equipped with an organ capable of registering pain or well-being; and no assemblage of human beings, great or small, possesses any such collective equipment. As I have said elsewhere, no community has ever fallen in love or suffered from toothache.

References to the "sick society," therefore, or to "the community as the patient" make sense only as shorthand descriptions of a social environment thought to be inimical to the mental health of the individuals who live under it. In that context psychiatry can properly be said to be social, insofar as it seeks to evaluate various social institutions in terms of their effect upon individual mental health.

The prospect of achieving such an evaluation certainly has great attractions. Psychiatrists may indeed be dazzled with visions of being able to pinpoint noxious social institutions with the confidence with which their colleagues in the public health service condemn insanitary buildings or infected meat; but these images are still for the most part creatures of a dream world. . . .

It is, I submit, imperative that the concept of mental health should be emptied of ethical content. Ethical judgments are the concern of the whole community, and acquire no special authority if they happen to emanate from persons qualified in psychological medicine. On what authority, one may ask, can medical science establish that the values of the Pentagon are "healthier" than those of the beatnik or that the break-up of a marriage has necessarily anything to do with the mental health or sickness of the parties concerned? In the assessment of physical health the same criteria are applicable alike to Americans, Russians, Chinese and Africans, although the diseases to which each of these groups is particularly vulnerable may differ. Yet so long as a moral and social component is introduced into the concept of mental health, we get the absurd result that millions of contemporary Chinamen must be regarded as mentally sick inasmuch as their Communist doctrine certainly runs counter to the "togetherness of middle class American life." Such a conclusion can only be avoided if conformity to the culture in which a man finds himself is accepted as proof of his mental health—a proposition hardly likely to commend itself to any society which owes as much to its rebels and objectors as does the Western world. Nor should it be overlooked that, in so far as psychiatry succeeds in usurping the right to make moral judgments, the layman's freedom to assert his own moral standards is correspondingly restricted. For once we are persuaded that, say, racial prejudice is a symptom of mental ill-health, it becomes as meaningless to denounce such prejudice as immoral as it would be to blame a man for developing cancer. In other words, every incursion of sickness into territory previously occupied by sin means a further concession to a philosophy of determinism. Indeed the persistence of the "stigma" that clings to mental illness is perhaps at least in part to be explained by the man in the street's instinctive resistance to any determinist encroachment on his personal responsibility.

Where then do we go from here in search of an ethically and socially neutral concept of mental disorder? Physical analogies suggest that the crucial feature of an illness is that it lowers the efficiency of an organism in the achievement of that organism's own purposes; and mental disorder may likewise be defined in terms of impairment of function. Such a definition carries no social or ethical overtones; and it covers not only the grosser forms of mental derangement, but also depressions, obsessions and phobias. Persons who suffer from these conditions may, I suggest, legitimately be regarded as sick, while those who are not so troubled must be classified as healthy, no matter how grossly their behaviour may diverge from the accepted norms of the society in which they live. To Dr. Szasz, of course, this terminology would still be objectionable; but perhaps he will find its use forgivable, inasmuch as even his categorical disbelief in mental illness does not, apparently, prevent him from using his professional skills to translate into intelligible form the communications which in his view the mentally "sick" are struggling to convey. In short, while Dr. Szasz would deny to sufferers from mental illness the full privileges of the sick, he is nevertheless willing to give them what he regards as appropriate help.

Certainly the spirit of the times favours the view that mental and physical illness are closely cognate, and encourages the public to see them in that light. In Britain the Royal College of Physicians, in evidence before a Royal Commission in 1954, strongly emphasised that "the procedure for the treatment of the mentally ill should approximate as far as possible to that of the physically ill," and subsequent legislation has provided that "informal" (i.e. voluntary) patients should be admitted to hospital without any formalities beyond those that are customary in cases of physical illness; and in this connection it should be remembered that to-day in Britain some 80% of all admissions of mental patients are on a voluntary basis. In the same spirit, also, psychiatric wards are now frequently attached to general hospitals, while even the institutions that cater for particularly difficult or dangerous patients have been re-christened "special" in place of "mental" hospitals. In short, the keynote of contemporary policy is abolition of the "stigma" attached to mental illness.

The distinction between mental and physical disorder is moreover now in process of attrition, so to speak, from both ends. On the one hand, more and more physical diseases are thought to be of psychosomatic origin; while, on the other side, the discovery of new psychotropic drugs encourages the belief that mental aberrations may be of physical origin and subject to physical control. Already the distinction between functional and organic disorders is held by some to be nothing more than a moving line separating the unknown from the known; and it is significant, also, that illnesses in which mental derangement is the accompaniment of obvious physical disturbance, as, for example, in cases of delirium due to high fever, are normally regarded as physical rather than mental. From this it could be argued that, as the relation between mental and physical illness may be destined eventually to disappear altogether, diagnosis and treatment alike being expressed in purely physical terms.

In the meantime, however, the dualism remains and it must be admitted that the concept of impairment of function, even as related to an organism's own goals, is still far from precise. It is, for instance, not easy to decide whether a schizophrenic patient suffers from inability to attain his own goals or whether he has merely chosen to adopt somewhat unusual objectives. In less dramatic cases of mental disturbance, moreover, as also in the assignment of physical ailments to the psychosomatic category, the inevitably subjective element in the physician's judgment to which I have already referred plays havoc with any attempt to relate mental disorders to social environment. For purely practical reasons, therefore, I would suggest that in the present state of knowledge studies in the epidemiology of mental disorders should work within a still narrower definition, and record only those cases in which the impairment is sufficiently serious to prevent the patient from following his usual occupation. Admittedly the use of this standard would leave out of account a wide range of cases in which sufferers from depressions or other psychoneuroses are still able, in spite of their disability, to go about their ordinary business. But so long as we are so lamentably unable to measure the size of the submerged portion of the iceberg, modesty as well as prudence suggests that attention should be concentrated upon the visible area.

It will not, I think, have escaped your notice that my formula would have the effect of excluding from the field of psychiatry large areas in which it is at present active. In particular, psychopathy or sociopathy would fail to qualify as mental illnesses since it cannot be said that the psychopath's disorder inhibits him from doing what he wants to do. The trouble is that what he wants to do is socially unwelcome, and that he often keeps on doing it in face of repeated punishment and severe social disapproval: yet, at the same time he may exhibit no other unusual symptoms of any kind.

The hypothesis that the psychopath is not a sick man is, I need hardly say, highly unorthodox. The trend of contemporary opinion tends to enlarge the notion of psychopathic illness rather than to restrict or to do away with it. Thus in Britain "psychopathy" is defined in the Mental Health Act of 1959 in remarkably wide terms as "a persistent disorder or disability of mind (whether or not including subnormality of intelligence) which results in abnormally aggressive or seriously irresponsible conduct on the part of the patient, and requires or is susceptible to medical treatment." Persons in whom this condition is diagnosed may be compulsorily committed to hospital, provided that they are under twenty-one years of age; but they may not be detained after the age of twenty-five, unless they are regarded as a danger to themselves or other people. Committal to hospital on a diagnosis of psychopathy "by reason only of promiscuity or other immoral conduct" is, moreover, expressly excluded. In the context this presumably means immorality of a sexual character.

Liberally interpreted, these provisions could result in the transfer from the ranks of the blameworthy into the category of the mentally afflicted of large numbers of young persons who drink to excess, take drugs, get into fights or use motor vehicles in a dangerous fashion. Actually, however, the number compulsorily detained as suffering from psychopathy, not in conjunction with any other disorder, is still small, though it is increasing rapidly, committals under these provisions having risen steadily from 377 in the first thirteen months of the Act's operation to an estimated 836 in 1965. No information is officially available as to the nature of the aggressive or irresponsible conduct which has led to the detention of these cases; but from such private enjuiries as I have been able to make, I would gather that the degree of deviance which they exhibit is generally considerable.

However, in spite of the wide terms of the Mental Health Act's definition, not every psychiatrist will admit psychopathy to be an illness. Particularly outspoken is Dr. Peter Hays of St. George's Hospital, London, who has roundly declared that psychopathy is "regarded inaccurately as a disease" and that the psychiatrist who deals with a psychopath "calls what he does 'treatment' out of habit, calls the psychopath a 'patient' because he is accustomed to label his clients in this way, and calls psychopathy 'a diagnosis' because most of the labels he attaches are diagnoses and it does not occur to him to except this one." According to Dr. Hays, research into psychopathy really involves investigation of two distinct and not necessarily allied problems, namely personality deviation and social nonconformity; and he concludes that owing to the "double-headed" nature of the problem, "the psychopath is not ideal material for the study of psychopathy" . . . .

As in the treatment of psychopaths, so also in the fields of law, government, education and industry . . . the activities of contemporary psychiatrists extend far beyond that of restoring the patient's impaired functions. Indeed it could be said that in these areas the role of social psychiatry is often reversed. Instead of seeking to discover and to create environments favourable to mental health, psychiatrists follow the opposite course of trying to promote the adjustment of the individual psyche to the world in which it has to live. Undoubtedly such activities are quite extraneous to, even if not in active conflict with, an ethically and socially neutral conception of mental health closely parallel to the physical concept of health as functional efficiency; for where is the evidence that Nature intended us to be good soldiers or law-abiding citizens or contented and productive workmen? and in what sense are we justified in regarding such people as more healthy than those in the opposite categories?

Nevertheless the fact has to be accepted that psychiatrists are well-established in these fields and certainly have no intention of allowing themselves to be dislodged. What matters, therefore, is, I submit, that we should recognise that psychiatrists who occupy themselves with the rehabilitation of criminals, the promotion of industrial peace or the selection of officers for the forces are taking on roles which have nothing to do with the healing function traditionally associated with medicine;

and that we should all be alive to the very real dangers involved in this metamorphosis. Dr. Szasz' warning that in all these activities, the doctor-patient relationship is fundamentally changed, if not actually destroyed, must not go unheeded. For the doctor who employs psychiatric techniques in the rehabilitation of criminals, has become an agent of the State and a part of the machinery of law enforcement. His function is no longer to minister to the needs and to cure the ills of his patient, but to induce conformity to the State's demands—a very different matter. So also the psychiatrist who advises managements on questions of personnel or of business organisation has become the agent of an industrial corporation, and must identify himself with the values of that corporation. In all such cases the skills employed may be psychological; but inasmuch as the concern of psychiatry is health and healing, they are misnamed psychiatric.

Particularly perplexing are the problems raised by the incursion of psychiatry into criminal and penal matters; and these are of concern alike to the profession itself and to the community at large. First and most conspicuous of the problems are those associated with questions of criminal responsibility. Psychiatrists who find themselves called upon to give evidence in the courts upon these questions are notoriously ill at ease . . . the truth is, I suggest, that this conflict cannot be resolved so long as a lawyer sees the function of the criminal courts as essentially punitive, and so long as the word "punishment" is constantly on the lips of even the most progressive and humane members of the legal profession. Punishment implies responsibility: it would be patently immoral to punish a man who could not help doing what he has done, and perhaps did not even realise that he had done it. In a punitive system, therefore, it is imperative to fix the limits of responsibility, and it is for help in that task that the lawyer invokes the specialised knowledge of the psychiatrist.

As is only too well known, the attempt to fix those limits has produced over the years a formidable body of legal decisions of rival formulae and of learned treatises. . . . As a result of this monumental labour on the part of both lawyers and psychiatrists, the legal concept of responsibility has been profoundly modified. Nevertheless, I find the history of this matter a melancholy spectacle of misplaced intellectual ingenuity. For the truth is that, although it is possible to hold opinions about responsibility, it is wholly impossible to validate these opinions scientifically. A psychiatrist may personally be convinced that, in terms of the Durham formula, a particular criminal act is the product of mental disease, but where is he to turn to for proof of the correctness of this opinion? Certainly, the psychiatrist who interests himself in criminological questions has a much wider experience than most of us of the behaviour of offenders, and he should, therefore, be in a better position than the layman to make predictions as to the probable future course of any particular criminal's career. But the question how a man is likely to act is entirely distinct from the question whether his action is responsible in the sense that he could have acted otherwise than as he did. That issue cannot, in the nature of things, be put to the test of experience. Indeed, it might well be argued that on that issue, the psychiatrist's judgment, for all his experience, is no better than that of anyone else.

So long, however, as the criminal courts concern themselves primarily with the imposition of punishment upon those who deserve it, they are bound to search for some criterion by which to distinguish the deserving from the undeserving, and into that search . . . many a psychiatrist has allowed himself to be lured. Dr. Sheldon Glueck has indeed hinted at what he calls the "twilight of futile blameworthiness": but even he contemplates that should the criminal law some day concern itself with matters of behaviour alone, special tribunals of psychiatrists and psychologists would still deal with questions of intent, premeditation and so forth. Yet anyone who has studied the desperate efforts of psychiatric witnesses in the courts to draw tenable distinctions between the wicked and the mentally irresponsible must view with profound scepticism Dr. Leighton's proud boast that "the psychiatrist can differentiate the pathological from the merely disagreeable." For no matter how firmly this differentiation may be established in the psychiatrist's own mind, the objective evidence by which it can be implanted in the minds of others is never forthcoming. In the end the hard fact must be faced, that on the issue of responsibility and culpability psychiatrists are required by the courts to answer inherently unanswerable questions. It is, I submit, high time that they said so in loud and unmistakable terms.

The employment of psychiatrists in the service of the criminal courts raises also important issues of personal liberty. In one form or another such issues concern the citizens of every state in the Union. As it happens, however, they have been illustrated with particular vividness by the Committee appointed in 1961 by the Judicial Conference of the District of Columbia Circuit to examine the problems arising from pre-trial mental examination in criminal cases; and I shall draw mainly upon the findings of that Committee in order to call attention to the risks involved.

Since the Durham case, pre-trial mental examinations in the District of Columbia may relate either to the accused's competence to stand trial or to his responsibility for the offence with which he is charged. Such examinations appear to be, at least by British standards, remarkably frequent. In the twelve months ended 30 June 1963, a motion for a pre-trial mental examination was made in the case of one in every six defendants. As is to be expected in the great majority of such cases it is the defendant's attorney who initiates the request for such an examination. But in a by no means negligible proportion of cases, the initiative is taken by the prosecution, or, very occasionally, by the court itself; and it is in these cases that serious issues of personal liberty can arise. For instance, a mental examination involves incarceration in a mental hospital, at one time for as much as 90 days, and more recently for a period of sixty days. How can such deprivation of liberty be justified in the case of a man who has not himself put his mental state in issue? Again, what rights has a defendant who himself disputes a psychiatric report that he is not competent to stand trial? In the state of New York, at least according to Dr. Szasz, the defendant's own plea to stand trial might, in such a case "be overruled solely on the basis of the opinion of government psychiatrists." And what is the position of the defendant who refuses to co-operate in the pretrial mental examination ordered by the court either on the motion of the prosecutor or on its own initiative? In the District of Columbia "no formal sanctions" are apparently "available to compel a defendant to co-operate in a mental examination, whether he or the prosecution requests it." But it is more than a little alarming to learn in this context that "a failure to co-operate" may "itself be a symptom of mental disorder." Equally alarming also is it to learn that, in the state of New York a charge of contempt of court can apparently be brought against anyone who refuses co-operation in a mental examination.

To those of us who come from Britain such provisions cannot but appear startling. They certainly confer upon psychiatrists powers far beyond those enjoyed by their British colleagues. In Britain a psychiatrist's opinion on fitness to stand trial cannot be conclusive: the issue must be determined by a jury. In charges of murder, prison medical officers (who may have some psychiatric training but are unlikely to be fully qualified psychiatrists) regularly supply pre-trial medical reports, in which some attempt is made to assess the accused's responsibility for his actions; but in all other cases questions of criminal responsibility are normally raised only after conviction, except that in committing for trial magistrates . . . can make it a condition of bail that the accused should present himself for such examination by a psychiatrist. But even after conviction the idea that a sixty-day remand in custody might be necessary for enquiry into an offender's mental condition is quite unheard of: indeed summary courts have no power to order custodial remands for medical examination for more than three weeks at a time. Perhaps, however, all this is merely evidence that we in Britain are very old-fashioned?

Finally, something must be said about the attitude of psychiatrists employed in the penal service to practices which are not easy to reconcile with the ethics of their profession. I refer to the use of surgery or drugs or aversion therapy. The ethical problems involved in brain surgery are too obvious to need elaboration, and in Britain at any rate the authorities responsible for the penal system are very much alive to possible charges of experimenting upon criminals. . . .

In the part of the world that I know best, recourse to drugs as a means of controlling anti-social behaviour is more talked about than actually practised, except in cases of gross mental disturbance which would be likely to receive similar treatment outside any penal context. Elsewhere, however, and notably in the United States, there has been a number of experiments upon juveniles. Summarising these Professor Eysenck reports that "the treatment consisted of medication with one of the stimulant drugs, usually amphetamine, and observations were made of the behaviour of the children and juveniles concerned. There were no particular attempts to alter their moral and ethical behaviour and no attempts at psycho-therapy. The success of the treatment, which was usually continued over a period of weeks, was quite astonishing . . . there was a considerable, almost immediate, improvement in the behaviour of the patients concerned. They became much more amenable to discipline and much more socialised in their pattern of activities; often they ceased to show behaviour problems. Usually the improvement ceased when the drug treatment itself was stopped, but sometimes the improvement in behaviour continued well beyond this point and seemed to become an enduring feature of the individual." It all sounds engagingly simple. Yet the prospect that drugs may be used to induce social conformity conjures up visions of a Brave New World contemplation of which cannot but be disquieting. And in the meantime, to a magistrate such as myself, who is constantly required to convict, and to impose penalties upon, young people for the possession of amphetamine tablets, there is something paradoxical in the discovery of the virtue-producing qualities of this very drug.

But of all the new developments in penal treatment, aversion therapy holds . . . the most sinister possibilities. True, these are limited by the fact that this treatment cannot be applied to an unco-operative patient; but there are ways and ways of obtaining co-operation, not least of which might be the prospect of release from detention. At all events interest in the potential application of the technique of aversion therapy to "patients who have been diagnosed either in law courts or in psychiatric practice as delinquents" has reached the point at which it was the subject of a special symposium, subsequently reported in the *British Journal of Criminology*. Among the cases described was that of a man convicted of many offences of damaging handbags and perambulators.

This patient was injected with apomorphine, and just before nausea resulted, he was shown a collection of handbags and prams together with coloured illustrations of similar objects. The treatment was given every two hours day and night, no food was allowed and the patient was kept awake by stimulant drugs. Not surprisingly it was not long before he felt sick at the mere sight of a handbag or a pram, and after a course of such treatments it is reported that his fetichism disappeared and had not recurred some two years later. Similar treatments, as is well known, have been applied to transvestists, to alcoholics and to certain sexual deviants; though the nature of the unpleasant stimulus used varied in different cases, "mild electric shock to the patient's feet" being on occasion substituted for nausea-producing drugs. Drivers who cannot resist exceeding the permitted speed limits have also, according to a recent newspaper report been subjected by a British psychiatrist to electric shocks of up to 70 volts, while watching a film of fast driving, with shots of speed limit signs and speedometer readings, and the psychiatrist in question, who is said to have used similar methods in the cure of compulsive gamblers, is reported to be "appealing for volunteers."

At the symposium just now mentioned one psychiatrist at least, Dr. H. M. Holden reacted vehemently against such procedures. Not only did he uncompromisingly reject the suggestion that it is a doctor's function to modify behaviour so as to suit the requirements either of the law or of a particular system of ethics, but he went on boldly to describe the techniques of aversion therapy as simply highly sophisticated forms of punishment, which indeed is what they are. It was a welcome outburst and a salutary reminder of the moral pitfalls which await the psychiatrist who strays beyond the doctor's traditional and humane obligation to devote himself to the relief of suffering.

Having said my say, I am conscious that what I have presented to you is a catalogue not so much of comments as of heterodoxies, strung together into what may well appear to have been a somewhat discursive lecture. Perhaps, therefore, in conclusion, I may recapitulate what to me is the essential theme. Psychiatry ranks as one among many medical specialisms, not as a church or a religion; and its status as such is contingent upon a fundamental analogy between mental and physical health. No one disputes that physical health is a morally neutral condition, equally compatible with vice or virtue; yet the link with medicine will be broken if mental health is not defined in similar terms. As medical men, psychiatrists cannot afford to appear to be the architects of social conformism or to allow moral judgments to masquerade in medical dress. Indeed on moral questions there is no reason to suppose that the judgments of doctors are superior to those of anybody else; and on social policy their expertise extends only to assessment of the possible impact of policies upon health as above defined. Finally, the psychiatrist who takes service as an agent of the state makes an inevitable breach with the medical profession's therapeutic tradition: but not, one hopes, with the dictates of common humanity.

THE ROLE OF THE MENTALLY ILL
AND THE DYNAMICS OF MENTAL DISORDER:
A RESEARCH FRAMEWORK
Thomas J. Scheff

. . .

One source of immediate embarrassment to any social theory of "mental illness" is that the terms used in referring to these phenomena in our society prejudge the issue. The medical metaphor "mental illness" suggests a determinate process which occurs within the individual: the unfolding and development of disease. It is convenient, therefore, to drop terms derived from the disease metaphor in favor of a standard sociological concept, deviant behavior, which signifies behavior that violates a social norm in a given society.

If the symptoms of mental illness are to be construed as violations of social norms, it is necessary to specify the type of norms involved. Most norm violations do not cause the violator to be labeled as mentally ill, but as ill-mannered, ignorant, sinful, criminal, or perhaps just harried, depending on the type of norm involved. There are innumerable norms, however, over which consensus is so complete that the members of a group appear to take them for granted. A host of such norms surround even the simplest conversation: A person engaged in conversation is expected to face toward his partner, rather than directly away from him; if his gaze is toward the partner, he is expected to look toward his eyes, rather than, say, toward his forehead; to stand at a proper conversational distance, neither one inch away nor across the room, and so on. A person who regularly violated these expectations probably would not be thought to be merely ill-bred, but as strange, bizarre, and frightening, because his behavior violates the assumptive world of the group, the world that is construed to be the only one that is natural, decent, and possible.

From *Sociometry,* Vol. 26 (December 1963), 436-53. Reprinted by permission.

The culture of the group provides a vocabulary of terms for categorizing many norm violations: crime, perversion, drunkenness, and bad manners are familiar examples. Each of these terms is derived from the type of norm broken, and ultimately, from the type of behavior involved. After exhausting these categories, however, there is always a residue of the most diverse kinds of violations, for which the culture provides no explicit label. For example, although there is great cultural variation in what is defined as decent or real, each culture tends to reify its definition of decency and reality, and so provide no way of handling violations of its expectations in these areas. The typical norm governing decency or reality, therefore, literally "goes without saying" and its violation is unthinkable for most of its members. For the convenience of the society in construing those instances of unnamable deviance which are called to its attention, these violations may be lumped together into a residual category: witchcraft, spirit possession, or, in our own society, mental illness. In this paper, the diverse kinds of deviation for which our society provides no explicit label, and which, therefore, sometimes lead to the labeling of the violator as mentally ill, will be considered to be technically *residual deviance*.

THE ORIGINS, PREVALENCE AND COURSE OF RESIDUAL DEVIANCE

The first proposition concerns the origins of residual deviance. *1. Residual deviance arises from fundamentally diverse sources.* It has been demonstrated that some types of mental disorder are the result of organic causes. It appears likely, therefore, that there are genetic, biochemical or physiological origins for residual deviance. It also appears that residual deviance can arise from individual psychogical peculiarities and from differences in upbringing and training. Residual deviance can also probably be produced by various kinds of external stress: the sustained fear and hardship of combat, and deprivation of food, sleep, and even sensory experience. Residual deviance, finally, can be a volitional act of innovation or defiance. The kinds of behavior deemed typical of mental illness, such as hallucinations, delusions, depression, and mania, can all arise from these diverse sources.

The second proposition concerns the prevalence of residual deviance which is analogous to the "total" or "true" prevalence of mental disorder (in contrast to the "treated" prevalence). *2. Relative to the rate of treated mental illness, the rate of unrecorded residual deviance is extremely high.* There is evidence that grossly deviant behavior is often not noticed or, if it is noticed, it is rationalized as eccentricity. Apparently, many persons who are extremely withdrawn, or who "fly off the handle" for extended periods of time, who imagine fantastic events, or

who hear voices or see visions, are not labeled as insane either by themselves or others. Their deviance, rather, is unrecognized, ignored, or
rationalized. This pattern of inattention and rationalization will be called
"denial."

In addition to the kind of evidence cited above there are a number of
epidemiological studies of total prevalence. There are numerous problems in interpreting the results of these studies; the major difficulty is
that the definition of mental disorder is different in each study, as are
the methods used to screen cases. These studies represent, however, the
best available information and can be used to estimate total prevalence.

A convenient summary of findings is presented in Plunkett and Gordon. This source compares the methods and populations used in eleven
field studies, and lists rates of total prevalence (in percentages) as 1.7,
3.6, 4.5, 4.7, 5.3, 6.1, 10.9, 13.8, 23.2, 23.3, and 33.3.

How do these total rates compare with the rates of treated mental
disorder? One of the studies cited by Plunkett and Gordon, the Baltimore study reported by Pasamanick, is useful in this regard since it includes both treated and untreated rates. As compared with the untreated
rate of 10.9 per cent, the rate of treatment in state, VA, and private
hospitals of Baltimore residents was .5 per cent. That is, for every mental
patient there were approximately 20 untreated cases located by the survey. It is possible that the treated rate is too low, however, since patients
treated by private physicians were not included. Judging from another
study, the New Haven study of treated prevalence, the number of patients treated in private practice is small compared to those hospitalized:
over 70 per cent of the patients located in that study were hospitalized
even though extensive case-finding techniques were employed. The over-
all treated prevalence in the New Haven study was reported as .8 per
cent, which is in good agreement with my estimate of .7 per cent for the
Baltimore study. If we accept .8 per cent as an estimate of the upper
limit of treated prevalence for the Pasamanick study, the ratio of treated
to untreated cases is 1/14. That is, for every treated patient we should
expect to find 14 untreated cases in the community.

One interpretation of this finding is that the untreated patients in the
community represent those cases with less severe disorders, while those
patients with severe impairments all fall into the treated group. Some of
the findings in the Pasamanick study point in this direction. Of the untreated patients, about half are classified as psychoneurotic. Of the psychoneurotics, in turn, about half again are classified as suffering from
minimal impairment. At least a fourth of the untreated group, then, involved very mild disorders.

The evidence from the group diagnosed as psychotic does not support
this interpretation, however. Almost all of the cases diagnosed as psy-

chotic were judged to involve severe impairment, yet half of the diagnoses of psychosis occurred in the untreated group. In other words, according to this study there were as many untreated as treated cases of
psychoses.

On the basis of the high total prevalence rates cited above and other
evidence, it seems plausible that residual deviant behavior is usually
transitory, which is the substance of the third proposition. *3. Most residual deviance is "denied" and is transitory.* The high rates of total
prevalence suggest that most residual deviancy is unrecognized or rationalized away. For this type of deviance, which is amorphous and uncrystallized, Lemert uses the term "primary deviation." Balint describes
similar behavior as "the unorganized phase of illness." Although Balint
assumes that patients in this phase ultimately "settle down" to an "organized illness," other outcomes are possible. A person in this stage may
"organize" his deviance in other than illness terms, e.g., as eccentricity
or genius, or the deviant acts may terminate when situational stress is
removed.

The experience of battlefield psychiatrists can be interpreted to support the hypothesis that residual deviance is usually transistory. Glass reports that combat neurosis is often self-terminating if the soldier is kept
with his unit and given only the most superficial medical attention.
Descriptions of child behavior can be interpreted in the same way. According to these reports, most children go through periods in which at
least several of the following kinds of deviance may occur: temper tantrums, head banging, scratching, pinching, biting, fantasy playmates or
pets, illusory physical complaints, and fears of sounds, shapes, colors,
persons, animals, darkness, weather, ghosts, and so on. In the vast majority of instances, however, these behavior patterns do not become
stable.

If residual deviance is highly prevalent among ostensibly "normal"
persons and is usually transitory, as suggested by the last two propositions, what accounts for the small percentage of residual deviants who
go on to deviant careers? To put the question another way, under what
conditions is residual deviance stabilized? The conventional hypothesis
is that the answer lies in the deviant himself. The hypothesis suggested
here is that the most important single factor (but not the only factor) in
the stabilization of residual deviance is the societal reaction. Residual
deviance may be stabilized if it is defined to be evidence of mental illness,
and/or the deviant is placed in a deviant status, and begins to play the
role of the mentally ill. In order to avoid the implication that mental
disorder is merely role-playing and pretence, it is first necessary to discuss the social institution of insanity.

SOCIAL CONTROL: INDIVIDUAL AND SOCIAL
SYSTEMS OF BEHAVIOR

In *The Myth of Mental Illness,* Szasz proposes that mental disorder be viewed within the framework of "the game-playing model of human behavior." He then describes hysteria, schizophrenia, and other mental disorders as the "impersonation" of sick persons by those whose "real" problem concerns "problems of living." Although Szasz states that role-playing by mental patients may not be completely or even mostly voluntary, the implication is that mental disorder be viewed as a strategy chosen by the individual as a way of obtaining help from others. Thus, the term "impersonation" suggests calculated and deliberate shamming by the patient. . . .

The present paper also uses the role-playing model to analyze mental disorder, but places more emphasis on the involuntary aspects of role-playing than Szasz, who tends to treat role-playing as an individual system of behavior. In many social psychological discussions, however, role-playing is considered as a part of a social system. The individual plays his role by articulating his behavior with the cues and actions of other persons involved in the transaction. The proper performance of a role is dependent on having a co-operative audience. This proposition may also be reversed: having an audience which acts toward the individual in a uniform way may lead the actor to play the expected role even if he is not particularly interested in doing so. The "baby of the family" may come to find this role obnoxious, but the uniform pattern of cues and actions which confronts him in the family may lock in with his own vocabulary of responses so that it is inconvenient and difficult for him not to play the part expected of him. To the degree that alternative roles are closed off, the proffered role may come to be the only way the individual can cope with the situation.

One of Szasz's very apt formulations touches upon the social systemic aspects of role-playing. He draws an analogy between the role of the mentally ill and the "type-casting" of actors. Some actors get a reputation for playing one type of role, and find it difficult to obtain other roles. Although they may be displeased, they may also come to incorporate aspects of the type-cast role into their self-conceptions, and ultimately into their behavior. Findings in several social psychological studies suggest that an individual's role behavior may be shaped by the kinds of "deference" that he regularly receives from others.

One aspect of the voluntariness of role-playing is the extent to which the actor believes in the part he is playing. Although a role may be played cynically, with no belief, or completely sincerely, with wholehearted belief, many roles are played on the basis of an intricate mixture of belief and disbelief. During the course of a study of a large public mental hospital, several patients told the author in confidence about their cynical use of their symptoms—to frighten new personnel, to escape from unpleasant work details, and so on. Yet these *same* patients, at other times, appear to have been sincere in their symptomatic behavior. Apparently it was sometimes difficult for them to tell whether they were playing the role or the role was playing them. . . . In accordance with what has been said so far, the difficulty is probably that the patient is just as confused by his own behavior as is the observer.

This discussion suggests that a stable role performance may arise when the actor's role imagery locks in with the type of "deference" which he regularly receives. An extreme example of this process may be taken from anthropological and medical reports concerning the "dead role," as in deaths attributed to "bone-pointing." Death from bone-pointing appears to arise from the conjunction of two fundamental processes which characterize all social behavior. First, all individuals continually orient themselves by means of responses which are perceived in social interaction: the individual's identity and continuity of experience are dependent on these cues. Secondly, the individual has his own vocabulary of expectations, which may in a particular situation either agree with or be in conflict with the sanctions to which he is exposed. Entry into a role may be complete when this role is part of the individual's expectations, and when these expectations are reaffirmed in social interaction. In the following pages this principle will be applied to the problem of the causation of mental disorder.

What are the beliefs and practices that constitute the social institution of insanity? And how do they figure in the development of mental disorder? Two propositions concerning beliefs about mental disorder in the general public will now be considered.

4. *Stereotyped imagery of mental disorder is learned in early childhood.* Although there are no substantiating studies in this area, scattered observations lead the author to conclude that children learn a considerable amount of imagery concerning deviance very early, and that much of the imagery comes from their peers rather than from adults. The literal meaning of "crazy," a term now used in a wide variety of contexts, is probably grasped by children during the first years of elementary school. Since adults are often vague and evasive in their responses to questions in this area, an aura of mystery surrounds it. In this socialization the grossest stereotypes which are heir to childhood fears, e.g., of the "boogie man," survive. These conclusions are quite speculative, of course, and need to be investigated systematically, possibly with tech-

niques similar to those used in studies of the early learning of racial stereotypes.

Assuming, however, that this hypothesis is sound, what effect does early learning have on the shared conceptions of insanity held in the community? There is much fallacious material learned in early childhood which is later discarded when more adequate information replaces it. This question leads to hypothesis No. 5. 5. *The stereotypes of insanity are continually reaffirmed, inadvertently, in ordinary social interaction.*

Although many adults become acquainted with medical concepts of mental illness, the traditional stereotypes are not discarded, but continue to exist alongside the medical conceptions, because the stereotypes receive almost continual support from the mass media and in ordinary social discourse. In newspapers, it is a common practice to mention that a rapist or a murderer was once a mental patient. This negative information, however, is seldom offset by positive reports. An item like the following is almost inconceivable:

> Mrs. Ralph Jones, an ex-mental patient, was elected president of the Fairview Home and Garden Society in their meeting last Thursday.

Because of highly biased reporting, the reader is free to make the unwarranted inference that murder and rape occur more frequently among ex-mental patients than among the population at large. Actually, it has been demonstrated that the incidence of crimes of violence, or of any crime, is much lower among ex-mental patients than among the general population. Yet, this is not the picture presented to the public.

Reaffirmation of the stereotype of insanity occurs not only in the mass media, but also in ordinary conversation, in jokes, anecdotes, and even in conventional phrases. Such phrases as "Are you crazy?", or "It would be a madhouse," "It's driving me out of my mind," or "It's driving me distracted," and hundreds of others occur frequently in informal conversations. In this usage insanity itself is seldom the topic of conversation; the phrases are so much a part of ordinary language that only the person who considers each word carefully can eliminate them from his speech. Through verbal usages the stereotypes of insanity are a relatively permanent part of the social structure. . . .

According to the analysis presented here, the traditional stereotypes of mental disorder are solidly entrenched in the population because they are learned early in childhood and are continuously reaffirmed in the mass media and in everyday conversation. How do these beliefs function in the processes leading to mental disorder? This question will be considered by first referring to the earlier discussion of the societal reaction to residual deviance.

It was stated that the usual reaction to residual deviance is denial, and that in these cases most residual deviance is transitory. The societal reaction to deviance is not always denial, however. In a small proportion of cases the reaction goes the other way, exaggerating and at times distorting the extent and degree of deviation. This pattern of exaggeration, which we will call "labeling," has been noted by Garfinkel in his discussion of the "degradation" of officially recognized criminals. Goffman makes a similar point in his description of the "discrediting" of mental patients. Apparently under some conditions the societal reaction to deviance is to seek out signs of abnormality in the deviant's history to show that he was always essentially a deviant.

The contrasting social reactions of denial and labeling provide a means of answering two fundamental questions. If deviance arises from diverse sources—physical, psychological, and situational—how does the uniformity of behavior that is associated with insanity develop? Secondly, if deviance is usually transitory, how does it become stabilized in those patients who became chronically deviant? To summarize, what are the sources of uniformity and stability of deviant behavior?

In the approach taken here the answer to this question is based on hypotheses Nos. 4 and 5, that the role imagery of insanity is learned early in childhood, and is reaffirmed in social interaction. In a crisis, when the deviance of an individual becomes a public issue, the traditional stereotype of insanity becomes the guiding imagery for action, both for those reacting to the deviant and, at times, for the deviant himself. When societal agents and persons around the deviant react to him uniformly in terms of the traditional stereotypes of insanity, his amorphous and unstructured deviant behavior tends to crystallize in conformity to these expectations, thus becoming similar to the behavior of other deviants classified as mentally ill, and stable over time. The process of becoming uniform and stable is completed when the traditional imagery becomes a part of the deviant's orientation for guiding his own behavior.

The idea that cultural stereotypes may stablize primary deviance, and tend to produce uniformity in symptoms, is supported by cross-cultural studies of mental disorder. Although some observers insist there are underlying similarities, most agree that there are enormous differences in the manifest symptoms of stable mental disorder *between* societies, and great similarity *within* societies.

These considerations suggest that the labeling process is a crucial contingency in most careers of residual deviance. Thus Glass, who observed that neuropsychiatric casualties may not become mentally ill if they are kept with their unit, goes on to say that military experience with psychotherapy has been disappointing. Soldiers who are removed from their unit to a hospital, he states, often go on to become chronically impaired. That is, their dèviance is stabilized by the labeling process, which is implicit in their removal and hospitalization. A similar interpretation can be made by comparing the observations of childhood disorders among Mexican-Americans with those of "Anglo" children. Childhood disorders such as *susto* (an illness believed to result from fright) sometimes have damaging outcomes in Mexican-American children. Yet the deviant behavior involved is very similar to that which seems to have high incidence among Anglo children, with permanent impairment virtually never occurring. Apparently through cues from his elders the Mexican-American child, behaving initially much like his Anglo counterpart, learns to enter the sick role, at times with serious consequences.

From this point of view, then, most mental disorder can be considered to be a social role. This social role complements and reflects the status of the insane in the social structure. It is through the social processes which maintain the status of the insane that the varied deviancies from which mental disorder arises are made uniform and stable. The stabilization and uniformization of residual deviance are completed when the deviant accepts the role of the insane as the framework within which he organizes his own behavior. Three hypotheses are stated below which suggest some of the processes which cause the deviant to accept such a stigmatized role.

6. *Labeled deviants may be rewarded for playing the stereotyped deviant role.* Ordinarily patients who display "insight" are rewarded by psychiatrists and other personnel. That is, patients who manage to find evidence of "their illness" in their past and present behavior, confirming the medical and societal diagnosis, receive benefits. This pattern of behavior is a special case of a more general pattern that has been called the "apostolic function" by Balint, in which the physician and others inadvertently cause the patient to display symptoms of the illness the physician thinks the patient has. Not only physicians but other hospital personnel and even other patients, reward the deviant for conforming to the stereotypes.

7. *Labeled deviants are punished when they attempt the return to conventional roles.* The second process operative is the systematic blockage of entry to nondeviant roles once the label has been publicly applied. Thus the ex-mental patient, although he is urged to rehabilitate himself in the community, usually finds himself discriminated against in seeking to return to his old status, and on trying to find a new one in the occupational, marital, social, and other spheres. Thus, to a degree, the labeled deviant is rewarded for deviating, and punished for attempting to conform.

8. *In the crisis occurring when a primary deviant is publicly labeled,*

the deviant is highly suggestible, and may accept the proffered role of the insane as the only alternative. When gross deviancy is publicly recognized and made an issue, the primary deviant may be profoundly confused, anxious, and ashamed. In this crisis it seems reasonable to assume that the deviant will be suggestible to the cues that he gets from the reactions of others toward him. But those around him are also in a crisis; the incomprehensible nature of the deviance, and the seeming need for immediate action lead them to take collective action against the deviant on the basis of the attitude which all share—the traditional stereotypes of insanity. The deviant is sensitive to the cues provided by these others and begins to think of himself in terms of the stereotyped role of insanity, which is part of his own role vocabulary also, since he, like those reacting to him, learned it early in childhood. In this situation his behavior may begin to follow the pattern suggested by his own stereotypes and the reactions of others. That is, when a primary deviant organizes his behavior within the framework of mental disorder, and when his organization is validated by others, particularly prestigeful others such as physicians, he is "hooked" and will proceed on a career of chronic deviance. . . .

The last three propositions suggest that once a person has been placed in a deviant status there are rewards for conforming to the deviant role, and punishments for not conforming to the deviant role. This is not to imply, however, that the symptomatic behavior of persons occupying a deviant status is always a manifestation of conforming behavior. To explain this point, some discussion of the process of self-control in "normals" is necessary.

In a recent discussion of the process of self-control, Shibutani notes that self-control is not automatic, but is an intricate and delicately balanced process, sustainable only under propitious circumstances. He points out that fatigue, the reaction to narcotics, excessive excitement or tension (such as is generated in mobs), or a number of other conditions interfere with self-control; conversely, conditions which produce normal bodily states, and deliberative processes such as symbolization and imaginative rehearsal before action, facilitate it.

One might argue that a crucially important aspect of imaginative rehearsal is the image of himself that the actor projects into his future action. Certainly in American society, the cultural image of the "normal" adult is that of a person endowed with self-control ("will-power," "backbone," "strength of character," etc.). For the person who sees himself as endowed with the trait of self-control, self-control is facilitated, since he can imagine himself enduring stress during his imaginative rehearsal, and also while under actual stress.

For a person who has acquired an image of himself as lacking the ability to control his own actions, the process of self-control is likely to break down under stress. Such a person may feel that he has reached his "breaking-point" under circumstances which would be endured by a person with a "normal" self-conception. This is to say, a greater lack of self-control than can be explained by stress tends to appear in those roles for which the culture transmits imagery which emphasizes lack of self-control. In American society such imagery is transmitted for the roles of the very young and very old, drunkards and drug addicts, gamblers, and the mentally ill.

Thus, the social role of the mentally ill has a different significance at different phases of residual deviance. When labeling first occurs, it merely gives a name to primary deviation which has other roots. When (and if) the primary deviance becomes an issue, and is not ignored or rationalized away, labeling may create a social type, a pattern of "symptomatic" behavior in conformity with the stereotyped expectations of others. Finally, to the extent that the deviant role becomes a part of the deviant's self-conception, his ability to control his own behavior may be impaired under stress, resulting in episodes of compulsive behavior.

The preceding eight hypotheses form the basis for the final causal hypothesis. 9. *Among residual deviants, labeling is the single most important cause of careers of residual deviance*. This hypothesis assumes that most residual deviance, if it does not become the basis for entry into the sick role, will not lead to a deviant career. Most deviant careers, according to this point of view, arise out of career contingencies, and are therefore not directly connected with the origins of the initial deviance. Although there are a wide variety of contingencies which lead to labeling rather than denial, these contingencies can be usefully classified in terms of the nature of the deviant behavior, the person who commits the deviant acts, and the community in which the deviance occurs. Other things being equal, the severity of the societal reaction to deviance is a function of, first, the degree, amount, and visibility of the deviant behavior; second, the power of the deviant, and the social distance between the deviant and the agents of social control; and finally, the tolerance level of the community, and the availability in the culture of the community of alternative nondeviant roles. Particularly crucial for future research is the importance of the first two contingencies (the amount and degree of deviance), which are characteristics of the deviant, relative to the remaining five contingencies, which are characteristics of the social system. To the extent that these five factors are found empirically to be independent determinants of labeling and denial, the status of the mental patient can be considered a partly ascribed rather than a completely achieved status. The dynamics of treated mental illness could then be profitably studied quite apart from the individual dynamics of mental disorder. . . .

SCHIZOPHRENICS IN THE COMMUNITY

Benjamin Pasamanick, Frank R. Scarpitti,
and Simon Dinitz

The following description summarizes a three-year experimental study
on the feasibility of caring for schizophrenics, not by the traditional
method of hospitalization, but by maintaining them in the community on
the new psychoactive drugs. Since schizophrenia is one of the most
prevalent psychotic disorders and schizophenics constitute perhaps the
majority of patients in mental hospitals, the findings of the study have
important implications for the care of patients in the future.

RECAPITULATION

. . . The Institute Treatment Center (ITC) was established in downtown Louisville, Kentucky in the latter half of 1961. The staff included
a director, a part-time psychiatrist, a psychologist, a social worker and
five nurses with public health nursing experience. Only one of the nurses
had any prior training or experience in psychiatric nursing. A psychiatrist was employed at the hospital to do the initial screening of patients
to determine their eligibility for inclusion in the program. Newly admitted state hospital patients had to meet the following criteria to be
admitted to the project: a diagnosis of schizophrenia, non-suicidal or
homicidal, be between 19 and 60 years of age, have residence in Louisville or surrounding countries and a family or relative willing to provide
supervision of the patient at home. State hospital admissions who met
these criteria were sent to the Institute Treatment Center for further
evaluation. If the ITC staff psychiatrist confirmed the diagnosis and
deemed the patient suitable for the program and the family agreed to
cooperate, the patient was accepted. Using a deck of random cards, the
study director then assigned the patient to one of three groups as follows: home on drugs (40 percent), home on placebo or on inert medication (30 percent) or hospital care (the control group, 30 percent).

State hospital schizophrenic patients do not, of course, include all
schizophrenics. Many schizophrenic patients, because their symptoms
are not especially florid and can therefore be tolerated more readily,

From *Schizophrenics in the Community: An Experimental Study in the Prevention of Hospitalization*, pp. 248-71. Copyright © 1967 by Appleton-Century-
Crofts, Inc. Reprinted by permission.

typically remain in the community and are not hospitalized. To tap this population as well, particularly for the purpose of determining the effectiveness of drug medication, referrals from community sources other than the state hospital and from private physicians were welcomed. In order to qualify for inclusion in the study, those referrals had equally to meet the same diagnosis, age, residence, family and other requirements. The only difference from the aforementioned study group resulted from their "ambulatory" status. Their random assignment permitted just two categories: home on drug or home on placebo.

Shortly after each patient returned home, the public health nurse assigned to the case visited the patient and family. The same nurse made weekly calls the first three months, bi-monthly visits during the second three months and monthly visits thereafter. On every visit she left the medication prescribed by the staff psychiatrist. She also completed a written report on the status of the patient which was reviewed by the ITC psychiatrist. Patients and families experiencing difficulties were free to call the treatment center and speak to or make appointments to see the social worker and psychiatrist. Usually, however, it was the nurse who arranged for such consultation.

In all, 152 state hospital patients were involved in the project, 57 drug home care patients, 41 placebo home care cases and 54 hospital controls. All were followed up for a period ranging from well over six months at the least to 30 months. In addition, 29 community drug home care cases and 23 community referred placebo home care patients were in the project for from six to 27 months.

The principal substantive findings were these:

1. Over 77 percent of the drug home care patients but only some 34 percent of the placebo cases remained in the community throughout their participation in the project. All controls, of course, were hospitalized. Not only did the program, by averting hospitalization, save a considerable amount of patient bed time, but this saving permitted in theory at least of the possibility of more intensive care for the fewer patients hospitalized.

2. Drug and placebo home patients in the project for a longer time period were no less successful than those in the program for shorter periods. Thus, it is fair to speak of *prevention* of hospitalization as such rather than merely of *delay* in institutionalization.

3. Patients who failed (13 drug and 27 placebo) and had to be hospitalized usually failed soon after acceptance into the program. Nearly all failures occurred within six months.

4. Even after initial hospitalization averaging 83 days and the presumable remission of the grosser symptoms, the *hospital controls failed*

more often at the termination of treatment than did the home care patients.

5. When home care patients failed it was frequently of the "last straw" variety. Either patient behavior was bizarre or dangerous, or the responsible relatives could no longer cope with the patient and his needs. Changes in the family situation sometimes resulted in a lack of supervision of the patient and so precipitated failure.

6. On the more subjective evaluation level—that is according to the nurses, psychiatrist and relatives—patients improved in mental status, psychological test performance, domestic functioning and social participation. These gains were considerable and frequently significant statistically. *In all of the very many specific measures, home care patients were functioning as well or better than the hospital control cases.*

7. *Most of the improvement in performance occurred in the first six months in the study.* Thereafter functioning improved very little, if at all. In other words, once the acute signs and symptoms abated and functioning returned to a pre-episode level, there was little more gain to be made.

8. At their best, some of these patients still showed considerable problems in performing at what might be termed an adequate level. Some of the home care patients as well as of the controls were still exhibiting low quality performance. Perhaps this is really all one might realistically expect, however, from a chronically impaired population.

9. Regarding the community referred drug and placebo patients, nearly 76 percent of the drug and 61 percent of the placebo cases succeeded on home care. Length of time on the project was not a major correlate of failure. In instances of hospitalization, failure occurred early and the precipitants were generally of the same nature. As for the state hospital patients functioning improved, and most of the gains in the psychiatric, psychological, and social functioning measures were registered between intake and the sixth month's testing.

IMPLICATIONS

. . . From a practical standpoint this research has important implications fo rseveral areas of concern but particularly for schizophrenia, and the community mental health center.

1. SCHIZOPHRENIA

It would have been far less complicated to have selected either a cross-section of the mentally ill or a non-psychotic population to test the feasibility of a home care program. Instead, schizophrenics were deliberately chosen for a variety of compelling reasons. First, there is clear professional agreement that the schizophrenias are chronic and disabling disorders, not merely the consequence of difficulties experienced in the everyday process of living and adjusting. If ever a case can be made for mental illness as a disease, schizophrenia would be one of the prime illustrations. Unlike the characterological disorders, the neuroses, the psychosomatic problems and other clinical entities, there is almost no dispute that schizophrenia fits, by almost any conventional definition, the disease model. This point is important. If so severe an illness as schizophrenia, accounting for about half of all mental hospital resident patients, and nearly a fourth of the new admissions, can be controlled and treated effectively in a community setting, other difficult behavioral problems presumably can also be managed without recourse to institutionalization, except in extreme cases.

Second, it is well to note, too, that all of the "loading" or biasing in this study was in the direction of selecting sicker rather than less impaired schizophrenic patients for study. Two psychiatrists evaluated each patient—one in the state hospital at admission of the patient and the other in the treatment center. Only when both agreed on the diagnosis as schizophrenia was the patient accepted into the program. For this reason, it is likely that very few, if any, non-schizophrenics were included in this investigation.

Third, the layman's concept of "cure" in the sense of complete remission of symptoms and the absence of later pathology is wholly inadequate. Instead, a more accurate assumption is that schizophrenics are sick continually and that this illness is, at times, exacerbated. On such occasions, hospitalization usually results. When the acute phase passes the patient continues to be ill but at a level which often permits him to return to the community and remain there until the next major episode.

Our home care data on the state hospital patients offers reasonably good evidence of this. Once the florid symptoms had passed, the patients settled into a routine which showed almost no superior functioning on any level and mostly just barely minimal functioning on all levels. . . .

In short, they are sick persons who require continuing attention not only when their symptoms peak but also when the peaks have flattened. Up to now, attention in or out of the hospital has been largely reserved for those patients whose symptoms were exaggerated and who were acutely ill. With limited resources and personnel, the more floridly ill were the most likely to receive what attention was available. Home care offers to all patients continuous management not otherwise possible.

Present evidence from drug and other studies indicates that care given to schizophrenic patients only in times of acute episodes is far from adequate treatment. Indeed, continued drug and other treatment is exceedingly important not only in the control of acute flareups but in reducing the frequency or eliminating entirely the periodic episodes normally resulting in hospitalization. *This type of continuous care, then, in the absence of knowledge of the etiology or specific treatment of schizophrenia may be, and probably is, the only type of prevention available to us now.* Such secondary prevention is clearly preferable to releasing patients back home without follow-up care and treatment and with the certain knowledge that many will return again for another round of hospitalization. *Thus, in hard terms, nearly half of the hospital control patients, 25 of 54, after an average initial period of 83 days in the state hospital had to be rehospitalized.* This is not only uneconomic but unnecessary since, as this study indicated so definitively, much of both the initial institutionalization and the rehospitalization could have been prevented by even a modest home care program.

It is instructive to compare the community home care approach with the historic hospital treatment accorded the schizophrenic. In the hospital, between acute episodes, patients are mostly left alone to stare vacantly into space, to walk down the corridors and back again, to sit, rock, and hallucinate, or to partake of inmate culture. In time, this lack of normal stimulation—intellectual, interpersonal, even physical—has usually resulted in deterioration and impairment of functioning which was wholly unnecessary. Between episodes, many of these patients could have been released had there been any provision for supervision and aftercare. As a result, because such patients were lost in the institutional process and were not frequently returned to the world outside the hospital walls, schizophrenia became identified in the public (and even often in the professional) mind with hopelessness and despair. In the past, instead of questioning the necessity for continued and prolonged hospitalization, the focal point of concern was the humanizing of the institution itself. Hardly anyone, before the advent of the psychoactive drugs plus the other changes described at the outset of this volume, was foolhardy enough to seriously propose that hospitalized schizophrenics could survive the pressures of living in a normal family setting without harm to themselves or to others. Whatever else may eventuate from this investigation and related studies, one conclusion seems warranted: in the absence of considerable deterioration, an acute episode or grossly exaggerated symptoms, no special reason exists for keeping schizophrenic patients hospitalized. Community facilities, now being established and those already in existence, are reasonable, preferable and necessary.

2. THE COMMUNITY MENTAL HEALTH CENTER

In the past one of the major drawbacks to community programs was the presumed risk involved in keeping disturbed persons outside a custodial setting. Families were afraid to take such risks, physicians were not enthusiastic either, and the police and courts were certainly not willing to propose any such reorientation. The ITC study, and other posthospital outcome investigations, have shown that the risks to patient, family and community are certainly well within the range of tolerance and acceptance. Actually, once the very high risk patients are screened out, the remaining patients are seldom dangerous. It may even be possible to return potentially aggressive and violent patients to home care once they have been given very short term and intensive therapy as inpatients and treated continuously thereafter as outpatients. Of the patients seen by the ITC staff and found otherwise eligible for study inclusion by diagnosis, age, and place of residence, only five percent were deemed suicidal or too disturbed to warrant risking their admission to the program. Also, during the 30 months of the program, two patients (both placebo) attempted suicide through an overdose of medication and the behavior of several of the failure cases necessitated calling the police. Surely, these negative experiences are no worse than those encountered in a posthospital population or conceivably for that matter even in a general population.

At the present time patients and their families are very likely to defer seeking care because such treatment means being "put away," voluntarily or by commitment, in a custodial mental hospital. In removing the fears and images long associated with almost automatic institutionalization of schizophrenics and possibly also of other psychotics, the community mental health center and its diverse facilities should encourage earlier identification and earlier treatment of disturbed persons in a community. The anxieties of the patient and the guilt of the families in having played an active role in the removal of the patient would also largely be eliminated. This, in turn, would create a spiral effect. Once the fears, anxieties and guilt are gone, the mental patient may come to be viewed as not very much different from other chronically ill, ineffective and inadequate people. The age old chain which made the mentally ill into social pariahs—feared, shunned, and isolated—will then be broken. In analogical terms, what psychoanalysis did to alter attitudes and to facilitate the acceptance of the non-psychotic disorders, the newer drugs and community mental health center care will almost certainly do for the psychotic and other more serious disorders. . . .

. . . Experience in the ITC home care project confirmed the need for a much more inclusive, integrated and broadly based program than the general hospital could conceivably offer. The treatment of the ITC patients with drugs and public health nursing care, although very successful in keeping them at home, left much to be desired. In the daily operation of the Center . . . a very sizeable number of patients needed specialized services which were either not readily available or too costly for them. These included both general and specialized medical and dental care, vocational counseling and guidance, family counseling, and homemaking services.

Male patients, although generally better in their functioning than before admission to the study, were still all too often inadequate as employees. Not only did they need vocational evaluation, guidance and placement services but many could have benefited from a more or less pressure free job environment such as that in a sheltered workshop situation. Since productive work is the central role of the male, it is difficult to see how patients can be returned to normal functioning unless some provision is made for them to be gainfully employed and stimulated within the limits of their abilities and tolerance levels for stress. Thus, community program planners need seriously consider establishing or utilizing existing sheltered workshops not only to serve patients who may some day be employable but for those whose employability will be problematic in the foreseeable future.

On the other side of the coin, many female patients, if they are to remain in the community for protracted periods, will require help with child care, cooking, shopping, cleaning, and in the performance of routine household tasks. Since most families cannot afford to employ domestic help even when confronted with the prolonged, or even the temporary inability of the wife and mother to assume her responsibilities, any comprehensive program must somehow incorporate such services—if only for the sake of the other family members and the functioning of the household.

Similarly, family members need, want, and deserve professional advice as well as reassurance in their relationships with the patient. Unfortunately, there is and can be no manual on how to deal with a disturbed person in the household. Still, questions do arise and decisions must be made. The ITC nurses were continually beseiged with questions about patient management, prognosis and treatment. The nurses were frequently as baffled as the family members in fielding these questions. The staff psychiatrist and, more immediately, the staff social worker provided many of the answers to the nurses, who then relayed them to the families. Family counseling personnel and services would have great value in reassuring and helping the families cope with troublesome and worrisome patient behavior. Even beyond this immediate gain, state hospital schizophrenic patients and many community referred cases, too, come from multi-problem families and settings that are hardly conducive to patient welfare. While family counseling cannot resolve these difficulties or generate improvement in the low socioeconomic status of the families, it can be of great utility when combined with more specific services such as job placement, providing homemaking help and remedying or at least alleviating some of the economic problems.

Thought ought also be given to relieving part of the load of patient supervision which now falls exclusively to family members. Even the most tolerant, accepting and loving husband, wife, or parent will almost inevitably become disenchanted with home and community treatment unless the burdens and worries and stress can at times be relaxed. Again, the case histories as well as the reports of the public health nurses amply document the need to work out arrangements which would give the responsible family members occasional respite from the unceasing concern with patient care. There are a number of ways this can be achieved. For example, a community mental health facility might well include a day care center featuring recreational activities, social participation in organized groups and occupational therapy. Equally or even more valuable would be a night hospital facility or even a less pretentious hostel where patients can be sent for overnight care and housing on those occasions when they become too difficult and disruptive. Such a facility would have made a very important contribution to the ITC program and possibly conserved several of the failures whose families were still willing but no longer able to tolerate the never ending stress of having the sick member constantly at home. . . .

. . . In the course of the 30 months of home care of schizophrenic patients it became abundantly clear why planning for community mental health centers had to be predicated on the criteria of continuous, coordinated and comprehensive services. According to these guidelines essential elements in such a facility should include: inpatient and outpatient services, partial hospitalization facilities such as day care or night care or both, emergency 24 hour services, and consultation and education services to professional personnel and community agencies. Beyond these essential services an adequate or more complete center would also provide diagnostic and evaluative services, rehabilitative activities such as vocational programs, pre- and after-care services, training and research.

Had the ITC program continued to operate beyond its experimental expiration date, the nature, intensity and quality of the problems of the schizophrenic patients would have compelled a broader and more inclusive array of services, more closely interwoven with other welfare and health agencies in the community, and providing more continuous (longitudinal) services. . . .

VII DILEMMAS IN DEVIATION

13 CONTROVERSIAL ISSUES IN THE CONTROL OF DEVIATION

Whatever their content at any moment in time, three perennial and controversial issues are involved in deviation. What behaviors are to be included as deviant and how are these to be defined? How is society to control these behaviors? And, what shall be public policy toward deviation? Stated otherwise, the central issues involve three aspects: definition, control, and general public policy. All of the preceding chapters have contained articles and essays devoted to these concerns. This was most evident in the sections on delinquency and on mental illness. The purpose of this final chapter is not to retrace our steps or belabor these issues, important as they are. Instead, we are concerned in this chapter with problem areas that are just emerging and therefore exemplify dissensus and conflict over methods of control and public policy. The four articles that follow deal respectively with pornography, the invasion of privacy, the rights of suspects in crime, and the control of firearms. All are being contested in the political arena. Most importantly, all involve questions of values—of individual rights and societal welfare; of one conception of social order and public morality versus another. There are, unfortunately, no scientific answers to value dilemmas and differing normative conceptions, and these articles reflect this fact.

In the first selection, "Pornography—Raging Menace or Paper Tiger," Professors Gagnon and Simon discuss three major Supreme Court decisions concerning the definition of pornography. In the most important of the three—the Ginzburg decision—an earlier test of pornography was reaffirmed. This test argues that the determination of pornography depends on "whether to the average person, applying contemporary standards, the dominant theme of the material taken as a whole appeals to a prurient (lustful) interest." Still, the Court also said that regardless of the content of the material itself, advertising which appeals and emphasizes the sexually provocative aspects of the material may be decisive in deciding whether the content is obscene. The implications of this and the other decisions are discussed in detail.

The article is also concerned with the various views of the effects of pornography and principally with the sexual arousal and safety value themes. In truth, the social context within which the obscene material is consumed is probably the most important element in what the consumer derives from it. Gagnon and Simon illustrate the importance of the social setting through the differential role of the stag film for its chief users—college boys and upper- and lower-middle-class males. The author also describe the pornographic fringeland—the pulps, girlie magazines, the pinups and "dirty" pictures, and the national tabloids.

The issue, then, is how to define the problem since pornography is tied to prevailing community standards and these vary widely from the cosmopolitan areas to the rural, Bible belt communities. Art, adult, and certain foreign films may be perfectly acceptable in the former and totally violative of the prevailing standards in the latter. A discussion of the elusive standards through which these divergent definitions might be reconciled concludes this essay.

Supreme Court Justice Louis Brandeis, a staunch defender of individual rights, wrote in 1928:

> The makers of our Constitution undertook to secure conditions favorable to the pursuit of happiness. They recognized the significance of man's spiritual nature, of his feelings, and of his intellect. They knew that only a part of the pain, pleasure, and satisfaction in life are to be found in material things. They sought to protect Americans in their beliefs, their thoughts, their emotions, and their sensations. They conferred, as against the Government, the right to be let alone.

Little could Justice Brandeis imagine the extent to which the invasion of privacy would become a major enterprise in American society in less than half a century after he expressed these thoughts. This enterprise is not at all restricted to the various agencies of government—the F.B.I., the Internal Revenue Service, the Post Office Department, for example. Snooping of one sort or another is also carried on by private investigators of every degree of integrity. Even the telephone company was once in the act. In 1965 it was estimated that 39 million telephone conversations were monitored across the country.

In addition to wiretaps and bugs, which are the most common of the devices intruding on personal privacy, many other techniques are utilized. The peephole has, for example, been replaced by the more sophisticated two-way mirror and hidden TV camera. Secret dossiers and closed files have yielded to computers which collect, collate, and store information on each of us.

The second selection, taken from the book, *The Intruders* by Edward N. Long of Missouri, is based, in large measure, on testimony presented in hearings of the United States Senate Subcommittee on Administrative Practice and Procedure on the problem of invasion of privacy by government agencies and others. Not only does former Senator Long describe the issues and problems but he presents a long list of suggestions for the regulation and control of wiretapping and bugging.

Few controversies have so agitated the public as the series of recent Supreme Court decisions concerning "due process" in criminal cases. The "Warren Court" has been charged, by everybody from J. Edgar Hoover to the newest sheriff's deputy in counties with only a handful of recorded crimes a year, with hindering law enforcement and protecting criminals at the expense of law-abiding citizens. Apart from the heat which has been generated, there is consensus that the individual rights of the criminal and of all others must be protected. The issue, then, is not one of principle but rather of the legitimacy of some practical measures used in law enforcement. In principle, all are agreed on the undesirability of illegal search and seizure, dragnet arrests, arrests for interrogation only, denial of the right of counsel, and all of the other specifics dealt with in the Supreme Court and lower court decisions. It is the implementation of these principles, in the face of increasing urbanization and of crime, that vexes and irritates law-enforcement people and others.

In the next article Judge George Edwards of the United States Court of Appeals (Sixth Circuit), former Police Commissioner of Detroit and former Justice on the Supreme Court of Michigan discusses the four major Supreme Court decisions that have occasioned and been responsible for most of the controversy. Probably the only person in the United States to serve both as a justice on a high court and as a police commissioner, Judge Edwards is surely qualified to describe the antecedents and implications of the Mallory, Mapp, Gideon, and Escobedo cases.

Since the assassination of President John F. Kennedy with a mail-order rifle, the desirability of controlling access to firearms has been voiced by many members of Congress, nearly all law-enforcement people and, if public-opinion polls are accurate, by a majority of the public. More than four years after the assassination no control bill has been passed by the Congress. As things stand, it may be a long time before such legislation is passed in view of the tremendous and well-organized opposition of the National Rifle Association and associated groups.

The fourth article, then, deals with the problem of controlling firearms in a society which is somewhat nostalgic about the Wild West tradition of gun toting and violence as well as distrustful of government regulation and intervention in general. The President's Commission on Law Enforcement and the Administration of Justice deals with almost all facets of firearms regulation: guns and crime, present control laws, the reasons for the limited effectiveness of indifferent or nonexistent state regulation, public opinion, and firearms control, and the views of opponents regarding gun control laws. The Commission report concludes with a series of recommendations which, in effect, urge the states, and if necessary the federal government, to outlaw the possession of military type firmarms such as bazookas, antitank guns, and mortars; prohibit some types of persons from buying, owning, or possessing firearms; require the registration of all hand guns and related weapons; and require a permit before a person can carry or possess a hand gun. Finally, the Commission recommends that mail-order and interstate sales of hand guns be forbidden.

The United States is now the only highly industrialized country in the world with a laissez-faire approach to lethal weapons. It therefore appears likely that, in time, state and federal policy will follow the model of the western European nations. It nothing else, the racial disturbances in our ghettos since 1965 almost ensure some type of gun legislation in the future.

A problem less important than the firearms, invasion of privacy, or other control measures, but nevertheless a very difficult one, involves the mass media. The problem is one of balancing the public's right to know, and of the free press's to publish, and the individual's to be protected from public display. This delicate balance, and how it may best be maintained, has been the subject of serious study by the American Bar Association, the mass media, and other concerned agencies.

In our final article, Professor Geis reviews the history and present status of identifying delinquents in the press. He discusses the pros and cons of such identification and uses the so-called Loble Law to illustrate the dilemma involved. He concludes that there exists very little unimpeachable data upon which to make judgments concerning the effects on behavior of the publication of the names of delinquents. A great deal would depend on the size of the community, the amount of delinquency, and whether the offenders are likely to be personally known to many residents in the community. After weighing these and other considerations, Professor Geis is of the opinion that the publication of names is likely to do more harm than good.

PORNOGRAPHY—RAGING MENACE
OR PAPER TIGER?

John H. Gagnon and William Simon

Since the task of defining pornography has fallen more and more on the Supreme Court—and since not much research exists on what effect por-

From *Trans-Action,* Vol. 4, No. 3 (July-August 1967), 41-8. Reprinted by permission.

nography has on the social actions of individuals—what standard is the court using?

The Supreme Court seems to be erecting a more complex standard for judging pornography to replace the old concern with individual morality. Some interesting insights into the confusion surrounding the topic can be drawn from three court decisions of March 21, 1966: *Ginzburg* v. *United States, Mishkin* v. *New York,* and *Memoirs of a Woman of Pleasure* v. *Massachusetts.* Although this set of decisions was almost immediately accorded distinction as a landmark by the public, the Nine Old Men themselves did not seem quite so sure of the meaning of the affair. The justices produced among them 14 separate opinions in the three cases. Only three judges were in the majority in all cases. The decisions were divided, respectively, 5-4, 6-3, and 6-3.

Ginzburg is the key decision. The court reversed the suppression of *Memoirs,* better known as *Fanny Hill,* under the Roth test of 1957—that is, "whether to the average person, applying contemporary standards, the dominant theme of the material taken as a whole appeals to a prurient interest." The conviction of Edward Mishkin, owner of the Main Stem and Midget book stores in New York City, was upheld. In the words of the court, Mishkin "was not prosecuted for anything he said or believed, but for what he did." What he did was commission; publish, and sell such illustrated books as *Mistress of Leather, Cult of Spankers,* and *Fearful Ordeal in Restraintland* for an audience interested in sadomasochism, transvestitism, fetishism.

Ralph Ginzburg was being tried on postal charges of obscenity for three publications: *The Housewife's Handbook of Selective Promiscuity,* an issue of the biweekly newsletter *Liaison,* and a volume of the hardbound magazine *Eros.* In this case the court departed from earlier rulings by considering not the obscenity of the specific items, but rather the appeal to prurient interest made in the advertising campaigns. The court remarked, "Where the purveyor's sole emphasis is on the sexually provocative aspects of his publications, that fact may be decisive in the determination of 'obscenity.' "

To the court, one of the proofs of Ginzburg's motives was his request for second-class mailing privileges at Intercourse or Blue Ball, Pennsylvania, before obtaining them at Middlesex, New Jersey. One of the indicators of the social worth of *Fanny Hill,* conversely, was the translation of the book into braille by the Library of Congress.

Three of the justices voting for reversal filed written dissents in which they argued that the court was creating a new crime—that of pandering, exploitation, or titillation—which Ginzburg could not have known existed when he committed it. Furthermore, the dissenters said, if a statute creating such a crime had come before the court, it would be found unconstitutional.

It is the Ginzburg decision that gives us the primary thread to follow in seeking to understand "obscenity" as it is now seen by the Supreme Court and the sexual arousal caused by what is conventionally termed pornography. With this decision the court has moved—in a way that may be inimical to the conception of law as abstract principle—toward a more realistic determination of the factors relevant to triggering a sexual response. The court's sociological discovery—whether intentional or not—is that in sex the context of the representation is significant. That is, sex as a physical object or symbolic representation has no power outside a context in which the erotic elements are reinforced or made legitimate.

In doing this, the court did not change the rules under which any work will be considered outside its context. If a book is charged—as *Fanny Hill* was—with being obscene under the Roth decision, it will be treated in exactly the same way as it would have been in the past. When aspects of the context of advertising or sale—the acts of labeling—are included in the original charges, then the Ginzburg rules will be applied. This was demonstrated in the court's decision this May [1967] on a number of girlie magazines. Obscenity convictions against the magazines were overturned because, as the court stated, "In none was there evidence of the sort of pandering which the court found significant in *Ginzburg* v. *United States*."

Whether the majority of the court was aware of the significance of the change it made in the definition of obscenity is not clear. From the tone of the opinions, it is obvious the court felt it was dealing with a problem of nuisance behavior—not only to the public, but to the court itself—quite anologous to keeping a goat in a residential area, or urinating in public. By making the promotion of the work a factor in determining its obscenity, the court was reinforcing the right of the person to keep his mailbox clean and private, not to mention the likelihood that it was cutting down the amount of misleading advertising.

TWO FACES OF PORNOGRAPHY

The court apparently considers pornography to have two major dimensions. The first can be defined as dealing with sexual representations that are offensive to public morality or taste, which concerned the court most importantly in the Ginzburg case. The second centers on the effect of pornography on specific individuals or classes, which is the focus of most public discussions and prior court decisions on pornography. This dimension was mentioned only twice in the array of decisions of 1966, but much of the confusion in discussions of pornography reflects a difficulty in distinguishing between these dimensions or a tendency to slip from one to the other without noting the change.

The first dimension—offenses to a public morality—not only appears more objective, but also has a cooler emotional tone. The problem becomes one of tolerating a public nuisance, or defining what constitutes a public nuisance. This issue becomes complex because the heterogeneity of an urban society makes it difficult to arrive at a consensus on what the limits of public morality might be. We might also add the complicating factor of our society's somewhat uneven libertarian tradition that affirms the theoretical existence of the right to subscribe to minority versions of morality. These obviously touch upon important issues of constitutional freedoms. As important as the implicit issues may be, however, the explicit issue is public nuisance, a misdemeanor, usually bringing only a fine or, at most, up to a year in the county jail. Talk of offense to public morality or public taste is relatively remote from the old fears of serious damage to the community or its members.

The second dimension—effects upon persons exposed to pornographic productions—generates more intense emotions. Claims are made that exposure to pornography results in infantile and regressive approaches to sexuality that can feed an individual's neuroses or, at the other extreme, that exposure tends to fundamentally and irreversibly corrupt and deprave. The latter argument asserts that exposure to pornography either awakens or creates sexual appetites that can only be satisfied through conduct that is dangerous to society. More simply stated: Pornography is a trigger mechanism that has a high probability of initiating dangerous, antisocial behavior. There also exists what can be called a major counterargument to these, but one that shares with them a belief in the effectiveness of pornography. This argument is that pornography serves as an alternative sexual outlet, one that releases tensions that might otherwise find expression in dangerous, antisocial behavior. For the proponents of this view, pornography is seen as a safety valve or a psychological lightning rod.

The very act of labeling some item as pornographic or obscene creates a social response very close to that brought on by pornography itself. The act of labeling often generates sexual anticipation centered on fantasies about the business of pornography and the erotic character of those who produce it. How else could such benign and hardly erotic productions as family-planning pamphlets and pictures of human birth have come under the shadow of the pornography laws? As with other unconventional sexual expressions, in public consideration of pornography even the dreary details of production, distribution, and sale are matters for erotic speculations. This simplification—defining as totally sexual that which is only marginally connected with sexuality—is perhaps one of the major sources of the public concern over pornography.

Labeling can also be done by individuals, who can thus make pornographic the widest range of materials—*Studs Lonigan, Fanny Hill, Play-*

boy, the Sears Roebuck catalog. This ability leads to the assumption that sexual fantasy and its agent, pornography, have a magical capacity to commit men to overt sexual action. In this view the sexual impulse lies like the beast in every man, restrained only by the slight fetters of social repression. This assumption, founded on the enlightenment's notion of a social contract, undepins most of our discussions of sex and its sideshow, pornography.

These serious views of pornography can lead directly to the formulation of an empirically testable question. Unfortunately, no one has provided an answer acceptable as the outcome of reliable and systematic research procedures.

WHAT EFFECT—IF ANY?

Of the data that are available on the effects of pornography, the best remain those provided by the investigations of the Institute for Sex Research. Kinsey and his associates indicate that the majority of males in our society are exposed, at one time or another, to "portrayals of sexual action." So are a smaller proportion of females. Further, 77 percent of males who had exposure to "portrayals of sexual action" reported being erotically aroused, while only 32 percent of women reported feelings of arousal. What is significant is that, arousal notwithstanding, no dramatic changes of behavior appeared to follow for those reporting both exposure and arousal. Perhaps even more significant is the fact that Paul H. Gebhard and his colleague in their book *Sex Offenders* report:

> It would appear that the possession of pornography does not differentiate sex offenders from nonsex offenders. Even the combination of ownership plus strong sexual arousal from the material does not segregate the sex offender from other men of a comparable social level.

Summing up their feeling that pornography is far from being a strong determinant of sexual behavior and that the use of pornography tends to be a derivative of already existing sexual commitments, the authors observe: "Men make the collections, collections do not make the men."

However, given the intensity and frequency with which the argument of pornography's corrupting powers is raised, one might wonder whether thinking about pornography has not itself given rise to sexual fantasies, developing an image of men and women as being more essentially sexual than they may in fact be.

The two major dimensions—public offense versus public corruption—result in two different images of the pornographer. Projected through the rhetoric of public corruption we see him as someone self-consciously evil, a representative of the antichrist, the Communist conspiracy, or at the very least, the Mafia. We also tend to see him in terms of the obscenity of ill-gotten wealth as he deals in commodities that are assumed to generate high prices.

Though of as a public nuisance, he appears in somewhat more realistic hues. Here we find not a sinister villain but a grubby businessman producing a minor commodity for which there is a limited market and a marginal profit and which requires that he live in a marginal world. Here our collective displeasure may be derived from his association with a still greater obscenity—economic failure. However, whether the pornographer is Mephistopheles or a Willie Loman, he is one of the few in our society whose public role is overtly sexual, and that is perhaps reason enough to abandon any expectations of rationality in public discussions of the role.

THE FANTASY OF THE STAG FILM

We tend to ignore the social context within which pornography is used and from which a large part of its significance for the individual consumer derives. The stag film is an excellent case in point. Out of context it is rarely more than a simple catalogue of the limited sexual resources of the human body. Stag films are rarely seen by females and most commonly by two kinds of male groups: those living in group housing in colleges or universities and those belonging to upper-lower-class and lower-middle-class voluntary social groups. The stag film serves both similar and different functions for the two major categories of persons who see them.

For the college male they are a collective representation of mutual heterosexual concerns and—to a lesser degree—they instruct in sexual technique. For this group the exposure is either concurrent with, or prior to, extensive sociosexual experience. Exposure comes later in life for the second group; after marriage or, at the very least, after the development of sociosexual patterns. For this audience the group experience itself provides validation of sexual appetites in social milieus where other forms of validation, such as extramarital activity, are severely sanctioned. The films primarily reinforce masculinity and only indirectly reinforce heterosexuality. This reinforcement of heterosexuality is reflected in the way the films portray the obsessive myths of masculine sexual fantasy. They emphasize, for example, that sexual encounters can happen at any moment, to anyone, around almost any corner—a belief that is a close parallel to the romantic love fantasy so very characteristic of female arousal. In the case of the male, however, sex replaces love as the central element. These films also reaffirm the myth of a breed of women who are lusty and free in both surrender and enjoyment. Last, given the kind of social context within which the films are shown, there is little reason to assume that their sexual arousal is not expressed through appropriate sexual or social actions.

Pictorial representations of sexual activity lend themselves to the same approach. Unlike films and more like written materials, their use is essentially private. Nonetheless, patterns of use remain congruent with other patterns of social life and process; they represent anything but the triggering mechanisms through which the social contract is nullified and raging, unsocial lust (whatever that might be) is unleashed. The major users of pictorial erotica are adolescent males. If these materials have any use, it is as an aid to masturbation. There is no evidence, however, that the availability of dirty pictures increase masturbatory rates among adolescents. This is a period in life when masturbatory rates are already extremely high, particularly for middle-class adolescents. Indeed, in the absence of hard-core pornography, the boys create their own stimulation from mail-order catalogues, magazine ads, and so on. In middle-class circles, many young men and the majority of females may grow up without ever having seen hard-core pornography.

If exposure to this kind of pornography, while facilitating masturbation, does not substantially affect masturbatory rates, it is still possible that such materials may shape the content of the masturbatory fantasy in ways that create or reinforce commitments to sexual practices that are harmful to the individual or to others. In this area little is known. It may be observed that most pornographic materials share with the masturbatory fantasy a sense of omnipotence, but the acts represented are rarely homosexual, nor are they sadistic beyond the general levels of violence common in contemporary kitsch. Once again, one suspects a reinforcing or facilitating function rather than one of initiation or creation.

The pornographic book, in contrast to photographs and films, represents a very different social situation. Few books are read aloud in our society, and it is very unlikely that this would occur with a book of descriptions of overt sexual activity. In fact, prosecutors take advantage of this by reading allegedly obscene books aloud in court with the aim of embarrassing the jury into a guilty verdict. The privately consumed erotic book merely provides fantasy content or reinforcement of fantasy that is already established. Few books lead to overt action of any kind, and the erotic book is unlikely to be an exception.

PORNOGRAPHIC FRINGELAND

The most difficult problem in considering pornography is the fringeland found on newsstands: the pulp books, national tabloids, men's magazines, and pinup collections which line the racks in drugstores, bus stations, and rail and air terminals. The girlie magazines are often under attack for nude pictures. The current magic line of censorship is pubic hair, though recently it was the bare breast or exposed nipple. Not so very long ago, navels were ruthlessly airbrushed away and Jane Russell's cleavage was an issue in gaining the censor's approval of the movie "Out-law." The Gay Nineties were made gayer with pinups of strapping beauties clad in tights revealing only the bare flesh of face and hands.

In our era the pulp book freely describes most sexual activity with some degree of accuracy, although less explicitly and more metaphorically than hard-core pornographic pulp books. Such books are clearly published for their capacity to elicit sexual arousal, and they are purchased by an audience that knows what it is buying.

To view these examples of fringe pornography exclusively in terms of a sexual function might well be misleading. Since we tend to overestimate the significance of sexual activity, we see the trends of representation in these works as indicators of sexual behavior in the community. An increase in works about homosexual love is taken as an indication of an incipient homosexual revolution or even as the cause of a homosexual revolution. If we find more books about adultery, sadomasochism, or fast-living teenagers, we believe that there must be more adulterers, sadomasochists, and fast-living teenagers in our midst. With a dubious logic reminiscent of primitive magic, many believe that if the number of such representations increases, so will the frequency of such acts, and conversely that the way to cut down on this antisocial behavior is to suppress the pornographic representations.

In the fringeland there is a greater attempt to place sexual activity in the context of a social script, with a greater concern for nonsexual social relations and social roles, and a more direct treatment of appropriate social norms. Some part of this, particularly its common trait of compulsive moralizing, is an attempt to establish a spurious—but defensible under the Roth decision—"redeeming context." This may also represent the producer's awareness that more than simple lust is involved, that the reader may bring to the work a complex of motives, many of which are nonsexual.

For example, the psychiatrist Lionel Ovesey links some of the fantasies of his homosexual patients not to their sexual commitments, but to their problems of managing other personal relations, particularly in their jobs. The management of dominance or aggression in nonsexual spheres of life or the management of ideologies and moralities of social mobility may be the organizing mechanisms of such fantasies while sexuality provides an accessible and powerful imagery through which these other social tensions may be vicariously acted upon. Possibly it is overly simplistic to view this marginal pornography merely as something exclusively sexual.

These items at the fringeland are of most concern in the formulation of community standards. The girlie magazine and the pulp book are visible and priced within the range of the mass market. The hardcover book available at a high price in a bookstore may well cause no comment until it goes on the drugstore racks in paperback. Because such items are sold at breaks in transportation or in locations that tap neighborhood markets, they are the most visible portion of the problem and are the source of the discontent among those who are committed to censorship.

ELUSIVE STANDARDS

The dilemma, then, becomes the formulation of community standards, and this has been the dilemma of the courts themselves. One interesting attempt to strengthen enforcement of conservative standards is the interpretation of federal law to allow prosecution of a seller in the jurisdiction in which materials are received rather than in the ones from which they are mailed. Thus in the rather liberal jurisdiction of New York, where the sale of obscene materials must be compared in the mind of the judge with all the other kinds of crimes that come before him, the seller may well be seen as a small-timer, his crime a misdemeanor. However, in a rural jurisdiction where religious standards are more conservative and a pornography offense is viewed more seriously—especially when compared with the strayed cows and traffic violations that make up the most of the court docket—the seller is a heinous criminal.

The Supreme Court may wish to establish a national standard, allowing some jurisdictions to be more liberal but none to be more conservative. Thus the Supreme Court may build a floor under the right of materials to be protected under the First Amendment, at the same time constraining, through the use of the Ginzburg decision, the importation of materials through wide mailing campaigns into conservative communities. In its more recent decision, the court indicated—somewhat Delphically—that its concern in the future would be with three areas, none of them directly concerned with the content of any works charged as pornographic. These were sales of smut to minors, obtrusive presentation, and "pandering" à la Ginzburg. The court's decisions, however, may well be too conservative in a period when a national society is being created through penetration by the mass media of larger and larger elements of the society. Indeed, it is likely that most legal revolutions have been imposed from above and that communities will fall back to the set floor, if allowed to do so. To trust to local innovation is to trust to nothing.

Pornography is as elusive as mercury. That of the past often no longer fills the bill. The use and users of contemporary pornography vary. Indeed, it might be said that sex itself would not change if there were no more pornography. Pornography is only a minor symptom of sexuality and of very little prominence in people's minds most of the time. Even among those who might think about it most, it results in masturbation or in the "collector" instinct.

What is most important about pornography is not that it is particularly relevant to sexuality, but that it elicits very special treatment when it confronts the law. In this confrontation the agencies of criminal justice, and especially the courts, behave in a very curious manner that is quite dangerous for the freedom of ideas as they might be expressed in other zones of activity such as politics, religion, or the family. Our best protection in this regard has been the very contradictory character of the courts which carefully excludes the consideration of sexual ideas from the general test of the expression of ideas: Do they give rise to a clear and present danger? Our problem is not that pornography represents such a danger—it is far too minor a phenomenon for that—but that the kind of thinking prevalent in dealing with pornography will come to be prevalent in controlling the advocacy of other ideas as well.

THE UNDECLARED WAR ON PRIVACY
Edward N. Long

One summer day in 1963, a federal agent entered a supermarket in a suburb of Kansas City, keeping close watch on a young couple who appeared to be doing their weekly grocery shopping. The couple stopped at a table where special dairy products were being shown. The young man told the two women demonstrators that he had seen one of their products, a milk substitute, advertised in the papers. He and his wife, he said, had a child who was allergic to milk. One of the demonstrators then handed him an explanatory brochure and suggested that he might wish to show it to the child's doctor.

The two demonstrators—both were moonlighting schoolteachers— could not know that their every move was being observed by a federal agent. Nor could they guess that outside the market, five more such agents were gathered around a car radio, listening to the conversation. Nor, again, that a recorder was preserving their words for possible future use. Finally, they could not know that the pleasant young parents worried about their allergic child were actually two more agents of the federal government.

This small army of government employees, equipped with electronic snooping gear, had been dispatched by the Kansas City office of the

From *The Intruders* by Edward N. Long, pp. 3-18 and 224-29. Copyright © 1967 by Frederick A. Praeger. Reprinted by permission.

Food and Drug Administration. Its purpose was to obtain a single copy of the brochure, and to record the conversation of the demonstrators. All this, of course, at the taxpayers' expense.

The most serious crime of which the two teachers could have been accused was poor judgment in their selection of a part-time employer, a company suspected of selling a milk substitute deficient in protein. Yet so ingrained is governmental mistrust of a citizen's ability to give a straight answer to a straight question that the FDA felt compelled to send a veritable expeditionary force of snoopers. Anyone who remembers the antics of the Keystone Cops will not be surprised at the result of this expenditure of time, effort, and federal money. When the FDA later brought the company to trial—a trial based in part on the point-of-sale brochure—the jury's verdict was Not Guilty.

The experience of the two supermarket demonstrators is far from unique in America today. People in every walk of life, innocent and guilty alike, are finding themselves the targets of the eavesdropper and the busybody. Most of the prying is done by professionals who are able to make use of equipment that might even surprise someone with Ian Fleming's imagination. In this field, as in many others, modern science and technology seem to have run far ahead of man's ability to handle his new knowledge wisely.

Our space and missile programs have produced electronic advances that have revolutionized the techniques of the rubberneck. Although the greatest strides have been made with transmitters, none of the eavesdroppers' other equipment has been slighted.

On February 18, 1965, the United States Senate Subcommittee on Administrative Practice and Procedure began hearings on the activities of government agencies that invade privacy. At the first of these hearings, one of the devices viewed with special interest was an olive with a toothpick in it. This ordinarily innocent object contained a tiny transmitter; the toothpick served as its antenna. Immersed in a martini, it could broadcast the length of a city block. Thus, a receiver, located anywhere within a hundred yards or so of a cocktail party, could monitor the conversation.

In addition to the olive, many other devices were on display at the Senate hearings. There were a cigarette box and a table lighter, each with a built-in transmitter. A lady's purse had a microphone built into its clasp that not only was suitable for transmitting street-corner conversation but, left conveniently behind on a desk or table, could transmit conversations taking place after its owner had gone out of the room.

The Subcommittee was also told of a device that is widely favored by those whose curiosity leads them to bug hotel and motel rooms; a picture frame that conceals a transmitter. This device is produced by one of the largest manufacturers of electronic snooping gear. It sells for a little over $200 on the open market, and is a bargain for anyone whose concept of human rights does not include privacy.

The testimony made it clear that the growing market in transmitter device's has provided the eavesdropper with a wide-open field of operations.

For example, in an office, a transmitter can be hidden in a stapler, a lamp, a desk, or almost any other piece of equipment or furniture.

There are virtually limitless opportunities for the wide-awake snooper in household electrical appliances, as well as in furniture. The radio, the television set, and even the ordinary wall socket are especially convenient for hiding a transmitter. Power for the transmitter can be obtained from the home's electrical system, thus freeing the snooper from worry about hiding or replacing batteries.

For outdoor work, in addition to the purse transmitter, several methods have been developed for hiding these devices on the person. Men working in warm climates are able to make use of a transmitter that is suitable for wear with a sport shirt.

An ingenious appliance makes it possible for the snooper to tune in on a meeting he cannot attend. If he can lay his hands on the coat of someone who is to attend the meeting, a miniature transmitter constructed on a piece of cloth can be sewn into the lining. There is little chance that the wearer will ever discover it has been especially tailored to someone else's design.

Electronic snooping flourishes in an open marketplace. Custom-made installations can now be devised to meet the needs of any situation, and the versatility of the miniature transmitter, as well as its potential for snooping, is noteworthy. Senator Wayne Morse, of Oregon, on June 11, 1954, described to the Senate his experience as the victim of such attentions:

"Last year a secret service agent conveyed to me his belief that a microphone was hidden in my office . . . or my home. . . . The agent was able to repeat conversations which took place across my desk in the Senate building and at home."

The Senator went on to describe a scene in which he, with the help of his administrative assistant and a newspaperman, explored the office "on our hands and knees" in search of the microphone. It could not be found there, even when the FBI sent in an expert to help. The Senator continued:

"The interesting thing is that the question was asked me, 'Have you sent a lamp from your home in recent days for repair, or have you sent a chair out to be repaired?' I said, 'I do not know. Let us call Mrs. Morse.' "

Mrs. Morse, it seemed, had sent out a lamp for repair only a few days before. The microphone was never discovered, but the FBI expert pointed out that it might well have been removed after it had served its purpose.

"I cite my experience," Senator Morse said, "as an example of the kind of suspicion and fear which is developing in America these days. It shows that even a public official may be advised, 'You had better be on guard, because . . . there is, or has been, a hidden microphone in your office or home.' "

In addition to the transmitter, the eavesdropper also has available the time-tested wiretap and the conventional wired microphone, as well as the newer miniature recorder that can be concealed in a brief case or in a shoulder holster worn under a suit coat. But even these devices are now considered relatively primitive by the wizards of modern snooping science.

A one-man manufacturer of electronic equipment, one of several such operations in the country today, told the Subcommittee of a unique device which he produces that converts an ordinary telephone into a potential bug able to pick up all conversations in a room. When it is installed, the room can be monitored from any place in the United States where long-distance direct dialing is possible. The eavesdropper can overhear everything said in the bugged room until an incoming call is received or an outgoing call is placed on the telephone. Either of these actions will automatically deactivate the bug. But the snooper can, by following the original procedure, resume his monitoring immediately after such breaks in the line. With direct dialing now in general use, an eavesdropper can do his snooping thousands of miles from his victim—and at no cost, since the automatic toll-charge equipment does not record such use of the line. There is, of course, no toll record to incriminate him.

A similar, though somewhat more involved technique, was brought to the attention of Congress several years ago. It requires not only the "fixing" of the target telephone but its cross-connection to another telephone line. The snooper can then monitor the bugged room by picking up any telephone and dialing the number to which the bugged telephone has been cross-connected. This set-up allows him to hear not only conversations in the room but any conversation taking place on the cross-connected instrument.

Another device, designed to be placed inside the base of a telephone, transmits all telephone conversations to an eavesdropper. And, when a small third wire is introduced, the instrument becomes a permanent microphone. The device is then able to transmit room conversations as well. At a Miami hearing, the Subcommittee was given evidence of an improvement on these techniques. A Florida company manufactures a small, clear-plastic piece, similar to the one found inside each telephone mouthpiece, that contains a tiny transmitter. It takes only a few seconds to exchange the two pieces, and then even an amateur can tap a telephone.

With a fine show of democracy, these modern devices are used to pry out corporate as well as personal secrets. An experience of Schenley Industries, Inc., confirms this. Officers of the company had been working for some time on confidential plans for future operations. However, bits and pieces of these closely guarded plans began to come back to the president of the corporation from outside sources. Suspecting the use of wiretaps or bugs, he decided to call in experts with the latest in detection equipment.

The technicians began their search in the Florida home of the company's president. In the study, where many confidential business conferences had been held, they discovered a small transmitter concealed in the bar. The device was still broadcasting when found. The search also revealed a tap on the lines leading to the president's private office telephone, which had been converted into a microphone that picked up everything said in his office. The eavesdropper had total coverage of all conversations in the president's office, including his personal as well as business telephone calls.

It might be concluded that, to insure a private, unrecorded conversation, persons must talk in a rowboat in the middle of a lake, dressed in swimsuits. But even these precautions will not stop the eavesdropper who knows his business. He can always use the parabolic microphone or the telescope microphone, capable of picking up distant conversation.

The Subcommittee investigation has established that purchases of such equipment have been made by official agencies at all levels of government, by private detectives, and by anyone else willing to pay for it. Mass marketing has brought many expensive items down to prices low enough for them to be enjoyed by the average citizen. Unfortunately, this merchandising advance has also benefited snoopers. The cost of many of these devices was originally high, but mass-marketing techniques, also used by the distributors of imported devices, have made prices of some items quite reasonable.

Richard Gerstein, District Attorney of Dade County, Florida, displayed before the Subcommittee a wide selection of such equipment purchased without difficulty. Included were telephone transmitting devices, bug transmitters, wireless microphones, and a series of different types of room bugs. All devices had been purchased either by telephone or across the counter. "With the exception of one shop owner," Gerstein said, "who stated that the equipment would only be sold to persons having identification as private investigators, there were no questions asked."

Ralph Ward, Vice President of Mosler Research Products, a manufacturer of electronic snooping devices, testified that his company's distribution was somewhat more restricted: "For ten years, our distribution
was limited to law-enforcement agencies." But then, he said, "About two
years ago, we opened this up to sell to law-enforcement agencies *and
licensed detectives, mainly because the field is spreading into industry
now* [italics added]."

Even with this vast array of new equipment to choose from, many
eavesdroppers find the older methods useful. A special agent of the
Internal Revenue Service, recognized as its technical specialist in the
Boston area, testified in 1965 that some of his activities were a practical
blend of the old and the new. He had received training in the use of
"technical investigative aids," at a school run by the Treasury Department. The very existence of this school introduces a curiously paradoxical note: Since 1938, the IRS has prohibited wiretapping, by specific
regulation. Despite this, it has trained at least 125 of its agents in the
installation and use of wiretaps.

The Boston electronics man went to work for the IRS in 1961. In the
next four years, he installed numerous wiretaps and bugs, not only for his
own agency but for others as well. For instance, in 1962, U.S. Treasury
agents called on him to help with a betting-tax investigation in the Boston suburbs. Employing the ingenuities so carefully taught him at the
Department school, he picked the lock of an office that was under
suspicion, entered, and installed a tap. . . .

And what was accomplished by these violations? In the agent's own
words, "Nothing came of this. It was unsuccessful."

In another betting-tax case, this same specialist went to work with a
pen register. This is a small device developed to record the numbers
dialed by a particular telephone. It is attached to the telephone line exactly like a wiretap. However, rather than recording conversations, it
merely prints a tape listing the numbers called. This kind of information helps to determine what contacts have been made by those using
the telephone under surveillance.

This same man was also adept at installing bugs. In June, 1962, he
concealed a microphone in a conference room at the IRS offices in Boston. He explained to the Subcommittee that the microphone was not
installed for the purpose of overhearing conversations between lawyers
and their taxpayer clients while they were alone in the room. To the
best of his knowledge, it had never been so used. Other testimony indicated, however, that the bug came close to being used for that purpose
on at least one occasión.

On July 26, 1965, the Commissioner of Internal Revenue himself submitted to the Subcommittee a list of twenty-two cities in which concealed microphones had been installed in IRS conference rooms. In May, he had ordered the removal of all permanent installations. But he did not prohibit the installation of hidden microphones in conference rooms for specific interviews. In other words, it was a case of *this will never happen again—except when I think it necessary.*

The bugs and wiretaps of this Boston specialist do not add up to a great many over a four-year period, but one must consider the number of people whose conversations were aired at each installation. Also, this list concerns only one technician out of 125 similiarly skilled persons that the IRS has at its disposal. When one realizes that the IRS is only one of the many investigative agencies on the federal level alone, the individual citizen is justified in his measure of concern and moral outrage, especially if he remembers those values for which our country is supposed to stand.

One federal agency, the Federal Bureau of Investigation, has publicly admitted its use of wiretapping year after year. During the past few years, it has usually acknowledged fewer than a hundred taps in operation on the reporting date. Assurances have always been given that these are limited to national-security matters and kidnaping cases, where human life is in danger. Assurances have also been given that each tap is authorized in writing by the Attorney General.

The FBI's use of bugs, however, does not seem to have been so strictly limited. The Division Security Supervisor of the Southwestern Bell Telephone Company told the Senate Subcommittee at a hearing in Kansas City that, on two occasions in 1961, the telephone company received requests from the FBI for the installation of certain leased lines. Such lines function, in effect, as private direct lines between two locations. In response to the first request, two direct lines were set up between the local FBI office and a telephone pole at the rear of a night club. In response to the other request, a direct line was put in between the FBI office and a local shop. In the second case, a public telephone was installed just outside the shop, and an extra line was run to it for use by the FBI.

The Bell Telephone supervisor testified that he understood these arrangements were made in connection with gambling investigations. With the use of appropriate listening devices tied to the leased lines, the FBI was in a position to do its monitoring from the convenience of its own offices. It was also the supervisor's understanding that these installations had been approved by the Attorney General. The Bell Telephone employee revealed at least nine other instances in which leased lines had been set up at the request of the FBI. One of these did actually involve national security.

According to the witness, the telephone company did not have a similar arrangement with any other federal agency. But he substantiated earlier testimony that special company information valuable for wiretapping would, on occasion, be made available to the Kansas City Police Department in cases of kidnaping, blackmail, or other crimes where human life was threatened.

This revelation of FBI bugging was substantiated in July, 1966, when the United States Solicitor General filed a memorandum with the Supreme Court admitting that "for a period of years prior to 1963, and continuing into 1965" the FBI had used bugging devices in the interest of internal security or national safety, which included the investigation of organized crime.

As with the IRS Boston man, the number of eavesdropping installations revealed here does not appear large for a five-year period. But again we are dealing with only one government agency out of many, and the specific office is only one of many in that agency. Then, of course, there is no way to be sure that in any of these investigations the whole story has ever been told. By its very nature, eavesdropping flourishes underground; it turns away from the public light and is nourished in maximum secrecy. In view of this, the Subcommittee has been fortunate to unearth as many witnesses as it has.

We are entitled to ask a few questions at this point. For instance: Who have been the victims of this electronic shadowing? Whose privacy has been invaded by the seemingly inexhaustible variety of listening devices?

Here are some answers: In Kansas City, the victims were gambling suspects and two schoolteachers. In Washington, D.C., it was Senator Wayne Morse. In Miami, it was the president of a large corporation. In Boston, it was suspected tax-law violators. And this is only a sampling of the number and variety of Americans who have been spied upon by public and private agents.

The guilty and the innocent alike have shared the anonymous attentions of snoopers. The famous and the infamous, the rich and the poor, the most respected and the least—all may come within range of a secret ear. In 1961, in Baton Rouge, Louisiana, the telephones of a rabbi, a Baptist minister, and the local director of the American Friends Service Committee were tapped. These three generally respected men had committed the crime—in someone's judgment—of trying to improve racial understanding.

Innocence is not necessarily a safeguard against eavesdropping, nor is physical security. The most carefully guarded family in our country is that of the President, and yet there have been stories of wiretaps on

When neither party to the telephone call has consented, law-enforcement officers should be prohibited from wiretapping. Both interception and divulgence here, too, should be considered crimes.

In the court-order situations here indicated, provision should be made, where a prosecution is brought, to notify the subject of the tap that his conversation has been seized. This should be done in adequate time before trial for him to challenge the order. In all cases, returns should be made to the issuing judge without delay to inform him of the action taken under authority of his order. In view of its limited nature, the court should not have difficulty in reviewing the results.

In national security cases involving a clear danger, the President, as Commander-in-Chief, would have authority to order tapping, at least so long as the Olmstead decision remains in effect. Information so obtained would not be admissible in court. Should Olmstead be overruled at some future time, then the Constitution would require that national-security taps be subject to the same restrictions as other law-enforcement taps.

This recommended federal legislation should be made applicable to federal and state law-enforcement officers, and federal and state courts. It protects privacy to the full extent of the Fourth Amendment, and at the same time allows law-enforcement use of wiretaps in the crimes where the technique has proved most useful.

As for bugging, because few legislative efforts have been made to regulate it, less evidence has been presented to support the need for its use in law enforcement. It is claimed to be of value in the following situations:

To record bribe offers to government agents or public officials.

To record transactions, involving narcotics or other contraband, between undercover agents or informers and a suspect.

To record bets placed by undercover agents or informers, as well as conversations in suspected gambling centers.

To record spiels of "medicine men" or other sellers of fraudulent health products and devices.

To coordinate raids and arrests.

To provide protection for undercover agents and informers.

To maintain general surveillance of the home or office of a suspected criminal.

It would appear from all this that bugging is a useful law-enforcement tool. But it will be noted that in many of the situations listed here, the bug serves only to support the word of a government agent or informer. It hears no more than he can hear himself.

The possibility of court orders for bugging which meet the requirements of the Fourth Amendment also seems to be limited. A wiretap picks up all conversation on a specific wire, while a planted bug will pick up all conversation in a particular area. It is not possible to limit its seizure to a specific conversation, and even if it were, the conversation normally would only be evidence per se. Also, there is the problem of a continuing seizure. The Fourth Amendment seems to preclude the use of all bugs where a physical intrusion would necessarily accompany their installation. In any case, they are similar to the wiretap in that their use falls short of the demands of our democratic traditions.

Because of the jurisdictional gap, it is not possible for Congress alone to protect privacy against all electronic snoopers. But there is a suggested approach to the problem.

The use of electronic devices by law-enforcement officers and informers should be allowed with court orders if the government agent is a participant in the monitored conversation or has the consent of one party to the conversation. Requirements similar to those enumerated for wiretap court orders should be imposed. This would call for both federal and state legislative action.

Congress should ban the use of radio devices by private citizens to monitor private conversation, and the states should similarly prohibit the use of wired bugs and recorders. An exception should be provided where all parties to the conversation consent to the monitoring or recording. The prohibition must be limited to private conversations or it could seriously interfere with radio and television coverage of public events. Private conversations accidentally and unavoidably heard under these circumstances would also be exempted. Again, both monitoring and divulgence should be considered crimes.

Telephone companies should be barred from leasing lines to government agencies for wiretapping or bugging. Advertisement of snooping devices should be prohibited. (Miniature recorders and transmitters have legitimate uses, and their advertisement for such purposes is entirely proper. But there is no reason to allow them to be promoted for private syping and snooping.) Manufacturers and distributors of such surveillance equipment should be licensed and their distribution regulated. It may be too early to tell if there is any value in extending licensing to owners of this kind of equipment. In view of the ease with which home-made devices of this kind can be put together, a licensing program might prove to be more trouble than it is worth. The experience of Maryland with its new law of this type should provide some facts on which to base a decision.

One final measure that should be considered by Congress is the framing of a Code of Conduct for federal investigators. This code would set out the do's and don't's in their relations with, and treatment of, both suspects and third parties. A code of this kind would have to be drawn up with extreme care so as not to interfere unnecessarily with the investigator's initiative. Actually, with adequate education programs and supervision, such a statutory code might not be necessary. This is especially likely if provision were made for all federal agency manuals to be reviewed by an independent authority, such as the Chairman of the Permanent Administrative Conference once he is appointed.

These recommendations do not cover all possible situations in which wiretaps and bugs may be used. Nor do they exhaust all ideas for control and regulation. But they suggest an approach that seems compatible with the Fourth Amendment and our democratic traditions, while recognizing the needs of law enforcement.

In addition to the above, the civil law should not be neglected in its capacity to protect the right of privacy against the intrusions noted here. It is recommended that each state survey its own civil law in this area. Legislation should be enacted to establish a comprehensive and actionable right of privacy, including punitive damages for any abuse of this right.

If the currently intensified war on privacy is to be stopped—or even slowed down—one final step is necessary: the full commitment of the American people. On this point, the Special Committee on Science and Law of the Association of the Bar of the City of New York, issued a call to arms on November 15, 1965: "[It] requires that our businessmen, our district attorneys, our journalists, our men of science—to mention only a few—be concerned with the human claim to privacy, as well as with their dominant respective concerns for the profitable enterprise, the enforcement of society's laws, the freedom of the press and the freedom of science." . . .

DUE PROCESS OF LAW IN CRIMINAL CASES
George Edwards

The phrase "due process of law" is fundamental to our American concepts of order and of liberty. It was first written into the Fifth Amendment to our Constitution by men who had had bitter experience with the arbitrary power of kings. It was made specifically applicable to the states at the end of the Civil War—the most bitter internal conflict in our history.

From *The Journal of Criminal Law, Criminology and Police Science*, Vol. 57, No. 2 (1966), 130-35. Reprinted by permission.

The Fourteenth Amendment language reads: "nor shall any State deprive any person of life, liberty, or property, without due process of law. . . ." The importance of this language to present legal problems is made more obvious by reference to Article VI: "This Constitution, and the Laws of the United States which shall be made in Pursuance thereof; and all Treaties made, or which shall be made, under the Authority of the United States, shall be the supreme law of the Land; and the Judges in every State shall be bound thereby, any Thing in the Constitution or Laws of any State to the Contrary notwithstanding."

At the outset, then, I deem it obvious that we in this country have chosen to bind ourselves to observation both in federal and state affairs of a national concept of "due process of law." And the legitimate area of debate concerns what is (or should be) included in that historic and meaningful phrase.

Let us then examine briefly where our law comes from and what it means to us. Basically, all good law is the codification of the wisdom and morality of past ages. It is never safe to deal long with a practical problem without relating it to a moral standard. Let me start with such a statement. In Romans, Chapter 13, we find these lines:

> Owe no man anything, but to love one another: for he that loveth another hath fulfilled the law.
>
> For this, Thou shalt not commit adultery, Thou shalt not kill, Thou shalt not steal, Thou shalt not bear false witness, Thou shall not covet; and if there be any other commandment, it is briefly comprehended in this saying, namely, Thous shalt love thy neighbor as thyself.
>
> Love worketh no ill to his neighbor; therefore love is the fulfilling of the law.
>
> And that, knowing the time, that now it is high time to awake out of sleep: for now is our salvation nearer than when we believed.
>
> The night is far spent, the day is at hand: let us therefore cast off the works of darkness, and let us put on the armour of light.

In this eloquent exhortation we find implicit the two ideals which we find so difficult to achieve. The ideal of an orderly society where each of us would be safe from trangressions such as assault, or theft, or murder, and the ideal which teaches that all people are our neighbors; that they are equal before our laws and entitled equally in the words of the Declaration of Independence to "life, liberty, and the pursuit of happiness."

A more succinct summary would be simply: order and individual liberty. Put in these terms, it is easy to recognize that these principles are frequently in conflict with each other and are never easy to reconcile.

Order has been the keynote of every organized government from the beginning of history. But our American government, while plainly designed to preserve order, made the signal contribution to history by also avowing, as a government objective, the achievement of individual liberty for its citizens.

No one needs to remind me that the statement of the objective has not created the reality. What I am seeking to do is to outline both the importance and the difficulty of the topics we deal with.

The nature of liberty is easier to describe than to define. Freedom on the frontier is one thing. Freedom in a metropolis is another. In relation to the man of the frontier, liberty could almost be defined as the right to do without hindrance what one wished. In the big city, liberty can be more accurately referred to as the maximum freedom of choice consistent with the maintenance of similar freedom for the other members of society.

In the days of Daniel Boone, there would be little point to a traffic light at a crossing of foot trails. Today, we accept the interference with our liberty represented by traffic signals because we know that without them all of us would be snarled in hopeless traffic jams.

When, a generation ago, a farm boy on a spring day yelled, ran, picked up a rock and threw it—who cared? He was a boy. But today—with perhaps no more basic motivation than the animal spirits which moved his rural grandfather—this same conduct would almost inevitably produce a police call and a police statistic.

In earlier days few people would be bothered by the bitter and violent words uttered by a pioneer to a few companions around a camp fire, but in today's hot summer city streets, words of equal violence addressed to a Ku Klux-minded crowd in St. Augustine, or to a Muslim-minded crowd in Philadelphia could prove to be a major public hazard.

These examples are provided only to remind us that law enforcement in a rural society, and law enforcement in our modern urban society are vastly different. Most of America today lives in metropolitan areas, where millions of people who do not know one another nevertheless live and work in close proximity, with greatly increased chances for conflict. At least partly out of necessity—and frequently without recognizing what we have done—we have turned over to the police officer of our big cities many functions which used to be among the most important duties of the individual and the family. Today the policeman's tour of duty is full of radio runs which require him to correct the conduct of children, mediate family quarrels, determine the right of way between overeager drivers, care for the injured on the streets, protect our homes at night and our persons in the daytime—all, hopefully, with the concern of a social worker, the wisdom of a Solomon, and the prompt courage of a combat soldier.

For the moment let us leave the frontline defender of law—the police officer—and turn abruptly to another agency of our law—the Supreme

Court of the United States. Hold your breath, for having said something good about our police, I am not in the next breath about to attack the Supreme Court. In fact, I may be the only judge or lawyer you will ever hear praise the police and the Supreme Court in the same discussion.

For over a decade our Supreme Court has been engaged in leading this country toward making effective the high ideals of our American Constitution. We should remember that our Constitution in Article III makes the Supreme Court the interpreter of our constitutional ideals. This Supreme Court has certainly taken that obligation seriously. It has been setting ever higher standards of due process of law.

The court has told us that deprivation of human liberty is essentially a decision for the judiciary. Absent a judicial warrant or probable cause, there cannot be a lawful arrest; and illegal detention for "investigation" may invalidate a confession.

The Supreme Court has reminded us also that it is equally fundamental under our Constitution not to compel a person to testify against one's self.

When a person is being questioned in police custody after arrest for a crime, he should be told of his constitutional right not to be compelled to testify against himself. Absence of such a warning may be an important factor in holding a confession inadmissible.

The Supreme Court has told us that the Fourth Amendment prohibition on "unreasonable searches and seizures" will be enforced—even against convictions based on procedures held consistent with state law.

The Court has acted to preserve the right to be confronted by an accuser and to be allowed effectively to cross-examine him.

And the court has held that the Sixth Amendment and the Due Process Clause of the Fourteenth Amendment give indigent defendants a right to counsel in at least all felony prosecutions—whether state or federal.

These principles do not really sound very shocking to us. We are fully familiar with all of them and we unhesitatingly subscribe to them when they are recited as legal platitudes. We become concerned only when they are applied to a specific case—where constitutional disregard or violation results in a retrial or the freeing of someone whom we deem to be guilty.

Let us then look at the four cases which have occasioned most of the current controversy over the United States Supreme Court. The names are all familiar—*Mallory, Gideon* and *Escobedo*.

The headnotes of *Mallory* tell its story:

> Petitioner was convicted in a Federal District Court of rape and sentenced to death after a trial in which there was admitted in evidence a

confession obtained under the following circumstances: He was arrested early in the afternoon and was detained at police headquarters within the vicinity of numerous committing magistrates. He was not told of his right to counsel or to a preliminary examination before a magistrate, nor was he warned that he might keep silent and that any statements made by him might be used against him. Not until after petitioner had confessed, about 9:30 p.m., was an attempt made to take him before a committing magistrate, and he was not actually taken before a magistrate until the next morning. . . .

The rationale of the court's order of reversal follows:

The purpose of this impressively pervasive requirement of criminal procedure is plain . . . The awful instruments of criminal law cannot be entrusted to a single functionary. The complicated process of criminal justice is therefore divided into different parts, responsibility for which is separately vested in the various participants upon whom the criminal law relies for its vindication. Legislation such as this, requiring that the police must with reasonable promptness show legal cause for detaining arrested persons, constitutes an important safeguard—not only in assuring protection for the innocent but also in securing conviction of the guilty by methods that commend themselves to a progressive and self-confident society. For this procedural requirement checks resort to those reprehensible practices known as the "third degree" which, though universally rejected as indefensible, still find their way into use. It aims to avoid all the evil implications of secret interrogation of persons accused of crime.

The holding in *Mallory* (a unanimous one) was:

We cannot sanction this extended delay, resulting in confession, without subordinating the general rule of prompt arraignment to the discretion of arresting officers in finding exceptional circumstances for its disregard.

In *Mapp* the defendant was convicted of possession of lewd and lascivious pictures and books. Her house had been forcibly entered after her refusal to admit police. "No search warrant was ever produced at the trial nor was the failure to produce one explained." The State of Ohio Supreme Court upheld the conviction though "based primarily upon . . . evidence . . . unlawfully seized during an unlawful search of defendant's home." The Supreme Court reversed and held that "all evidence obtained by searches and seizures in violation of the Constitution is, by that same authority, inadmissible in a state court."

Subsequently the Supreme Court held, in *Linkletter v. Walker,* that the exclusionary role of *Mapp* did not "operate retrospectively upon cases finally decided . . . prior to *Mapp.*"

In *Gideon* the defendant was charged with breaking and entering a poolroom—a felony under Florida law. At his trial he asked the right to appointed counsel. This was refused by the trial judge. In reversing the conviction the Supreme Court held: "The right of one charged with crime to counsel may not be fundamental and essential to fair trial in some countries, but it is in ours." The decision was unanimous. Incidentally, Gideon was retried with competent counsel and found "not guilty."

In *Escobedo* the defendant was convicted of the murder of his brother-in-law. Eleven days after the shooting he was arrested. He asked to see his lawyer and was refused such permission. The lawyer, who was present in the building, asked to see Escobedo and was refused access to his client. No advice as to his constitutional rights was given by the police. Questioned persistently, Escobedo made damaging statements which were admitted at his trial.

The Supreme Court held:

> [W]here, as here, the investigation is no longer a general inquiry into an unsolved crime but has begun to focus on a particular suspect, the suspect has been taken into police custody, the police carry out a process of interrogations that lends itself to eliciting incriminating statements, the suspect has requested and been denied an opportunity to consult with his lawyer, and the police have not effectively warned him of his absolute constitutional right to remain silent, the accused has been denied "the Assistance of Counsel" in violation of the Sixth Amendment of the Constitution as "made obligatory upon the States by the Fourteenth Amendment," . . . and that no statement elicited by the police during the interrogation may be used against him at a criminal trial.

I have sought carefully to outline to you the actual holdings of these cases. It is these holdings which are law and must be followed. We are not required to follow the fears (or hopes) as to some future case which these opinions have stimulated in the breast of some lawyer or law professor.

Now, which of us really can conscientiously disagree with the actual holdings of these cases? Do we not want the police to be required to get a search warrant before breaking into any home? Should a poor person be tried on a felony charge without a lawyer? Do we not want the police to follow both the Constitution and the law in arrest and interrogation? I think your answers and mine would be the same on these questions. But these cases do seem to me to afford these suggestions to all concerned with law enforcement:

(1) They suggest more police emphasis on investigation before rather than after arrest. There should be less reliance upon efforts to sweat a confession out of a suspect even where no violence is employed.

(2) There should be more reliance upon establishing by other evidence than confessions the facts which point to the suspect's guilt.

(3) There should be a concern for having in mind what really moves an officer to make an arrest or search. Description of his conduct as based on a "hunch" will not convince a court. But where that "hunch" actually is based on prior knowledge of a crime recently committed, and the suspicious conduct of the party under observation, it may well represent legal probable cause.

(4) They suggest increased use of the judiciary to issue warrants for arrest and search.

(5) They suggest compliance with state and federal statutes requiring prompt appearance before a judge of a person arrested for crime.

(6) They suggest prompt measures by every bar association in the United States to devise ways and means to provide counsel for indigents.

Even if we do agree theoretically with the principles of these new Supreme Court cases and recognize that they advance our concepts of constitutional law, there may be still another question in your minds. What about the argument that the police cannot enforce the law and maintain public peace and follow these rules?

Well, I would have to answer that this simply is not so. After service for some six years on the Supreme Court of Michigan, in 1961 I resigned from the court to take the post of Police Commissioner of the City of Detroit. The basic motive for such a move (and I assure you I regarded it as extraordinary) was to seek to quiet the then explosive conflict between the Police Department and the Negro community of our city— before it blew into the sort of catastrophe which recently shook Los Angeles. That is another story for another day. But I must confess that a subsidiary interest—and concern—was whether or not insistence on constitutional law enforcement (to which I was thoroughly committed) would indeed hamper effective law enforcement.

We followed *Mallory* and *Mapp* and *Gideon* and *Escobedo*—and the rest. No case that I have talked about to you today was really new to Michigan. For my state's courts had long since adopted every one of the principles we have talked about—not under United States Supreme Court duress, but as a matter of state law. But my comment is meant to indicate that the Detroit Police Department sought to follow these rules in actual practice. For those of you who know that most police Commissioners are carefully screened from the facts of life, let me add that I tried with every means at my command (and they were considerable) to know the actuality of our police practices and to conform it to the law.

It wasn't exactly easy. Some days I felt as if I was wading ankle deep in blood—a good deal of it my own. But we stopped "alley court" and "falling on the precinct steps" and the "merry-go-round" of prisoners from one precinct to another. And we did take prisoners promptly before a judge. And the town did not fall apart. Murder and pillage did not run rampant. In fact—doubtless by happy coincidence—murders went down. And we markedly increased arrests resulting in prosecutions, even though we eliminated investigative arrests.

It would be nice to tell you that we solved all the problems. But it would also be untrue. What I think I can tell you is that we made law enforcement a bit more effective and we convinced most of the people of Detroit that we were moving toward making it more nearly equal in its application to all people, regardless of race or color.

In those two years, Detroit did not have anything approaching a race riot, nor has it in the period that has followed. [until the summer of 1967].

We did not end crime. Nor do I think that any police department ever can. Unorganized crime stems from the most degraded and deprived portions of our society. As we better living circumstances for these—as we increase opportunities for jobs, and education, and housing, and normal family life, we strike directly at the deep roots of crime. As is obvious, these are not police tasks.

I certainly believe that higher quality of law enforcement—such as that mandated by the ideals of our Constitution and by the mandates of the Supreme Court—does demand new practical measures of support for law enforcement. By saying this I do not by any means intend to join the [Joseph] McCarthy-like tone of some national comment on this problem. Impeach Earl Warren signs, attacks on the Supreme Court, cries for police "crackdowns" with their implications of dragnet arrests and arrests for investigation only, shed much more heat than light.

Our city police officers are the front line of defense of law enforcement. Generally we have lampooned them, paid them badly, assigned them a relatively low social status, and appreciated them only when faced with an individual emergency. With this kind of attitude and the new demands for higher standards of police performance, our police may not be able to do an acceptable job. Something else must be added.

For the next decades acceptable standards of law enforcement will require: (1) Higher status for police officers; (2) More police officers; (3) Higher pay for police officers; (4) Better training for police officers; (5) More public support for law enforcement; (6) Greater coordination between the agencies of our government concerned with law enforcement.

The great majority of police officers want no part of any abusive practices. They want and will support higher standards of training, of pay, and of performance in their profession.

I look forward to the time, probably not too distant in history, when police induction requirements will include two years of college and when the fully trained and qualified police officer will command a salary of $10,000 a year.

Federal assistance in relation to some of these local police needs should be sought—particularly, I believe, in relation to a National Police Training College, organized, staffed and financed at a level to make it comparable in police work to a West Point or an Annapolis. Such an institution could do more to enhance the level of local law enforcement than any other single program I can think of.

In addition to better trained police officers for the next two decades, we will also need more of them—probably in substantial percentage terms. This is demanded by higher standards of performance. (The third degree and the tipover raid are repugnant to our ideals of American justice, but they are certainly economical of police man-hours!)

More police are demanded too by present day problems and standards of public safety. One of major proportions is the fact that history has moved hundreds of thousands of our most deprived citizens from isolated areas where officialdom made little effort at law enforcement and planted them in the heart of our greatest cities.

I would like to see more public concern about police work—not less. I would like to see citizens feel that they have a tremendous stake in how their police department operates and feel a duty to support it in the proper discharge of its duties. I would like to see them willing to "get involved."

What about the woman murdered in New York some months ago within sight or hearing of 38 people, not one of whom called the police? They didn't want to "get involved."

What about the police officer engaged in a desperate struggle to prevent a would-be suicide from throwing himself off an expressway bridge recently in Detroit? When the officer asked for help in trying to lift the man to safety, one citizen gave it. Others passed by, not wanting to become involved.

What commentaries these are on our civilization!

The effort to involve citizen support for law enforcement is basic in a democratic society. Without it the police effort can degenerate into an occupation army attitude. With citizen support the police are the community's right arm in fighting the evils which make city living difficult.

Lastly, a few words as to coordination of law enforcement efforts. In many states the Attorney General is constitutionally described as the chief law enforcement officer of the state. Is there not a greater role for him to play in law enforcement than merely to act as lawyer for the state when the state is a litigant?

In our country there are 40,000 separate and autonomous police jurisdictions. Generally, it may be said that they tend to operate strictly on their own. Yet the police chief who is most jealous of his powers would be likely to welcome guidance on United States and state constitutional problems. And it would be hard to conceive of an honest department that would not welcome state aid in dealing with the great and formidable challenge of organized crime.

Two measures might be suggested as a beginning of concern on the part of Attorneys General. Would it not be desirable to have all local police regulations reviewed and approved as to constitutionality and legality by the Attorney General's office? Would it not be desirable for the Attorney General's office to establish a continuing effort to prosecute organized crime, which moves so easily across local and county boundaries?

Let us return directly then to "due process of law." It is this concept which has given us what Justice Cardoza described as "our American system of ordered liberty." . . .

CONTROL OF FIREARMS
The President's Commission on Law Enforcement and the Administration of Justice

The assassination of President John F. Kennedy with a mail-order rifle offered a grim and tragic illustration of what can result when firearms are easily available to anyone in the United States. The Commission strongly believes that the increasing violence in every section of the Nation compels an effort to control possession and sale of the many kinds of firearms that contribute to that violence.

During 1963, 4,760 persons were murdered by firearms. During 1965, 5,600 murders, 34,700 aggravated assaults and the vast majority of the 68,400 armed robberies were committed by means of firearms. All but 10 of the 278 law enforcement officers murdered during the period 1960-65 were killed with firearms. And statistics, of course, cannot even indicate the personal tragedy each of these offenses caused.

The issue of firearms control has been debated heatedly throughout the country in the past few years. Many millions of the estimated 50 million privately owned guns in the United States belong to hunters, gun collectors, and other sportsmen. Their representative organizations resist controls over the present easy accessibility of rifles and shotguns. Many

From The Task Force Report, *The Challenge of Crime in a Free Society,* February 1967, pp. 239-43.

other millions of firearms—pistols, revolvers, rifles, and shotguns—are owned by citizens determined to protect their families from criminal attack and their property from loss to burglars. In a nationwide sampling conducted for the Commission by the National Opinion Research Center, 37 percent of the persons interviewed said that they kept firearms in the household to protect themselves. Some citizens who fear assault and robbery in the streets of our cities carry firearms about for self-protection. Many of these firearms owners contend that control over the purchase and possession of firearms conflicts with the need and right to defend themselves, their families, and their property.

Although the Commission believes that controls at all levels of government must be strengthened in order to reduce the probability that potential criminal offenders will acquire firearms, it agrees that the interests of persons desiring such weapons for legitimate purposes must be preserved as much as possible. No system of control, of course, can guarantee that society will be safe from the misuse of firearms, but the Commission is convinced that a strengthened system can make an important contribution to reducing the danger of crime in the United States.

EXISTING FIREARMS CONTROL LAWS

Regulation of firearms in the United States is based upon three Federal laws, various kinds of State legislation, and a large number of local ordinances.

The first of the Federal laws, the National Firearms Act of 1934, applies to machine guns, short-barreled and sawed-off rifles and shotguns, mufflers and silencers, and concealable firearms—not including pistols. The 1934 act requires that possessors register all of these weapons and devices with the Treasury Department, and it imposes annual taxes on firearms manufacturers, importers, and dealers. Taxes ranging from $5 to $200 are also imposed on the transfer of registered weapons and other equipment.

The Federal Firearms Act of 1938 requires the licensing of all manufacturers and dealers who use the facilities of interstate or foreign commerce. It prohibits the knowing transportation of firearms in interstate commerce to, or receipt by, any person who has been convicted of a felony, or who is a fugitive from justice. The law requires that most kinds of firearms imported into or manufactured in the United States bear serial numbers, and it prohibits the interstate transportation of stolen firearms, or those with mutilated serial numbers. The 1938 law also prohibits the licensed manufacturers and dealers from transporting firearms into States in violation of State laws requiring a permit to purchase firearms.

The third Federal law regulating firearms is the Mutual Security Act of 1954, which authorizes the President to regulate the export and import of firearms. Administration of the act has been delegated to the Department of State.

The Department of Defense, which formerly disposed of its surplus firearms through commercial and other private channels, suspended all such sales several months ago. It is now considering the advisability of destroying surplus or obsolete weapons in the future.

There is a wide diversity in the purpose and scope of State gun control laws:

Twenty-five States require a license to sell handguns at retail, 8 require a permit (or the equivalent) to purchase a handgun, 11 require a waiting period between purchase and delivery of a handgun, 1 requires a license to possess a handgun, 29 require a license to carry a handgun, 19 prohibit the carrying of a concealed handgun, 18 require a license to carry a handgun in a vehicle, 22 prohibit the carrying of a loaded firearm in a vehicle, and 4 States require the registration of firearms.

New York State's Sullivan law is the most stringent firearms control regulation in the United States. The laws of several States require that anyone carrying concealable firearms have a license, but the Sullivan law prohibits anyone from keeping a pistol or revolver in his home or place of business without a license. Further, no one may even purchase a pistol or revolver until he has obtained either a license to possess or a license to carry such a weapon. The New York law does not require a license to possess or carry rifles and shotguns, but does state that they cannot be carried in an automobile or a public place when loaded.

In addition to the State laws, there are many county, city, town, and village ordinances that require licenses for the possession or purchase of firearms.

LIMITED EFFECTIVENESS OF PRESENT LAWS

At first glance, the combined regulatory machinery established by these firearms laws may appear to provide sufficient control. This appearance is misleading. A 1966 Federal Bureau of Investigation survey of the chief administrators of police departments in 10 large cities discloses that all but one believe that the easy accessibility of firearms is a serious law enforcement problem.

On the Federal level, the statutes do little to control the retail and mail-order sale of handguns, rifles, and shotguns. The provision of the Federal Firearms Act of 1938 prohibiting Federal licenses from transporting firearms into States in violation of State laws requiring a permit to purchase firearms has an extremely limited effect. Only eight States have enacted permit laws. If there are local ordinances within a State, but no State law, the Federal provision does not apply. The prohibition against transport of firearms to, or receipt by, felons or fugitives applies only to direct interstate shipment and does not prevent such persons from buying firearms locally after they have been transported from another State. Despite the Federal laws, therefore, practically anyone—the convicted criminal, the mental incompetent, or the habitual drunkard— can purchase firearms simply by ordering them in those States that have few controls.

Strict controls by one State or city are nullified when a potential criminal can secure a firearm merely by going into a neighboring jurisdiction with lax controls, or none at all. While information is sparse, there are strong indications that mail-order houses and other out-of-State sources provide a substantial number of guns to those who commit crimes. One study by the Massachusetts State Police showed that 87 percent of concealable firearms used during the commission of crimes in Massachusetts in a recent year were obtained from sources outside the State.

In order to prevent criminal use of firearms, the police must have some way of following weapons into the hands of the ultimate consumer. But only in four States do police agencies have a method of determining who owns firearms and where they are located. The requirement that each person register firearms—a tool available to law enforcement in almost every industrial nation in the world—has been compared with the State control of automobiles and drivers. At a time when there were very few automobiles, registration was not thought necessary. When automobiles became so numerous that they posed a serious physical threat to society, comprehensive registration was felt to be essential.

A final failing in the present system of control is the ease with which extremely low-priced, and therefore widely available, surplus weapons are brought into the United States from foreign countries. At the present time it is estimated that at least 1 million such weapons are reaching the civilian market each year. During the recent hearings of the Senate Subcommittee on Juvenile Delinquency, law enforcement officials testified that foreign imports accounted for a significant percentage of the total number of firearms coming into their possession as a result of having been used in the commission of crimes. The figures ranged from a low of 18 percent in Washington, D.C., to a high of 80 percent in Atlanta, Ga. . . .

PUBLIC OPINION ABOUT FIREARMS CONTROL

Public opinion on the subject of firearms control has been sampled several times in the last few years by the Gallup Poll. According to the 1966 poll, a substantial majority of persons interviewed—67 percent— said they favored "a law which would require a person to obtain a police permit before he or she could buy a gun." Even when the same question was put to firearms owners, a majority—56 percent—indicated that they favored police permits to purchase guns.

A second question asked by the Gallup Poll was directed to the problem of guns and juveniles. "Which of these three plans would you prefer for the use of guns by persons under the age of 18—forbid their use completely; put strict regulations on their use; or continue as at present with few regulations?" In response, 27 percent of those questioned and 17 percent of firearms owners said they favored completely forbidding the use of guns by persons under 18; 55 percent of all persons and 59 percent of gun owners said they favored strict regulation; and 15 percent of all persons and 22 percent of the gun owners wanted to continue as at present.

On the question of outlawing all handguns except for police use (a question last asked in 1959) 59 percent of the sample were in favor and 35 percent were opposed.

THE CONTROVERSY ABOUT FIREARMS CONTROL

While the majority of the public favors reasonable firearms control, the National Rifle Association and other citizen groups have provided an effective legislative lobby to represent those hunters, gun collectors, and other persons who oppose additional regulation. Many arguments are offered by this opposition.

The most emotional position—one this Commission must reject outright—is that licensing and registration provisions for handguns, rifles, and shotguns would disarm the public and thus render it easy prey for violent criminals, or an invading or subversive enemy. In fact, all proposals for regulation would permit householders and shopkeepers to continue to possess firearms. Licensing and registration for the legitimate firearms owner would merely add a small measure of inconvenience to the presently largely unregulated mail-order and over-the-counter sales of firearms. It is this inconvenience that appears to be the underlying reason for the opposition to more firearms control. Opponents suggest that laws calling for registration would penalize the law-abiding citizen, who would comply—while not touching criminals who would not comply. They thus conclude that such laws do not address themselves to the real problem of firearms misuse.

Those supporting stricter control of firearms agree that many potential criminal offenders will obtain firearms even with additional laws. But they point to the conclusion of the Senate Subcommittee on Juvenile Delinquency, which found that criminals, for the most part, purchase their firearms through the mails or in retail stores, rather than stealing them. One police chief from a large western city told an FBI survey that, after permissive State legislation had preempted local controls, there were "several instances of homicide committed within 30 minutes of the time a short firearm was purchased by a person who would not have been granted a permit to purchase one under the former legislation."

During the first year's operation of a Philadelphia ordinance requiring a permit to obtain a firearm, 73 convicted persons were prohibited from purchasing firearms in the city. Federal Bureau of Investigation statistics demonstrate that a higher proportion of homicides are committed with firearms in those areas where firearms regulations are lax, than in those areas where there are more stringent controls. In Dallas, Tex., and Phoenix, Ariz., firearms regulations are fairly weak. In Dallas in 1963, 72 percent of homicides were committed with firearms; in Phoenix 65.9 percent were committed with firearms. In Chicago, where regulations are more strict, 46.4 percent of the homicides were committed with firearms. In New York City, with the most stringent gun controls of any major city in the United States, only about 25 percent of the homicides are committed with firearms.

Opponents of additional controls contend that firearms are dangerous only if misused and that the appropriate legal remedy is to punish illegal use of firearms—not to hamper ownership. Supporters of control argue that it is not enough to rely on the deterrent effect of punishing the wrongdoer after the act to prevent others from misusing guns. They maintain that firearms should be kept out of the hands of those who intend to use them wrongfully.

Opponents of firearms control legislation also rely upon the Second Amendment's guarantee of "the right to bear arms." The Second Amendment, in its entirety, states:

> A well regulated Militia, being necessary to the security of a free State, the right of the people to keep and bear Arms, shall not be infringed.

The U.S. Supreme Court and lower Federal courts have consistently interpreted this Amendment only as a prohibition against Federal interference with State militia and not as a guarantee of an individual's right to keep or carry firearms. The argument that the Second Amendment prohibits State or Federal regulation of citizen ownership of firearms has no validity whatsoever.

COMMISSION RECOMMENDATIONS

Since laws, as they now stand, do not accomplish the purposes of firearms control, the Commission believes that all States and the Federal Government should act to strengthen them. Any legislative scheme should maximize the possibility of keeping firearms out of the hands of potential criminal offenders, while at the same time affording citizens ample opportunity to purchase such weapons for legitimate purposes. It is appropriate to ban absolutely the sale of those weapons no citizen has a justifiable reason for owning.

The Commission recommends:

Federal and State Governments should enact legislation outlawing transportation and private possession of military-type firearms such as bazookas, machine guns, mortars, and antitank guns.

In addition, dangerous or potentially dangerous persons should be prohibited from purchasing firearms.

The Commission recommends:

States should enact laws prohibiting certain categories of persons, such as habitual drunkards, drug addicts, mental incompetents, persons with a history of mental disturbance, and persons convicted of certain offenses, from buying, owning, or possessing firearms.

Prevention of crime and apprehension of criminals would be enhanced if each firearm were registered with a governmental jurisdiction. A record of ownership would aid the police in tracing and locating those who have committed or who threaten to commit violent crime. Law enforcement officers should know where each gun is an who owns it.

The Commission recommends:

Each State should require the registration of all handguns, rifles, and shotguns. If, after 5 years, some States still have not enacted such laws, Congress should pass a Federal firearms registration act applicable to those States.

Government regulation to prevent those with criminal purposes from purchasing firearms cannot be effective as long as mail-order sales and retail sales to persons living outside the seller's States are not controlled. It is essential, also, to reduce and to regulate the importation into the United States of large numbers of cheap firearms. Since sporting weapons such as rifles and shotguns apparently present less danger of criminal use than do handguns, control over the latter should be more stringent. A truly effective system of regulation requires a meshing of State and Federal action.

The Commission recommends:

Each State should require a person to obtain a permit before he can either possess or carry a handgun. Through licensing provisions, Federal law should prohibit mail-order and other interstate sales of handguns and should regulate such sales of rifles and shotguns.

Federal legislation to implement these goals should prohibit the inter-state shipment of handguns except between federally licensed importers, manufacturers, and dealers. A Federal license should also be prohibited from selling handguns to an individual not living in the State of the seller. The interstate shipment of shotguns and rifles should be delayed a sufficient time for law enforcement authorities in the buyer's home-town to examine his sworn statement concerning age and other factors affecting his eligibility to purchase such a weapon, and the consent of these authorities should be required before the weapon may be shipped. Antique dealers could continue to operate under reasonable regulations. Stats may also want to prohibit firearms sales to persons under a certain age, such as 18 or 21, or require parental approval for firearms registra-tion in a minor's name.

IDENTIFYING DELINQUENTS IN THE PRESS
Gilbert Geis

Much can be told about a society and its people by the tactics they choose in dealing with persons whom they officially label as deviants. "The mood and temper of the public with regard to the treatment of crime and criminals," wrote Winston Churchill more than half a century ago, "is one of the most unfailing tests of the civilization of any country." Churchill may have had in mind the varying degrees to which certain cultures permitted the anger and the selfrighteousness of the exemplary to be exerted against the less-than-exemplary throughout time, and the long and noxious catalog of punitive horrors visited upon persons who offended against various standards of conduct.

In these terms, it is worth a moment to place the fervor often demon-strated these days in favor of providing newspaper readers with names, pictures, and other personal details concerning juvenile delinquents and their families into brief historical and psychological perspective. The intensity and persistence of the drive to identify delinquents in the mass media and the long and painful record of similar endeavors to label devi-ants would suggest that such moves have an underlying source.

It does not seem unlikely that placing discernible and ineradicable signs upon the wayward reflects a basic desire to demonstrate by con-tinuously visible reminders one's own decency as opposed to the deg-

From *Federal Probation,* Vol. 29, No. 4 (December 1965), 44-9. Reprinted by permission.

radation of others. In ancient times, various stigmata were taken to represent divine permission to accentuate by harshness and lack of compassion the isolation originally imposed by physical or behavioral idiosyncrasy. When the legitimacy of sanctified brutality was brought into ethical and theological question, new tactics were readily devised so that the good would be provided with human fare to enhance their own self-satisfaction. There is a storehouse of literary exemplars of such procedures, including Jean Valjean with his yellow passport, a testament to his former status as a convict, which he was obligated to display at the mayor's office whenever he entered a new town, and Hester Prynne with the scarlet "A" embroidered upon her garment to provide the not unpleasant excitement of vicarious lechery for the well-behaved.

The irony of such tactics lies, of course, in the fact that the presumably well-meant attempts of the powerful to protect themselves against the contamination of sinners and the outrages of predators by spotlighting such malefactors so that they will be unable to camouflage themselves as often as not—and probably much more often than not—serves to reinforce and cement the objectionable behavior. It is also disconcerting to learn that such labeling by public proclamation of the individual often provides him with precisely that attention and those personal and tangible testimonials of accomplishment and recognition that elicited the original act.

There is something to be understood in this respect from the wry tale of the exhibitionist who always managed to arouse a shocked and screaming reaction from those privy to his performance. On one occasion, however, he encountered a rather blase young lady, whose response to his exhibit was a nonchalant: "So what?" Thus regarded, the act of exhibitionism, it is said, totally lost its appeal for the performer. With considered exceptions, the same lesson would seem to apply regarding children who throw temper tantrums, employ obscene language, and appear before the juvenile courts.

IMPORTANT TO AVOID TAGGING

It would be quite naive, of course, to assume that delinquency will evaporate amiably in the face of indifference to it. There are a vast number of other reinforcing mechanisms involved in its production and perpetuation. But it merits incessant emphasis that a vital procedure for altering human behavior is the allowance and provision of alternative self-definitions for the individual. Hesitancy in tagging a person, and reluctance in confirming him in his image of himself as one capable of and likely to reproduce undesired behavior is perhaps the most fundamental desideratum for providing a climate for the growth of more acceptable kinds of behavior.

The structuring of such a climate can, perhaps, be illustrated by the rather unusual approach of an interviewer intent upon detouring an offender from formalizing a view of himself as a confirmed deviant. Rather than standard guilt-arousing inquiries, he takes the line: "This certainly is not the kind of behavior you're accustomed to engaging in. You must be feeling pretty bad about it."

Such an approach would be patently absurd, of course, with a dyed-in-the-wool alcoholic check writer or with a similar recidivistic offender. But we have firm data that virtually all juvenile delinquents are not persistent or confirmed malefactors; that they drift in and out of delinquent situations; that they are quite plastic and malleable creatures at this stage of their existence. In fact, this is the major reason why we have an institution such as the juvenile court. It should also be the major reason why we will not permit the publication of the names or other identifying data about young persons who appear before the juvenile court or who are arrested for offenses constituting juvenile delinquency.

The point may perhaps be further emphasized by noting the strategies employed by groups attempting to inculcate desired kinds of self-images and consequent behavior among their members. The United States Marine Corps, for example, continuously reminds its members of the stirring history of their group, and provides them with a plethora of reinforcements, many of them wrapped persuasively in ceremonial garb, so that they will come unfailingly to think of themselves as representatives of a special tradition and will automatically behave in the manner that persons with the internalized label "Marine" are expected to behave. Many "delinquents" obviously will also respond to similar reinforcement tactics, which include public proclamation of their status and deeds, by reproducing the behavior associated with the accorded label. "We're cruddy juvenile delinquents," the gang boys in *West Side Story* note, "so that's what we'll give them."

The campaign to publicize the names of juvenile delinquents has gathered increasing momentum in the United States during the past several years. Before 1961, the issue showed no deep stirrings nor any clear-cut pattern of resolution. Primarily the question of publicity in regard to delinquents was at the option of the individual judge, and most judges had reached an agreement, however uneasy, with local editors to refrain in most instances from printing identifying material. In these years, occasional states would make it mandatory that such information not be divulged while, sometimes in the same year, other states would repeal mandatory no-disclosure laws, or would enact special variants on previous procedures. In Georgia, for instance, the 1957 legislature passed an act requiring that the names of all second and subsequent offenders be released for public consumption.

Many people, however, were stirring uneasily in the face of statistics indicating a striking rise in the amount and the kind of delinquent behavior taking place. Scapegoating subtle underlying social forces offered little satisfaction to persons confronted with behavior which appeared exasperating in its unwillingness to respond to admonition and frightening in its threat of physical violence and harm. Nor was it much relief to work one's way through academic disputation regarding the validity of reported statistics on delinquency, or through abstract theories insisting that what had changed was not the amount but the visibility of delinquency in a society in which ecological class barriers were disappearing. The seeming dimunition of religious control over juvenile standards could be mourned, the schools could be whipped, and the apparently lax and irresponsible family group, especially its working mother, flagellated. But none of these was really eminently satisfactory, since they did not provide direct and tangible targets, things, and people that could be named and excoriated specifically and individually.

THE "LOBLE LAW" COMES FORTH

It was into such a climate that a fiery and zealous Montana judge unloosed an almost prophet-like cry for the publication of the names of juveniles and their parents as a solution to the problem of delinquency. Judge Lester Loble of Helena, from a jurisdiction encompassing two counties with a combined population of about 31,000 persons, had almost single-handedly pushed an amendment through the 1961 Montana legislature requiring the release to newspapers of the names of juvenile offenders convicted of acts which, had they been committed by adults, would be felonies. Quite soon, the "Loble law," now accorded a glow of legitimacy by the addition of a set of statistics presumably indicating its striking efficacy, had gained widespread attention through personal appearances by the juror and by means of several glowing articles concerning him and his program in nationally circulated periodicals. Public frustration, impatience, and hostility in the face of seemingly intransigent juvenile delinquents had now been given the necessary ingredients for a crusade.

Newspaper coverage of Judge Loble's proposal was extensive, though the press could hardly be regarded as a totally disinterested party in the matter. In San Bernardino, California, the *Sun* was given the details of the Loble platform by the chief of police who asked for its local introduction as a matter of "common sense in the courts." A Boston *Sunday Globe* reporter, after repeating the oft told Loble story, noted in a manner representing something other than the objective impartiality generally considered part of the ethos of the American press, that "Judge Loble considers himself anything but a tyrant—and rightly so." Columnist

Robert C. Ruark told his readers that Judge Loble had been "responsible for a 50 percent decrease in juvenile crime over the past 5 years" and that Helena "used to be called 'Little Chicago' because of the war between the juves and the law." Ruark endorsed the Judge's proposal on publicity though he was disappointed that it did not go far enough. "The technique is milder than the one I used to advocate," Ruark noted, "which was the shaving of heads and a day's immolation in old-fashioned stocks for all the other wise guys to watch and be warned." Soon unsigned printed cards began to arrive in the mail of juvenile court workers extolling the "bold experiment," pointing out that "Montana scrapped its juvenile courts 2 years ago" and, in one instance, demanding to know in large bold-face letters: 'Why Not Michigan To!" *(sic)*.

A few more considered judgments appeared here and there. Perhaps the most colorful was an editorial in a rural Idaho newspaper. After summarizing Loble's views, it noted that "only a small handful of Idaho's 44 probate judges have seen fit to follow this course, although it's been open to them for years." The editor suggested two possible explanations for this state of affairs:

> Perhaps that's because, as Loble suggests, they are a sickeningly protective bunch, who cringe from the dispensation of justice.
> Or perhaps it's because many of them long ago recognized the old "let's print their names" bromide for the fraud it is—a slick cure-all which actually cures nothing and merely compounds the problem.

NCCD INVESTIGATES IN MONTANA

Attempts to provide some evidence for or against the claims from Helena led the National Council on Crime and Delinquency to undertake a field investigation as the Loble campaign picked up speed and support. The Council's research report, issued during the past year, indicates that instead of the 49 percent decrease invariably credited to the Loble measure, there had actually been a 58 percent increase in delinquency cases coming before his court since passage of the new law. Figures secured from the Helena police department further showed that there had been an increase in arrests of juveniles in Helena between 1962 and 1963 from 69 to 90. Perhaps the most ignoble outcome of the Loble law survey was the disclosure that the judge, despite his fervid campaign for open, well-publicized hearings, had refused to allow Council representatives to examine his court records so that they could ascertain the accuracy of his claims.

The Loble crusade would hardly evaporate overnight, even in the face of such disconcerting statistical scrutiny. Matters such as it have a way of surviving well beyond the point of their intellectual burial. In New Jersey, for instance, the State Supreme Court on September 13,

1965, altered its rules to permit press coverage of juvenile hearings at the discretion of the individual judge and to allow publication of names and photographs of the young offenders. The rather plaintive language in the announcement of the charge indicates the kind of pressures that served to bring about the new rationale in the State:

> The philosophy of the juvenile court is to rehabilitate the juvenile, with a view toward preventing future acts of delinquency and developing him into a law-abiding adult, rather than merely punishing him.
> But many people say in the press and elsewhere that the court is very soft on juveniles, or that the juvenile offender merely gets a pat on the wrist and is told to go home and not come back again.
> This is not so. Perhaps if the press is present and sees what is actually going on in court, the public will understand.

Following its scuttling of the Montana claims, the National Council on Crime and Delinquency released *Guides for Juvenile Court Judges on News Media Relations,* which reiterated the Council's official stand in favor of anonymity for delinquents appearing in juvenile courts. The report placed considerable stress at the same time on the idea that representatives of the news media should be cultivated assiduously in efforts to provide support and understanding for the work of the juvenile court, and that they should be welcomed to its sessions.

JUVENILE PUBLICITY: PROS AND CONS

Putting the empirical claims from Montana to the side—where they belong—it continues to be necessary to address various questions concerning the likely impact of publication of their names on juvenile offenders. Obviously the curtailment of the traditionally free-ranging penetration of the press into public business should be undertaken only with great reluctance and only if the best available evidence indicates that social values of contravening and superior importance are likely to be served by such a policy. Various claims bearing on this issue may be examined in turn:

(1) One reason often put forward in favor of the publication of the names of offending delinquents is that such publication puts the community on guard against further depredations by such youths. A family will come to learn of the boy in its neighborhood involved in a rape offense and thus be able to warn its daughter against association with this individual. "You may never know if you live next door to a criminal," the New York Society of Newspaper Editors warned the public when it campaigned for publication rights in juvenile courts.

It is notable that this argument offers no particular hope of protection to the community at large, but only to those elements within it which see and act upon the information imparted by the press. It is not alleged that the delinquent will not commit a subsequent offense, but only that some members of the community may avoid that offense being committed in regard to persons or things important to them. This hardly seems to be a very appealing social policy, but rather represents a social lottery. The delinquent behavior is not deterred, but merely channeled elsewhere. The best protection to the community would not appear to be the identification of the malefactor so that he can be shunned, but the reform of the offender so that he can be trusted. Constant vigilance may be the price of eternal security, but it is a very high price, and in the area of delinquency, at least, an unrealistic one that should not be paid unless other procedures are inadequate.

(2) The complaint of some youths that they themselves are indiscriminately labeled delinquents because of the anonymity afforded their violating brethren also seems to be rather spurious. Sailors will continue to be scorned because some of their shipmates behave less well than a community desired, and Negroes will suffer discrimination even though a comparatively small number may fit the stereotype that the majority group has seized upon to justify its bigotry. It would not help if individual deviating sailors or offending Negroes were identified for public consumption, but only if basic attitudes toward these groups were altered. Teenagers will continue to reap the general attitudes and opinions in the society about them whether or not particular delinquents are singled out for newspaper identification. In fact, it might be hypothesized that the more that individual delinquents are identified, the more the public attitude toward all teenagers as real or potential menaces will be reinforced. Furthermore, of course, the obverse of this prepublication view also merits attention: It would seem particularly unfortunate for nonoffending brothers and sisters of the identified delinquent to have to suffer the abuse so characteristically accorded their vulnerable classmates by school children.

(3) There is a strong claim made for the fact that publication would serve as a deterrent to other youngsters who would now comprehend the notoriety and shame ensuant upon any delinquent behavior they may have had in mind. Such a prospect will obviously not be effective with juveniles who will be acclaimed for their publicized feats; quite the contrary. It also does not appear unreasonable to assume that those juveniles who will behave only because of the likelihood of scorn from persons upon whom they rely for emotional satisfaction and support will almost behave just as well without the overhanging threat of publication. Effective deterrence against delinquency has in most instances been built into their very being.

(4) In terms of the control of further delinquency by the person who

has offended and found himself written up in the newspapers, the evidence all points in a single direction, and that direction is contrary to the idea of publication as a deterrent. If a considerable segment of delinquency is conceived theoretically as a lower-class attempt to achieve benefits offered to all segments of the society, then publicity, ironic as it might appear, may be seen as a form of social recognition, a recognition somewhat hostile and grudging on the part of the upper echelons of the society, but replete with outright admiration when accorded by the delinquent's peer.

To those juveniles who do not take enthusiastically to the publicity, the resultant shame and humiliation also seems unlikely to produce only conforming behavior. If they do bring about such behavior, it does not seem unreasonable to attempt to assess the cost of the product. It is most important to keep in mind that delinquency, however reprehensible and irritating it may be, is not, by far, necessarily the worst manifestation of human nonconformity. Frightened and self-abnegating creatures may be more readily tolerated in our society, for instance, and may cause less trouble for others, but it would be difficult to maintain that they are "better off" than delinquents or that society is better off producing them in the place of delinquents.

(5) It is worth noting, in addition, a number of other undesirable results which might be brought about by publication of the identity of juvenile offenders. The "punishment" involved in such a procedure could conceivably provide a relief from guilt so that the cycle of delinquent behavior could be resumed. Work opportunities, often crucial in inhibiting delinquency, could be dried up as the juvenile becomes notorious in the community. If juvenile delinquency is a hostile reaction and a response to fear, then publication would presumably increase that fear. Finally, if shame is related to delinquency in some fashion, and this seems a likely hypothesis, publicity would likely accentuate such shame. Delinquents do not in a large number of cases appear to steal because they are impoverished, but because they have come to define their situation as undesirable and, perhaps, shameful. Taylor provides historical support for the thesis that humiliation may be more devastating than seemingly harsher punishments and may produce various unanticipated consequences with the information that infanticide increased notably in Scotland when adulterers and fornicators were punished by having to appear in church each week for 6 or more months to be harrangued by the minister. "Women who had illegitimately become pregnant," he notes, "preferred to risk the capital penalty for infanticide rather than admit the facts and suffer such extreme public humiliation."

CONCLUSIONS

There exists, unfortunately, a paucity of clearcut and unimpeachable data upon which to base a judgment concerning the precise relationship between the publication of the names of juvenile delinquents and the impact of this policy upon their behavior. It is obvious that the question itself has never really been stated adequately: A more sophisticated reformulation would inquire concerning the impact of such a policy on different kinds of offenders in different kinds of communities. Rural settings obviously present different conditions than urban areas, conditions which favor the spread of information about delinquents whether the facts are officially reported or not. The likelihood that the offender is personally known to most residents of the community would also appear to be of substantial importance in evaluating the potential impact of a publication policy on behavior.

With these and cognate considerations in mind, it still appears reasonable to maintain in summary that a program involving the publication of identifying information about youths appearing before the juvenile court is likely to cause more social and individual harm than it is likely to eliminate. The further alienation of the individual from those segments of the society seeking to inculcate their standards in him would seem to be of great importance in opposing identification. Disavowal of the offender and formalization of his delinquent status represent the processes most deplored. The elements and the consequences of such practices were clearly stated more than 250 years ago in words that constitute the theme of this article. In 1709, the *Tatler,* an eminent English journal of manners and morals, carried the following striking observation:

> When crimes are enormous, the delinquent deserves little pity, yet the reporter may deserve less.
>
> A discovery of this kind serves not to reclaim, but enrages the offender, and precipitates him into further degrees of ill. He that once stumbles may yet, by a check of that bridle, recover again; but when by public detection, he is fallen under that infamy he feared, he will then be apt to discard all caution, and to think he owes himself the utmost pleasures of vice.
>
> Nay perhaps he advances farther, and sets up a reversed sort of fame, being eminently wicked, and he who before was but a clandestine disciple becomes a doctor of impiety.